APPLIED INFORMATION SECURITY LABS

A HANDS-ON APPROACH

Second Edition

RANDALL BOYLE, Ph.D.

Longwood University

JEFFREY G. PROUDFOOT

University of Arizona

Editor in Chief: Stephanie Wall
Executive Editor: Bob Horan
Program Manager Team Lead: Ashley Santora
Program Manager: Denise Vaughn
Editorial Assistant: Kaylee Rotella
Executive Marketing Manager: Anne K. Fahlgren
Project Manager Team Lead: Judy Leale
Project Manager: Ilene Kahn
Procurement Specialist: Michelle Klein

Creative Director: Jayne Conte
Cover Designer: Bruce Kenselaar
Cover Image: Kundra/Shutterstock
Media Project Manager: Lisa Rinaldi
Printer/Binder: Edwards Brothers Malloy
   BAR/Jackson
Cover Printer: Edwards Brothers Malloy
   BAR/Jackson

Credits and acknowledgments borrowed from other sources and reproduced, with permission, in this textbook appear on the appropriate page within text.

Microsoft and/or its respective suppliers make no representations about the suitability of the information contained in the documents and related graphics published as part of the services for any purpose. All such documents and related graphics are provided "as is" without warranty of any kind. Microsoft and/or its respective suppliers hereby disclaim all warranties and conditions with regard to this information, including all warranties and conditions of merchantability, whether express, implied or statutory, fitness for a particular purpose, title and non-infringement. In no event shall Microsoft and/or its respective suppliers be liable for any special, indirect or consequential damages or any damages whatsoever resulting from loss of use, data or profits, whether in an action of contract, negligence or other tortious action, arising out of or in connection with the use or performance of information available from the services.

   The documents and related graphics contained herein could include technical inaccuracies or typographical errors. Changes are periodically added to the information herein. Microsoft and/or its respective suppliers may make improvements and/or changes in the product(s) and/or the program(s) described herein at any time. Partial screen shots may be viewed in full within the software version specified.

Microsoft® and Windows®, and Microsoft Office® are registered trademarks of the Microsoft Corporation in the U.S.A. and other countries. This book is not sponsored or endorsed by or affiliated with the Microsoft Corporation.

Many of the designations by manufacturers and sellers to distinguish their products are claimed as trademarks. Where those designations appear in this book, and the publisher was aware of a trademark claim, the designations have been printed in initial caps or all caps.

Library of Congress Cataloging-in-Publication Data
Boyle, Randall.
   [Applied information security.]
   Applied information security labs : a hands-on approach / Randall Boyle, Ph.D., Longwood University ; Jeffrey G. Proudfoot, University of Arizona. -- Second edition.
      pages cm
   ISBN 978-0-13-354743-6
   1. Computer security. 2. Computer networks--Security measures. I. Proudfoot, Jeffrey G. II. Title.
   QA76.9.A25B693 2014
   005.8--dc23
                                                                          2013037911

10 9 8 7 6 5 4 3 2 1

ISBN 10: 0-13-354743-4
ISBN 13: 978-0-13-354743-6

Randall Boyle, Ph.D.
College of Business & Economics
Longwood University
201 High Street
Farmville, VA 23909
Phone: 434-395-4913
E-mail: BoyleRJ@Longwood.edu

Jeffrey G. Proudfoot
Department of Management Information Systems
University of Arizona
Center for the Management of Information
McClelland Hall Room #427
1130 East Helen Street
Tucson, AZ 85719
E-mail: jproudfoot@cmi.arizona.edu

New in this Edition:

1. Microsoft® Windows 7® Professional compliant.
2. Additional chapter projects in existing chapters.
3. New chapters on Microsoft Windows, Web-based applications, Mobile applications, etc.
4. Project Questions require students to identify key concepts, information, or functionality within each project. Project questions can be assigned to students and turned in along with their screenshots.
5. Cheat-proof projects which include timestamps and unique identifiers in each project.
6. Updated software versions (all projects).
7. Chapter objectives and outlines.

ABOUT THE AUTHORS

Dr. Randall Boyle is an associate professor at the College of Business and Economics at Longwood University. He received his Ph.D. in Management Information Systems (MIS) from Florida State University in 2003. He also has a master's degree in Public Administration, and a B.S. in Finance.

His research areas include deception detection in computer-mediated environments, information assurance policy, the effects of IT on cognitive biases, and the effects of IT on knowledge workers. He has published in journals such as *Journal of Management Information Systems*, *International Journal of E-Collaboration*, and *Journal of International Technology and Information Management*.

Dr. Boyle has received various teaching awards at the University of Alabama in Huntsville, the University of Utah, and Longwood University, including the Marvin J. Ashton Excellence in Teaching Award, and the Excellence in Education Award. He has taught a variety of classes including Information Security, Cyber Security, Advanced Cyber Security, Telecommunications, Systems Analysis and Design, Decision Support Systems, Web Servers, and Introductory MIS courses. He is the author of *Applied Information Security*, *Applied Networking Labs*, and *Corporate Computer Security* 3rd Ed.

Jeffrey Proudfoot is currently pursuing a Ph.D. in Management Information Systems (MIS) at the University of Arizona. He is working under the direction of Dr. Jay F. Nunamaker Jr. in the Center for the Management of Information (CMI) as well as the National Center for Border Security and Immigration (BORDERS), a Department of Homeland Security (DHS) Center of Excellence. He has a master's degree in MIS, with an emphasis in security, as well as a B.S. in MIS, both from the University of Utah.

His research interests include automated credibility assessment, information privacy and security, the influence of technology on learning, behavioral sensor research, and border security issues. He has been directly involved in securing and completing research grants totaling more than $1.3 million, and has presented research to United States Congressmen, military intelligence officers, international border security experts, and top Customs and Border Protection (CBP) officials at DHS headquarters in Washington D.C.

Jeff has received teaching awards at the University of Utah as well as the University of Arizona. He has taught a number of courses including Using and Managing Information Systems, Computer Essentials, and Detecting Deception and Intent.

DEDICATION

To Courtney Boyle, thank you for your patience, kindness, and perspective on what's most important in life.

-Randy Boyle

To Leah, my wife and best friend, everything I do is for you. To my parents, Harold and Mary, your encouragement and support have made all of this possible. To Eddie, our yellow lab, thanks for your companionship in the office at all hours of the night.

To Randy, thank you for yet another opportunity to collaborate.

-Jeffrey Proudfoot

ACKNOWLEDGEMENTS

We would like to thank the reviewers of the prior edition. They have used this book for years and know it well. Their suggestions, recommendations, and criticisms helped shape this edition. This book really is a product of a much larger community of academics.

We would also like to thank the industry experts who contributed to this edition. Their expertise and perspective added a real-world perspective that can only come from years of practical experience. Thank you to Matt Christensen and Taylor Jones for your generous help. Thanks go to our editor Bob Horan for his support and guidance. A good editor can produce good books. Bob is a great editor who produces great books. And he has done so for many years. We feel privileged to be able to work with Bob.

Special thanks go to Denise Vaughn at Pearson. Most readers won't fully appreciate the hard work and dedication it takes to transform the "raw" content provided by authors, into the finished copy you're holding in your hands. Denise's commitment and attention to detail have made this into a great looking book.

Randy Boyle

Jeffrey Proudfoot

Contents

ABOUT THE AUTHORS IV
DEDICATION V
ACKNOWLEDGEMENTS V

INTRODUCTION X
DESCRIPTION X
INTENDED AUDIENCE X
WARNING X
FOR THE INSTRUCTOR XI

GETTING STARTED XIII
TAKING SCREENSHOTS XIII
FREE WINDOWS-BASED SOFTWARE XIII
COMPUTER SCANNING INSTRUCTIONS XIV
SOFTWARE, SUPPLEMENTS, AND UPDATES..XIV
REMOTE TEST MACHINES XV
DOS PROMPT XV
SOFTWARE INSTALLATION AND UN-INSTALLATION XV
CREATE A VIRUS-SCAN EXCEPTION FOLDER XV
COMPRESSED (ZIP) FILES XVI

CHAPTER 1: DOS COMMANDS 1
1.1   DOS BASICS 2
1.2   IPCONFIG 6
1.3   PING 9
1.4   TRACERT 11
1.5   NETSTAT 13
1.6   NSLOOKUP 16
1.7   FTP 17
1.8   POWERSHELL® 22
1.9   HASHING 30
1.10 SDELETE® 33

CHAPTER 2: WINDOWS SECURITY 37
2.1   LOCAL SECURITY POLICY 38
2.2   WINDOWS FIREWALL® 40
2.3   CONFIGURING BACKUP 43
2.4   WINDOWS UPDATE® 46
2.5   USER MANAGEMENT 48
2.6   MICROSOFT SECURITY ESSENTIALS® 51

CHAPTER 3: WEB SECURITY 55
3.1   WEB BROWSER HISTORY...56
3.2   COOKIES..57
3.3   TRACKING (GHOSTERY®)..61
3.4   ANONYMOUS BROWSING 62
3.5   WEB PROXY 64
3.6   ADBLOCK PLUS® 65
3.7   HTTPS EVERYWHERE® 66
3.8   FLAGFOX® 68
3.9   WEB OF TRUST® (WOT) 69
3.10 ONION ROUTING (TOR®)...70

CHAPTER 4: PORN & SPAM FILTERS 73
4.1   K-9® 74
4.2   EMAIL FILTER (OUTLOOK®) 75
4.3   BLOCK SENDERS (OUTLOOK) 78
4.4   JUNK EMAIL (HOTMAIL) 80

CHAPTER 5: MONITORING SOFTWARE 83
5.1   REFOG® KEYLOGGER 84
5.2   SPECTOR 360® 86
5.3   UNTANGLE® 87
5.4   PREY® 88

CHAPTER 6: PASSWORD AUDITORS 93
6.1   JOHN THE RIPPER® (JTR) 94
6.2   LOCAL PASSWORD AUDIT 98
6.3   FREE WORD AND EXCEL PASSWORD RECOVERY 103
6.4   CAIN & ABLE® (PASSWORDS) 105
6.5   DEFAULT PASSWORDS 109
6.6   PASSWORD EVALUATOR 109
6.7   PASSWORD GENERATORS 110
6.8   RAINBOW TABLES 111
6.9   RAINBOWCRACK® 114

CHAPTER 7: WIRELESS 118
7.1   WI-FI INSPECTOR® 119
7.2   INSSIDER® 120
7.3   WIFIDENUM® 122
7.4   WIGLE.NET® 123
7.5   EKAHAU HEATMAPPER® 126

CHAPTER 8: SECURITY READINGS 130
8.1   THE REGISTER®, NAKED SECURITY®, & COMPUTERWORLD® 131
8.2   SANS® & SECURITY POLICIES 132
8.3   PONEMON INSTITUTE & PWC 135

CHAPTER 9: INFORMATION GATHERING 138
9.1   TRACE ROUTE TO THE SOURCE 139
9.2   TRACE A PHONE NUMBER 140
9.3   WHOIS® LOOKUP TO SOURCE NETWORK 141
9.4   LOCATE AN IP ADDRESS SOURCE 143
9.5   LOCATE AN EMAIL SOURCE 144
9.6   SAM SPADE® 146

CHAPTER 10: PACKET SNIFFER 150
10.1   PACKET CAPTURE (WIRESHARK I) 151
10.2   CAPTURE WEB TRAFFIC (WIRESHARK II) 154
10.3   CAPTURE AN EMAIL (WIRESHARK III) 157
10.4   DISPLAY FILTERING (WIRESHARK IV) 159
10.5   COMMAND-LINE PACKET SNIFFING (WINDUMP®) 163

CHAPTER 11: PORT & VULNERABILITY SCANNERS 170
11.1   PORTQRY® 171
11.2   NMAP® (ZENMAP®) 174
11.3   ADVANCED IP SCANNER 176
11.4   NESSUS® 178
11.5   APPSCAN® 181

11.6   SHIELDS UP® 184

CHAPTER 12: HONEYPOTS AND IDS 186
12.1   HONEYBOT® 187
12.2   NST®, SNORT® (IDS), & BASE® 194

CHAPTER 13: FILE INTEGRITY CHECKERS & SYSTEM MONITORS 203
13.1   HASHCALC® 204
13.2   PROCESS MONITOR® (FILEMON) 206
13.3   FILEVERIFIER++® 208
13.4   WINDOWS EVENT VIEWER® (LOGS) 210
13.5   SNARE® FOR WINDOWS 212

CHAPTER 14: ALTERNATE DATA STREAMS 215
14.1   CREATE AN ADS 216
14.2   ADS EXECUTABLE 218
14.3   ADS SPY® 222

CHAPTER 15: DATA RECOVERY & SECURE DELETION 225
15.1   FILE RECOVERY (RECUVA®) 226
15.2   SECURE DELETION (ERASER®) 228
15.3   CLEAN UP (CCLEANER®) 230
15.4   DISK WIPE® 232

CHAPTER 16: CRYPTOGRAPHY 235
16.1   LOCKNOTE® 236
16.2   AXCRYPT® 238
16.3   COMPRESS AND ENCRYPT (7-ZIP®) 240
16.4   ENIGMA® 242
16.5   TRUECRYPT® 244
16.6   CRYPTOOL V2® 246
16.7   ENCRYPTED USB (TRUECRYPT®) 253
16.8   ENCRYPTED EMAIL (HUSHMAIL®) 256

CHAPTER 17: STEGANOGRAPHY 261
17.1   DIGITAL WATERMARKING 262
17.2   INVISIBLE SECRETS 2.1® 263
17.3   STEGDETECT® 267
17.4   OPENPUFF® 269

CHAPTER 18: FORENSICS 273
18.1   BGINFO® 274
18.2   METADATA (TAGVIEW®) 275
18.3   CAINE® 277

CHAPTER 19: APPLICATION SECURITY 285
19.1   CONCURRENCY FLAWS 286
19.2   CROSS-SITE SCRIPTING (XSS) 289
19.3   AUTHENTICATION ERRORS 291
19.4   SQL INJECTION 294

CHAPTER 20: LINUX PRIMER 301
20.1   LINUX INSTALLATION (FEDORA®) 302
20.2   COMMAND-LINE PRIMER (FEDORA) 310
20.3   SOFTWARE INSTALLATION (UBUNTU) 319
20.4   NET-TOOLS AND NETWORKING COMMANDS (UBUNTU) 326
20.5   SYSTEM TOOLS AND CONFIGURATION (UBUNTU) 333

20.6 **USER AND GROUP MANAGEMENT (MINT®)** 342
20.7 **NETWORK CLI UTILITIES (MINT)** 352
20.8 **FILE CLI UTILITIES (MINT)** 359
20.9 **TCPDUMP (PC-BSD®)** 375
20.10 **NETCAT (PC-BSD)** 387
20.11 **HPING3 (PC-BSD)** 392
20.12 **PORTABLE LINUX (DEBIAN)** 396

CHAPTER 21: SECURING WEB SERVERS 402
21.1 **INSTALL APACHE®, CREATE A WEBSITE, AND HOST PAGES**......................................403
21.2 **INTERNET INFORMATION SERVICES (IIS) INSTALLATION** 409
21.3 **PHISHING AND HOSTS FILE** 413
21.4 **AUTHENTICATION, LIMITS, AND BLOCKING** 422
21.5 **REQUEST FILTERING AND LOGS** 426

CHAPTER 22: UTILITIES & OTHER 435
22.1 **PORTABLE APPLICATIONS** 436
22.2 **REMOTE DESKTOP®** 440
22.3 **PROCESS EXPLORER®** 443
22.4 **CHANGE MAC ADDRESS** 445
22.5 **BINDERS (IEXPRESS®)** 447
22.6 **BUFFER OVERFLOW** 451
22.7 **FILE SPLITTING** 453
22.8 **USB LOCK (PREDATOR®)** 455

CHAPTER 23: IT SECURITY DISTRIBUTIONS 458
23.1 **KALI® LINUX I** 459
23.2 **KALI LINUX II** 465
23.3 **CAIN & ABLE** 469

CHAPTER 24: MOBILE SECURITY 473
24.1 **SCREENSHOT (DROIDATSCREEN)** 474
24.2 **MOBILE SECURITY (LOOKOUT®)** 476
24.3 **WARDRIVING (WIGLE WIFI®)** 479
24.4 **TETHERING** 481
24.5 **MOBILE NET TOOLS (FING®)** 482
24.6 **ENCRYPTED CALLS (REDPHONE®)** 485
24.7 **ENCRYPTION (FILE LOCKER®)** 487

APPENDIX A: ANTIVIRUS 489
A.1 **CREATING A VIRUS SCAN EXCEPTION FOLDER (MCAFEE)** 490

APPENDIX B: SOFTWARE LINKS 492
B.1 **SOFTWARE LINKS** 493

INTRODUCTION

DESCRIPTION

Applied Information Security Labs guides students through the installation and basic operation of IT security software. The software presented is widely used in the IT security industry. The primary audience is upper-division BS majors in Information Systems, Computer Science, and Computer Information Systems.

This book is also intended for graduate students in MSIS, MIS, MBA, MACC, or other MS programs who are seeking a broader applied knowledge about IT security. This book can also be used in executive training programs, or by anyone interested in learning the practical side of IT security.

IT security is a rapidly growing area within the information systems landscape. Students hear about security incidents on the news, and watch movies (or TV programs) that popularize the use of IT security. Students are often motivated to take an IT security course to learn more about what they have been exposed to in the media. This book gives students hands-on experience with some of the tools they may have heard about.

This book covers a wide range of IT security software. Several thousand pieces of software were reviewed for possible inclusion in this edition. In each category, the best free Windows-based software was chosen.

INTENDED AUDIENCE

This book was written for students with limited computer experience. Typically, students have already taken an introductory course about information systems or computer science. College-aged juniors enrolled in an IT security class will use this book along with an IT security textbook like Boyle and Panko's *Corporate Computer Security*, Whitman and Mattord's *Principles of Information Security*, Pfleeger's *Security in Computing*, Goodrich and Tamassia's *Introduction to Computer Security*, or Stallings' *Computer Security: Principles and Practice*.

This book gives students real-world experience using actual software that may not be presented in a traditional textbook. Both practical and theoretical books are necessary to adequately train a student to be able to add value to an organization. This book focuses on the practical side of IT security.

WARNING

This book is NOT a "hacking" book. This book is designed to provide students interested in IT security with the tools necessary to secure their computers and information systems. It is not designed to give them the tools necessary to break into other systems. Anyone familiar with IT security software will attest to the fact that the software demonstrated in this book is relatively benign. Malicious software does exist and was intentionally left out.

Students are discouraged from using software illegally, inappropriately, or immorally. Do NOT scan any machine that is not your own. Using these programs to gain unauthorized access to other computer systems, or harm them in any way, is illegal.

There programs are set up to monitor illegal computer activity and you will eventually get caught if you engage in illegal behavior. If you are uncertain about what you are doing, please STOP. Ask your instructor for more direction. Curiosity is admirable, but you may find that going to jail is no fun at all.

The author, publisher, and instructor have given, and will continue to give, strong warnings against all illegal use of the software presented here. Any illegal or inappropriate use of the software listed in this book is the sole responsibility of the reader.

FOR THE INSTRUCTOR

Applied Information Security Labs reduces the amount of preparation an instructor has to do because it provides him or her with approximately 145 homework assignments ready to give to his or her students. These projects have been tested in both undergraduate and graduate classes for several years. Many students say that doing hands-on projects is the best part of the class.

Students learn how to use the tools they will need when they start working in the real world. This gets them more excited about the class. Throughout this book, students learn to use software in a building-block fashion. It introduces them to progressively more complicated software. Later chapters refer to skills learned in earlier chapters. A step-wise learning method increases memory retention and integration across software categories.

One of the main criticisms of IT security classes is that they are "too theoretical." Students hear "security" and they think it's going to be a really fun class. Sometimes, however, they are disappointed when they are presented with a class that deals exclusively with theoretical concepts and lists of suggested guidelines. A healthy dose of real-world software projects that reinforce in-class lectures can change students' attitudes right away.

GRADING

Each project contains instructions to take a screenshot by pressing Alt-PrtScn or Ctrl-PrtScn at specific points in the project to show that students have completed the project. Each project also includes Project Questions that require students to provide information about the project.

Screenshots and Project Questions can be put into a document and emailed to the instructor. Grading an entire semester of projects can be done in a couple of minutes.

Using this book along with a traditional IT security textbook will reduce the time and effort required to prepare a security course. It will also get students excited about the course, and give them hands-on experience using real-world IT security tools.

CHEATING

Cheating is virtually impossible because screenshots and Project Questions will be unique to each student. Each project will require students to produce a unique timestamp, file name, or hardware configuration. For example, a student will likely have a unique IP address, MAC address, and default gateway when he or she uses the `ipconfig` command at the DOS prompt. Any sharing or cheating will be obvious.

Projects can be used across multiple semesters and years without the possibility of academic dishonesty. Each student must produce a set of screenshots unique to him or her during that semester. Sharing of information between students across different semesters wouldn't yield any more information than the screenshots shown in this book. The result is that the projects are essentially cheat-proof.

A SANDBOX

If possible, it's a good idea to give students a safe environment to complete these projects. A secured "sandbox" can help students feel more comfortable about experimenting with the software. It will also benefit the instructor because it will reduce compatibility issues, hardware conflicts, etc. A dedicated computing lab or remote virtual machines are both effective solutions. They can be quickly re-imaged for subsequent semesters.

GETTING STARTED

Sometimes, the more knowledgeable you are about a given topic area, the harder it is to effectively teach it to others. This is especially true of IT security. It takes a lot of time and effort to really understand the fundamentals of information security. It requires an in-depth understanding of networking, databases, a variety of operating systems, programming, and IT hardware. You also need plenty of curiosity, a strong desire to learn, and the ability to learn on your own.

There isn't a single person on the planet who knows everything about information security. You don't need to know everything. You just need to know one thing. You can decide what that is and then become an expert in that particular part of the IT security field. It just takes time and hard work.

HANDS-ON EXPERIENCE

This book was designed to give you experience using a broad array of IT security tools. It will help give you an idea of the types of tools IT security experts might use on a daily basis. It will also equip you with a repertoire of useful tools that you could use on your first IT security job. Too many students graduate with a degree in IS from well-known colleges and only know what they were taught — theory and hand waving. This book will introduce you to a broad array of practical IT security tools and how to use them.

There is a great deal more to learn about each piece of software presented in this book. Entire books could be written about each one. Please feel free to take time to become more familiar with them. We will introduce each tool and show you its basic functionality. You won't become an expert by completing these projects.

TAKING SCREENSHOTS

To show that you have completed each project, you will be required to take screenshots of your work, answer Project Questions, or answer Thought Questions. You will take screenshots at specific points in each project to show that you have completed each part of the project. These screenshots, along with the Project Questions and Thought Questions, will be pasted into a document and submitted to your instructor.

If you need a word-processing program, you can download a free copy of the LibreOffice® suite (http://www.libreoffice.org/). You will then turn in your project screenshots to your instructor. Instructors will choose the quantity and variety of projects to assign.

To get a screenshot of the current window, press Alt-PrtScn. To get a screenshot of the whole computer screen, press Ctrl-PrtScn. You can also get freeware such as Screenshot Pilot (http://www.colorpilot.com/screenshot.html), which comes with additional screen capturing functionality. Microsoft Windows 7® comes with a Snipping tool that can be used to manually select the screenshot area.

FREE WINDOWS-BASED SOFTWARE

The software in this book is freeware and will run on any computer with Microsoft Windows 7® Professional (64-bit). If you have Microsoft Windows XP® or Microsoft Windows Vista® operating systems, some of these programs may not work. If you have Mac OS X®, you can run a Windows virtual machine using VMware Fusion® (www.vmware.com), Boot Camp® (www.apple.com), Parallels® (www.parallels.com), or Oracle VM VirtualBox® (www.virtualbox.org).

This is not intended to be a comprehensive manual for all IT security software. There are many other great pieces of software that were not included due to space limitations. Each piece of software is worth exploring more thoroughly. Online help manuals for each piece of software are available at the links listed throughout the book.

The objective of this book is to help beginners have a good first experience with a wide breadth of security software. A few of the best pieces of software in each category were selected to represent the whole category. More experienced users may find some of the projects presented in this book simplistic.

COMPUTER SCANNING INSTRUCTIONS

For projects that require scanning, your instructor will provide you with an IP address of a test machine. If you aren't familiar with what an IP address is, please ask your instructor. If you are working on this book without attending a formal course, you are welcome to scan your own computer by using the IP address 127.0.0.1 or your real IP address, which you will learn about later.

Some of the examples below use the author's IP address (155.97.74.45) at the time this book was written. Please do not use this IP address for any of the exercises in this book. This IP address range runs several honeypots and intrusion detection systems (some of which you will learn about) to monitor various activities. All scans on this IP address range will be logged. Please obtain a valid target IP address from your instructor or use your own IP address.

You will need to know your own IP address for some of the projects. Your IP address may change over time. You can find out what your own IP address is by going to http://whatismyipaddress.com/, or you can use the loopback adapter address (127.0.0.1). If your instructor gives you a different IP address to use, please use that address. Do NOT scan the Department of Defense, FBI, CIA, NSA, or any other site that hasn't given you permission to do so.

SOFTWARE, SUPPLEMENTS, AND UPDATES

The software you are going to use in this book will be available for download on the Internet, or will be available on WebCT®/Blackboard®, if your teacher chooses to upload them. If one of the links listed doesn't appear to be working, please check Google or WebCT/Blackboard for a current link. Almost all of the programs listed below can be found by searching Google®. They are all well known and virus/worm free. All of the programs in this manual were tested on a Microsoft Windows 7 Professional (64-bit) desktop machine.

We recommend you make a folder labeled "**security**" on your C: drive to store all the software that you will download. Creating this folder will make software organization and operation easier. This book is written with the understanding that you did create a security folder on your C: drive. All the programs in this manual will match the directions in the book if you create the C:\security folder on your C: drive.

The list of good, free software will change every year as new software becomes freeware. If you know of a piece of *free* Windows-based software that is more *useful* and *easier to use* than the ones listed below, please feel free to email a link to BoyleRJ@Longwood.edu and it may get included in the next edition. Please do not send emails about shareware, trial versions, or anything from which you are trying to make money.

REMOTE TEST MACHINES

If you do not want to load the software listed in this book onto your own computer, your instructor can set up a standard Microsoft Windows 7 computer for you to use remotely as a test machine. You can use Windows Remote Desktop® (included with Windows 7) to remotely access the test machine and complete the projects.

If your instructor doesn't know how to enable multiple, concurrent Remote Desktop connections, you can find the instructions online and give them to him/her. Hopefully your network administrator already has several remote machines set up for your class to use. Instructions on how to use Remote Desktop are shown in a later project.

Having a safe environment where you, as a student, can test software is nice because you don't have to worry about causing problems on your own computer. You will also have fewer installation issues, downloading problems, and hardware conflicts. Overall, it will save your instructor countless hours answering emails if he/she sets up a remote test machine.

DOS PROMPT

Some of the projects use DOS-based programs and will require you to run them in a DOS window from a specific directory. When you download the programs in this book, you can put them in the C:\security\ directory (mentioned earlier) and run them from there. When you are asked to run a program, you will go to **C:\security** and then type in the command. For example, C:\security\john.exe hackme.txt.

There are also several projects that require you to run the command prompt with administrator privileges. To start a command prompt with administrator privileges, you must right-click the command prompt icon and then select "Run as administrator." Some of the projects will not work if you did not select the "Run as administrator" option.

SOFTWARE INSTALLATION AND UN-INSTALLATION

Some of the programs will require administrator privileges before they can be installed. Most users are administrators on their own computers. If you are not, you'll have to ask the owner of the computer to create an administrator account for you.

Once you have completed a project, please feel free to uninstall or delete the software. Most of the software listed below can be automatically uninstalled. You can also go to Control Panel, Add/Remove Software, and then select the software you want to uninstall.

IMPORTANT: If you are a beginning computer user, it's highly recommended that you uninstall every piece of software that you use in this book after you are done. Newbies (people new to computers) tend to blame the IT security software in these projects for unrelated external problems such as a city-wide power outage, their spouse spilling Coke® on their router, or their ISP failing to offer service that day. Uninstalling the software in this book may help reduce your anxiety level.

CREATE A VIRUS-SCAN EXCEPTION FOLDER

None of the programs listed in this book are viruses, worms, or malware. If your anti-virus software gives you a warning that any of the programs are viruses, you'll need to create an exception folder. The antivirus program will not scan the files/programs in the exception folder you will create. Instructions on how to get McAfee® and Norton® anti-virus scanners to create exception folders are listed in Appendix A.

Most common anti-virus scanners will have the ability to create an exception folder. If they don't have this option, you may want to get a better anti-virus scanner. It may take a small amount of effort to figure out how to make an exception folder if you are using an anti-virus scanner that is not listed in the Appendix.

COMPRESSED (ZIP) FILES

Many of the files you will open, and subsequently install, will be compressed (or "zipped"). Windows 7 comes with a standard zip/unzip program. There are a variety of compression programs including WinZip® (http://www.winzip.com/index.htm), 7-Zip® (http://www.7-zip.org/), etc. We recommend you use 7-Zip or the built-in Windows zip program. We will use both in this book.

chapter 1

Below are a few DOS commands that are widely used by security professionals on a daily basis. Although DOS commands may seem archaic to those who grew up on Windows, many useful programs still use a command-line interface. Learning command-line will become easier with practice. Knowing how to use a command prompt will make transitioning from Windows to Linux much easier.

These projects cover just a few of the DOS commands available. A larger list is available by typing "help" at the DOS prompt. One of the main advantages of using DOS commands is that they will work on all current versions of Windows in a command prompt. An administrator can run DOS commands on any Windows machine without installing additional software. This will save him/her time and money.

All versions of Windows will have a command prompt where you can run DOS commands. Windows 7 includes PowerShell, which has extended capabilities including being able to run many Linux/Unix/Mac commands. To pull up a command prompt, you can go through the start menu by clicking Start, All Programs, Accessories, Command Prompt. Alternatively, you can click Start, Run, and then type cmd.

For this book, we will use CMD.exe because it is included in both Windows XP and Windows 7. As Windows 7 becomes more widely adopted, users will be able to take advantage of the additional functionality in PowerShell. A short PowerShell primer is included in this chapter.

Time required to complete this chapter: 20 minutes.

Chapter Objectives

Learn how to:
1. Navigate the Windows file system via the command prompt.
2. Obtain basic host configuration parameters.
3. Identify active hosts on the Internet.
4. Trace a route across the Internet.
5. Obtain relevant network information.
6. Use command-line FTP.
7. Use PowerShell.
8. Create hashes.
9. Securely delete a file.

Chapter Projects

Project:
1.1 DOS Basics
1.2 IPconfig
1.3 Ping
1.4 Tracert
1.5 Netstat
1.6 NSlookup
1.7 FTP
1.8 PowerShell
1.9 Hashing
1.10 Sdelete

1.1   DOS BASICS

This project will cover a few basic DOS commands. For later projects in this book, you will need to create directories (or folders), move between directories, create files, edit files, move/copy/delete files, etc. You are going to run through a couple of quick commands that you might already know. For beginning users, these may be entirely new. Repetition is the key to knowing when and how to use these commands.

The dir command gives you a listing of the files, programs, and subdirectories in the current directory. Directories (called folders in Windows) are shown with a <DIR> before the name of the directory. Files and programs (or executables) are shown with their file size. For example, notice in the screenshots below that Adobe is a directory and Fport.exe is a program. You can also see the identical listing of directories, programs, and files in both DOS and Windows Explorer. (See Figure 1-1 and Figure 1-2.)

1. Click Start.
2. In the search box type **cmd**
3. Press Enter. (This will open a command prompt.)
4. Type **dir**
5. Press Enter. (This will show a listing of the files and directories.)
6. Type **time**
7. Press Enter twice. (This will display the current time and provide a timestamp for your project.)
8. Take a screenshot. (See Figure 1-1.)

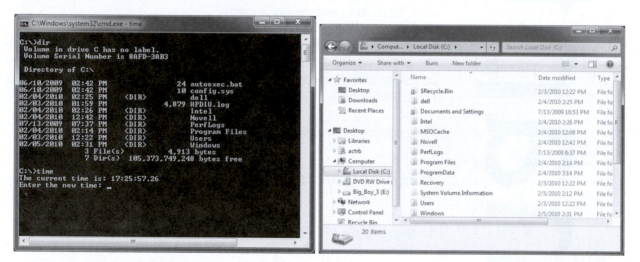

Figure 1-1: Contents of C:\ in a DOS prompt.   Figure 1-2: Contents of C:\ in Windows Explorer.

9. Type **dir /?**
10. Press Enter. (This will show the help listing for the **dir** command.)
11. Type **dir /w**
12. Press Enter. (This will show a listing of the directories and files with no other information.)
13. Type **dir /ad**
14. Press Enter. (This will show a listing of just directories. See Figure 1-3.)
15. Type **time**
16. Press Enter twice. (This will add a timestamp.)
17. Take a screenshot.

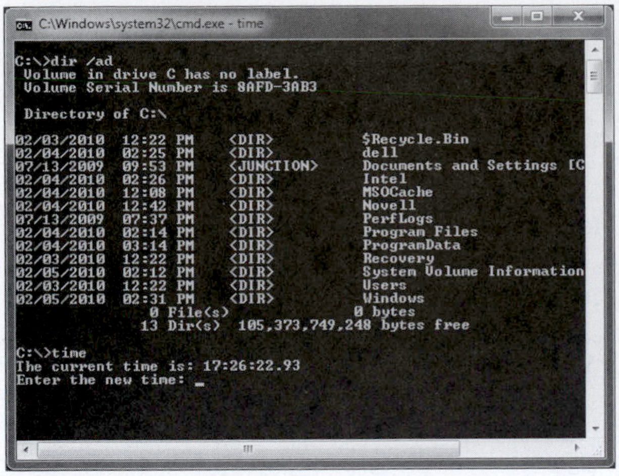

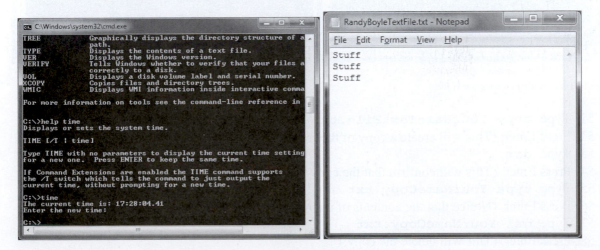

Figure 1-3: Output from the dir /ad command. 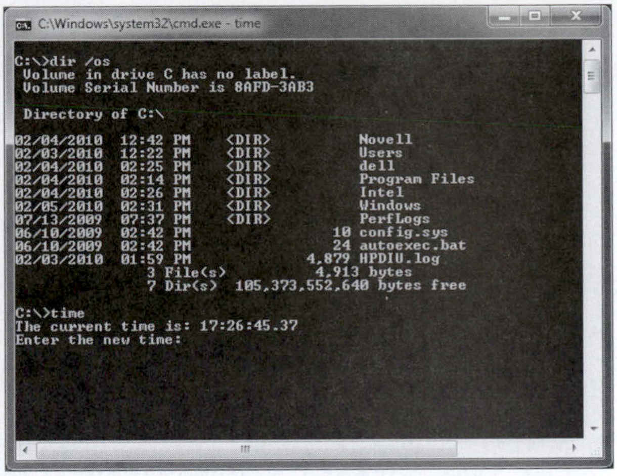   Figure 1-4: Output from the dir /os command.

18. Type **dir /oe**
19. Press Enter. (This will sort by file type.)
20. Type **dir /o-s**
21. Press Enter. (This will sort by file size, largest first.)
22. Type **dir /os**
23. Press Enter. (This will sort by file size, smallest first. See Figure 1-4.)
24. Type **time**
25. Press Enter twice. (This will add a timestamp.)
26. Take a screenshot.
27. Type **help**
28. Press Enter. (This will get a listing of DOS commands.)
29. Type **help time**
30. Press Enter. (To see the help for the **time** command.)
31. Type **time**
32. Press Enter twice. (This will add a timestamp.)
33. Take a screenshot. (See Figure 1-5.)

Figure 1-5: Output from the help command.   Figure 1-6: Editing a text file.

34. Type **cls**
35. Press Enter. (This will clear the screen.)

In the next command, you will replace YourName with your first name and last name. The screenshots will show RandyBoyle (the author's name). Many examples throughout this book will use the YourName example; any time you see YourName, please type your first and last name as a combined word.

36. Type `mkdir YourName`
37. Press Enter. (This will create a directory [folder] labeled YourName.)
38. Type `cd YourName`
39. Press Enter. (This will change to the newly created directory. It should be C:\YourName\ if you entered the command when you were at C:\. If you were not at C:\, then you can use the "`cd..`" command to keep moving up one directory. You will eventually get to C:\.)
40. Type `dir`
41. Press Enter.
42. Type `notepad YourNameTextFile.txt`
43. Press Enter. (This will create a new text file and open it for editing.)
44. Type the word "Stuff" into the newly opened text file and press Enter three times.
45. Take a screenshot. (See Figure 1-6.)
46. Press Alt-F-S.
47. Press Alt-F-X.
48. Type `dir`
49. Press Enter. (The newly created file YourNameTextFile.txt should be showing.)
50. Take a screenshot. (See Figure 1-7.)

Figure 1-7: Output after creating a text file.   Figure 1-8: Copying and deleting a text file.

51. Type `copy YourNameTextFile.txt YourNameCopy.txt`
52. Press Enter. (This will create a copy of the text file.)
53. Type `dir`
54. Press Enter. (This will confirm that the copy was successful.)
55. Type `type YourNameCopy.txt`
56. Press Enter. (Notice that the contents of the newly copied file match the original file.)
57. Type `del YourNameCopy.txt`
58. Press Enter. (This will delete the copy.)
59. Type `dir`
60. Press Enter. (This will confirm the deletion.)
61. Take a screenshot. (See Figure 1-8.)

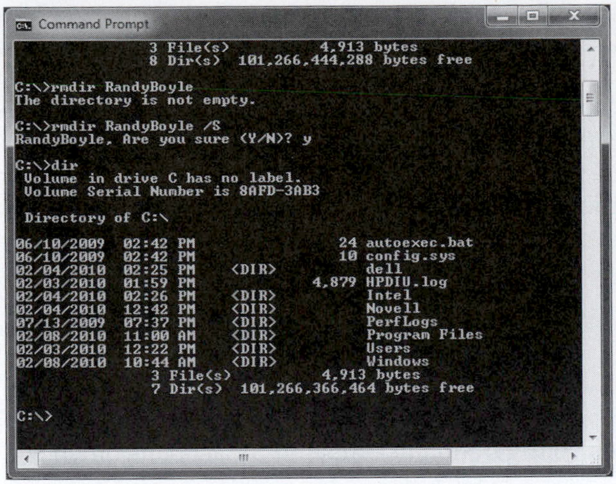

Figure 1-9: Deleting a directory.

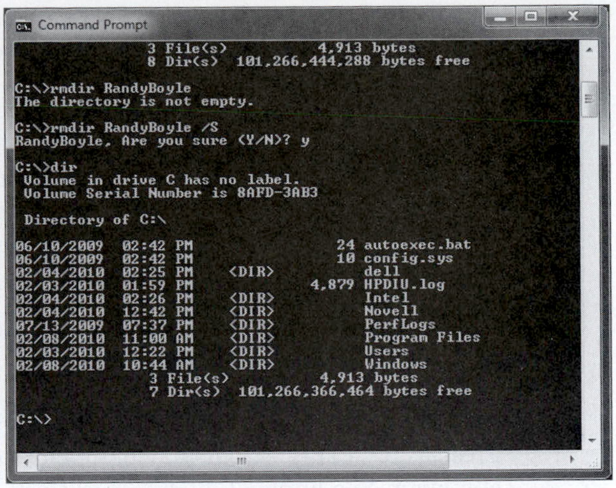

Figure 1-10: Selecting a previously used command.

62. Type **cd ..**
63. Press Enter. (This will move back one level to C:\.)
64. Type **dir**
65. Press Enter. (This will confirm you are at C:\.)
66. Type **rmdir YourName**
67. Press Enter. (This will try to delete the directory labeled YourName but fail to do so.)
68. Type **rmdir YourName /S**
69. Press Enter. (This will force the deletion of the directory labeled YourName.)
70. Type **Y**
71. Press Enter.
72. Type **dir**
73. Take a screenshot. (See Figure 1-9.)
74. Press F7. (You can also keep pressing the up arrow key.)
75. Arrow up until you get to the command labeled **mkdir YourName**
76. Take a screenshot. (See Figure 1-10.)
77. Press Enter.

PROJECT QUESTIONS

1. What was the creation date of your Windows directory?
2. What was the largest file in that directory?
3. What was the smallest file in that directory?
4. What was the complete command used to delete your directory?

THOUGHT QUESTIONS

1. Can you use the DIR command to show only executables? How?
2. What happens if you start typing part of an existing file name and then press the Tab key?
3. Can you start programs from the command prompt? How?
4. What happens if you drag-and-drop a file from Windows Explorer onto the DOS window?

1.2　IPCONFIG

This command will give you a listing of your basic IP information for the computer you are using. You will get your IP address, subnet mask, and default gateway (the computer that connects you to the Internet). You will use your IP address for scanning, remote administration, testing, and so forth. Ipconfig will also allow you to manage your DNS resolver cache and renew your IP address with the DHCP server.

1. Click Start.
2. In the search box type `cmd`
3. Press Enter.
4. Type `ipconfig`
5. Press Enter. (This will display basic network configuration information for adapters on your computer. See Figure 1-11.)
6. Type `ipconfig /all`
7. Press Enter. (This will display extended network configuration information for all adapters on your computer.)
8. Take a screenshot. (You can press Alt-PrtScn for the current window or Ctrl-PrtScn for the entire computer screen. See Figure 1-12.)

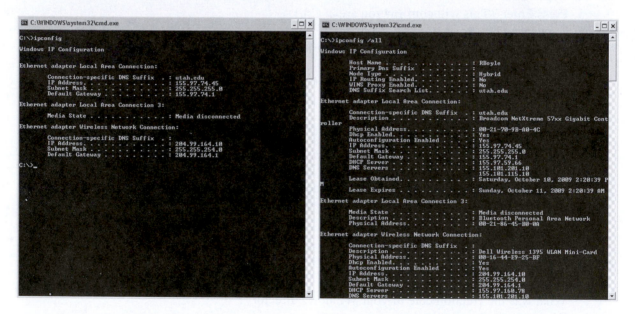

Figure 1-11: Output from the ipconfig command.　　　　Figure 1-12: Output from the ipconfig /all command.

In the second command, you used the `/all` option to get more information about each adapter. Note that this computer has three ways of connecting to different networks. There is a regular NIC to connect to the LAN, a wireless card, and a Bluetooth adapter. You now know the following about this LAN card:

The IP address for this computer is: `155.97.75.45`

The MAC address for this computer is: `00-21-70-9B-A0-4C`

The computer that connects to the Internet (Default Gateway) is: `155.97.74.1`

9. Type `ipconfig /flushdns`

10. Press Enter. (This will flush all DNS entries.)
11. Type **ping www.google.com**
12. Press Enter.
13. Type **ipconfig /displaydns**
14. Press Enter. (See Figure 1-13.)
15. Scroll down until you see the entry for www.Google.com.
16. Take a screenshot. (See Figure 1-14.)

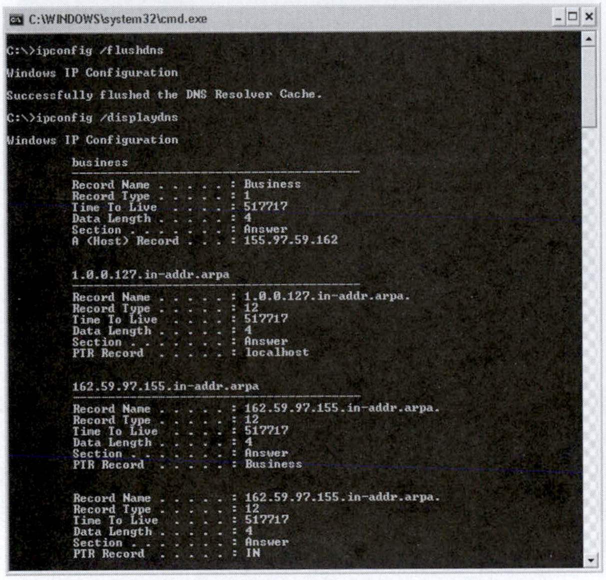

Figure 1-13: Output from the displaydns command.

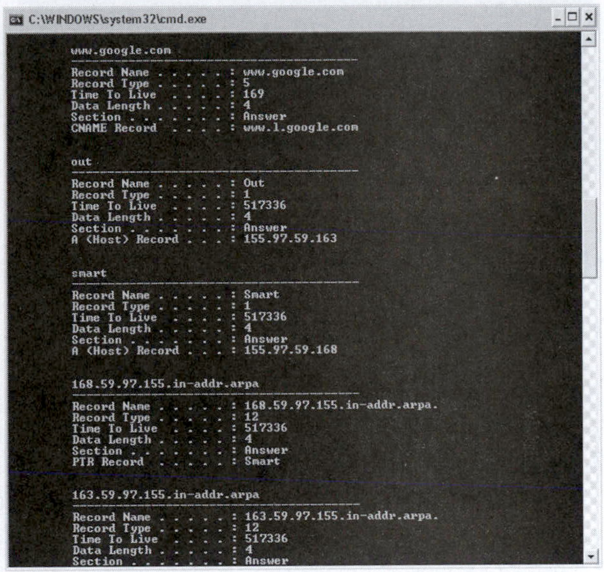

Figure 1-14: Output showing the entry for www.Google.com.

17. Type **ipconfig /all**
18. Press Enter.
19. Take a screenshot. (See Figure 1-15.)
20. Type **ipconfig /renew**
21. Press Enter. (This will renew all network adapters on your computer.)
22. Type **ipconfig /all**
23. Press Enter.
24. Take a screenshot. (See Figure 1-16.)

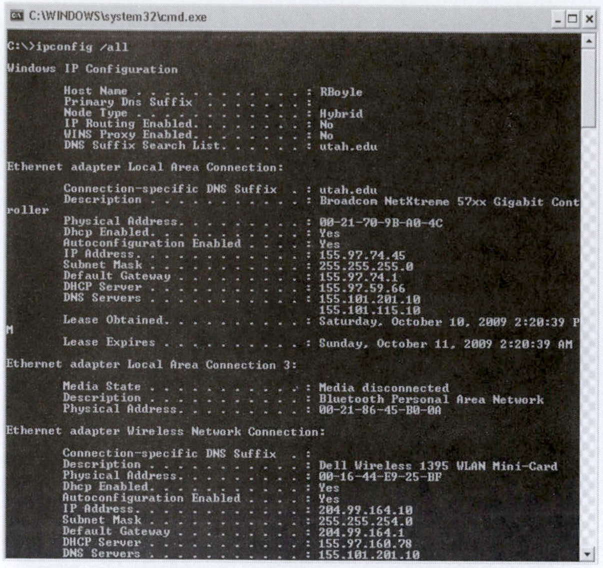

Figure 1-15: Showing lease time before renewal.

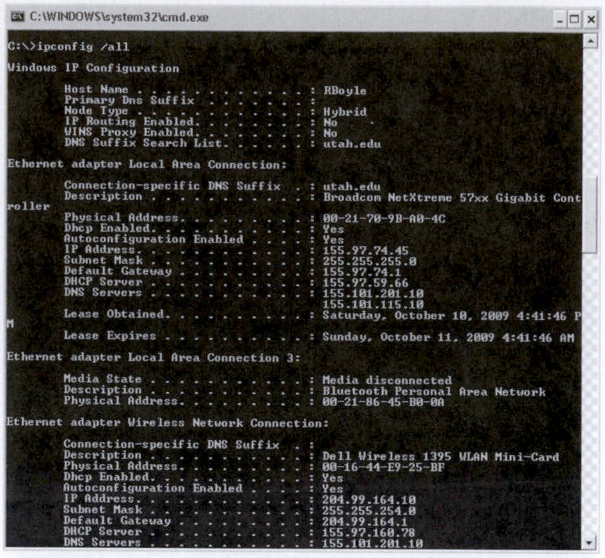

Figure 1-16: Showing lease time after renewal.

The DHCP server loaned you an IP address for a given amount of time. (In this case it was one day.) By renewing your IP address, you can reserve this same IP address for a longer amount of time. The information provided by the ipconfig command will come in handy when you do the rest of the projects. If you want a listing of all the possible options available for a given DOS command (ipconfig), you can just type the name of the command followed by a question mark.

25. Type **ipconfig /?**
26. Type **time**
27. Press Enter twice.
28. Take a screenshot. (See Figure 1-17.)

Figure 1-17: Displaying help for ipconfig.

PROJECT QUESTIONS

1. What was your IP address?
2. What was your MAC address?
3. What was the IP address of your default gateway?
4. What was your subnet mask?

THOUGHT QUESTIONS

1. What is the practical difference between an IP address and a physical (MAC) address?
2. What is the Default Gateway?
3. What do DNS servers do?
4. What is a subnet mask?

1.3   PING

Ping is a command that will tell you if a host is reachable and alive. It works just like pings in submarines (think back to the movie *The Hunt for Red October*). It sends out a packet that asks the target computer to send it back a message saying it's actually there. It also tells you how long it took to get back and if any of the packets were lost. This is very useful if you need to see whether a server/computer is running. You can also diagnose latency and/or packet loss issues.

This example pings www.utah.edu repeatedly. Feel free to ping your own university or website of your choice. Instead of using "www.utah.edu", please use "www.YourUniversity.edu." Timestamps will also be included at the end of each example.

1. Click Start.
2. In the search box type `cmd`
3. Press Enter.
4. Type `ping www.utah.edu`
5. Press Enter. (This will ping www.utah.edu with four packets.)
6. Type `time`
7. Press Enter twice.
8. Take a screenshot. (See Figure 1-18.)

Figure 1-18: Output from ping command.   Figure 1-19: Output from the ping -t command.

9. Type **ping www.utah.edu -t**
10. Press Enter.
11. Press Ctrl-Break after about 5 replies.
12. Press Ctrl-Break again after about 5 replies.
13. Press Ctrl-C to stop sending packets.
14. Type **time**
15. Press Enter twice.
16. Take a screenshot. (See Figure 1-19.)
17. Type **cls**
18. Press Enter. (This clears the screen.)
19. Type **ping www.utah.edu –n 6**
20. Press Enter.

Note: The following command uses the lowercase of the letter "L," not the number one (1). The characters look similar (**l vs 1**), but you will need to use the lowercase letter "l" in the following command.

21. Type **ping www.utah.edu –l 50**
22. Press Enter.
23. Type **time**
24. Press Enter twice.
25. Take a screenshot. (See Figure 1-20.)

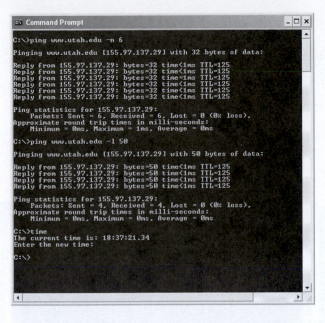

Figure 1-20: Output from the ping -n command.

PROJECT QUESTIONS

1. Which hostname did you ping?
2. What was the IP address of the hostname you pinged?
3. How long did one of your pings take?
4. What was the TTL value?

THOUGHT QUESTIONS

1. Can you adjust the number of packets that are sent? How?
2. What did the -t, -n, and -l, options do?
3. Why would you experience packet loss?
4. Why would you want to send larger packets?

1.4   TRACERT

Trace route (tracert in Windows and traceroute in Linux) is a command that allows you to see every computer (including routers) between your computer and a target host of your choosing. You can type in the name of the computer (e.g. www.utah.edu) or the IP address of the computer (155.97.137.29). Tracert can be used to diagnose routing problems, latency issues, or network bottlenecks. Pathping combines the statistics from ping and the route tracing function from tracert.

Tracert can also provide you with information about the route packets that are taking over a network. It can be surprising how many hops there are between you and a website that you visit. Oftentimes, the route a packet takes is not the shortest geographical distance. This example uses www.utah.edu repeatedly. Feel free to use the hostname of your own university or any other website. Instead of using "www.utah.edu", please use "www.YourUniversity.edu."

1. Click Start.
2. In the search box type `cmd`

3. Press Enter.
4. Type **tracert www.utah.edu**
5. Press Enter. (This will list every computer on the route between your computer and www.utah.edu.)
6. Type **tracert www.google.com**
7. Press Enter. (This will list every computer on the route between your computer and www.Google.com.)
8. Type **time**
9. Press Enter twice.
10. Take a screenshot. (See Figure 1-21.)

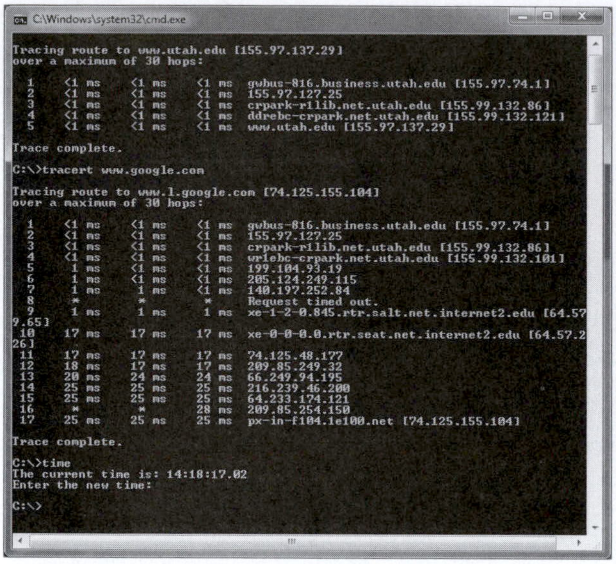

Figure 1-21: Output from tracert command.

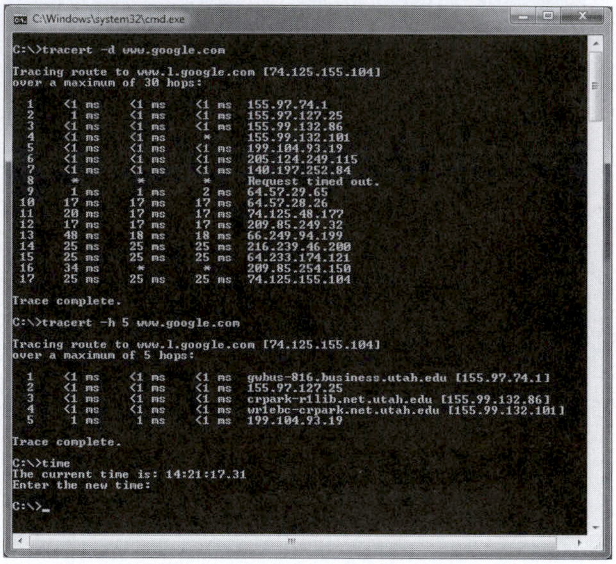

Figure 1-22: Output from tracert -d and tracert -h commands.

11. Type **tracert -d www.google.com**
12. Press Enter.
13. Type **tracert -h 5 www.google.com**
14. Press Enter.
15. Type **time**
16. Press Enter twice.
17. Take a screenshot. (See Figure 1-22.)
18. Type **pathping -q 5 -w 5 www.utah.edu**
19. Press Enter.
20. Type **time**
21. Press Enter twice.
22. Take a screenshot. (See Figure 1-23.)
23. Type **pathping -q 5 -w 5 www.google.com**
24. Press Enter.
25. Type **time**
26. Press Enter twice.
27. Take a screenshot. (See Figure 1-24.)

Figure 1-23: Output from pathping -q -w command.

Figure 1-24: Output from pathping -q -w command to Google.com.

At the time the route was traced, there were 14 computers or routers between this host and www.Google.com. None of the nodes along the way timed out and most of the packets took less than 50 ms (milliseconds) to come back.

PROJECT QUESTIONS

1. How many entries were between you and www.Utah.edu?
2. How many entries were between you and www.Google.com?
3. What was the IP address of the computer after yours?
4. How long did pathping gather statistics?

THOUGHT QUESTIONS

1. Why would you use the -d option?
2. If you had several nodes "time out," how would the -w option help?
3. Why would a network administrator only want to see part of the route?
4. How would the pathping results change if you didn't use -q 5 in the command?

1.5   NETSTAT

Netstat is the command that lists all current network connections, connection statistics, and routing tables on your computer. The default netstat command will give you a listing of all the ports open on your computer as well as the foreign address of the computer you're connected to.

Ports are like doors on your house. Information packets are addressed to a specific IP address (or location) and port number (or point of entry). Your house works the same way. It has an address (location) and door (point of entry) where packages are delivered. Netstat can tell you which programs are sending/receiving information to/from your computer.

1. Click Start.
2. In the search box type **cmd**

3. Press Enter.
4. Type **netstat**
5. Press Enter.
6. Type **time**
7. Press Enter twice.
8. Take a screenshot. (See Figure 1-25.)

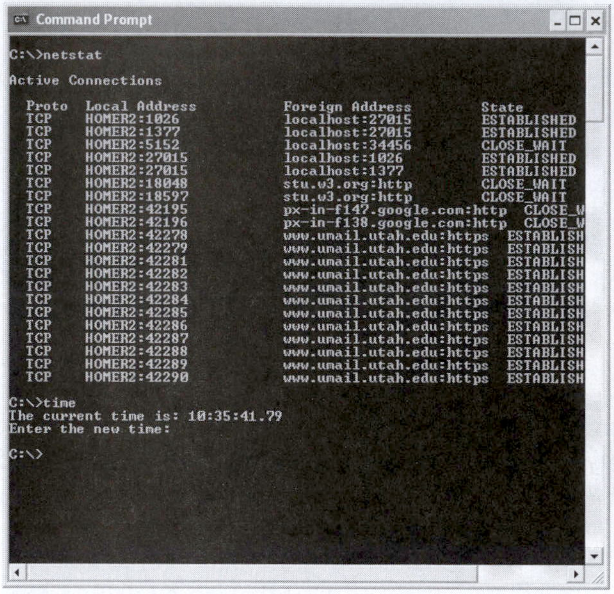

Figure 1-25: Output from netstat command.

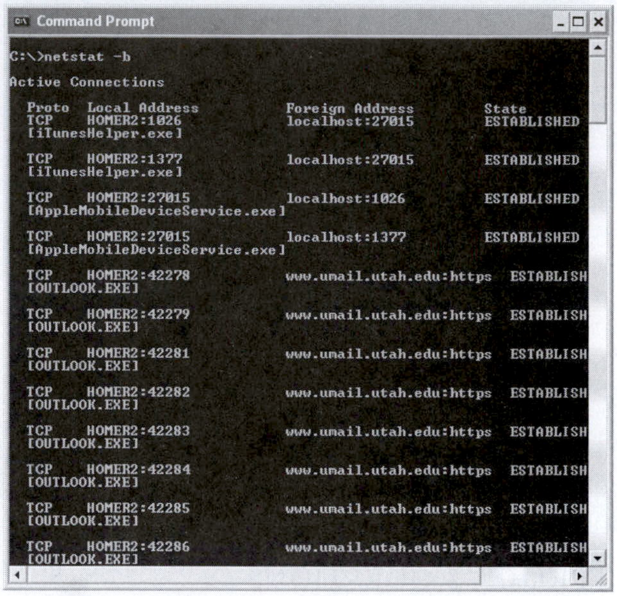

Figure 1-26: Output from netstat -b command.

In this example, you can see multiple ports open with the www.umail.utah.edu:https server (Microsoft Outlook® is open). The only problem is that you don't know which program is opening all of those ports. You can use the -b option to get information about which program is opening each port.

The -a option will show all of the ports (including UDP ports) that may be open on your machine. The -n option will show the local and foreign addresses for each connection. The -e option will display statistics about the number of packets sent/received, errors, and packets that were discarded.

9. Type **cls**
10. Press Enter.
11. Type **netstat -b**
12. Press Enter.
13. Take a screenshot. (See Figure 1-26.)
14. Type **netstat -a**
15. Press Enter.
16. Take a screenshot. (See Figure 1-27.)

In the screenshot above, you can see that Outlook.exe is opening a lot of ports to send/receive email. Using the -b option, you can find out if a rogue program is opening a port. This is useful when you want to identify programs that are sending/receiving information. You don't want rogue programs sending/receiving information.

17. Type **cls**
18. Press Enter.

19. Type **netstat -n**
20. Press Enter.
21. Take a screenshot.
22. Type **netstat -e**
23. Press Enter.
24. Take a screenshot. (See Figure 1-28.)

Using the -n option, you can see which external computers are connected to your computer and which port(s) they are using. Knowing which foreign address your computer is connecting to can be helpful if you want to be sure where your data is going to or coming from. The -e option is a quick way to tell if you are sending/receiving packets and if you are getting a large number of errors. This will help you identify a bad network card, cable, or configuration issue.

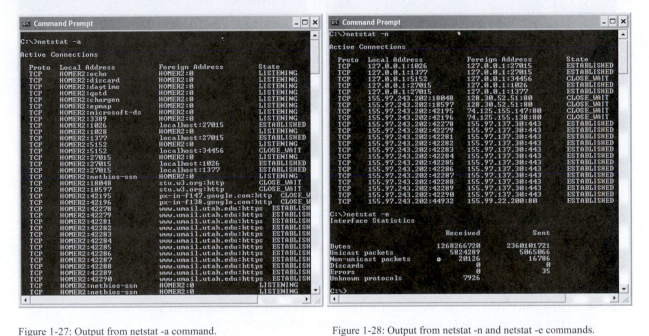

Figure 1-27: Output from netstat -a command.   Figure 1-28: Output from netstat -n and netstat -e commands.

25. Type **cls**
26. Press Enter.
27. Type **netstat -e 5**
28. Press Enter.
29. Let it run for about 15 seconds.
30. Press Ctrl-C to stop sending packets.
31. Type **time**
32. Press Enter twice.
33. Take a screenshot. (See Figure 1-29.)
34. Type **netstat -s**
35. Press Enter.
36. Take a screenshot. (See Figure 1-30.)

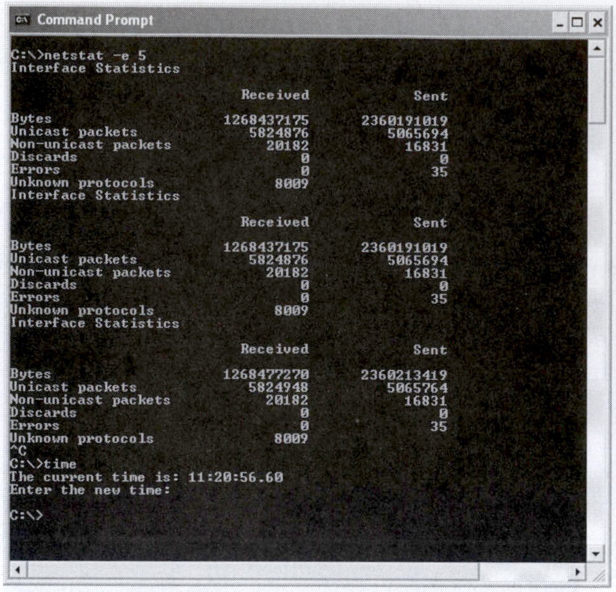

Figure 1-29: Output from netstat -e command.

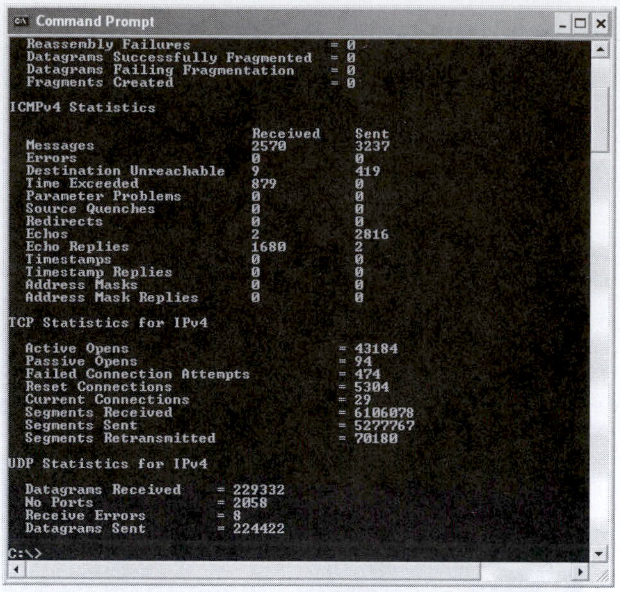

Figure 1-30: Output from netstat -s command.

PROJECT QUESTIONS

1. What was the first local port listed when you entered `netstat`?
2. Approximately how many active TCP connections did you have?
3. Approximately how many bytes had you sent (hint: `netstat -e`)?
4. Did you have any Echo Replies? How many?

THOUGHT QUESTIONS

1. How can netstat help you track the information coming in and out of your computer?
2. How can netstat help you diagnose network problems?
3. How would the routing table (`netstat -r`) be useful?
4. Why would someone need different statistics for IP, IPv6, ICMP, TCP, UDP, etc.?

1.6   NSLOOKUP

Nslookup is a command that will give you all of the IP addresses that are associated with a given domain name from the local DNS server (like an Internet phone book). For example, if you wanted to find the IP addresses of www.CNN.com, you could use nslookup to identify them. Nslookup is also useful for solving DNS problems.

There are two modes for using nslookup -- non-interactive and interactive. You will use the non-interactive mode for this exercise and can learn more about the interactive mode here: http://support.microsoft.com/kb/200525.

1. Click Start.
2. In the search box type **cmd**
3. Press Enter.
4. Type **nslookup www.utah.edu**
5. Press Enter. (You can substitute www.Utah.edu for your school's hostname.)

6. Type **nslookup www.cnn.com**
7. Press Enter.
8. Type **nslookup www.google.com**
9. Press Enter.
10. Type **time**
11. Press Enter twice.
12. Take a screenshot. (See Figure 1-31.)

Figure 1-31: Output from nslookup command.

PROJECT QUESTIONS

1. What was the IP address for www.Utah.edu?
2. What did the various IP addresses for www.CNN.com have in common?
3. What was the IP address listed for www.Google.com?
4. What was the alias for www.Google.com?

THOUGHT QUESTIONS

1. Why are there multiple IP addresses associated with a single domain name (e.g., www.CNN.com and www.Google.com)?
2. Why did Nslookup query fiber1.utah.edu instead of querying www.CNN.com directly?
3. Why does www.Google.com use an alias?
4. How do domain names and IP addresses get registered?

1.7 FTP

File Transfer Protocol (FTP) is a way to transfer files from one computer to another. While it may be a little more convenient to use a modern FTP client, it's still valuable to learn command-line FTP. Some systems/servers use a command-line interface exclusively. This makes FTP an important skill to have in your repertoire.

FTP has both interactive and non-interactive modes. You will look at the differences between the two in this exercise. In this project, you will download some images from NASA. Some of the file names and/or directories on the NASA FTP server may change over time. You can download any images from any of the directories to complete this project. The important part is to learn how to use command-line FTP.

First, you are going to make a folder on C:\ to store the images. Then you will FTP into the server and practice transferring images to your local machine.

1. Click Start.
2. In the search box type **cmd**
3. Press Enter.
4. Type **cd ..**
5. Press Enter. (Repeat **cd ..** command multiple times until you get to C:\.)
6. Type **mkdir images**
7. Press Enter.
8. Type **time**
9. Press Enter twice.
10. Type **ftp nssdcftp.gsfc.nasa.gov**
11. Press Enter.
12. Type **anonymous**
13. Press Enter.
14. Press Enter again.
15. Type **ls**
16. Press Enter. (See Figure 1-32.)

Note: If you get a popup message about your Windows Firewall, you can click Allow Access.

17. Type **cd photo_gallery**
18. Press Enter. (See Figure 1-33.)

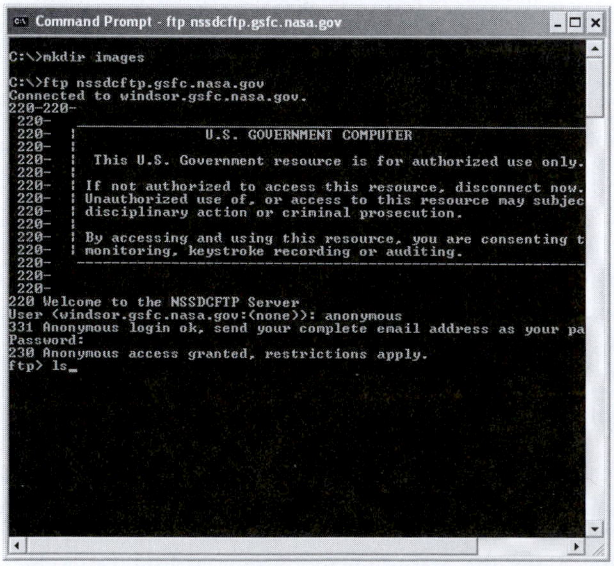

Figure 1-32: Accessing a FTP server.

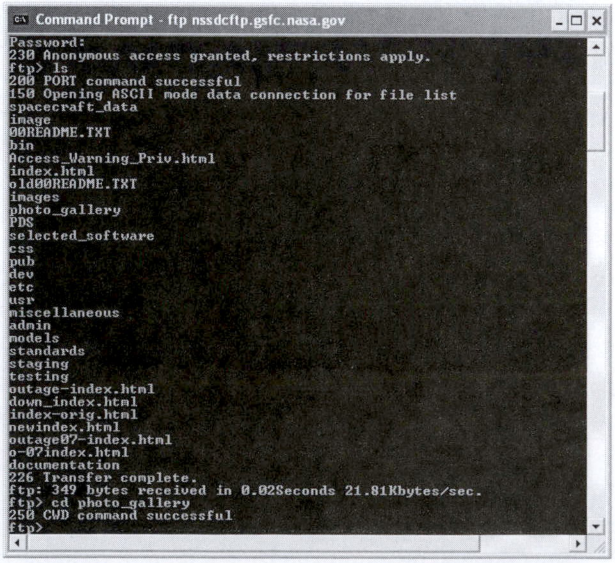

Figure 1-33: Listing directories on FTP server.

19. Type **ls**
20. Press Enter.

21. Type **cd image**
22. Press Enter.
23. Type **ls**
24. Press Enter.
25. Type **cd astro**
26. Press Enter.
27. Type **ls**
28. Press Enter. (See Figure 1-34.)
29. Type **binary**
30. Press Enter.
31. Type **lcd C:\images**
32. Press Enter.
33. Type **get hst_crab_nebula.jpg**
34. Press Enter. (You can get any image you want.)
35. Type **status**
36. Press Enter.
37. Take a screenshot. (See Figure 1-35.)

Figure 1-34: Listing files on FTP server.　　　　Figure 1-35: Transferring file from FTP server.

38. Type **quit**
39. Press Enter.
40. Type **cd images**
41. Press Enter.
42. Type **dir**
43. Press Enter.
44. Type **hst_crab_nebula.jpg**
45. Press Enter. (See Figure 1-36.)
46. Take a screenshot of the Crab Nebula image. (See Figure 1-37.)

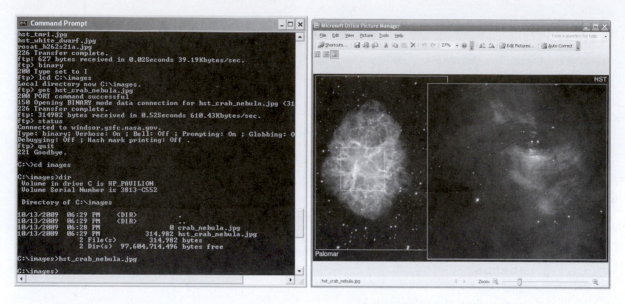

Figure 1-36: Quitting the FTP server.   Figure 1-37: Image downloaded from FTP server.

47. Return to the DOS prompt.
48. Type `time`
49. Press Enter twice.
50. Press the up arrow key until you get to the following command:

    `ftp nssdcftp.gsfc.nasa.gov`

51. Press Enter.
52. Type `anonymous`
53. Press Enter.
54. Press Enter again.
55. Take a screenshot.
56. Type `ls`
57. Press Enter.
58. Type `cd photo_gallery/image/astro`
59. Press Enter.
60. Type `ls`
61. Press Enter.
62. Type `binary`
63. Press Enter.
64. Type `prompt`
65. Press Enter. (See Figure 1-38.)
66. Type `mget *`
67. Press Enter.
68. Take a screenshot. (See Figure 1-39.)

Figure 1-38: Transferring entire directory from FTP server.

Figure 1-39: Files transferred.

69. Type **prompt**
70. Press Enter.
71. Type **quit**
72. Press Enter.
73. Type **dir**
74. Press Enter.
75. Type **time**
76. Press Enter twice.
77. Take a screenshot. (See Figure 1-40.)
78. Type **hst_pillars_m16.jpg**
79. Press Enter.
80. Take a screenshot. (See Figure 1-41.)

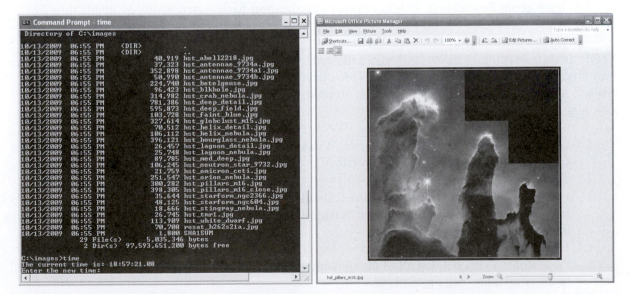

Figure 1-40: Displaying downloaded files on local host.

Figure 1-41: Downloaded image.

PROJECT QUESTIONS

1. How big was the hst_pillars_m16.jpg file?
2. Approximately how long did it take to transfer the image?
3. What was your username?
4. What was the name of the directory in which you stored the image?

THOUGHT QUESTIONS

1. What would have happened if you had run the `mget *` command in interactive mode (i.e., without entering "prompt" first)?
2. Is transferring files with FTP faster than using HTTP?
3. What effect did the `binary` command have on the file transfer? Was it necessary?
4. Why did you use the `lcd` command?

1.8 POWERSHELL®

This project will provide you with a quick introduction to Windows PowerShell®. PowerShell is a command-line interface similar to DOS but with expanded functionality. You can use all of the DOS commands (`dir`, `cd`, `ipconfig`, etc.), many Linux/Unix commands (`ls`, `cd`, `ifconfig`, etc.), and new cmdlets (pronounced command-lets). In fact, DOS and Linux/Unix commands are actually aliases for cmdlets. You will see an example of how to do this using just one of over 100+ cmdlets.

One of the key distinctions between DOS and PowerShell is that DOS is text-based, whereas PowerShell uses cmdlets as objects. Using cmdlets, you can direct output from one object to another object. You will see how to do this later in this project. Powershell also provides .NET integration and a custom scripting environment. You can create your own custom cmdlets.

Powershell provides extensive help documentation via the Get-Help cmdlet. You will learn how to use the help pages (similar to man pages in Linux/Unix) to perform a variety of tasks. You will see that there is much to learn about PowerShell. This is a primer into the most basic functionality available through PowerShell.

STOP: If you are using Windows XP, you will need to download and install PowerShell before you can start this project. Instructions on how to download and install PowerShell are given at the end of this project. After installing PowerShell, you can proceed. If you have Windows 7, you don't have to install anything.

1. Click Start, All Programs, Accessories, Windows PowerShell, and Windows PowerShell. (You can also press ⊞+r and enter "powershell".)
2. Type `cd C:\images`
3. Press Enter. (This will take you to the C:\images\ directory you created earlier in the FTP project. If you don't have a directory labeled "images," you can create one and put a copy of any text file in the directory.)
4. Type `dir`
5. Press Enter. (This will list all of the files and subdirectories. This is a Windows/DOS command listed as an alias. See Figure 1-42.)
6. Type `ls`
7. Press Enter. (This will list all of the files and subdirectories. This is a Linux/Unix command listed as an alias for the Get-ChildItem cmdlet.)

8. Type `gci`
9. Press Enter. (This will list all of the files and subdirectories. This is a PowerShell alias for the Get-ChildItem cmdlet.)
10. Type `Get-ChildItem`
11. Press Enter. (This will list all of the files and subdirectories.)
12. Type `get-childitem`
13. Press Enter. (Note that cmdlets are NOT case-sensitive.)
14. Take a screenshot. (See Figure 1-43.)

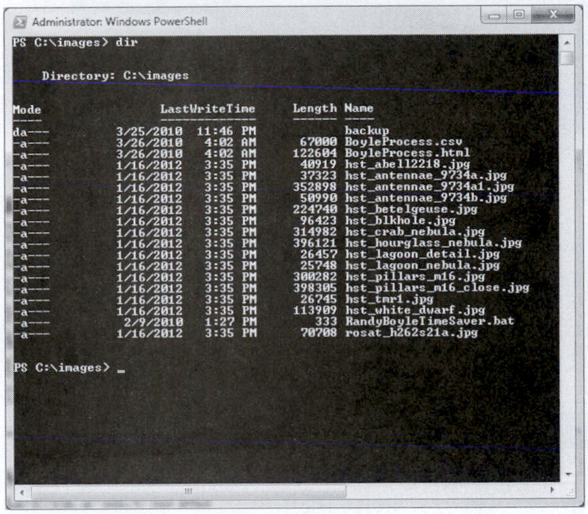

Figure 1-42: Directory listing in PowerShell.

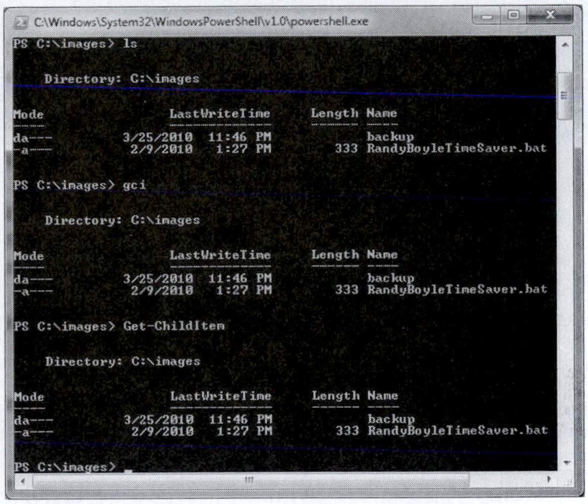

Figure 1-43: Aliases for Get-ChildItem.

Note: In PowerShell, the commands `dir`, `ls` and `gci` are all aliases for the Get-ChildItem cmdlet. They all returned the same results. Next, you will see all the aliases for the `dir` command and create your own alias. This alias will last until you end the current PowerShell session. You can make your new alias permanent. However, you won't be shown how to do that in this tutorial.

15. Type `Get-Alias dir`
16. Press Enter. (This will show that the dir command is an alias for the Get-ChildItem cmdlet.)
17. Type `Get-Alias –definition Get-ChildItem`
18. Press Enter. (This will get all of the aliases for the Get-ChildItem cmdlet.)
19. Type `Set-Alias YourNameList Get-ChildItem`
20. Press Enter. (This will create a custom alias called "YourNameList" for the Get-ChildItem cmdlet. This alias will only last until you close the PowerShell window. In this case, the alias was RandyBoyleList. See Figure 1-44.)
21. Type `YourNameList`
22. Press Enter. (This will list all of the files and subdirectories using your custom alias. In this case, it was RandyBoyleList.)
23. Take a screenshot. (See Figure 1-45.)

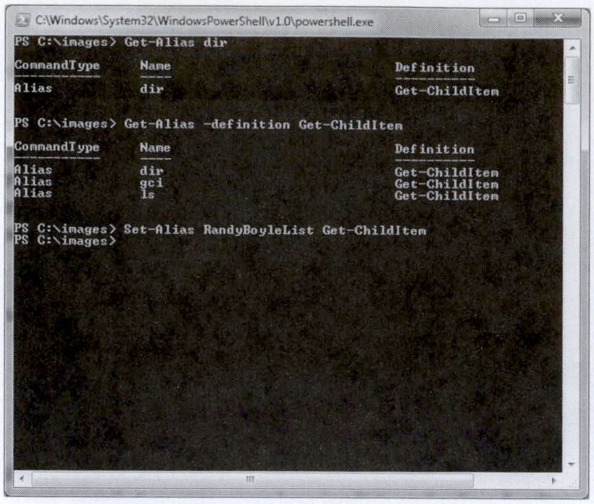

Figure 1-44: Listing aliases for Get-ChildItem.

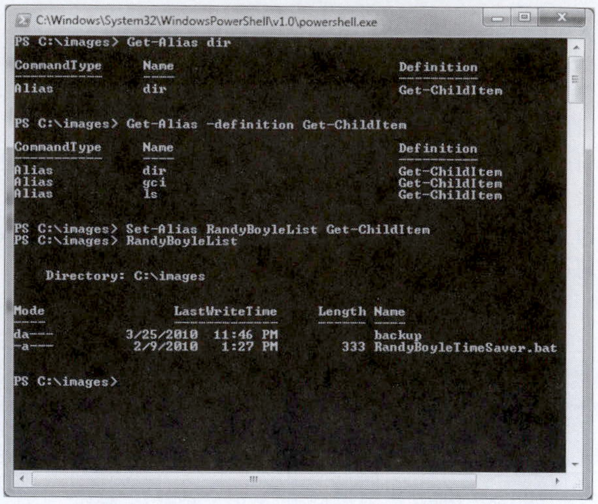

Figure 1-45: Creating a custom alias.

Note: Below is Table 1-1, showing a few of the aliases from DOS/Windows, Linux/Unix, and PowerShell. You will learn more about the Linux/Unix commands in a later project. You can use the Get-Alias cmdlet to get aliases for individual commands.

DOS, Windows	Linux, Unix, Mac	PowerShell - Cmdlet	PowerShell - Aliases
Dir	ls	Get-ChildItem	dir, ls, gci
Help	Man	Get-Help	help, man
tasklist	ps	Get-Process	ps, gps

Table 1-1: Aliases for cmdlets in PowerShell.

In the next part of this project, you are going to explore the Get-Help cmdlet. This will show you what each cmdlet can do and give you examples of how to use them. You will also learn how to list all PowerShell cmdlets and sort them by function.

PowerShell cmdlets are named using the "verb-noun" convention. In other words, *nouns* (Process, Help, ChildItem, etc.) are preceded by *verbs* (Get, Set, Stop, etc.). You will sort all PowerShell cmdlets by specific verbs or nouns to narrow your search. Later you will see how to list all the methods and functions associated with a cmdlet.

24. Type **Get-help Get-ChildItem**
25. Press Enter. (This will display the help file for the Get-ChildItem cmdlet. You can also use the help and man commands.)
26. Press the space bar to page through the help file.
27. Type **Get-help Get-ChildItem -examples**
28. Press Enter. (This will display examples for Get-ChildItem.)
29. Type **help dir –examples | more**
30. Press Enter. (This will also display examples for Get-ChildItem. This displays the same result as the previous command. The commands help and dir are aliases for Get-Help and Get-ChildItem respectively. See Figure 1-46.)

Note: The "| more" addition makes the output come page by page. That is NOT the lowercase letter "l" or the number 1. It is the vertical bar "|" (a.k.a., pipe). It may appear as "|" on your keyboard. Piping sends the results from one cmdlet to another cmdlet. You can press the space bar to page through to the end or press q to quit.)

31. Type **Get-Command**

32. Press Enter. (This will display a list of all of the cmdlets, aliases, and functions. There are a lot of cmdlets. That's why it's called PowerShell. You can use "| more" if you want to page through the entire list.)

33. Type **Get-Command –verb Get**

34. Press Enter. (This will display a list of all of the cmdlets starting with "Get.")

35. Type **Get-Command –verb Set**

36. Press Enter. (This will display a list of all of the cmdlets starting with "Set.")

37. Type **Get-Command –noun Process**

38. Press Enter. (This will display a list of all of the cmdlets ending with "Process.")

39. Type **Get-Command –noun Service**

40. Press Enter. (This will display a list of all of the cmdlets ending with "Service.")

41. Type **Get-Date**

42. Press Enter. (This will display the date and time.)

43. Take a screenshot. (See Figure 1-47.)

Figure 1-46: Contents of a help file.   Figure 1-47: Listing of Process and Service cmdlets.

Note: In the next part of this project, you will look more closely at one cmdlet (Get-Process). You will look at the methods and properties associated with this cmdlet (or object). You will pipe the output from one cmdlet to another cmdlet and then to an HTML document. The concept of "objects" can be confusing if you haven't done a lot of programming.

The following example may help. Think of an object (cmdlet) like an iPod®. Your IPod has *properties* associated with it (e.g., color, size, capacity, etc.) and things it can do (e.g., play, stop, turn on, turn off, etc.). The things your IPod® can do are called *methods*. Output (e.g., music) from your IPod can be "piped" through other objects (e.g., your car, stereo, computer, etc.).

This modularity is advantageous because you can use a single IPod rather than having multiple players in your car, computer, etc. Piping output from cmdlets works the same way. Add custom scripting into the equation and you have a very powerful tool.

44. Type **Get-Process | Get-Member**

45. Press Enter. (This will display a listing of all of the properties and methods associated with the Get-Process cmdlet. The Get-Member cmdlet is helpful when you want to know what you can do with a specific cmdlet.)
46. Type `Get-Process | Get-Member –membertype method`
47. Press Enter. (This will display all of the methods associated with the Get-Process cmdlet. In other words, these are things the Get-Process object can do. See Figure 1-48.)
48. Type `Get-Process | Get-Member –membertype properties`
49. Press Enter. (This will display all of the properties associated with the Get-Process cmdlet. In other words, these are the attributes of the Get-Process object.)
50. Type `Get-Process | Get-Member –membertype AliasProperty`
51. Press Enter. (This will display all of the alias properties associated with the Get-Process cmdlet. In other words, these are the aliases for the properties.)
52. Take a screenshot. (See Figure 1-49.)

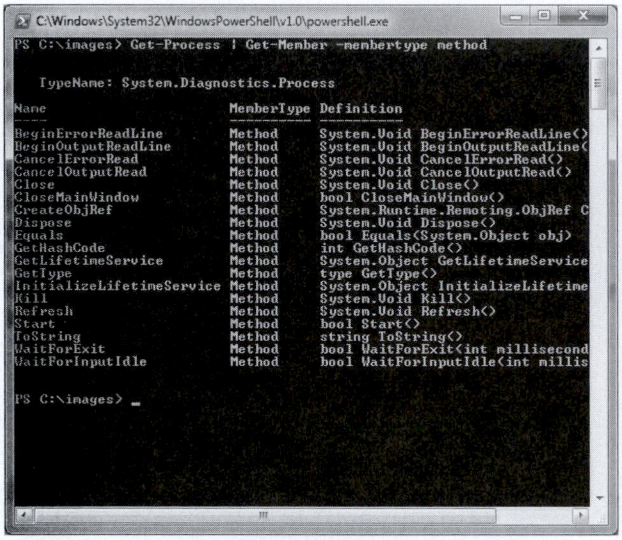

Figure 1-48: Listing of the methods associated with Get-Process.   Figure 1-49: Listing of the alias properties for Get-Process.

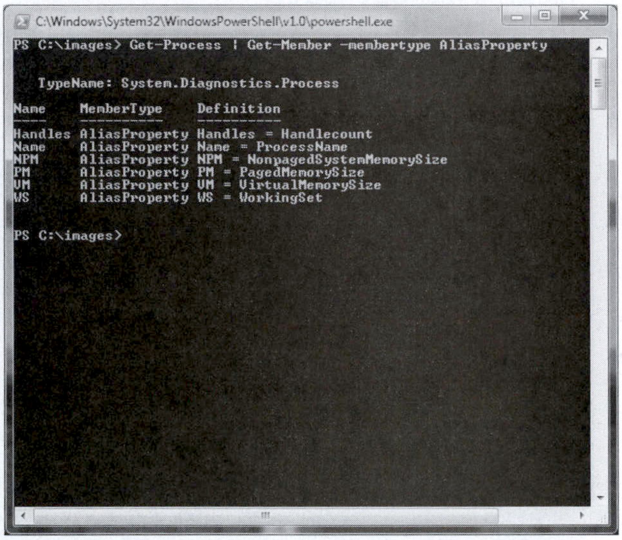

Note: In this part of the project, you will use the Get-Process cmdlet to list and sort all of the processes currently running on your computer. You will open the Windows Task Manager to see the GUI equivalent of Get-Process. You may realize that the Get-Process cmdlet offers a great deal more functionality than is available in Windows Task Manager.

53. Type `Get-Process`
54. Press Enter. (This will display all of the processes currently running on your computer. See Figure 1-50.)
55. Right-click the task bar.
56. Select Start Task Manager. (In Windows XP you will select Task Manager.)
57. Click on the Processes tab. (This will also display all processes running on your computer. See Figure 1-51.)

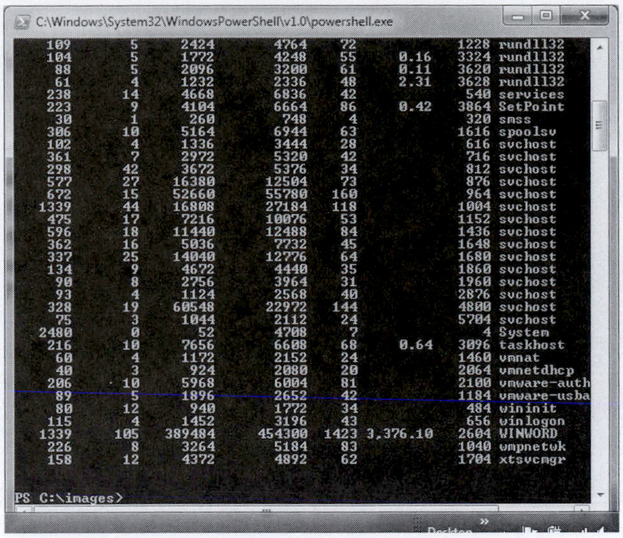

Figure 1-50: List of processes.

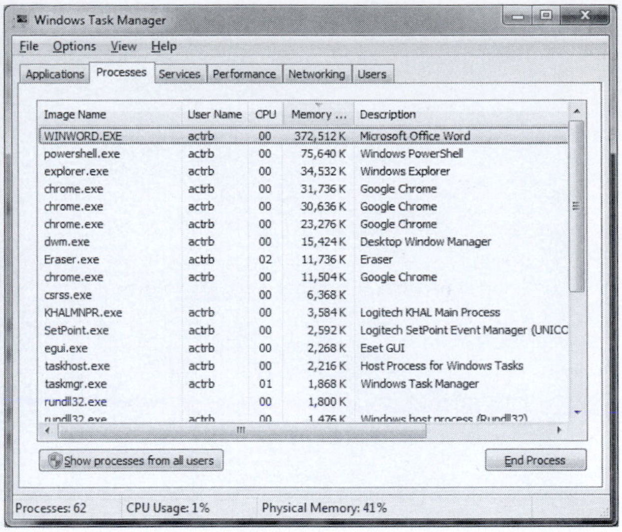

Figure 1-51: Running processes displayed in Windows Task Manager.

58. Return to your PowerShell window.

59. Type `Invoke-Item C:\windows\system32\notepad.exe`

60. Press Enter. (This will start Notepad.)

61. Type `Get-Process notepad -FileVersionInfo`

62. Press Enter. (This will display all of the information available about the notepad process. This is helpful in identifying a process you may not immediately recognize.)

63. Type `Get-Process | Group-Object Name`

64. Press Enter. (This will display processes grouped by name. Note that "Name" is listed as one of the alias properties for the Get-Process cmdlet. Also note that there were four Chrome processes grouped together in this example. Grouping and sorting are different. You will see the effects of sorting next. See Figure 1-52.)

65. Type `Get-Process | sort WS`

66. Press Enter. (This will sort the processes by the amount of memory [Working Set] they are using.)

67. Type `Get-Process | sort CPU`

68. Press Enter. (This will sort the processes by the amount of processor time they have used.)

69. Take a screenshot. (See Figure 1-53.)

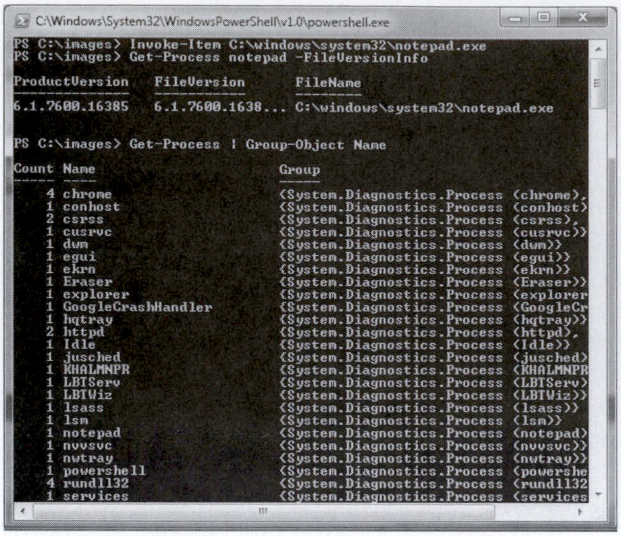

Figure 1-52: Grouping processes by process name.

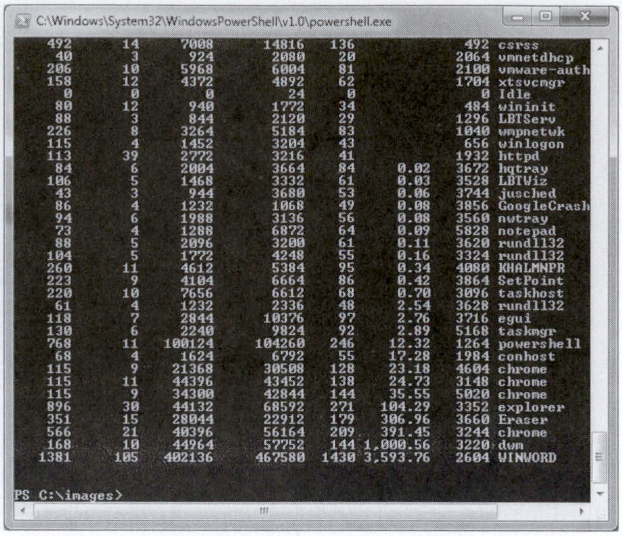

Figure 1-53: Sorting processes by CPU usage.

70. Type **Get-Process | ConvertTo-Html | out-file "LNameProcess.html"**
71. Press Enter. (This will convert a list of currently running processes to an HTML file. Replace LName with your last name. In this case, it was BoyleProcess.html.)
72. Type **Get-Process | ConvertTo-CSV | out-file "LNameProcess.csv"**
73. Press Enter. (This will convert a list of currently running processes to a CSV file. Replace LName with your last name. In this case, it was BoyleProcess.csv.)
74. Type **dir**
75. Press Enter. (This will confirm that the files were created. See Figure 1-54.)
76. Type **Invoke-Item LNameProcess.html**
77. Press Enter. (This will open the HTML file showing all of the currently running processes. Replace LName with your last name. In this case, it was BoyleProcess.html.)
78. Take a screenshot. (See Figure 1-55.)

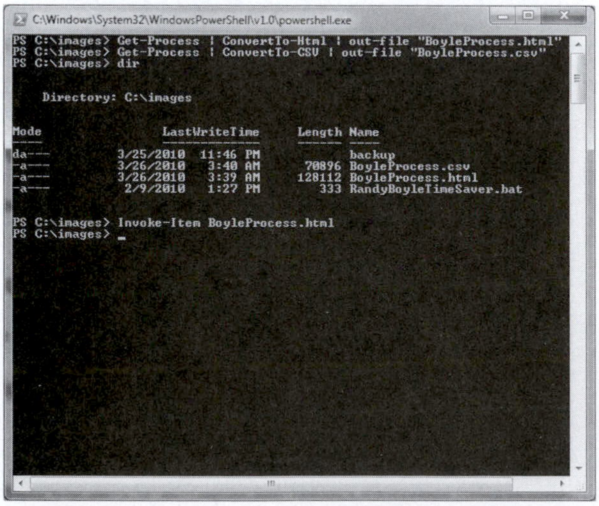

Figure 1-54: Piping process information to HTML and CSV files.

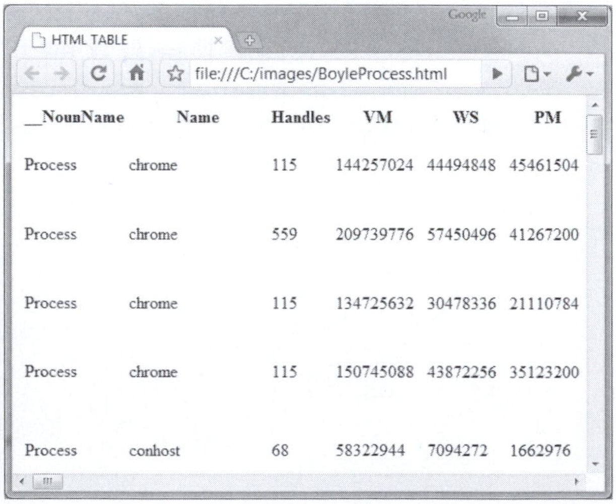

Figure 1-55: HTML page showing process information.

79. Type **Get-Process n***
80. Press Enter. (This will display all of the processes starting with the letter "n".)
81. Type **Stop-Process -name notepad**
82. Press Enter. (This will stop the notepad process.)
83. Type **Get-Process n***
84. Press Enter. (This will confirm that notepad was stopped. See Figure 1-56.)
85. Take a screenshot.
86. Type **Get-History**
87. Press Enter. (This will list a history of the most recent commands you entered.)
88. Take a screenshot. (See Figure 1-57.)

Figure 1-56: Stopping a process.   Figure 1-57: History of commands entered.

Note: Windows XP and Windows Vista users will have to download and install PowerShell (instructions below) before they can start this project. Windows 7 comes with PowerShell preinstalled. If you are using Windows 7, you do not have to download or install PowerShell.

1. Download Microsoft PowerShell from: http://www.microsoft.com/powershell.
2. Click the Downloads tab at the top of the page. (See Figure 1-58.)
3. Click the link labeled "Download Windows PowerShell 2.0".
4. Click the link labeled "Download the Windows Management Framework Core for Windows XP and Windows Embedded package now." (See Figure 1-59.)
5. Click Download.

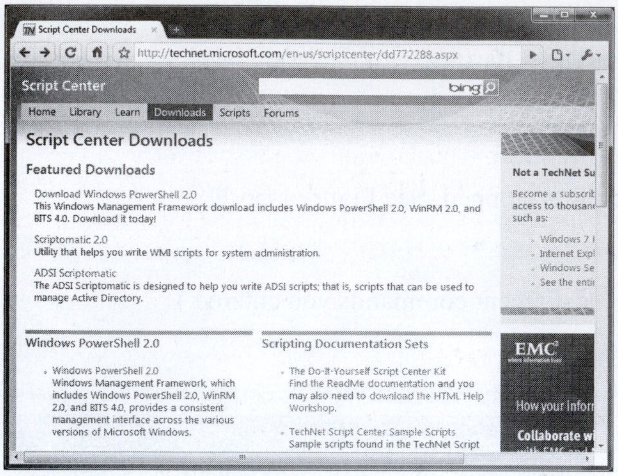

Figure 1-58: Microsoft Script Center.

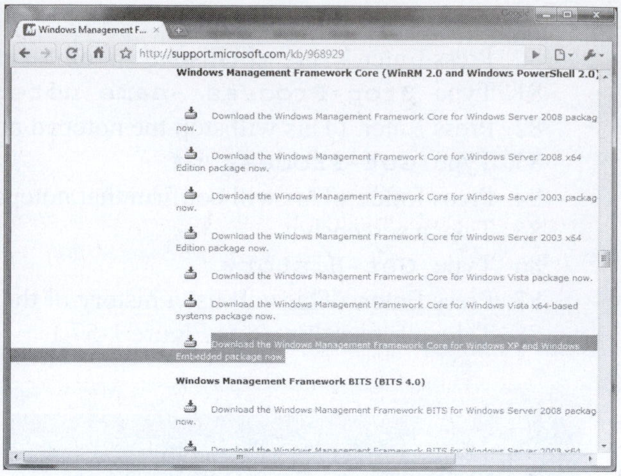

Figure 1-59: Download for PowerShell.

6. Click Save.
7. Select the C:\security folder (If you haven't already created the "security" folder on your C:\, you will have to do so now.)
8. If the program doesn't automatically open, browse to C:\security.
9. Right-click WindowsXP-KB968930-x86-ENG.exe.
10. Complete the installation process.
11. Return to the start of this project.

PROJECT QUESTIONS

1. What was the name of the cmdlet you created?
2. What was the name of the HTML file you created?
3. What was the name of the CSV file you created?
4. What was one of the processes that had the letter "n" in it?

THOUGHT QUESTIONS

1. Could you use the Invoke-Command to start a process on a remote computer?
2. In what instances would you use the Measure-Object cmdlet?
3. Which cmdlet would you use to stop a service?
4. Pwd is an alias for which cmdlet?

1.9   HASHING

A hash is a fixed-size string of numbers; for example, 128 numbers. A hashing function can take any file (text, audio, video, program, etc.) and produce a unique hash based on that file. The resulting hash is a string of numbers unique to that file. Even a small change in the file will produce an entirely different hash value.

In some ways, a hash is similar to a fingerprint. Fingerprints are unique shapes on people's fingers that uniquely identify them. Hashes work in a similar manner. Hashes uniquely identify files.

Suppose you had a text file with the word "password" in it. If you ran it through a hashing function (e.g., MD5), it would produce a specific hash value (in this case, 5f4dcc3b5aa765d61d8327deb882cf99). If you changed the text file so it had the word "passwords" (note the "s" at the end), it would produce an entirely different hash (in this case, 48cccca3bab2ad18832233ee8dff1b0b). Because the file is different, it has its own unique hash.

Hashes are used in many different ways. You may have seen a hash value when you downloaded a piece of software. Software producers post hash values so users can verify the integrity of their software. After you download a piece of software, you can calculate its hash value. If this hash value matches the value on the website, then you know it has not been tampered with. If it does not match, you should not use the software.

In later chapters, you will see how hashes can be used as part of an intrusion detection system. The hashes will tell us which files have been tampered with. This project will have you calculate a couple of hashes, make a small change to a text file, and note the differences in the hash values.

1. Download Microsoft File Checksum Integrity Verifier® (FCIV) utility from: http://support.microsoft.com/kb/841290.
2. Click on the Download link midway down the page.
3. Save the file in your C:\security directory.
4. Open Windows Explorer.
5. Browse to C:\security.
6. Right-click the executable labeled "windows-kb841290-x86-enu.exe".
7. Select Run as administrator.
8. Click Yes, Yes, and Browse.
9. Select your C:\security folder.
10. Click OK, OK, and OK. You should now have the fciv.exe executable and a ReadMe.txt file in your C:\security directory.
11. Click Start.
12. In the search box, type `cmd`
13. Press Enter.
14. Type `cd ..`
15. Press Enter. (Repeat this until you get back to your C:\ prompt.)
16. Type `cd security`
17. Press Enter.
18. Type `dir`
19. Press Enter
20. Type `fciv.exe ReadMe.txt`
21. Press Enter.
22. Type `fciv.exe ReadMe.txt -md5`
23. Press Enter.
24. Type `fciv.exe ReadMe.txt -sha1`
25. Press Enter.
26. Type `fciv.exe ReadMe.txt -both`
27. Press Enter.
28. Take a screenshot. (See Figure 1-60.)

Figure 1-60: Calculating hash values.

29. Type **notepad ReadMe.txt**
30. Type your name at the top of the ReadMe.txt file.
31. Save your changes and exit.

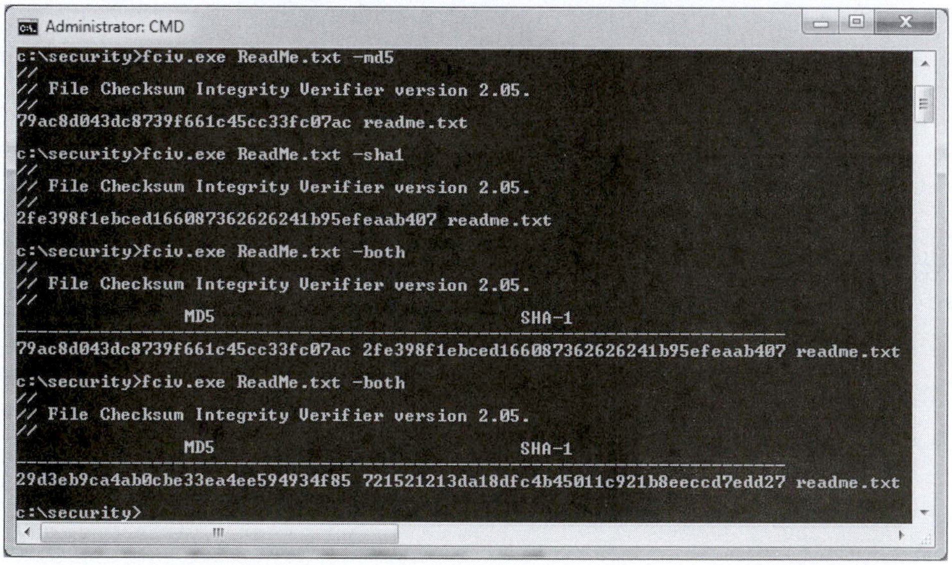

Figure 1-61: Comparing hash values after a change to the text.

32. Return to the Command prompt and type **fciv.exe ReadMe.txt -both**
33. Press Enter.
34. Take a screenshot. (Note that the hashes are now different. See Figure 1-61.)
35. Type **fciv.exe C:\security**
36. Press Enter.
37. Take a screenshot. (See Figure 1-62.)

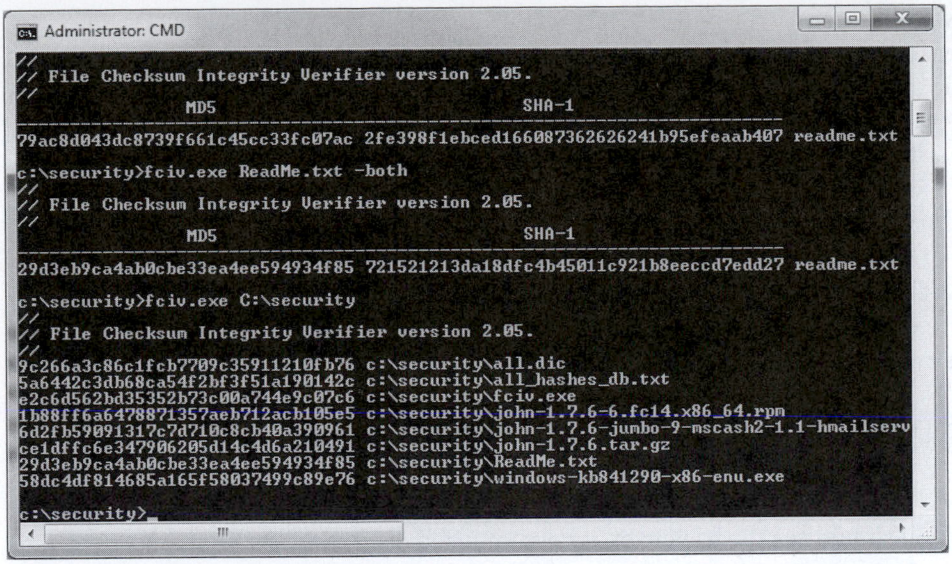

Figure 1-62: Calculating hash values for the files in a directory.

PROJECT QUESTIONS

1. What was the MD5 hash before you made the change?
2. What was the MD5 hash after you added your name to the text file?
3. What was the SHA1 hash after you added your name to the text file?
4. What was the hash of the fciv.exe executable?

THOUGHT QUESTIONS

1. What does the `-v` option do? (Hint: `fciv /?`)
2. Can you store the hashes in a database? How?
3. Which is better, MD5 or SHA1? Why?
4. Are longer hashes better? Why?

1.10 SDELETE®

When you delete a file, it doesn't permanently delete the file. It just removes the pointer for that file and marks the file's location as "free space." The file still exists and it can be recovered as long as it hasn't been overwritten. Only secure deletion actually permanently deletes the file.

Secure deletion is important for more than just your personal privacy. Secure deletion is used on a daily basis to prevent data loss (accidental or intentional). Corporations, hospitals, government agencies, and financial institutions all have confidential data. Most of these organizations are compelled by the force of law to *securely* delete all data.

The following is a simple example of how to securely delete a file. Later chapters will discuss more advanced deletion software. You'll also learn how to recover data that has not been securely deleted.

1. Download the SDelete® utility from: http://technet.microsoft.com/en-us/sysinternals/bb897443.
2. Click on the Download SDelete link.
3. Save the file in your C:\security directory.

4. Open Windows Explorer.
5. Browse to C:\security.
6. Right-click the zipped file labeled "SDelete.zip".
7. Select Extract All.
8. Click Extract. (It should extract two files to a folder labeled "SDelete".)
9. Click Start.
10. In the search box, type `cmd`
11. Press Enter.
12. Type `cd ..`
13. Press Enter. (Repeat this until you get back to your C:\ prompt.)
14. Type `cd security`
15. Press Enter.
16. Type `cd SDelete`
17. Press Enter.
18. Type `dir`
19. Press Enter. (You should see the sdelete.exe program listed.)
20. Type `notepad YourNameSecrets.txt`
21. Press Enter.
22. Type "secret stuff" into the text file.
23. Save your changes and exit.
24. Type `dir`
25. Press Enter.
26. Take a screenshot. (See Figure 1-63.)
27. Type `sdelete.exe -p 7 YourNameSecrets.txt`
28. Press Enter.
29. Type `dir`
30. Press Enter.
31. Take a screenshot. (See Figure 1-64.)

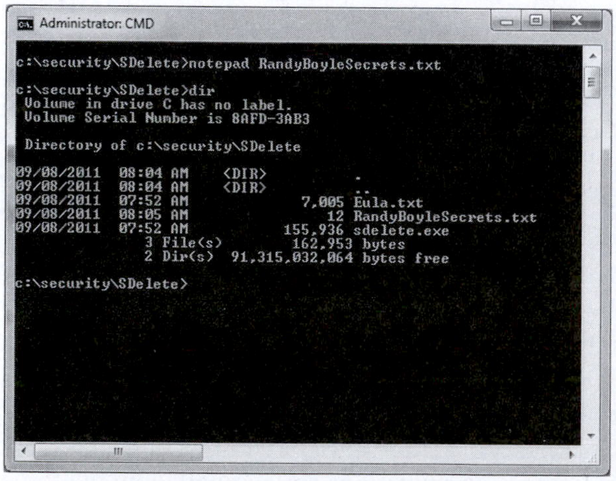

Figure 1-63: Creating a text file for secure deletion.

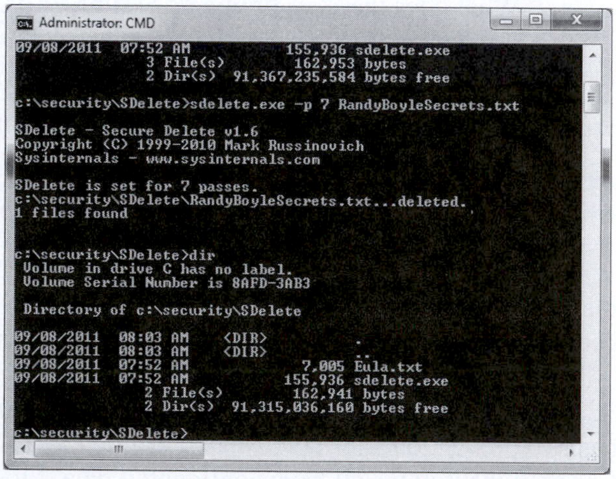

Figure 1-64: Securely deleting a text file.

PROJECT QUESTIONS

1. What was the name of your text file?
2. How long did it take to securely delete the text file?
3. How many passes did it take?
4. Who made this program?

THOUGHT QUESTIONS

1. Which option would clean the free space?
2. Which option would zero the free space?
3. How does secure deletion differ from normal deletion?
4. What is "free space"?

chapter 2

Microsoft Windows is the most popular desktop operating system currently in use. Its popularity makes it a common target for attackers. Desktop computers can be used for a variety of malicious purposes. This might include stealing a person's identity, storing illicit images or pirated music, being used as part of a bot net, or part of a pre-planned cyberwar.

This chapter includes projects that will help protect a Microsoft Windows desktop from a variety of attacks. These projects include implementing a security policy, configuring Windows Advanced Firewall®, configuring an automated backup, configuring automatic updates, managing user accounts, and installing a free malware scanner.

This chapter is not a comprehensive Microsoft Windows security guide. This chapter covers a few of the basic IT security skills each user should know in order to protect his or her personal computer. The ubiquity and general target-attractiveness of the Microsoft Windows operating system necessitate a chapter devoted to securing it.

Time required to complete this chapter: 40 minutes

Chapter Objectives

Learn how to:
1. Implement a local security policy.
2. Configure a host firewall.
3. Configure an automated backup.
4. Configure automatic updates.
5. Manage user accounts.
6. Run a scan for malicious software.

Chapter Projects

Project:
2.1 Local Security Policy
2.2 Windows Firewall
2.3 Configuring Backup
2.4 Windows Update
2.5 User Management
2.6 Microsoft Security Essentials

2.1   LOCAL SECURITY POLICY

In this project, you are going to make changes to a few settings related to your local password policy and account lockout policy. Security policies are not a set of universally agreed upon rules. Rather, they are written for individual organizations (or users) with different requirements. Security policies will vary between organizations.

You are going to change three password policy settings in this project. You will set values for maximum password age and minimum password length, and enable password complexity requirements. Password complexity requirements are a set of rules about the structure of passwords as defined by Microsoft. They can only be enabled or disabled.

In addition to changing the settings for your local password policy, you will also change the settings for your account lockout policy. More specifically, you will set your account lockout threshold and account lockout duration. You will take an initial screenshot before any changes are made. You can roll back any changes to their orgional settings at the end of the project.

1. Click Start, Control Panel, System and Security, Administrative Tools, and Local Security Policy.
2. Click Account Policies, and Password Policy. (See Figure 2-1.)
3. Double-Click Enforce password history.
4. Change the number of passwords remembered to a value greater than 5. (Choose any number greater than 5.)
5. Click OK. (See Figure 2-2.)

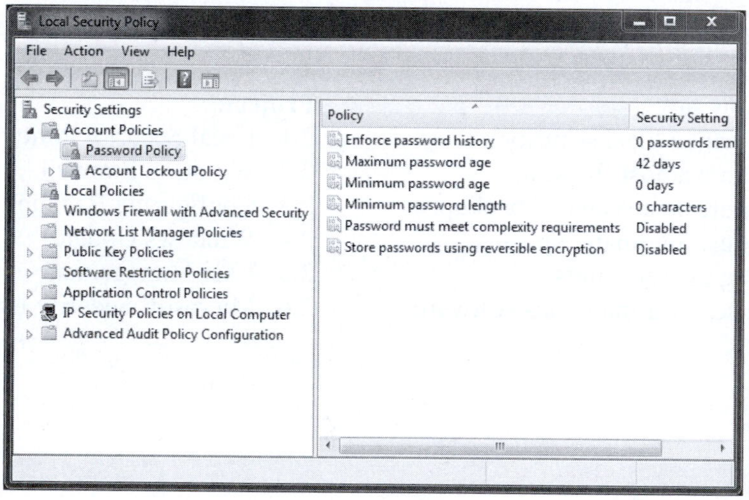

Figure 2-1: Local security policy.

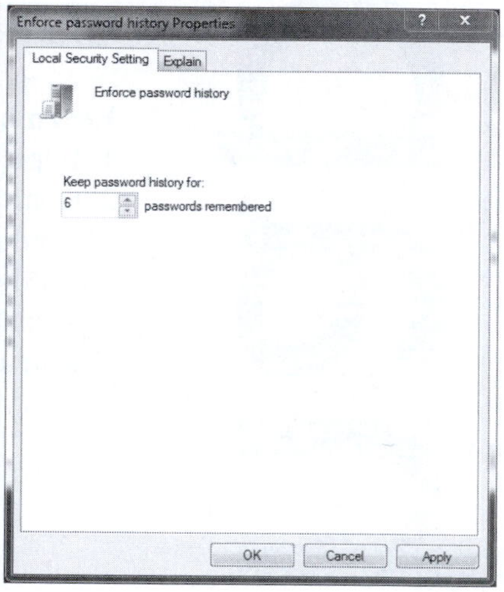

Figure 2-2: Setting the number of passwords remembered.

6. Double-Click Maxiumum password age.
7. Change the maximum password age to a value greater than 60. (Choose any number greater than 60.)
8. Click OK. (See Figure 2-3.)
9. Double-Click Minimum password length.
10. Change the maximum password age to a value greater than 10. (Choose any number greater than 10.)
11. Click OK. (See Figure 2-4.)

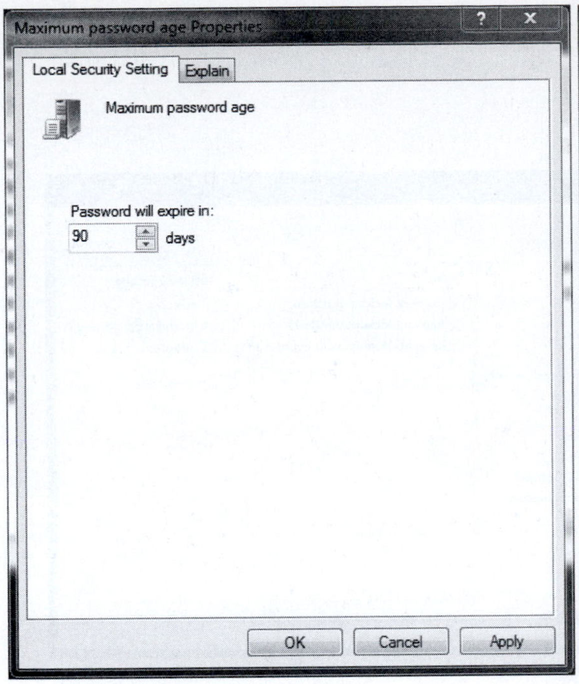

Figure 2-3: Maximum password age.

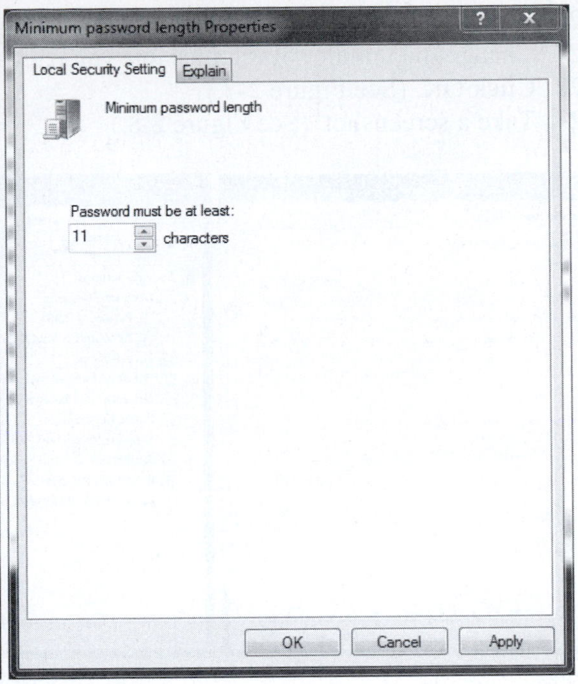

Figure 2-4: Minimum password length.

12. Double-Click Passwords must meet complexity requirements. (The complexity requirements are set by Microsoft. These requirements ensure that passwords are longer than 6 characters, do not contain the user's screen name or user name, and must contain a combination of at least three of the following: uppercase, lowercase, letters, numbers, and symbols.)
13. Select Enable.
14. Click OK.
15. Take a screenshot. (See Figure 2-5.)
16. Click on Account Lockout Policy.
17. Double-Click Account lockout threshold.
18. Change the number of invalid logon attempts to a value greater than 3. (Choose any number greater than 3.)
19. Click OK. (See Figure 2-6.)

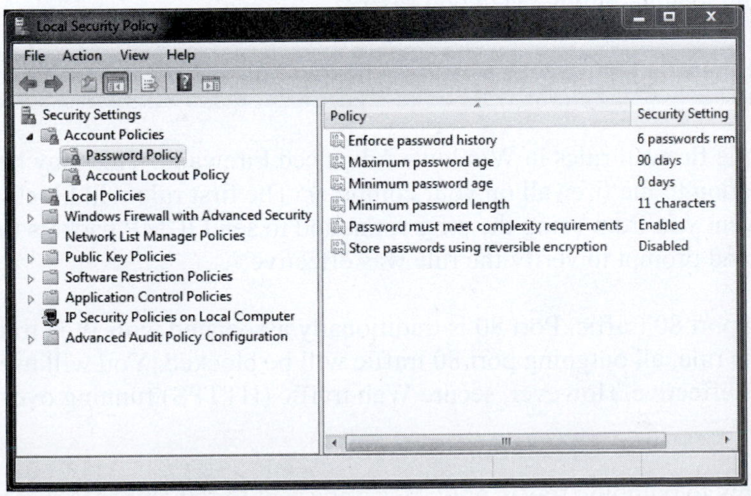

Figure 2-5: Password policies changed.

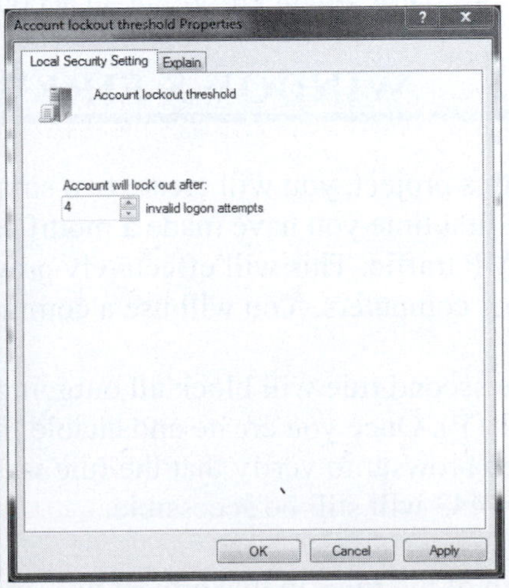

Figure 2-6: Account lockout threshold.

20. Double-Click Account lockout duration.
21. Change the number of minutes to a value greater than 5. (Choose any number greater than 5.)
22. Click OK. (See Figure 2-7.)
23. Take a screenshot. (See Figure 2-8.)

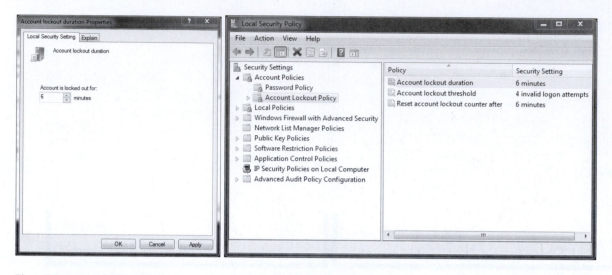

Figure 2-7: Account lockout duration.   Figure 2-8: Account lockout policy.

PROJECT QUESTIONS

1. How many invalid logon attempts did you allow?
2. How long was your account lockout?
3. What was the minimum password length you chose?
4. What was the maximum password age you chose?

THOUGHT QUESTIONS

1. How might enforcing a password history make you safer?
2. How might enforcing a minimum password length make you safer?
3. How might enforcing password complexity requirements make you safer?
4. How might enforcing an account lockout policy make you safer?

2.2   WINDOWS FIREWALL®

In this project, you will create two simple firewall rules in Windows Advanced Firewall®. This may be the first time you have made a modification to the firewall on your computer. The first rule will block all ICMP traffic. This will effectively prevent you from using the ping command to send ICMP packets to other computers. You will use a command prompt to verify the rule was effective.

The second rule will block all outgoing port 80 traffic. Port 80 is traditionally associated with Web traffic (HTTP). Once you create and enable the rule, all outgoing port 80 traffic will be blocked. You will use a Web browser to verify that the rule was effective. However, secure Web traffic (HTTPS) running over port 443 will still be accessible.

Both of the rules in this project will apply to outgoing traffic only. It is important to remember to disable the rules at the end of the project so your ICMP and port 80 traffic will not be blocked.

1. Click Start.
2. In the search box, type `cmd`
3. Press Enter.
4. Type `ping www.google.com`
5. Press Enter. (This will ping www.Google.com.)
6. Type `time`
7. Press Enter twice.
8. Take a screenshot. (See Figure 2-9.)
9. Click Start, Control Panel, System and Security, and Windows Firewall. (See Figure 2-10.)

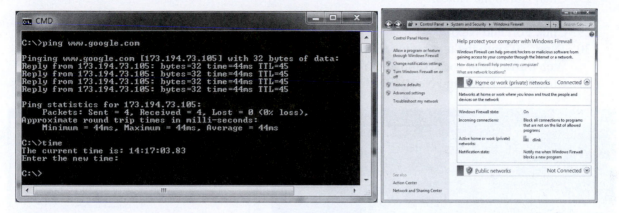

Figure 2-9: Pinging www.Google.com.   Figure 2-10: Windows Advanced Firewall.

10. Click Advanced settings.
11. Click Outbound Rules.
12. Click New Rule (right-hand pane).
13. Click Custom, Next, and Next.
14. Change the dropdown box to ICMPv4. (See Figure 2-11.)
15. Click Next, Next, Next, and Next.
16. Name the rule YourName_Block_ICMP. (Replace YourName with your first and last names. In this case, it was RandyBoyle_Block_ICMP.)
17. Click Finish. (See Figure 2-12.)

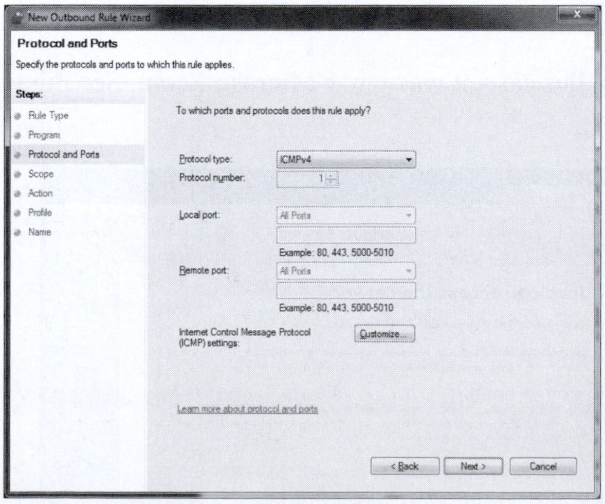

Figure 2-11: Blocking a protocol. 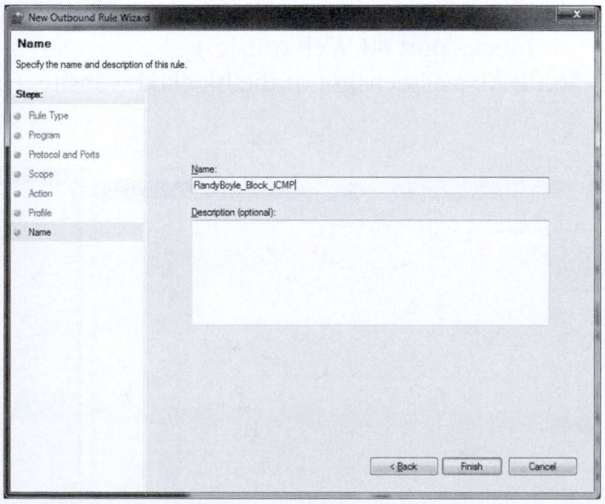   Figure 2-12: Naming the new rule to block ICMP.

18. Return to your command prompt.
19. Type `ping www.google.com`
20. Press Enter. (This will ping www.Google.com. You should get a "General failure" error.)
21. Type `time`
22. Press Enter twice.
23. Take a screenshot. (See Figure 2-13.)
24. Open a Web browser.
25. Browse to www.Google.com. (This will verify that you do have Internet access.)
26. Return to the Windows Advanced Firewall window.
27. Click Outbound Rules.
28. Click New Rule (right-hand pane).
29. Click Port and Next.
30. Type "80" into the text box for Specific remote ports. (This will effectively block all outgoing Web traffic from your computer. You will disable or delete this rule later.)
31. Click Next, Next, and Next. (See Figure 2-14.)

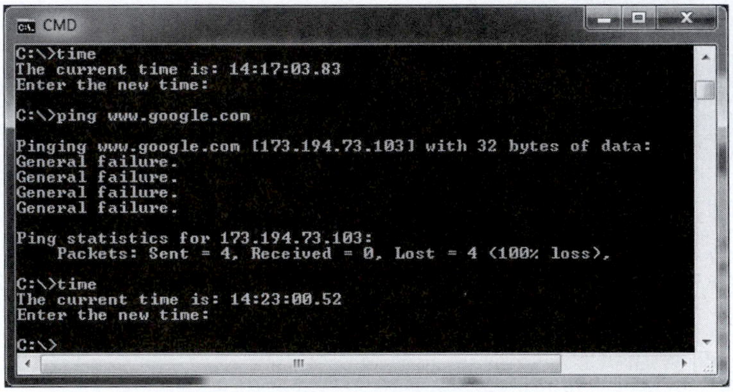

Figure 2-13: Confirming blocked ICMP packets.

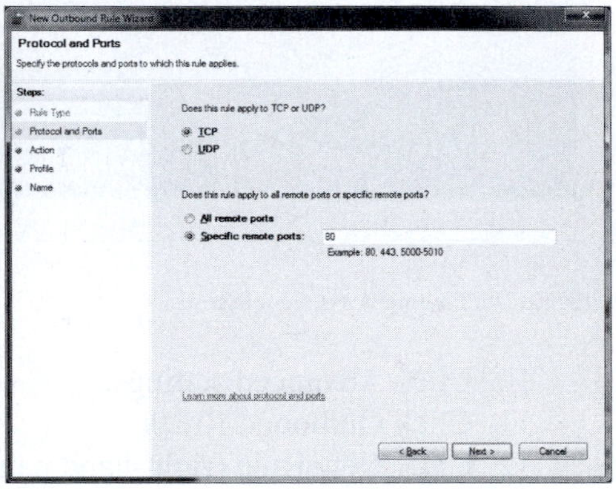

Figure 2-14: Blocking port 80.

32. Name the rule YourName_Block_Port_80. (Replace YourName with your first and last names. In this case, the rule was named RandyBoyle_Block_Port_80.)
33. Click Finish. (See Figure 2-15.)
34. Return to your Web browser.
35. Browse to any non-secure (not HTTPS) website of your choosing. (You can browse to any website as long as it does not make an HTTPS connection [port 443]. The rule you made only blocks port 80 Web traffic.)
36. Take a screenshot of the blocked website. (In this case, it was www.Microsoft.com. See Figure 2-16.)

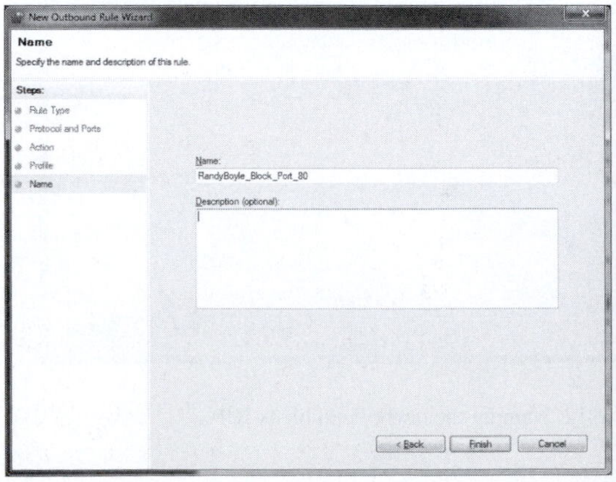

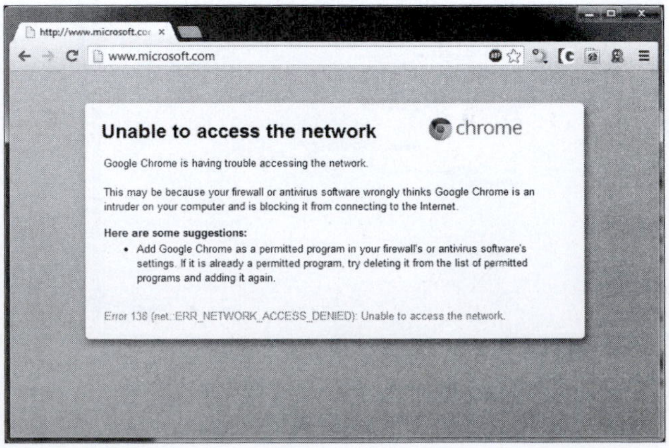

37. Return to the Windows Advanced Firewall window.
38. Select both of the rules you created.
39. Right-click the selected rules.
40. Click Disable Rule. (If you don't disable the rules, your ICMP and Web traffic will still be blocked.)
41. Take a screenshot of your disabled rules. (See Figure 2-17.)

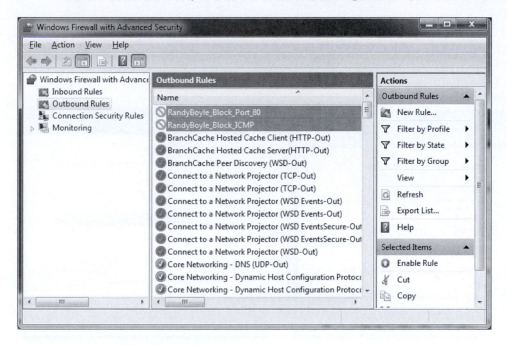

Figure 2-17: New firewall rules.

PROJECT QUESTIONS

1. What was the name of the rule you created to block ICMP traffic?
2. What was the name of the rule you created to block port 80 traffic?
3. What website did you visit to test the port 80 rule?
4. What time did you run the second ping command?

THOUGHT QUESTIONS

1. Could you still access some websites with your port 80 rule enabled? Why?
2. Why would you want to allow incoming (not outgoing) port 443, but block incoming port 80?
3. How could blocking all ICMP traffic protect you?
4. How could blocking all ICMP traffic hurt you?

2.3   CONFIGURING BACKUP

In this project, you are going to configure a backup of a single directory on your computer. You are not going to back up your whole computer in this project. You will need a USB drive to complete this project.

If you were actually configuring a backup of your entire computer, you should use a larger external USB drive with enough capacity.

There are many different ways to back up your data, applications, and operating system. You could simply back up a single file. Or you could create an image of your entire hard drive. For simplicity, this project will only back up a single directory. People who have lost a substantial amount of data have learned to back up often. They also store copies of their backups in different locations.

1. Insert a USB drive into your computer. (In this case, it was a 16GB USB drive named Boyle_USB.)
2. Click Start, Control Panel, System and Security, and Backup and Restore.
3. Click Set up backup. (See Figure 2-18.)
4. Select your USB drive. (In this case, it was the H: drive named Boyle_USB.)
5. Click Next. (See Figure 2-19.)

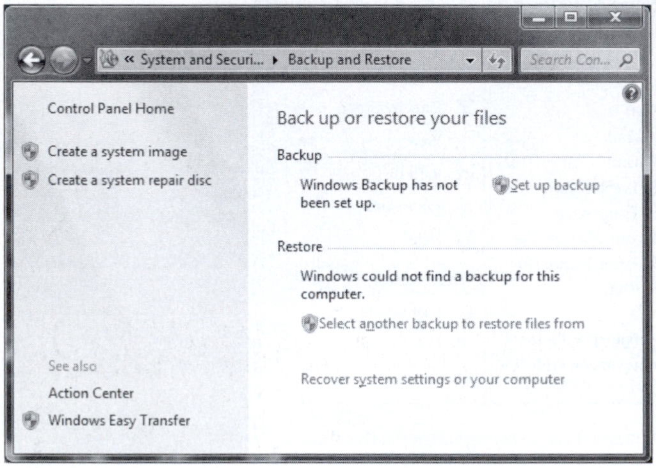

Figure 2-18: Windows Backup and Restore. 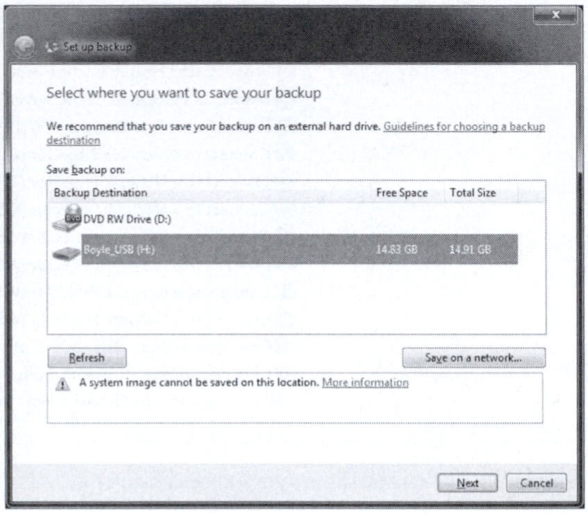 Figure 2-19: Selecting your USB drive as the backup location.

6. Click Let me choose.
7. Click Next.
8. Expand the tree under your username.
9. Deselect all check boxes except the Documents Library for your username. (Note here that you have the option to select any directory on your C: drive.)
10. Take a screenshot. (See Figure 2-20.)
11. Click Next.
12. Click Change schedule. (See Figure 2-21.)

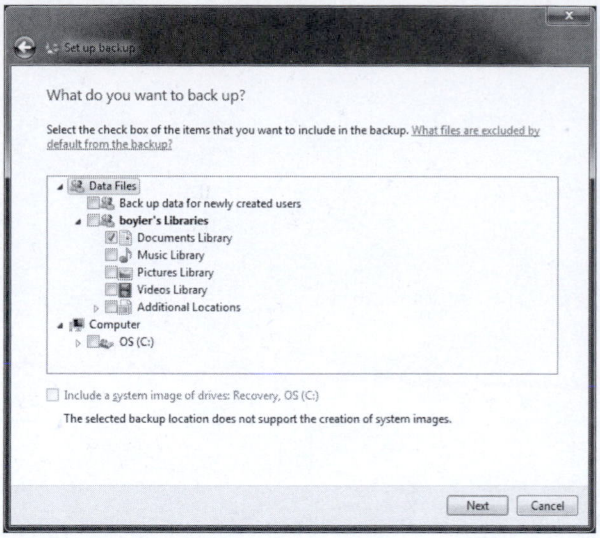

Figure 2-20: Selecting a directory to backup.

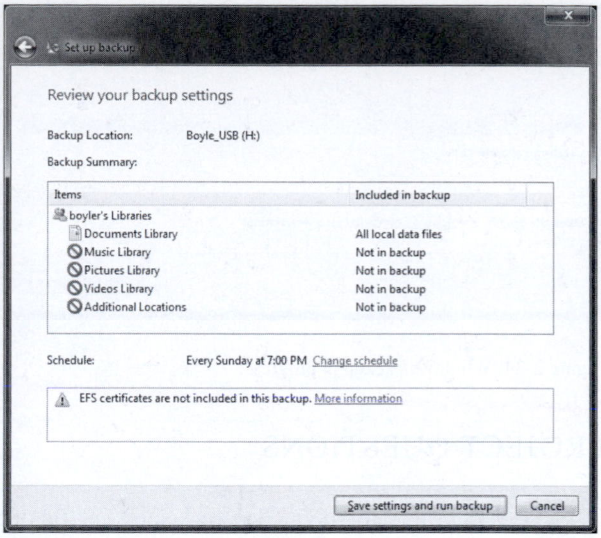

Figure 2-21: Documents Library is selected.

13. Set the backup day and time to a period when you will likely not be using your computer. (In this case, it was Wednesday at 3:00 AM.)
14. Take a screenshot. (See Figure 2-22.)
15. Click OK.
16. Click Save settings and run backup. (See Figure 2-23.)

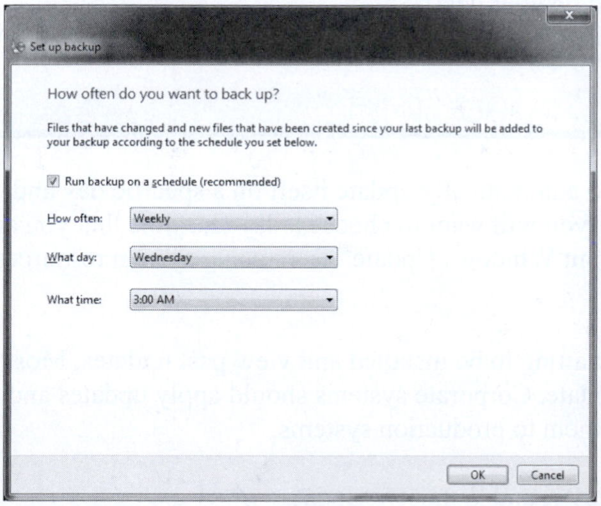

Figure 2-22: Changing the backup schedule.

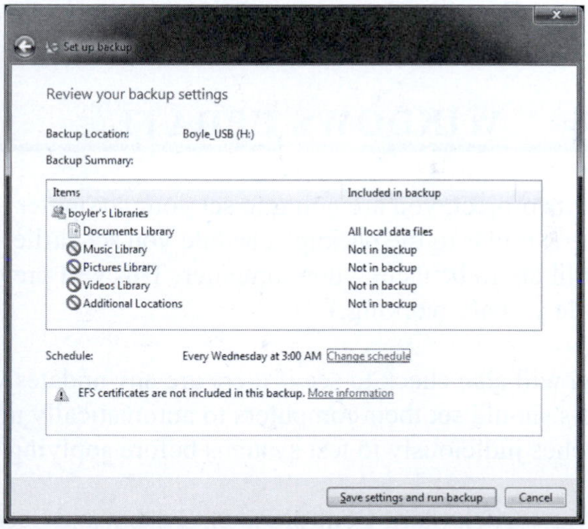

Figure 2-23: Backup schedule is changed.

17. Click View details.
18. Take a screenshot. (See Figure 2-24.)
19. Click Stop backup if you do not want to complete the backup at this time. (It will run at a later time if you keep the same configuration.)

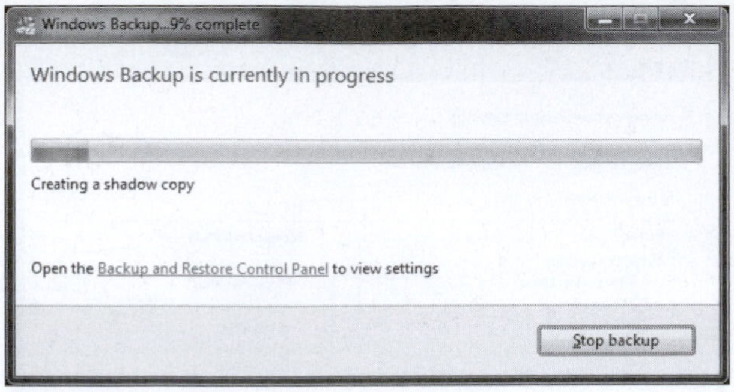

Figure 2-24: Windows backup in progress.

PROJECT QUESTIONS

1. How big was the USB you used for this project?
2. What was your username?
3. What day did you choose to run your backup?
4. What time of day did you choose to run your backup?

THOUGHT QUESTIONS

1. How much data would you lose if your hard drive failed right now?
2. How long would it take to restore your data?
3. How long has it been since you have backed up your data?
4. Would a cloud-based backup solution be wise? Why or why not?

2.4   WINDOWS UPDATE®

In this project, you are going to set your computer to automatically update itself on a specific day and time. Similar to the backup schedule you set earlier, you will want to choose a day and time that you are not likely to be using your computer. This will prevent Windows Update® from using system resources while you are working.

You will also check to see if there are any updates waiting to be installed and view past updates. Most end users should set their computers to automatically update. Corporate systems should apply updates and patches judiciously to test systems before applying them to production systems.

1. Click Start, Control Panel, System and Security, and Windows Update.
2. Click Change settings in the left-hand panel. (See Figure 2-25.)
3. Change the drop box to "Install updates automatically (recommended)".
4. Change the day and time to a period when you will likely not be using your computer. (In this case, it was Wednesday at 3:00 AM.)
5. Take a screenshot. (See Figure 2-26.)

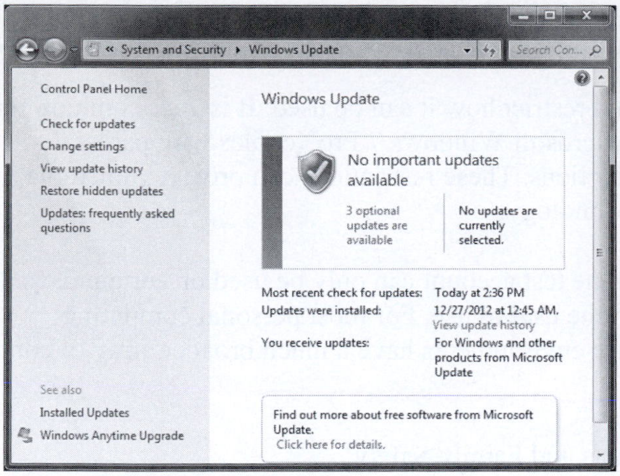

Figure 2-25: Windows Update.

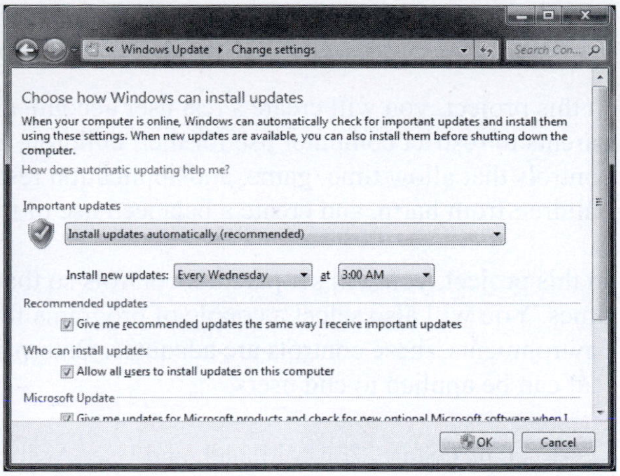

Figure 2-26: Setting a day and time to install new updates.

6. Click OK.
7. Click Check for updates.
8. Take a screenshot while it is checking for updates. (See Figure 2-27.)
9. Click View update history in the left-hand panel.
10. Take a screenshot. (See Figure 2-28.)

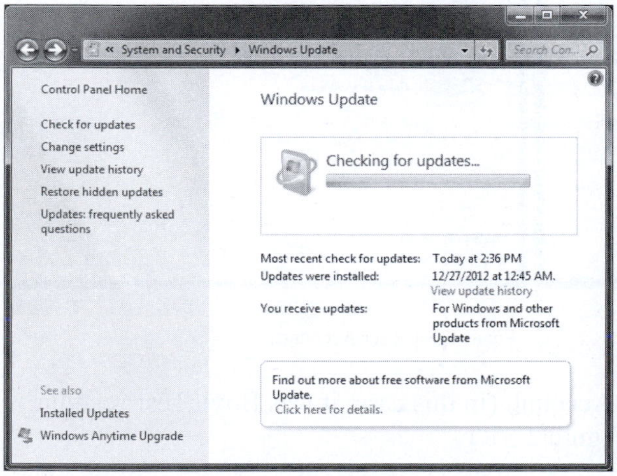

Figure 2-27: Checking for updates.

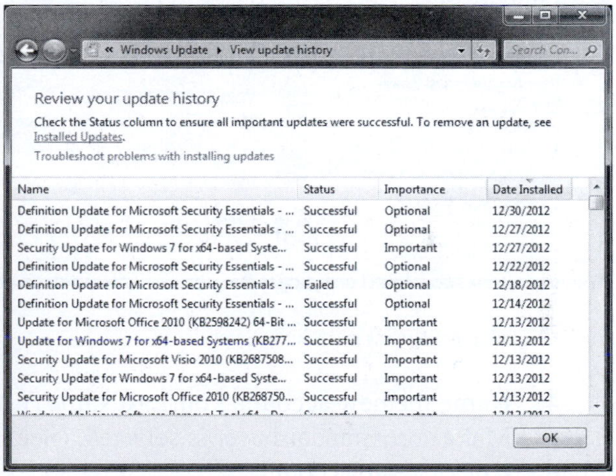

Figure 2-28: Update history.

PROJECT QUESTIONS

1. When were updates most recently installed on your computer?
2. What day did you choose to run your updates?
3. What time of day did you choose to run your updates?
4. Were there any pending updates? How many?

THOUGHT QUESTIONS

1. How can updates make your computer more secure?
2. Could updates cause problems? Why?
3. Should all updates be applied? Why or why not?
4. How do large organizations control updates for hundreds, or thousands, of computers?

In this project, you will create a test user account and restrict how it can be used. It is very common for parents to restrict computer use for their children. Microsoft Windows 7 Pro® comes with parental controls that allow time, game, and application restrictions. These restrictions can protect vulnerable children from harm, and create a balanced use of technology.

In this project, you will set parental controls so that the test account can only be used on certain days and times. You will also select a couple of programs for the user to use. For most personal computing environments, these controls are adequate. Enterprise environments have a much broader array of controls that can be applied to end users.

1. Click Start, Control Panel, and User Accounts and Family Safety.
2. Click Add or remove user accounts. (See Figure 2-29.)
3. Click Create a new account. (See Figure 2-30.)

Figure 2-29: User Accounts and Family Safety.   Figure 2-30: User Accounts.

4. Name the new account YourLastNameTestAccount. (In this case, it was BoyleTestAccount.)
5. Make sure Standard user is selected. (See Figure 2-31.)
6. Click Create account.
7. Click Set up Parental Controls at the bottom of the window. (See Figure 2-32.)

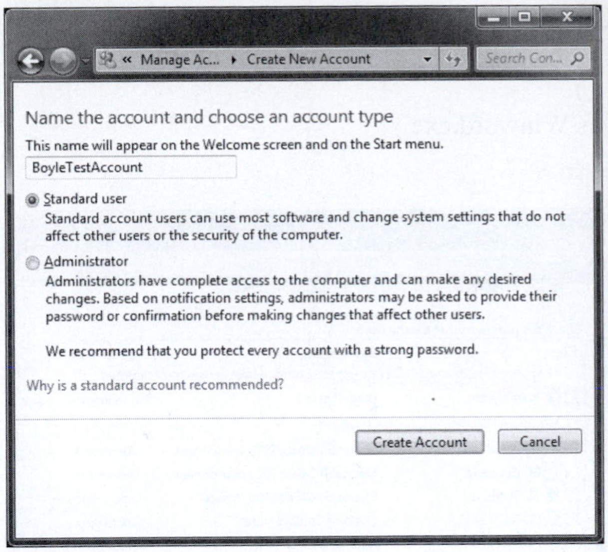

Figure 2-31: Creating a standard user.

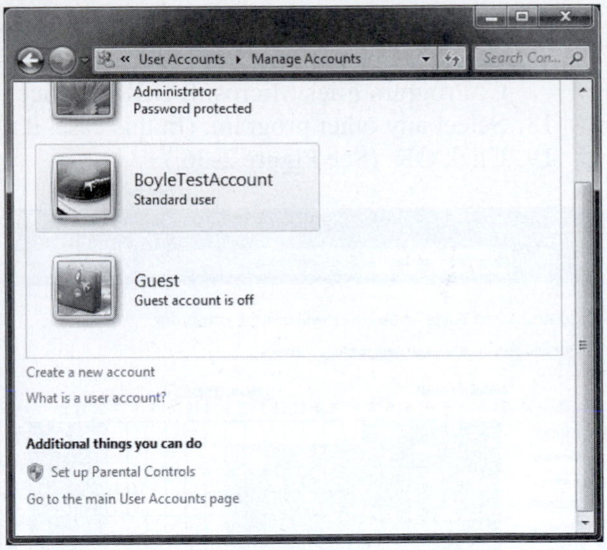

Figure 2-32: User account created.

8. Click on the test account you just created (YourLastNameTestAccount) to set controls for this account. (In this case, the account was BoyleTestAccount. See Figure 2-33.)
9. Click On, enforce current settings. (See Figure 2-34.)

Figure 2-33: Choosing an account for parental controls.

Figure 2-34: Enabling parental controls.

10. Click Time limits.
11. Select all of the available days and times by clicking and dragging.
12. Select a few days and times you feel would be appropriate for this test user to be able to use your computer. (In this case, available hours were weekdays from 3:00 PM to 10:00 PM, and weekends from 8:00 AM to 8:00 PM. You can set any days and times of your choosing.)
13. Take a screenshot. (See Figure 2-35.)
14. Click OK.
15. Click Allow and block specific programs.
16. Click YourLastNameTestAccount can only use the programs I allow.

17. Scroll down until you get to the listing for your word processing suite (Microsoft Office®, Libre Office®, Open Office®, etc.) and select one of the programs. (In this case, it was Excel.exe in C:\Program Files\Microsoft Office\Office14.)
18. Select any other program. (In this case, it was Winword.exe.)
19. Click OK. (See Figure 2-36.)

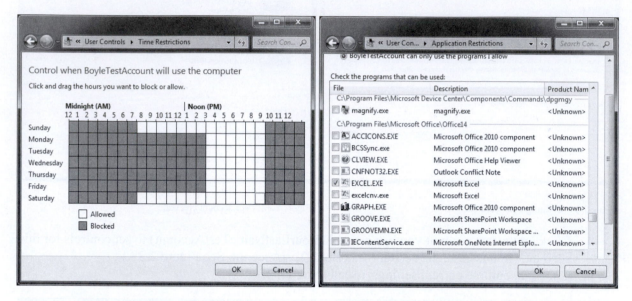

Figure 2-35: Setting time restrictions.   Figure 2-36: Setting application restrictions.

20. Take a screenshot showing the parental controls for your test account. (See Figure 2-37.)
21. Click OK. (You can delete this account after completing this project.)

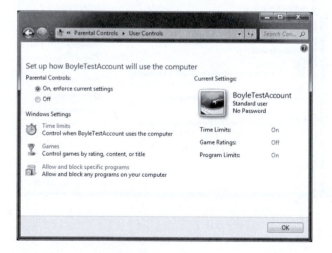

Figure 2-37: Parental controls set.

PROJECT QUESTIONS

1. What was the name of the user account you created?
2. Which days did you allow for use?
3. Which times did you allow for use?
4. Which programs did you allow for use?

1. How do parental controls protect users (children)?
2. How do time controls protect users (children)?
3. How do application controls protect users (children)?
4. How might a user circumvent parental controls?

2.6 MICROSOFT SECURITY ESSENTIALS®

In this project, you are going to download and install Microsoft Security Essentials®. This is a free malware (i.e., viruses, spyware, etc.) scanner that uses minimal resources. It updates itself with the latest virus signature files used to identify malware, and can be set to run at non-peak times. It has been shown to be effective at catching most viruses.

There are many different antivirus scanners available. Some are free. Others must be purchased. Not all antivirus software is created equal. Some have a much richer feature set. There are cases where a feature-rich product is desirable and it may be worth purchasing premium antivirus software. However, some users may just need a simple antivirus scanner. This project will walk you through installing a free (simple) malware scanner.

1. Download Microsoft Security Essentials from: http://windows.microsoft.com/en-US/windows/security-essentials-download.
2. Select the version of your operating system. (In this case it was 64-bit Windows.)
3. Click Download.
4. Save the file in your C:\security directory.
5. Open Windows Explorer.
6. Browse to C:\security. (See Figure 2-38.)
7. Right-click the downloaded executable. (In this case the executable was labeled "mseinstall.exe".)
8. Click Run as administrator.
9. Click Yes, if prompted.
10. Click Next, and I accept. (See Figure 2-39.)

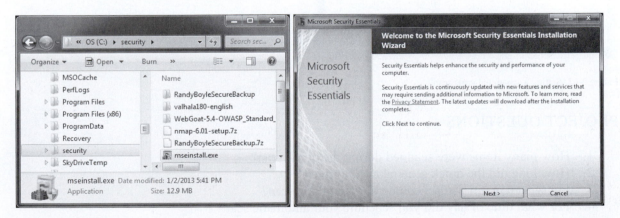

Figure 2-38: Microsoft Security Essentials executable.   Figure 2-39: Installing Microsoft Security Essentials.

11. Click I do not want to join the program at this time.
12. Click Next, Next, Install, and Finish. (A quick antivirus scan will run after you click Finish. See Figure 2-40.)

13. Take a screenshot when the scan completes. (The scan may take several minutes to complete. In this case, it took about 10 minutes. See Figure 2-41.)

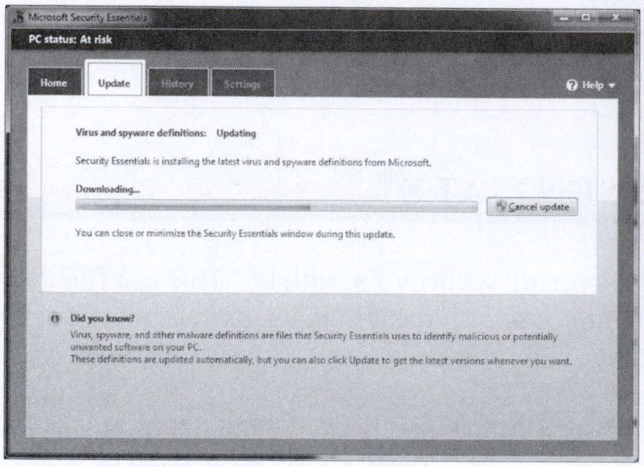

Figure 2-40: Updating virus signature files.

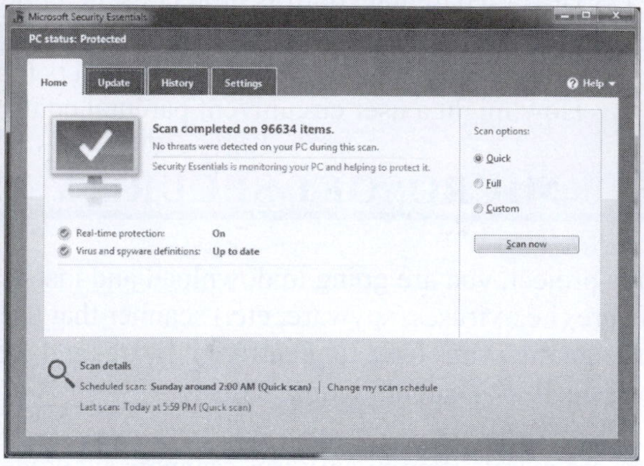

Figure 2-41: Virus scan complete.

14. Click the Settings tab.
15. Change the scheduled scan time to a period when you will likely not be using your computer. (In this case, it was Wednesday at 4:00 AM.)
16. Take a screenshot. (See Figure 2-42.)
17. Click Save changes.

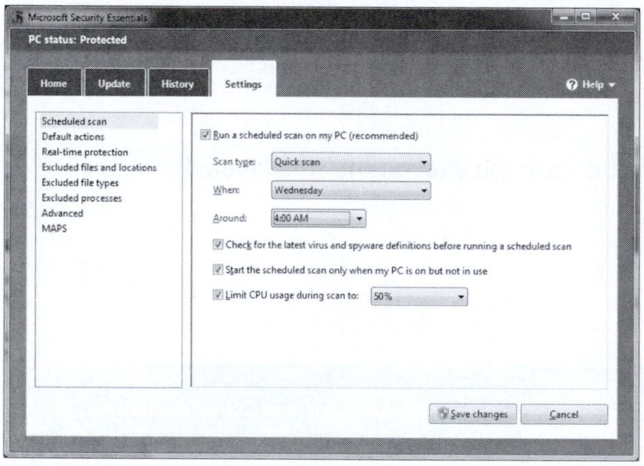

Figure 2-42: Setting a scheduled virus scan.

PROJECT QUESTIONS

1. How many items were scanned during the quick scan?
2. How long did the quick scan take to complete?
3. For what day did you schedule your automatic scan?
4. For what time of day did you schedule your automatic scan?

THOUGHT QUESTIONS

1. Why is malware produced?
2. Should you run multiple antivirus scanners? Why or why not?
3. Can malware scanners misidentify software as harmful? Why or why not?

4. How does Microsoft Security Essentials ensure you are protected against the most current threats?

chapter 3

Users spend a considerable amount of time surfing the Internet. Unfortunately, they usually don't think about how secure their Web browsing activities might be. In most cases, everything you do on the Web can be monitored, tracked, and logged.

This chapter focuses on Web security. It deals with the practical steps users can take to secure their Web browsing activities. The tools in this chapter will show you how to securely and safely browse the Web.

You will first look at how much information is being logged about your Web activities and kept on your own computer. You will learn how to manage your cookies and temporary Internet files. You will also learn how to browse the Internet using "private browsing" and a Web proxy.

You will then learn how to remove Web advertising, use secure connections (HTTPS), identify trustworthy websites, and get information about those websites.

Finally, you will use Tor® to create completely secured and anonymous Internet connections.

Time required to complete this chapter: 60 minutes

Chapter Objectives

Learn how to:
1. Manage your Web browser history.
2. Manage your Web cookies.
3. Identify Web trackers.
4. Browse the Web anonymously.
5. Use a Web proxy.
6. Block Web advertising.
7. Force HTTPS connections.
8. Gather information about websites you are visiting.
9. Identify trustworthy websites.
10. Use Tor routing.

Chapter Projects

Project:
3.1   Web Browser History
3.2   Cookies
3.3   Tracking (Ghostery)
3.4   Anonymous Browsing
3.5   Web Proxy
3.6   AdBlock Plus
3.7   HTTPS Everywhere
3.8   Flagfox
3.9   Web of Trust (WOT)
3.10 Onion Routing (TOR)

3.1   WEB BROWSER HISTORY

Computer newbies commonly ask how they can see which websites their spouse, son, daughter, significant other, roommates, etc. have been looking at. They are unaware that most Web browsers have built in logging functions to keep track of all websites visited. It's surprising how many people don't know this tracking occurs.

In the following exercises, you'll see that there is a tremendous amount of information logged about your Web activities. It's turned on by default in most Web browsers. This exercise will use Internet Explorer®. Chrome® and Firefox® have similar tracking functions.

1. Open Internet Explorer. (You can run the `iexplore` command from the Start menu.)
2. Press Ctrl-H to see your browser's history (Internet Explorer, Firefox, and Chrome). (See Figure 3-1.)
3. Take a screenshot.
4. Open up a folder from a prior day.
5. Take a screenshot.
6. Right-click any one of the prior days (or today) and click Delete. (See Figure 3-2.)

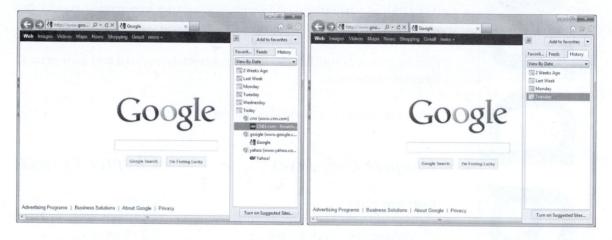

Figure 3-1: Internet Explorer browser history.   Figure 3-2: Deleted browser history.

7. In Internet Explorer, click Tools (the gear symbol), Internet Options, and Settings under Browsing history.
8. Adjust your browser history from 90 days to 10 days.
9. Take a screenshot. (See Figure 3-3.)
10. Click OK.
11. Click Delete under Browsing history.
12. Click Delete.
13. In your browser, Press Ctrl-H to see your browser's history. (It should be empty.)
14. Take a Screenshot. (See Figure 3-4.)

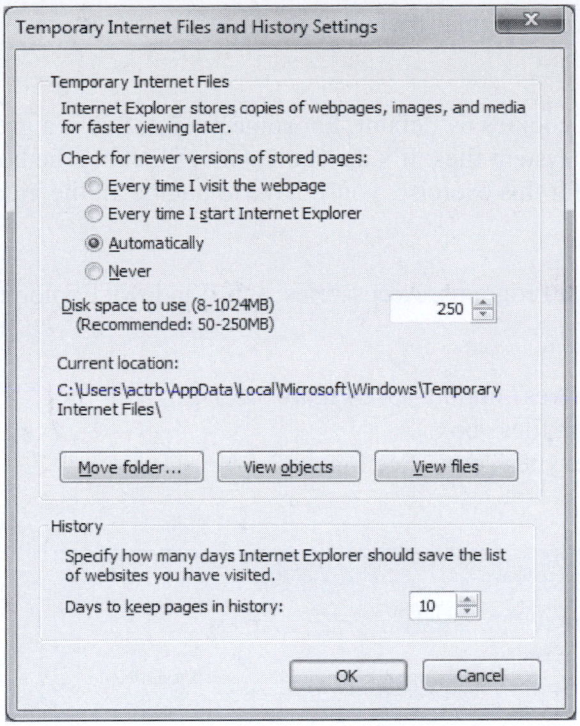

Figure 3-3: Adjusting Web browser history.

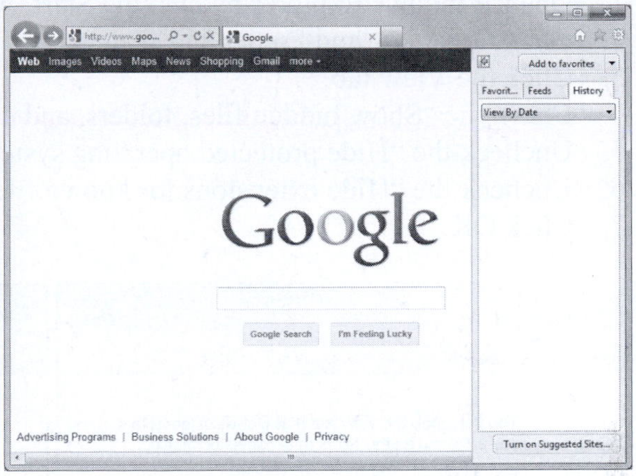

Figure 3-4: Empty browsing history.

PROJECT QUESTIONS

1. What was the most recent website in your browser history?
2. According to your browser history, about how many websites do you visit each day?
3. Approximately how far back did your browser history go?
4. In your opinion, how many days of browser history should be kept?

THOUGHT QUESTIONS

1. Why do you want to keep your browser history?
2. Do the benefits of having a browser history outweigh the potential costs of it being used inappropriately?
3. How could someone use your browser history for malicious purposes?
4. Could you edit the history file manually to show any browsing history you want?

3.2   COOKIES

Some people are aware of the fact that your browser saves a history of all websites visited. However, they may not be aware that hundreds of "cookies" are being stored on your computer. Cookies are placed on your computer by your Internet browser when you visit websites. They store information about you and the websites you've visited. Most people are shocked when they see how many cookies are being kept on their computer.

Invariably, people also ask why cookies are necessary. It turns out that cookies can be beneficial in certain situations. For example, cookies can be helpful for beginning computer users who don't want to keep re-entering their passwords every time they visit a site. However, in the end, the risks of allowing cookies may outweigh the benefits. Deleting cookies on a regular basis is a good idea. Let's see how many cookies are on your computer.

Most new computers hide your system files and your cookies by default. For some people, this is a great idea because it keeps them from damaging important system files. It's the equivalent of locking the hood of your car so you can't get to the engine. However, for this exercise, you'll have to unhide all the hidden files on your computer.

1. Open Windows Explorer by clicking Start, All Programs, Accessories, and Windows Explorer.
2. Click Organize, and Folder and search options.
3. Click the View tab.
4. Check the "Show hidden files, folders, and drives" option. (See Figure 3-5.)
5. Uncheck the "Hide protected operating system files" box.
6. Uncheck the "Hide extensions for known file types" box. (See Figure 3-6.)
7. Click OK.

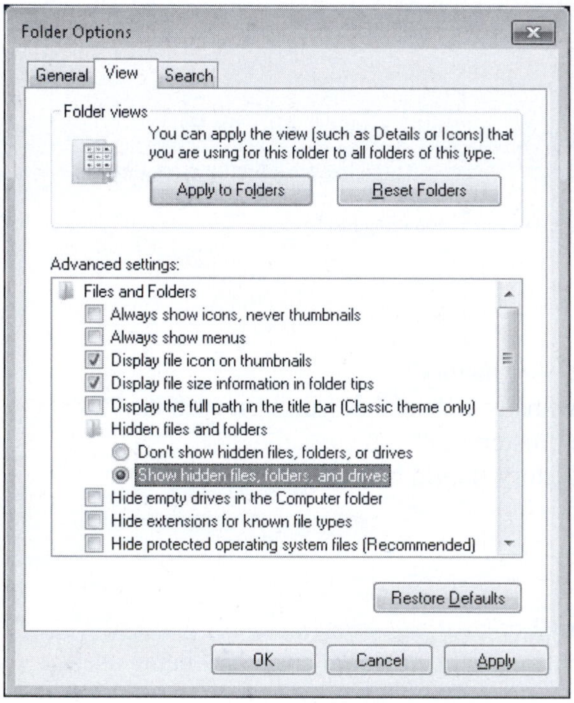

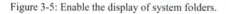

Figure 3-5: Enable the display of system folders. 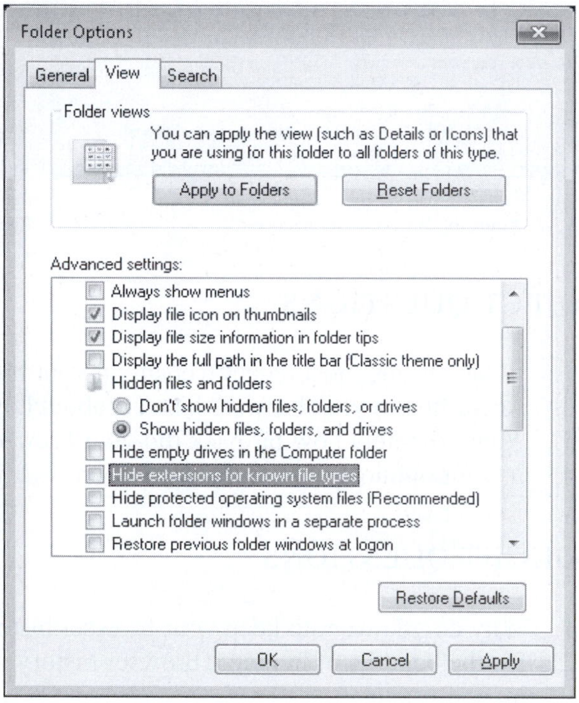　　　　Figure 3-6: Show hidden files and folders.

8. Go to C:\Users\[your user name]\AppData\Roaming\Microsoft\Windows\Cookies\Low (without brackets). In Windows XP they will be in C:\Documents and Settings\[your user name]\Cookies (without brackets). (See Figure 3-7.)
9. Double-click one of the cookies to open it. (If you don't see any cookies, you may have to open Internet Explorer and visit a couple of Web pages. You should see the cookies start populating the folder automatically.)
10. Take a screenshot. (See Figure 3-8.)

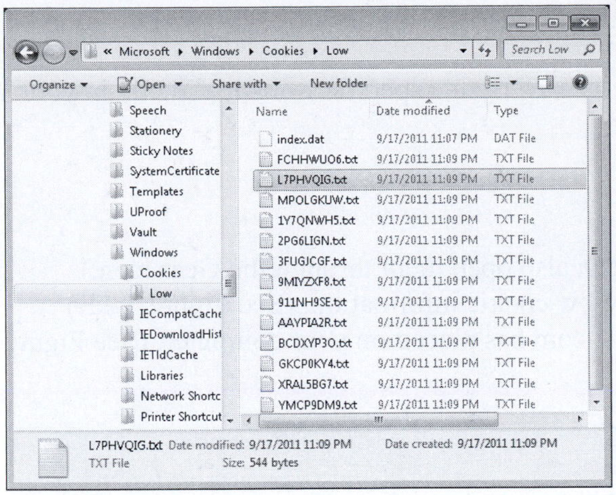

Figure 3-7: View cookies on your hard drive.

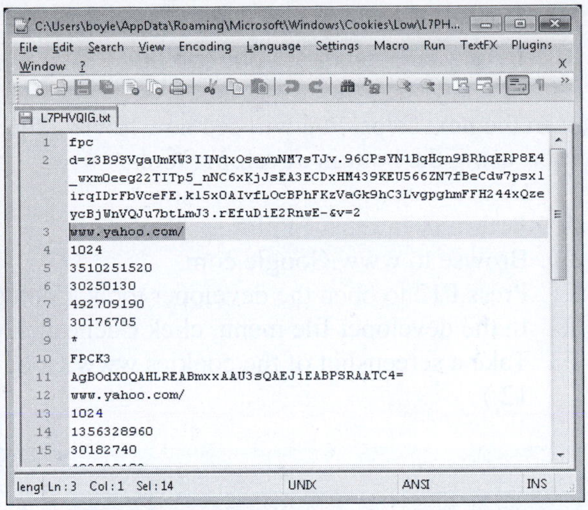

Figure 3-8: Cookie from Yahoo.com.

Note: Your computer also stores other files as temporary Internet files (i.e., icons and their URLs). The following steps will show you how to view the temporary Internet files stored by Internet Explorer.

11. In Internet Explorer, click the Gear icon (or Tools in older versions of IE), and Internet options.
12. Under the sub-section marked "Browsing history," click Settings.
13. Click View Files. (See Figure 3-9.)
14. Click the Type column to sort the temporary files by file type.
15. Scroll to the bottom (or top) to see your cookies listed as Text Documents. (See Figure 3-10.)

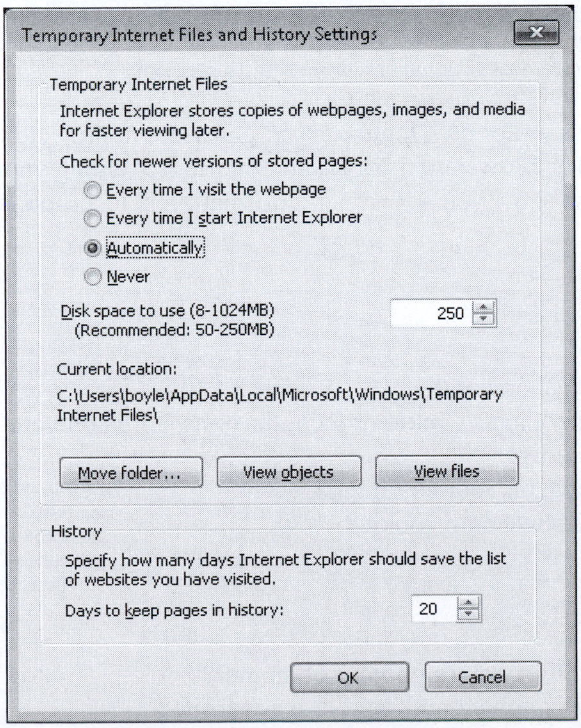

Figure 3-9: Temporary Internet files settings.

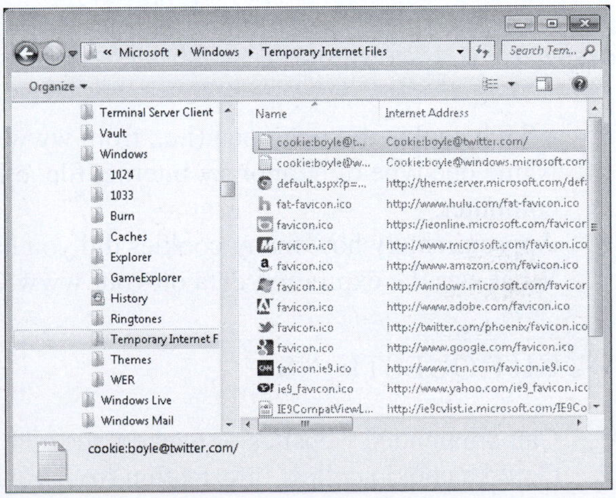

Figure 3-10: Listing of temporary Internet files.

16. Double-click one of the cookies to open it.

17. If a pop-up asks you if you want to open it, click Yes.
18. Take a screenshot of your cookie.

Note: In the next steps, you will see how to view the cookies from a specific website directly in your Web browser, using the built in developer tools.

19. Return to Internet Explorer.
20. Browse to www.Google.com.
21. Press F12 to open the developer tools. (You can also open them through the Gear icon.)
22. In the developer file menu, click Cache and View cookie information. (See Figure 3-11.)
23. Take a screenshot of the cookies www.Google.com has placed on your computer. (See Figure 3-12.)

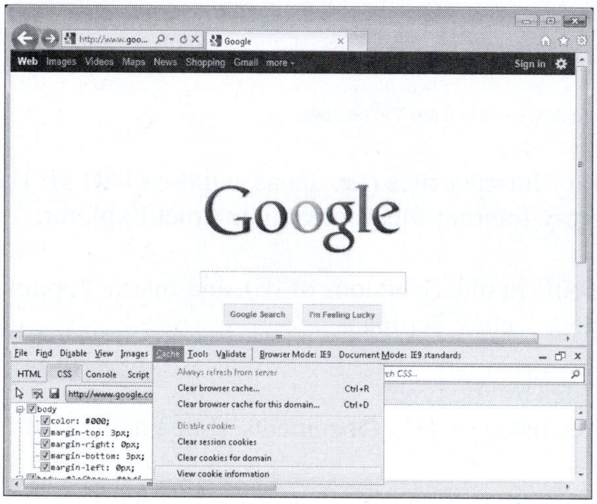

Figure 3-11: Developer tools in Internet Explorer.

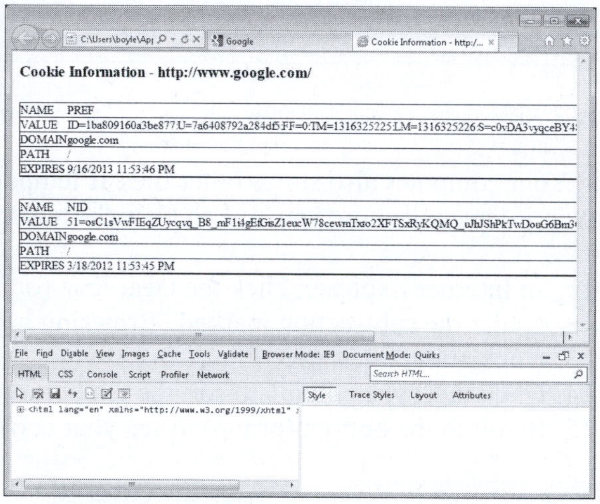

Figure 3-12: Cookie information for www.Google.com.

It's a good idea to delete all your cookies and temporary files on a regular basis. Subsequent projects will show you how to delete all the cookies, temporary files, browsing history, and other logs. Wiping your machine once a week is not only prudent, but will also show you how much information is recorded in such a short period of time.

PROJECT QUESTIONS

1. Which cookie did you open (i.e., from www.Yahoo.com)?
2. Name one type of temporary Internet file, other than a cookie or icon, that was stored on your computer.
3. Approximately how many cookies did you have on your computer?
4. What was the expiration data on your www.Google.com cookie?

THOUGHT QUESTIONS

1. Can unintended websites or hackers see all of the cookies on your computer?
2. Could a cookie collect information from your computer and send it to a website?
3. Do certain websites require cookies? Why would they require cookies?
4. Why are so many cookies from online advertisers? Why do they want information put on your computer?

There are a lot more than just cookies being passed around the Web. For example, Web bugs can track your browsing behavior across multiple websites. Thus, your behavior across multiple websites can be analyzed. It's interesting to know which websites are using certain cookies, Web bugs, or common advertising networks.

Ghostery® is an add-on that can be added to your Web browser that will automatically give you a list of sources (i.e., companies) tracking you as you visit each website. For this project, we will use the Firefox Web browser.

1. Download and install the latest version of Firefox from http://www.mozilla.org/.
2. Open Firefox.
3. Click on the Firefox menu, and then Add-ons. (You can also press Ctrl-Shift-A.)
4. In the Search box, enter "Ghostery".
5. Press Enter.
6. Click Install for the Ghostery add-on. (See Figure 3-13.)

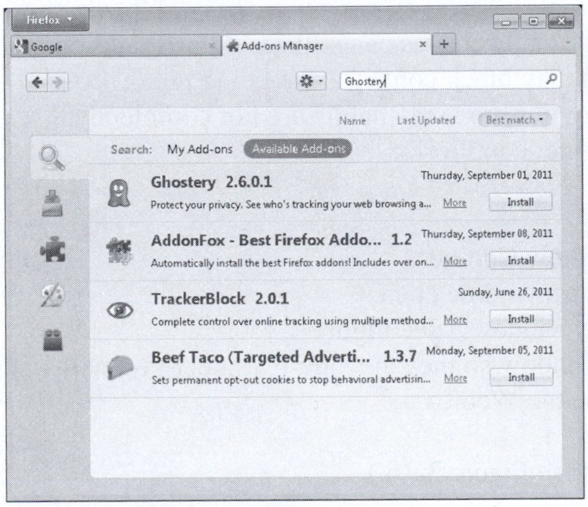

Figure 3-13: Search for Ghostery.

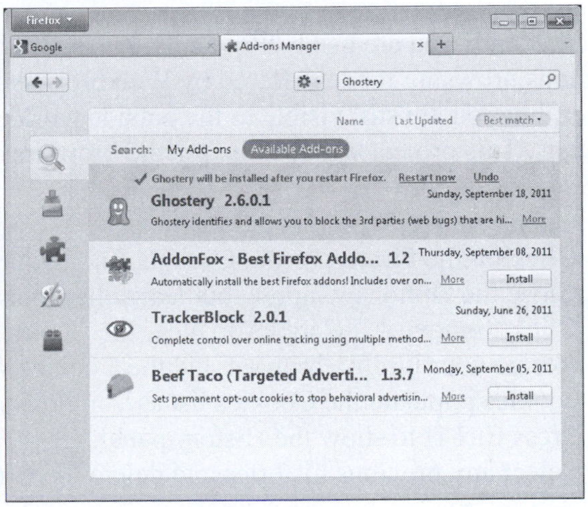

Figure 3-14: Ghostery is installed.

7. Click Restart now. (See Figure 3-14.)
8. After Firefox restarts, browse to www.Microsoft.com.
9. Note the Ghostery notice in the top right-hand corner of your Web browser.
10. Take a screenshot of any trackers Ghostery may have found.
11. Visit a few well-known news websites. (News websites such as www.CNN.com, www.MSNBC.msn.com, www.FoxNews.com, www.ABCNews.go.com, etc. will have a dozen or so trackers.)
12. Take a screenshot of the website that has the most trackers.
13. Browse to your university main page (e.g., www.Longwood.edu).
14. Click on the Ghostery icon to read about any trackers that your university may be using.
15. Enter your name in the Firefox search box.
16. Take a screenshot.

PROJECT QUESTIONS

1. Which news website had the most trackers?
2. Was your university using any trackers? Which ones?

3. How many trackers were found at www.Microsoft.com?
4. Name one tracker that you saw at two or more websites. (Hint: Compare the well-known news websites.)

THOUGHT QUESTIONS

1. What are ad networks?
2. Would websites share tracking information? Why?
3. What is a white list?
4. Why would websites be interested in tracking your behavior?

3.4   ANONYMOUS BROWSING

Most well known Web browsers have the ability to allow users to browse the Web anonymously. Individual Web browsers may label it as "Private Browsing," "Incognito Mode," or "InPrivate Browsing." In general, the idea is that your Web browser will allow you to visit websites anonymously without keeping a history, cookies, or temporary Internet files.

However, even if you are using "Private Browsing," external websites can still see your IP address. Anonymous browsing modes offered by Web browsers may block content from being put on your computer, but you are still visible to the outside world. Your browsing habits are not completely anonymous. This project will test the private browsing mode in Firefox.

1. Open Firefox.
2. Click on the Firefox menu, Options, and then Show Cookies.
3. Close the Options window, but leave the Cookies window open.
4. Click Remove All Cookies to clear the Cookies window. (See Figure 3-15.)
5. Resize your Firefox browser and the Cookies window so they are side-by-side. (You will watch cookies populate the Cookies list as you browse the Web.)
6. Press Ctrl-H to show the History panel.
7. Select any previous histories and delete them. (See Figure 3-16.)

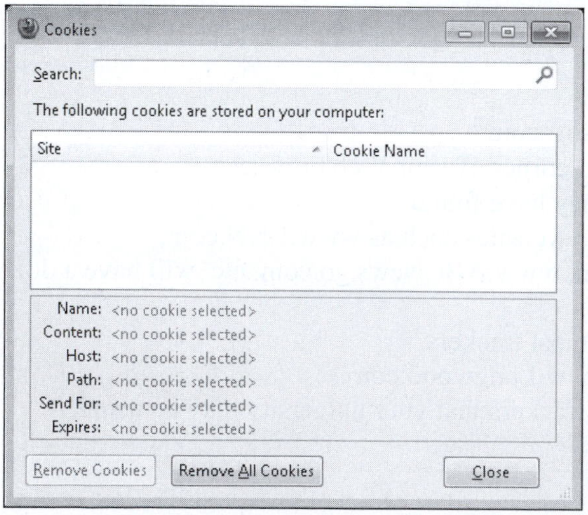

Figure 3-15: Empty cookies in Firefox.

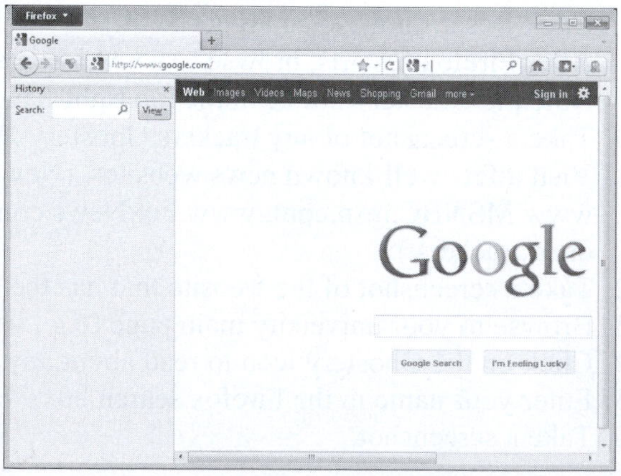

Figure 3-16: Empty browser history in Firefox.

8. Browse to www.Google.com. (You should see cookies recorded, and an entry in your browsing history logged.)

9. Search www.Google.com for the term "my IP address".
10. Click on the first search result.
11. Take a screenshot of the page showing your current IP address.

Note: You have now shown that during a typical browsing session cookies are stored, a browsing history is logged, and your IP address is known to external websites. We are now going to turn on Private Browsing.

12. Browse back to www.Google.com.
13. Delete any prior browsing history in the History panel.
14. Press Remove All Cookies in the Cookies window. (Both the Cookies window and the browsing history should be blank.)
15. Click on the Firefox menu and select Start Private Browsing (again, if prompted to do so).
16. Press Ctrl-H to show the History panel. (See Figure 3-17.)

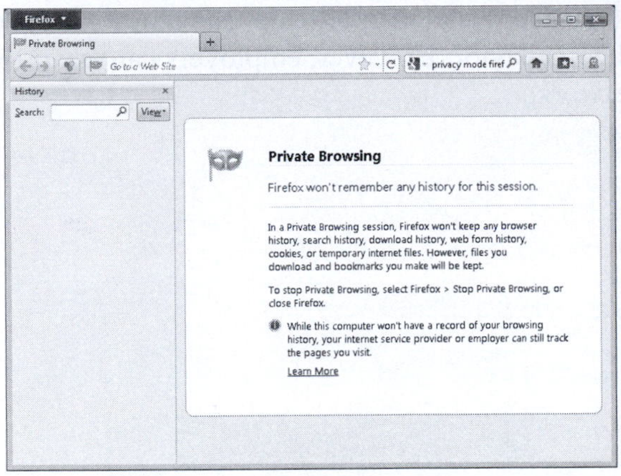

Figure 3-17: Private Browsing in Firefox.

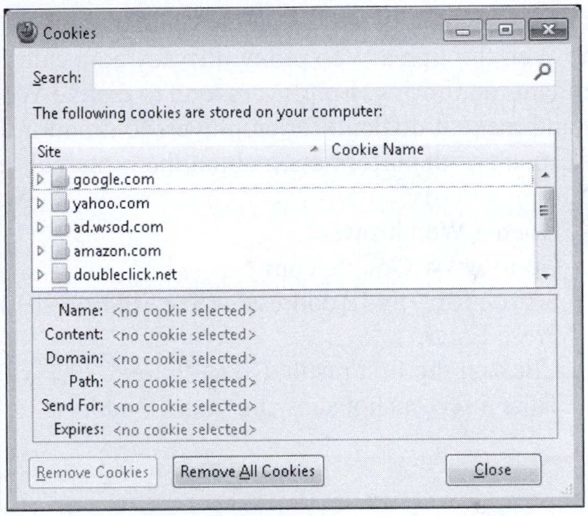

Figure 3-18: Cookies recorded during privacy browsing.

17. Browse to www.Google.com.
18. Search www.Google.com for the term "my IP address".
19. Click on the first search result.
20. Take a screenshot of the page showing your current IP address.
21. Take a screenshot of the Cookies window showing the cookies that were collected. (At this point, you can choose to browse a few other websites. See Figure 3-18.)
22. Click on the Firefox menu and select Stop Private Browsing. (Note that the cookies recorded have now been purged, and no browsing history was retained.)
23. Browse to www.Google.com.
24. Enter your name in the search box.
25. Take a screenshot.

PROJECT QUESTIONS

1. What was your IP address?
2. What was the name of the website that displayed your IP address?
3. Did Ghostery (from a prior project) still show trackers?
4. For what purpose would you use private browsing?

1. What would be a legitimate use for private Web browsing?
2. What effect does private Web browsing have on online retailers?
3. How could you have true anonymity when you browse the Web?
4. Could your employer still monitor your Web surfing if you are using Private Browsing? How?

3.5   WEB PROXY

A proxy is a person who can act on your behalf. For example, you can make someone your proxy if you can't make it to a meeting but still want to cast your vote. Another example would be giving your lawyer power of attorney. Computers can also have proxies. Essentially, one computer has another computer do tasks for it. Proxies have their good and bad uses.

In this project, you will use a Web proxy. You will see that your IP address will appear differently if you surf the Web through a Web proxy. Privacy advocates argue that proxies protect them from undue government monitoring. Employers tend to dislike Web proxies because employees can abuse Internet access and make it difficult for employers to monitor their behavior. However, employers can use proxies to mask much of the information about their internal networks.

1. Open a Web browser.
2. Go to www.Google.com.
3. Search for "my IP address". (See Figure 3-19.)
4. Press Enter.
5. Click on the first result. (See Figure 3-20.)
6. Take a screenshot showing your IP address.

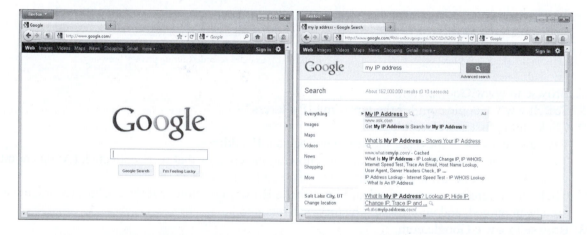

Figure 3-19: Search for your IP address.   Figure 3-20: Results for "my IP address" search.

7. Go to the Web proxy at https://Proxify.com. (If this Web proxy is not available, you can get a list of other Web proxies by searching www.Google.com for "web proxy".)
8. Enter "www.Google.com" as the Web address you'd like to visit.
9. Click Proxify. (The results will show www.Google.com's main page in a lower panel.)
10. Search the lower www.Google.com panel for "my IP address".
11. Press Enter.
12. Click on the first result.
13. Take a screenshot showing the IP address as it shows through the proxy. (It should be different.)

PROJECT QUESTIONS

1. What was your IP address without using the Web proxy?
2. Which Web proxy did you use?
3. Could the Web proxy handle HTTPS connections (i.e., a connection to a bank)?
4. What was your IP address when you used the Web proxy?

THOUGHT QUESTIONS

1. Can a proxy server really hide your identity?
2. Could a company block any/all traffic to/from a proxy server?
3. Could a company use a proxy server to hide confidential information about an internal network from hackers? How?
4. Would your employer become suspicious if you were using a proxy server?

3.6   ADBLOCK PLUS®

Adblock Plus® is a Web browser add-on that can block advertisements. It can also block trackers and domains that are known to be sources of malware. It also allows you to create custom filters that can block specific Web content.

Not only can Adblock Plus make Web surfing safer, it can also make it more enjoyable – no more annoying ads. In this project, you will compare the same website in two browsers. You will install Adblock Plus in Firefox. You'll then compare the filtered website to an unfiltered version in Internet Explorer.

1. Open Internet Explorer and browse to www.Amazon.com.
2. Fill the right-hand side of your screen with your IE browser by pressing the Window key and right arrow (⊞+→).
3. Open Firefox and browse to www.Amazon.com.
4. Fill the left-hand side of your screen with your Firefox browser by pressing the Window key and left arrow (⊞+←). (You should now have both browsers side-by-side.)
5. In your Firefox browser, type your name into the Amazon search box, but don't press Enter. (Note the number of trackers found by Ghostery. Adblock Plus will reduce this number substantially.)
6. Take a screenshot.
7. Click the Firefox menu, and Add-ons.
8. Click Get Add-ons.
9. In the search box, enter "Adblock Plus". (See Figure 3-21.)
10. Press Enter.
11. Click Install for the latest version of Adblock Plus. (See Figure 3-22.)
12. Click Restart now.

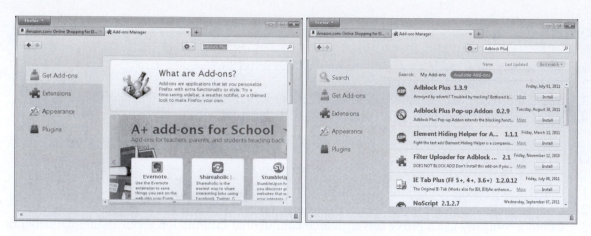

Figure 3-21: Searching for Adblock Plus.   Figure 3-22: Installing Adblock Plus.

13. Refresh the www.Amazon.com Web page in your Firefox browser. (You can press F5 or the Refresh button.)
14. Enter your name in the Amazon search bar in your Firefox browser, but don't press Enter. (Note the reduced number of trackers and ads along the right-hand side when compared to the exact same page in your Internet Explorer browser.)
15. Take a screenshot of your entire desktop by pressing Ctrl-PrintScreen.
16. Go to another website in both browsers that you know has advertising. (Major news websites typically have lots of ads and trackers.)
17. Take another screenshot of your entire desktop, showing the difference in browsers.

PROJECT QUESTIONS

1. How many trackers did Ghostery find before Adblock Plus was installed?
2. How many trackers did Adblock Plus block on the same page?
3. How many ads did Adblock Plus block?
4. What was the second website you visited? Did Adblock Plus stop ads there too?

THOUGHT QUESTIONS

1. Would online retailers dislike Adblock Plus? Why?
2. Some websites pay for their operations through ad revenue. Could Adblock Plus put them out of business?
3. Can you make exceptions (i.e., not block content) for specific websites?
4. What are filter subscriptions?

3.7   HTTPS EVERYWHERE®

Most of the websites you visit are not secure. Anyone between you and the website you are visiting can see the contents of the packets you are sending. Hypertext Transfer Protocol Secure (HTTPS) provides secure communication between hosts. It encrypts the traffic between the two hosts and provides Web server authentication.

Most websites do not provide HTTPS connections because of costly certificates, integration issues with virtual hosts, limits on caching across regions, and performance issues. All of these issues can be resolved, but it does add costs.

This project will have you install HTTPS Everywhere®, an add-on from www.EFF.org. This add-on checks to see if the website you are visiting offers an HTTPS connection. Many of the larger Web services do offer HTTPS connections, if requested.

1. Open your Firefox Web browser. (Firefox can be downloaded from www.Mozilla.org.)
2. Browse to the following four websites to show that they are NOT already providing a default HTTPS main page: www.Google.com, www.Facebook.com, www.Twitter.com, and www.en.Wikipedia.org. (See Figure 3-23.)
3. Browse to https://www.eff.org/https-everywhere to get HTTPS Everywhere.
4. Click Encrypt the Web: Install HTTPS Everywhere.
5. Click Allow, on the Firefox popup.
6. Click Install Now.
7. Click Restart Now. (You should see an HTTPS Everywhere icon in the top-right corner of your browser after it restarts.)
8. Browse to the following four websites to show that they are not already providing a default HTTPS main page: www.Google.com, www.Facebook.com, www.Twitter.com, and www.en.Wikipedia.org.
9. Browse to www.Google.com.
10. Enter your name into the search box at the encrypted site.
11. Take a screenshot with your name showing. (See Figure 3-24.)

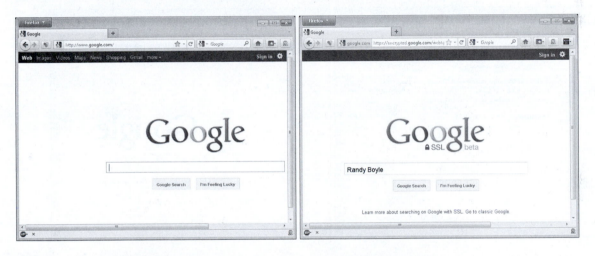

Figure 3-23: Unencrypted Google.com.   Figure 3-24: Encrypted Google.com.

PROJECT QUESTIONS

1. What was the first website listed in the search results for your name?
2. Were the links to the search results encrypted?
3. Which website do you visit most often? Does it offer HTTPS?
4. Do you use HTTPS when you send email?

THOUGHT QUESTIONS

1. Why don't all websites offer HTTPS connections?
2. Would an employer not like you using HTTPS connections? Why?
3. What would you need in order to start offering HTTPS on a website?
4. Is HTTPS only needed when you buy things, or do online banking?

When you are surfing the Internet, it can be difficult to accurately gauge the legitimacy of websites. It's hard to know who really runs a site, where they are located, if they are reputable, if other people trust them, and what other websites they run. Essentially, you want to know if you should trust that website.

Flagfox® is a Firefox add-on that will provide you with information about the websites you are visiting. It uses a variety of applications and services to give you loads of information about the page you are currently visiting. You can even customize the application to provide more information. Flagfox is a simple tool that helps you determine the legitimacy of a website.

1. Open Firefox.
2. Click the Firefox menu and Add-ons.
3. Search for "Flagfox".
4. Click Install (Flagfox), and Restart now. (You should see a small flag in the navigation bar.) (See Figure 3-25.)
5. Browse to www.Google.com.
6. Click on the small flag (Flagfox). (See Figure 3-26.)
7. Take a screenshot. (You should see a map showing www.Google.com's location.)

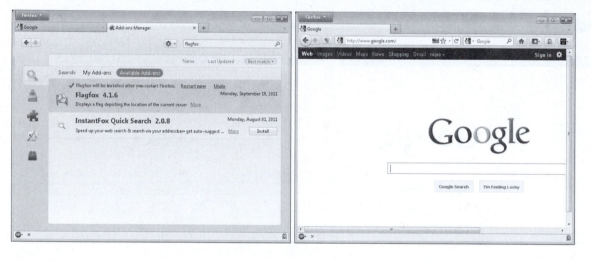

Figure 3-25: Adding the Flagfox add-on.   Figure 3-26: Firefox with Flagfox add-on.

8. Return to the tab showing www.Google.com.
9. Browse to www.BBC.co.uk. (Note that the flag changed.)
10. Right-click the Flagfox icon and select Whois. (Note the registrant information.)
11. Click on the Site Profile tab.
12. Take a screenshot.
13. Return to the tab showing www.BBC.co.uk.
14. Right-click the Flagfox icon and select Alexa. (Note the Alexa Traffic Rank in Great Britain and the world.)
15. Click on the Search Analytics tab that is slightly further down the page.
16. Scroll down until you see a listing of ranked Search Query terms.
17. Take a screenshot.
18. Return to the tab showing www.BBC.co.uk.
19. Right-click the Flagfox icon and select Options.
20. Scroll down and select the option labeled "Same IP".
21. Click Close.

22. Right-click the Flagfox icon and select Same IP.
23. Take a screenshot of the listing showing any other websites being hosted on the same IP address.
24. Return to the tab showing www.BBC.co.uk.
25. Right-click the Flagfox icon and select My Info.
26. Take a screenshot.

PROJECT QUESTIONS

1. What was the closest major city near the location of www.Google.com?
2. Who was the registrant for www.BBC.co.uk?
3. What was the Alexa Traffic Rank for www.BBC.co.uk Great Britian?
4. Who is listed as your Internet Service Provider (ISP)?

THOUGHT QUESTIONS

1. How can two hostnames use the same static IP address?
2. Why is it important to online retailers to know the keywords used to find them?
3. What information does "Whois" return?
4. From a security point of view, why would it be important to know the origin of a website?

3.9   WEB OF TRUST® (WOT)

Most users want an easy way to identify which websites are trustworthy, and which websites they should avoid. Web of Trust® (WOT) provides a "scorecard" for each website you visit. This scorecard gives you a summary of four ratings: trustworthiness, vendor reliability, privacy, and child safety. The values shown on the scorecard are based on ratings from members of the WOT community who have contributed their evaluations of that website.

After installing WOT, you will notice a slight addition to the search results from major search engines (e.g., Google, Bing, and Yahoo). You will see a WOT evaluation at the end of each search result. This evaluation provides a scorecard for each website displayed in the search results. The WOT evaluation can serve as a quick visual indicator of websites to avoid.

1. Open Firefox.
2. Click the Firefox menu, and Add-ons.
3. Search for "WOT".
4. Click Install (WOT), and Restart now. (You should see a small flag in the navigation bar.)
5. Browse to www.Google.com. (You can turn off HTTPS Everywhere if desired.)
6. Click on the WOT icon near your navigation bar. (It looks like a little green circle. You should see a WOT evaluation for www.Google.com.)
7. Enter your name into www.Google.com.
8. Press Google Search.
9. Take a screenshot of the results. (Notice the WOT icons next to each of the search results. See Figure 3-27.)

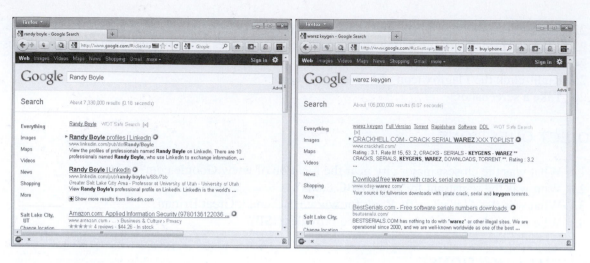

Figure 3-27: Search results with WOT evaluations.   Figure 3-28: WOT evaluations for "warez keygen" search.

10. Click on the WOT icon for one of the search results. (This will show you the WOT scorecard for that specific website.)
11. Browse back to www.Google.com.
12. Search for "warez keygen" without quotes. (You should get a few websites with red circles, meaning they have a poor reputation. See Figure 3-28.)
13. Click on the WOT icon for that website's WOT scorecard.
14. Take a screenshot.
15. Click on another website that you frequently visit, but may not be well known nationally.
16. Click on the WOT icon for that website.

PROJECT QUESTIONS

1. Which website did you look at that you frequently visit?
2. Did that website have a good scorecard?
3. Were there any bad reports showing when you searched for your name?
4. What was the name of the website that had a bad scorecard when you searched for "warez keygen?"

THOUGHT QUESTIONS

1. How does WOT get the values for their website scorecards?
2. Can you evaluate websites using WOT?
3. Where is the WOT service provider (www.mywot.com) located? (Hint: Use Flagfox.)
4. How could WOT help protect you while you surf the Internet?

3.10 ONION ROUTING (TOR®)

It is a common misconception that HTTPS provides anonymous Web browsing. This is not the case. A secured HTTPS connection can ensure confidentiality (i.e., what you're sending can't be read by others) and authentication (i.e., the website you're visiting is really who they say they are). However, it does not provide anonymity. Eavesdroppers cannot see *what* you are sending, but they can see that you are sending *something* to that website.

Onion routing can provide anonymity via an encrypted network of "relay" servers. Computers around the world pass your fully encrypted traffic. The intermediary relay servers do not know the entire path of the onion network. Requests that come from you appear to originate from around the world. You have complete anonymity.

It's still a good idea to use a secured end-to-end HTTPS connection because the connection between the last relay server and the website you are visiting is not encrypted. An HTTPS connection is still necessary. You can read more about onion routing, and its most popular implementation (Tor®) at www.TorProject.org. This project will use Tor to illustrate onion routing.

1. Open a Web browser.
2. Go to http://www.google.com/.
3. Search for "my IP address". (See Figure 3-29.)
4. Press Enter.
5. Click on the first result. (See Figure 3-30.)
6. Take a screenshot showing your IP address.

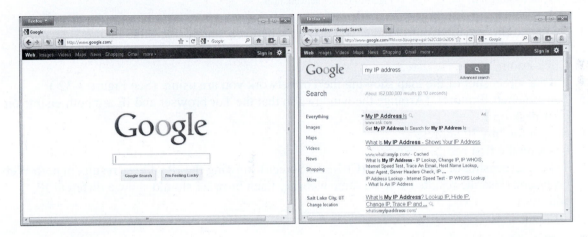

Figure 3-29: Search for your IP address.   Figure 3-30: Results for "my IP address" search.

7. Go to www.TorProject.org.
8. Click Download.
9. Click on the link for Windows 7 under Tor Browser Bundle.
10. Save the file in your C:\security folder.
11. Browse to your C:\security folder.
12. Right-click the Tor executable and select Run as administrator.
13. Click Yes, and Extract.
14. Browse to the C:\security\Tor Browser folder.
15. Right-click the executable labeled "Start Tor Browser.exe" and select Run as administrator.
16. Click Yes. (A new Web browser window should open.)
17. Within the Web browser, go to www.Google.com.
18. Search for "my IP address".
19. Click on the first result. (If you get a warning about an "Untrusted" connection, just click I Understand the Risks, Add Exception, and Confirm Security Exception.)
20. Take a screenshot showing the new IP address. (This is someone else's IP address.)

Figure 3-31: Vidalia control panel.   Figure 3-32: Tor network map.

21. Switch to the Vidalia Control Panel that opened when you started Tor. (See Figure 3-31.)
22. Click on View the Network.
23. Click Zoom To Fit.
24. Take a screenshot of the map showing the Tor network you are using. (See Figure 3-32.)
25. Start Internet Explorer. (Arrange the windows so that the Tor browser and IE are both visible on your desktop.)
26. Search for "my IP address".
27. Click on the first result.
28. Take a screenshot of your desktop (Ctrl-PrintScreen) showing the IP address results in both Web browsers. (Use the results from the same website. Each browser should show a different IP address.)

PROJECT QUESTIONS

1. What was your real IP address?
2. What was the IP address shown when you used Tor?
3. A list of relay servers was shown next to the Tor Network Map. Where was the first relay server from?
4. Approximately how many countries did your Tor network go through?

THOUGHT QUESTIONS

1. What do relay servers do in a Tor network?
2. Could you act as a relay server? How?
3. Can the relay servers read the traffic being sent through them?
4. Do you still need HTTPS if you are using Tor? Why or why not?

chapter 4

One of the increasingly important pieces of software people ask about is application layer filters (i.e., porn filters, spam filters, etc.). More specifically, individuals are seeking solutions to keep their children safe. Companies are looking for ways to keep their employees productive while on the clock. Application layer filters can solve both of these problems.

Talking about porn filters is not regular conversational fare. In fact, it makes some people uncomfortable to even talk about it. However, once you broach the subject, people are interested and will likely want to implement a solution right away. The response from parents can be overwhelming. They want to protect their children but are just not sure how to do it.

Spam is easier to talk about, but people tend to be less motivated to devote resources to solve this problem. Employers are more likely to want a strong spam filter. The larger your organization is, the more likely you are to need a spam filter. Spam, unlike porn, is illegal. However, the enforcement of the existing spam laws has been anemic at best. Companies have been forced to defend themselves against this electronic plague. There are some excellent commercial products available.

Companies are becoming aware that they can, and often are, held liable when one of their employees creates a hostile work environment by viewing porn at work or sending pornographic emails. In the past ten years, companies have really started to crack down on employees who view porn at work. Not only is viewing porn at work illegal, but it also reduces employee productivity.

We will only look at personal application filters in this book (e.g., porn and spam filters). If your organization needs a commercial porn/spam filter, you should test a variety of products before you buy.

Time required to complete this chapter: 30 minutes.

Chapter Objectives

Learn how to:
1. Configure a Web filter.
2. Create an email filter.
3. Block email senders.
4. Configure spam settings.

Chapter Projects

Project:
4.1 K-9
4.2 Email Filter (Outlook)
4.3 Block Senders (Outlook)
4.4 Junk Email (Hotmail)

K-9® is a free porn filter that allows users to block Internet content that they feel is inappropriate. Users can make exceptions, block/unblock whole categories, and override any filtering. Only the administrator can make changes to the program settings and the account is locked with a password. If someone tries to access the administrator account (sometimes people foolishly try to guess passwords), it will send the administrator an email telling him or her that someone is trying to make changes to the account. This is a great feature for parents with persistent children.

Using a porn filter is great for adults too. It assures that you will avoid potentially embarrassing situations. For example, a business professional can feel confident that he or she won't accidentally hit a pornographic page during an important presentation. You only have to have one important meeting go badly to see the value of a good porn filter. You can always override it, but it's nice to know that it's there, keeping you safe.

Parents are typically very interested in using porn filters. Porn is prevalent and one of the most profitable industries on the Internet. We'll test the filter after we are done, to see how effective it is at filtering porn. Let's walk through an installation.

1. Click on the following link: http://www1.k9webprotection.com/getk9/index.php.
2. Fill in a first name, last name, and a valid email address. (In this example, we used John Doe.)
3. Click the Request License button and an email will arrive in about 5 minutes with the license code to activate the software.
4. Click on the email link to get the download: http://www1.k9webprotection.com/getk9/download-software.php.
5. Click on the Download for Windows button.
6. Click Run, and then Run again, if prompted to do so. (Make sure you run the setup program with administrator-level access.)
7. Click Next, I Agree, and Next.
8. Copy the license code from the email you received and paste it into the box labeled "License". (One of the codes I got was K9USERFE43; this one is already used and won't work again.)
9. Enter a password that only you will know, or one given to you by your instructor, if you are using a remote machine. (This password will allow you to override the Web filter and change its settings.)
10. Write this password down. (REMEMBER YOUR PASSWORD!)
11. Enter the same password in both boxes.
12. Click Next, Next, Install, and Finish. (This completes the installation and will restart your computer.)
13. Open K9 by clicking Start, All Programs, Blue Coat K9, and Blue Coat K9.
14. Take a screenshot.
15. Click Setup.
16. Enter your administrator password.
17. Feel free to select/deselect any categories.
18. Take a screenshot.
19. Click View Internet Activity at the top of the screen.
20. Take a screenshot.
21. Open your Web browser and test the porn filter to see if it is effective by entering www.playboy.com or www.sex.com.
22. Take a screenshot. (Hopefully, it blocked the request.)
23. You can enter your password to temporarily override the block.
24. Open K9 again and click on View Internet Activity.
25. Take a screenshot.

26. Click on the Pornography link to view the details for that category.
27. Take a screenshot.

PROJECT QUESTIONS

1. What was your license code?
2. In your Activity Summary, how many Web Advertisements were blocked?
3. In your Activity Summary, how many Pornography requests were blocked?
4. In the View Activity Detail screen, what was the date listed when it blocked the pornography websites?

THOUGHT QUESTIONS

1. Can you put in custom exceptions for specific pages that are blocked by default?
2. How does the filter make the list of "blocked" pages?
3. Does the filter work for foreign languages? Slang?
4. What other things would you want to block/filter? Could you filter IM, chat, specific photos, or songs?

4.2   EMAIL FILTER (OUTLOOK®)

Corporations and homes are inundated with about 100 billion illegal spam emails every day (CAN-SPAM Act of 2003). Billions of dollars ($11–20B depending on the survey you look at) are lost each year from decreased productivity. Not to mention the fact that it is annoying. Don't purchase anything from spam email. It just encourages more bad behavior.

Many large companies use their own spam filters on their mail servers to reduce the workload on end users. However, they don't want to accidently delete valid emails. Setting up spam filtering rules can be tricky. To solve this dilemma, many companies add a special tag (e.g., [SPAM]) to the subject line of a potential spam email. This additional tag indicates that the email may be spam. Users can then make a custom filter using this [SPAM] tag to send offending emails to a "junk" folder. Ask your administrator if your employer is using a server-level spam filter with this capability.

Below are instructions to create a filtering rule in Microsoft Outlook®. We will take care of spam in a later project. It's important to learn how filters work so you can get an idea of how email can be filtered. Most in-boxes are wildly out of control and need to be managed.

Many people give out the *same* email address to both work associates, and friends. This project will show you how to make a filter to automatically separate emails into different folders. First, we will create a "Friends" folder. Next, we will make a filtering rule to send all emails you receive from a friend to the Friends folder.

Note: If you don't have access to Outlook, you can skip the projects that require it. Later projects use Hotmail® and/or Gmail®.

1. Open Outlook.
2. Right-click on Mailbox.
3. Select New Folder.
4. Enter "Friends" in the Name text box. (See Figure 4-1.)
5. Click OK.

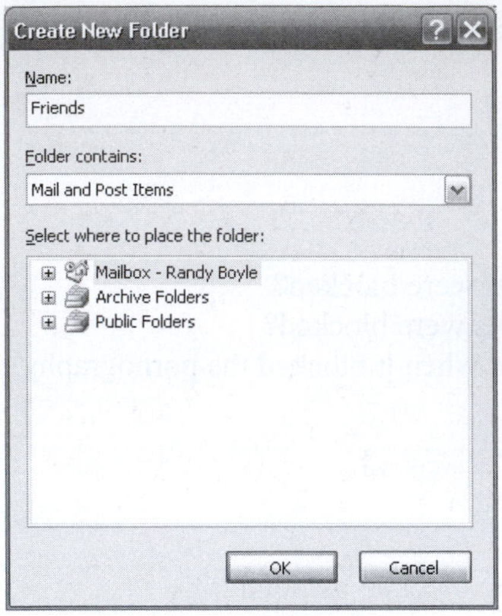

Figure 4-1: Manage Outlook mail folders.

6. Click Tools, and Rules and Alerts.
7. Click New Rule. (See Figure 4-2.)
8. Select "Move messages from someone to a folder". (See Figure 4-3.)
9. Click Next.

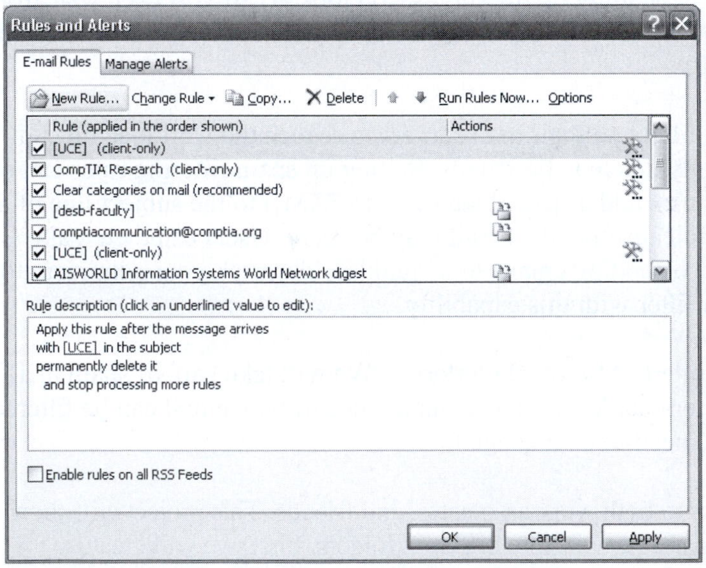

Figure 4-2: Manage Outlook rules and alerts.

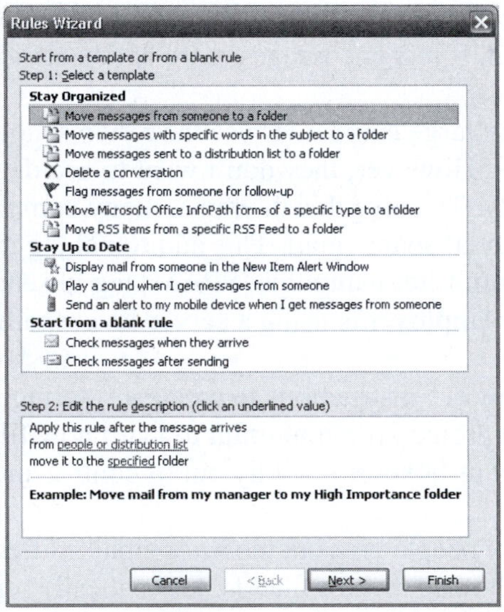

Figure 4-3: Outlook rules wizard.

10. Click on the highlighted text in the bottom pane (Step 2) labeled "people or distribution list". (See Figure 4-4.)
11. Double-click on anyone in your Address Book (preferably a friend). (See Figure 4-5.)

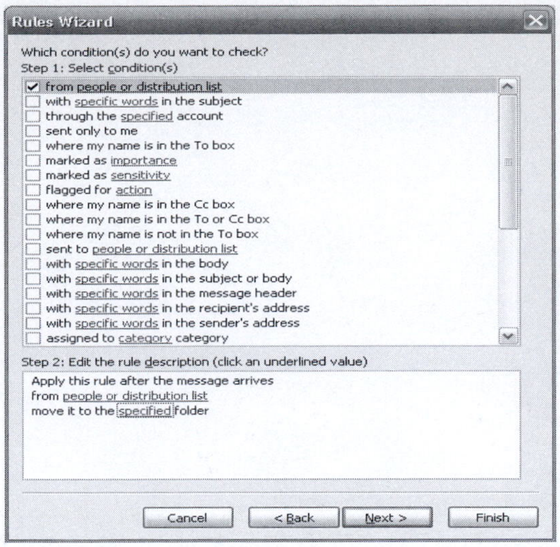

Figure 4-4: Select conditions to filter.

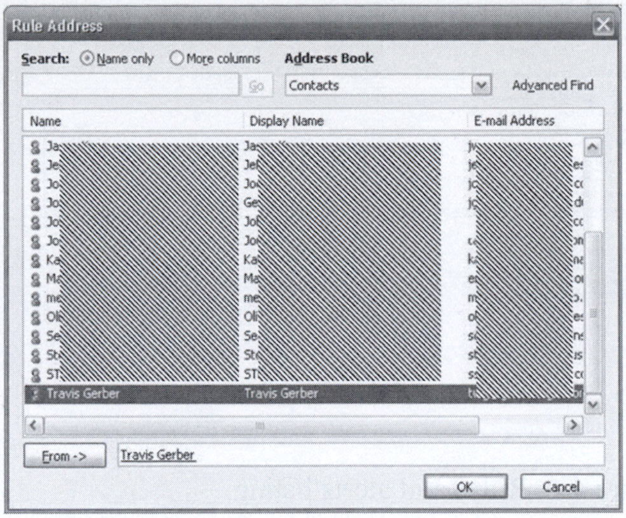

Figure 4-5: Select source contact to filter.

12. Click OK.
13. Click Next.
14. Click on the highlighted text in the bottom pane (Step 2) labeled "specified". (See Figure 4-6.)
15. Double-click on the Friends folder.
16. Take a screenshot. (See Figure 4-7.)

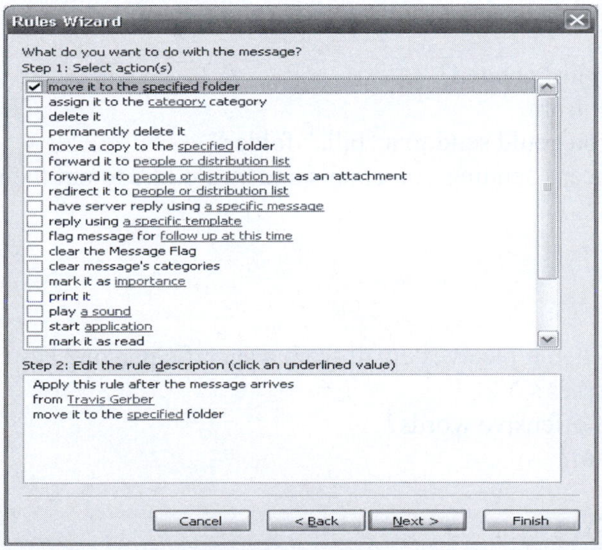

Figure 4-6: Action to take with email.

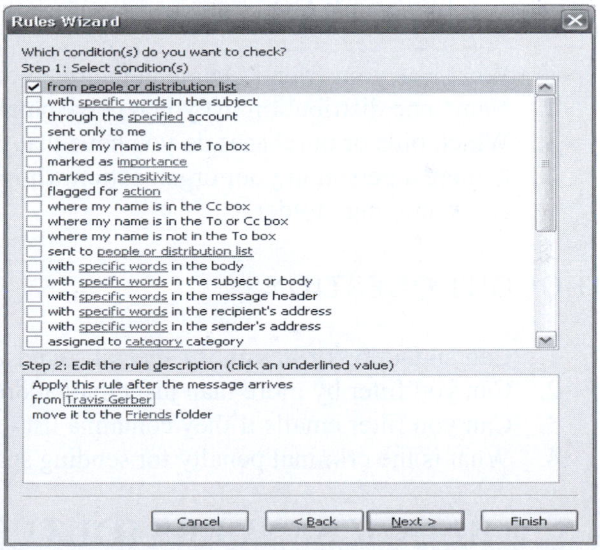

Figure 4-7: Conditions for filtering.

17. Click Next, Next, Next (no exceptions), and Finish.
18. Take a screenshot. (See Figure 4-8.)
19. Click OK.

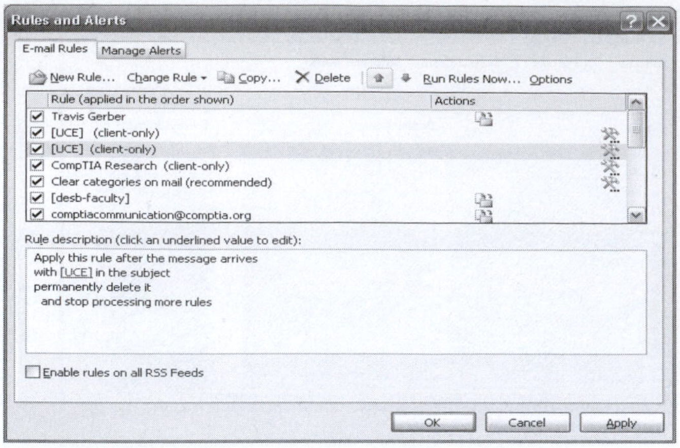

Figure 4-8: Rules and alerts listing.

The next time you get an email from the person you selected in the list, the email should go into your Friends folder. You can repeat this procedure for all your friends. You can also create new folders for notices, bills, clients, or a specific organization.

Taking a few minutes to set up some basic email rules will help you take control of your Inbox, and save you a lot of time in the future. Nothing is worse than seeing an Inbox with 100+ emails in it.

PROJECT QUESTIONS

1. What was your friend's name in the rule you just created?
2. Name one distribution list you receive email from.
3. Which bills or purchases do you have that you could send to a "bills" folder?
4. Is there a person in your organization who keeps sending you emails and you'd like to put them in an "Annoying" folder?

THOUGHT QUESTIONS

1. Can an Outlook filter play a special sound when it receives email from a specific person? How?
2. Can you filter by more than just email addresses?
3. Can you filter emails if they contain a list of offensive words?
4. What is the criminal penalty for sending spam?

4.3   BLOCK SENDERS (OUTLOOK)

You will inevitably get a gaggle of annoying emails from individuals who believe they have the right to force you to accept their emails. Luckily, it is possible to automatically ignore these petulant spammers.

Blocking people from sending you emails is quick and easy. However, if you are getting a lot of junk emails, you should consider changing to a different email provider. You don't have to sit there and waste your time blocking emails that the administrator should be taking care of. Gmail and Hotmail have gotten much better at blocking spam over the years. Let's look at an example of how to block a sender in Outlook.

1. Open Outlook.
2. Click on the Inbox folder.

3. Select an email or send yourself an email that we will block. (Don't worry, we will show you how to unblock it later.)
4. Take a screenshot. (See Figure 4-9.)
5. Click Actions, Junk E-mail, and Add Sender to Blocked Senders List. (You can also right-click the email.) (See Figure 4-10.)
6. Click the Junk E-mail folder.
7. Take a screenshot.

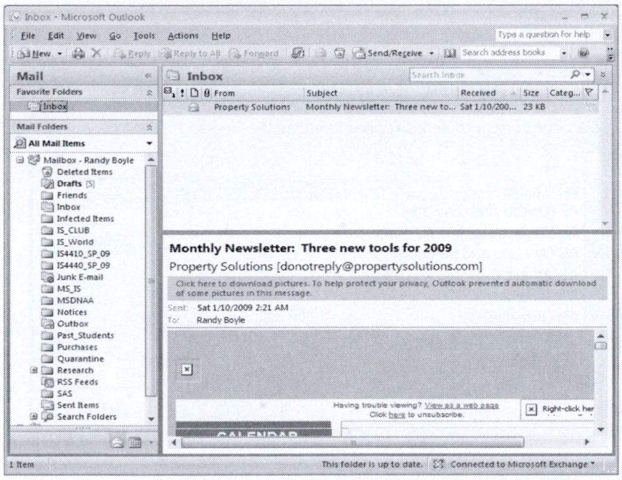

Figure 4-9: Select sender to block. 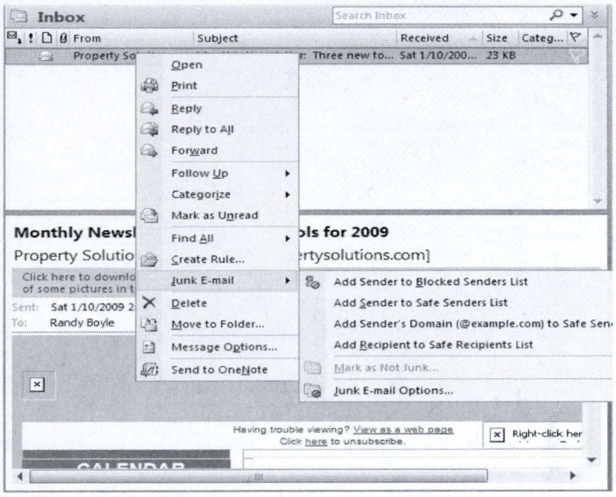   Figure 4-10: Junk email.

8.   Click Actions, Junk E-mail, and Junk E-mail Options.
9.   Click on the Blocked Senders tab.
10. Select the email address you just blocked.
11. Take a screenshot. (See Figure 4-11.)
12. If you blocked your own email address, select your email address and click Remove.
13. Click on the International tab.
14. Click Blocked Top-Level Domain List.
15. Select any three of the countries listed.
16. Take a screenshot. (See Figure 4-12.)

Note: Several countries are notorious for sending spam. Blocking emails from a given country is really easy. Unfortunately, the spammers have caught on and now only send emails that look like they are coming from internal domains.

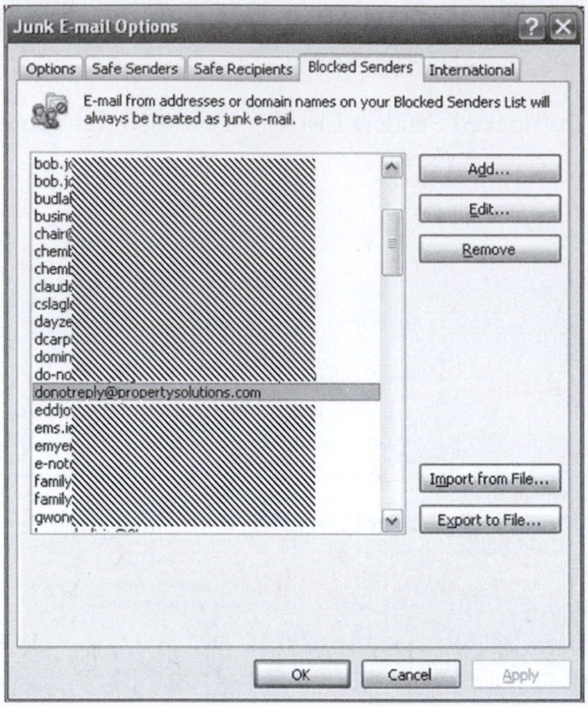

Figure 4-11: List of blocked senders.

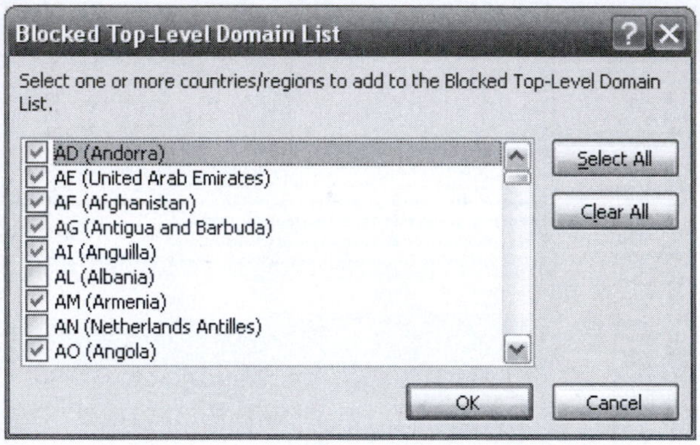

Figure 4-12: Block emails from top-level domains.

PROJECT QUESTIONS

1. What was the email address you blocked?
2. Name one other email address you would block?
3. Which three countries did you block on the Top-Level Domain List?
4. Which country in the Top-Level Domain List do you think sends the most spam?

THOUGHT QUESTIONS

1. Who is in charge of tracking down and arresting spammers?
2. Is sending spam from a fake email address possible? Easy?
3. How much does spam cost corporations each year?
4. Which countries send the most spam per capita?

4.4   JUNK EMAIL (HOTMAIL)

Most people should have at least three email addresses. You should have one for friends, one for work, and one for Internet use (in case you are required to give a real email address for a download). It's a good idea to keep your personal emails from bouncing off work email servers. All the email going over company servers is considered company property and can be read anytime.

Most email programs can check multiple email accounts at the same time, so three accounts is not a big deal. They just take some time to set up. In this project, you will sign up for an online email account and set up some junk mail preferences. They use similar settings that you saw in the Outlook project. If you already have a Hotmail account, you can skip down to step 7.

1. Go to www.hotmail.com.

2. Click Sign up. (See Figure 4-13.)
3. In the Windows Live ID box, enter your FirstNameLastName12345. (The author's was RandyBoyle12345.)
4. Click Check Availability.
5. Enter fake information for the rest of the text boxes. (See Figure 4-14.)
6. Click I Accept to log in.
7. Take a screenshot of your inbox showing your new email address. (See Figure 4-15.)

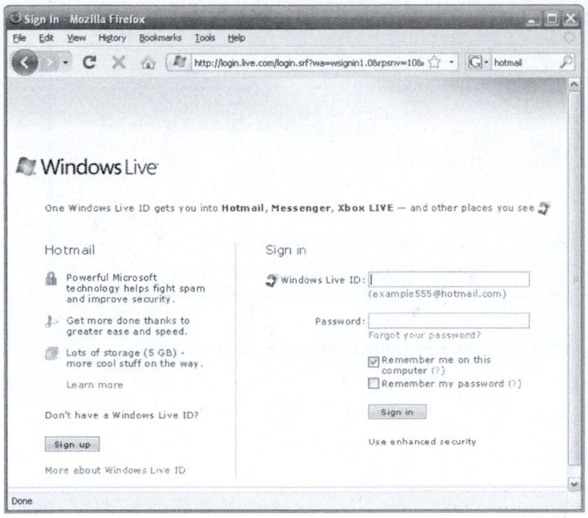

Figure 4-13: Hotmail sign-in.

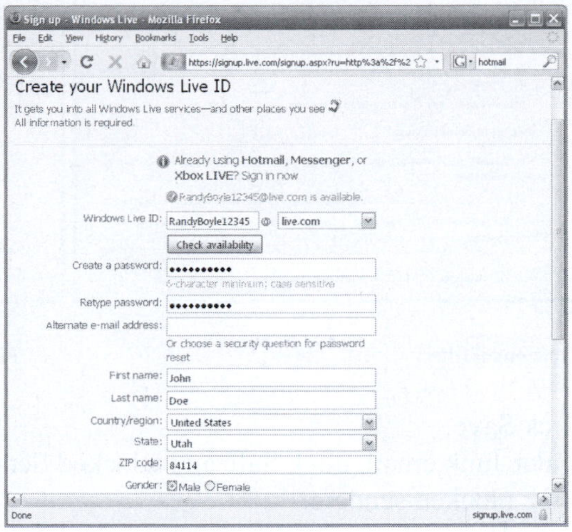

Figure 4-14: Creating a Windows Live ID.

8. Click Options on the right-hand of the screen.
9. Click More options.
10. Under Junk email, click Filters and reporting. (See Figure 4-16.)
11. Under Delete junk email, select Immediately. (You'll likely never see spam.)
12. Under Report junk message, select Report junk. (You'll help get rid of spam.)
13. Take a screenshot. (See Figure 4-17.)

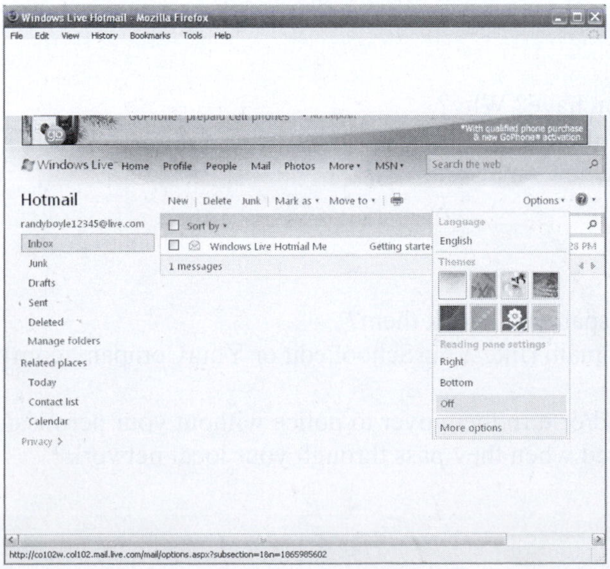

Figure 4-15: Hotmail inbox.

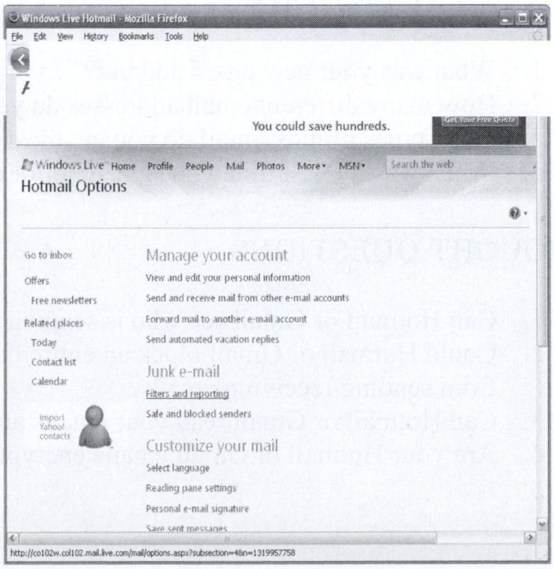

Figure 4-16: Hotmail configuration options.

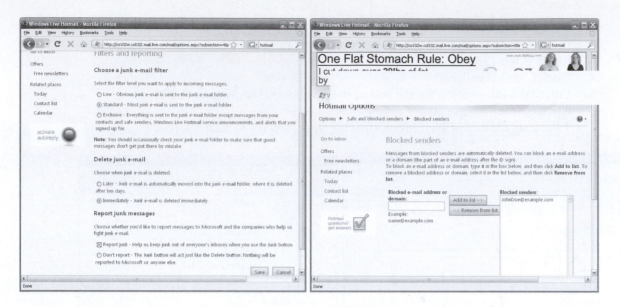

Figure 4-17: Junk email filter.   Figure 4-18: Blocked senders configuration screen.

14. Click Save.
15. Under Junk email, click Safe and Blocked Senders.
16. Click blocked senders.
17. In the Blocked e-mail address box, enter JohnDoe@example.com.
18. Click Add to List.
19. Take a screenshot. (See Figure 4-18.)

If you use Gmail, you will have even more control over filtering emails. Gmail has similar filtering mechanisms that you may have used in Outlook. You won't have to do another project using Gmail. If you were able to work through the prior two examples, you are more than capable of setting up the Gmail email filters.

PROJECT QUESTIONS

1. What was your new email address?
2. How many different email addresses do you have? Why?
3. What types of junk email do you get most often?
4. When was the last time you signed up for a new email address?

THOUGHT QUESTIONS

1. Can Hotmail or Gmail see who is sending spam and block them?
2. Could Hotmail or Gmail block an entire domain (like YourSchool.edu or YourCompany.com) from sending/receiving emails?
3. Can Hotmail or Gmail read your emails and/or turn them over to police without your permission?
4. Are your Hotmail or Gmail emails encrypted when they pass through your local network?

chapter 5

There are many ways to monitor a user. Monitoring user behavior will increase productivity and prevent undesired behaviors. It may also prevent illicit user behavior for which a corporation could be held liable. This chapter will look at a few pieces of software that can be used to monitor user behavior.

A keylogger is a piece of software or hardware that records all keystrokes on a computer. Over the years, keyloggers have added functionality and become much more than just a tool to capture keystrokes. As a result, many people have tried to come up with new terms to convey the fact that these new products have added functionality. However, most people still use the term "keylogger" to mean a piece of software that monitors a person's activity on a computer.

Keyloggers can be hidden from users. A certain sequence of keys can be pressed to reveal the keylogger program and configuration screen. Information gathered from logging sessions can be stored in encrypted files and/or sent to a pre-specified email account at regular intervals. Keyloggers can also hide themselves from anti-virus scans.

Keyloggers can be used by concerned parents wanting to monitor Internet activity, spouses worried about infidelity, employers suspicious of employees, and hackers capturing passwords on compromised systems. Users can use keyloggers on their own computers to ensure that no one else is using their machine for malicious purposes.

Time required to complete this chapter: 60 minutes

Chapter Objectives

Learn how to:
1. Configure a keylogger.
2. Understand the capabilities of enterprise-level monitoring software.
3. Understand the filtering and monitoring capabilities of open-source software.
4. Configure loss prevention and monitoring software.

Chapter Projects

Project:
5.1 Refog Keylogger
5.2 Spector 360
5.3 Untangle
5.4 Prey

Refog® is a really good keylogger with a simple interface. There are monitoring suites available that have more functionality, but the downside is that they cost anywhere from $50 to $100 or more. Refog is one of the few GUI-based keyloggers that is free. Most keyloggers will be free to download, but will then require you to pay $20–$70 to get full functionality. Refog has a trial version, and you can get the full version by completing an online offer.

Refog can stay completely hidden until you press the specific key sequence to recall the main window. It can automatically load the keylogger and hide it from users. It also monitors programs, websites, chat, and can take screenshots at specified time intervals.

WARNING Do NOT load a keylogger on any computer that is not your own. You can get in trouble. It's not worth the risk of loading a keylogger onto a machine that is not your own.

Important Your anti-virus may tell you that these keyloggers are a virus. Windows Defender® should give you a couple of notices that this keylogger is a virus. Although these keyloggers are not viruses, it is actually comforting to see your anti-virus software doing its job. It's good to know that your computer could actually keep someone else from installing a keylogger without your knowledge.

If your anti-virus program recognizes these files as viruses, you will need to create an exception folder to store your files. Appendix A shows you how to create an exception folder using McAfee or Norton.

1. Download Refog from http://www.refog.com.
2. Click Download for the REFOG Keylogger.
3. Click Download Keylogger Trial Version.
4. Click Save.

**Important ** Your anti-virus may tell you that this keylogger is a virus. It is not a virus. You may have to make an exception to allow the download to proceed.

5. Select the C:\security folder.
6. If the program doesn't automatically open, browse to C:\security.
7. Right-click refog_keylogger.exe.
8. Select Run as administrator.
9. Click Yes, if prompted.
10. Click Install.
11. Click OK, Next, I Agree, Next, Next, Next, Install, and Finish.
12. Click Start, All Programs, REFOG Keylogger, and REFOG Keylogger. (You can also click on the desktop shortcut.)
13. Click Buy Later.
14. Click Next, Next, Next, Next, Next, and Finish.
15. Click the green Play button to start monitoring.
16. Press the Hide button. (It has a little eye on it.)
17. Click OK. (Note that you will need to run "runrefog," or press Ctrl+ Shift+Alt+K to get to the Refog screen again.)

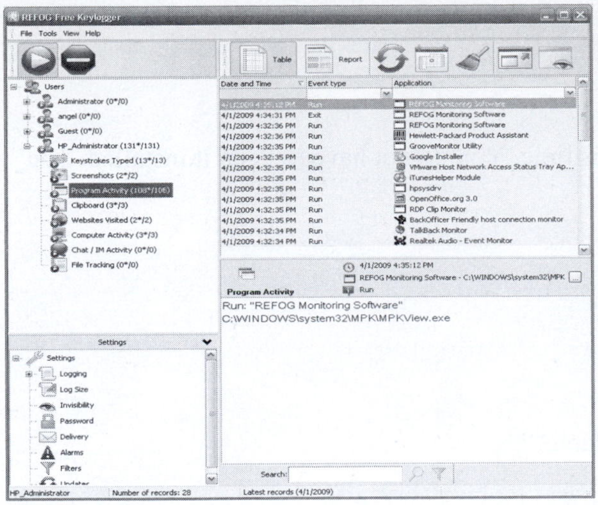

Figure 5-1: Monitoring program activity.

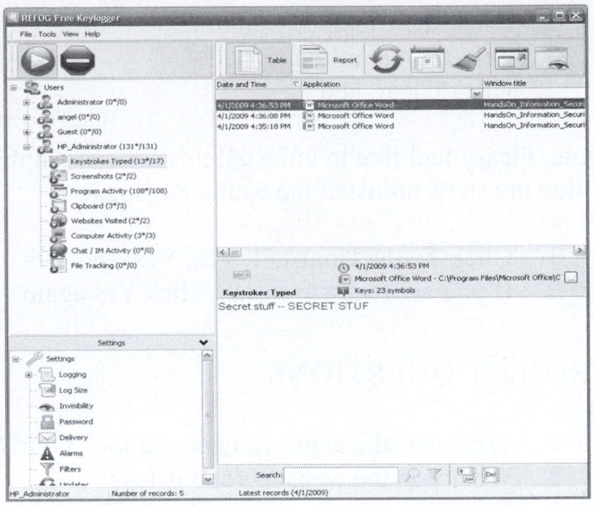

Figure 5-2: Results from monitoring keystrokes.

18. Make a Word document or send yourself an email with the words "YourName, Credit card number, SSN, and Secret Stuff." (Replace "YourName" with your first and last name. In this case, it was Randy Boyle.)

19. Open a Web browser and visit a couple of websites.

20. Click Start and in the Run box type "runrefog" to get the Refog Keylogger window to show again. (You may also be able to press Shift+Ctrl+Alt+K or Ctrl+Shift+Alt+K to get the program to show again. Students have had mixed success with the keystroke shortcuts.)

21. Click on Program Activity under your username.

22. Take a screenshot. (See Figure 5-1.)

23. Click on Keystrokes Typed under your username.

24. Take a screenshot. (See Figure 5-2.)

25. Scroll through the bottom window to see all the words you just typed.

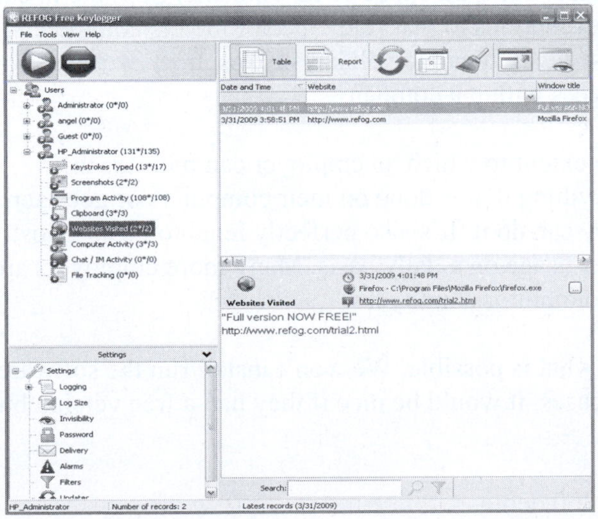

Figure 5-3: Websites visited.

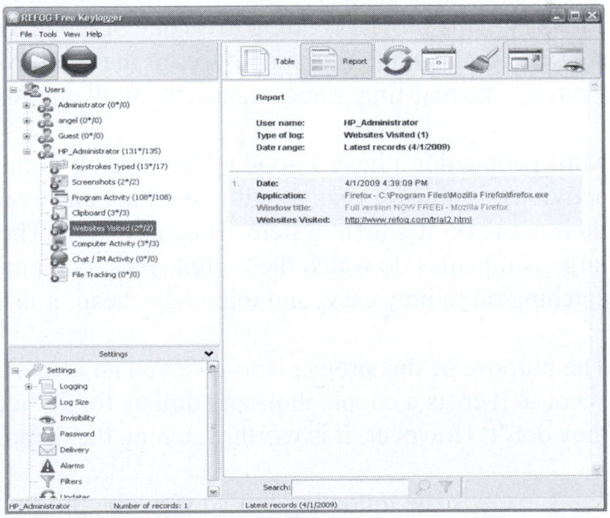

Figure 5-4: Details for websites visited.

26. Click on Websites Visited.

27. Take a screenshot. (See Figure 5-3.)

28. Click on the Report button at the top of the screen.

29. Take a screenshot. (See Figure 5-4.)

30. Click the Clear Logs button.
31. Select Clear all logs.
32. Click Clear, and Yes.

Note: Please feel free to uninstall this software at this time. You do not have to keep it installed. The following steps uninstall the Refog Keylogger.

1. Click Tools, Uninstall, Yes, Yes, and Yes.
2. If you are ready to restart, click Yes again.

PROJECT QUESTIONS

1. What was the name you entered for "YourName"?
2. What was the website you visited?
3. What programs were listed under Program Activity?
4. What was the time/date you typed in your last keystrokes?

THOUGHT QUESTIONS

1. Does your employer/spouse/roommate monitor your activities with a keylogger? Are you sure?
2. What would happen if your employer/spouse/roommate found out you were using a keylogger to monitor their activities?
3. Why would someone want to install a keylogger on his or her own computer?
4. How would you know if you had a keylogger on your computer? How would you get rid of it?

5.2   SPECTOR 360®

This book was written to give beginning students practical experiences with real-world security software. We have focused on free Windows-based software that shows the range of functionality possible in each category. This project is going to be one of the few exceptions to that rule. Spector360® is commercial software that can monitor employees at the enterprise level. It can log all keystrokes, track websites visited, take real-time screenshots, etc. of all employees within a company.

Most people don't have a good understanding of the extent to which an employer can monitor their activities. Employers can monitor anything and everything that is done on their computers or goes across their network. It's their system. They pay for it. They can do it. It's also perfectly legal to do so. Most large companies do watch their employees' computer usage on a daily basis. Many more employers are catching on to how easy, and relatively cheap, it is to monitor employees.

The purpose of this project is to give you an idea of what is possible. We won't install/run the software because it costs a couple thousand dollars for 25 licenses. It would be nice if they had a free version but they don't. However, it is worth watching the demo.

1. Click the following link to view the Spector360 demo:
    http://www.spector360.com/Resources/OnlineDemos/.
2. Click View Demo for the Product Overview Demonstration (8 minutes).
3. Take a screenshot while it's playing.
4. Click View Demo for the Recording Tools Demonstration.
5. Click on one of the Recording Tools you find interesting.
6. Take a screenshot while it's playing.
7. Click View Demo for the Internet Filtering and Employee Monitoring.

8. Take a screenshot while it's playing.

PROJECT QUESTIONS

1. What surprised you most about Spector 360's monitoring ability?
2. What do you think about Spector 360's reporting capabilities?
3. Would you change any of your behaviors at work? Which ones?
4. Which policy violation do you think is violated most often at your workplace?

THOUGHT QUESTIONS

1. Could this software help reduce wasted time at work? How?
2. Could this software help protect the company from being sued? How?
3. Could this software hurt employee morale and lead to other negative behaviors?
4. What industries or types of companies could really benefit from this software?

5.3 UNTANGLE®

Untangle® is an application that integrates a variety of open-source monitoring software into a single management console. It can monitor all traffic that passes over a network. It also has the ability to filter out unwanted traffic.

The Untangle Lite® Package is free and uses open-source software. In this project, you won't install Untangle because it requires additional hardware that you may not have (i.e., a server that will pass traffic between your internal network and your gateway). If you have access to a testing server, it's well worth the effort to install and configure Untangle.

In this project, you will watch a couple of videos exploring Untangle's functionality, its value to businesses, and reporting ability. You will see that Untangle is extraordinarily easy to use. It also combines monitoring and filtering functions. Most importantly, it's completely free.

1. Open a Web browser.
2. Browse to http://www.untangle.com/video-intro/.
3. Click on the Intro to Untangle video (2 minutes).
4. Take a screenshot while it's playing. (See Figure 5-5.)
5. Browse to the following link to view the Untangle videos: http://www.untangle.com/videos/.
6. Click on the Application Control link (10 minutes). (Watching them in full-screen mode makes it easier to see the presentation.)
7. Take a screenshot while it's playing. (See Figure 5-6.)

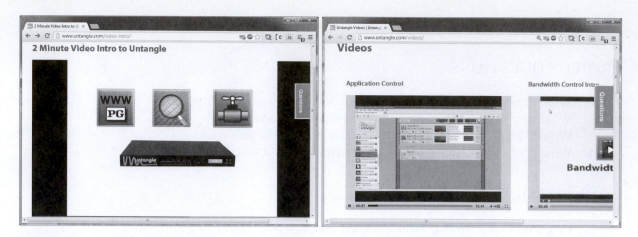

Figure 5-5: Intro to Untangle video.   Figure 5-6: Application Control video.

8. Click on the Reports link (11 minutes).
9. Take a screenshot while it's playing. (See Figure 5-7.)

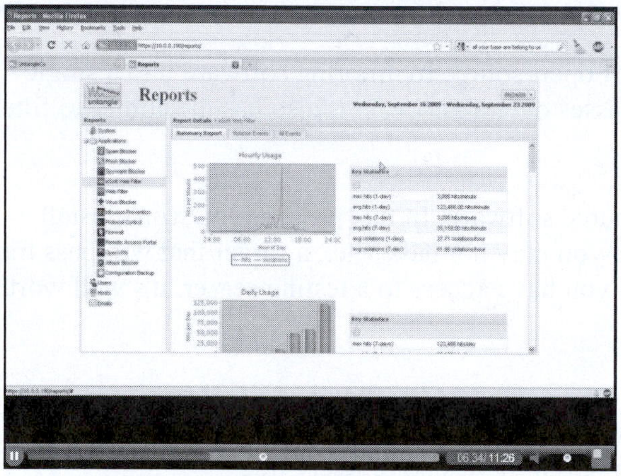

Figure 5-7: Untangle Reports video.

PROJECT QUESTIONS

1. Which Untangle report do you think would be most valuable? Why?
2. Realistically, how long do you think it would take you to set up an Untangle server to manage your network?
3. What is displayed in your screenshot for the Untangle Platform Overview?
4. Which application in Untangle would add the most value where you work? Why?

THOUGHT QUESTIONS

1. How can Untangle add value to a business?
2. Why would open-source applications, like those used in Untangle, be attractive to businesses?
3. Is it difficult to add functionality to Untangle? Why?
4. Could Untangle be used to stop policy violations? How?

5.4   PREY®

Prey® is an application that allows you to monitor your computer – after it is stolen! It allows a user to geographically locate a laptop or cell phone through a web interface after it has been stolen. Prey also allows a user to take a screenshot of the stolen device, take a webcam picture of the thief, and completely lock down the device.

Prey is completely free, and can help reduce the staggering amount of corporate property theft. Most people can identify with the horrible feeling they experienced after having property stolen. If you have Prey installed, it can give you hope that your device will be recovered if stolen. Oftentimes, it can be recovered in a couple of hours.

1. Download Prey from http://preyproject.com/.
2. Click Download now.
3. Click Save.
4. Select the C:\security folder.
5. If the program doesn't automatically open, browse to C:\security.
6. Right-click the Prey installation program (prey-0.5.3-win.exe). (The version number will vary depending on how often new versions of Prey are released. Your file name will likely be different.)
7. Click Run, Next, I Agree, Next, Install, and Finish.
8. Click OK, Next, Next, and Next. (See Figure 5-8.)
9. Enter your name, an email address, and password.
10. Take a screenshot. (See Figure 5-9.)
11. Click Create, OK, and OK.

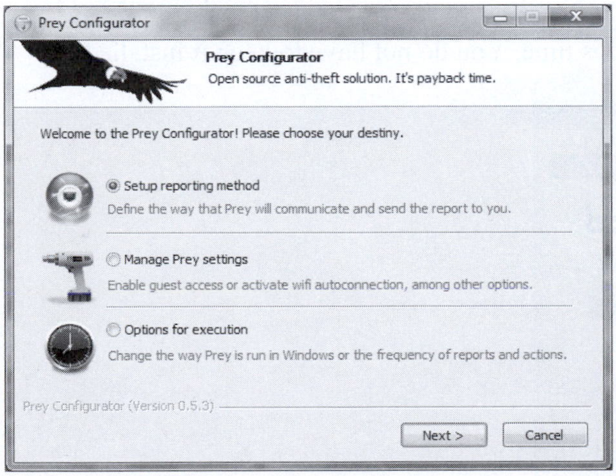

Figure 5-8: Prey setup.

Figure 5-9: Creating a Prey account.

12. Check your email for a confirmation email.
13. Click on the account activation link in the Prey email.
14. Enter the username and password you chose for your Prey installation.
15. Take a screenshot. (See Figure 5-10.)
16. Click Log in.
17. Click on the laptop icon.
18. Change the frequency of reports to 10 minutes, and the Missing status to YES.
19. Click Save Changes. (See Figure 5-11.)
20. Click on the Devices link in the upper left-hand corner of the Web page.

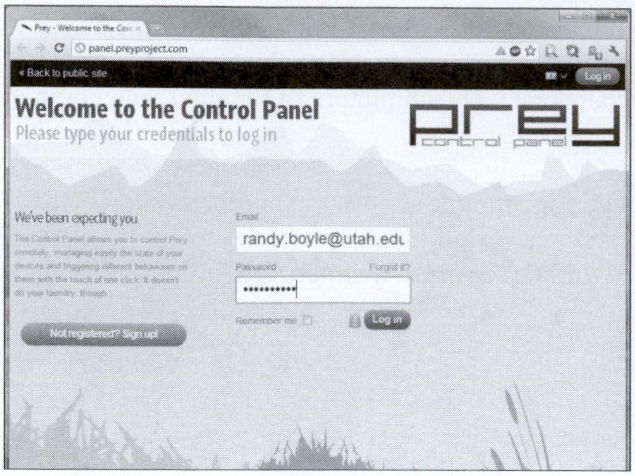

Figure 5-10: Logging into the Prey website. 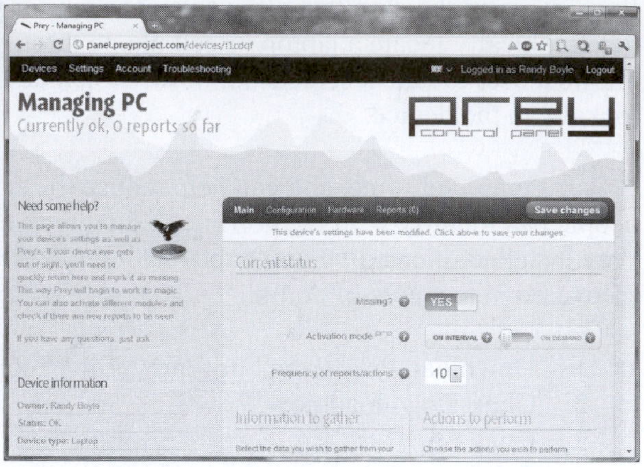   Figure 5-11: Changing Prey status.

21. In about 10 minutes you will get a Prey report about your "stolen" computer. Click on the email link to the report.

Note: It may take as long as 15 minutes to issue the first report. You don't have to sit and wait for the report. You can move on to another project or take a well-deserved break. If you have a webcam, don't be surprised if it automatically activates. It will take a picture. This is part of the Prey recovery process.

22. Take a screenshot of the Prey report. (See Figure 5-12.)

Note: Please feel free to uninstall this software at this time. You do not have to keep it installed.

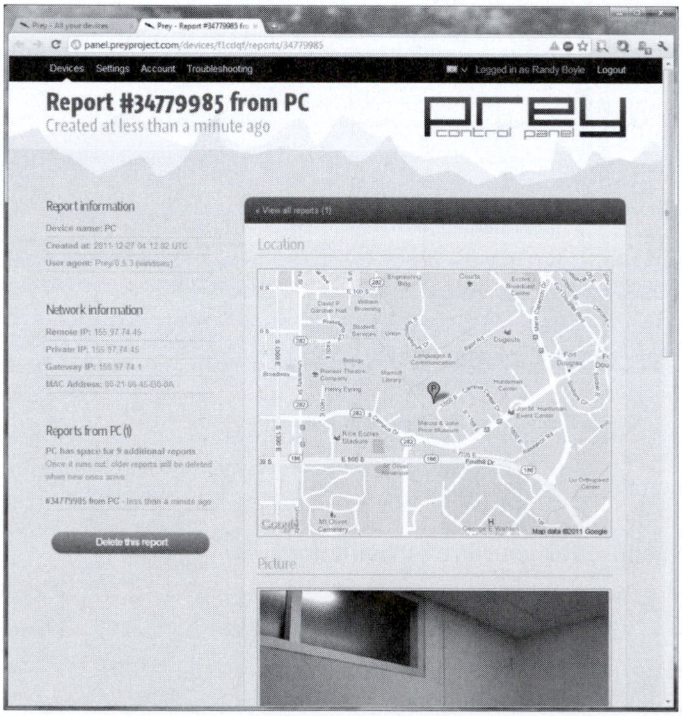

Figure 5-12: Prey report.

PROJECT QUESTIONS

1. What location was mapped in the report?
2. What time was the report created?
3. What was displayed on the screenshot of your computer?
4. What was your IP address at the time the report was issued?

THOUGHT QUESTIONS

1. How could a business or organization use Prey to reduce property theft?
2. Does Prey collect other information about your computer?
3. Could the prey report be used as evidence in court?
4. Can Prey remotely wipe all the passwords and lock your stolen laptop?

CHAPTER 6: PASSWORD AUDITORS

chapter 6

All major corporations run password audits to ensure that users have strong passwords. If just one user has a weak password, the entire company is at risk. Criminals only need one weak password to access an entire computer system.

A password audit will identify those weak passwords. Network administrators will notify users that they need to change their weak passwords. Password audits are a critical part of an overall corporate security policy.

Below are some of the most well known password auditors (or "crackers") available and in use today. You will run them on your own passwords to see how secure they are. You will run brute force and dictionary attacks. You will also create a rainbow table and use it to crack a random password.

You will also see how to make secure passwords. Using secure passwords will help protect your computer, data, online accounts, and cell phone. Secure passwords will also help ensure your privacy.

Time required to complete this chapter: 60 minutes

Chapter Objectives

Learn how to:
1. Crack passwords.
2. Dump your local passwords.
3. Audit an Excel password.
4. Perform a dictionary attack.
5. Look up default passwords.
6. Evaluate the strength of a password.
7. Generate a strong password.
8. Create rainbow tables.
9. Use rainbow tables to crack passwords.

Chapter Projects

Project:
6.1 John the Ripper (JtR)
6.2 Local Password Audit
6.3 Free Word & Excel Password Recovery
6.4 Cain & Able (passwords)
6.5 Default Passwords
6.6 Password Evaluator
6.7 Password Generators
6.8 Rainbow Tables
6.9 Rainbow Crack

One of the most well known password auditing programs in use today is John the Ripper® (JtR). It has been used for many years and has proven to be robust, efficient, and easy to use. You can read more about JtR at http://www.openwall.com/john/.

Once you have downloaded JtR, you will have a folder called "john" followed by a version number (e.g., 179) in the security directory. JtR is a command-line program. You will run JtR in the command prompt (DOS). You can read more about how to use JtR at www.openwall.com.

1. Download JtR from http://www.openwall.com/john/.
2. Scroll down and click on the link labeled "John the Ripper 1.7.9 (Windows)". (Download the latest version available.)
3. Click Save.
4. Select your C:\security folder. (If you haven't already created this folder, you will need to do so now.)
5. If the program doesn't automatically open, browse to C:\security.
6. Right-click on john179w2.zip. (If a later version was available, this file may have a slightly different name.)
7. Select Extract All, and Extract. (See Figure 6-1.)
8. Download the sample password database labeled "hackme.txt" from www.pearsonhighered.com/boyle/. (The files may be listed under Companion Website, Student Resources, and Student Project Files.)
9. Extract all of the student project files (including hackme.txt) into the C:\security folder.
10. Copy the "hackme.txt" file from the student project folder to C:\security\john179w2\john179\run. (It is important that the hackme.txt file be in the "run" directory with the JtR executable. See Figure 6-2.)

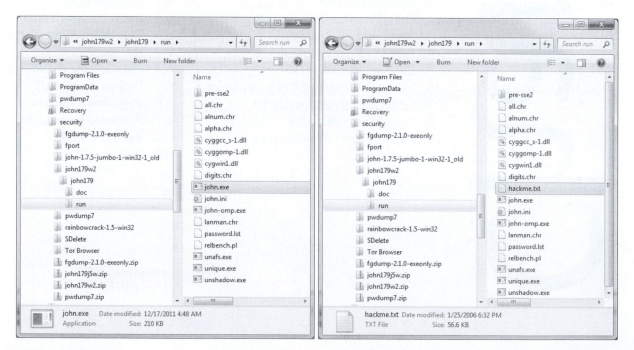

Figure 6-1: JtR executable.   Figure 6-2: Sample password file (hackme.txt).

11. Click Start.

12. In the search box, type `cmd`
13. Press Enter. (This will open a command prompt.)
14. Type `cd ..`
15. Press Enter. (This will move up one directory.)
16. Type `cd ..`
17. Press Enter. (This will move up one directory. You should now be at the C:\)
18. Type `cd security`
19. Press Enter. (This will move you into the C:\security directory.)

Note: As newer versions of JtR come out, the version numbers may change. The instructions below are written to help you navigate to the "run" directory for the version mentioned above. The steps below may need to be slightly modified if you downloaded a different version of JtR. You can refer to Chapter 1 for a review of how to navigate between directories.

20. Type `cd john179w2`
21. Press Enter. (This will move you into the C:\security\john171w2 directory.)
22. Type `cd john179`
23. Press Enter. (This will move you into the C:\security\john171w2\john1701 directory.)
24. Type `cd run`
25. Press Enter. (This will move you into the C:\security\john171w2\john1701\run directory. See Figure 6-3.)

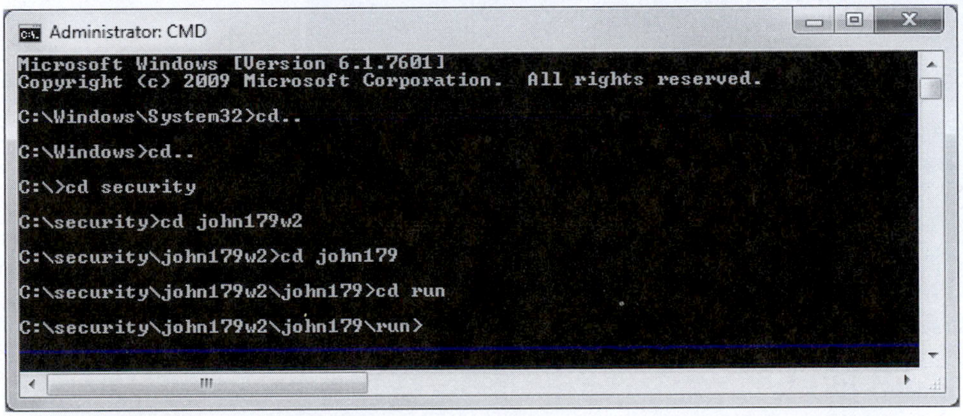

Figure 6-3: Navigating to the "run" directory

26. Type `dir`
27. Press Enter. (This will give you a listing of the files in the "run" directory. You can confirm that both *john.exe* and *hackme.txt* are in this directory.) (See Figure 6-4.)

Note: You need to make sure you have a copy of the hackme.txt file in the run directory. You need to give john.exe something to crack. After the passwords are cracked, they will be stored in a file called john.pot in the C:\security\john179w2\john179\run directory. You can delete john.pot and run it again to show a friend what you've learned.

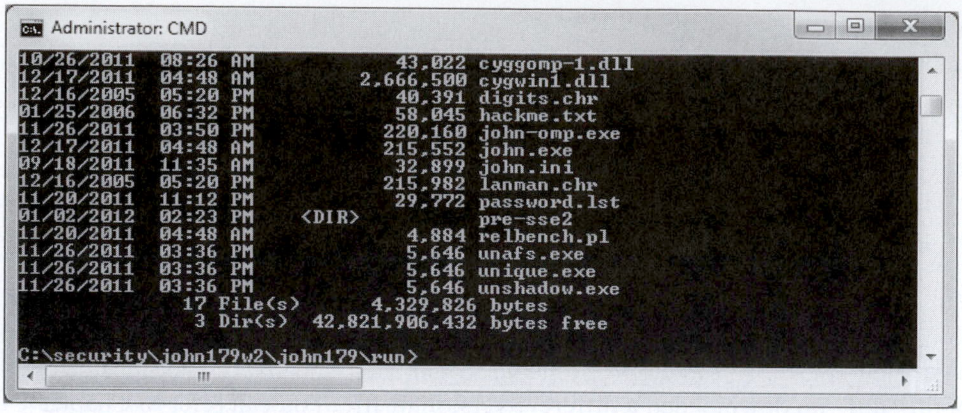

Figure 6-4: Listing of the "run" directory.

28. Type `john.exe -wordlist=password.lst hackme.txt`
29. Press Enter. (This will start a dictionary attack using a built-in dictionary [password.lst] that came with JtR. Note that the extension on password.lst is an abbreviation of the word "list". See Figure 6-5.)

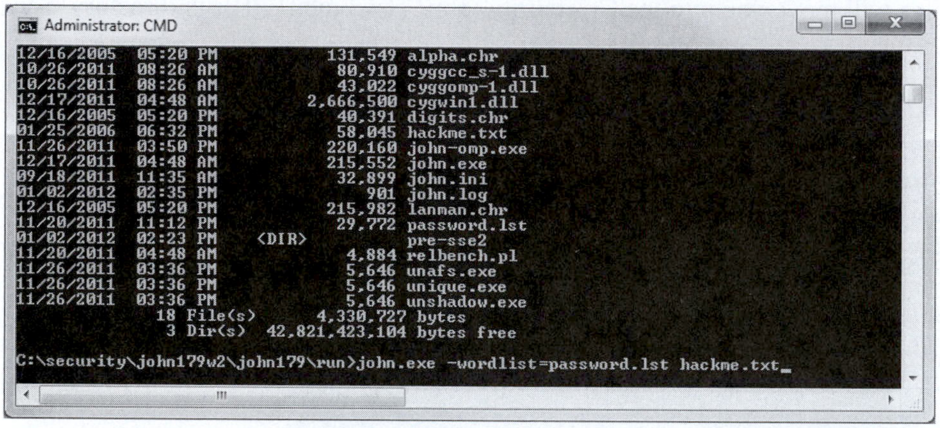

Figure 6-5: Syntax to start JtR.

30. Type `time`
31. Press Enter twice. (This will provide a timestamp.)
32. Take a screenshot. (See Figure 6-6.)

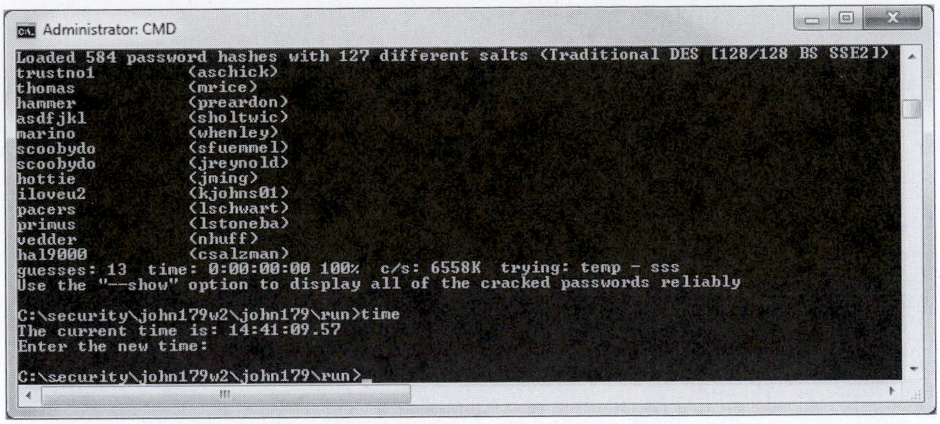

Figure 6-6: Cracking passwords from a dictionary attack.

33. Type **john.exe hackme.txt**
34. Press Enter. (This will start a brute force attack. JtR will start trying all possible combinations until it cracks all of the passwords. The passwords you see were cracked *in addition to* the ones found during the dictionary attack.)

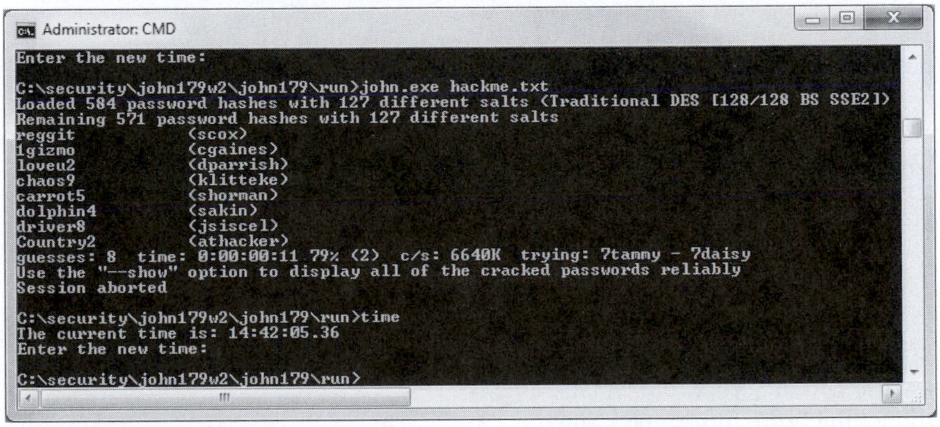

Figure 6-7: Cracking passwords from a brute force attack.

35. Stop the brute force attack by pressing Ctrl-C. (You can let it run for a couple of minutes.)
36. Type **time**
37. Press Enter twice. (This will provide a timestamp. See Figure 6-7.)
38. Take a screenshot.
39. Type **notepad john.pot**
40. Press Enter twice. (This will open the john.pot file where the cracked passwords are stored.)
41. Take a screenshot showing hashes and passwords you have cracked. (See Figure 6-8.)

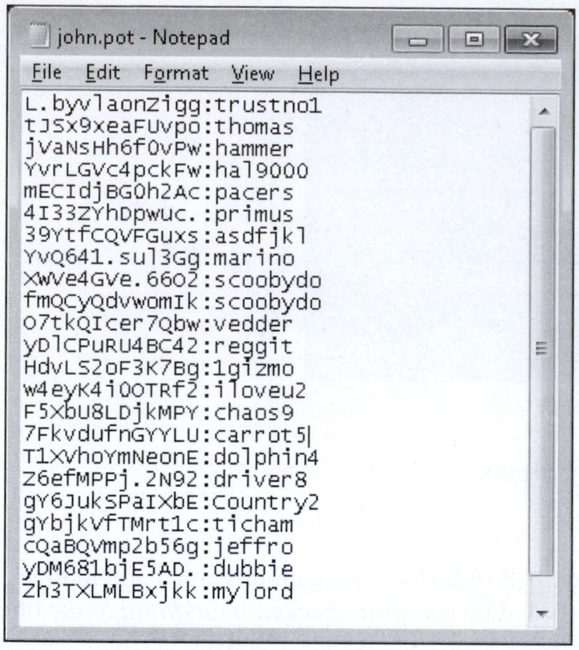

Figure 6-8: Cracking passwords.

You just did your first password audit. You ran both a dictionary attack and a brute force attack. You can run additional dictionary attacks using sample dictionary files (e.g., martok.dic and puffs.dic) in the student project files from www.pearsonhighered.com/boyle/. Additional dictionary files can be found on the Internet. You can also delete john.pot and run JtR on the same sample password file to get more practice.

PROJECT QUESTIONS

1. How many passwords did the dictionary attack crack?
2. How many passwords did the brute force attack crack?
3. How long did you let the brute force attack run?
4. Approximately how many "guesses" per second did it make? (Hint: c/s)

THOUGHT QUESTIONS

1. How does the cracking program actually "crack" the password?
2. Can a cracking program like JtR crack any password?
3. If you used a larger dictionary, would it crack the passwords faster?
4. Can you use foreign language wordlists?

6.2   LOCAL PASSWORD AUDIT

In this project, you will dump the usernames and password hashes from your local computer using Pwdump7®. Then you will use Ophcrack® to "crack" the passwords. Ophcrack will try to find matches to the dumped password hashes from your computer in pre-indexed hash tables called rainbow tables.

Pwdump7 is a utility for dumping passwords on Windows machines. You will dump your usernames and password hashes into a text file. You can then open the text file with Ophcrack and crack your passwords.

Your anti-virus program may errantly believe Pwdump7 is malware. It is not malware. You must have administrator access on your computer to do this exercise.

Ophcrack is a password auditing tool that can use rainbow tables to crack passwords. In certain situations, it can yield quicker results than a dictionary attack or a brute force attack. The writers of Ophcrack explain it this way: "Ophcrack is a Windows password cracker based on a time-memory trade-off using rainbow tables. This is a new variant of Hellman's original trade-off, with better performance. It recovers 99.9% of alphanumeric passwords in seconds.[1]"

You must have a high-speed connection to complete this project. You will download a large file from the Internet. A typical home Internet connection will take about an hour to download the entire file. Downloading it at your university will be much faster.

1. Download Pwdump7 from http://www.tarasco.org/security/pwdump_7/index.html. (Download a later version, if it is available.)
2. Click Download pwdump.
3. Click Save.
4. Select the C:\security folder.
5. If the program doesn't automatically open, browse to C:\security.
6. Right-click pwdump7.zip.
7. Select Extract All, and Extract.
8. Browse to C:\security\pwdump7\.
9. Confirm that PwDump7.exe is in this folder.
10. Open a command prompt by clicking Start, All Programs, Accessories, and then right-clicking the Command Prompt icon and selecting Run as administrator.
11. In the command prompt, go to C:\. (If necessary, review the `cd` command in the DOS tutorial from Chapter 1.)
12. Change directory to C:\security\pwdump7\. (You can get there directly by typing: **cd security\pwdump7**)
13. Type **dir** to get a listing of all the files in the current directory. (This will verify that the PwDump7.exe is in the directory. See Figure 6-9.)

---

[1] Phillipe Oechslin, Ophcrack project page accessed September 9, 2013. http://sourceforge.net/projects/ophcrack/.

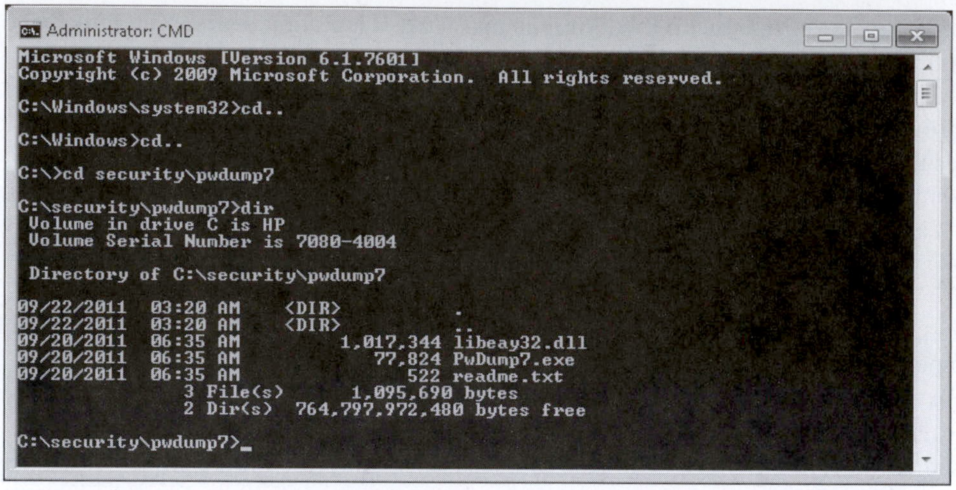

Figure 6-9: Verify that PwDump7.exe is in the directory.

14. Type `pwdump7`

Note: This will show you the usernames and passwords that are going to be saved into the text file in the next step. The hashes below have been intentionally blocked out. See Figure 6-10. In the next step, replace "YourName" with your first and last name. In this example, it was RandyBoyle.

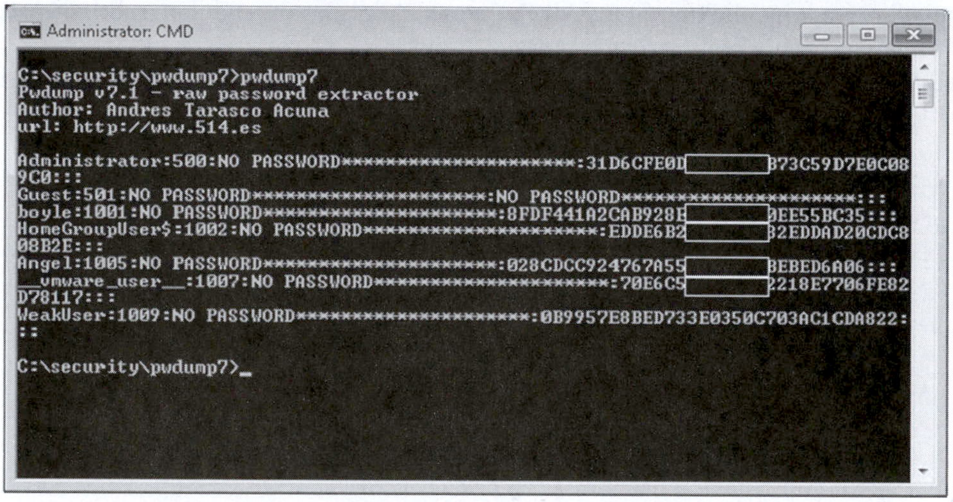

Figure 6-10: Displaying passwords with PwDump7.exe.

15. Type `pwdump7 > YourName.pwdump`
16. Type `dir` to get a listing of all the files in the current directory.
17. Take a screenshot. (You should see a pwdump file with your first and last name displayed. See Figure 6-11.)

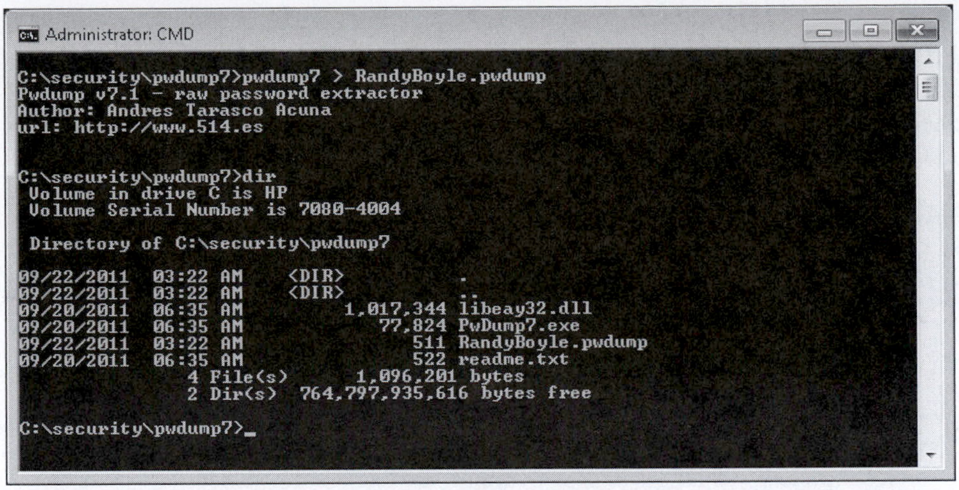

Figure 6-11: Dumping passwords with PwDump7 into a text file.

Note: You now have dumped all the encrypted passwords from your local machine into a file called YourName.pwdump and it is saved in the current directory. You are now going to download, install, and run Ophcrack. You'll also get a rainbow table.

18. Download Ophcrack from http://ophcrack.sourceforge.net/.
19. Click Download ophcrack.
20. Click on ophcrack-win32-installer-3.4.0.exe. (Download the latest version available.)
21. Click Save.
22. Select the C:\security folder.

Note: Your anti-virus program may block this download because it says it's a virus. It is not a virus. You may need to make an exception to allow it to download.

23. If the program doesn't automatically open, browse to C:\security.
24. Right-click on ophcrack-win32-installer-3.4.0.exe and select Run as administrator.
25. Click Next, Next, Next, Install, Next, and Finish. (You may get a 404 error window saying it wasn't able to download part of the application. You can ignore this error.)

Note: You are now going to download and extract the rainbow table.

26. In your Web browser, return to the Ophcrack website at http://ophcrack.sourceforge.net/.
27. Click Tables.
28. Scroll down and click on Vista Free.
29. Click Save.
30. Select the C:\security folder. (This will take 3-5 minutes depending on the speed of your Internet connection.)
31. Browse to C:\security.
32. Right-click on tables_vista_free.zip.
33. Select Extract All, and Extract.

Note: You are now going to run Ophcrack, load the rainbow tables, load your password hashes (YourName.pwdump), and then attempt to crack them.

34. Right-click the Ophcrack icon on your desktop and select Run as administrator. (It can also be started by clicking Start, Programs, Ophcrack, and Ophcrack. See Figure 6-12.)

35. Click Tables.
36. Select Vista Free.
37. Click Install.
38. Browse to C:\security\tables_vista_free.
39. Click OK, and OK.

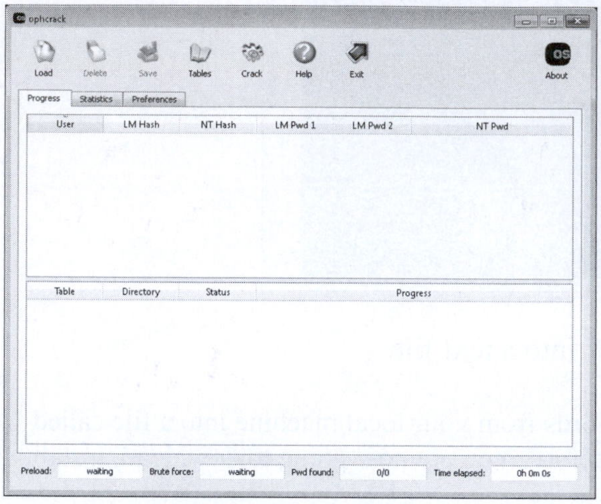

Figure 6-12: Ophcrack interface.

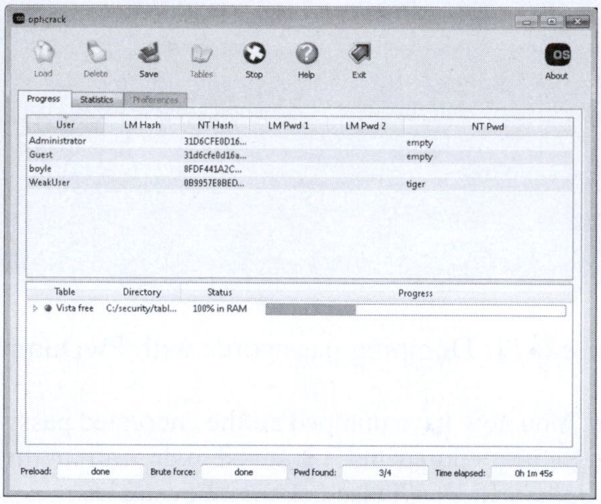

Figure 6-13: Cracking passwords with Ophcrack.

40. Click Load, and PWDUMP file. (This is the file you created earlier.)
41. Browse to C:\security\pwdump7.
42. Select the file named YourName.pwdump. (In this case, it was RandyBoyle.pwdump.)
43. Click Open
44. Click Crack.
45. Take a screenshot while it is running. (See Figure 6-13.)
46. Let it run for a couple of minutes and see if it cracks your password. (It will crack some fairly strong passwords. In this example, WeakUser's password was found to be "tiger." You can create your own temporary user with a generic dictionary password to test the rainbow table's effectiveness.)
47. Don't take a screenshot of your cracked passwords. Just make a note that it may have cracked some of your passwords.

PROJECT QUESTIONS

1. How many password hashes did you load into Ophcrack?
2. How long did it take to run Ophcrack against your hashes?
3. On the Statistics tab, how many hashes did it indicate were loaded?
4. Was your password an LM hash or NT hash?

THOUGHT QUESTIONS

1. How do rainbow tables differ from dictionary or brute force attacks?
2. If you had a faster computer, would it crack the passwords faster?
3. Could someone get the password database from your computer?
4. Could someone remotely access your password database?

Security professionals get requests from individuals on a regular basis asking them for help unlocking Word®, Excel®, and Access® files. Individuals are worried about security, so they try to secure their documents with the built-in features in Microsoft products. However, they sometimes forget the passwords they use.

There are a large number of products on the market that can help you recover your passwords if you used a Microsoft product. Below is a free version that can help you. This project will use both dictionary and brute force password attacks.

1. Download Free Word and Excel Password Recovery® Wizard from http://www.freewordexcelpassword.com/index.php?id=download.
2. Click on Download Free Word / Excel password recovery wizard now.
3. Click Save.
4. Select the C:\security folder.
5. If the program doesn't automatically open, browse to C:\security.
6. Right-click on FreeWordExcelPasswordrecoverywizard.zip.
7. Select Extract All, and Extract.
8. Browse to C:\security\FreeWordExcelPasswordrecoverywizard\.
9. Right-click on setup.exe and select Run as administrator.
10. Click OK, Next, I accept, Next, Next, Create a desktop icon, and Next
11. Deselect any additional offers.
12. Click Next, Install, and Finish.
13. Download the sample password-protected Excel file from www.pearsonhighered.com/boyle/. (Click on Companion Website for this book, Student Resources, and then Student Project Files.)
14. Click Save.
15. Select the C:\security folder.
16. Extract the downloaded file. (You should now have all the project files necessary for the remaining projects. You'll only have to download this once.)
17. Double-click the Free Word / Excel Password Wizard on your desktop. (It might already be open.)
18. Click Next.
19. Click Browse.
20. Browse to your C:\security folder where you have the student project files.
21. Select the file called CrackMe_1234.xls. (You can also create a blank Excel spreadsheet and protect it with the password "1234".)
22. Click Open. (See Figure 6-14.)
23. Click Next.
24. Click Brute Force Attack.
25. Change the character set to "0-9, a-z" in the drop-down box.
26. Change the password length from 1 to 6.
27. Click Next. (See Figure 6-15.)

Figure 6-14: Select a file to recover.

Figure 6-15: Select a character set.

28. Click Go. (See Figure 6-16.)
29. Take a screenshot. (See Figure 6-17.)
30. Click OK.

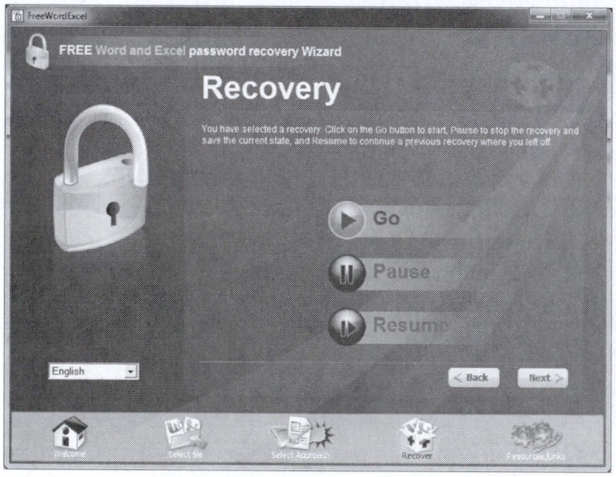

Figure 6-16: Ready to start the password recovery.

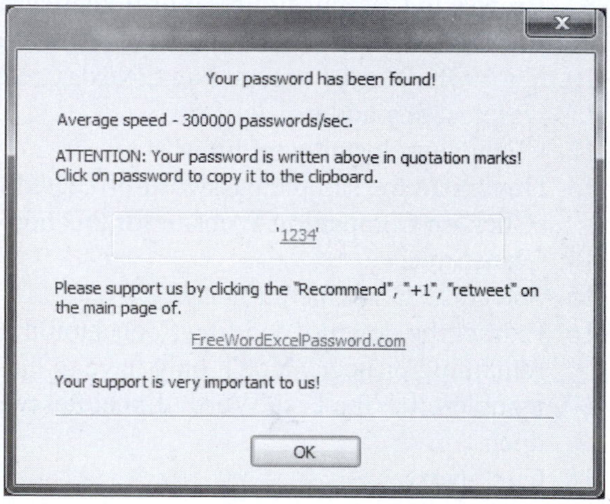

Figure 6-17: Recovered password.

PROJECT QUESTIONS

1. What was the password on the example Excel file?
2. What was the name of the dictionary file you used?
3. What was the maximum password length in the Brute Force Attack setting? (You will have to click Back to see the brute force attack options.)
4. This software supports two languages. One is English. What is the other language?

THOUGHT QUESTIONS

1. Are there additional programs that can "recover" your passwords more quickly?
2. Is the password system used in this Microsoft application inherently and intentionally weak?
3. Would third-party encryption software keep your documents safer?
4. Are there options that could speed up the cracking process?

When people see Cain & Able® for the first time, they start clicking buttons wildly. This is an *extremely* bad idea. Cain & Able comes with a great deal of functionality that most beginning students are not ready to use. Yes, you can cause problems on your network and get into trouble. Do *not* run Cain & Able at your workplace or in school labs. Only run it on your personal computer or on a computer set up by your instructor.

Please feel free to click on any of the tabs and look at the functionality available. However, it would be best for you to go through the rest of the projects in this book before you do anything else. Cain & Able integrates a wide array of functionality into a single piece of software.

A longer project using Cain & Able is shown at the end of this book. It's introduced at this point because it has a handy cracking feature for Microsoft Access databases. It also has an integrated password cracker. We will go through a project showing how to use the Microsoft Access cracker and leave the other features for later projects.

1. Download Cain & Able from http://www.oxid.it/cain.html.
2. Select Download Cain & Abel v4.9.42 for Windows NT/2000/XP. (Download the latest version available.)
3. Click Save.
4. Select the C:\security folder.
5. Browse to C:\security.
6. Right-click on ca_setup.exe and select Run as administrator.
7. Click Next, Next, Next, Next, and Finish.
8. Install WinPCap, if you haven't already installed it.
9. Download the sample Access database file from http://www.pearsonhighered.com/boyle/ or from your instructor (via Canvas, Blackboard, or other learning management system). This file is password protected. You are going to recover the password that was used to lock this database. You should have already downloaded this file in a prior project. (If you are downloading the student project files for the first time, be sure to save them in the C:\security folder.)
10. Run Cain & Able from Start, All Programs, Cain, and Cain. (There should also be a shortcut on your desktop. See Figure 6-18.)
11. Click OK if you see a warning about Windows Firewall. (You can make an exception for Cain & Able in Windows Firewall if you want to use additional features later. This project will not require an exception in your firewall.)

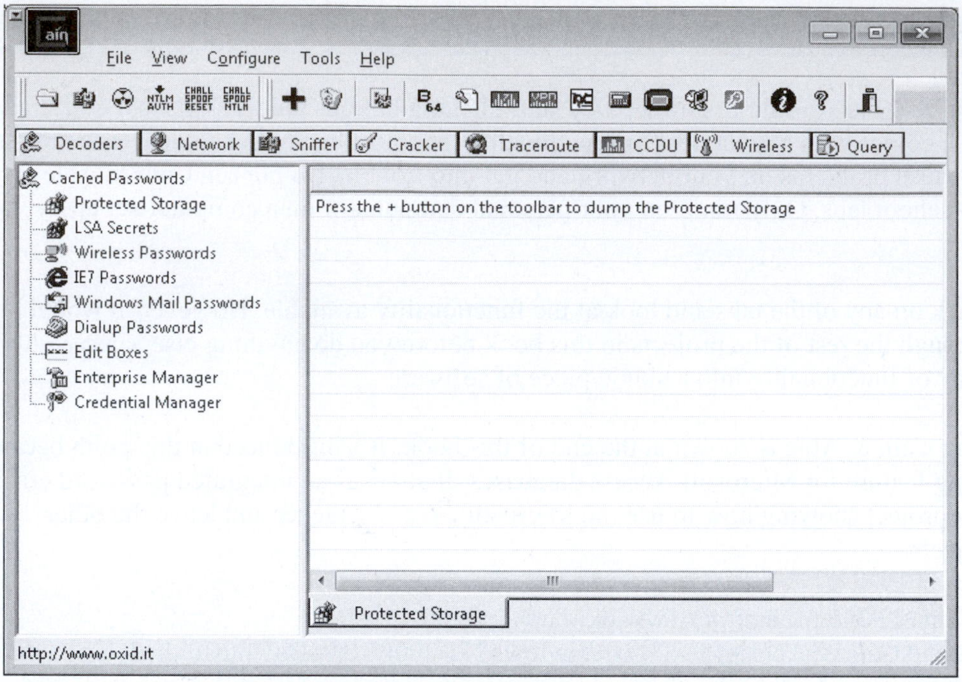

Figure 6-18: Cain start page.

12. Click Tools, Access Database Password Decoder. (See Figure 6-19.)
13. Click on the "…" browse button to the right.
14. Select the file called HackMe_tiger1234.mdb that you downloaded earlier. (You can also create your own Microsoft database and set the password to "tiger1234" without quotes.)

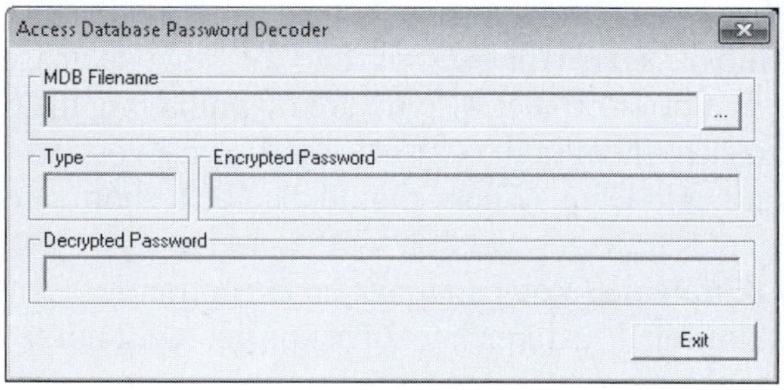

Figure 6-19: Database decoder.

Figure 6-20: Decoded password.

15. Click Open.
16. Take a screenshot of the decoded password. (See Figure 6-20.)
17. Click Exit.

Note: In the next step, you are going to change the password for the sample database. In order to change the password, you have to open the database "exclusively." This means you will need to first start Access *without* opening the HackMe_tiger1234.mdb database. You will open Access and then click File, Open, and select the database.

Important You MUST click on the menu arrow on the Open button. DO NOT click the Open button itself. If you do, you will have to repeat these steps. When you click on the menu arrow on the Open button, you will select "Open Exclusive." After you have opened it exclusively, you will be able to click File, and Unset Database Password. You will then be prompted for a new password.

18. Open the database and change the password to your last name followed by any number sequence.
19. Repeat the decoding process starting at step 12 and see if it cracks your new password.
20. Take a screenshot.

Note: Now you are going to explore the built-in password cracker in Cain & Able. You will create three hashes based on your first name, last name, and the word "tiger." You'll enter these hashes into Cain & Able's cracker. Then you will load the martok.txt dictionary and see if it finds the passwords associated with these hashes.

21. Click on the Cracker tab.
22. Click on MD5 Hashes in the left-hand pane. (See Figure 6-21.)
23. Click Tools, and Hash Calculator. (You can also press Alt-C to open the hash calculator, or press the hash calculator icon that looks like a little green calculator.)
24. Type your *first* name in the text box labeled Text to hash in all lower-case letters.
25. Click Calculate. (This will display a list of hashes based on your first name.)
26. Take a screenshot. (See Figure 6-22.)

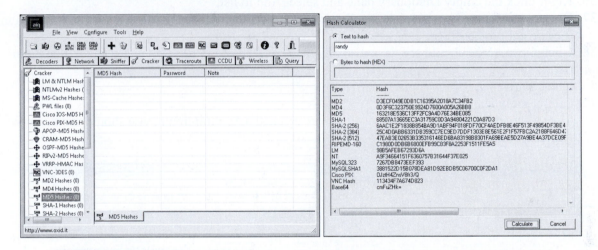

Figure 6-21: Password cracker in Cain & Able.   Figure 6-22: Hash Calculator.

27. With your mouse, select the MD5 hash for your first name.
28. Press Ctrl-C to copy the hash to the clipboard.
29. Click Cancel to exit the Hash Calculator.
30. Click File, and Add to list.
31. Press Ctrl-V to paste the hash into the MD5 Hash box.
32. Click OK. (You should now see the hash listed in the table. See Figure 6-23.)
33. Repeat this process and create hashes for your *last* name and the word "tiger" in lower-case letters. Enter them into the MD5 Hash pane. (You will have three hashes listed when you are done. See Figure 6-24.)

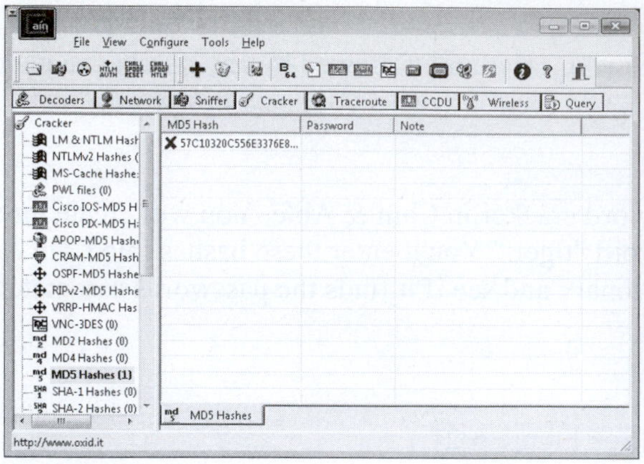

Figure 6-23: First hash is loaded.

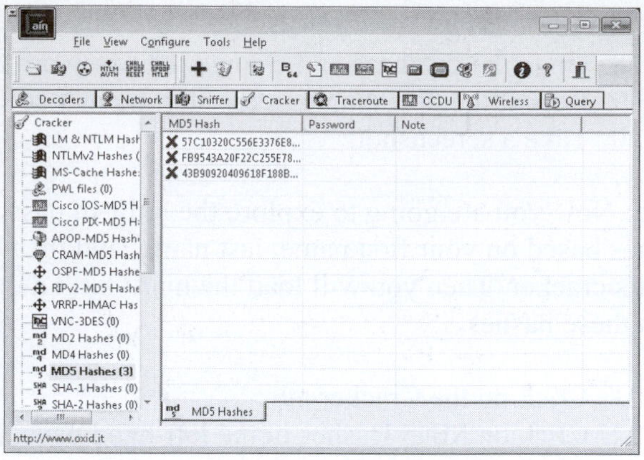

Figure 6-24: All MD5 hashes are loaded.

34. Select all three hashes in the MD5 Hash pane using the Shift key.
35. Right-click the selected hashes and select Dictionary Attack.
36. Right-click the empty Dictionary pane and select Add to list.
37. Browse to C:\security and select the dictionary labeled "martok.txt." (This file will be included in the student project files.)
38. Click Open. (You should see the martok dictionary file listed in the Dictionary panel. See Figure 6-25.)
39. Click Start.
40. Click Exit when it finishes.
41. Take a screenshot of any passwords that were cracked. (At a minimum, you should see the word "tiger" listed. See Figure 6-26.)

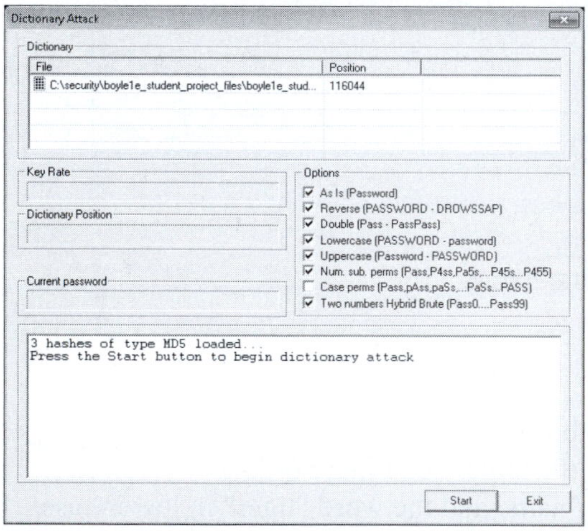

Figure 6-25: Dictionary Attack options.

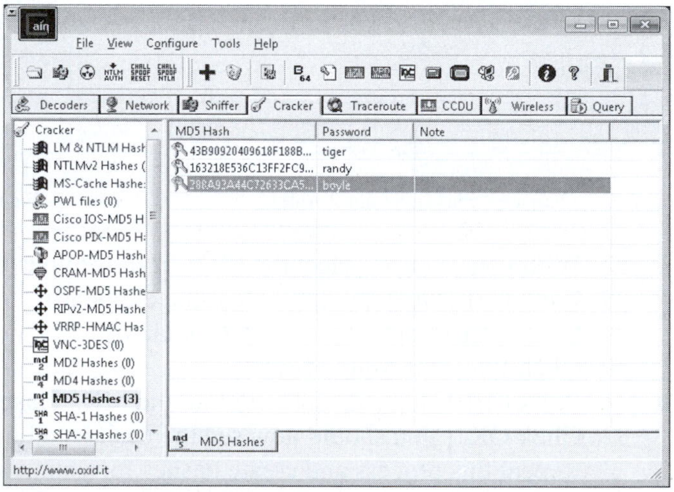

Figure 6-26: Cracked MD5 password hashes.

Again, don't click on any of the additional features in Cain & Able until you know what they do. Randomly clicking on buttons can be harmful. You will learn more about Cain & Able later.

PROJECT QUESTIONS

1. What was the new password you used for the database file?
2. What were the first four characters in the hash of your first name?
3. What were the first four characters in the hash of your last name?

4. Which checkbox was *not* selected in the Dictionary Attack Options box?

THOUGHT QUESTIONS

1. Did the length or strength of the password slow down the cracking of the database password?
2. Why did Cain & Able crack the password so quickly?
3. Would a stronger password help?
4. Does Cain & Able integrate a password cracker with other security tools?

6.5   DEFAULT PASSWORDS

Many people are surprised to know that their computers, routers, and printers may come with a default password. Sometimes people do not change the default password for their computers, routers, and printers. This may open them up to an attack from an outsider. There are also lists of "backdoor" passwords on some devices that will always work regardless of what you make the new password.

This project is not intended to give access to all default/backdoor password lists. Rather, its intent is to show the reader that these lists do exist and it is absolutely necessary to change the default password on any new devices (e.g., a new wireless router). Failing to do so will unnecessarily open your system up to a potential attack.

1. Go to http://www.phenoelit-us.org/dpl/dpl.html for a limited list of default passwords.
2. Search the left-most column for the manufacturer of your computer, router, printer, etc.
3. Take a screenshot.
4. If there is more than one device that you own shown, take additional screenshots.

PROJECT QUESTIONS

1. What is the brand of your computer?
2. Was there a default password listed for your computer?
3. What is the brand of your router?
4. Was there a default password listed for your router?

THOUGHT QUESTIONS

1. Why have default passwords?
2. Do all devices have default passwords (e.g., routers, switches, firewalls, desktops, cars, vending machines, alarm systems, etc.)?
3. Is there any way to disable default passwords?
4. Does "flashing" the device remove new passwords?

6.6   PASSWORD EVALUATOR

This project will evaluate your current password to see how good it really is. Having a strong password can save you from headaches. It can reduce the chances of a criminal being able to break into your computer at home or at work. Just because a criminal steals your password database does not mean he or she automatically knows your password. The criminal still has to crack it.

A strong password can keep your computers, systems, and data safe even if they are stolen. George Shaffer has written several online tools that help users learn more about strong passwords. These are great tools to help users understand the difference between strong and weak passwords.

1. Go to http://geodsoft.com/cgi-bin/pwcheck.pl.
2. Enter a variation of a password that you use on a regular basis. (Don't enter your real password. Include a minor change. You might end up changing to a stronger password anyway.)
3. Click Submit.
4. Take a screenshot.
5. Take note of the problems with your password. (In my case, a number sequence and a dictionary word.)
6. Try submitting a password you might actually use and you think is strong.
7. Take a screenshot of the results.
8. Try submitting a word from a dictionary twice (e.g., "picklepickle").

PROJECT QUESTIONS

1. How many characters was your normal password?
2. How many characters was your strong password?
3. Did your normal password include a number at the beginning or end?
4. Did the password with a repeated word have issues? Why?

THOUGHT QUESTIONS

1. Why did you choose the password you currently have?
2. Could others follow the same logic and choose a similar password?
3. Do hackers/crackers know that users follow these same patterns when they choose their passwords?
4. Do you use the same password for multiple accounts?

6.7   PASSWORD GENERATORS

It is difficult to create a good password. Weak passwords are typically easier to remember. However, it is possible to create a strong password that is fairly easy to remember. The following website will show you some strong passwords. George Shaffer has written another good tool that will automatically generate strong passwords.

If you want to make sure you have a strong password, you might want to consider using one of the passwords generated by this website. They will be difficult to crack. If you don't see a password that you could easily remember, keep clicking the Submit button.

1. Go to http://geodsoft.com/cgi-bin/password.pl.
2. Click Submit several times and watch the passwords at the top change.
3. Write down a password that you think would be easy for you to remember.
4. Take a screenshot.

Note: The following password generator takes *simple* words (like "tiger") and automatically creates a *difficult* password based on that word. It will create the same difficult password every time you enter the same simple word. The difficult password could then be used on a website. Each time you revisited the website, you would enter the easy password into the password generator, copy the output, and paste it into the password field on the website. If the website's password database were ever stolen, your password would not be cracked.

5. Download Phrase Password Generator® from http://www.vaultmate.com/freewaregifts.php.
6. Click Download Now under the listing for Phrase Password Generator 2. (Download the latest version available.)
7. Click Save.
8. Select the C:\security folder.
9. Browse to C:\security.
10. Right-click on Passgen2-installer.exe and select Run as administrator. (The filename may change slightly if you downloaded a newer version.)
11. Click Next, Next, and Next.
12. Uncheck the box labeled Create a Quick Launch icon.
13. Click Next, Install, and Finish.
14. Type the word "tiger" into the source phrase text box. (You should see asterisks shown in both boxes. It displays asterisks so anyone trying to look over your shoulder can't see your password.)
15. Check both Show boxes.
16. Keep typing the letter "r" at the end of the word tiger. (Notice that the output password changes, but doesn't increase in length.)
17. Clear the source phrase text box.
18. Enter YourName into the source phrase text box. (In this case, it was RandyBoyle.)
19. Click the up arrow to increase the length of the output password to 16.
20. Take a screenshot.
21. Click the Options tab.
22. Select Special symbols.
23. Click on the General tab. (Notice that the output password changed. This would be a *very* strong password. You can copy the output password by clicking on the adjacent Copy button. You could then paste it into any password field.)
24. Take a screenshot.

PROJECT QUESTIONS

1. Which strong password would you have chosen from the Geodsoft.com website?
2. What was the 8-character password for your name?
3. What was the 16-character password for your name without special characters?
4. What was the 16-character password for your name with special characters?

THOUGHT QUESTIONS

1. Do you think one of these passwords would be easy for you to remember?
2. Why are these good passwords?
3. Why do special characters (e.g., @#$%^&*) make passwords difficult to crack?
4. Why does a change of case help make a stronger password?

6.8   RAINBOW TABLES

Rainbow tables are tables of precomputed hashes that have been indexed in order to reduce the amount of time it takes to crack a password. A simple way to think of how rainbow tables work is to compare them to a phone book.

Let's say you started walking down the street, asking every person you met for his or her name and phone number. You wrote them down in the order that you met each person. You eventually walked long enough to meet everyone in the world. You now have a very long list of names and phone numbers.

Now, let's say a friend asks you to look up a phone number. Someone called your friend, but only left their phone number. They want to know who called them without having to calling them back. You could check each number on your list, but that would take a very long time (e.g., brute force attack). It would be much more efficient to index your list by phone number. Then you could look up the number very quickly.

Rainbow tables work the same way. They create a list of all possible passwords (i.e., a person's name) and hashes (i.e., a person's phone number). The rainbow table is then indexed based on the hash value. A password hash is cracked by looking up its value in a rainbow table and returning the plaintext password.

Rainbow tables can substantially reduce the amount of time it takes to crack a password. However, there is a tradeoff. You have to store all of the indexed passwords and hash values. You also have to index all of the passwords. This means you have to store a great deal of data. As password length increases, so does the size of the rainbow table required to crack it.

This project will create a small rainbow table for all numbers with six or fewer characters. You will be able to crack any MD5 password hash from a six character (or less) numeric password. You will use this rainbow table to crack a password in the next project.

1. Download Winrtgen from http://www.oxid.it/projects.html.
2. Click on Winrtgen.
3. Click Save.
4. Select the C:\security folder.
5. Browse to C:\security.
6. Right-click on winrtgen.zip and select Extract All, and Extract.
7. Browse to C:\security\winrtgen.
8. Right-click on winrtgen.exe and select Run as administrator.
9. Click Add Table.
10. Set the hash to MD5.
11. Set the Max Length to 6.
12. Set the Chain Length to 2400.
13. Set the Chain Count to 40000.
14. Set the Charset to numeric.
15. Click Benchmark. (Note the success probability, table precomputation time, and cryptanalysis time.)
16. Take a screenshot. (See Figure 6-27.)
17. Change the Charset to mixalpha-numeric-symbol14.
18. Click Benchmark. (Note the change in the success probability.)
19. Take a screenshot. (See Figure 6-28.)

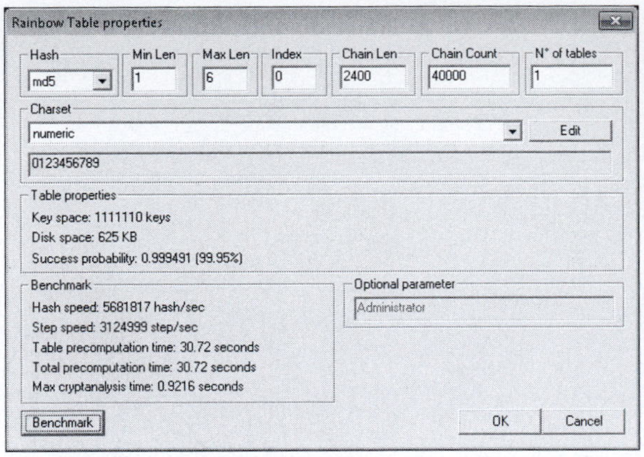

Figure 6-27: Rainbow table settings.

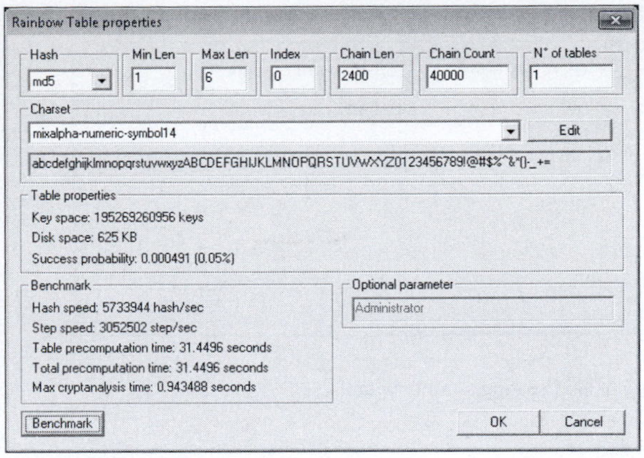

Figure 6-28: Changed character set.

20. Change the Charset back to numeric.
21. Change the Max Length from 6 to 10.
22. Click Benchmark. (Note the change in success probability. See Figure 6-29.)
23. Increase the Chain Count from 40,000 to 400,000,000.
24. Click Benchmark. (Note the change in success probability, disk space, and precomputation time. See Figure 6-30.)

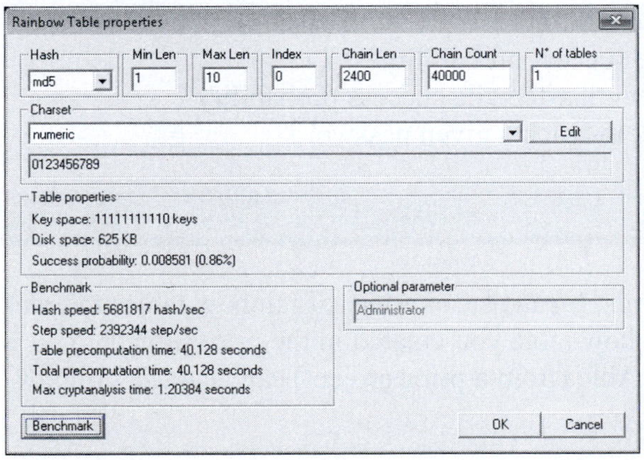

Figure 6-29: Increased maximum password length.

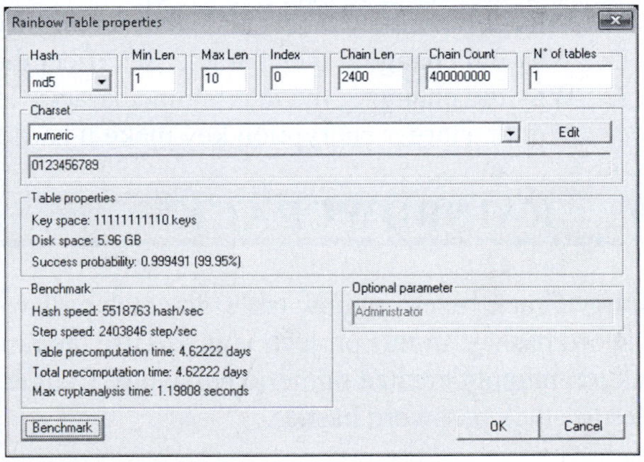

Figure 6-30: Increased size of rainbow table.

25. Change the Max Length from 10 to 6.
26. Change the Chain Count from 400,000,000 to 40,000. (This should return the settings back to the original configuration.)
27. Click OK, and Start. (It should take about 30 seconds to create the table. The table will be in your C:\security\winrtgen directory. See Figure 6-31.)
28. Browse to your C:\security\winrtgen directory. (You should see the newly created table titled "md5_numeric#1-6_0_2400x40000_oxid#000.rt".)
29. Add your last name to the END of the table name by right-clicking on the table and selecting Rename. (e.g., md5_numeric#1-6_0_2400x40000_oxid#000_LAST NAME.rt.)
30. Take a screenshot of your newly named rainbow table.

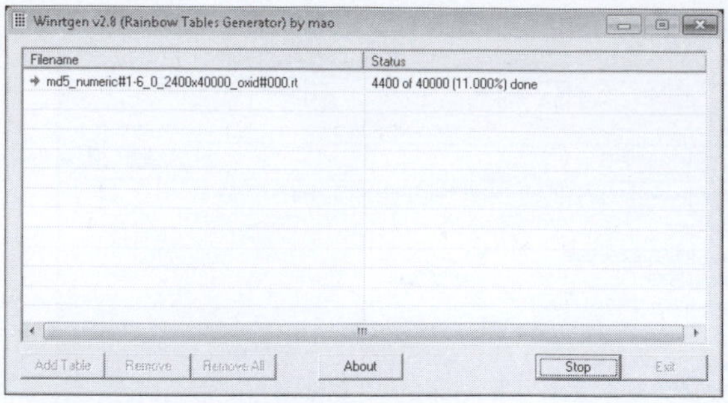

Figure 6-31: Creating a rainbow table.

PROJECT QUESTIONS

1. What was the maximum cryptanalysis time for the table you created?
2. What was the success probability for the table you created?
3. What was the size of the rainbow table you created?
4. What was the size of the key space for the rainbow table you created?

THOUGHT QUESTIONS

1. What are rainbow tables and what do they look like?
2. Why did changing the character set affect the success probability?
3. Why did changing the maximum character length affect the success probability?
4. Would a larger encryption key make it harder to crack a given password?

6.9   RAINBOWCRACK®

RainbowCrack® uses rainbow tables to crack passwords. It can use a variety of rainbow tables to crack password hashes. In this project, you will use the rainbow table you created in the prior project. You will crack a randomly created numeric password. Cain & Able (from a prior project) can also use rainbow tables to crack password hashes.

1. Download RainbowCrack from http://project-rainbowcrack.com/.
2. Click on the link for the latest version of RainbowCrack. (You will likely want to choose the Windows 64-bit version of RainbowCrack. You can determine if you have a 32-bit or 64-bit machine by clicking on your Computer properties in the Start menu.)
3. Click Save.
4. Select the C:\security folder.
5. Browse to C:\security.
6. Right-click on rainbowcrack-1.5-win64.zip and select Extract All, and Extract. (The file name might be slightly different if a newer version is available.)
7. Browse to C:\security\rainbowcrack-1.5-win64\rainbowcrack-1.5-win64.
8. Right-click on rcrack_gui.exe and select Run as administrator.
9. Open Cain & Able.
10. Click Tools, and Hash Calculator.
11. Enter any six random numbers into the Text to hash box. (In this case, it was 568135.)
12. Click Calculate. (See Figure 6-32.)
13. Copy the resulting MD5 hash. (In this case, it was 1CE493EE8F0C1F8C9372FF9365115D14.)
14. Return to RainbowCrack.
15. Click File, and Add Hash.

16. Paste in the MD5 hash you copied from Cain & Able's Hash Calculator.
17. Enter your name into the Comment box.
18. Click OK.
19. Take a screenshot. (Your name and MD5 hash should be visible. See Figure 6-33.)

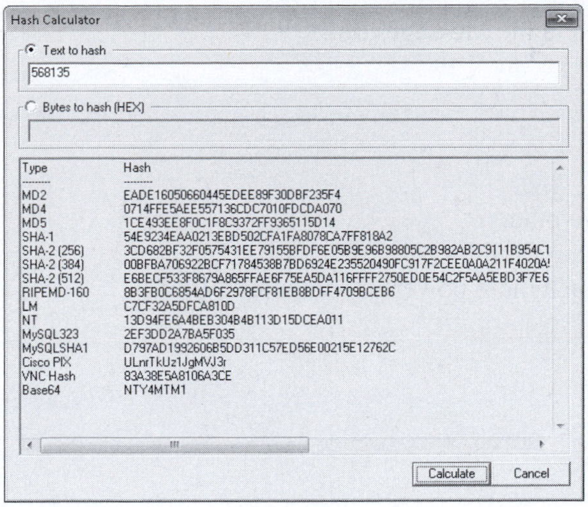

Figure 6-32: Generating random six-digit MD5 hash. 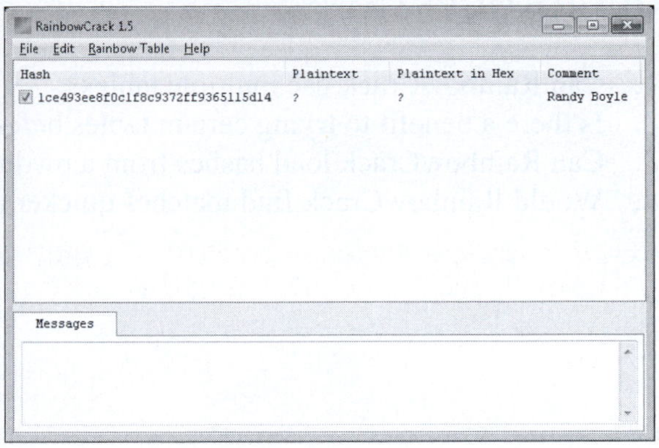   Figure 6-33: MD5 hash is loaded.

20. Click Rainbow Table, and Search Rainbow Tables.
21. Browse to your C:\security\winrtgen directory.
22. Select the rainbow table you created in the prior project. (If you haven't done the prior project, you will need to complete it at this time. You cannot complete this project without creating the rainbow table in the prior project. In this case, the rainbow table was titled "md5_numeric#1-6_0_2400x40000_oxid#000_Boyle.rt".)
23. Click Open.
24. Take a screenshot. (The random number you chose for the hash should be visible. See Figure 6-34.)

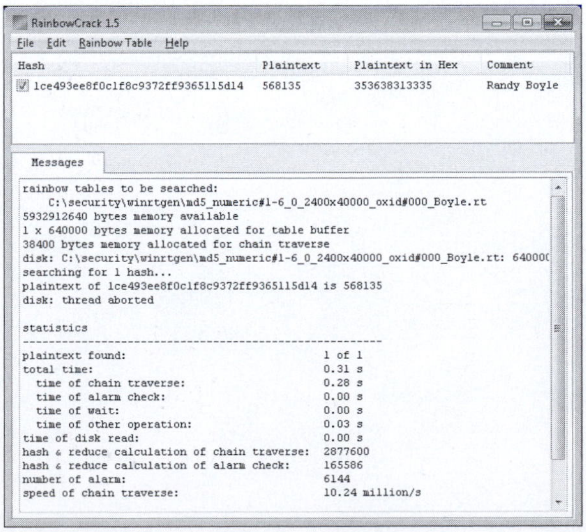

Figure 6-34: Cracked password with a rainbow table.

PROJECT QUESTIONS

1. What was the random six-digit number you chose?
2. What was the hash value for that six-digit number?
3. How long did it take to find the plain text match?
4. What was the "speed of chain traverse" shown in the Messages box?

THOUGHT QUESTIONS

1. Can RainbowCrack use multiple tables?
2. Is there a benefit to trying certain tables before others?
3. Can RainbowCrack load hashes from a pwdump file?
4. Would RainbowCrack find matches quicker on a more powerful computer? Why?

Wireless networks are hard to secure and difficult to monitor. Wireless technology has had some well known problems of which hackers are well aware. Administrators must fight to keep control of wireless networks that are ripe for the picking.

Wired networks are much easier to protect. You can physically secure wires and keep people from attaching to the network. Wireless is much more difficult because radio waves can't be seen by the human eye.

Do you know who is on your wireless network at all times? Could someone drive by and steal your data? Could a naïve VP plug in a wireless router and punch a gaping hole in your security perimeter? There are many ways to intentionally hack a wireless network, or unintentionally open your network to unauthorized users.

The 802.11 standard is hard enough to manage. Administrators are now starting to worry about potential security issues with cell phones. Cell phones are starting to include almost all the functionality you find in regular desktop computers.

Wireless computers and cell phones will be a big challenge for IT security professionals for at least the next 15 years. This chapter will look at some of the basic wireless tools that are available for Windows machines.

Time required to complete this chapter: 60 minutes

Chapter Objectives

Learn how to:
1. Identify wireless networks.
2. Gather wireless network information.
3. Identify wireless card drivers.
4. Find wireless networks within a city.
5. Spatially map a wireless network.

Chapter Projects

Project:
7.1   Xirrus Wi-Fi Inspector
7.2   InSSIDer
7.3   WiFidenum
7.4   Wigle.net
7.5   Ekahau Heatmapper

Xirrus® Wi-Fi Inspector® by Xirrus Inc. gives information about how wireless networks are configured and the relative signal strength from your computer to nearby access points (APs). Wi-Fi Inspector is a great tool for diagnosing wireless network problems, like weak signal strength, relative distance, dead zones, faulty APs, and causes of interference in a network's wireless signal.

Wi-Fi Inspector can also help find rogue APs. Often a new employee with limited knowledge about how wireless works will simply plug in an unsecured wireless router. This has the potential to open a serious security hole in a company's wireless network. This happens more often than you might think. Wi-Fi Inspector can help identify those uninformed users and keep an internal network safe.

1. Download Wi-Fi Inspector from http://www.xirrus.com/Products/Wi-Fi-Inspector.aspx.
2. Click the download link for Wi-Fi Inspector. (Download the latest version.)
3. Click Save.
4. Select the C:\security folder.
5. If the program doesn't automatically start, browse to the C:\security folder.
6. Double-click the XirrusWiFiInspectorSetup.1.2.0.exe program. (The program version number may appear differently if a new version has been released.)
7. Click Run, Next, Next, Install, and Finish.
8. Click Start, All Programs, Xirrus, and Xirrus Wi-Fi Inspector. (See Figure 7-1.)
9. Take a screenshot.

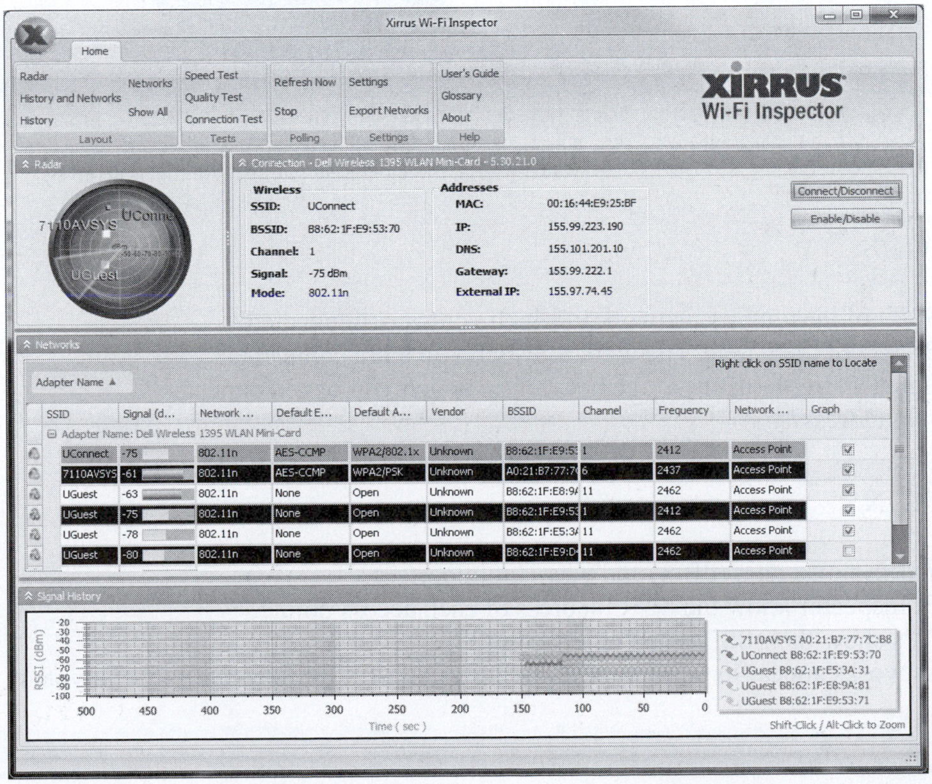

Figure 7-1: Xirrus Wi-Fi Inspector showing all available wireless networks. Source: Xirrus Wi-Fi Inspector - Xirrus Inc, 2013 All Rights Reserved.

10. Select several networks in the Network pane to start graphing below.
11. Click on the History button in the ribbon. (See Figure 7-2.)

12. Take a screenshot.
13. Click on the Show All button in the ribbon.
14. Right-click the network you are connected to, and select Locate [SSID of the network you are connected to]. (It should be highlighted in orange. You can stop the continuous beeping by clicking the Exit Locate button on the right-hand side of your screen.)
15. Pick up your laptop and physically move toward the access point you are connected to. (The beeping will get more frequent as you get closer to the access point.)
16. Once you get as close as you can, click on the Radar button in the ribbon. (See Figure 7-3.)
17. Take a screenshot.
18. Press the Exit Locate button on the right-hand side of your screen.

Figure 7-2: Signal strength for a close network. Source: Xirrus Wi-Fi Inspector - Xirrus Inc, 2013 All Rights Reserved.

Figure 7-3: Signal strength for a more distant network. Source: Xirrus Wi-Fi Inspector - Xirrus Inc, 2013 All Rights Reserved.

PROJECT QUESTIONS

1. What was the SSID of the wireless network to which you were connected?
2. What was the BSSID of the wireless network to which you were connected?
3. What was the signal strength (dBm) of the network to which you were connected?
4. What was your IP address?

THOUGHT QUESTIONS

1. What is the signal-to-noise ratio (dBm) and why is it important?
2. How does Wi-Fi Inspector know the MAC address of each access point?
3. Why do some APs show their SSIDs and others don't?
4. Why do some networks appear to be encrypted but others don't? Are they really unencrypted?

7.2   INSSIDER®

InSSIDer® is another useful wireless LAN scanner with the same basic functionality as Wi-Fi Inspector, but with some additional integrated graphing functions, network filtering, and GPS mapping. The relative signal strengths of various APs are easier to see using the inSSIDer graphical format. This can improve proper placement of your AP and avoid excessive overlap.

Both inSSIDer and Wi-Fi Inspector display the encryption type used on a specific network. This is important information if you are doing a penetration test or a security audit. If your company is using wired equivalent privacy (WEP), it would be wise to switch to Wi-Fi protected access (WPA) or WPA2, which is even better. Running a quick scan of your network using inSSIDer may help you determine if you need to make changes to your network.

1. Download inSSIDer from http://www.metageek.net/products/inssider/.
2. Click Download inSSIDer for Windows.
3. Click Save.
4. Select the C:\security folder.
5. If the program doesn't automatically start, browse to the C:\security folder.
6. Double-click on Inssider-Installer-2.1.6.1394.exe. (The version number might be slightly different than the one shown here. Always download the latest version.)
7. Click Next, Next, Next, and Close.

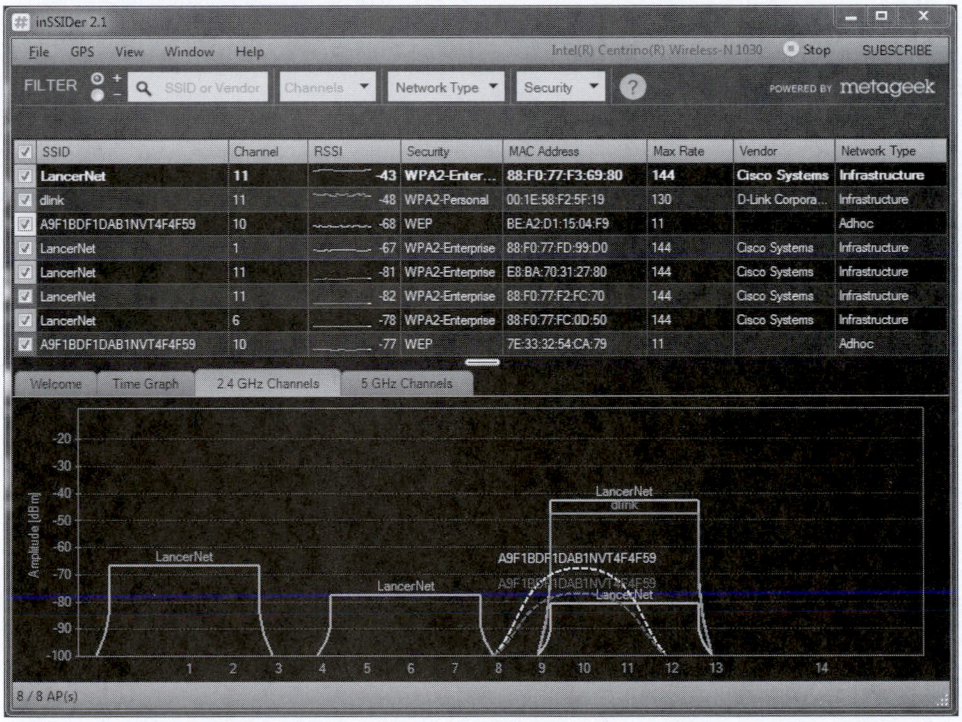

Figure 7-4: InSSIDer showing available wireless networks and their relative signal strengths.

8. Click Start, All Programs, MetaGeek, and inSSIDer.
9. Select your wireless network card from the drop-down menu if it isn't already selected.
10. Click Start Scanning.
11. Click on the 2.4 GHz Channels tab in the lower pane. (See Figure 7-4.)
12. Take a screenshot.
13. Click on the 5 GHz Channels tab in the lower pane. (This tab may be empty if your laptop does not support 5 GHz channels.)
14. Take a screenshot.

PROJECT QUESTIONS

1. What channel was your AP using?

2. Were there any other APs using the same channel? Which ones?
3. What was the MAC address of the AP to which you were connected?
4. What was the SSID address of the AP to which you were connected?

THOUGHT QUESTIONS

1. What are channels? Would one be better than another?
2. Why is WEP considered cryptographically weak?
3. What is the difference between WPA and WPA2?
4. Why do some networks run at 11 Mbps and others at 54 Mbps?

7.3 WIFIDENUM®

One of the ways hackers can access your wireless network is by exploiting vulnerabilities in your wireless network driver. Even if you are using WPA or WPA2, your network can still be compromised. You don't even have to be on a network to be attacked. Your firewall and Intrusion Prevention System may not be able to protect you from this type of attack.

WiFiDEnum® will scan your local wireless network card and retrieve its driver information. It will tell you the driver version, date, manufacturer, and if there are any known vulnerabilities. It's a good idea to keep your drivers updated if they are available. Unfortunately, updating drivers is not a common occurrence and can cause substantial problems if done incorrectly. Let's see if you have any driver issues with your wireless network card.

1. Download WiFiDEnum from https://labs.arubanetworks.com/wifidenum.
2. Click on Security Tools.
3. Scroll down and click on WiFiDEnum 1.2.0.
4. Click Save.
5. Select the C:\security folder.
6. If the program doesn't automatically start, browse to the C:\security folder.
7. Right-click on wifidenum-1.2.zip.
8. Select 7-Zip, and Extract to wifidenum-1.2\. (If you don't have 7-Zip installed, you can download it from www.7-zip.org.)
9. Browse to C:\security\wifidenum-1.2\wifidenum-1.2.
10. Right-click on WiFiDEnum.exe and select Run as administrator.

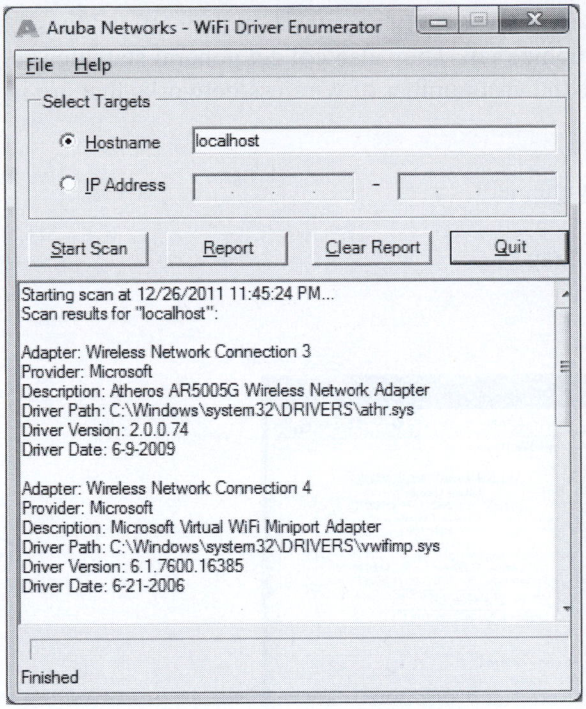

Figure 7-5: WiFiDEnum scanning the local computer.

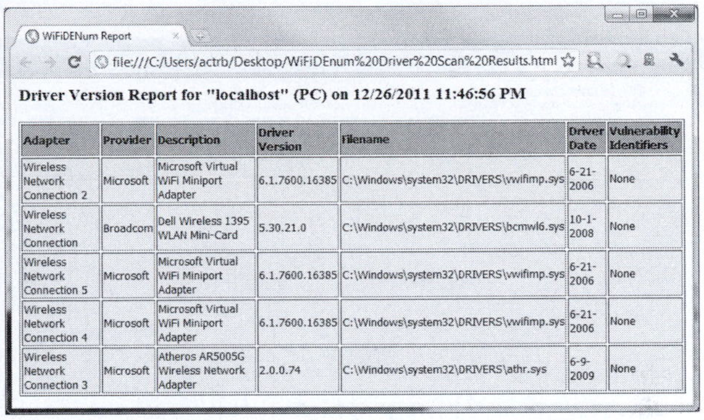

Adapter	Provider	Description	Driver Version	Filename	Driver Date	Vulnerability Identifiers
Wireless Network Connection 2	Microsoft	Microsoft Virtual WiFi Miniport Adapter	6.1.7600.16385	C:\Windows\system32\DRIVERS\vwifimp.sys	6-21-2006	None
Wireless Network Connection	Broadcom	Dell Wireless 1395 WLAN Mini-Card	5.30.21.0	C:\Windows\system32\DRIVERS\bcmwl6.sys	10-1-2008	None
Wireless Network Connection 5	Microsoft	Microsoft Virtual WiFi Miniport Adapter	6.1.7600.16385	C:\Windows\system32\DRIVERS\vwifimp.sys	6-21-2006	None
Wireless Network Connection 4	Microsoft	Microsoft Virtual WiFi Miniport Adapter	6.1.7600.16385	C:\Windows\system32\DRIVERS\vwifimp.sys	6-21-2006	None
Wireless Network Connection 3	Microsoft	Atheros AR5005G Wireless Network Adapter	2.0.0.74	C:\Windows\system32\DRIVERS\athr.sys	6-9-2009	None

Figure 7-6: WiFiDEnum vulnerability report.

11. Click Start Scan. (See Figure 7-5.)
12. Click Report, Save, and Yes to view the report. (See Figure 7-6.)
13. Take a screenshot.

Note: Sometimes a computer will show the bottom panel in WiFiDEnum as all black. The results of the scan are being displayed, you just need to highlight them. WiFiDEnum works just fine on other computers. Both the lower pane and the HTML report show the same information.

PROJECT QUESTIONS

1. What was listed under the description of your wireless card (i.e., the manufacturer)?
2. What was the driver version of your wireless card?
3. What was the driver date listed for your wireless card?
4. Were there any vulnerabilities listed for your wireless card driver?

THOUGHT QUESTIONS

1. What would you do if your driver listed a known vulnerability?
2. Have you ever updated your drivers?
3. What does a driver do exactly?
4. What tool would a hacker use to exploit a vulnerability associated with a wireless network card?

7.4 WIGLE.NET®

Wigle.net® is a website that gives you geographical maps with locations of wireless networks. It has recorded over 16 million networks from almost a billion observations since 2001. It has maps for almost every single street in the United States. It also has maps for Europe, Asia, and the Middle East.

Supporters of Wigle.net drive around and collect observations automatically. Then they upload these observations to Wigle.net to be included in the geographic map. They also collect general statistics about the network observations. This is a fun website to see the vast number of wireless networks that are in operation where you live.

1. Open a Web browser and go to http://www.wigle.net/.
2. Click on Web Maps at the top of the page.
3. Enter your zip code into the text box labeled "Zip."
4. Press Enter. (See Figure 7-7.)
5. Take a screenshot.

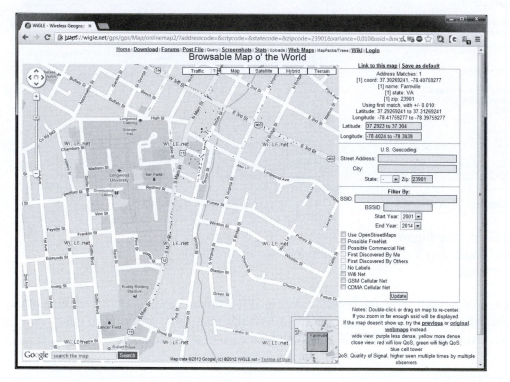

Figure 7-7: Wigle.net map of Longwood University in Virginia.

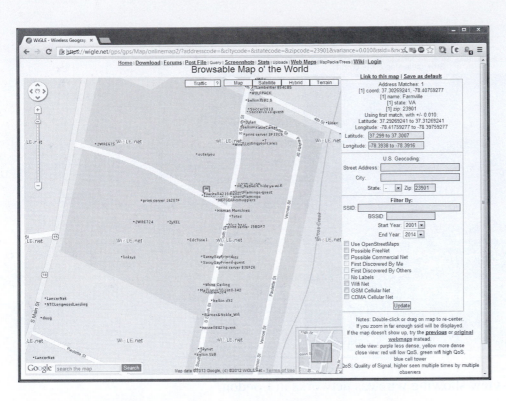

Figure 7-8: Showing wireless networks in Farmville, Virginia.

6. Drag the screen so it is approximately centered over your location.
7. Click the Zoom In button (+) about 4 to 5 times so you can zoom in and see the SSIDs. (See Figure 7-8.)
8. Take a screenshot.
9. Click the Zoom out button (-) about 12 times. (You should be able to see the world map.)
10. Zoom in to London (in the United Kingdom) until you can see the names of the wireless networks listed. (See Figure 7-9.)
11. Click the Hybrid button at the top of the map.
12. Take a screenshot.

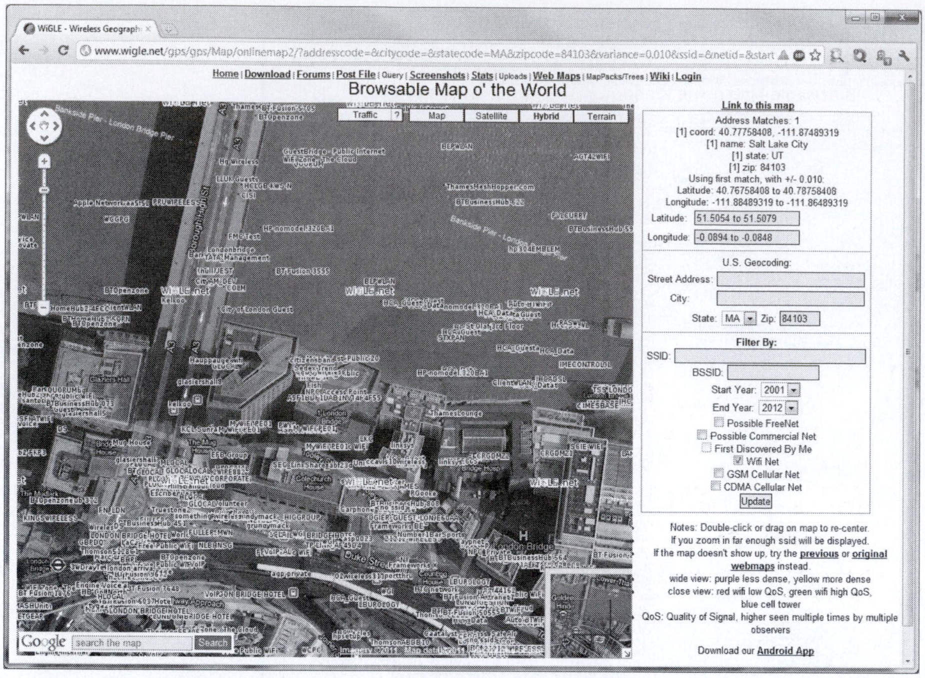

Figure 7-9: Street-view showing wireless networks in London.

PROJECT QUESTIONS

1. Can you see a street name in your map of London? Which one?
2. What was your zip code?
3. What were the approximate coordinates for your zip code?
4. Give the name of one wireless network *other than your own* within your zip code.

THOUGHT QUESTIONS

1. Who collects all these data points?
2. What equipment would you need to contribute to this website?
3. Does Wigle.net keep statistics on the number of networks with WEP, WPA, etc.?
4. Which manufacturer is listed most frequently in all submissions?

7.5 EKAHAU HEATMAPPER®

Ekahau HeatMapper® shows you the location of access points and relative signal strength of a wireless network on a map. This is a tremendous advantage to network administrators because they can identify dead zones, locate rogue access points, and map coverage areas.

Small wireless networks are easy to set up. Large wireless networks, on the other hand, are notoriously difficult to implement correctly. Placement of multiple access points to cover a specific geographic area can be difficult due to 1) variations in building materials in the walls/floors, 2) integrating different wireless standards (e.g., 802.11b, 802.11g, 802.11n), 3) the number of users in a given area, and 4) accounting for 3-dimensional buildings.

HeatMapper allows you to use your own custom map (e.g., building, campus, neighborhood, etc.) to pinpoint access points and wireless coverage. It's also free and easy to use.

1. Download Ekahau HeatMapper from: http://www.ekahau.com/products/heatmapper/overview.html.
2. Fill in any information in the required fields. (The download will start automatically, so you do not have to put in your personal email address.)
3. Click Download.
4. Click Save.
5. Select the C:\security folder.
6. If the program doesn't automatically start, browse to the C:\security folder.
7. Double-click on Ekahau_HeatMapper-Setup.exe.
8. Click Next, I Agree, and Install.
9. Click Install Driver Software if you are prompted.
10. Click Finish.
11. Click I don't have a map.

Note: You are going to be walking around for this project. Be careful. You are going to be marking waypoints every few steps. It's important to keep your directions so the map is accurate. You can use the grid to help estimate your distance. You can use each block as five steps. You might get better results if you make a change in direction.

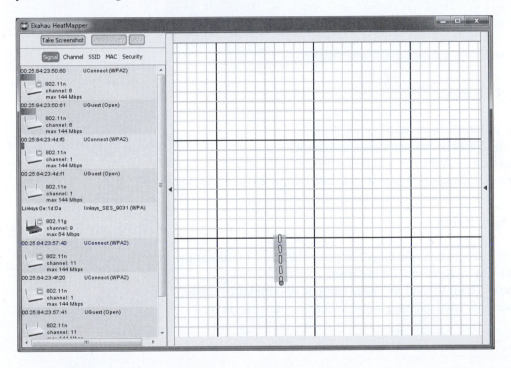

Figure 7-10: Setting waypoints using HeatMapper.

12. Click any point on the map as your first waypoint. (You are going to click several, so it's a good idea to start at the bottom. See Figure 7-10.)
13. Walk 5 to 20 paces in one direction and stop.
14. Click another point on the grid. (In this example, every square on the grid was five paces.)
15. Make at least three more waypoints, including one change of direction.
16. Right-click the grid after you have clicked your last point. (It won't map this last point if you right-click the point. Once enough data is collected, HeatMapper will automatically map the access points and draw the map showing signal strength.)
17. Take a screenshot showing all access points and signal strength mapping. (See Figure 7-11.)

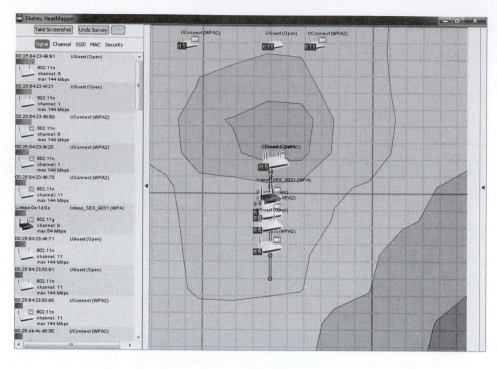

Figure 7-11: Mapped APs and relative signal strength using HeatMapper.

PROJECT QUESTIONS

1. How many points did you map?
2. What was the SSID of the nearest access point?
3. How would you describe the wireless coverage?
4. Did you see any access points that you didn't know existed? Which ones?

THOUGHT QUESTIONS

1. How does the program know where to place the icons representing other networks?
2. What do the colors represent on the map?
3. Would it be difficult to map an entire campus or corporate location?
4. Can you use your own existing map? Where would you get it?

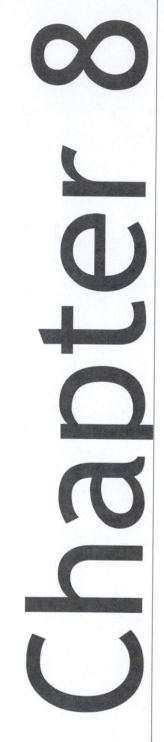

The IT industry moves quickly. Five years in the IT world is equivalent to 25 years in other industries. Software, processes, functionality, connectivity, and capacity (e.g., CPU, memory, storage, etc.) are changing at a dizzying rate. As a result, IT security changes quickly too.

Multiple new viruses are reported every day. Criminal hackers are coming up with creative and devious forms of malware. The variety of criminal behaviors occurring on computers is increasing rapidly. Identity theft, credit card fraud, DOS attacks, phishing scams, corporate espionage, financial fraud, laptop theft, employee abuse, system penetration, and intellectual property theft are all serious concerns.

The same is true of exploits. Every time a new page of code is written, there is the possibility of new vulnerabilities. There are billions of pages of code currently in use today. This creates a substantial number of possible vulnerabilities. Hackers are becoming more adept at automating tools to take advantage of these vulnerabilities.

It's impossible for you to know everything about IT security. However, you can choose to study a specific topic area in depth by reading books, whitepapers, and research articles about your area of interest. It is also wise to be aware of industry-wide trends. A good way is by reading current IT security news at least one hour every day.

Below are just a few websites that provide information about current IT security developments. This is not a comprehensive list. Due to space limitations, we are unable to include many good websites and blogs. It's worth the time to search out those websites and blogs that interest you.

Time required to complete this chapter: 20 minutes

Chapter Objectives

Learn how to:
1. Find current security readings.
2. Find and modify security policy templates.
3. Find information and statistics about broad trends in IT security.

Chapter Projects

Project:
8.1 The Register, Naked Security, & Computerworld
8.2 SANS & Security Policies
8.3 Ponemon Institute & PWC

8.1   THE REGISTER®, NAKED SECURITY®, & COMPUTERWORLD®

If you are new to the IT security field, or just want a more accessible (i.e., less technical) news feed, you might want to read the Security sections of The Register®, Naked Security® (Sophos®), or Computerworld®. Sometimes you are just plain busy and will only have time to look at a few articles.

The Register is based in the UK and gives excellent worldwide coverage. You may want to sign up for their RSS feed too. Naked Security gives a good synopsis of some of the more important IT security developments in an easy-to-read format. Computerworld is another well known site that is worth visiting. If it's an important security article, it's probably on one of these sites.

1. Open a Web browser and go to www.theregister.co.uk/security/. (See Figure 8-1.)
2. Click on an article that interests you. (See Figure 8-2.)
3. Take a screenshot.
4. Under the Security section, click on Enterprise Security.
5. Click on an article that interests you.
6. Take a screenshot.
7. Under the Security section, click on Malware.
8. Click on an article that interests you.
9. Take a screenshot.
10. In the Search box, enter "DDoS" and press Enter.
11. Click on an article that interests you. (See Figure 8-3.)
12. Take a screenshot.

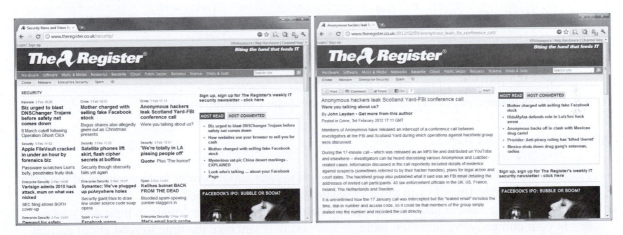

Figure 8-1: The Register security section.   Figure 8-2: An article on The Register.

13. Open a Web browser and go to http://nakedsecurity.sophos.com. (See Figure 8-4.)
14. Click on an article that interests you.
15. Take a screenshot.

Figure 8-3: DDoS article.   Figure 8-4: Security article from Naked Security.

16. Open a Web browser and go to http://www.computerworld.com/.
17. Click on the Topics drop-down menu and select Security.
18. Click on an article that interests you.
19. Take a screenshot.
20. Under the Security section, click Data Security.
21. Click on an article that interests you.
22. Take a screenshot.

PROJECT QUESTIONS

1. What was the topic of the article from The Register?
2. What was the topic of the article from Naked Security?
3. What was the topic of the article from Computerworld?
4. What was the topic of the data security article from Computerworld?

THOUGHT QUESTIONS

1. How much time does your employer give you to read about current events related to your job?
2. How much free time do you think IT security professionals have?
3. Does reading current news articles really help IT security professionals in their daily jobs?
4. Is your company/organization more or less secure if you take the time to read about current events?

8.2   SANS® & SECURITY POLICIES

SANS® is a great source for information about current IT security trends. It also has an excellent collection of security-related whitepapers to help keep you current. If you are planning to work in the IT security field, it would be a good idea to look into their RSS feeds. SANS also has several ready-made templates to help you write a good security policy for your business or organization.

We will look at just a few of the resources on the SANS website. It's worth taking a few minutes to click through the entire website to see all of the resources available to you. As you learn more about IT security, you may find that SANS has some great resources that can help you with your career development.

1. Open a Web browser and go to www.sans.org. (See Figure 8-5.)
2. Click Resources, and Top 20 Critical Controls. (See Figure 8-6.)
3. Take a screenshot.
4. Click Resources, and Additional Resources.
5. Scroll down and click on 20 Coolest Careers.
6. Scroll down to the description of a career that interests you. (See Figure 8-7.)
7. Take a screenshot.
8. Click Resources, and Reading Room.
9. Click Top 25 Papers Based on Views.
10. Click on a paper that interests you. (See Figure 8-8.)
11. Take a screenshot.

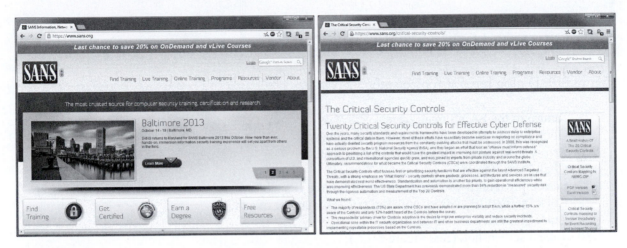

Figure 8-5: SANS main page.

Figure 8-6: Top 20 Critical Controls.

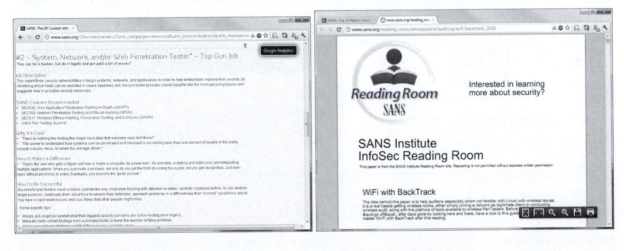

Figure 8-7: SANS 20 Coolest Careers.

Figure 8-8: SANS Reading Room.

12. Return to the SANS main page.
13. Click Resources, and Security Policy Project.
14. Click Email Security Policy.
15. Scroll down and click Download Email Policy (Word Doc).
16. Open the email policy document you just downloaded.
17. In the Microsoft Word window, press Ctrl-H.
18. Click on the Replace tab. (See Figure 8-9.)
19. In the Find what text-box, enter "<COMPANY NAME>".

20. In the Replace with text-box, enter "Your Name Company". (Replace Your Name with your first and last names. In this case, it was Randy Boyle Company.)
21. Click Replace All.
22. Take a screenshot of your new policy. (See Figure 8-10.)

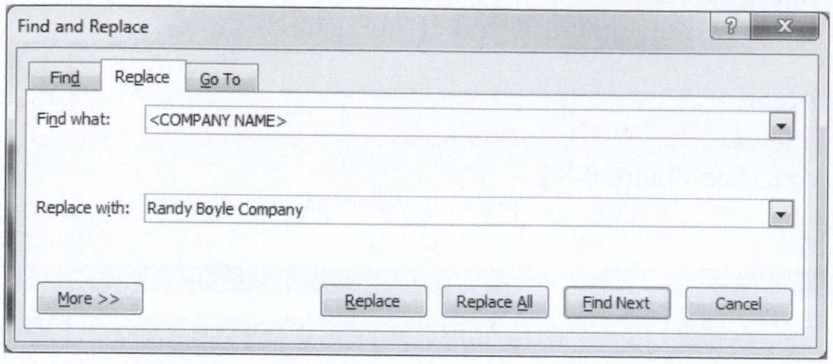

Figure 8-9: Dialog box for replace tab.

23. Return to the SANS main page.
24. Click Resources, and Additional Resources.
25. Scroll down and click Internet Storm Center.
26. Click Data/Reports.
27. Scroll down until you see the Top 10 Source IPs table.
28. Click the first IP address with the greatest number of attacks.
29. Click Summary for [IP address].
30. Take a screenshot. (See Figure 8-11.)

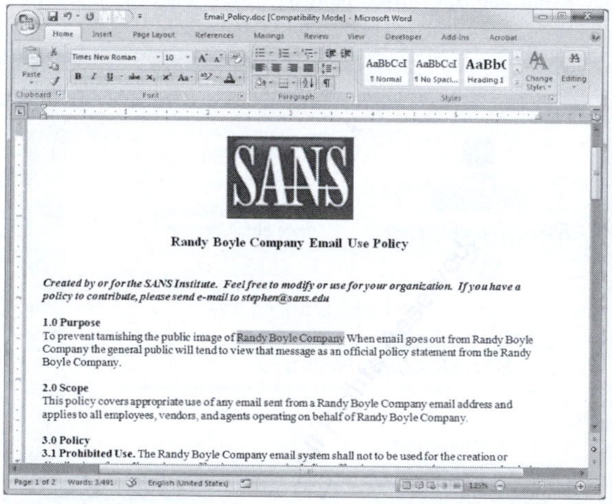

Figure 8-10: Security policy.

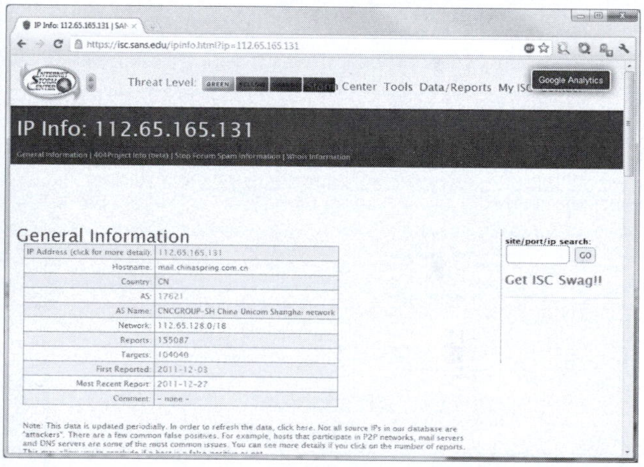

Figure 8-11: SANS Internet Storm Center.

PROJECT QUESTIONS

1. What was the top IP address listed in the Top 10 Sourced IPs list?
2. Where was the IP address from?
3. What was the title of the career you chose?
4. What was the title of the SANS paper you chose?

THOUGHT QUESTIONS

1. Where does SANS get all of the information about attacks that are occurring?
2. Who contributes to the SANS Reading Room?
3. What type of training or certification does SANS provide?
4. What does the SANS Top 20 Critical Controls list tell you?

8.3 PONEMON INSTITUTE & PWC

The Ponemon Institute is a research center that performs studies on IT security and privacy related topics. The research studies and white papers produced by the Ponemon Institute are widely cited and quoted in the news. They are an excellent way to get "hard data" in a field that is rapidly changing.

Many C-level executives (i.e., CEOs, CIOs, or CSOs) require reliable data about security related issues before they authorize large capital expenditures in order to protect against them. For example, a Chief Information Officer (CIO) may want to look at industry-wide statistics related to the average cost of a data breach before hiring additional IT security personnel.

The PricewaterhouseCoopers® (PWC) Global State of Information Security Survey® is an annual survey of information security threats and protection practices across a variety of industries. It is an invaluable tool because it looks at what corporations are doing to protect themselves. It also reports how effective they are at implementing their respective security plans.

Together, the research studies from the Ponemon Institute and the Global State of Information Security Survey from PWC can help IT security professionals explain to non-technical managers how investments in IT security will protect them. It gives them an idea of how big the threats really are and how vulnerable their companies may be.

1. Open a Web browser and go to http://www.ponemon.org. (See Figure 8-12.)
2. Click on Research, Research Studies & White Papers, and Security. (See Figure 8-13.)
3. Click on any one of the research paper links that interest you.
4. Take a screenshot.

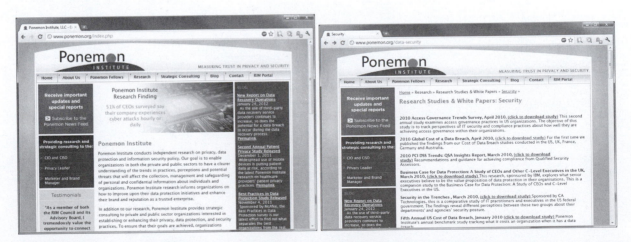

Figure 8-12: Ponemon Institute mainpage. Figure 8-13: Research Studies and White Papers.

5. Return to the listing of research studies and white papers.
6. Click on another research study that interests you.

7. Take a screenshot.
8. Go to http://www.pwc.com/gx/en/information-security-survey or search for "PWC Global State of Information Security Survey" at www.Google.com. (The link above will likely change when newer surveys become available. Searching for the name of the survey may be the most effective way to find the survey.)
9. Click on Explore key findings.
10. Expand the key findings.
11. Take a screenshot.
12. Click on Explore the data.
13. Change the Question dropdown to a question in which you're interested.
14. Select a few industries in which you're interested. (You could select Aerospace, Education, and Energy.)
15. Take a screenshot of the new graph.

PROJECT QUESTIONS

1. What was the topic of the first Ponemon research study?
2. What was the topic of the second Ponemon research study?
3. What key finding did you read about in the PWC survey?
4. What question did you look at in the "Explore the data" section of the PWC survey?

THOUGHT QUESTIONS

1. How could a research study about the cost of data breaches help a CIO plan for information security expenditures?
2. Why might it be difficult to get information about security breaches?
3. Who pays for these studies?
4. How could identifying new security trends and threats help a CIO, or CSO?

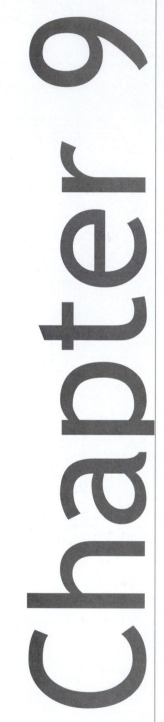

To physically enter the United States, you need a passport. However, you can enter it electronically without a passport of any kind. You can be the nastiest criminal mastermind in the world and enter the United States electronically without any questions asked. In some ways, the cyber world is like the Old West. People can easily move between countries without documentation. Enforcement of existing electronic laws is scarce. In order to hold people accountable for their actions done through computer networks, we need to know who they are and where they live.

Tracing tools may be some of the more useful tools you will learn about in this book. You will be able to actually determine the physical location of a person, a company, a website, etc. Sometimes users see a Web address (i.e., a URL) like www.CNN.com and they have no idea where it's physically located. Just because the Web address sounds like an English word, it does not mean the website is physically hosted within the United States. The website may be located in a country with completely different laws governing electronic communications (or worse… no laws at all). It can be valuable to know the actual physical location of an online company or hacker.

Email is also fairly anonymous to the uninformed computer user who just doesn't know how email really works. IT security professionals are getting more and more requests to track down the source of an email. Typically, the person got flamed, conned out of money, keeps getting spammed, or wants to verify the sender's identity. Anonymity does have its place in society. However, email is increasingly being used for deleterious purposes.

In general, getting information about the actual source of data is becoming much easier. Websites are tying data sources together and triangulating data to yield previously confidential information. This may be good or bad. Either way, it's accelerating at a rapid rate. Let's look at a few examples.

Time required to complete this chapter: 40 minutes

Chapter Objectives

Learn how to:
1. Trace the route a packet takes.
2. Trace a phone number.
3. Look up information about an IP address.
4. Map the source of an IP address.
5. Locate the source of an email.
6. Obtain DNS and network information about a host name.

Chapter Projects

Project:
9.1 Trace Route to the Source
9.2 Trace a Phone Number
9.3 WHOIS Lookup to Source Network
9.4 Locate an IP Address Source
9.5 Locate an Email Source
9.6 Sam Spade

Let's look at a hypothetical example using the author's alma mater, Florida State University. Suppose you are hard at work and all of a sudden your intrusion detection system (IDS) goes off. It turns out that someone from the IP address **128.186.6.14** just scanned your machine to see if you had port 25 open. You have no idea who it is or where they're located. You may also be unsure what service runs over port 25. (This didn't really happen; it's just an example.)

There is a great online trace route tool that maps the physical location of every computer between you and the IP address you enter. YouGetSignal.com® has several useful tools that are worth exploring. Having them online is also nice because the tools are not operating system dependent. You just need to make sure your Internet connection doesn't go down. Let's trace an IP address.

1. Go to the tracing tool hosted by YouGetSignal.com at http://www.yougetsignal.com/tools/visual-tracert/.
2. Enter 128.186.6.14 in the Remote Address text box. (You can also try www.FSU.edu, or www.UCONN.edu, etc.)
3. Click Host Trace, from www.yougetsignal.com to your target. (See Figure 9-1.)
4. Take a screenshot.
5. Click Proxy Trace, from you to www.yougetsignal.com to your target. (See Figure 9-2.)
6. Take a screenshot.

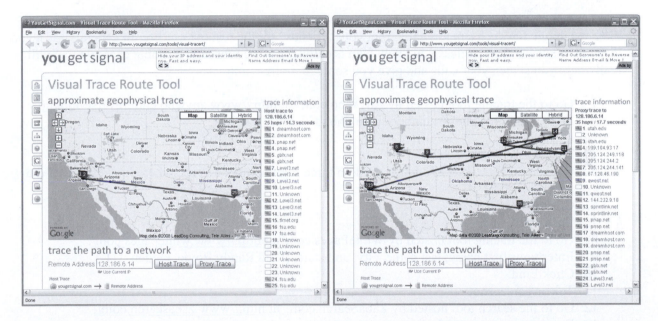

Figure 9-1: Tracing a route.   Figure 9-2: Tracing a route with a proxy.

Not only did you learn the actual physical location of the remote computer (i.e., Florida State University in Tallahassee, FL), but you can also see that information doesn't always take a straight line between hosts. The information between these two computers took what appears to be a wildly inefficient path from the University of Utah to Florida State University. This was likely the "best" path for the information to take depending on the metric used.

Information traveling through the Internet moves quickly and passes through many different computers. Trace route programs are also useful in diagnosing network problems (i.e., determining slow points in a network). It is worth the time and effort to become well acquainted with a trace route program. Network administrators use them every day.

1. What was your IP address?
2. Approximately how many nodes did the trace go through?
3. Did your trace backtrack at all?
4. What was the first node after your computer?

THOUGHT QUESTIONS

1. Could any person along the route look at your information? How?
2. How could you keep someone from looking at your information as it is passed along the Internet?
3. Who owns the routers that forward your information?
4. How does the program map the IP addresses of the routers to their physical location?

9.2   TRACE A PHONE NUMBER

It's highly likely that you have seen a number show up on your phone that you didn't know. This project will show you how to look up the number and see who is calling you before you answer the call. You don't have to blindly answer the phone and be forced to talk to someone. You can also get their general location mapped!

Some people find phones to be a nuisance. Once someone knows you are "good at computers," you'll likely be dogged by tech support calls from your "friends" for the rest of your life. In general, it is a good idea not to answer a call unless you know who is calling. Let's go through a simple example that will really help you screen your calls and give you some more free time.

1. Go to the tracing tool hosted by AnyWho.com® at http://www.anywho.com/reverse-lookup.
2. Enter a landline phone number in the Phone Number text box.
3. Click Find.
4. Take a screenshot.
5. Change the area code to another random three-digit number and see where it takes you. (I did 507.)
6. Click Find.
7. Take a screenshot.
8. Go to the tracing tool hosted by WhitePages.com® at http://www.whitepages.com/.
9. Enter your first name, last name, city, and state. (I did Randy Boyle, Ogden, UT.)
10. Click Find.
11. Take a screenshot.
12. Go to the search tool hosted by ZabaSearch.com® at http://www.zabasearch.com/.
13. Enter your first name, last name, and state.
14. Click Free People Search.
15. Take a screenshot.

Not only did you find out who called, but you also know where they live and possibly who their relatives are. There are many other tools that are used to collect information, but we will stop here. If we showed you all the tools used to gather information, and the implications of that information, it might surprise you. Most hackers/crackers spend quite a bit of time and energy just gathering information as a first step. It's easy and no one notices.

The integration of these information sources is disconcerting from a security point of view. For example, website A may be restricted by law from giving out a certain piece of information. However, website B can take the information from websites A, C, and D to triangulate, calculate, or estimate the prohibited information. Laws governing information use are still in the dark ages. You need to take steps to protect yourself.

The following are some useful guidelines to help you keep your privacy:

✓ Don't give personal information to anyone unless you absolutely have to.

✓ Learn the phrase "**I don't give out that information**" and repeat it every time you are asked for your phone number, Social Security number, zip code, address, etc.

✓ NEVER give out your Social Security number. The only exceptions to this rule would be if you were being admitted to the hospital, or applying for a loan or credit card.

PROJECT QUESTIONS

1. What was the phone number you searched for?
2. What was the approximate geographic location of the phone trace?
3. Did the people trace tool find any of your family members or relatives? Which ones?
4. Did the ZabaSearch find any of your prior residences? Was it accurate?

THOUGHT QUESTIONS

1. Why doesn't your cell phone have an application just like this?
2. Can someone fake his or her phone number to make it appear that it is coming from a different number?
3. Who controls the exchange of information between different private companies?
4. How could you get your information taken out of other companies' directories? Do you own your information?

9.3   WHOIS® LOOKUP TO SOURCE NETWORK

Oftentimes an IP Address will show up in an IDS or honeypot log and you don't know exactly which individual caused the log entry. You can't see a specific person associated with the log entry because there is currently no lookup service to resolve an IP address into a specific person's name, though it's possible that there will be one in the future.

IP addresses can be "loaned" out to several individuals throughout the day. It may be important to know who had which IP address at a given time, but without cooperation from the network administrator, you can't tell who was using the computer at the time of the log entry. However, you can tell who the network administrator is (i.e., the person in charge of managing that range of IP addresses) and get his or her contact information.

Hackers do questionable things to IT security professionals' computers all the time. In general, you can email the network administrators about an incident, but you will typically get an automated response in return. Once in a while, you will get an actual email from the administrator in charge of a particular address range. If you get a log entry for a network outside the United States, you'll likely be wasting your time trying to contact the network administrator about it. They'll probably get a good laugh out of your email.

Alternatively, you may get an IDS log entry, email the network administrator, and get a thank you email in return because it turns out that he or she didn't even know that a certain machine had been "lost" (i.e., hacked). The administrator may walk down, shut the machine off, and send you an email thanking you for bringing it to his or her attention. However, this is usually the exception, not the rule. Let's see how to find out who is in charge of an IP address range.

1. Go to the WHOIS Lookup Tool® hosted by YouGetSignal.com at http://www.yougetsignal.com/tools/whois-lookup/.
2. Enter your IP address in the Remote Address text box.
3. Click Check. (See Figure 9-3.)
4. Take a screenshot.
5. Enter this IP address: 155.97.243.201.
6. Click Check.
7. Take a screenshot.
8. Enter a random IP address. (Make sure each octet value is below 254.)
9. Click Check.
10. Take a screenshot.

Figure 9-3: Looking up an IP address.

Now you have the contact information for the network administrator for the University of Utah. If you get an IP address in the 155.97.X.X range that tries to break into your machine, you can email the administrator. Just don't email them too often.

This is another good project that reinforces the need to be cautious when using IT security software. Your actions may alarm your administrator and cause him/her to take legal action against you. Your network administrator will likely know which computer has a specific IP address at any given time. Your network administrator knows who you are and has your home address.

PROJECT QUESTIONS

1. What was the first IP address you entered?
2. What was the OrgName shown in the results for the first IP address?
3. Where was the organization located?
4. For the random IP address you entered, where was the organization located?

THOUGHT QUESTIONS

1. If we can trace the IP addresses of people trying to break into our computers, why is it so hard to catch hackers?
2. Can someone fake an IP address?
3. Who decides ownership over a given IP address range?
4. What can you do if the hacker is coming from outside the United States?

9.4   LOCATE AN IP ADDRESS SOURCE

One of the most common tasks that IT security professionals perform on a daily basis is to track down an external IP address. IDS and honeypot logs are slowly being filled with IP addresses of individuals doing things they shouldn't be doing. A good tool that can trace their physical location is necessary. If they are outside the United States, there is little you can do. However, if they are from the network of a competing company or from an internal network, you do have some recourse. It's fun to see where these people are.

Most IT security professionals have seen log entries from almost every single country in the world. (If you get one from Antarctica, you should feel extremely lucky.) Administrators will also see log entries from all major U.S. universities and a surprising number of local/state governments. It's understandable that students are bored and/or curious, but the number of local and state government log entries is surprising. You will load your own honeypot in the next section, and you'll be able to start recognizing possible scans/attacks. Let's try a couple of examples.

1. Go to the IP address lookup tool hosted by WhatIsMyIpAddress.com® at http://whatismyipaddress.com/.
2. Enter your IP address in the Remote Address text box. (It may already be displayed.)
3. Click Additional IP Details. (See Figure 9-4.)
4. Take a screenshot.
5. Enter the IP address, 155.97.243.201.
6. Click Lookup IP Address.
7. Take a screenshot.
8. Change the first octet (155) to a random number less than 255 and see where the network is located. (In this example, we used 140 and got London.) (See Figure 9-5.)
9. Take a screenshot.

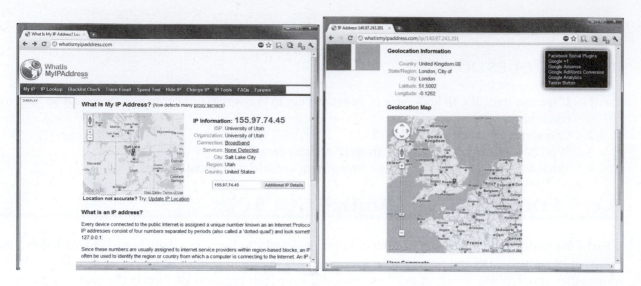

Figure 9-4: Finding your location based on IP address.　　　Figure 9-5: Locating the source of an IP address.

PROJECT QUESTIONS

1. What was your IP address?
2. Did it map your location correctly?
3. What was the random IP address you chose?
4. Where was the random IP address located?

THOUGHT QUESTIONS

1. What is a proxy server and can it really hide one's identity?
2. How does a proxy server work?
3. Can someone (company, law enforcement, government) track everything that is sent to/from one's computer?
4. Do I have to have an IP address to send/receive information?

9.5　　LOCATE AN EMAIL SOURCE

Occasionally, a network administrator will have an individual come and ask if it is possible to trace an email back to its source. Almost 99% of the time, he or she has gotten a nasty email from someone and wants to find out who it was. Whether or not they deserved it is another story. There are other reasons for wanting to track down the source of an email, but this is a fairly common occurrence.

It's surprisingly easy to get most of the information. Let's look at an example that uses the email's header to trace it back to the source. The header, which is typically hidden, contains all of the routing information for that specific email. Finding the header information will be the hardest part. Most people are unaware that emails even have headers. Below is a really good tool by Butterfat.net®. There are other websites that have similar tools.

1. Open Outlook. (Hotmail and Gmail also have header information.)
2. Open any email message, preferably from someone who lives in another state or country. (See Figure 9-6.)
3. Click on Message Options.

Note: If you're using the MS ribbon feature, you need to click on the little arrow next to the word "Options." Yes, this can be confusing. Before Office 2007, it was easier to view an email header. If you are using another email program, you may have to look around for some option that allows you to view the email header. Most email accounts, like Hotmail and Gmail, have this option.

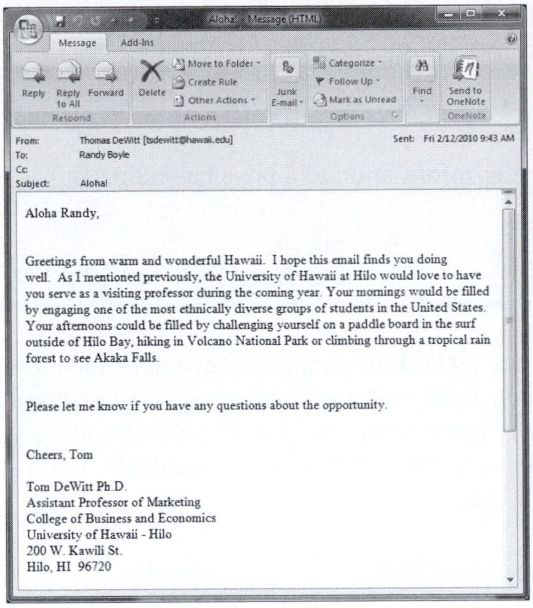

Figure 9-6: Any email.

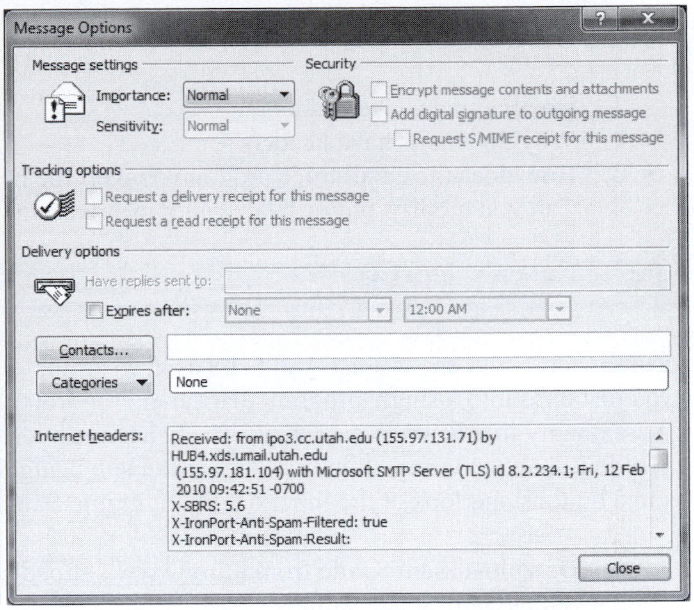

Figure 9-7: Email header information.

4. Select ALL of the header information in the bottom text box (Ctrl-A). (See Figure 9-7.)
5. Copy all of the information you just selected (Ctrl-C).
6. Go to the Email Trace tool hosted by Butterfat.net at http://map.butterfat.net/emailroutemap/. (You can also go to http://www.ip-adress.com/trace_email/.)
7. Paste all of the information you just copied from Outlook into the text box at the bottom of the page.
8. Take a screenshot.
9. Click Do it.
10. Take a screenshot.

This email came from Dr. Tom DeWitt on Hawai'i. Even if you didn't know the actual name of the person sending the email, you would still have their IP address. Knowing a person's IP address can be better than knowing their name. As you've seen from prior examples, once you have one piece of information, you can gather any additional information quickly.

The moral of this story is simple: don't send "flaming" emails. Most people don't really have a strong grasp of the IP addressing system, how routers work, how mail servers work, or how email works. These are unknowns that can get you into trouble. Nowadays, almost all electronic messages are copied, logged, and tracked. This includes the emails *you* send to other people.

There are many information gathering tools that could be demonstrated, but it is best to stop here. It might shock you to learn the types and quantities of information available on the Internet.

PROJECT QUESTIONS

1. Whom did the email come from that you used in this project?

2. Did the trace accurately map the location of the person's mail server?
3. What was one of the IP addresses listed in the results, located below the box you pasted the header information into?
4. If you traced your own email, where do you think the source would be located?

THOUGHT QUESTIONS

1. Do all emails have headers?
2. Why do emails have headers?
3. How does the email trace program convert the header information to a physical address?
4. Can you modify and/or fake header information?

9.6   SAM SPADE®

Sam Spade® is an easy-to-use tool that has been around since 1997. It incorporates several of the tools you just used into a single program that can be run from your local machine. It also has some additional functionality that is worth exploring. The benefit of a locally installed application like Sam Spade is that you don't have to worry about the remote website being down and the tools being unavailable. Let's click some buttons and look at the functionality built into Sam Spade.

1. Download Sam Spade from http://www.softpedia.com/get/Network-Tools/Network-Tools-Suites/Sam-Spade.shtml.
2. Click Download.
3. Click Softpedia Mirror.
4. Save the file to your C:\security folder. (You can make one at this point if you don't already have one.)
5. If the installation program doesn't automatically start, browse to C:\security.
6. Double-click the spade114.exe program to install Sam Spade.
7. Click Run, Next, Next, Next, and Install.
8. Click Yes to update HTML help.
9. Click OK, and Finish.
10. Click Start, All Programs, Blightly Design, and Sam Spade 1.14.
11. Enter your IP address in the text box in the upper left-hand corner. (You can also use a hostname like www.Longwood.edu.)
12. Press Enter or the purple arrow next to the text box. (See Figure 9-8.)
13. Take a screenshot.
14. Enter www.Google.com into the text box in place of your IP address.
15. Click the Ping, DNS, Whois, and IP Block buttons on the left-hand side of the screen. (See Figure 9-9.)
16. Take a screenshot.
17. Click Trace. (See Figure 9-10.)
18. Take a screenshot.

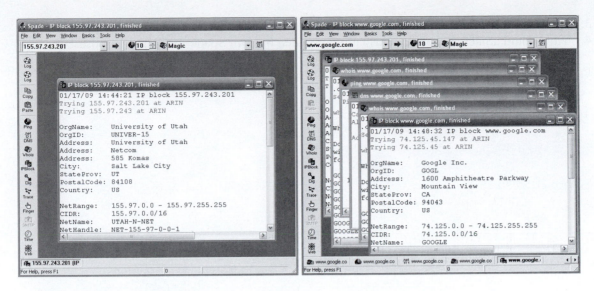

Figure 9-8: Sam Spade reverse lookup.

Figure 9-9: Sam Spade utilities.

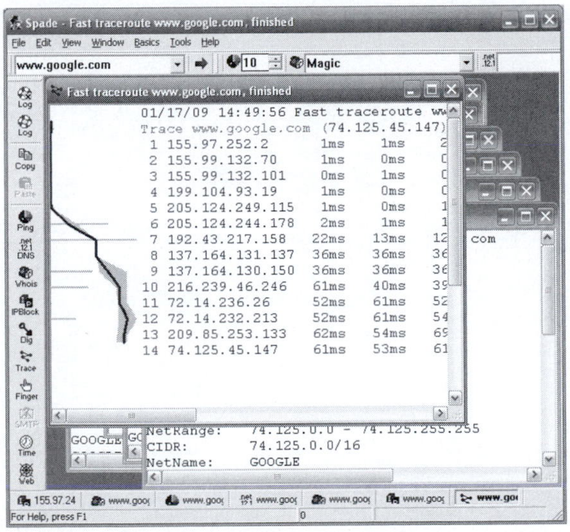

Figure 9-10: Sam Spade trace route.

Sam Spade has several other useful built-in tools. Feel free to test all of Sam Spade's functionality. For a tool that has been around for over a decade, Sam Spade is still quite useful for getting information about a specific URL or IP address.

PROJECT QUESTIONS

1. What was your IP address?
2. What IP address was displayed for www.Google.com when you pressed the Ping button?
3. What was the first IP address listed for www.Google.com when you pressed the DNS button?
4. How many hops were recorded in the traceroute from your computer to www.Google.com?

THOUGHT QUESTIONS

1. What does the Whois tool do?
2. What does the Crawl Website command do?

3. What legitimate uses would a network administrator have for the tools in Sam Spade?
4. How could a hacker use the information provided by Sam Spade for illegal purposes?

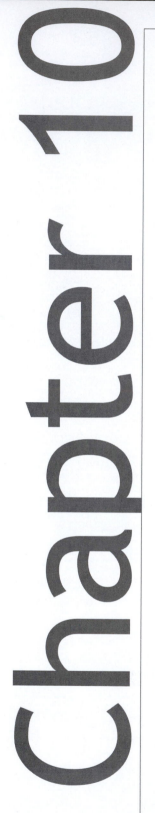

Packet sniffers are used to analyze intercepted network traffic as it is travels across a network. You can pick up packets of information that may or may not be intended for your computer. Packet sniffers are an extremely valuable tool for network administrators and IT security personnel. Network administrators use them to diagnose a wide array of everyday problems on both wired and wireless networks.

Packet sniffers are used to gather information about potential targets or hackers, watch hackers send traffic over a network (i.e., data loss prevention), watch for illicit or unauthorized traffic, manipulate man-in-the-middle attacks, perform penetration testing, etc. It would be well worth your time to learn all the functionality of the packet sniffer called Wireshark®.

In this chapter, you will do a couple of basic exercises to learn how packet sniffers work on a fundamental level. Most people are shocked when they first see a packet sniffer because they didn't realize 1) that there were so many packets going across a network, 2) that a single packet had so much information in it, and 3) that someone else could look at their packets.

Seeing a packet sniffer work for the first time can be overwhelming. The trick is to go slow and try to understand each part.

There are several other packet sniffers available on the market today that you could learn how to use. Wireshark was chosen because it has excellent functionality and beginning students find it easy to use. Learning how to actually use a packet sniffer is a critical skill for anyone interested in a career in IT security.

Time required to complete this chapter: 40 minutes

Chapter Objectives

Learn how to:
1. Capture network traffic.
2. Capture specific types of traffic.
3. Read captured traffic.
4. Filter captured traffic.
5. Capture traffic using the command line.

Chapter Projects

Project:
10.1 Packet Capture (Wireshark I)
10.2 Capture Web Traffic (Wireshark II)
10.3 Capture an Email (Wireshark III)
10.4 Display Filtering (Wireshark IV)
10.5 Command-line packet sniffing (Windump®)

Wireshark (formerly named Ethereal®) is one of the most well known packet sniffers in use today. It is a flexible and powerful tool. Any IT security professional worth his or her salt will know how to use Wireshark. Wireshark has been getting better and better with each release. It will likely remain the industry standard packet sniffer for many years.

In this project, you will install Wireshark and capture some network traffic. In addition to loading Wireshark, you will also load WinPCap® in order to actually capture the packets being sent over your network.

1. Download Wireshark from http://www.wireshark.org/download.html.
2. Click Download Windows Installer. (Download the latest stable release.)
3. Click Save.
4. Save the file in your C:\security folder. (You can create a security directory if you haven't already created one.)
5. If the program doesn't automatically open, browse to C:\security.
6. Double-click on Wireshark-setup-1.8.5.exe. (The software version numbers will be slightly different as newer versions are released.)
7. Click Next, I Agree, Next, Next, Next, and Install.
8. Click Next to install WinPCap.
9. Click Next, I Agree, Install, and Finish.
10. Click Next, and Finish.
11. Double-click the Wireshark icon on your desktop. (You can also access it through your Start menu.)
12. Click Interface List. (This will display a list of all available network interfaces on your computer.)
13. Note the interface with the most traffic. (You will select this interface in the following steps. If there are duplicate names for the Network Interface Card [NIC], you can use the last 3 or 4 values of the MAC address to identify the appropriate NIC.)
14. Close the Capture Interfaces window.
15. Click Capture, and Options. (See Figure 10-1.)
16. Select your Network Interface Card if it is not already selected. (See Figure 10-2.)
17. Take a screenshot.

Note: Your NIC will undoubtedly have a different name. If you don't know which NIC is your active network card, you should keep trying them all until one of them works. Then memorize the model name and number of your NIC. If you are still looking for a Broadcom® NIC, like the one shown in the screenshots above, please stop and ask your instructor for help.

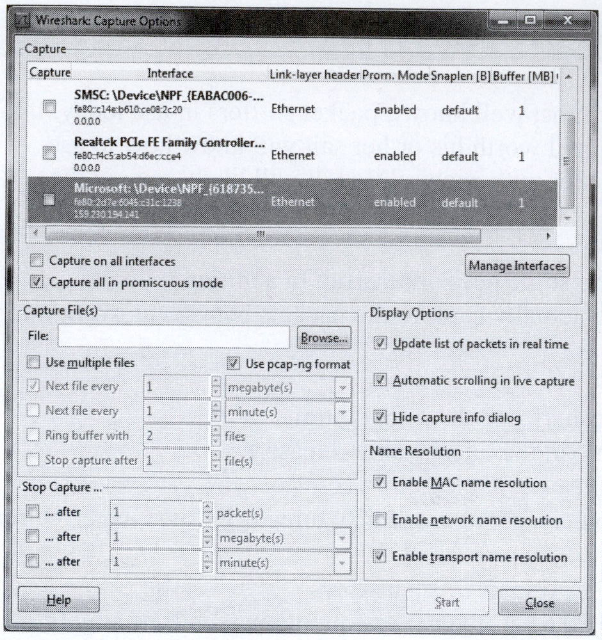

Figure 10-1: Wireshark capture options.

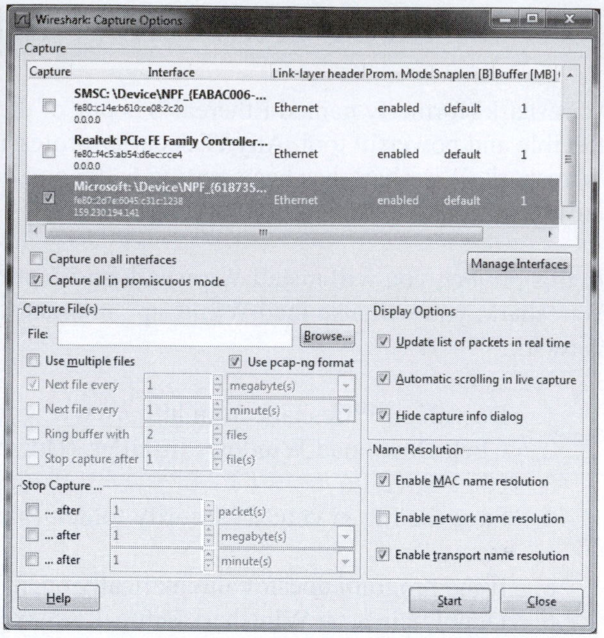

Figure 10-2: Network card is selected.

18. Close ALL other programs you currently have open *except* your word processing program (e.g., MS Word, LibreOffice Writer®, etc.). (You can download a free copy of the LibreOffice suite from www.LibreOffice.org.)
19. Click Start.
20. Let it run for 10 seconds.
21. While you are waiting, open a Web browser and go to www.Google.com.
22. Return to your Wireshark window.
23. In the file menu, click Capture and Stop (or use the keyboard shortcut—Ctrl+E).
24. Scroll up until you see a green and blue area. (These are the packets you captured when you requested Google's main page.)
25. Take a screenshot. (See Figure 10-3.)

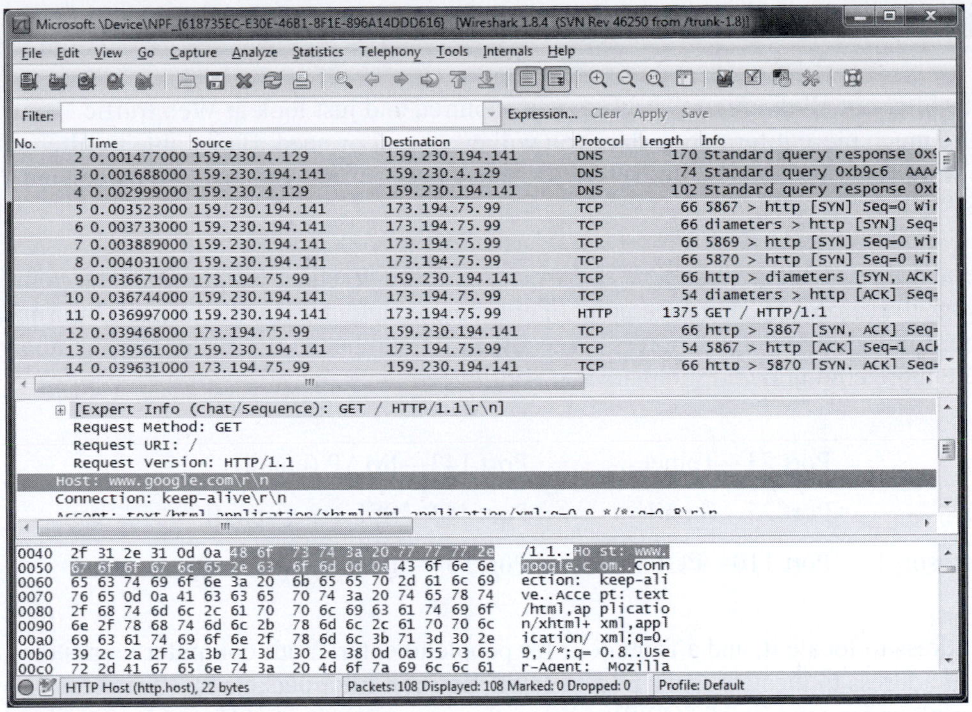

Figure 10-3: Captured packets.

26. Scroll down until you see a line that has GET / HTTP/1.1. (You may have to try more than one until you get to the packet that shows "www.google.com" in the bottom pane.)
27. Select that row.
28. In the bottom pane, you will see a bunch of numbers to the left. (It's the packet's contents in hexadecimal.) Just to the right, you will see the content of the packet in a column.
29. Select this text: www.google.com.
30. Take a screenshot.

You just picked packets off your network and looked at their contents. There may have been lots of traffic that you couldn't interpret. Don't worry about the information on your screen that is difficult to understand. As you learn more about IT security and TCP/IP, it will begin to make more sense. In the next project, you will use a filter to capture only Web traffic going over port 80.

PROJECT QUESTIONS

1. What was your IP address?
2. What was one of the remote IP addresses with which your computer was communicating?
3. How many packets did you capture?
4. What was the protocol type for the blue colored entries?

THOUGHT QUESTIONS

1. What do the different colors mean?
2. Why does your computer get packets that are addressed to another machine?
3. How many packets does your computer send/receive in a single mouse click when you visit a website?
4. Could you organize or filter the traffic to make it easier to understand?

Now you are going to filter out all the "extra" packets you captured and just look at Web traffic. Too often, you will capture much more information than you will ever want or need. Being able to filter out the traffic you don't want is an important skill. Before you can filter packets, you need to understand a little bit about "ports."

Your house has several points of entry, like doors and windows, through which people can enter your house. Computers work the same way, and each point of entry on a computer is called a port. Information comes into a computer through a port. Each port is given a specific number so it's easier to remember. Below are some of the more common port numbers that you'll need to know:

Port 80—Web	Port 23—Telnet	Port 143—IMAP (email)
Port 20—FTP (data)	Port 25—Email	Port 443—SSL (encrypted)
Port 21—FTP (supervisory)	Port 110—POP (email)	Port 53—DNS

Your house has an address to locate it, and a front door for people to enter. Your computer works the same way. It has an IP address to locate it and a port to enter. You can filter packets by IP address or by port number. A thorough understanding of TCP/IP will greatly aid your understanding of how packet filtering works. There are many great tutorials available on the Web that will teach you the basics.

Below are instructions on how to filter out all packets *except* Web traffic by creating a filter for just port 80. This will capture all the Web traffic going to all the computers on your local network. Reread the last sentence. Yes, you read that correctly, it will even capture Web traffic intended for other computers on your network. This is one of the reasons why packet sniffers are important to learn.

1.   With Wireshark open, click Capture, and Options.
2.   If you haven't already done so, select your Network Interface Card. (Your NIC will undoubtedly have a different name than the one shown below.)
3.   Double-click the interface you have selected. (This will allow you to enter a capture filter.)
4.   Click Capture Filter. (See Figure 10-4.)
5.   Type "YourName_TCP_port_80" for the filter name. (Replace YourName with your first and last name. In this case, the filter name was RandyBoyle_TCP_port_80.)
6.   Type "tcp port 80" in the filter string text box.
7.   Take a screenshot. (See Figure 10-5.)
8.   Click OK.

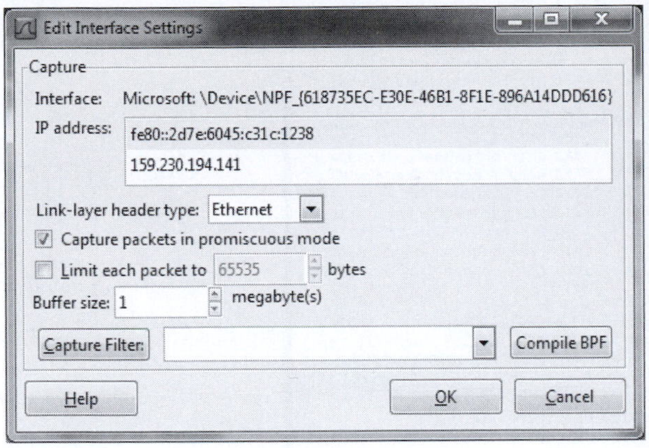

Figure 10-4: Wireshark Edit Interface Settings.

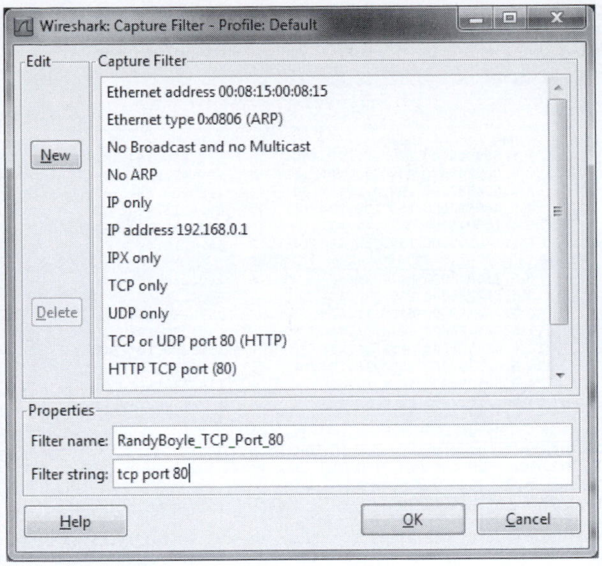

Figure 10-5: Configuring a TCP port 80 traffic capture.

9. Close ALL other programs you currently have open *except* your word processing program (e.g., Microsoft Word, OpenOffice Writer®, etc.).
10. Click OK. (You should see the capture filter set. See Figure 10-6.)
11. Click Start.
12. Click Continue without Saving, when prompted. (You can always click Continue without Saving, because you won't be saving any of the captures in these projects. See Figure 10-7.)

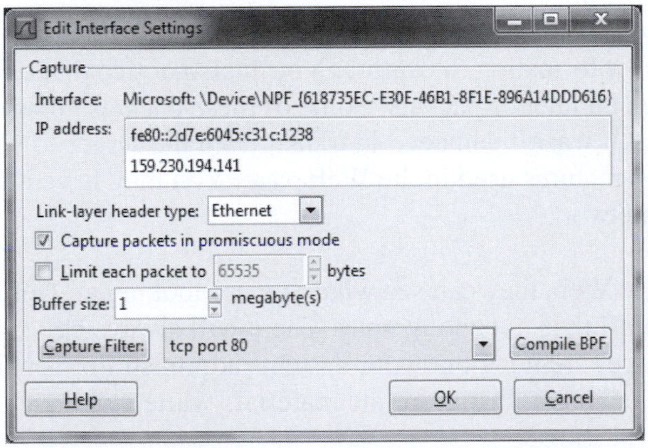

Figure 10-6: Capture filter is set.

Figure 10-7: Not saving captured packets.

13. Open a Web browser and go to www.Microsoft.com.
14. Return to your Wireshark window.
15. Click Capture, and Stop.
16. Scroll down until you see a line that has GET / HTTP/1.1. (You may have to try more than one until you get to the www.Microsoft.com packet.)
17. Select that row.
18. In the bottom pane, you will see a bunch of numbers to the left. (It's the contents of the packet in hexadecimal. Just to the right, you will see the content of the packet in a column.)
19. Select the "www.microsoft.com" text.
20. Take a screenshot. (See Figure 10-8.)

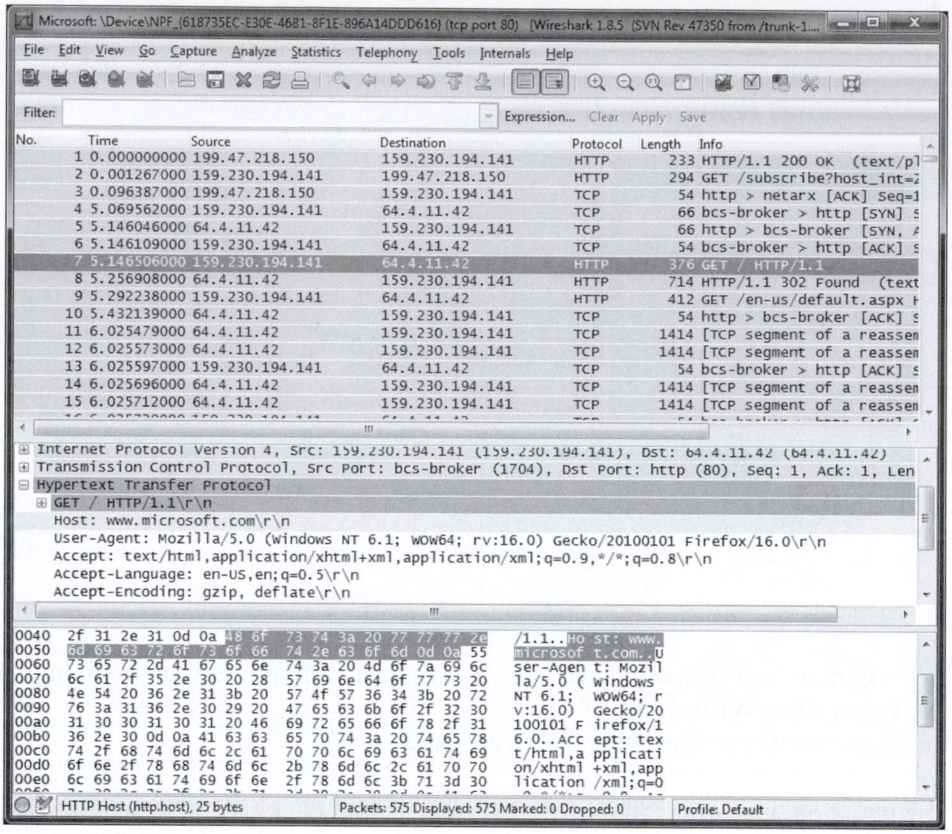

Figure 10-8: Viewing the contents of a packet.

By filtering only Web traffic (port 80) there was *less* information to capture. You'll also notice that one simple visit to www.Microsoft.com generates a large number of packets. Some of these packets are used to guarantee that you received the Web page and that it wasn't damaged in transit from the server to your computer. Other packets are used to transfer text and pictures used in the Web page. You may have also captured packets going to other computers on your network.

If you can see what other people are looking at on the Web, they can see what you are looking at. Doing this project helps individuals understand that Web surfing is not anonymous. There will always be someone who can see what you are looking at. Chances are good that your systems administrator is able to see *exactly* what you are looking at. That is why looking at inappropriate materials while you are at work is the acme of foolishness.

Many systems administrators watch employees' Web surfing activities during work hours. It's completely legal. Employees have been fired for viewing inappropriate material at work. It's well within a company's rights to do so. There are commercial software products that track all employee Web surfing activities.

PROJECT QUESTIONS

1. How many total packets did you capture?
2. What row (number) contained the GET request?
3. What was the source port (Src Port) on your GET request?
4. What was your IP address for this project?

THOUGHT QUESTIONS

1. Why does your computer send so many packets? Why not send just one big packet?
2. What do SYN, ACK, FIN, and GET mean?
3. Why do some packets have sequence numbers?
4. Why does your computer send packets to the Web server from which you requested data?

10.3   CAPTURE AN EMAIL (WIRESHARK III)

In this project, you will capture a packet and look at its contents. You will use Wireshark to capture packets containing an email message. You will send an email to a generic Hotmail account and capture it as it's going over the network. Then you will look at the contents of the email without opening it in an email client.

Most email traffic has traditionally not been encrypted. However, many providers are starting to make encrypted email an option for their users. A packet sniffer allows you to look at the contents of many different types of packets.

1. With Wireshark open, click Capture, and Options.
2. If you haven't already done so, select your Network Interface Card. (Your NIC will undoubtedly have a different name than the one shown below.)
3. Double-click the interface you have selected. (This will allow you to enter a capture filter.)
4. Click Capture Filter.
5. Make sure the capture filter is set to "tcp port 80" from the prior project. (This filter will capture Web-based email. Use port 80 for Web-based email, or port 25 for email if you are using a local client like Outlook. See Figure 10-9.)
6. Click OK.
7. Close ALL other programs you currently have open *except* your word processing program (e.g., MS Word, LibreOffice Writer) and your Web browser.
8. Direct your Web browser to www.Hotmail.com. (If you already have a Hotmail account, skip to step 12.)
9. Click Sign Up. (This will sign you up for a free Hotmail email account.)
10. Enter information for the required fields. (Fake information is fine to enter. Write down the information you entered. The email address on this account was boyle12345678@hotmail.com.)
11. Click I accept. (See Figure 10-10.)

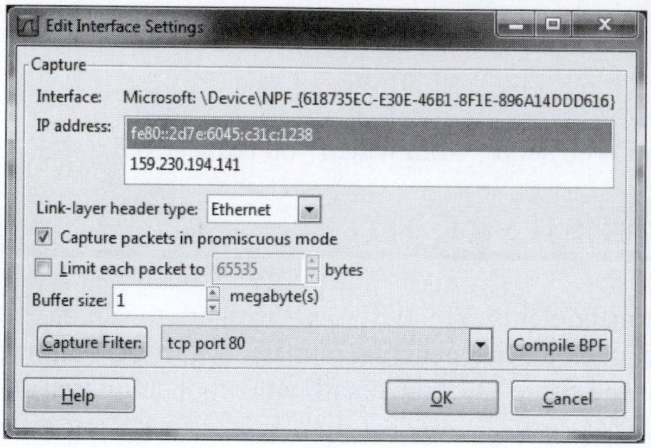

Figure 10-9: Configuring Wireshark to capture port 80 packets.   Figure 10-10: Hotmail.com inbox.

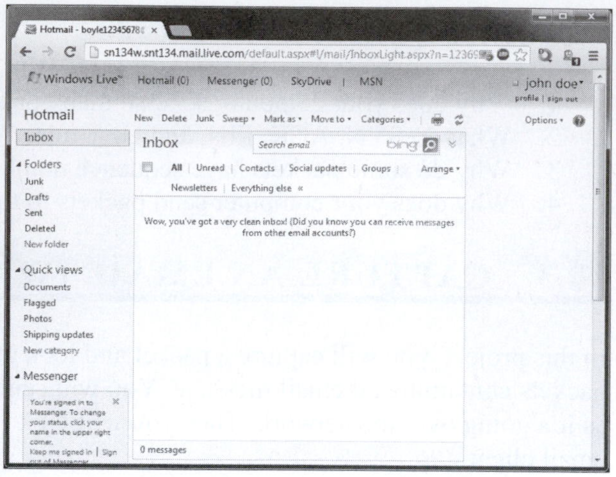

12. Click New. (This will create a new email.)
13. In the To field, put your real email address or the same email address you just created.
14. In the Subject line, put Your Name. (Replace Your Name with your first and last name. In this case, it was Randy Boyle.)
15. In the body of the email, put the words "Your Name" and copy/paste it until it fills up the body of the email message. (This will help us identify the packet when we see it. In this case, it was Randy Boyle. The more you fill the page with your name, the easier it will be to identify the packet after it is captured. See Figure 10-11.)
16. Go back to Wireshark and click Start. (You can also start a capture by clicking Capture and then Start through the file menu.)
17. Go back to your Hotmail account and click Send. (You may be prompted to type in a CAPTCHA to stop spammers. After you complete the CAPTCHA, you can go back and send the email.)
18. Go back to Wireshark and click Capture and then Stop in the file menu.
19. Click on the line that has Post/mail/SendMessageLight in the Info field. (In this case, it was the eleventh packet. The contents of the email were about three quarters of the way down, in the bottom pane. If you captured a lot of packets, it might be easier to find a line with "Post" in the Info line and then press the info column header to sort by that column. It will group all of the packets with "Post" together. This will make it easier to find the packet. You may see some HTML tags like "<div>" next to your name.)
20. Click on the bottom window pane where you see a column of words saying Your Name. (In this case, the body of the message contained "Randy Boyle," along with some HTML tags. It was the eleventh packet.)
21. Take a screenshot. (See Figure 10-12.)

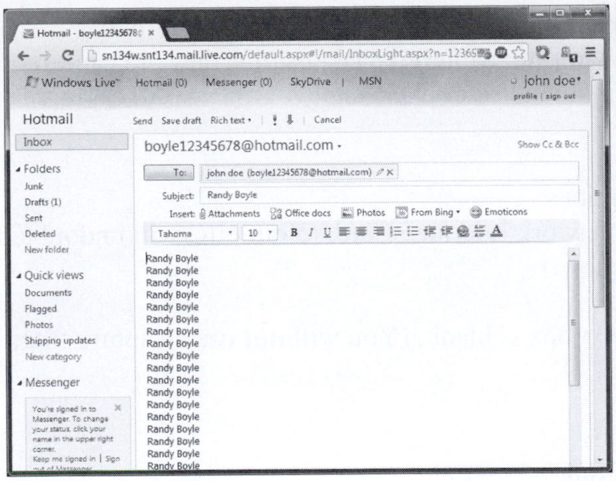

Figure 10-11: Sending a test email.

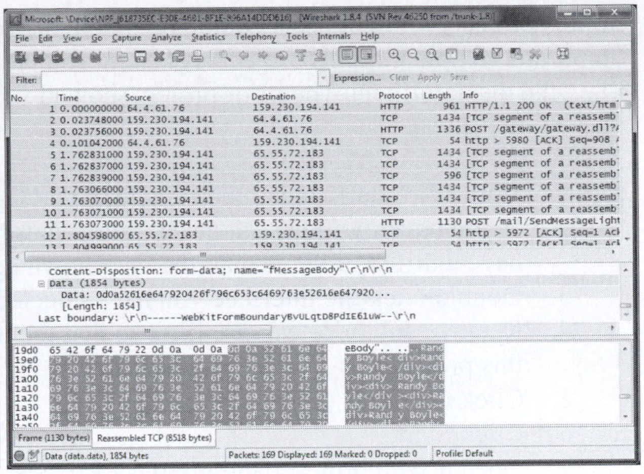

Figure 10-12: Viewing the contents of the captured email.

You just picked up your email off the network that was on its way to www.Hotmail.com. Unless specified, your emails are *not* encrypted. Most people are unaware of this and send confidential information on a regular basis over unencrypted email systems. Do *not* send sensitive information by email.

It's important to understand that Wireshark picked up your email from the network. It can just as easily pick up *all* email traffic going over your network. One of the main concepts you will learn by doing these projects is that you may not fully understand how computers (or information systems) work. Hopefully, knowing more about computers, networks, and information systems will help protect you.

PROJECT QUESTIONS

1. What was your Hotmail email address?
2. Which packet (or packet number) contained the contents of your email?
3. What was the IP address of the Hotmail server to which you connected?
4. Do you use secure email?

THOUGHT QUESTIONS

1. How many people do you think are unaware that their emails may be unencrypted?
2. Why wouldn't email be encrypted by default?
3. Can you look at Web content just as easily as Web traffic?
4. Can you look at information being sent to/from your bank?

10.4 DISPLAY FILTERING (WIRESHARK IV)

It is important to show beginning users the *filtering* capabilities in Wireshark. By now you have noticed that there are many packets flowing through a network. It takes a great deal of mental energy to sift through all those packets to get the ones you are looking for. Filtering can make it less onerous. Once you learn how to use all the functionality built into Wireshark, your life will be much easier.

In the prior projects, you learned to use *capture* filters to reduce the number of packets you collected. You can also apply *display* filters after you have captured a large number of packets. Using display filters ensures that you capture all relevant data while still reducing the processing load.

In this project, you will use a couple of simple display filters to sort the packets you capture. It's important to note that this project will show you how to filter captured packets *after* they are captured (i.e., the display filter). The prior project showed you how to filter packets *before* they were captured (i.e., the capture filter).

1. With Wireshark open, click Capture, and Options.
2. If you haven't already done so, select your Network Interface Card. (Your NIC will undoubtedly have a different name than the one shown below.)
3. Double-click the interface you have selected.
4. Remove any prior capture filter so that the text box is blank. (You will **not** use a capture filter in this project.)
5. Click OK.
6. Click Start.
7. Open a Web browser and go to www.CNN.com.
8. Return to the Wireshark window.
9. Click Capture, and Stop.
10. Take a screenshot. (See Figure 10-13.)
11. Notice that you likely have several packets that may not be intended for you. (In this example, lots of extra traffic was picked up from a router that wasn't intended for this computer. Overall, almost 2,000 packets were captured.)

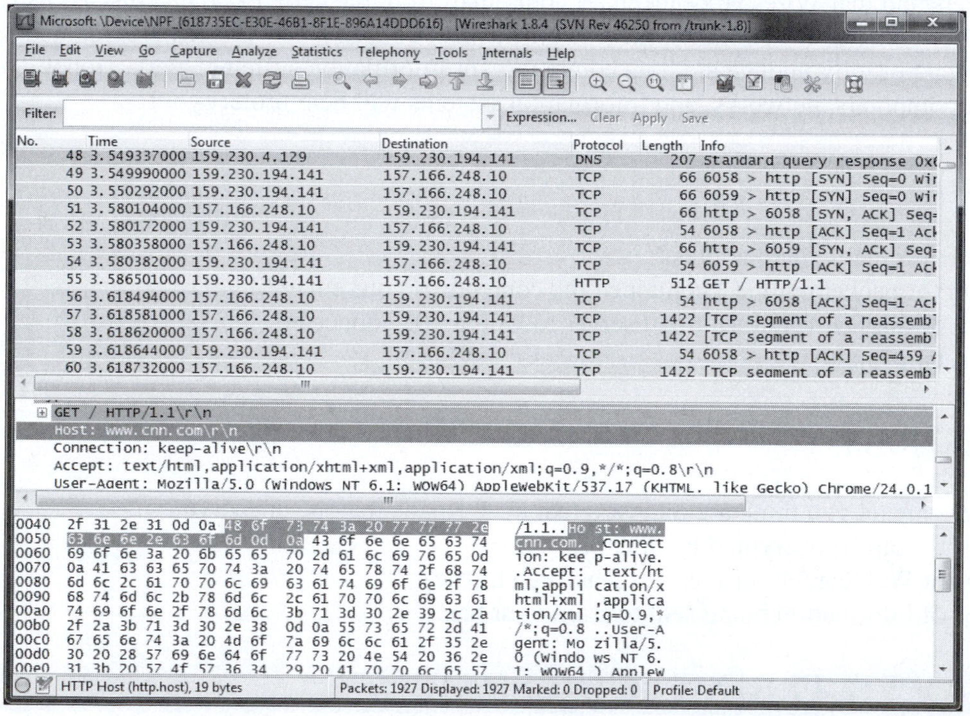

Figure 10-13: Captured packets from CNN.com.

Note: The following steps will show you how to filter the packets you have just captured. You are not going to recapture packets. You are going to filter the packets you just captured.

12. Type the following into the *display filter* text box located below the row of icons: `ip.src ==` `[enter your IP address without the brackets]`.
13. Press Enter. (In this case the display filter was `ip.src == 159.230.194.141`.)

14. Take a screenshot. (You have filtered out all packets except those packets where the source IP address is your own. See Figure 10-14.)

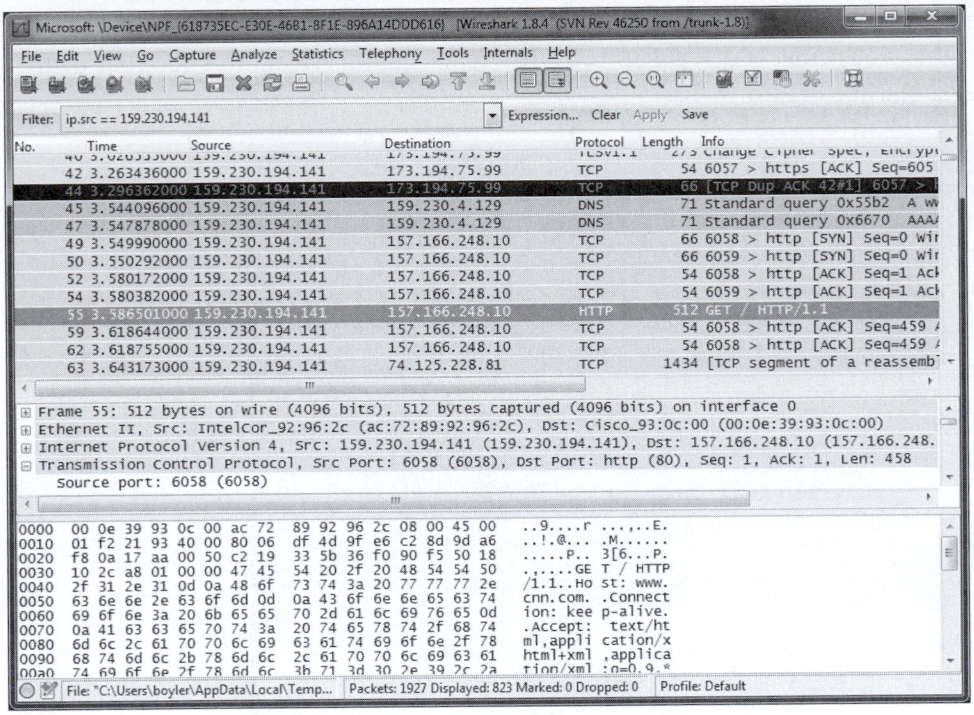

Figure 10-14: Filtering packets based on IP address.

15. Click on the Expression button to the right of the filter box.
16. Scroll down until you see TCP – Transmission Control Protocol.
17. Click on TCP to expand the TCP tree.
18. Click on the tcp.port field name.
19. Click ==.
20. Enter 80 for the value (to view only Web traffic). (See Figure 10-15.)
21. Click OK.

Note: The filter box will be red, indicating incorrect syntax. After you fix the syntax in the next step, the box will turn green. (See Figure 10-16.)

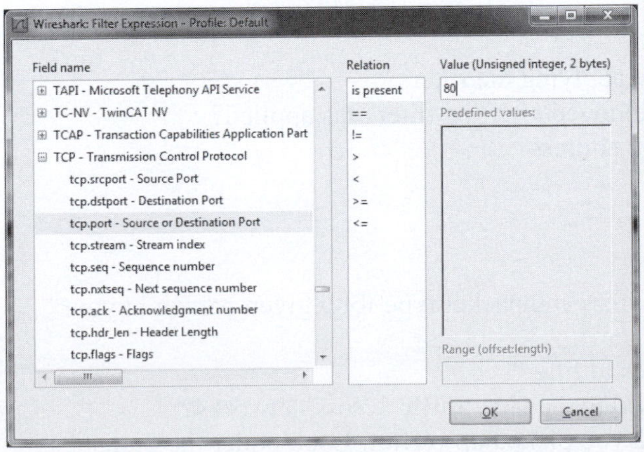

Figure 10-15: Creating a filter expression.

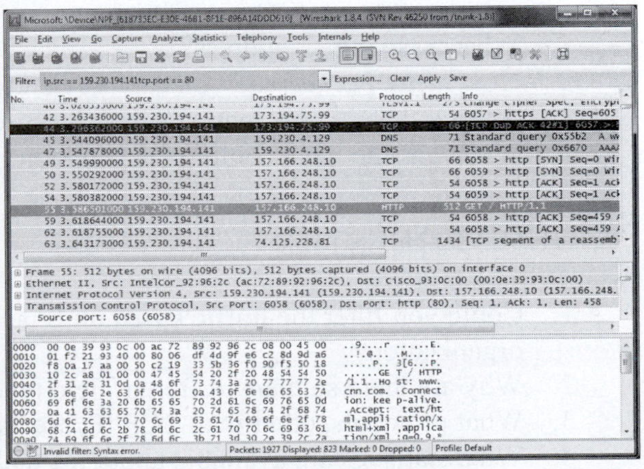

Figure 10-16: Filter without "and" in the expression.

22. Add an "and" to the syntax, so that both the prior filtering rule and the new rule are applied together. (The filter box will turn green when you have the syntax correctly entered.)
23. Re-enter the correct syntax if you didn't get it to work correctly (`ip.src == 159.230.194.141 and tcp.port == 80`), replacing this IP address for your own.
24. Take a screenshot. (See Figure 10-17.)

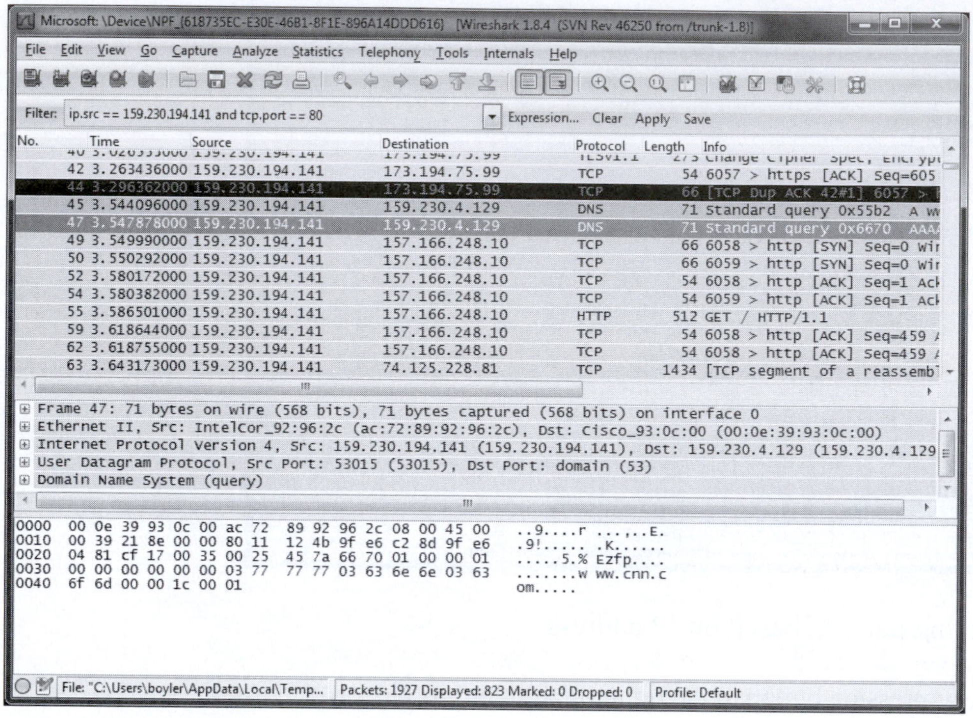

Figure 10-17: Filter packets by IP address and port 80.

You are now looking at only Web traffic that is coming from your computer. It's important to point out that we have only scratched the surface with these projects. Wireshark is a powerful program with many features. It's highly recommended that you explore all of the functionality built into Wireshark. You may have to do some additional research and/or read the manual, but it will be well worth it.

PROJECT QUESTIONS

1. What was your IP address?
2. How many packets did you capture before applying the filters?
3. Approximately how many packets were removed after the filter was applied?
4. What was the most common destination IP address?

THOUGHT QUESTIONS

1. Could you filter the traffic based on IP address and packet type for a given person in your organization?
2. Why are there so many different field types to filter?
3. What protocols, other than TCP/IP, are used to manage traffic across networks?
4. What statistics are available about the data you picked up? (Hint: Look under the Statistics menu.)

WinDump® is a command-line packet sniffer. The original version, called tcpdump, is still widely used on Linux/UNIX systems. Similar to Wireshark, it can be used as a packet sniffer to read network traffic, or as a packet analyzer to identify and resolve networking issues. Learning how to use WinDump at the command prompt is valuable because similar commands can be used on Windows-based and Linux-based systems. It is also quick and easy to use once you are familiar with the general syntax.

1. Download WinDump from: http://www.winpcap.org/.
2. Click on Download Get WinPcap. (You will need to download and install WinPcap before you install WinDump.)
3. Click on Download Get WinPcap (again).
4. Save the file in your C:\security directory.
5. Click on the WinDump link at the top of the page.
6. Click on Download Get WinDump.
7. Click on Download Get WinDump (again).
8. Save the file in your C:\security folder.
9. Open Windows Explorer.
10. Browse to your C:\security folder.
11. Right-click on WinPcap_4_1_2.exe. (Always download the latest version of WinPcap. The name of the executable will change as newer versions are released.)
12. Select Run as administrator.
13. Click Next, Next, I agree, Install, and Finish.
14. Click Start.
15. In the search box type **CMD**
16. Press Enter.
17. Type **cd ..**
18. Press Enter. (Repeat this until you get back to C:\)
19. Type **cd security**
20. Press Enter.
21. Type **dir**
22. Press Enter.

Note: If you type the command "windump" without options, it may appear that your command prompt has "locked up." This is not the case. Windump is actually running. You can press Ctrl+C to cancel the current windump task. It will return you to your command prompt.

23. Type **windump -D**
24. Press Enter. (This will display all of the available network adapters on your computer. See Figure 10-18.)

Note: You will need to be able to determine which adapter you are using for the remainder of the project. In this case, the wired adapter was #6 on the list. The remaining steps will use adapter #6. However, it is likely that you are using a different adapter. You can see a listing of the available adapters in the Control Panel here: Control Panel\Network and Internet\Network Connections.

Figure 10-18: Displaying available network adapters.

25. Type **windump -i 6**
26. Press Enter. (This will capture all packets on network interface 6. Your adapter may be different. Use the adapter that has Internet access. See the note above and make sure you are using the correct network adapter.)
27. Open a Web browser and go to any website.
28. Press Ctrl+C to stop capturing packets.
29. Type **windump -i 6 host www.longwood.edu**
30. Press Enter. (This will only capture packets that have a source or host name of www.Longwood.edu. You can substitute another URL if you'd like.)
31. In your Web browser, go to www.Longwood.edu. (Note that no packets were captured *until* you went to www.Longwood.edu.)
32. Press Ctrl+C to stop capturing packets.
33. Take a screenshot. (See Figure 10-19.)

Figure 10-19: Capturing packets for a specific host.

Note: In the following steps, you will enter your computer's IP address. In this example, the computer's IP address was 155.97.74.45. Your IP address will be different. Use the IPconfig command from Chapter 1 to determine your IP address. It may even be a local IP address (e.g., 192.168.X.X). Replace [type your IP address] with your actual IP address *without* brackets.

34. Type **windump -i 6 host [type your IP address]**
35. Press Enter. (This will capture packets on interface 6 that have a specified *source* or *destination* IP address. In this case, it was 155.97.74.45. Your IP address will be different than the one shown.)
36. In your Web browser, refresh the page you are on. (Note that only packets with your IP address were captured.)
37. Press Ctrl+C to stop capturing packets.
38. Type **windump -i 6 src [type your IP address]**

39. Press Enter. (This will capture packets on interface 6 that have a specified *source* IP address. In this case, it was 155.97.74.45.)

40. In your Web browser, refresh the page you are on. (Note that only packets listing your IP address as the *source* were captured.)

41. Press Ctrl+C to stop capturing packets.

42. Type **windump -i 6 dst [type your IP address]**

43. Press Enter. (This will capture packets on interface 6 that have a specified *destination* IP address. In this case, it was 155.97.74.45.)

44. In your Web browser, refresh the page you are on. (Note that only packets listing your IP address as the *destination* were captured.)

45. Press Ctrl+C to stop capturing packets.

46. Take a screenshot. (See Figure 10-20.)

Figure 10-20: Capturing packets with a destination IP address.

47. Type **windump -i 6 port 53**

48. Press Enter. (This will capture DNS packets.)

49. In your Web browser, type in any URL. (In this example, it was www.Google.com.)

50. Press Ctrl+C to stop capturing packets.

51. Type **windump -i 6 src port 53**

52. Press Enter. (This will capture DNS packets listing 53 in their *source* port field.)

53. In your Web browser, type in any other URL. (In this example, it was www.Yahoo.com.)

54. Press Ctrl+C to stop capturing packets.

55. Take a screenshot. (See Figure 10-21.)

Figure 10-21: Capturing packets with a source port of 53.

56. Type `windump -i 6 dst port 53`

57. Press Enter. (This will capture DNS packets listing 53 in their *destination* port field.)

58. In your Web browser, type in any other URL. (In this example, it was www.Facebook.com.)

59. Press Ctrl+C to stop capturing packets.

60. Type `windump -i 6 udp dst port 53`

61. Press Enter. (This will capture only UDP DNS packets listing 53 in their destination port field.)

62. In your Web browser, type in any other URL. (In this example, it was www.Twitter.com.)

63. Press Ctrl+C to stop capturing packets.

64. Type `windump -n -i 6 udp dst port 53`

65. Press Enter. (The "-n" option will force Windump to *not* resolve host names.)

66. In your Web browser, type in any other URL. (In this example, it was www.CNN.com. Note that IP addresses are now displayed instead of hostnames.)

67. Press Ctrl+C to stop capturing packets.

68. Type `windump -tn -i 6 udp dst port 53`

69. Press Enter. (The "-t" option will remove timestamps.)

70. In your Web browser, type in any other URL. (In this example, it was www.Longwood.edu. Note on the right-hand side you can see some of the hostnames that were being requested.)

71. Press Ctrl+C to stop capturing packets.

72. Take a screenshot. (See Figure 10-22.)

Figure 10-22: Capturing packets with timestamps removed.

73. Type `windump -Xtn -i 6 udp dst port 53`

74. Press Enter. (The "-X" option will display the contents of the packets.)

75. In your Web browser, type in any other URL. (In this example, it was www.Yahoo.com.)

76. Press Ctrl+C to stop capturing packets.

77. Type the following command:

```
windump -tn -i 6 tcp dst port 80 and src [type your IP address]
```

78. Press Enter. (This will capture TCP packets with destination port 80 [Web traffic], and a specific source IP address. In this case, it was 155.97.74.45.)

79. In your Web browser, type in any other URL. (In this example, it was www.Google.com.)

80. Press Ctrl+C to stop capturing packets.

81. Take a screenshot. (See Figure 10-23.)

Figure 10-23: Capturing Web traffic from a specific IP address.

82. Type **windump –i 6 –c 5 dst port 53**
83. Press Enter. (The "-c" option will capture a specific number of packets. In this case, it will capture 5 DNS packets. It will stop capturing packets after it captures the first five.)
84. In your Web browser, type in any other URL. (In this example, it was www.Twitter.com.)
85. Type **windump –i 6 –c 5 –w YourNameCapture.txt dst port 53**
86. Press Enter. (The "-w" option will write the captured packets to a file [YourNameCapture.txt]. Replace "YourName" with your first and last names. In this case, it was RandyBoyleCapture.txt.)
87. In your Web browser, type in any other URL. (In this example, it was www.Google.com.)
88. Type **windump –r YourNameCapture.txt**
89. Press Enter. (This will read the saved text file you just created. The five packets you captured will be displayed on the screen.)
90. Take a screenshot. (See Figure 10-24.)

Figure 10-24: Reading a capture file.

PROJECT QUESTIONS

1. What was your IP address for this project?
2. What was the name of your text file containing the captured packets?
3. Did your IP address resolve into another host name? If so, what was it?
4. Were you able to see any of the hostnames sent for DNS resolution? Which ones?

THOUGHT QUESTIONS

1. Why would it be important to be able to capture only port 53 traffic?
2. Why would a network administrator want to only capture traffic from a specific IP address?
3. Could WinDump be used to capture packets and write them to a text file for later analysis?
4. How could WinDump be used to prevent internal phishing scams?

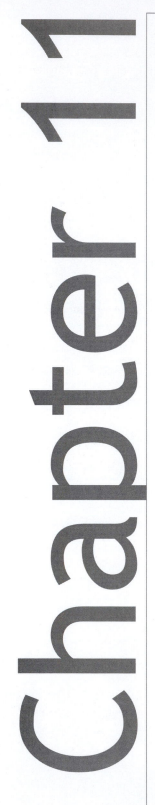

Port scanners are programs that determine how many possible open ports there are on your computer. It's like walking around a house and listing all the possible ways you could get in (e.g., doors and windows). Ports allow information to flow in and out of your computer. Programs on your computer open ports when they want to send/receive information.

For example, when you open a Web browser, your computer opens at least one port to send/receive information to/from the server at the other end of the connection (e.g., www.Yahoo.com). Any number of programs can open/close ports on your computer. It's important to know which ports are open and why they are sending and/or receiving information. Just like doors or windows on your house, every port is a potential vulnerability point for hackers.

Vulnerability scanners have all the functionality of port scanners and much more. They give additional information about open ports, the target application, or the target operating system. For example, a port scanner may tell you that a server has port 80 open. A vulnerability scanner will tell you the name of the Web server (e.g., Apache, IIS, etc.) running on that port, and its specific version number. You typically won't get this information from a simple port scanner.

WARNING Remember, only scan your own computer or those designated by your instructor. Do NOT start randomly scanning computers. Network administrators are watching, and they will see you scan their machines. They will not be happy, and you may get in trouble.

Hopefully this was a strong enough warning.

If you are still considering scanning a machine other than your own, please re-read the above paragraph until the desire goes away. If you want to scan another machine, ask a classmate for permission to scan his or her IP address.

Time required to complete this chapter: 60 minutes

Chapter Objectives

Learn how to:
1. Scan individual ports.
2. Scan a range of ports.
3. Run a vulnerability scan.
4. Run a vulnerability scan on a website.

Chapter Projects

Project:
11.1 PortQry
11.2 Nmap (Zenmap)
11.3 Advanced IP Scanner
11.4 Nessus
11.5 AppScan
11.6 Shields Up

PortQry Command Line Port Scanner® is a simple command-line port scanner from Microsoft. If this is the first time you've used a port scanner, it's a good idea to start slow and learn the basics. Once you learn how port scanners work, you can move on to more advanced port scanners with greater functionality. You could inadvertently cause yourself problems (i.e., get in trouble) if you start randomly clicking buttons on an advanced port scanner.

This project will walk you through the basics of port scanning. You can scan your own local computer, another home computer, or a classmate's computer (with permission). Do NOT scan anyone else's computer without permission.

1. Download PortQry from
    http://www.microsoft.com/download/en/details.aspx?displaylang=en&id=17148
2. Click Download.
3. Click Save.
4. Select your C:\security folder. (You will need to create a "security" folder on your C: drive if you have not already created one.)
5. If the program doesn't automatically open, browse to C:\security.
6. Right-click on PortQryV2.exe. (The version number may be slightly different as newer versions are released.)
7. Select Run as administrator.
8. Click Yes.
9. Change the directory to C:\security. (See Figure 11-1.)
10. Click Unzip, OK, and Close.

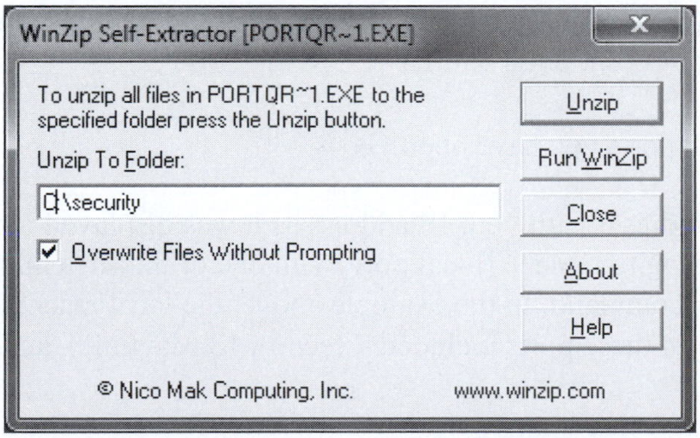

Figure 11-1: Extracting PortQry.exe.

11. Open Windows Explorer and browse to C:\security.
12. Verify that PortQry.exe is in the C:\security directory.
13. Close all other programs except your word processing program. If other programs are connecting to the Internet, you will see more ports displayed.
14. Click Start.
15. In the search box type `cmd`
16. Press Enter. (This will open a command prompt.)
17. Type `cd..`
18. Press Enter. (This will move you up or back one level in your file system.)
19. Repeat the prior two steps until you are at your C:\ directory.
20. Type `cd security`
21. Press Enter. (This will move you into your security directory.)

22. Type `dir`
23. Press Enter. (This will display the contents of the directory. Verify that PortQry.exe is listed.)
24. Type `ipconfig`
25. Press Enter. (This will display your current IP address. In this case, it was 155.97.74.45. Your IP address will not be the same as the one displayed below. Your IP address may even start with 192.168. You will need to know your IP address for part of this project. See Figure 11-2.)

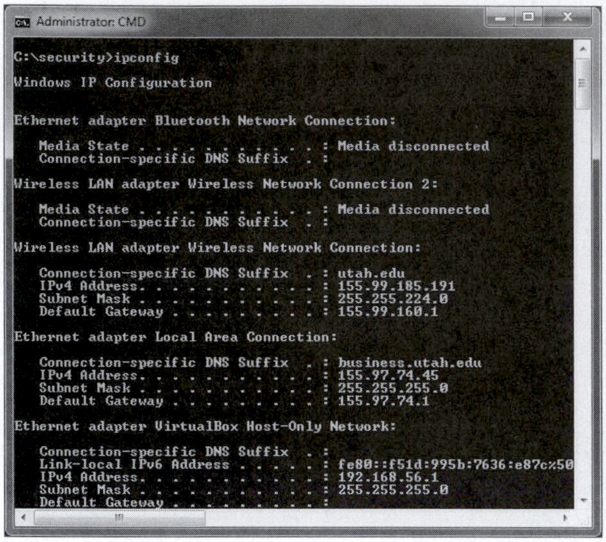

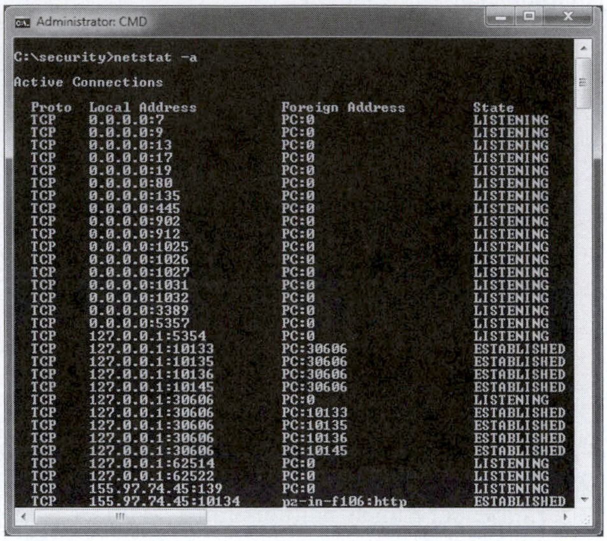

Figure 11-2: Using ipconfig to display Windows IP configuration.   Figure 11-3: Listing open ports.

26. Type `netstat -a`
27. Press Enter. (This will show you which ports you have open. The "listening" ports will be at the top of the listing. See Figure 11-3.)
28. Type `portqry -local`
29. Press Enter. (This will also show you which ports you have open.)

In the next step, you are going to replace [your IP address] with your IP address as it was displayed when you entered the ipconfig command. You are also going to replace [local port] with one of the "listening" ports shown when you entered the `netstat -a` command. In the example above, the local machine (155.97.74.45) and had many ports listening. Some of these ports included 7 (echo), 13 (daytime), and 80 (HTTP).

30. Type `portqry -n [your IP address] -e [local listening port]`
31. Press Enter. (Remember to replace your IP address and local port number. In this example, the following was entered: `portqry -n 155.97.74.45 -e 7`. This command will scan to see if port 7 is open on your local machine. Remember, pressing the up arrow within the command prompt will scroll through prior commands. This may save you time.)
32. Type `time`
33. Press Enter twice. (This will display the current time and provide a timestamp for your project.)
34. Take a screenshot. (See Figure 11-4.)
35. Type `portqry -n [your IP address] -r 1:80`
36. Press Enter. (Remember to replace your IP address and local port number. In this example, the following was entered: `portqry -n 155.97.74.45 -r 1:80`. This command will scan all ports from 1 to 80 on your machine. Remember, pressing the up arrow within the command prompt will scroll through prior commands. This may save you time.)
37. Type `time`

38. Press Enter twice. (This will display the current time and provide a timestamp for your project.)
39. Take a screenshot. (See Figure 11-5.)

Figure 11-4: Scanning a single port.   Figure 11-5: Scanning multiple ports.

Note: Figure 11-6 shows a similar port scan to the one you just completed. The only difference is that the machine is running a honeypot, which pretends to have numerous ports open. Figure 11-7 shows that it has about one thousand ports open. You'll learn how to install and configure a honeypot in a later project. In general, it's better to have fewer open ports because it makes life more difficult for hackers by limiting their potential entry points.

WARNING Do not scan any machine without permission. Most good network administrators watch for network and port scans. The safe bet is to just scan your own machines and/or the ones designated by your instructor.

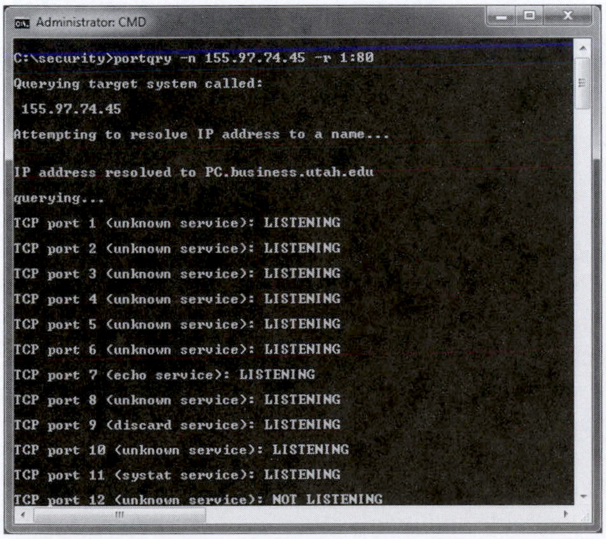

Figure 11-6: Port scanning a honeypot. 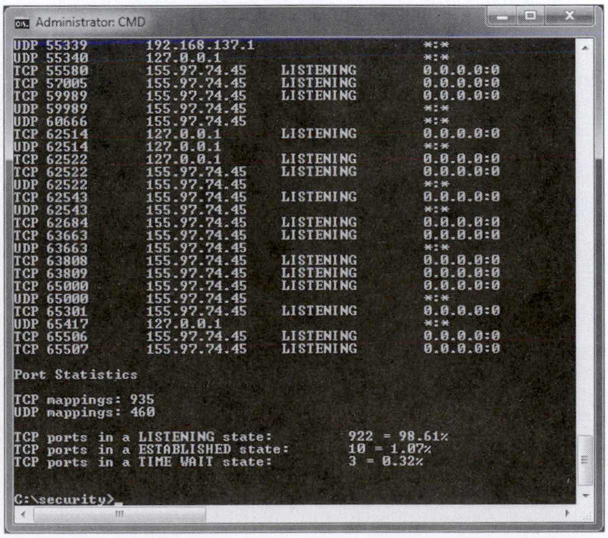   Figure 11-7: Many open ports.

PROJECT QUESTIONS

1. What was your IP address?
2. Approximately how many ports were designated as "listening" when you entered the netstat –a command?
3. Which ports were open when you scanned ports 1 through 80?
4. Were there any "listening" ports that you were unaware of? Which ones?

THOUGHT QUESTIONS

1. How many ports are there on a single computer?
2. What programs (or services) run over each port?
3. Can hackers use ports to spread malware?
4. How do you close ports that may already be open?

11.2 NMAP® (ZENMAP®)

Another well known port scanner that has been around for many years and is available on a variety of operating systems is called Nmap®. It also has a GUI interface that makes it more user-friendly to introductory IT security students. Nmap can tell you which operating system a machine is running, which services are available, and can give you a graphical representation of a network. The GUI interface also gives a command-line option for those users who are accustomed to using the traditional CLI (command-line interface).

Nmap has long been an industry staple for IT security professionals. It's well worth the time to become familiar with Nmap. Insecure.org has a good reference by Gordon "Fyodor" Lyon that can help answer many questions about port scanning (http://nmap.org/book/toc.html). Let's look at a simple example using Nmap.

1. Download Nmap from http://nmap.org/download.html.
2. Click on nmap-6.01-setup.exe. (It's likely that a newer version will be available. Download the latest version. Mac and Linux versions are also available further down the page. If you are uncertain which version to get, please ask your instructor.)
3. Click Save.
4. Select your C:\security folder.
5. Browse to C:\security.
6. Double-click on nmap-6.01-setup.exe.
7. Click Run, and Run.
8. Click I Agree, Next, Install, and Yes (if you are asked to replace WinPcap).
9. Click Next, Close, Next, Next, and Finish.
10. Click I Agree, Install, and Close.
11. Double-click the Nmap-Zenmap® icon on your desktop.
12. Enter the IP address of another computer on your home network, a classmate's computer (with permission), or a computer designated by your instructor into the Target text box.

Note: The IP address used in this example (10.0.1.11) belongs to a computer the author uses on an internal system. Do not scan this IP address. It is non-routable and won't return correct results. Ask your instructor for an IP address if you are unsure what to enter as your target.

13. Take a screenshot. (See Figure 11-8.)
14. In the Profile box, select Regular Scan.
15. Press Scan.

16. Take a screenshot after the scan completes. (See Figure 11-9.)

Note: If you get an error, you can get the latest version of WinPcap from
http://www.winpcap.org/install/default.htm. Nmap should work correctly after you install WinPcap. You may have to close Nmap to get WinPcap to install correctly. You will need to restart Nmap once you have installed WinPcap.

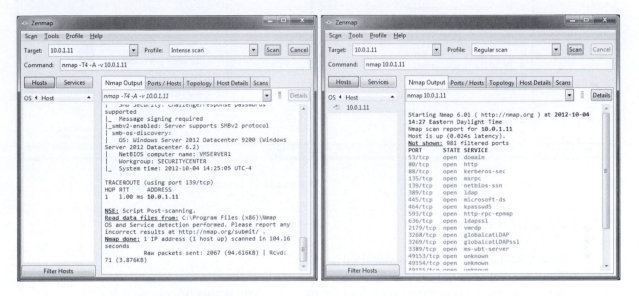

Figure 11-8: Zenmap configuration.   Figure 11-9: Results from a Zenmap scan.

17. Click on the Ports/Hosts tab.
18. Take a screenshot. (See Figure 11-10.)
19. Click on the Host Details tab.
20. Take a screenshot. (See Figure 11-11.)
21. Swap IP addresses with another classmate/friend and scan his or her computer.
22. Take a screenshot.

Note: You only port scanned one IP address at a time in this project. You can port scan entire blocks of IP addresses at one time. Nmap is a powerful tool with much more functionality than you have seen here. Additional documentation for Nmap can be found here: http://nmap.org/book/man.html.

Warning Remember to scan ONLY your own computers or machines designated by your instructor. Many organizations (e.g., corporations, governments, universities, etc.) have intrusion detection systems that will notice these scans. You will set up honeypots and IDSs later and test them with these port scanners.

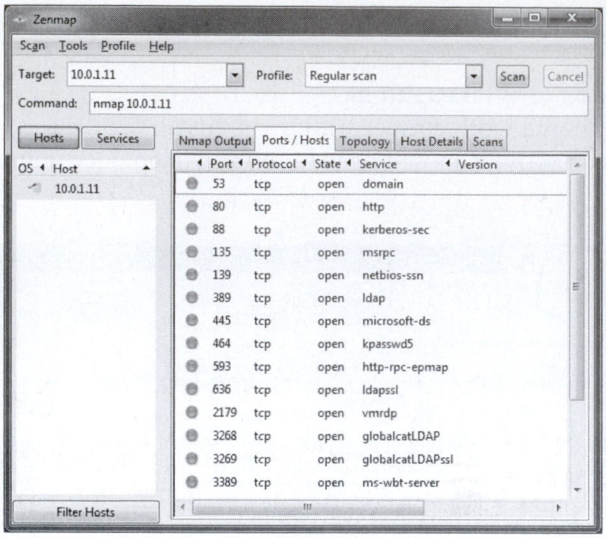

Figure 11-10: Ports identified from a port scan.

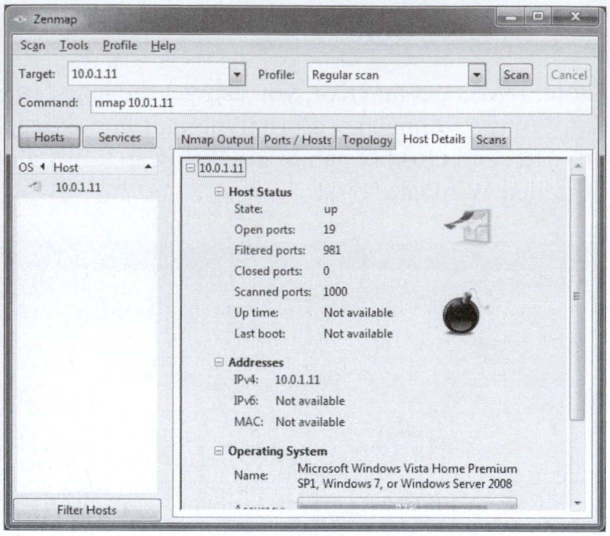

Figure 11-11: Host details from a port scan.

PROJECT QUESTIONS

1. What was the first IP address you used?
2. What was the second IP address you used?
3. How many open ports were on each of the machines you scanned?
4. How long did the first scan take to complete?

THOUGHT QUESTIONS

1. What is the difference between "Regular" and "Intense" scans?
2. Why does Nmap fail to identify some operating systems on certain machines?
3. Why does a port show up at all if it is closed?
4. Can you protect yourself from port scans? How?

11.3   ADVANCED IP SCANNER

Another easy-to-use port scanner is Advanced LAN Scanner®. It can yield more detailed results in some cases. If you are looking for an easy-to-use scanner, this is it. You just enter the IP address or host name of the machine you want to scan and press the Scan button.

You need to be careful when you open Advanced LAN Scanner, as it sets the target range as your entire C block of IP addresses. C blocks are groupings of about 255 IP addresses. You do *not* want to scan an entire C block of IP addresses because scanning multiple machines can make some network administrators nervous. Scan *only* those machines designated by your instructor.

1. Download Advanced LAN Scanner from http://www.radmin.com/products/ipscanner/.
2. Click Download.
3. Click Save.
4. Select your C:\security folder.
5. Browse to C:\security.
6. Double-click on ipscan21.exe.
7. Click Run, Run, Install, Next, I Accept, Next, Next, Install, and Finish.

8. Click Start, All Programs, Advanced IP Scanner v2, and Advanced IP Scanner.
9. Click Settings, and Options.
10. Check all options under Resources.
11. Click Apply.
12. Enter your IP address in the text box next to Scan.
13. Press Scan.
14. Take a screenshot. (See Figure 11-12.)
15. Enter another IP address (e.g., a classmate's or friend's IP address) in the Scan text box separated by a comma and space. (In this example, three IP addresses were entered.)
16. Press Scan.
17. Take another screenshot. (See Figure 11-13.)

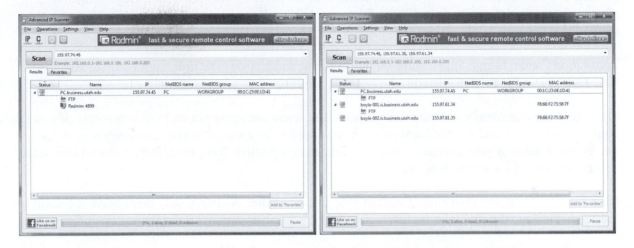

Figure 11-12: Results from a port scan.   Figure 11-13: Results from scanning multiple computers.

Again, you can see all ports open on your computer that are potential entry points for hackers. You may actually see more ports with this port scanner than you did with the other port scanners. You can also see that Advanced LAN Scanner shows your computer's name, network name (this network is named Simpsons), and possibly other users logged into your machine. Use these port scanners with caution.

PROJECT QUESTIONS

1. What was your IP address?
2. What was the other IP address you entered?
3. What was the MAC address displayed for the second IP address you scanned?
4. Did it resolve your NetBIOS name? What was it?

THOUGHT QUESTIONS

1. Can you enter an IP address (e.g., 209.85.173.99) in a Web browser and open a Web page directly without entering the domain name (e.g., www.Google.com)?
2. Once hackers know which ports you have open, what do they do next?
3. Which ports should you have open for your home PC, a Web server, an email server, etc.?
4. Web servers typically use port 80 to serve requests. Could they use a port other than port 80?

Tenable's Nessus® is a well known vulnerability scanner that has been around for a long time. It is fast and thorough. Many companies, universities, organizations, and governments use it every day. A single scan can put over 1000 entries on an intrusion detection system. The additional information provided from a vulnerability scan can be helpful to network administrators, penetration testers, and hackers alike. It tells you which machines have software running that may need to be patched and are currently vulnerable to attack.

As previously mentioned, Nessus is like any other security tool. It can be used for good or bad. This has nothing to do with the tool and everything to do with the person running the tool. Beginning and advanced user guides can be found at the following URLs, through www.Tenable.com. They are great recreational reading.

Installation Guide: http://static.tenable.com/documentation/nessus_5.0_installation_guide.pdf
User Guide: http://static.tenable.com/documentation/nessus_5.0_user_guide.pdf

Most users are completely unaware that vulnerability scans are being run on their computers. If you take your laptop to work and use the local network, you need to be aware that your company may run a vulnerability scan on your personal computer. Some organizations have mandatory vulnerability scans written into their IT security policies.

Let's install Nessus and do a simple scan of your local machine. As previously mentioned, the scans are thorough and can take several minutes.

1. Download Nessus 5 from http://www.tenable.com/products/nessus/nessus-download-agreement.
2. Click Agree.
3. Click on Nessus-5.0.1-amd64.msi (Download Nessus-5.0.1-i386.msi if you have a 32-bit system. Download the latest version available. It's very likely a newer version is available).
4. Click Save.
5. Select your C:\security folder.
6. If the program doesn't automatically open, browse to C:\security.
7. Double-click on Nessus-5.0.1-x86_64.msi.
8. Click Run, Next, I Accept, Next, Next, Next, Install, and Finish. (This should open a Web browser.)
9. Click "Get Started" in the Web page that opened.
10. Enter a username and password for the administrator account. (In this case, the administrator username was "admin.")
11. Click Next. (See Figure 11-14.)
12. Click on the following link to register and obtain an activation code: http://www.nessus.org/register/.
13. Click Select on the HomeFeed subscription. (See Figure 11-15.)
14. Click Agree.

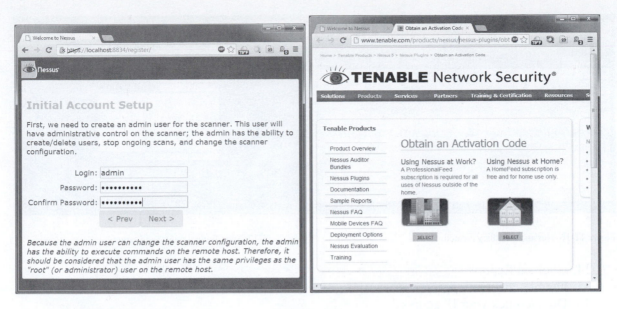

Figure 11-14: Nessus initial account setup.　　　　　　　　Figure 11-15: Obtaining an activation code.

15. Enter any first name, last name, and valid email address. (You'll need to retrieve the activation code to get Nessus to work.)
16. Click Register.
17. Open the email that Nessus.com just sent you.
18. Copy/paste the activation code from the email to the Plugin Feed Registration page that asked for your activation code.
19. Click Next.
20. Click Download plugins.
21. Wait for the plug-ins to update. (This could take a while. Plug-ins are what give Nessus the ability to do an effective vulnerability scan. You only need a large update like this once. You could move on to another project, and then come back to this project after it finishes updating.)

Note: You may get an error message when Nessus starts updating. It may just sit there and say it is updating, but won't show any progress. You will need to create an exception for Nessus on your Windows Firewall. You can allow Nessus through your firewall by clicking Start, Control Panel, System and Security, Allow a program through Windows Firewall, Change settings, and Allow another program. Browse to C:\Program Files\Tenable\Nessus. Select the files named "nessus.exe" and "nessusd.exe". Click Open, Add, and OK.

22. Enter the username and password you created for your administrator login.
23. Click Login. (Click OK if you see a popup warning.)
24. Click Policies, and Add.
25. Enter YourName in the Name text box. (In this case, it was RandyBoyle.)
26. Select TCP Scan on the right if it is not already selected.
27. Click Next, Next, Next, and Submit.
28. Take a screenshot. (See Figure 11-16.)
29. Click Scans and Add.
30. In the Name text box, type YourNameScan. (In this case, it was RandyBoyleScan.)
31. Change the Policy dropdown to the policy you just created.
32. In the Scan Targets box, enter your IP address. (Enter 127.0.0.1 if you don't know your IP address. See Figure 11-17.)
33. Click Launch Scan. (The scan could take 5 minutes or more to complete.)

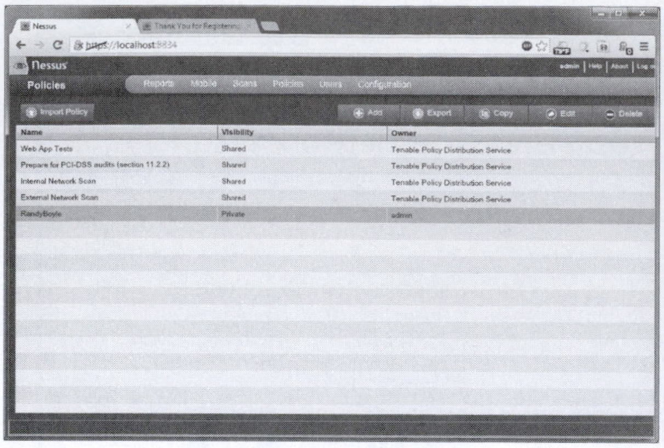

Figure 11-16: Nessus test policy created.

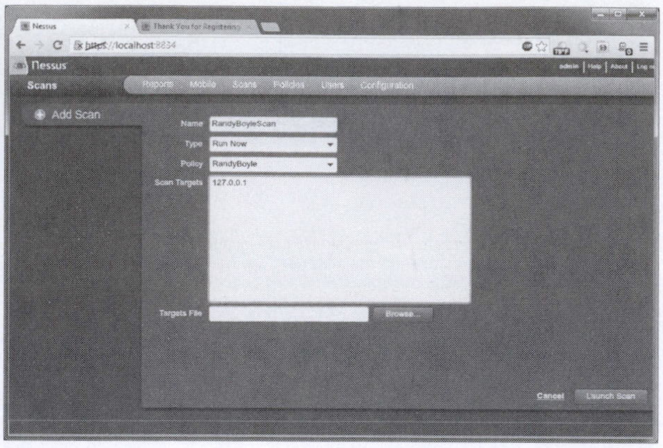

Figure 11-17: Specifying a policy and target.

34. Click on Reports.
35. Double-click your report.
36. Double-click your IP address.
37. Take a screenshot. (See Figure 11-18.)
38. Click on any of the open ports on the left to see the detailed information. (You will likely see an entry for TCP port 7 [echo] that you could click on.)
39. Click on any of the entries listed.
40. Take a screenshot. (See Figure 11-19.)
41. Repeat the scan using one of your friend's/classmate's IP address. (Do NOT scan anyone else.)
42. Take a screenshot.

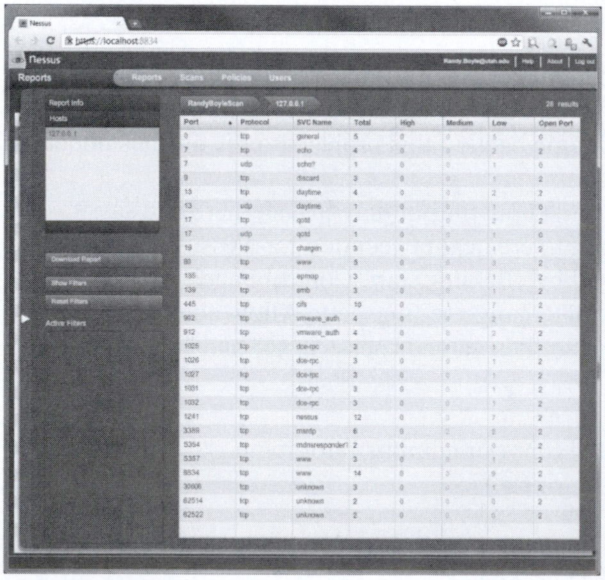

Figure 11-18: Nessus test policy created.

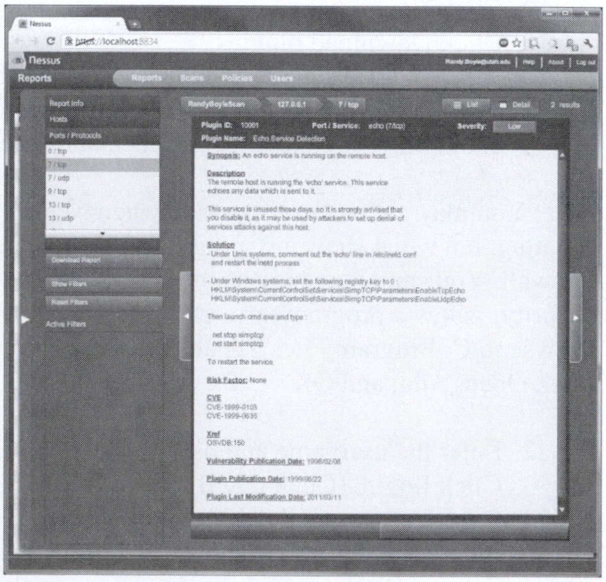

Figure 11-19: Specifying a policy and target.

Notice that the Nessus scanner yields much more information than a port scanner. For example, Nessus can indicate that this machine has a medium risk factor related to port 161 using SNMP. Information about this system can be obtained, including network shares, users, system information, network interfaces, services, processes, and software installed on this computer. All of this can be obtained by anyone with a Nessus scanner and a network connection.

A nice feature of Nessus is that it tells you how to protect your machine from intruders. It gives you solutions to the weaknesses noted on your computer. Overall, a vulnerability scanner will give you much more information than a simple port scanner. Nessus is an easy-to-use scanner that is well worth getting acquainted with.

PROJECT QUESTIONS

1. Did you have any high risk results? Which ones?
2. Did you have any medium risk results? Which ones?
3. What was the other IP address that you scanned?
4. When you ran Nessus on your friend's/classmate's computer, did you find any high risk weaknesses? Which ones?

THOUGHT QUESTIONS

1. Running the scan was fairly easy. Where could you go to get more information about understanding the results from the scan?
2. Who creates the plug-ins for Nessus and how do they decide which vulnerabilities to include?
3. How many vulnerabilities are reported each day?
4. Do all operating systems and applications have vulnerabilities? Which are less vulnerable?

11.5 APPSCAN®

IBM®'s AppScan® is a vulnerability scanner specifically focused on testing websites. This is the only commercial (read: not free) piece of software in the book. It is included in this book because you probably work for a company or organization that has a website that needs to be secured. Securing your company's website is likely more important than securing your personal computer. Your company's website may be a major source of revenue and may interact with mission-critical systems.

The AppScan demo shown below can help companies assess potential risks related to their Web server(s). At the writing of this book, a totally free Windows-based vulnerability scanner for websites with all the features that are built into AppScan was not available. There might be one available now.

You will use a fully functional version of AppScan, but it will only run on a test website that IBM has set up. It's worth using the free version to get exposure to this type of software and see how it works. It has good documentation and is easy to use. It is a good idea for companies running mission-critical Web servers to consider buying a vulnerability scanner to secure their electronic storefronts.

WARNING The way IBM hosts this application changes often. The instructions were accurate at the time this book was printed. You may have to follow slightly different instructions to get the download to work. Internet Explorer might be the best Web browser to use.

1. Download AppScan from http://www.ibm.com/developerworks/downloads/r/appscan/.
2. Click Download.
3. Click Register here.
4. Fill out their form with as many creative answers as you can dream up, but the email address has to be real. (They send the download link to that email account.)
5. Click Continue.
6. Fill out more creative information wherever you see an asterisk.
7. Click Submit.

8. Log in using the email address you provided and your fake password.
9. Click Continue.
10. Click on I Agree for "**IBM Rational AppScan Standard Edition V8.5 Windows Multilingual eAssembly.**"
11. Click Continue.
12. Fill out more creative information wherever you see an asterisk.
13. Deselect all of the Privacy options.
14. Select I Agree.
15. Click I Confirm.
16. Click on Download using http.
17. Right-click on Download now for "**IBM Rational AppScan Standard Edition V8.5 Evaluation Multilingual Windows.**"
18. Click Save.
19. Select your C:\security folder.
20. Click Save, and Close.
21. If the program doesn't automatically open, browse to C:\security.
22. Right-click on RATL_STD_ED_V8.5_EVAL_MP_ML.zip.
23. Select Extract All, Extract, and Finish.
24. Browse to C:\security\ RATL_STD_ED_V8.5_EVAL_MP_ML.
25. Double-click on AppScan_Setup.exe.
26. Click Run, OK, Next, I Accept, Next, Next, Next, Next, and Finish.

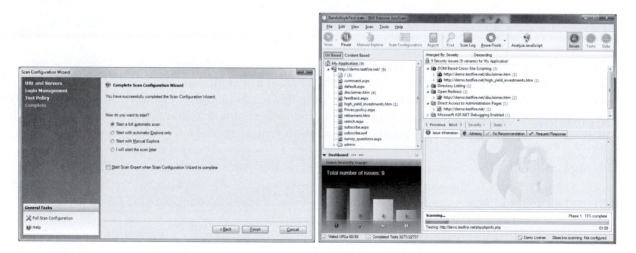

Figure 11-20: AppScan.   Figure 11-21: Running a scan.

27. Double-click the IBM Rational AppScan icon on your desktop.
28. Click Create New Scan.
29. Click on demo.testfire.net under Recent Templates.
30. Click Next, Next, Next, and Next.
31. Uncheck the option for selecting Start Scan Expert…
32. Click Finish. (See Figure 11-20.)
33. Click Yes to save the scan, and enter "YourNameTest" for the scan name. (In this case, it was RandyBoyleTest.)
34. Click Save.
35. Take a screenshot once the scan ends. (It will take 15 or more minutes to finish Phase 1 but it is fun to watch. You can pause the scan and continue on with the rest of the project after Phase 1 completes.) (See Figure 11-21.)

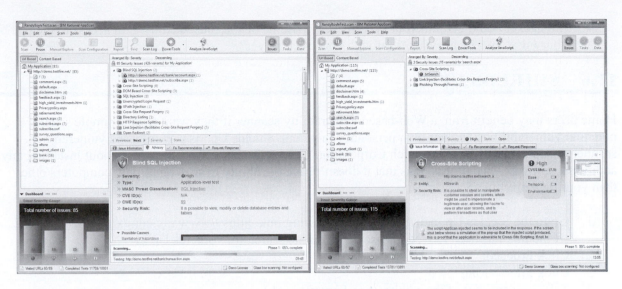

Figure 11-22: Results and details from a scan.   Figure 11-23: Details about cross-site scripting.

36. Click on the line that reads "Blind SQL Injection." (Expand the file tree, if necessary.)
37. Take a screenshot. (See Figure 11-22.)
38. Click on the bottom right pane that tells you about blind SQL injection.
39. Read about the blind SQL injection issue and how it works.
40. Click on another security issue that interests you, like Cross-Site Scripting.
41. Take a screenshot. (See Figure 11-23.)

As you can see, AppScan is a good tool that can analyze a large number of potential weaknesses in websites. If you are involved with e-commerce, it's probably worth the money to purchase a full copy. Not only does AppScan identify vulnerabilities in your website, but it also tells you how they work and how to fix them. For example, you may not have even known what SQL injection was before running this scan. Now that you are aware of what a SQL injection attack is, you are in a much better position to protect yourself.

AppScan also comes with several "power tools" that you can find in the Start menu. They are really useful if you take the time to understand how to use them. As this is an introductory book on information security software, we won't be using them. Please feel free to browse them (and hopefully learn them). These tools are fully functional and free.

PROJECT QUESTIONS

1. How many total issues did the scan find?
2. How many blind SQL injection issues did your scan find?
3. How many cross-site scripting issues did your scan find?
4. How long did it take to complete the entire scan, including Phase 2?

THOUGHT QUESTIONS

1. What would it take to fix your website so it's not vulnerable to an SQL injection attack?
2. What background training would you need to be able to fully understand all the attacks listed in AppScan (e.g., databases, SQL, HTML, programming, networking, TCP/IP, etc.)?
3. Do you think companies actually see SQL injection attacks? How often?

4. If a hacker could get into your Web server, could he or she subsequently gain access to the rest of your mission-critical systems through your Web server?

11.6   SHIELDS UP®

Home users may benefit from a Web-based vulnerability scanner if they want to do a simple scan of potential vulnerabilities on their own personal computers. Shields Up® is a Web-based vulnerability scanner, managed by Gibson Research Corporation®, that will scan your computer without installing any additional software. The downside is that it doesn't have the ability to scan additional computers other than your own machine.

1. Go to the Shields Up main page at the following link: https://www.grc.com/x/ne.dll?bh0bkyd2. (If the link has been moved, please do an online search for "Shields Up".)
2. Click Proceed.
3. Click File Sharing.
4. Take a screenshot of the results. (See Figure 11-24.)
5. Click Common Ports.
6. Take a screenshot of the results.

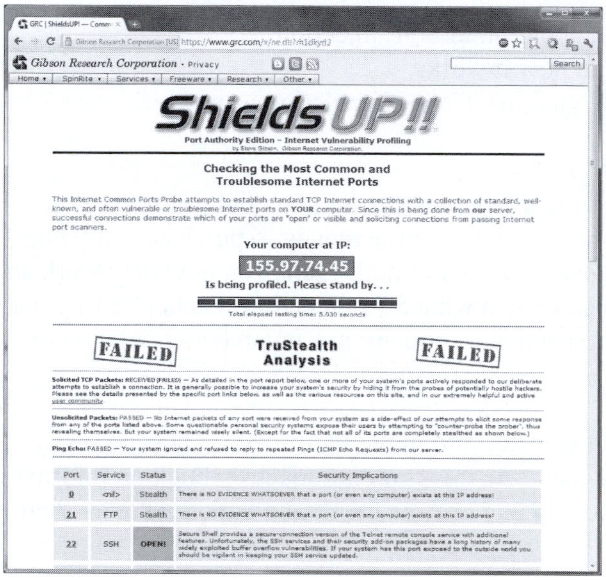

Figure 11-24: Results from a Shields Up scan.

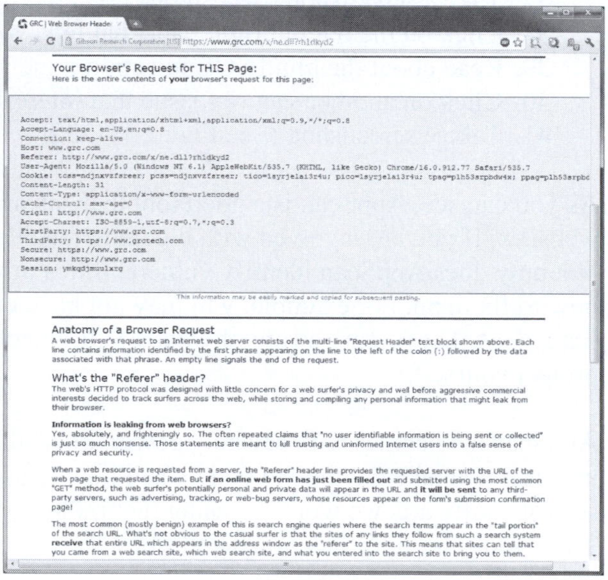

Figure 11-25: Contents from your Web browser request.

7. Click on any one of the ports that may have been open.
8. Take a screenshot of the explanation page.
9. Go back to the port results page.
10. Click All Service Ports. (This may take a couple of minutes.)
11. Take a screenshot of the results.
12. Scroll to the bottom of the page and click Messenger Spam.
13. Take a screenshot.
14. Click Spam Me with this Note.
15. Take a screenshot if a note appears.
16. Scroll to the bottom and click Browse Headers.
17. Take a screenshot of the box named "Your Browser's Request for THIS Page". (See Figure 11-25.)

Shields Up is an easy way to see common security vulnerabilities on your personal computer without installing or configuring new software. Running the scan is the easy part. The hard part is interpreting and understanding the results.

You also need to think about the eventual security implications of the page you see. Running the scan and looking at the results page only gives you an idea of how vulnerable your computer is. You need to make changes to your computer to actually make it safer. Shields Up provides a good explanation of the scans and their results if you are willing to do a little more reading. Please feel free to take the time to read and understand the results from the scans.

PROJECT QUESTIONS

1. What was your IP address for the scan?
2. Did you have any file sharing issues? Which ones?
3. Did you have any common port issues? Which ones?
4. Did you have any service port issues? Which ones?

THOUGHT QUESTIONS

1. Why isn't this functionality built into your operating system?
2. Do you have any ports open that you know shouldn't be open?
3. Could this functionality be built into websites that you visit and be used by the Web administrator to compromise your computer?
4. Could other tools listed in this book be written as a Web-based application?

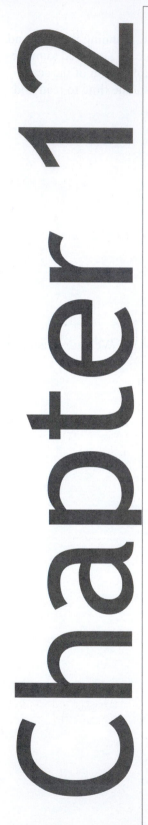

Honeypots are fun because they can attract hackers and log what they do to your computer without putting it at additional risk. For example, a hacker might want to break into a computer with a Web server running because it might serve as a potential launching platform for a future denial-of-service attack. A hacker might also want to store stolen software, host a phishing site, deface the legitimate website, steal valuable information, etc. A hacker will look for a computer with port 80 open because Web servers use that port to serve Web pages.

A honeypot will trick outsiders by making it look like port 80 is open on your computer. In reality, you won't be running a real Web server. It will be the equivalent of painting a door on a brick wall. A better way to think of honeypots is to remember back to the old Roadrunner cartoons. The Roadrunner would paint a picture of a tunnel on a rock wall. Then the Coyote would run right into it. The same basic principle applies here. It appears that you have a Web server running, but you really just painted a door on a brick wall.

Hackers waste a lot of time and clock cycles on honeypots. Honeypots are helpful in determining the real threat level for a given network, computer, and IP address range. It can give upper management an idea about the appropriate level of funding needed for IT security.

Intrusion detection systems (IDSs) are notoriously difficult to setup, configure, and maintain. They watch computers and the network to see what is happening. They are difficult to run because of the sheer number of programs, processes, protocols, ports, logs, attack signatures, etc. There are many different balls to keep bouncing to keep things running properly. IT security professionals must have a strong background in networking, databases, and programming just to understand the basics of what is going on inside an IDS.

Let's look at a couple of examples of a honeypot and an IDS. You'll find that IT security professionals have little regard for people who try to break into other people's computer systems. Hackers create headaches and problems, and make administrators look bad. Curiosity and testing one's skills is perfectly acceptable, but individuals should explore and test their own systems, not poke around someone else's critical infrastructure.

Time required to complete this chapter: 60 minutes

Chapter Objectives

Learn how to:
1. Configure and test a honeypot.
2. Configure and test an IDS.
3. View IDS logs.

Chapter Projects

Project:
12.1   HoneyBot
12.2   NST, Snort (IDS), & BASE

HoneyBOT® is a simple honeypot for beginners. Since this might be the first time you have seen a honeypot, it's good to start out with one that is easy to use. Honeypots can give you a good idea of how many people are probing your machine for weaknesses. Without a honeypot, you may not be able to tell if anyone is scanning your machine. It turns out that there is an active community of hackers interested in gaining access to a variety of computers.

Once the honeypot (or IDS) records the IP address of the remote machine that scanned your computer, you can use the previously mentioned tracing tools to see who they are. If you run a honeypot long enough, you will likely see scanning attempts from several continents, all of the countries in Europe and Asia, all 50 states, and every university in the United States. Let's look at a simple example of how HoneyBOT works. We will use a port scanner (Portqry) and a vulnerability scanner (Nessus) and see how the two might differ from a victim's point of view.

1. Download HoneyBOT from http://www.atomicsoftwaresolutions.com/honeybot.php.
2. Click on the Download link in the left-hand menu.
3. Click on the appropriate "here" link to download the latest version of HoneyBOT.
4. Click Save.
5. Select your C:\security folder.
6. Browse to C:\security.
7. Double-Click on HoneyBOT_018.exe. (The version number may be different as newer releases become available.)
8. Click Run, Next, I accept, Next, Next, and Next.
9. Check Create desktop icon.
10. Click Next, Install, and Finish.

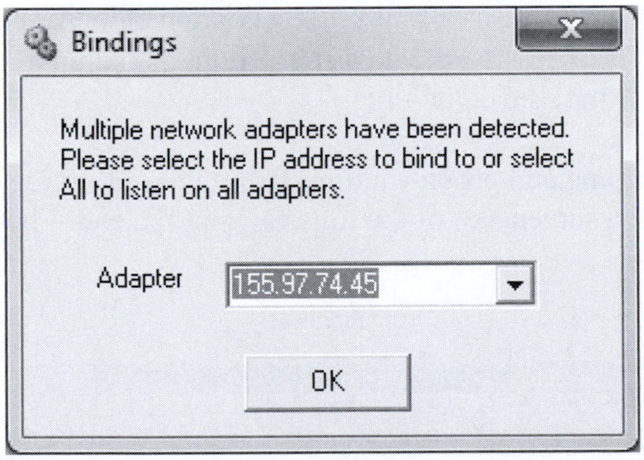

Figure 12-1: Designating an IP address.

11. Press the Start button or click File, and Start.
12. HoneyBOT may ask you to select an adapter if you have multiple NICs in your computer. Select your current IP address. (It could be a non-routable IP that starts with 192.168 or it could be a typical IP address. See Figure 12-1.)
13. Click OK.
14. Take a screenshot showing the total number of sockets loaded in the bottom status bar. (See Figures 12-2 and 12-3.)

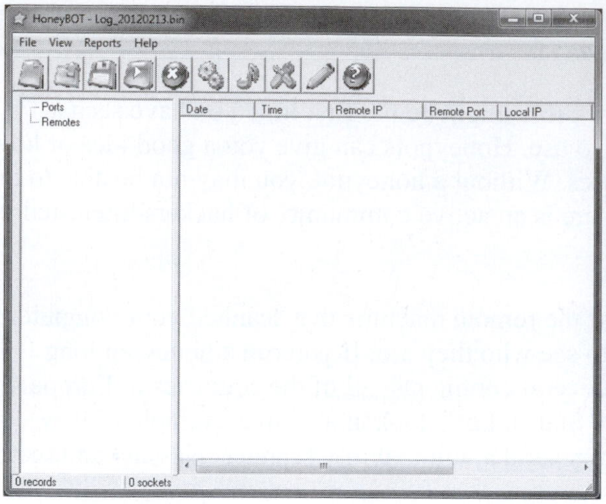

Figure 12-2: No sockets selected.

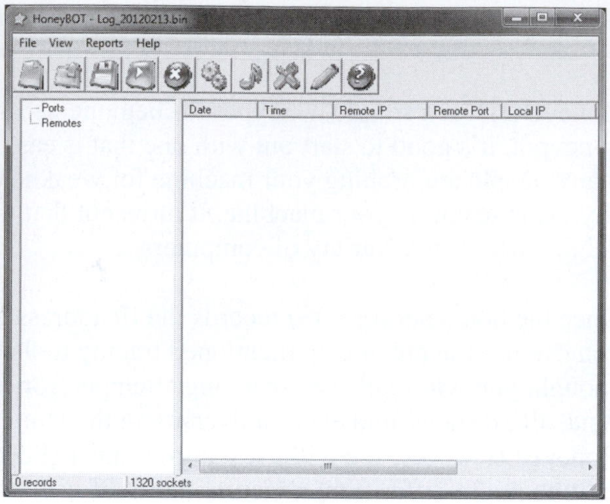

Figure 12-3: Multiple sockets selected.

15. Click Start.
16. In the search box, type `cmd`
17. Press Enter. (This will open a command prompt.)
18. Type `cd..`
19. Press Enter. (This will move you up one level in your file system.)
20. Repeat the prior two steps until you are at your C:\ directory.
21. Type `cd security`
22. Press Enter. (This will move you into your security directory.)
23. Type `portqry -n [your IP address] -r 1:80`
24. Press Enter. (Remember to replace your IP address and local port number. In this example, the following was entered: `portqry -n 155.97.74.45 -r 1:80`. This command will scan all ports from 1 to 80 on your machine. Remember, pressing the up arrow within the command prompt will scroll through prior commands. This may save you time.)
25. Type `time`
26. Press Enter twice. (This will display the current time and provide a timestamp for your project. There will be a long list of results. You can take a screenshot of the timestamp at the end. Figure 12-4 shows a sample port scan command.)
27. Take a screenshot. (See Figure 12-4.)

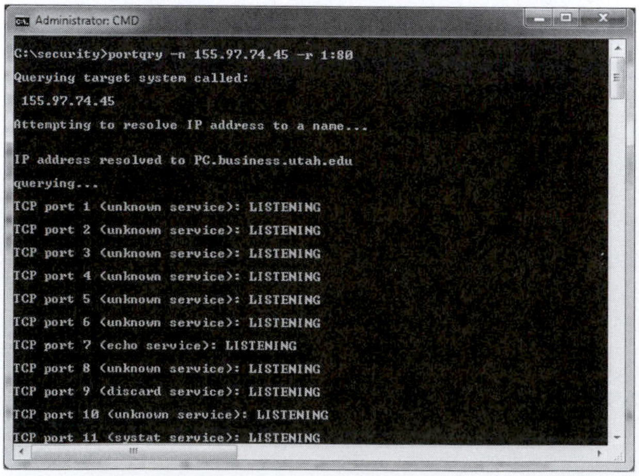

Figure 12-4: Port scan to test HoneyBOT.

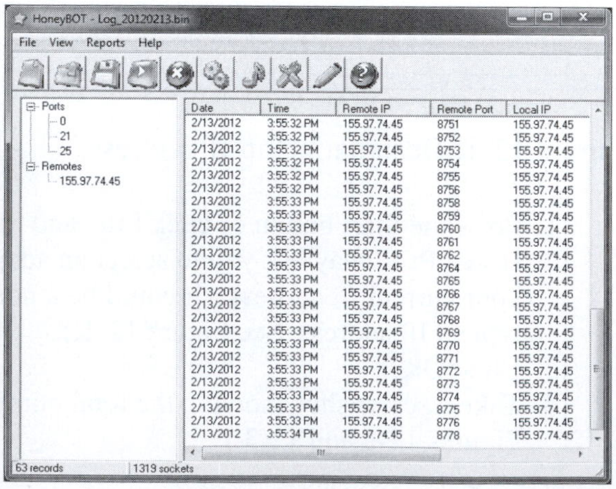

Figure 12-5: HoneyBOT results from portqry command.

28. Return to HoneyBOT.
29. Take a screenshot. (See Figure 12-5.)
30. Click File, New, and No. (This will refresh the logs so you can see the difference between the various scans.)
31. Open a Web browser and go to **ftp://[Your IP Address]**. (Replace Your IP Address with the IP address that is being used by HoneyBOT. In this example, it was ftp://155.97.74.45.)
32. When prompted for a username, enter your first name. (See Figure 12-6.)
33. Enter your last name for the password. (Entering your first and last name as username and password will record them in the HoneyBOT log. You don't really have an FTP server running. It's being "faked" by HoneyBOT.)

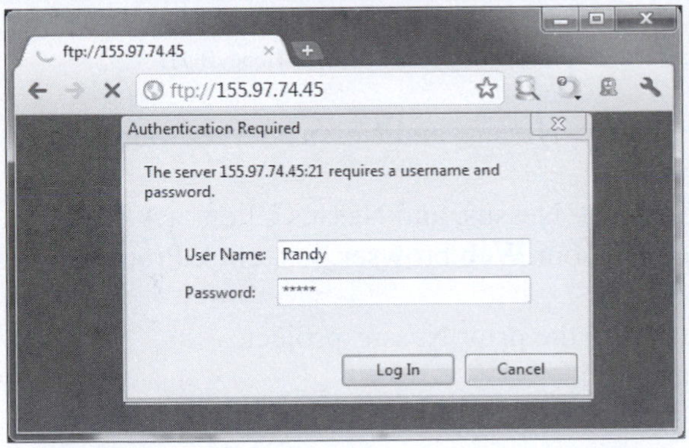

Figure 12-6: Authenticating with your fake FTP server.

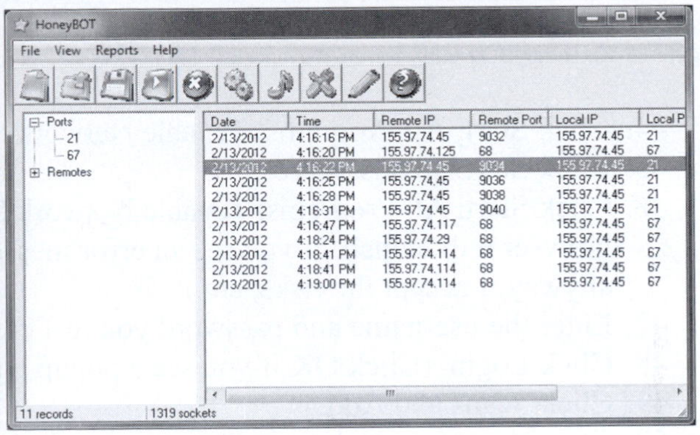

Figure 12-7: HoneyBOT results from attempted FTP access.

34. Return to HoneyBOT and take a screenshot. (See Figure 12-7.)
35. Double-click on one of the entries with the local port listing 21. (The remote IP and local IP should be the same.)
36. Take a screenshot of the HoneyBOT log entry showing your first and last name being used to access an FTP server. (See Figure 12-8.)

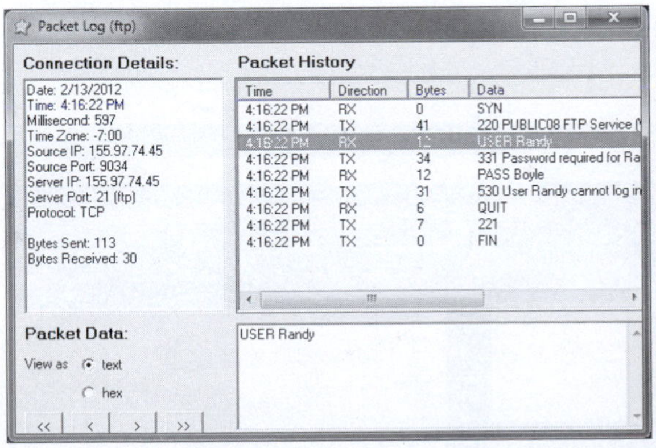

Figure 12-8: HoneyBOT entry for a false FTP connection attempt.

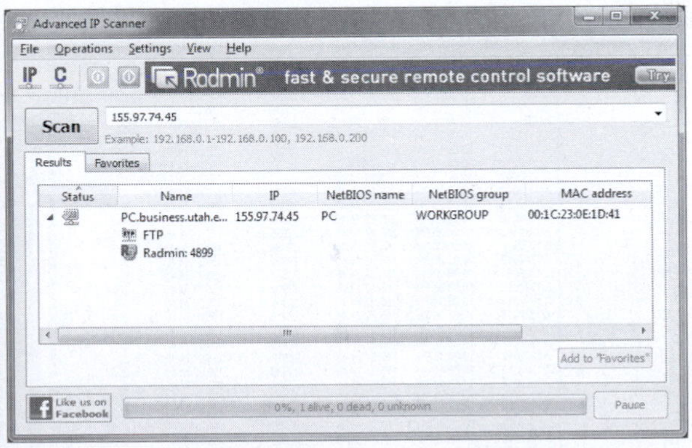

Figure 12-9: Advanced IP Scanner targeted at HoneyBOT.

37. In HoneyBOT, click File, New, and No. (This will refresh the logs so you can see the difference between the various scans.)
38. Click Start, All Programs, Advanced IP Scanner v2, and Advanced IP Scanner.
39. Enter your IP address in the text box next to Scan. (In this case, it was 155.97.74.45.)
40. Press Scan.
41. Take a screenshot. (See Figure 12-9.)
42. Return to HoneyBOT.
43. Take a screenshot of the results from the Advanced IP scan. (See Figure 12-10.)

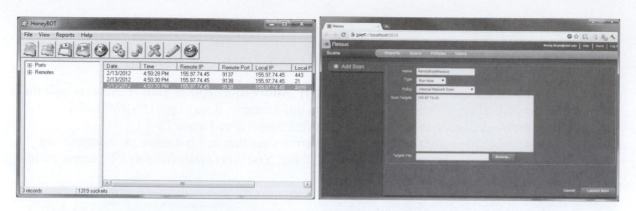

Figure 12-10: HoneyBOT entry for the Advanced IP scan.   Figure 12-11: Configuring Nessus to scan HoneyBOT.

44. Click Start, All Programs, Tenable Network Security, Nessus, and Nessus Server Manager.
45. Click Start Nessus Server.
46. Click Start, All Programs, Tenable Network Security, Nessus, and Nessus Client. (A Web browser will launch. If you see an error message in your Web browser, just click Proceed anyway, I accept the risks, etc.)
47. Enter the username and password you just created in the prior Nessus project.
48. Click Login. (Click OK if you see a popup warning.)
49. Click Scans and Add.
50. Type YourNameNessus in the name text box.
51. Change the policy drop-down to Internal Network Scan.
52. Type your IP address in the Scan Targets text box. (See Figure 12-11.)
53. Click Launch Scan. (Make sure HoneyBOT is cleared before you click Launch Scan. The whole scan could take up to 20-30 minutes to complete. The Nessus scan below created about 5500 entries on HoneBOT's logs. You can stop the scan early, but it might be interesting to let it run for 3-4 minutes.)

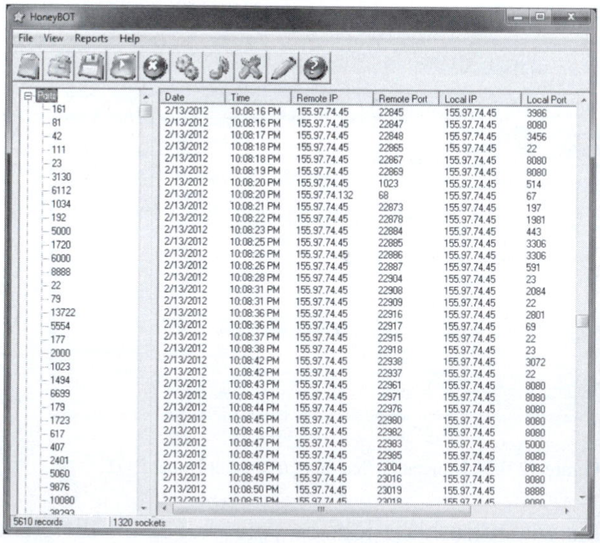

Figure 12-12: HoneyBot log from a Nessus scan. 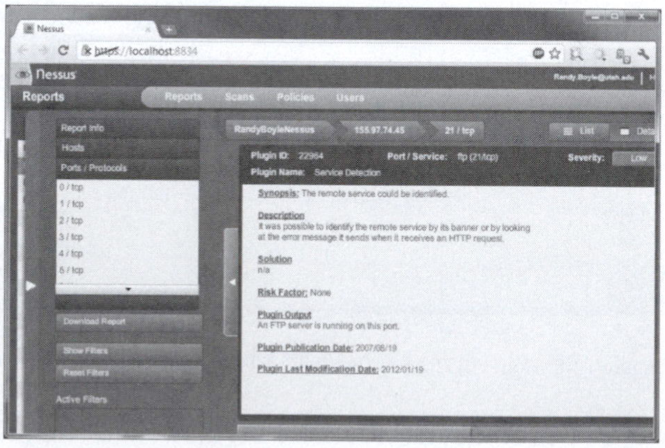   Figure 12-13: Nessus scan for target computer with HoneyBOT.

54. Take a screenshot of the results in HoneyBOT. (See Figure 12-12.)
55. Return to the Nessus Web interface.
56. Click on Reports.

57. Double-click the report you just ran. (You can stop it early if you want.)
58. Double-click your IP address. (It should be the only one displayed.)
59. Scroll down and click on port 21.
60. Click on one of the entries for port 21.
61. Take a screenshot of the results from the Nessus scan. (See Figure 12-13.)

As you can see, HoneyBOT is able to "fake" a lot of ports and applications. It is also able to provide detailed logging features. HoneyBOT is simple to use and gives users an idea of the extent to which external hackers/bots are scanning their machines. It also allows non-technical users to estimate the probability of any given attack. This is a great way to show non-technical people, such as business managers, how honeypots really work. They are usually amazed at the results.

The log entry for the scan recorded on July 11, 2008 is shown on the following two pages. (See Figure 12-14.) The log is copied using font size 6 to fit it on two pages. This partial log entry is shown to give you an idea of how thorough some of these automated scans can be.

This individual tried quite a few default usernames and passwords in an attempt to gain access to this fake Web server. It's likely that he or she has tried to access other Web servers on other networks. This log also gives you an idea of why IT security professionals really dislike hackers. They cause a great deal of additional work and trouble. How would you feel if someone stood in front of your house and kept turning the doorknob to see if the door was open?

PROJECT QUESTIONS

1. What was your IP address for this scan?
2. How many events did HoneyBOT record for the Advanced IP Scanner scan?
3. How many events did HoneyBOT record for the Nessus scan?
4. Did HoneyBOT record any other IP addresses while you had it open? Which ones?

THOUGHT QUESTIONS

1. What impact would more open ports have on the ability of your honeypot to attract hackers?
2. Can hackers tell that you have a honeypot running?
3. Are there honeypots for spammers that keep them from harvesting emails from your Web pages?
4. Do you think law enforcement agencies (e.g., CIA, FBI, NSA, etc.) in the United States run honeypots to track criminal behavior?

Fri Jul 11 12:43:08   HTTP empty request from 221.8.61.69
Fri Jul 11 13:03:31   HTTP request from 221.8.61.69: GET /manager/html
Fri Jul 11 13:03:31   HTTP authorization attempt from 221.8.61.69: user: , password:
Fri Jul 11 13:03:32   HTTP request from 221.8.61.69: GET /manager/html

Fri Jul 11 13:03:32   HTTP authorization attempt from 221.8.61.69: **user: admin, password: admin**

Fri Jul 11 13:03:32   HTTP request from 221.8.61.69: GET /manager/html
Fri Jul 11 13:03:32   HTTP authorization attempt from 221.8.61.69: user: admin, password: 147258369
Fri Jul 11 13:03:32   HTTP request from 221.8.61.69: GET /manager/html
Fri Jul 11 13:03:32   HTTP authorization attempt from 221.8.61.69: user: admin, password: 369258147
Fri Jul 11 13:03:32   HTTP request from 221.8.61.69: GET /manager/html
Fri Jul 11 13:03:32   HTTP authorization attempt from 221.8.61.69: user: admin, password: 258147
Fri Jul 11 13:03:32   HTTP request from 221.8.61.69: GET /manager/html
Fri Jul 11 13:03:32   HTTP authorization attempt from 221.8.61.69: user: admin, password: 147258
Fri Jul 11 13:03:32   HTTP request from 221.8.61.69: GET /manager/html
Fri Jul 11 13:03:32   HTTP authorization attempt from 221.8.61.69: user: admin, password: 258369
Fri Jul 11 13:03:32   HTTP request from 221.8.61.69: GET /manager/html
Fri Jul 11 13:03:32   HTTP authorization attempt from 221.8.61.69: user: admin, password: 369258
Fri Jul 11 13:03:32   HTTP request from 221.8.61.69: GET /manager/html
Fri Jul 11 13:03:32   HTTP authorization attempt from 221.8.61.69: user: admin, password: 159357
Fri Jul 11 13:03:32   HTTP request from 221.8.61.69: GET /manager/html
Fri Jul 11 13:03:32   HTTP authorization attempt from 221.8.61.69: user: admin, password: 12
Fri Jul 11 13:03:32   HTTP request from 221.8.61.69: GET /manager/html
Fri Jul 11 13:03:33   HTTP authorization attempt from 221.8.61.69: user: admin, password: 123
Fri Jul 11 13:03:33   HTTP request from 221.8.61.69: GET /manager/html
Fri Jul 11 13:03:33   HTTP authorization attempt from 221.8.61.69: user: admin, password: 1234
Fri Jul 11 13:03:33   HTTP request from 221.8.61.69: GET /manager/html
Fri Jul 11 13:03:33   HTTP authorization attempt from 221.8.61.69: user: admin, password: 12345
Fri Jul 11 13:03:33   HTTP request from 221.8.61.69: GET /manager/html
Fri Jul 11 13:03:33   HTTP authorization attempt from 221.8.61.69: user: admin, password: 123456
Fri Jul 11 13:03:33   HTTP request from 221.8.61.69: GET /manager/html
Fri Jul 11 13:03:33   HTTP authorization attempt from 221.8.61.69: user: admin, password: 1234567
Fri Jul 11 13:03:33   HTTP request from 221.8.61.69: GET /manager/html
Fri Jul 11 13:03:33   HTTP authorization attempt from 221.8.61.69: user: admin, password: 12345678
Fri Jul 11 13:03:33   HTTP request from 221.8.61.69: GET /manager/html
Fri Jul 11 13:03:33   HTTP authorization attempt from 221.8.61.69: user: admin, password: 123456789
Fri Jul 11 13:03:33   HTTP request from 221.8.61.69: GET /manager/html
Fri Jul 11 13:03:33   HTTP authorization attempt from 221.8.61.69: user: admin, password: 1234567890
Fri Jul 11 13:03:33   HTTP request from 221.8.61.69: GET /manager/html
Fri Jul 11 13:03:33   HTTP authorization attempt from 221.8.61.69: user: admin, password: 9876543210
Fri Jul 11 13:03:33   HTTP request from 221.8.61.69: GET /manager/html
Fri Jul 11 13:03:33   HTTP authorization attempt from 221.8.61.69: user: admin, password: 987654321
Fri Jul 11 13:03:33   HTTP request from 221.8.61.69: GET /manager/html
Fri Jul 11 13:03:33   HTTP authorization attempt from 221.8.61.69: user: admin, password: 98765432
Fri Jul 11 13:03:33   HTTP request from 221.8.61.69: GET /manager/html
Fri Jul 11 13:03:33   HTTP authorization attempt from 221.8.61.69: user: admin, password: 9876543
Fri Jul 11 13:03:33   HTTP request from 221.8.61.69: GET /manager/html
Fri Jul 11 13:03:33   HTTP authorization attempt from 221.8.61.69: user: admin, password: 987654
Fri Jul 11 13:03:33   HTTP request from 221.8.61.69: GET /manager/html
Fri Jul 11 13:03:33   HTTP authorization attempt from 221.8.61.69: user: admin, password: 98765
Fri Jul 11 13:03:33   HTTP request from 221.8.61.69: GET /manager/html
Fri Jul 11 13:03:33   HTTP authorization attempt from 221.8.61.69: user: admin, password: 9876
Fri Jul 11 13:03:33   HTTP request from 221.8.61.69: GET /manager/html
Fri Jul 11 13:03:33   HTTP authorization attempt from 221.8.61.69: user: admin, password: 987
Fri Jul 11 13:03:33   HTTP request from 221.8.61.69: GET /manager/html
Fri Jul 11 13:03:33   HTTP authorization attempt from 221.8.61.69: user: admin, password: 0123
Fri Jul 11 13:03:33   HTTP request from 221.8.61.69: GET /manager/html
Fri Jul 11 13:03:33   HTTP authorization attempt from 221.8.61.69: user: admin, password: 01234
Fri Jul 11 13:03:33   HTTP request from 221.8.61.69: GET /manager/html
Fri Jul 11 13:03:33   HTTP authorization attempt from 221.8.61.69: user: admin, password: 012345
Fri Jul 11 13:03:33   HTTP request from 221.8.61.69: GET /manager/html
Fri Jul 11 13:03:33   HTTP authorization attempt from 221.8.61.69: user: admin, password: 0123456
Fri Jul 11 13:03:33   HTTP request from 221.8.61.69: GET /manager/html
Fri Jul 11 13:03:34   HTTP authorization attempt from 221.8.61.69: user: admin, password: 01234567
Fri Jul 11 13:03:34   HTTP request from 221.8.61.69: GET /manager/html

Fri Jul 11 13:03:35   HTTP request from 221.8.61.69: GET /manager/html
Fri Jul 11 13:03:35   HTTP authorization attempt from 221.8.61.69: user: admin, password: administrator
Fri Jul 11 13:03:35   HTTP request from 221.8.61.69: GET /manager/html

Fri Jul 11 13:03:35   HTTP authorization attempt from 221.8.61.69: **user: admin, password: administrators**

Fri Jul 11 13:03:35   HTTP request from 221.8.61.69: GET /manager/html
Fri Jul 11 13:03:35   HTTP authorization attempt from 221.8.61.69: user: admin, password:
Fri Jul 11 13:03:35   HTTP request from 221.8.61.69: GET /manager/html
Fri Jul 11 13:03:35   HTTP authorization attempt from 221.8.61.69: user: admin, password: tomcat
Fri Jul 11 13:03:35   HTTP request from 221.8.61.69: GET /manager/html
Fri Jul 11 13:03:35   HTTP authorization attempt from 221.8.61.69: user: admin, password: tomcatcat
Fri Jul 11 13:03:35   HTTP request from 221.8.61.69: GET /manager/html
Fri Jul 11 13:03:35   HTTP authorization attempt from 221.8.61.69: user: admin, password: tomcattomcat
Fri Jul 11 13:03:35   HTTP request from 221.8.61.69: GET /manager/html
Fri Jul 11 13:03:36   HTTP authorization attempt from 221.8.61.69: user: admin, password: manager
Fri Jul 11 13:03:36   HTTP request from 221.8.61.69: GET /manager/html
Fri Jul 11 13:03:36   HTTP authorization attempt from 221.8.61.69: user: admin, password: tomcatadmin
Fri Jul 11 13:03:36   HTTP request from 221.8.61.69: GET /manager/html
Fri Jul 11 13:03:36   HTTP authorization attempt from 221.8.61.69: user: admin, password: tomcatmanager
Fri Jul 11 13:03:36   HTTP request from 221.8.61.69: GET /manager/html
Fri Jul 11 13:03:36   HTTP authorization attempt from 221.8.61.69: user: admin, password: fackyou
Fri Jul 11 13:03:36   HTTP request from 221.8.61.69: GET /manager/html
Fri Jul 11 13:03:36   HTTP authorization attempt from 221.8.61.69: user: admin, password: fack
Fri Jul 11 13:03:36   HTTP request from 221.8.61.69: GET /manager/html
Fri Jul 11 13:03:36   HTTP authorization attempt from 221.8.61.69: user: admin, password: 1qaz
Fri Jul 11 13:03:36   HTTP request from 221.8.61.69: GET /manager/html
Fri Jul 11 13:03:36   HTTP authorization attempt from 221.8.61.69: user: admin, password: 1qaz2wsx
Fri Jul 11 13:03:36   HTTP request from 221.8.61.69: GET /manager/html
Fri Jul 11 13:03:36   HTTP authorization attempt from 221.8.61.69: user: admin, password: 1qaz2wsx3edc
Fri Jul 11 13:03:36   HTTP request from 221.8.61.69: GET /manager/html
Fri Jul 11 13:03:36   HTTP authorization attempt from 221.8.61.69: user: admin, password: 3edc4rfv
Fri Jul 11 13:03:36   HTTP request from 221.8.61.69: GET /manager/html
Fri Jul 11 13:03:36   HTTP authorization attempt from 221.8.61.69: user: admin, password: 5tgb6yhn
Fri Jul 11 13:03:36   HTTP request from 221.8.61.69: GET /manager/html
Fri Jul 11 13:03:36   HTTP authorization attempt from 221.8.61.69: user: admin, password: 7ujm8ik,
Fri Jul 11 13:03:36   HTTP request from 221.8.61.69: GET /manager/html
Fri Jul 11 13:03:36   HTTP authorization attempt from 221.8.61.69: user: admin, password: !@#!@#
Fri Jul 11 13:03:36   HTTP request from 221.8.61.69: GET /manager/html
Fri Jul 11 13:03:36   HTTP authorization attempt from 221.8.61.69: user: admin, password: !@#$%^&*()
Fri Jul 11 13:03:36   HTTP request from 221.8.61.69: GET /manager/html
Fri Jul 11 13:03:36   HTTP authorization attempt from 221.8.61.69: user: admin, password: !@#
Fri Jul 11 13:03:36   HTTP request from 221.8.61.69: GET /manager/html
Fri Jul 11 13:03:36   HTTP authorization attempt from 221.8.61.69: user: admin, password: !@#$
Fri Jul 11 13:03:36   HTTP request from 221.8.61.69: GET /manager/html
Fri Jul 11 13:03:36   HTTP authorization attempt from 221.8.61.69: user: admin, password: !@#$%^
Fri Jul 11 13:03:36   HTTP request from 221.8.61.69: GET /manager/html
Fri Jul 11 13:03:36   HTTP authorization attempt from 221.8.61.69: user: admin, password: !@#$%^&*
Fri Jul 11 13:03:36   HTTP request from 221.8.61.69: GET /manager/html
Fri Jul 11 13:03:36   HTTP authorization attempt from 221.8.61.69: user: admin, password: !@#$%^&*(
Fri Jul 11 13:03:36   HTTP request from 221.8.61.69: GET /manager/html
Fri Jul 11 13:03:36   HTTP authorization attempt from 221.8.61.69: user: admin, password: ~!@
Fri Jul 11 13:03:36   HTTP request from 221.8.61.69: GET /manager/html
Fri Jul 11 13:03:36   HTTP authorization attempt from 221.8.61.69: user: admin, password: ~!@#
Fri Jul 11 13:03:36   HTTP request from 221.8.61.69: GET /manager/html
Fri Jul 11 13:03:36   HTTP authorization attempt from 221.8.61.69: user: admin, password: ~!@#$
Fri Jul 11 13:03:36   HTTP request from 221.8.61.69: GET /manager/html
Fri Jul 11 13:03:36   HTTP authorization attempt from 221.8.61.69: user: admin, password: ~!@#$%
Fri Jul 11 13:03:36   HTTP request from 221.8.61.69: GET /manager/html
Fri Jul 11 13:03:36   HTTP authorization attempt from 221.8.61.69: user: admin, password: ~!@#$%^
Fri Jul 11 13:03:36   HTTP request from 221.8.61.69: GET /manager/html
Fri Jul 11 13:03:37   HTTP authorization attempt from 221.8.61.69: user: admin, password: ~!@#$%^&
Fri Jul 11 13:03:37   HTTP request from 221.8.61.69: GET /manager/html
Fri Jul 11 13:03:37   HTTP authorization attempt from 221.8.61.69: user: admin, password: ~!@#$%^&*

Fri Jul 11 13:03:34   HTTP authorization attempt from 221.8.61.69: user: admin, password: 012345678
Fri Jul 11 13:03:34   HTTP request from 221.8.61.69: GET /manager/html
Fri Jul 11 13:03:34   HTTP authorization attempt from 221.8.61.69: user: admin, password: 0123456789
Fri Jul 11 13:03:34   HTTP request from 221.8.61.69: GET /manager/html
Fri Jul 11 13:03:34   HTTP authorization attempt from 221.8.61.69: user: admin, password: 112233
Fri Jul 11 13:03:34   HTTP request from 221.8.61.69: GET /manager/html
Fri Jul 11 13:03:34   HTTP authorization attempt from 221.8.61.69: user: admin, password: 223344
Fri Jul 11 13:03:34   HTTP request from 221.8.61.69: GET /manager/html
Fri Jul 11 13:03:34   HTTP authorization attempt from 221.8.61.69: user: admin, password: 334455
Fri Jul 11 13:03:34   HTTP request from 221.8.61.69: GET /manager/html
Fri Jul 11 13:03:34   HTTP authorization attempt from 221.8.61.69: user: admin, password: 445566
Fri Jul 11 13:03:34   HTTP request from 221.8.61.69: GET /manager/html
Fri Jul 11 13:03:34   HTTP authorization attempt from 221.8.61.69: user: admin, password: 778899
Fri Jul 11 13:03:34   HTTP request from 221.8.61.69: GET /manager/html
Fri Jul 11 13:03:34   HTTP authorization attempt from 221.8.61.69: user: admin, password: 123123
Fri Jul 11 13:03:34   HTTP request from 221.8.61.69: GET /manager/html
Fri Jul 11 13:03:34   HTTP authorization attempt from 221.8.61.69: user: admin, password: 456456
Fri Jul 11 13:03:34   HTTP request from 221.8.61.69: GET /manager/html
Fri Jul 11 13:03:34   HTTP authorization attempt from 221.8.61.69: user: admin, password: 789789
Fri Jul 11 13:03:34   HTTP request from 221.8.61.69: GET /manager/html
Fri Jul 11 13:03:34   HTTP authorization attempt from 221.8.61.69: user: admin, password: 147123
Fri Jul 11 13:03:34   HTTP request from 221.8.61.69: GET /manager/html
Fri Jul 11 13:03:34   HTTP authorization attempt from 221.8.61.69: user: admin, password: 321321
Fri Jul 11 13:03:34   HTTP request from 221.8.61.69: GET /manager/html
Fri Jul 11 13:03:34   HTTP authorization attempt from 221.8.61.69: user: admin, password: 654654
Fri Jul 11 13:03:34   HTTP request from 221.8.61.69: GET /manager/html
Fri Jul 11 13:03:34   HTTP authorization attempt from 221.8.61.69: user: admin, password: 987987
Fri Jul 11 13:03:34   HTTP request from 221.8.61.69: GET /manager/html
Fri Jul 11 13:03:34   HTTP authorization attempt from 221.8.61.69: user: admin, password: 654654
Fri Jul 11 13:03:34   HTTP request from 221.8.61.69: GET /manager/html
Fri Jul 11 13:03:34   HTTP authorization attempt from 221.8.61.69: user: admin, password: 456456
Fri Jul 11 13:03:34   HTTP request from 221.8.61.69: GET /manager/html
Fri Jul 11 13:03:34   HTTP authorization attempt from 221.8.61.69: user: admin, password: 789789
Fri Jul 11 13:03:34   HTTP request from 221.8.61.69: GET /manager/html
Fri Jul 11 13:03:34   HTTP authorization attempt from 221.8.61.69: user: admin, password: 987987
Fri Jul 11 13:03:34   HTTP request from 221.8.61.69: GET /manager/html
Fri Jul 11 13:03:34   HTTP authorization attempt from 221.8.61.69: user: admin, password: 258369
Fri Jul 11 13:03:34   HTTP request from 221.8.61.69: GET /manager/html
Fri Jul 11 13:03:34   HTTP authorization attempt from 221.8.61.69: user: admin, password: 369147
Fri Jul 11 13:03:34   HTTP request from 221.8.61.69: GET /manager/html
Fri Jul 11 13:03:35   HTTP authorization attempt from 221.8.61.69: user: admin, password: 234567
Fri Jul 11 13:03:35   HTTP request from 221.8.61.69: GET /manager/html
Fri Jul 11 13:03:35   HTTP authorization attempt from 221.8.61.69: user: admin, password: 345678
Fri Jul 11 13:03:35   HTTP request from 221.8.61.69: GET /manager/html
Fri Jul 11 13:03:35   HTTP authorization attempt from 221.8.61.69: user: admin, password: 678910
Fri Jul 11 13:03:35   HTTP request from 221.8.61.69: GET /manager/html
Fri Jul 11 13:03:35   HTTP authorization attempt from 221.8.61.69: user: admin, password: 147369
Fri Jul 11 13:03:35   HTTP request from 221.8.61.69: GET /manager/html
Fri Jul 11 13:03:35   HTTP authorization attempt from 221.8.61.69: user: admin, password: 369369
Fri Jul 11 13:03:35   HTTP request from 221.8.61.69: GET /manager/html
Fri Jul 11 13:03:35   HTTP authorization attempt from 221.8.61.69: user: admin, password: 258258
Fri Jul 11 13:03:35   HTTP request from 221.8.61.69: GET /manager/html
Fri Jul 11 13:03:35   HTTP authorization attempt from 221.8.61.69: user: admin, password: 147147
Fri Jul 11 13:03:35   HTTP request from 221.8.61.69: GET /manager/html
Fri Jul 11 13:03:35   HTTP authorization attempt from 221.8.61.69: user: admin, password: admin3388
Fri Jul 11 13:03:35   HTTP request from 221.8.61.69: GET /manager/html
Fri Jul 11 13:03:35   HTTP authorization attempt from 221.8.61.69: user: admin, password: admin8888
Fri Jul 11 13:03:35   HTTP request from 221.8.61.69: GET /manager/html
Fri Jul 11 13:03:35   HTTP authorization attempt from 221.8.61.69: user: admin, password: admin3388

Fri Jul 11 13:03:37   HTTP request from 221.8.61.69: GET /manager/html
Fri Jul 11 13:03:37   HTTP authorization attempt from 221.8.61.69: user: admin, password: ~!@#$%^&*(
Fri Jul 11 13:03:37   HTTP request from 221.8.61.69: GET /manager/html
Fri Jul 11 13:03:37   HTTP authorization attempt from 221.8.61.69: user: admin, password: ~!@#$%^&*()
Fri Jul 11 13:03:37   HTTP request from 221.8.61.69: GET /manager/html
Fri Jul 11 13:03:37   HTTP authorization attempt from 221.8.61.69: user: admin, password: ^*$%^&#$%^@
Fri Jul 11 13:03:37   HTTP request from 221.8.61.69: GET /manager/html
Fri Jul 11 13:03:37   HTTP authorization attempt from 221.8.61.69: user: admin, password: asdfasdf
Fri Jul 11 13:03:37   HTTP request from 221.8.61.69: GET /manager/html
Fri Jul 11 13:03:37   HTTP authorization attempt from 221.8.61.69: user: admin, password: asdfg
Fri Jul 11 13:03:37   HTTP request from 221.8.61.69: GET /manager/html
Fri Jul 11 13:03:37   HTTP authorization attempt from 221.8.61.69: user: admin, password: qwer
Fri Jul 11 13:03:37   HTTP request from 221.8.61.69: GET /manager/html
Fri Jul 11 13:03:37   HTTP authorization attempt from 221.8.61.69: user: admin, password: qwertyuiop
Fri Jul 11 13:03:37   HTTP request from 221.8.61.69: GET /manager/html
Fri Jul 11 13:03:37   HTTP authorization attempt from 221.8.61.69: user: admin, password: asdfghjkl
Fri Jul 11 13:03:37   HTTP request from 221.8.61.69: GET /manager/html
Fri Jul 11 13:03:37   HTTP authorization attempt from 221.8.61.69: user: admin, password: zxcvbnm
Fri Jul 11 13:03:37   HTTP request from 221.8.61.69: GET /manager/html
Fri Jul 11 13:03:37   HTTP authorization attempt from 221.8.61.69: user: admin, password: 123qweasdzxc
Fri Jul 11 13:03:37   HTTP request from 221.8.61.69: GET /manager/html
Fri Jul 11 13:03:37   HTTP authorization attempt from 221.8.61.69: user: admin, password: 123qweasd
Fri Jul 11 13:03:37   HTTP request from 221.8.61.69: GET /manager/html
Fri Jul 11 13:03:37   HTTP authorization attempt from 221.8.61.69: user: admin, password: 123qwe
Fri Jul 11 13:03:37   HTTP request from 221.8.61.69: GET /manager/html
Fri Jul 11 13:03:37   HTTP authorization attempt from 221.8.61.69: user: admin, password: 1234qwer
Fri Jul 11 13:03:37   HTTP request from 221.8.61.69: GET /manager/html
Fri Jul 11 13:03:37   HTTP authorization attempt from 221.8.61.69: user: admin, password: 1234qwerasdf
Fri Jul 11 13:03:37   HTTP request from 221.8.61.69: GET /manager/html
Fri Jul 11 13:03:37   HTTP authorization attempt from 221.8.61.69: user: admin, password: 1234qwerasdfzxcv
Fri Jul 11 13:03:37   HTTP request from 221.8.61.69: GET /manager/html
Fri Jul 11 13:03:37   HTTP authorization attempt from 221.8.61.69: user: admin, password: 159753
Fri Jul 11 13:03:37   HTTP request from 221.8.61.69: GET /manager/html
Fri Jul 11 13:03:37   HTTP authorization attempt from 221.8.61.69: user: admin, password: microsoft
Fri Jul 11 13:03:37   HTTP request from 221.8.61.69: GET /manager/html
Fri Jul 11 13:03:37   HTTP authorization attempt from 221.8.61.69: user: admin, password: Microsoft
Fri Jul 11 13:03:37   HTTP request from 221.8.61.69: GET /manager/html
Fri Jul 11 13:03:37   HTTP authorization attempt from 221.8.61.69: user: admin, password: Server
Fri Jul 11 13:03:37   HTTP request from 221.8.61.69: GET /manager/html
Fri Jul 11 13:03:37   HTTP authorization attempt from 221.8.61.69: user: admin, password: server
Fri Jul 11 13:03:37   HTTP request from 221.8.61.69: GET /manager/html
Fri Jul 11 13:03:37   HTTP authorization attempt from 221.8.61.69: user: admin, password: Service
Fri Jul 11 13:03:37   HTTP request from 221.8.61.69: GET /manager/html
Fri Jul 11 13:03:37   HTTP authorization attempt from 221.8.61.69: user: admin, password: service
Fri Jul 11 13:03:37   HTTP request from 221.8.61.69: GET /manager/html
Fri Jul 11 13:03:37   HTTP authorization attempt from 221.8.61.69: user: admin, password: 2008
Fri Jul 11 13:03:37   HTTP request from 221.8.61.69: GET /manager/html
Fri Jul 11 13:03:38   HTTP authorization attempt from 221.8.61.69: user: admin, password: 2003
Fri Jul 11 13:03:38   HTTP request from 221.8.61.69: GET /manager/html
Fri Jul 11 13:03:38   HTTP authorization attempt from 221.8.61.69: user: admin, password: webserver
Fri Jul 11 13:03:38   HTTP request from 221.8.61.69: GET /manager/html
Fri Jul 11 13:03:38   HTTP authorization attempt from 221.8.61.69: user: admin, password: sqlserver
Fri Jul 11 13:03:38   HTTP request from 221.8.61.69: GET /manager/html
Fri Jul 11 13:03:38   HTTP authorization attempt from 221.8.61.69: user: admin, password: adminserver
Fri Jul 11 13:03:38   HTTP request from 221.8.61.69: GET /manager/html
Fri Jul 11 13:03:38   HTTP authorization attempt from 221.8.61.69: user: admin, password: 5201314
Fri Jul 11 13:03:38   HTTP request from 221.8.61.69: GET /manager/html
Fri Jul 11 13:03:38   HTTP authorization attempt from 221.8.61.69: user: admin, password: 1314520
Fri Jul 11 13:03:38   HTTP request from 221.8.61.69: GET /manager/html
Fri Jul 11 13:03:38   HTTP authorization attempt from 221.8.61.69: user: admin, password: 7758520

Figure 12-14: Honeypot log excerpt.

12.2   NST®, SNORT® (IDS), & BASE®

We mentioned at the start of this chapter that intrusion detection systems (IDSs) can be difficult to install, configure, and maintain because they look at more than just changes in local files. Intrusion detection systems also look at network traffic and use complex rules to try to identify attacks/scans that may be occurring on your network. Configuring an IDS to catch *all* intruders based on specific attack signatures is extremely difficult. New types of threats appear on a daily basis.

We are going to look at an IDS called Snort® that uses a GUI front-end called BASE® to analyze the log entries. Both of these tools are part of a larger suite of tools named Network Security Toolkit® (NST). NST incorporates many of the tools we have already looked at, including some advanced tools that we will not cover. It's worth the time to explore the NST image or download a bootable CD image from their website (http://networksecuritytoolkit.org/nst/index.html).

We will download a virtual image of the NST and run it inside Oracle's VirtualBox®. We will see an example of how virtual machines work later, but essentially you will be running a computer (Linux) within your existing computer (Windows). This might seem foreign at first, but you will quickly see how easy virtual machines are to use. Incidentally, you can also use VirtualBox to run a Windows on your Mac.

Snort (www.Snort.org) is one of the most well known free intrusion detection systems available. Most students are excited to learn Snort but quickly realize that it can be difficult to use if they are not familiar with Linux/Unix. Snort, like most security tools, was initially developed to run on Linux/Unix operating systems. There are many security tools available for Linux that cannot be run under Windows.

1. Download Oracle VirtualBox from https://www.virtualbox.org/.
2. Click Downloads.
3. Click on the download link for the latest version of Oracle VM VirtualBox for Windows. (At the time of writing, the latest version was VirtualBox-4.2.6.82870-Win.exe. Download the latest version of VirtualBox available. Versions for Mac OS X and Linux are also available.)
4. Click Save.
5. Select your C:\security folder.
6. If the program doesn't automatically open, browse to C:\security.
7. Double-click the VirtualBox-4.2.6.82870-Win.exe program. (The version number will likely be different as later versions are released.)
8. Click Run, Run, Next, Next, Next, Install, Next, and Finish. (This runs you through the installation process.)

Note: You have just installed VirtualBox. We will now download and start the virtual machine for NST.

9. Download the NST VM image from http://networksecuritytoolkit.org/nst/index.html.
10. Click Download NST on the right-hand side.
11. Click on Download nst-2.15.0-2515.i686.iso (1.4 GB). (The version numbers may be slightly different as newer software is released. Download the latest version.)
12. Click Save.
13. Select your C:\security folder. (This may take several minutes to download. It might be faster to get it from your instructor if a copy is available.)

Note: You just downloaded the NST image. You are now going to create a virtual machine using VirtualBox, and then install NST on that virtual machine.

14. Double-click the VirtualBox icon on your desktop, or run it from the Start menu by clicking Start, All Programs, Oracle VM VirtualBox, and Oracle VM VirtualBox.
15. Click New.

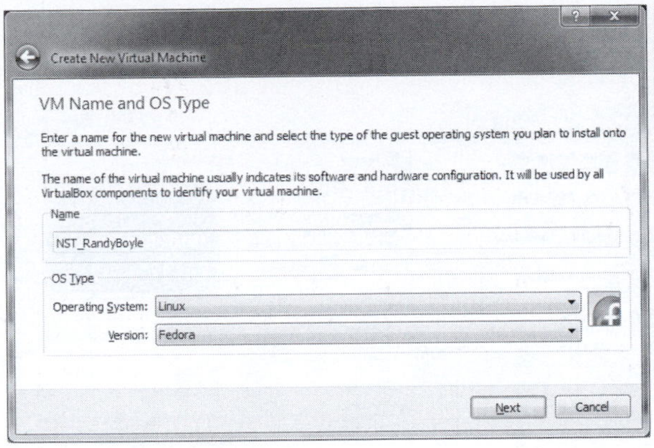

Figure 12-15: Selecting the vm OS.

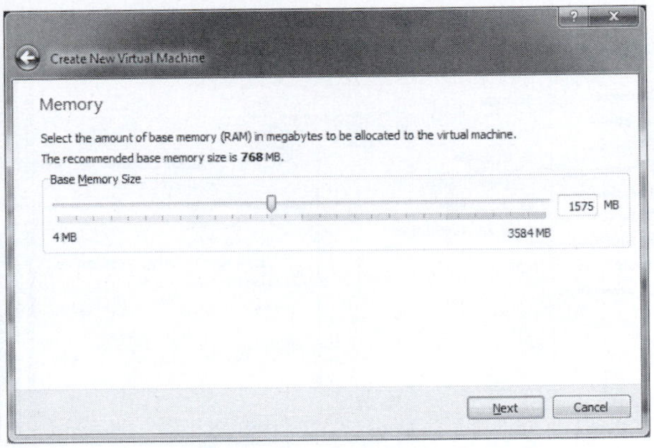

Figure 12-16: Allocating memory.

16. Enter "NST_YourName" for the Name. (In this case, it was NST_RandyBoyle.)
17. Select Linux for the Operating System.
18. Select Fedora (64) for the Version. (You can select just "Fedora" if you have a 32-bit system. See Figure 12-15.)
19. Click Next.
20. Increase the amount of memory to 1500 MB+. (See Figure 12-16.)
21. Click Next, Create, Next, and Next.

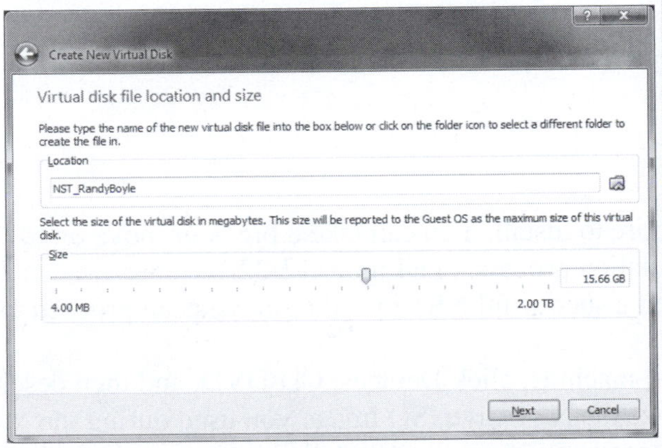

Figure 12-17: Naming your virtual disk.

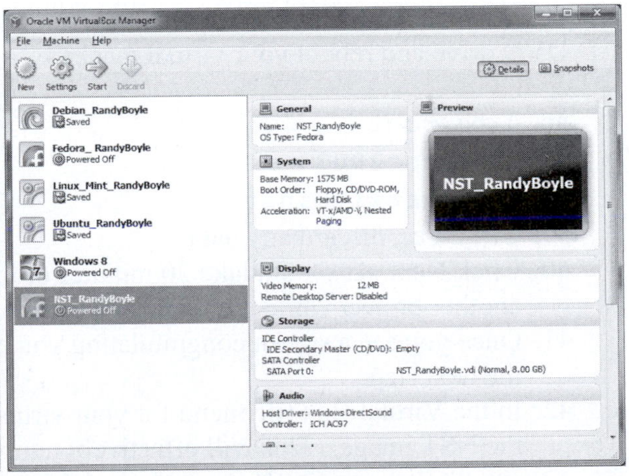

Figure 12-18: Virtual machine was created.

22. Increase the hard drive space to 15 GB or more. (See Figure 12-17.)
23. Click Create.
24. Select the Virtual machine labeled "NST_YourName". (See Figure 12-18.)
25. In the right-hand pane, click Storage.
26. Click on the IDE Controller labeled "Empty".
27. Click the browse button (it looks like a DVD disk) on the right-hand side of the screen next to CD/DVD Drive. (You are going to browse to the NST ISO image you downloaded earlier and mount it.)
28. Click Choose a Virtual CD/DVD disk file.
29. Browse to your C:\security directory where you saved the NST image.

30. Select the NST image you downloaded. (See Figure 12-19.)
31. Click OK.
32. Take a screenshot showing the new virtual machine. (See Figure 12-20.)
33. Click Start.

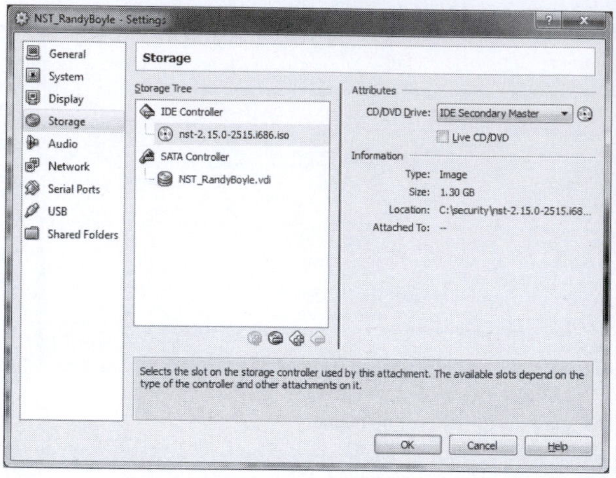

Figure 12-19: Capturing the downloaded .ISO image. 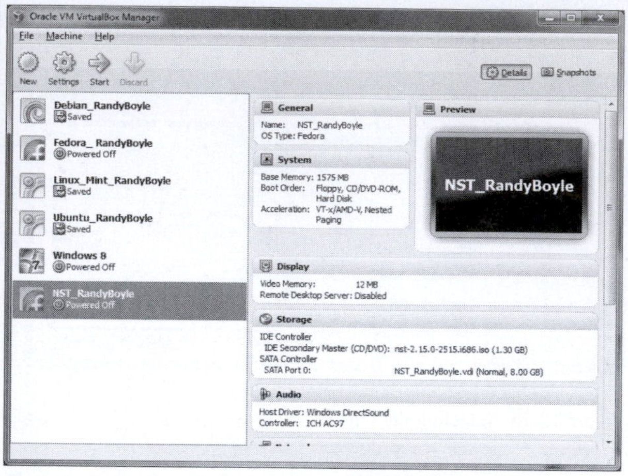   Figure 12-20: The vm is ready to start.

34. Make sure the NST Console option is selected.
35. Press enter.

Note: In the next few steps, you are going to enter a username (root), password (nst2003), and a command to install NST to your virtual hard drive (nstliveinst). (See Figure 12-21.) You will then walk through a couple of screens to finish the installation. You will then remove the NST image (ISO) from your virtual CD/DVD drive and reboot your virtual machine.

36. Type **root**
37. Type **nst2003**
38. Type **nstliveinst**
39. Click Yes, discard any data.
40. Click Next. (It should take 20 minutes or more to install. You can take a break or move on to another project while it completes the installation process. See Figure 12-22.)
41. Once you see a screen congratulating you on a successful NST installation, you can proceed to the next step.
42. In the Virtual Box file menu for your virtual machine, click Devices, CD/DVD, and then deselect the NST image. (This will effectively remove the NST Live ISO image you used during the installation process. You won't need this image because you just installed it to your virtual hard disk.)
43. Click Force Unmount if prompted.
44. Click Close.

Note: You may only have a few seconds to scroll down to the Graphical Desktop option in the boot menu. If you miss this option, you can always click Machine, and Reset, in the VirtualBox file menu.

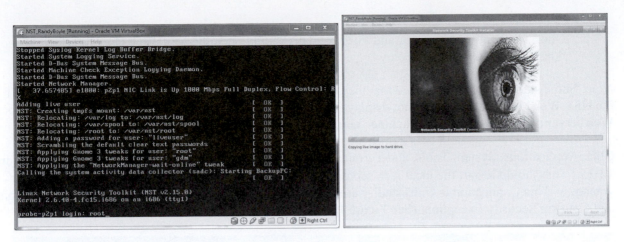

Figure 12-21: NST login.

Figure 12-22: NST installation.

45. In the VirtualBox file menu for your virtual machine, click Machine, and Reset.
46. Scroll down and select Graphical Desktop. (See Figure 12-23.)
47. Press Enter. (It will take a minute to get the virtual machine running. You can leave the virtual machine by holding down the right Ctrl key.)
48. Click Other.
49. Enter "root" for the username, without quotes.
50. Enter "nst2003" for the password, without quotes.
51. Click Log In. (See Figure 12-24.)

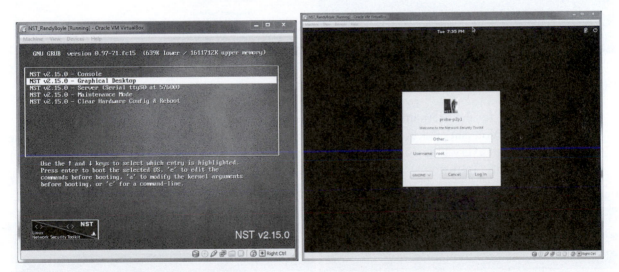

Figure 12-23: Selecting the graphical desktop for NST.

Figure 12-24: NST login screen.

Note: You may have to press the right Ctrl key to exit the virtual machine and then use Screenshot Pilot to take screenshots in VirtualBox. You can download Screenshot Pilot at the following link: http://www.colorpilot.com/screenshot.html.

Note: You can install VirtualBox Guest Additions to make the virtual machine run smoother (i.e., resize the virtual machine, better mouse integration, etc.). In the VirtualBox file menu for your virtual machine, click Devices, and Install VirtualBox Guest Additions. This will mount an ISO image in your virtual machine's CDROM drive. You can browse to the ISO image in the Ubuntu file manager. You should see a button labeled "Open Autorun Prompt" or you can run autorun.sh. Follow the prompts and then reboot your virtual machine.

52. Click Applications, Internet, and Firefox. (This should open the NST Web User Interface. If it doesn't open, see the note below.)

Note: Some students have mentioned that they could not see the NST interface in their Web browser. If the NST Web User Interface does not display (i.e., it gives you an error), you may need to restart the local Web server on your NST virtual machine. You can do this through a command-line terminal.

Click Applications, System Tools, and Terminal. Then type `service httpd restart`. (See Figure 12-25.) This should restart the local web server and give you access to the NST Web User Interface. If you see a "This Connection is Untrusted" warning, you can click I Understand the Risks, Add Exception, and Confirm Security Exception. (See Figure 12-26.)

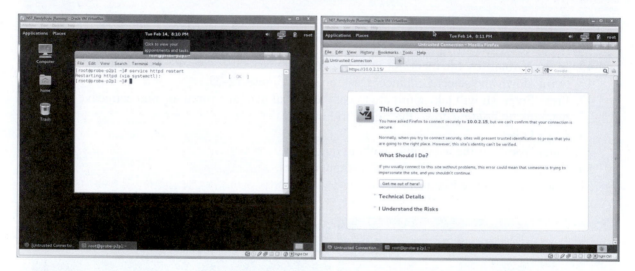

Figure 12-25: Restart httpd service.   Figure 12-26: Trusted connection screen.

53. Enter "root" for the username and "nst2003" for the password.
54. Click OK. (You can click Remember Password if you don't want to keep entering the username and password every time you want to access the NST Web User Interface.) (See Figure 12-27.)
55. Click Security, Intrusion Detection, and Snort IDS. (See Figure 12-28.)

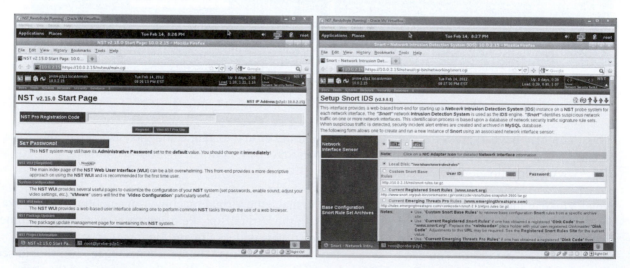

Figure 12-27: NST start page.   Figure 12-28: Snort setup page.

56. Scroll down and check the "Startup this instance of Snort immediately after setup" option in the Setup/Start Snort section. (See Figure 12-29.)
57. Scroll to the bottom of the page and click Setup/Start Snort.
58. Click the Check Status button. (See Figure 12-30.)

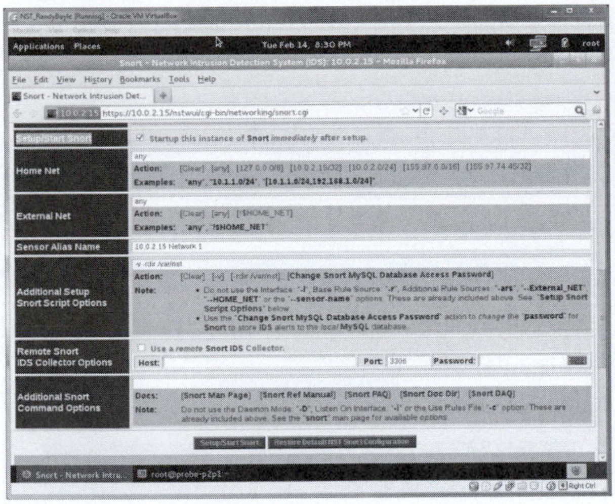

Figure 12-29: Configuring Snort to startup.

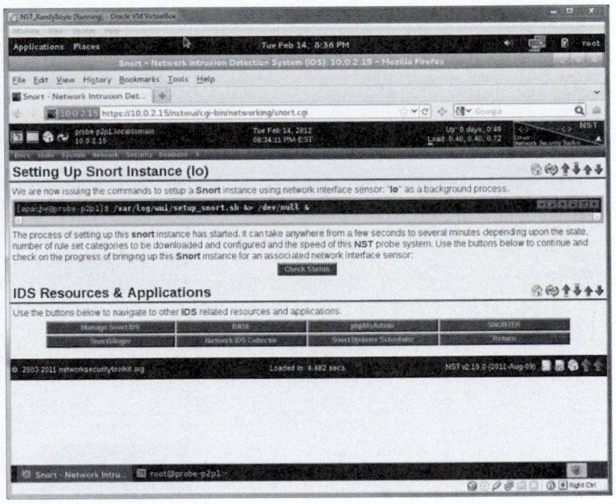

Figure 12-30: Check Status of Sort.

59. Scroll down and check to see that the mysqld and snortd services are running. (If not, press the corresponding Start buttons.) (See Figure 12-31.)
60. Scroll up to see the IP address associated with the virtual network adapter. (It will be shown in green font.) (See Figure 12-32.)
61. Write down the virtual IP address you see because you'll need it later.

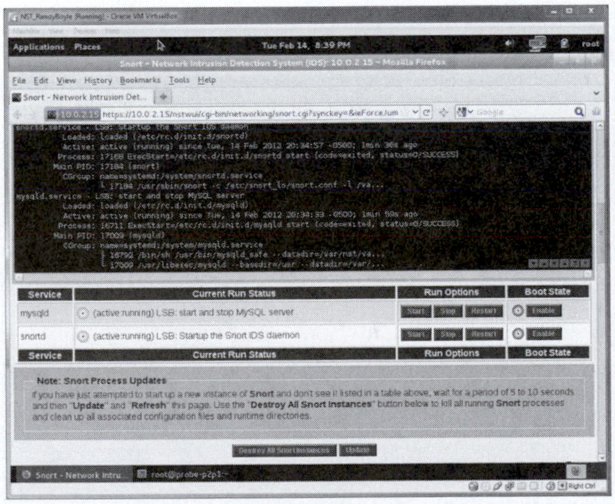

Figure 12-31: Check to see if mysqld and snortd are running.

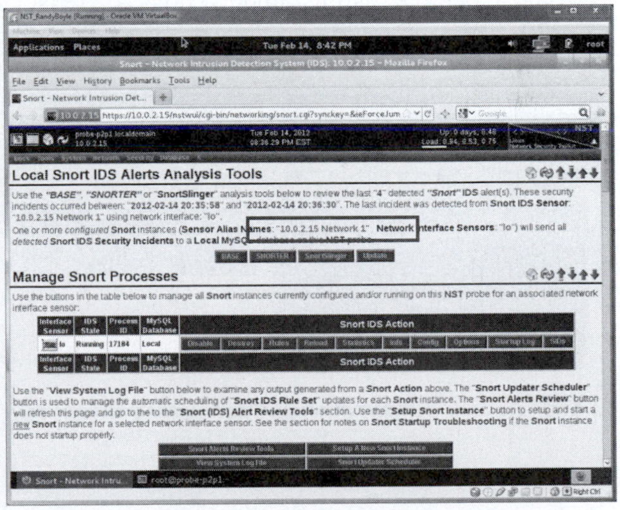

Figure 12-32: Snort analysis tool.

Note: In this example, the IP address was 10.0.2.15. Your IP address will not be the same but may appear like 192.168.X.X, where the Xs represent any number between 0 and 255). Make sure to write down the IP address shown.

62. Click Applications, Internet, and Zenmap (as root).

63. Enter the IP address you just wrote down into the Hostname/IP text box. (In this case, it was 10.0.2.15.)
64. Click the Scan button. (If it doesn't recognize a "live" host, you have entered an incorrect IP address.) (See Figure 12-33.)
65. Return to the NST Web User Interface.
66. Click Update under the Local Snort IDS Alerts Analysis Tools. (You should see the number of Snort IDS alerts jump up dramatically. In this example, they jumped from 9 to 805.)
67. Take a screenshot. (See Figure 12-34.)

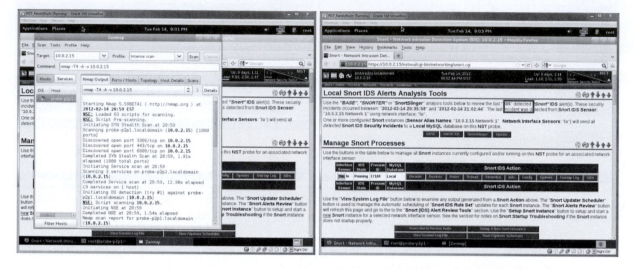

Figure 12-33: Zenmap scanner within a virtual machine.

Figure 12-34: Updated listing of Snort alerts.

68. Click Base, located just below the IP address you wrote down. (It's located to the left of the Update button.) (See Figure 12-35.)
69. Click on "listing" under Today's Alerts. (See Figure 12-36.)
70. Take a screenshot.

Figure 12-35: BASE main page.

Figure 12-36: BASE results from scan.

You can see that Snort recorded lots of information about the scan you just did. BASE provides excellent reporting and analysis tools to handle large numbers of log entries. Take some time to explore the graphical front-end to BASE. If you want to see a large number of log entries, run a "Slow comprehensive scan" in Zenmap, or run a Nessus scan.

It would also be worthwhile to look over the additional tools that are included with NST. Some of the tools you will recognize from prior projects. However, there are several tools included in NST that are not currently ported for Windows. We will look at a couple of other IT security suites similar to NST later.

Important If you plan on leaving NST installed, you should reset the password.

PROJECT QUESTIONS

1. What was the name of your virtual machine?
2. What was the IP address of your virtual machine?
3. How many Snort events were displayed *before* you ran the Zenmap scan?
4. How many Snort events were displayed *after* you ran the Zenmap scan?

THOUGHT QUESTIONS

1. Why are tools like Snort initially developed for Linux/Unix if there are more Windows users and potentially more customers?
2. Who makes the "rules" used by Snort?
3. What is the difference between Snort and a packet sniffer like Wireshark?
4. What would you do with the information you get from Snort/Base?

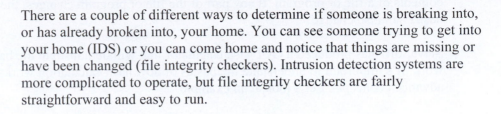

CHAPTER 13: FILE INTEGRITY CHECKERS & SYSTEM MONITORS

chapter 13

There are a couple of different ways to determine if someone is breaking into, or has already broken into, your home. You can see someone trying to get into your home (IDS) or you can come home and notice that things are missing or have been changed (file integrity checkers). Intrusion detection systems are more complicated to operate, but file integrity checkers are fairly straightforward and easy to run.

File integrity checkers basically take a snapshot of a file and then compare it to a later snapshot to see if anything has changed. There are several good file integrity checker programs on the market. We will start with the basics and move up from there. We will also look at software that monitors system activity and logs system events.

Time required to complete this chapter: 40 minutes

Chapter Objectives

Learn how to...
1. Calculate a hash.
2. Identify system events.
3. Detect changes to a file or directory.
4. Read Windows system logs.
5. Run automated system monitoring software.

Chapter Projects

Project:
13.1 HashCalc
13.2 Process Monitor (Filemon)
13.3 File Verifier++
13.4 Windows Event Viewer
13.5 Snare for Windows

13.1 HASHCALC®

HashCalc® is a program that will compute a checksum or message digest for any given file. Hashes can be confusing for beginners. You can think of a hash as a unique number that is generated based on the contents of a file or program. If any part of the file or program changes, then the unique number (the hash) will also change.

SlavaSoft® has produced a GUI hash calculator that will demonstrate the basic principles of how hashes work. It's important to understand the basics of how hash calculation works before you move on to more advanced concepts. Let's look at an example.

1. Download HashCalc from http://www.slavasoft.com/hashcalc/index.htm.
2. Click on the Download link for HashCalc 2.02.
3. Click Save.
4. Select your C:\security folder.
5. Browse to C:\security\.
6. Right-click on hashcalc.zip.
7. Select Extract All, and Extract.
8. Browse to C:\security\hashcalc\.
9. Double-click the setup.exe program.
10. Click Run, Next, I accept, Next, Next, Next, Next, Install, and Finish.
11. Open Windows Explorer.
12. In your C:\security folder, right-click and select New, and Text Document. (See Figure 13-1.)
13. Name the new text document YourNameHash.txt. (In this case, it was RandyBoyleHash.txt.)

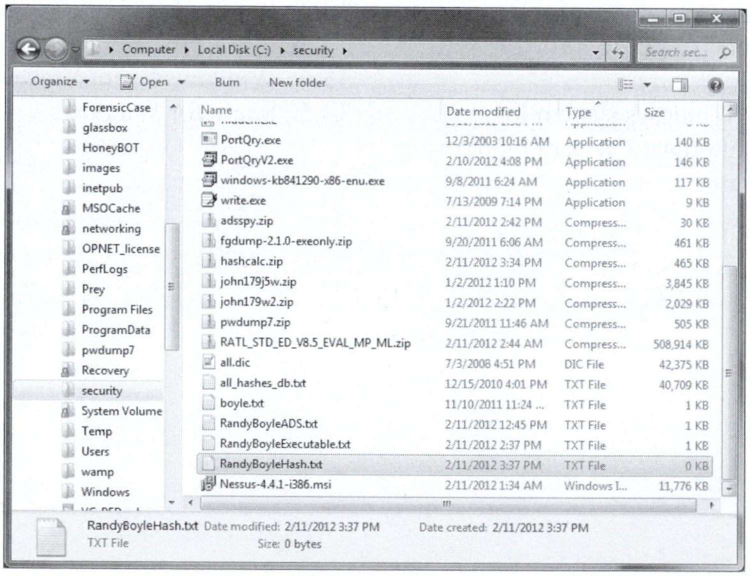

Figure 13-1: Select a file.

14. In the HashCalc window, click on the Find File button to the right of the Data text box.
15. Browse until you select the file you just created in C:\security named YourName.txt.
16. Click Open.
17. In the HashCalc window, click the Calculate button.
18. Take a screenshot.
19. Back in Windows Explorer, open the YourNameHash.txt file and type your name into the text file. (See Figure 13-2.)

Note: We now need to create a test file to determine if HashCalc really works. You are going to create a basic text file in the C:\security folder called YourName.txt. (In this case, it was RandyBoyle.txt.)

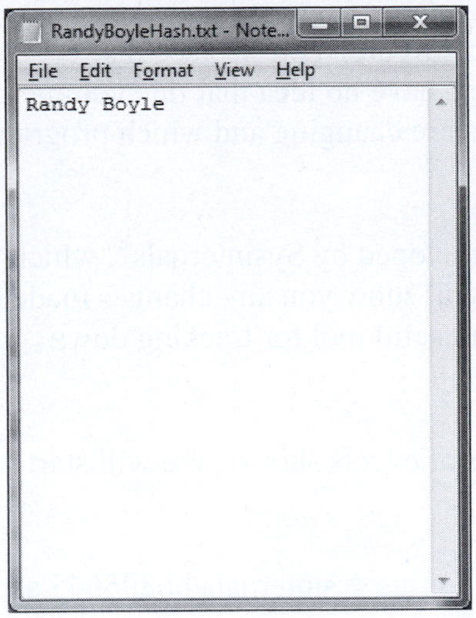

Figure 13-2: Change contents of file.

20. Click File, and Save, to save the changes in the YourName.txt file.
21. Click File, and Exit, to close the text file.
22. Back in the HashCalc window, click Calculate again. (The hashes should change because the text within your text file has changed.)
23. Take a screenshot.

You can clearly see that the MD5 hash is different after you changed the text file. You can do the same thing for any type of file or program on your computer. You can also use programs that will automatically note any/all changes made to files on your computer. This can be useful when you need to know which files have been changed after a possible intrusion.

You may have noticed that software authors/publishers post MD5 hashes along with their downloadable software. They do this so you can be sure that your download is authentic, not corrupted, and not infected with spyware/viruses. There are other hashing and message digest standards used depending on your specific security needs.

PROJECT QUESTIONS

1. What was the name of your text file?
2. What was your original MD5 hash before you changed the text file?
3. What was your MD5 hash after you changed the text file?
4. Which hashing algorithm produced the longest hash?

THOUGHT QUESTIONS

1. Why are there so many different hashing methods?
2. Is it possible to get the exact same hash out of two different files?
3. Is hashing the same thing as encrypting?
4. Can you de-hash?

13.2 PROCESS MONITOR® (FILEMON)

Now that you have seen how hashes work, we will get an idea of how often files are changed on your computer. This will give you an idea of why IDSs are so difficult to configure. You will see that thousands of files are changed on your computer every day. Most users have no idea that this volume of activity is occurring on their computers. It's good to know which files are changing and which program is making the changes.

Process Monitor® is a collection of tools available from Microsoft, developed by Sysinternals®, which give you real-time monitoring capabilities for your local machine. It will show you any changes made to files, the registry, network activities, and/or process activity. This is a useful tool for tracking down malicious programs that may be lurking on your computer.

This program can be overwhelming for many users due to the number of events shown. We will start with the component that tracks file changes, Filemon.

1. Download Process Monitor from http://technet.microsoft.com/en-us/sysinternals/bb896645.aspx.
2. Click Download Process Monitor.
3. Click Save.
4. Select your C:\security folder.
5. Browse to C:\security\.
6. Right-click on ProcessMonitor.zip.
7. Select Extract All, and Extract.
8. Browse to C:\security\ProcessMonitor\.
9. Double-click the procmon.exe program and click Run.
10. As it opens, click Cancel to close the smaller window.

Note: Process Monitor will start collecting large amounts of data immediately. It's collecting a variety of changes including changes to or by the registry, processes, and files. We need to stop all these log entries and only collect information about changes in files. You will see that there are a large number of entries. Knowing how to use filters will be a useful skill at this point. Let's stop everything before we move on.

11. In Process Monitor, click File, and Capture Events (Ctrl+E). (This should stop Process Monitor from capturing events.)
12. Click Edit, and Clear Display (Ctrl+X). (You can use the icons if you can decipher their meaning.)
13. Click Filter, and Reset Filter. (This will show all captured events.)
14. Click File, and Capture Events. (This will start capturing *many* events.) (See Figure 13-3.)

Figure 13-3: Process Monitor.　　　　　　　　　Figure 13-4: Filter only file system activity.

15. After about 5 seconds, click File, and Capture Events (Ctrl+E) to stop capturing events.
16. Note how many events were captured in the bottom left-hand side of the screen.
17. Deselect all of the depressed buttons in the middle of the Process Monitor Screen that act as basic filters. (This should make your screen blank.)
18. Press the Show File System Activity icon. (It looks like a file cabinet with a magnifying glass. Note the number of items displayed at the bottom of the screen.) (See Figure 13-4.)
19. Take a screenshot.
20. Open a Web browser (e.g., Internet Explorer, Firefox, Chrome, etc.) behind Process Monitor.
21. Make sure Process Monitor is reduced and your Web browser is maximized in the background, as shown in the screenshot. (See Figure 13-5.)

Figure 13-5: Process Monitor and Web browser.　　　　Figure 13-6: Events recorded for Web browser activity.

22. Click Edit, and Clear Display.
23. Click-and-drag the Include Process From Window icon (it looks like a cross-hair) from the Process Monitor window onto the Web browser window.
24. Click File, and Capture Events (to start capturing events).
25. In your Web browser, click on any link or reload the page.

26. In Process Monitor, click File, and Capture Events (to stop capturing events). (See Figure 13-6.)
27. Take a screenshot.

In the first part of this project, you captured events and filtered out all events happening on your computer except those that dealt with file system activity. In the second example, you directed Process Monitor to capture events but only show those events that were associated with your Web browser (e.g., Google Chrome).

Process Monitor is an excellent piece of software that can help you identify system changes or events due to malware. An intrusion into your computer or system may have already happened. You may have a virus, spyware, a keylogger, etc., and not even know it. This program can help you find those rogue programs and stop them. It may help prevent future intrusions.

PROJECT QUESTIONS

1. How many events were recorded when you first monitored system activity?
2. How many events remained after you applied the filters?
3. What website did you visit?
4. How many events were recorded that directly related to Chrome?

THOUGHT QUESTIONS

1. Why do programs make so many read/writes to the hard drive?
2. Can you stop programs from running or starting up?
3. Why are there so many entries for the registry? What is the registry?
4. What is the difference between a process and a thread?

13.3   FILEVERIFIER++®

FileVerifier++® is an excellent tool that will compute hashes on any single file or all of your files at once. It can also automatically check to see if there have been any changes to those files. It is intuitive and easy to use. Prior examples showed software that only checked individual files one at a time. FileVerifier++ can check the integrity of a large number of files at a single time.

FileVerifier++ could come in handy if you need to verify that a given set of files has not been changed or altered in any way. Certain professionals might find this tool to be useful if they are dealing with information-based products. If you find that your files are continually being changed, you may need third party encryption software. Encryption software will help ensure the integrity and confidentiality of your data. We will discuss encryption options in a later section. Let's look at a quick example.

1. Download FileVerifier++ from
   http://www.programmingunlimited.net/siteexec/content.cgi?page=fv.
2. Scroll down to the Download section.
3. Click on the [MSI] link for the latest stable version (v0.6.3.5830.msi). (Download the latest stable version available.)
4. Click Save.
5. Select your C:\security folder.
6. If the program doesn't automatically open, browse to C:\security\.
7. Double-click on fv-0.6.3.5830W.msi.
8. Click Run, Next, I agree, Typical, Install, and Finish.

9. Click Start, All Programs, FileVerifier++, and FileVerifier++.
10. In FileVerifier, click the Options button.
11. Change the Default Algorithm to MD5. (See Figure 13-7.)
12. Click OK.

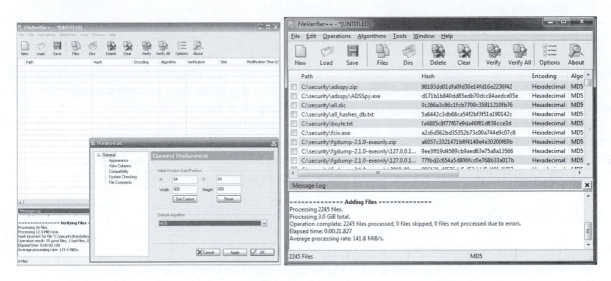

Figure 13-7: FileVerifier++ preferences.   Figure 13-8: Hashes calculated for files.

13. Click on the Dirs button to select the directories you want. (You can also select individual files.)
14. Browse to and select the C:\security directory.
15. Click OK.
16. Take a screenshot.
17. Click the Verify All button. (Browse to the C:\security directory if necessary.)
18. Click OK. (See Figure 13-8.)
19. Take a screenshot.
20. Open the text file labeled YourNameHash.txt that you created earlier in your C:\security directory. (You can create it now if you haven't already done so. It is a text file named YourNameHash.txt. In this case, it was RandyBoyleHash.txt.)
21. Add your name one more time to that text file. (See Figure 13-9.)
22. Save your changes to that text file by clicking File, and Save.
23. Close the text file.

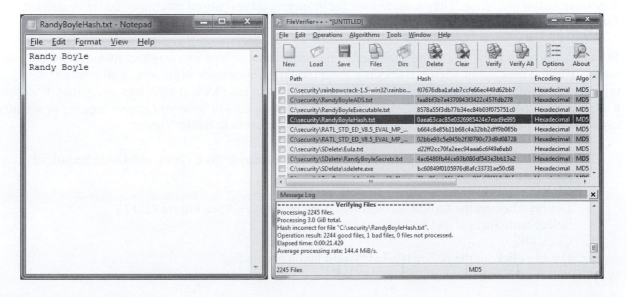

24. In the FileVerifier++ window, click Verify All again. (Browse to the C:\security directory if necessary.)
25. Scroll down until you can see the text file that you changed. (It should be highlighted in red.)
26. Take a screenshot. (See Figure 13-10.)

Note that the file you changed is now marked as "invalid" in red. Any change in a document or file will be recognized due to a non-matching hash. You can do this to any or all files on your system. This is a handy tool you can use to see which, if any, files were changed on your computer.

This is one way IT security professionals can detect a possible intrusion. They can see which files an intruder may have changed. The trick is in knowing which files are changed due to the normal operation of your computer and which files were changed due to an intrusion.

PROJECT QUESTIONS

1. What was the name of the text file you changed?
2. What were the first four characters of the hash for that text file *before* you changed it?
3. What were the first four characters of the hash for that text file *after* you changed it?
4. If you double-click the changed text file (shown in red), it will give more information about when it was changed. When was the text file changed?

THOUGHT QUESTIONS

1. How could a top-notch hacker keep you from knowing which files were changed?
2. Can you calculate a hash for a single file?
3. Can you tell what was changed in the file from the hash?
4. Should you use the longest hash possible? How long is good enough?

13.4   WINDOWS EVENT VIEWER® (LOGS)

Good administrators check their logs as soon as they get to work. They want to know what went on when they were out of the office. They need to look for intruders, compromised machines, stolen or deleted files, etc. The list of things to look for can be long depending on your role in the organization.

Windows Event Viewer® is a simple program that organizes these logs in a way that makes them easy to view. Learning how Event Viewer works is a great training platform for beginners. You need to understand how all the pieces fit together and how important it is to look at your logs every day. It's also a great way to diagnose problems on your machines. This project will have you enable logging of security events, log in and out of your machine, and then look up the event in Event Viewer.

1. Click Start, Control Panel, System and Security, Administrative Tools, and Local Security Policy. (See Figure 13-11.)
2. Click on Local Policies, and Audit Policy.
3. Double-click on the "Audit account logon events" policy. (See Figure 13-12.)
4. Select both Success and Failure.
5. Click OK.
6. Double-click on the policy labeled "Audit logon events."
7. Select both Success and Failure.

8. Click OK.
9. Take a screenshot.

Figure 13-11: Windows administrative tools.   Figure 13-12: Local security settings.

10. In the control panel, click System and Security, Administrative Tools, and Event Viewer.
11. Click Windows Logs, and Security.
12. Take a screenshot.
13. Log off your computer (you don't need to shut down) by clicking Start, the drop-down menu next to Shut Down, and Log Off.
14. Log onto your computer by clicking your username and entering your password.
15. In the control panel, click System and Security, Administrative Tools, and Event Viewer.
16. Click Windows Logs, and Security.
17. Take a screenshot. (See Figure 13-13.)
18. Double-click on the Logon/Logoff event that was just recorded.
19. Take a screenshot. (See Figure 13-14.)

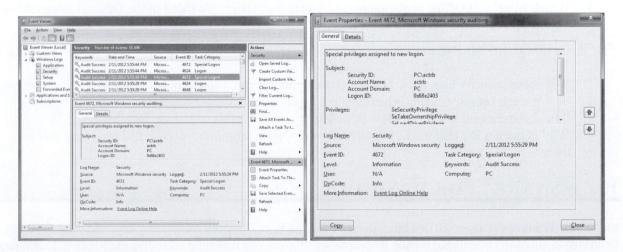

Figure 13-13: Security logs.   Figure 13-14: Details for logged security event.

20. Click Close.
21. Click Applications and Services Logs, and Microsoft Office Sessions.
22. Click on one of the log events.
23. Take a screenshot. (See Figure 13-15.)

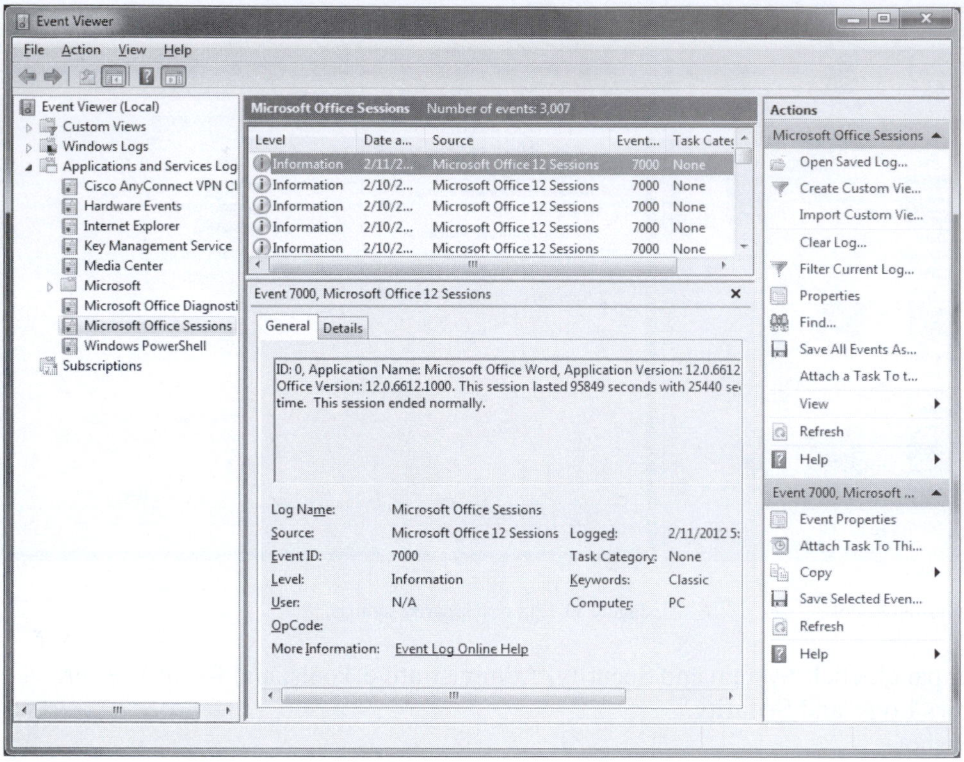

Figure 13-15: Log for Microsoft Office sessions.

PROJECT QUESTIONS

1. What time did you log off?
2. What time did you log on?
3. How long was your last Microsoft Office session?
4. Which Microsoft Office application were you using? (Hint: It's listed in the General information.)

THOUGHT QUESTIONS

1. Will these security logs track failed logon attempts? From remote machines too?
2. Will it track security events other than just logon/logoff events?
3. Can you use event viewer to view other logs?
4. Why is there a log that tracks which Microsoft Office programs you use and how long you use them?

13.5 SNARE® FOR WINDOWS

Snare® for Windows is a service that takes events from the Windows Event log subsystem and presents them in an easy-to-use interface through your Web browser. It gives you real-time custom event logging. It also has a remote administration feature that makes watching a large number of machines much easier.

It can filter events from your Security, Application, and System logs that we looked at earlier. It can provide you with custom rankings of the severity of logged events. This makes administering your computers much easier because you can automatically filter all logged events and only look at the ones that interest you. Let's look at a quick example.

1. Download Snare for Windows from http://www.intersectalliance.com/.
2. Click Snare Agents.
3. Scroll down and click on Snare Agent details.
4. Scroll down and click on Download Snare Agent for Windows.
5. Click Snare installation package.
6. Click Save.
7. Select your C:\security folder.
8. If the program doesn't automatically open, browse to C:\security\.
9. Double-click on SnareForWindows-4.0.1.2-MultiArch.exe.
10. Click Next, I accept, Next, Next, Next, and Next.
11. Select the two boxes labeled Enable Web Access and Local access only.
12. Enter a password you can remember.
13. Click Next, Next, Next, Install, Next, and Finish.
14. Click Start, All Programs, InterSect Alliance, and Snare for Windows.
15. Enter the username "SNARE" and the password you just set.
16. Click Latest Events. (See Figure 13-16.)
17. Take a screenshot.

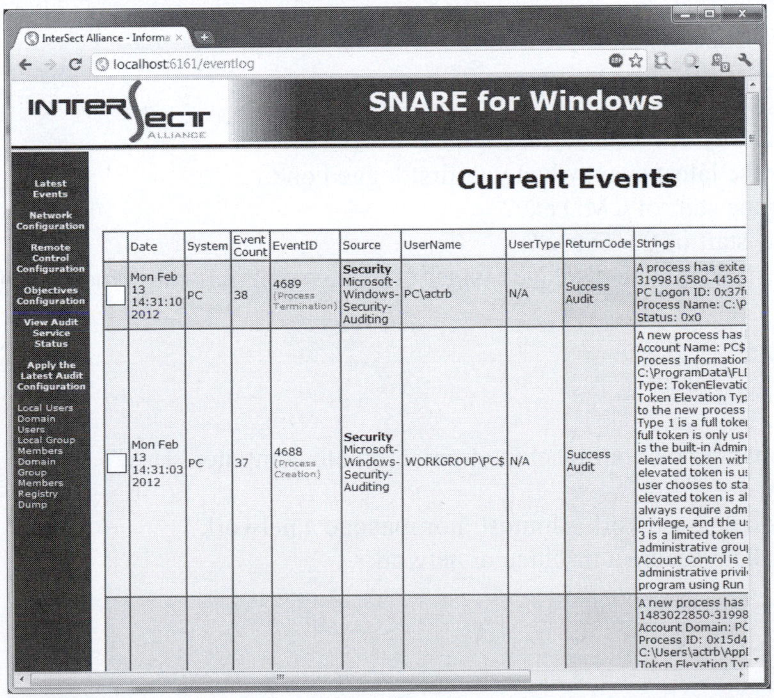

Figure 13-16: Current events.

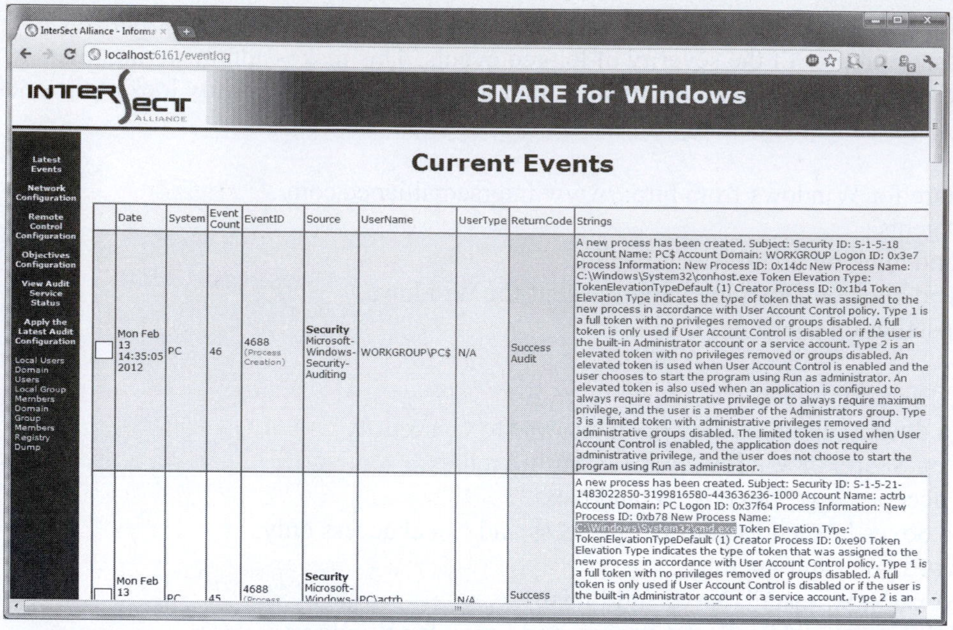

Figure 13-17: Events showing CMD run.

18. Click Start, Run, CMD, and OK.
19. Back in Snare for Windows, press F5 or Refresh. (See Figure 13-17.)
20. Take a screenshot.

PROJECT QUESTIONS

1. What time was displayed for the latest event when you first logged on?
2. What time was displayed for the start of CMD.exe?
3. What was the EventID for the start of CMD.exe?
4. What was your Security ID? (It should be displayed under in Strings column within the entry for the CMD.exe process.)

THOUGHT QUESTIONS

1. Can you view the events happening on your machine from a remote computer? How?
2. Can you add custom filters?
3. How can Snare for Windows help a network administrator manage a network?
4. How can Snare for Windows help secure a machine or network?

chapter 14

Alternate data streams (ADSs) are memory spaces linked to files. One of the purposes of an ADS is to store metadata about a file (i.e., file type, icon, etc.). However, they can be used to store more than just information specific to a file. You can store entire files within an ADS.

The problem IT security professionals have with ADSs is that they can be used to store malicious content. It's extremely easy to store a variety of files within an ADS belonging to a non-descript text file. In fact, viruses can be stored inside an ADS, making them difficult to detect.

In this section you, will learn how to create an ADS. You will also use software to detect the ADS you just created. You can scan your computer to see if you have any other hidden alternate data streams on your computer. An example will help you understand alternate data streams.

Time required to complete this chapter: 30 minutes

Chapter Objectives

Learn how to:
1. Create an ADS.
2. Store, run, and hide programs within an ADS.
3. Detect an ADS.

Chapter Projects

Project:
14.1   Create an ADS
14.2   ADS Executable
14.3   ADS Spy

This is a simple example showing you how to create an ADS. You won't need to download any additional software. You can create the new ADS within a DOS prompt. Alternate data streams are pretty easy to work with after you understand the syntax.

1. Click Start, All Programs, Accessories, and Windows Explorer.
2. Browse to C:\security on your computer.
3. Right-click inside your C:\security folder.
4. Select New, and Text Document.
5. Name the text document YourNameADS.txt. (In this case, it was RandyBoyleADS.txt.) (See Figure 14-1.)
6. Double-click the text file you just created to open it.
7. Type your name twice in the text file. (This is done to increase the file size.)
8. Click File, and Save.
9. In the C:\security folder, right-click the YourNameADS.txt file you just made. (In this example, it was named RandyBoyleADS.txt.)
10. Click Properties. (See Figure 14-2.)

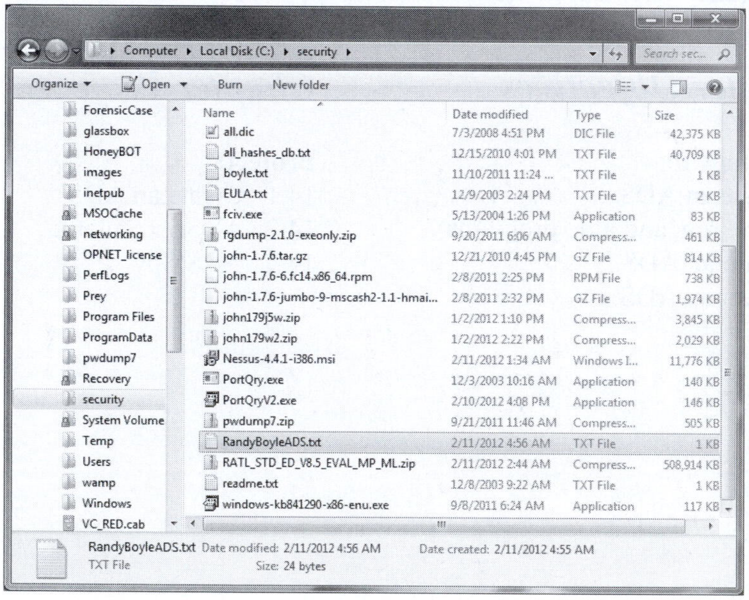

Figure 14-1: Create text file. 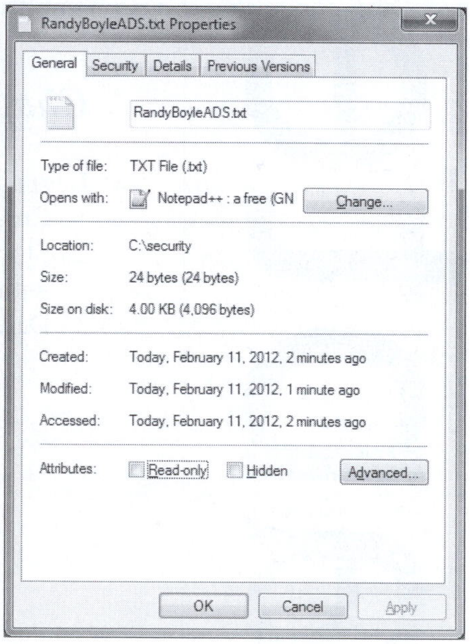   Figure 14-2: Properties of text file.

11. Take a screenshot and note the exact file size. (In this example, it was 24 bytes.)
12. Click Start, All Programs, Accessories, and Command Prompt.
13. In the DOS prompt, navigate to the C:\security folder. (Refer to the Dir & CD section in Chapter 1 if you need to refresh your memory.)
14. In the C:\security folder, type **dir** to get a directory listing. (Make sure you see YourNameADS.txt.) (See Figure 14-3.)
15. Type **notepad YourNameADS.txt**

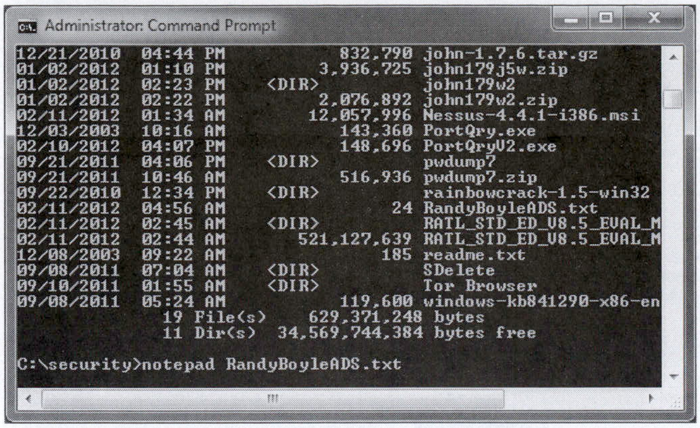

Figure 14-3: Opening the text file from the command prompt.

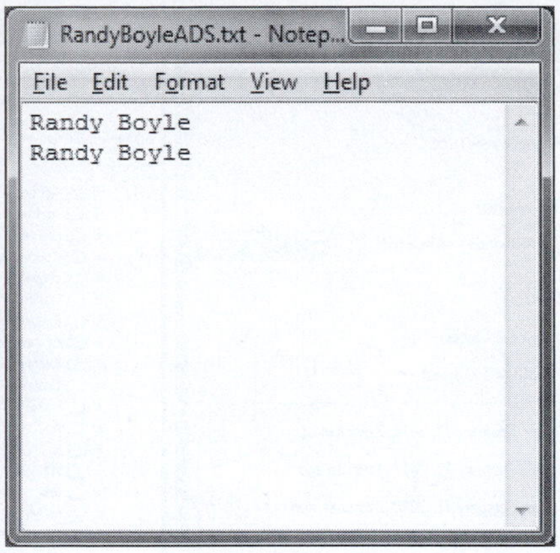

Figure 14-4: Modifying your original text file.

16. Note that you just opened the YourNameADS.text file with Notepad. (See Figure 14-4.)
17. Close the notepad document that just opened.
18. Type **notepad YourNameADS.txt:SecretStuff.txt**
19. Take a screenshot of the DOS prompt showing this command. (See Figure 14-5.)
20. Click Yes if prompted to create a new file.
21. Type "Secret Stuff" a few times in the new text document. (See Figure 14-6.)
22. Click File, and Save.
23. Click File, and Exit, to close this text document.

Figure 14-5: Make the ADS.

Figure 14-6: Enter text into the ADS.

24. In Windows Explorer, right-click the YourNameADS.txt file in C:\security.
25. Select Properties. (See Figure 14-7.)

Note: It's worth noticing that the file size of YourNameADS.txt did *not* change. If you look in Windows Explorer, you will also see that there is not a new text file named SecretStuff.txt. In fact, if you search the entire C:\ drive, you will not find a SecretStuff.txt file at all. (See Figure 14-8.)

26. In the command prompt, type **notepad YourNameADS.txt:SecretStuff.txt** to show the ADS with the SecretStuff.txt file again.
27. Take a screenshot of this SecretStuff.txt text document.

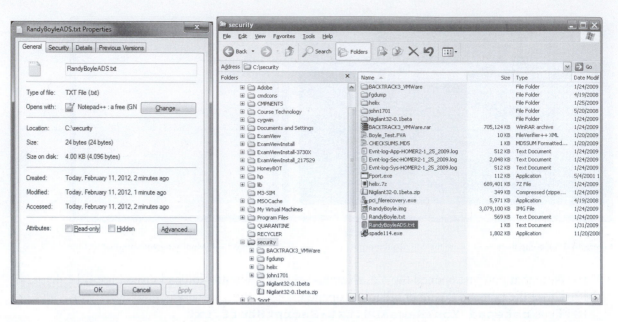

Figure 14-7: Check the properties of the text file.

Figure 14-8: Only the original text file appears to exist.

PROJECT QUESTIONS

1. What was the name of your ADS text file?
2. What was the creation time of your ADS text file?
3. How large was your ADS text file?
4. Did the SecretStuff.txt file appear in the directory? Why not?

THOUGHT QUESTIONS

1. Why do alternate data streams (or forks) exist?
2. Where does the operating system store them on the hard drive?
3. Can you store more than just text in an ADS? How?
4. If you move or copy the file to your USB, will you still be able to open the SecretStuff.txt ADS?

14.2   ADS EXECUTABLE

In the prior example, you created a simple ADS by hiding some text in another text document. In this example, we will hide a program ("write.exe") inside a text file. It's important to understand that even executables can be hidden in files, because virus writers can and do hide their malware in alternate data streams.

We will also create a symbolic link (or shortcut) to the hidden executable ("write.exe"), and then hide the symbolic link. That may sound complicated but it will make more sense after you walk through it. We will see how to search for and delete ADS in the next project.

1. Click Start, All Programs, Accessories, and Windows Explorer.
2. Browse to your C:\security directory on your computer.
3. Right-click inside the C:\security folder.
4. Select New, and Text Document.
5. Name the text document YourNameExecutableADS.txt. (See Figure 14-9.)

6. Double-click the text file that you just created to open it.
7. Enter the words "Executable" several times just to give the file some size. (This step is not necessary to make the ADS, but it's done to show that the file size will not change when the ADS is created.) (See Figure 14-10.)

Note: You can complete all of the previous steps in a single DOS command by typing the following command: `echo Executable Executable > YourNameExecutable.txt`

8. Click File, and Save.
9. Click File, and Exit.
10. In the C:\security folder, right-click the YourNameExecutableADS.txt file you just made. (In this example, it was named RandyBoyleExecutableADS.txt.)
11. Click Properties.
12. Note the exact file size. (In this example, it was 106 bytes.)

Note: It is important that you start the command prompt with administrator-level privaledges by right-clicking the command prompt link and selecting Run as administrator. The project may not work correctly if you don't.

13. Click Start, All Programs, and Accessories.
14. Right-click the Command Prompt link and select Run as administrator. (This is an important step that must be done correctly for the rest of the project to work.)
15. In the DOS prompt, navigate to the C:\security folder. (Refer to the Dir & CD section in the DOS Prompt section if you need a review.)
16. In the C:\security folder, type `dir` to get a directory listing. (Make sure you see YourNameExecutableADS.txt.)

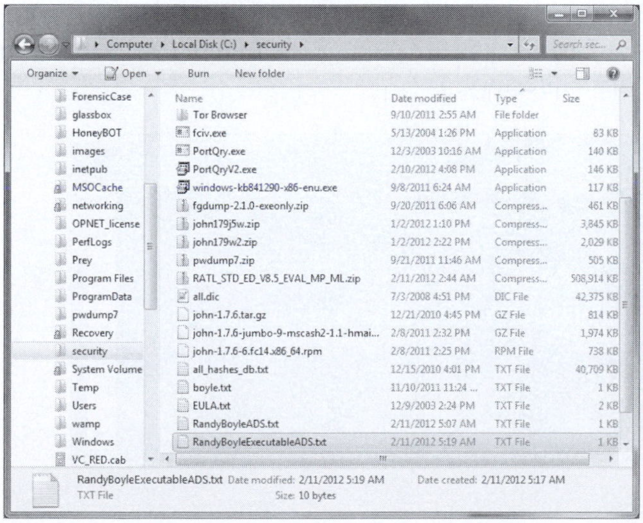

Figure 14-9: Creating a text file.

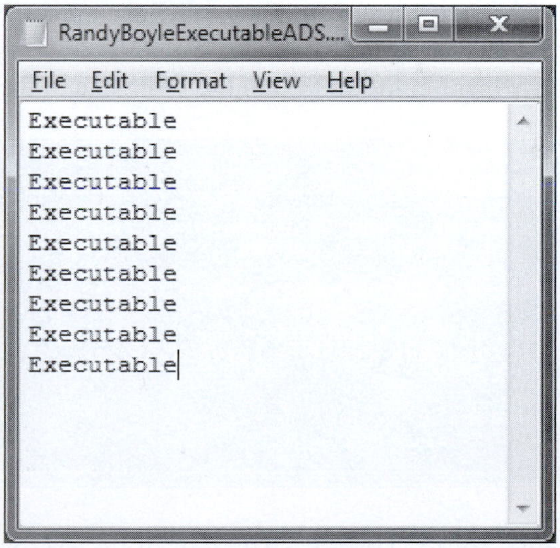

Figure 14-10: Entering text into your original text file.

17. Type `copy C:\Windows\System32\write.exe C:\security`

Note: The previous command copied write.exe into your C:\security directory. You will put write.exe into the ADS of the YourNameExecutable.txt file that you just created. Write.exe can also be found in C:\Windows\SysWOW64.

18. Type the following command including the word "type". (This will attach write.exe to your new text file. See Figure 14-11.)

```
type write.exe > C:\security\YourNameExecutableADS.txt:write.exe
```

Figure 14-11: Copying and hiding write.exe in the ADS.

Note: Windows 7 will not allow you to use the Start command for your hidden executable ("write.exe"). In prior versions of Windows you could use the Start command, but in Windows 7 you have to create a symbolic link first.

19. Type the following command. (This will create a symbolic link, or shortcut, called "hidden.exe" to write.exe within the new text file. See Figure 14-12.)

```
mklink hidden.exe C:\security\YourNameExecutableADS.txt:write.exe
```

20. Take a screenshot. (In the next step, you are going to delete write.exe. It's already in the ADS, so deleting it is ok to do. It also reinforces the fact that you are going to be running write.exe from within the ADS, not the write.exe in the main directory.)

Figure 14-12: Hiding write.exe in the ADS.

21. Type `del write.exe`
22. Type `dir`
23. Type `hidden`

Note: Write.exe should have launched when you typed "hidden." In the next few steps, we will go one step further and hide the hidden.exe link. This will mean that it won't be displayed in Windows Explorer, but you will still be able to start write.exe with the "hidden" command.

24. Take a screenshot of your entire desktop (Ctrl-PrintScreen) with the command prompt and write.exe displayed.
25. Return to Window Explorer in your C:\security directory.
26. Right-click on hidden.exe and select properties.
27. Click the General tab.
28. Select the Hidden option.
29. Click OK. (See Figure 14-13.)
30. Click Start, Control Panel, Appearance and Personalization, and Folder Options.
31. Click on the View tab.
32. Make sure "Don't show hidden files, folders, or drives" is selected. (You can always change this back later. It's a good idea to show all files, even if they are hidden.)
33. Click OK. (See Figure 14-14.)

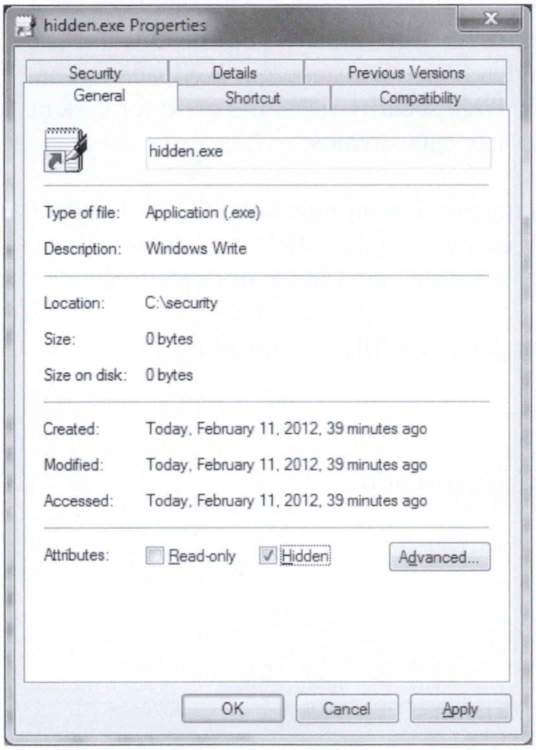

Figure 14-13: Hiding a file.

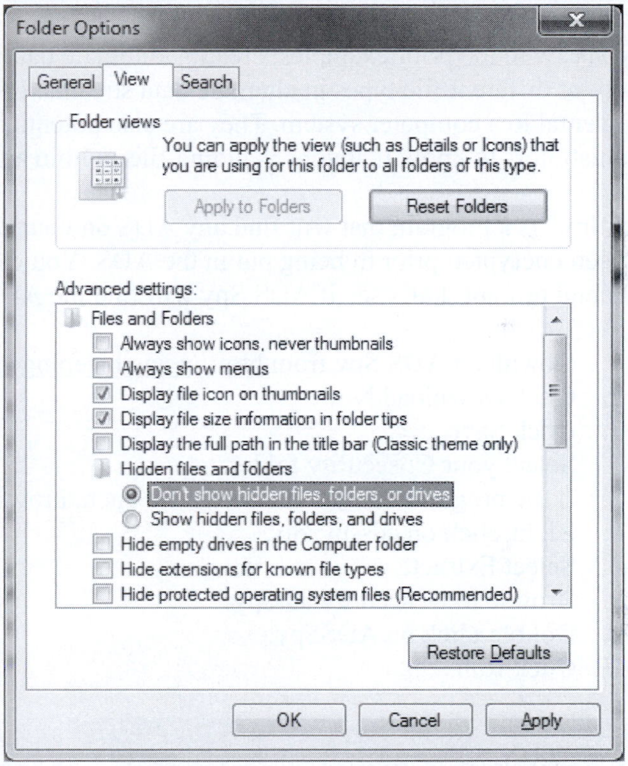

Figure 14-14: Hiding hidden files, folders, and drives.

34. Return to the DOS prompt and type **dir** to get a directory listing. (Hidden.exe should not be visible.)
35. Type **hidden**
36. Take a screenshot of your entire desktop (Ctrl-PrintScreen) with the command prompt and write.exe displayed.

It's interesting to note that you just ran an executable from your C:\security directory that is not visible. The executable itself ("write.exe") is in an ADS for a text file. It's clear that alternate data streams could be used for malicious purposes. In the next project, you will learn how to identify an ADS.

PROJECT QUESTIONS

1. What was the name of your text file?

2. How big was the text file?
3. Was your computer already set to hide all files marked as hidden?
4. Would you prefer to have hidden files always show, or allow them to be hidden? Why?

THOUGHT QUESTIONS

1. Did creating the ADS change the size of the YourNameExecutableADS.txt file?
2. How could a virus use alternate data streams to hide its payload?
3. Can you create an ADS for an executable file (i.e., hide a program within a program)?
4. Could criminals hide illicit material in alternate data streams? Could you get it out?

14.3   ADS SPY®

As you saw in the prior examples, creating alternate data streams is quite easy. You can also hide a variety of different file types in alternate data streams. Hidden files with dangerous payloads can be detrimental to a computer system. They are also potentially large security risks. It's good for systems administrators to know if anyone is hiding files within alternate data streams.

ADS Spy® is a program that will find any ADS on your computer. It won't open the file or decrypt it if it has been encrypted prior to being put in the ADS. You can easily open the ADS yourself from the command prompt. Let's see if ADS Spy will find the ADS we just created in the prior example.

1. Download ADS Spy from http://www.bleepingcomputer.com/files/adsspy.php.
2. Click Download Now.
3. Click Save.
4. Select your C:\security folder.
5. If the program doesn't automatically open, browse to C:\security.
6. Right-click on adsspy.zip.
7. Select Extract.
8. Browse to C:\security\adsspy.
9. Double-click on ADSSpy.exe.
10. Click Run.

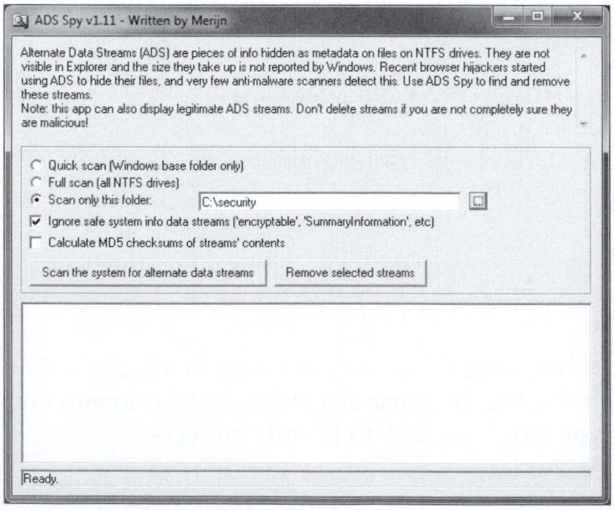

Figure 14-15: Select the folder or drive to scan. 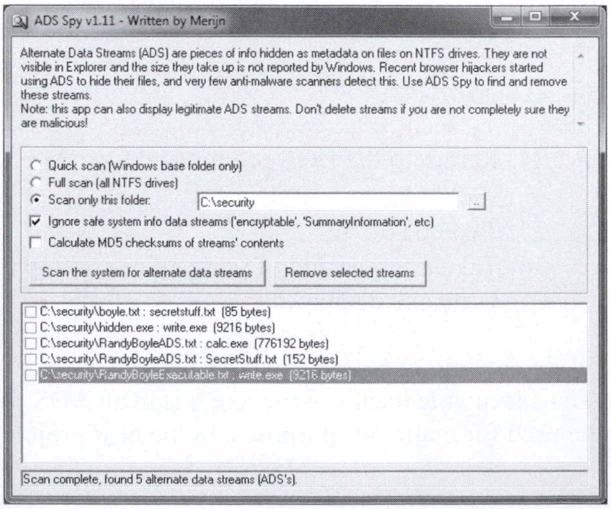   Figure 14-16: Files with ADS are shown.

11. Select the "Scan only this folder" radio button.
12. Browse to C:\security. (See Figure 14-15.)
13. Click OK.
14. Click Scan the system for alternate data streams.
15. Take a screenshot. (See Figure 14-16.)
16. Open a command prompt.
17. Navigate to your C:\security folder.
18. Type `dir /r`
19. Take a screenshot. (You should see all of the visible files, as well as the ADS you have created.) (See Figure 14-17.)

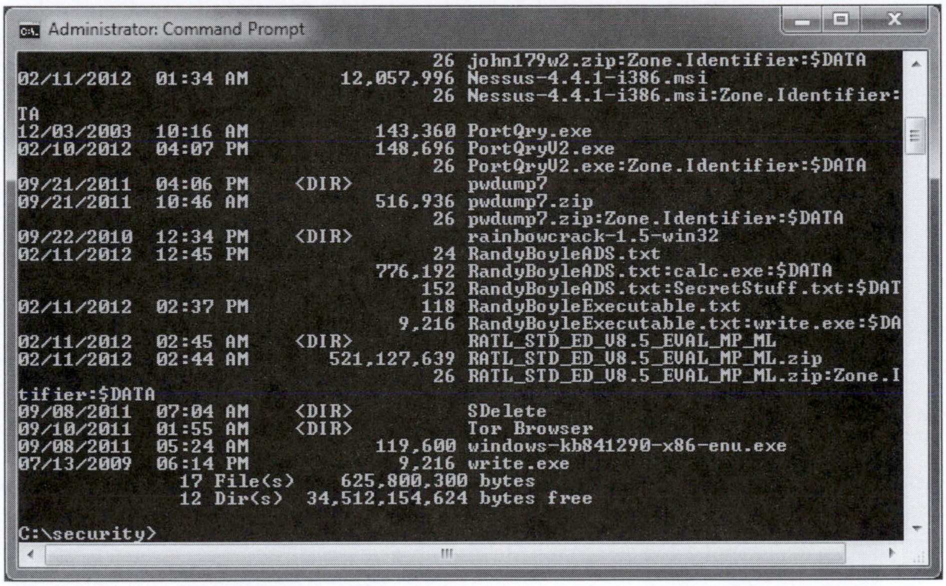

Figure 14-17: Displaying hidden files and ADS.

PROJECT QUESTIONS

1. How many ADSs were found in your C:\security directory?
2. Approximately how many ADSs were displayed in your C:\security directory when you used the dir /r command?
3. Were there other ADSs in your C:\security directory that you didn't create? Name one of them.
4. How big was the write.exe executable shown in your command prompt?

THOUGHT QUESTIONS

1. Do you have additional alternate data streams anywhere on your computer?
2. Why would ADS Spy have the option for calculating MD5 checksums for the stream's contents?
3. Are alternate data streams being used by legitimate system files?
4. Would law enforcement be interested in using ADS Spy? Why?

CHAPTER 15: DATA RECOVERY & SECURE DELETION

chapter 15

After taking an introductory course on IT security, most people say that one of the most useful skills they learned was how to recover a lost file. When a user deletes a file, the file is usually not permanently deleted. Deleting the file marks the space on the hard drive as "free space" where additional files can be written. That means the file is still there, but could be overwritten by a newer file. The programs below try to recover files, or parts of files, that have been deleted and marked as free space.

Whenever you are using a computer, it's a good idea to remember that pretty much everything you are doing can be recorded, logged, or monitored. It's highly likely that more information is being recorded about you than you would like. All your actions, data, secrets, and private information can be stored on a computer for a very long time. The same goes for electronic devices, including cell phones, digital cameras, iPads©, iPods©, etc.

All electronic devices need to be completely destroyed when you are disposing of them. Never throw away a computer or cell phone without pounding the hard drive with a hammer for a minimum of 2 minutes on each side.

The following are programs that can be used to recover data, delete tracking data (e.g., logs, temp files, etc.), and permanently wipe data from your computer. Many of these programs can also be used on other types of media connected to your computer, including USB drives, cameras, and external drives.

Time required to complete this chapter: 40 minutes

Chapter Objectives

Learn how to:
1. Recover deleted files.
2. Securely delete files.
3. Wipe unused HDD space.
4. Remove unwanted files.

Chapter Projects

Project:
15.1 File Recovery (Recuva)
15.2 Secure Deletion (Eraser)
15.3 Clean Up (CCleaner)
15.4 Disk Wipe

Recuva® is a useful program by Piriform®. In the past, file recovery software was somewhat expensive and not very user-friendly. It was a source of revenue for those individuals who had the software and knew how to run it. Their customers were extremely grateful to have their lost data recovered. Recuva scans the entire empty memory space for possible files to recover.

As mentioned above, most users errantly believe that data is gone forever when they empty it from the Recycle Bin. This is incorrect. It merely marks the space as open to be written over if another file needs to be stored. Your operating system writes over these open spaces and subsequently "damages" the previously deleted file. Knowing how a given file (e.g., document, image, database, etc.) is structured so you can easily recover the undamaged part of the file.

Below is a picture of Angel's Landing at Zion National Park in Utah (Figure 15-1). If it were partially written over by another program, it might look like the second image (Figure 15-2). Using a simple hex editor, you can recover partial files that may be damaged and not open automatically with the default application (Figure 15-3).

There is software available that will automatically recover partial images without using a hex editor, but they are not necessarily free. Learning to use a hex editor to recover partial files is beyond the scope of this introductory book, but it is a great skill to have. Let's look at a simple file recovery example using Recuva.

Figure 15-1: Original image.

Figure 15-2: Partial image.

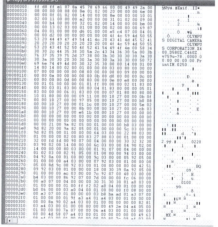
Figure 15-3: Hex editor.

1. Download Recuva from http://www.recuva.com/download.
2. Click Download from FileHippo.com.
3. Click Download Latest Version.
4. Click Save.
5. Select your C:\security folder.
6. If the program doesn't automatically open, browse to your C:\security folder.
7. Right-click the rcsetup142.exe installation program and select Run as administrator. (Due to different versions, the filename may be slightly different than the one listed here. Download the latest version.)
8. Select Run, Ok, Next, I Agree, Install, and Finish.
9. Click Start, Programs, Recuva, and Recuva. (You can also double-click the Recuva desktop icon.)

10. Select the drive from which you want to recover files. (Your C: drive will always work. You can use your USB if you have it handy. Your USB will finish much quicker than your C: drive.) (See Figure 15-4.)
11. Click Scan. (See Figure 15-5.)

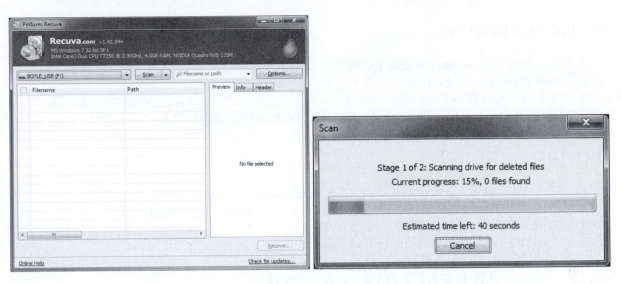

Figure 15-4: Select drive to scan.   Figure 15-5: Recuva scanning a drive.

12. After the scan completes, click on any of the recovered files listed with a graphic extension (e.g., .jpg or .bmp) until you see a picture on the right-hand side of the screen. (If you don't see an image file, you can put a file on your USB, delete it, and then run the scan again. Remember the name of the file you delete, so you can easily find it after you recover it.)
13. Take a screenshot. (See Figure 15-6.)

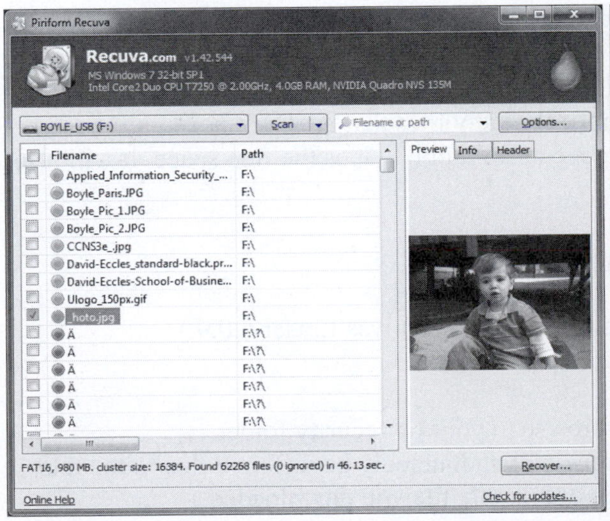

Figure 15-6: Recovered image that was previously deleted. 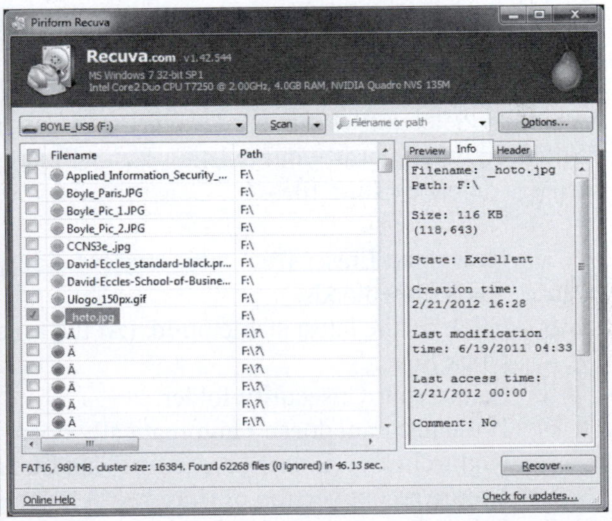   Figure 15-7: Details for a recovered image.

14. Click on the Info tab to see the details for the file.
15. Take a screenshot. (See Figure 15-7.)
16. Check one of the recoverable graphic files. (Even some of the "unrecoverable" files are actually recoverable.)
17. Click Recover.
18. Save it to your desktop.

19. Open the picture you recovered.
20. Take a screenshot.
21. Repeat this process on your USB to confirm that it can recover files on a removable drive.
22. Take a screenshot.

PROJECT QUESTIONS

1. How long did you let the scan run?
2. How many files did it find?
3. Did it recover files from other users?
4. Did you find any files that you thought were permanently deleted?

THOUGHT QUESTIONS

1. Would this work on your cell phone if it were connected to your computer?
2. What effect does the condition of the file have on its ability to be recovered?
3. What other recovery options come with Recuva?
4. Does Recuva have the ability to find a deleted file by its specific file name?

15.2   SECURE DELETION (ERASER®)

It can be disconcerting to learn that files you think were deleted might actually be recoverable. Most people errantly believe they are permanently deleting their files with simple deletion. After finding out how file recovery works, they immediately want to know how to permanently delete their files. It's not that they are trying to hide anything; they may just want to protect their privacy. They have the right to do so. Honestly, most of the people reading this book have visited a website they wish they hadn't.

Individuals and companies also need to make sure all confidential data are deleted from hard drives before they dispose of them. Recovering files from discarded hard drives is extremely easy. Going through someone's garbage is becoming a profitable activity for criminals. Eraser® will delete any previously deleted files on your hard drive. It will not delete any files that have not been previously deleted. In other words, your existing data will not get erased. It only wipes the free space. It will also securely delete existing files.

1. Download Eraser from http://eraser.heidi.ie/.
2. Click Downloads.
3. Click on the latest stable build. (At the time of this writing, it was Eraser 6.0.9.)
4. Click Save.
5. Select your C:\security folder.
6. If the program doesn't automatically open, browse to your C:\security folder.
7. Right-click on Eraser 6.0.9.exe. (This filename will undoubtedly be different due to the release of a more recent version of Eraser. Click on the executable file you downloaded.)
8. Select Run as administrator.
9. Click Next, Accept, Next, Typical, Install, and Finish.
10. Click Start, All Programs, and Eraser. (You can also click on the Eraser icon that was put on your desktop.)
11. Right-click the empty Eraser table and select New Task. (See Figure 15-8.)
12. Click Add Data.
13. Select Unused disk space.
14. Select the drive you want to clean. (A small USB works faster than your hard drive. This example used a small USB.) (See Figure 15-9.)

15. Click OK, and OK.

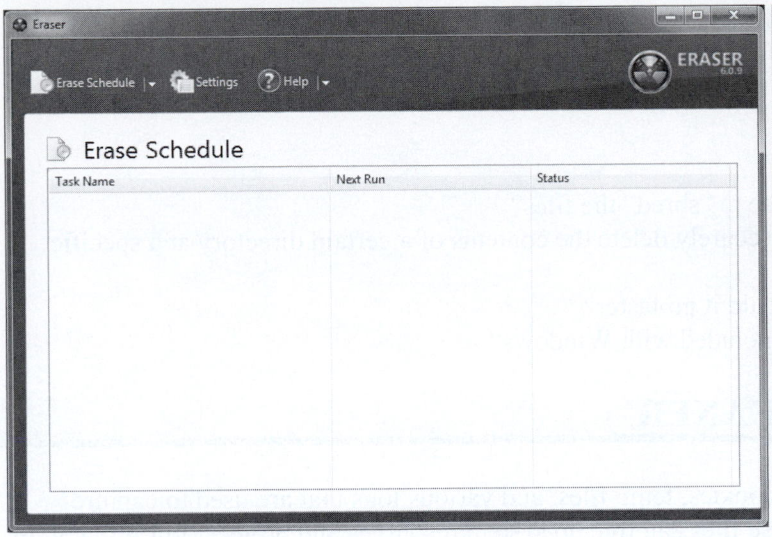

Figure 15-8: Eraser file shredder.

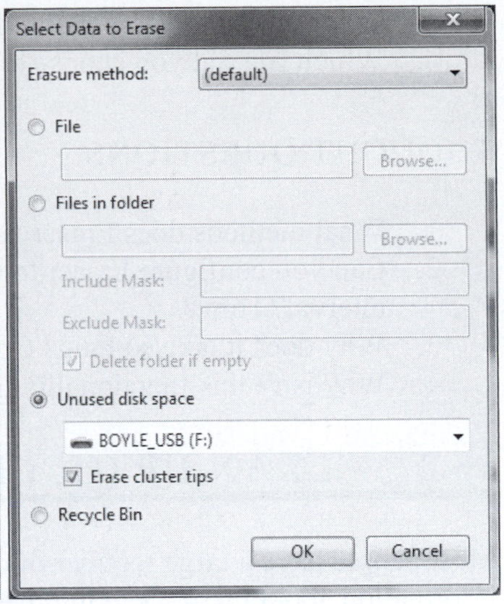

Figure 15-9: Drive selected to clean.

16. Right-click the "Unused disk space" task.
17. Select Run now.
18. Double-click the task labeled "Unused disk space" to see the progress of the wiping.
19. Take a screenshot while it is running. (If it takes too long, you can click Stop. If you selected your C: drive, it will take hours to complete. You can leave it running overnight if you choose.) (See Figure 15-10.)

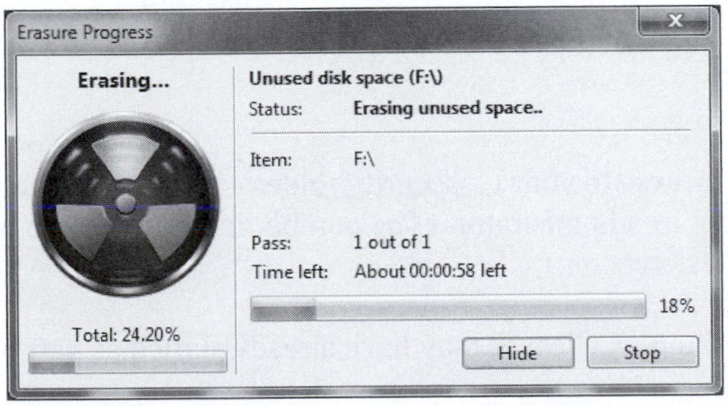

Figure 15-10: Wiping free disk space.

20. Open Windows Explorer (or your file browser). (You can run "explore" or press ⊞+e.)
21. Browse to your C:\security folder.
22. Right-click on any file you want to delete. (You can select any of the prior downloads.)
23. Select Eraser, and Erase.

Note: You won't have to worry about unauthorized data recovery if you pulverize your hard drive with a hammer. Never throw away a hard drive without thoroughly destroying it.

PROJECT QUESTIONS

1. Which drive did you choose?
2. How long did you let it run?
3. What secure deletion method was listed in the Settings menu?
4. Which file did you choose to delete?

THOUGHT QUESTIONS

1. What methods does Eraser use to "shred" the files?
2. Can you configure Eraser to securely delete the contents of a certain directory at a specific interval? How?
3. Why does it take so long? Could it go faster?
4. Why isn't this functionality included with Windows?

15.3   CLEAN UP (CCLEANER®)

Most people have a large number of cookies, temp files, and various logs that are used to capture information about them. Deleting these files can free up system resources and protect your privacy. In addition to deleting your browser history, CCleaner® will also empty your Recycle Bin, Clipboard, memory dumps, etc.

CCleaner is a great free tool that will delete all those annoying files that need to be cleaned up. If you change the configuration settings, CCleaner will delete those files permanently using secure deletion. None of these files will be recoverable after you run CCleaner with secure deletion. The DOD 5220.22-M standard is a sufficient secure deletion standard.

1. Download CCleaner from http://www.piriform.com/CCLEANER.
2. Click Download.
3. Click Download from FileHippo.
4. Click Save.
5. Select your C:\security folder.
6. If the program doesn't automatically open, browse to your C:\security folder.
7. Right-click on ccsetup315.exe and select Run as administrator. (The number in the file name will change with each version. Download the latest version.)
8. Click OK, Next, I Agree, Install, and Finish.
9. Double-click the CCleaner icon on your desktop. (CCleaner may have already started as part of the installation process.)
10. Click Analyze. (It may take several minutes if you are running it for the first time. You may have several files to delete.)
11. Take a screenshot. (See Figure 15-11.)

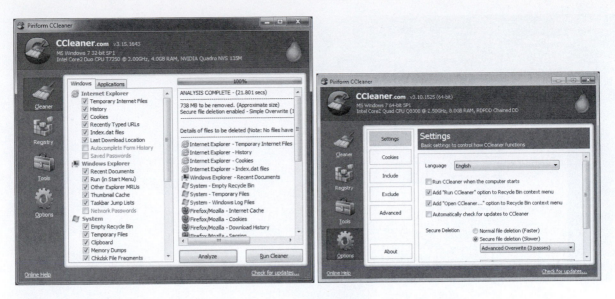

Figure 15-11: Cleaning files with CCleaner.   Figure 15-12: CCleaner settings.

STOP You can skip the next step (Step 12) if you do not wish to delete your temp files, cookies, etc. Temp files remember your passwords when you visit websites and help some pages load faster. Running CCleaner once a week is a good idea. Most people delete about 2 GB of information the first time they run CCleaner.

12. If you choose to delete these files, click Run Cleaner. (If it's your first time, it can take up to 30 minutes if you have lots of junk on your computer.)
13. Take a screenshot and look at how much it deleted. (If you chose not to run CCleaner, you won't take a screenshot.)
14. Click on Options, and Settings.
15. Select Secure file deletion using the Advanced Overwrite (3 passes) method. (See Figure 15-12.)
16. Open your Web browser and click on five of your most commonly visited websites.
17. Go to www.Google.com.
18. Close your Web browser.
19. Go back to CCleaner and click Analyze.
20. Click Options, and Cookies.
21. In the "Cookies to Delete" pane, select Google.com or www.Google.com and press the right arrow to keep the Google cookie. (You just created an exception for the Google cookie.)
22. Take a screenshot. (See Figure 15-13.)

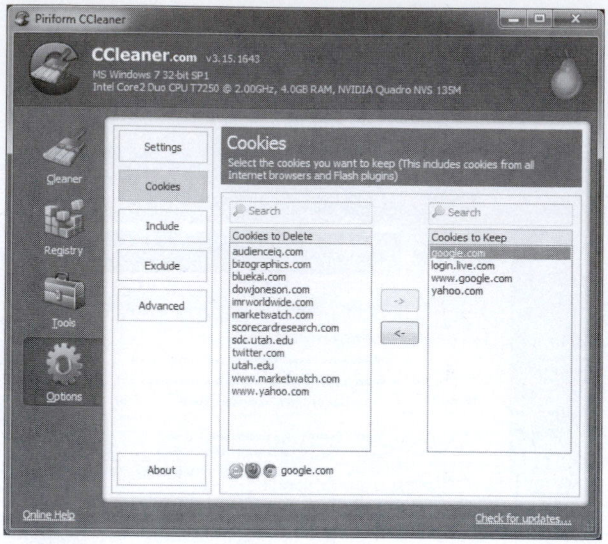

Figure 15-13: Making exceptions for cookies.

PROJECT QUESTIONS

1. From the first analysis you ran, how many MB was CCleaner going to delete?
2. Approximately how many cookies did CCleaner find on your computer?
3. Is there another cookie (e.g., from a bank) that you would want to keep?
4. Can you select specific directories for CCleaner to automatically clean? How?

THOUGHT QUESTIONS

1. Why isn't secure deletion an option included with Microsoft Windows 7?
2. Why are there different levels of secure deletion?
3. Can you set CCleaner to run automatically?
4. Will CCleaner delete other logs in different programs other than Web browsers?

15.4 DISK WIPE®

In prior projects, you learned how to securely delete files. In this project, you will learn how to securely delete (or "wipe") an entire drive. This project uses a USB drive rather than a larger hard drive. Using a USB drive will shorten the amount of time it takes to wipe the drive. You can use Disk Wipe® to wipe any attached drive. If you want to wipe your local hard disk, you may want to consider using a bootable disk like DBAN (Darik's Boot And Nuke).

You will need a USB drive for this project. A smaller USB drive will wipe more quickly than a larger USB drive. You will securely wipe your USB and all data will be lost. Before starting this project, you will need to backup any files on your USB that you may want to keep. After completing the project, you can move your files back to your USB drive.

1. Download Disk Wipe from http://diskwipe.org/.
2. Click Download at the top of the page.
3. Click on the "Click Here to download Disk Wipe" link.
4. Click Save.
5. Select your C:\security folder.

6. If the program doesn't automatically open, browse to your C:\security folder.
7. Right-click on DiskWipe.exe and select Run as administrator.

Important In the following steps, you will be wiping your USB drive. Before starting the following steps, you will need to back up all files from your USB to your local computer. Any files left on your USB will be permanently erased. You will not be able to recover them. You can copy the files back to your USB drive after you have completed the project.

8. Insert a USB drive into your computer.
9. Back up any files from your USB to your local computer. (Everything on your USB will be securely deleted. None of the files on your USB will be recoverable.)
10. Right-click your USB drive and select Rename.
11. Type YourName_USB for the new USB name. (In this case, it was Boyle_USB.)
12. Close Windows Explorer. (If Windows Explorer is still using your USB drive, it may not wipe correctly.)
13. In the Disk Wipe window, select your USB drive. (In this case, it was "Boyle_USB (F:)". Note the file system type.)
14. Click Wipe Disk.
15. Select the File System you would like. (This example changed the file system from FAT to FAT 32. NTFS is also a good option if you have a Windows-based computer.)
16. Deselect Perform Quick Format.
17. Click Next.
18. Select US Department of Defense DoD 5220.22-M(E) (3 passes-slow). (Note how many passes are used in the Guttman erasing pattern.)
19. Press Next.
20. Type "ERASE ALL" in the text box.
21. Click Finish, and Yes. (Make sure Windows Explorer is closed before you click Yes. It can't be accessing your USB drive at the same time.)
22. Take a screenshot while it is formatting your USB.
23. Take another screenshot when it completes. (The secure wiping process may take 10 or more minutes depending on the size and access speed of your USB. You can continue on to another project while it finishes. Formatting an entire hard drive can take many hours.)

PROJECT QUESTIONS

1. What was the name of your USB drive?
2. What was the serial number of your drive?
3. What was the capacity of your USB drive?
4. About how long did it take to format your USB drive?

THOUGHT QUESTIONS

1. Why is there more than one method of securely wiping a disk?
2. Do multiple passes imply more secure deletion? Why?
3. How long might a large hard drive take to securely wipe? Why?
4. Should you securely wipe your hard drive before you throw it away? Why?

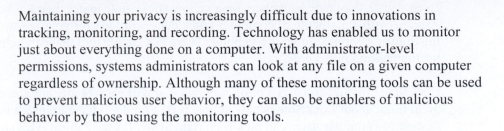

CHAPTER 16: CRYPTOGRAPHY

Maintaining your privacy is increasingly difficult due to innovations in tracking, monitoring, and recording. Technology has enabled us to monitor just about everything done on a computer. With administrator-level permissions, systems administrators can look at any file on a given computer regardless of ownership. Although many of these monitoring tools can be used to prevent malicious user behavior, they can also be enablers of malicious behavior by those using the monitoring tools.

As people learn more about the extent to which they are being monitored, they search out ways to protect their privacy. They don't necessarily have anything to hide, but are merely trying to maintain their privacy. In a business setting, there is often confidential information that must be kept secret to sustain a competitive advantage. There are many legitimate reasons for wanting privacy.

In the following section, we will look at some simple tools that can help you keep your information private. We will also look at an Enigma® simulator that works just like the original Enigma machines used in WWII.

There are many excellent books written about cryptography (e.g., Practical Cryptography by Bruce Schneier). This entire book could be filled with modern cryptography examples and projects. Cryptographers spend their entire lives studying cryptography and implementing cryptographic systems.

However, as this is an introductory IT security book, we will look at just a few basic examples. Hopefully they will inspire you to learn more about cryptography and how it works.

Time required to complete this chapter: 60 minutes

Chapter Objectives

Learn how to:
1. Access an encrypted file.
2. Encrypt files.
3. Compress and encrypt files.
4. Use an encryption device.
5. Create an encrypted virtual drive.
6. Encode and decode text.
7. Create encrypted external media.
8. Use encrypted email.

Chapter Projects

Project:
16.1 Locknote
16.2 AxCrypt
16.3 Compress and Encrypt (7-Zip)
16.4 Enigma
16.5 TrueCrypt
16.6 Cryptool 2
16.7 Encrypted USB (TrueCrypt)
16.8 Encrypted email (Hushmail)

Users often keep a list of their usernames and passwords written on a piece of paper near their computer. Even worse, they may keep them on a yellow sticky note under their keyboard. This is not a good idea. Anyone with a modicum of computer knowledge will look for your passwords under your keyboard or in the drawer right next to your computer. There is a simple tool that can help you remember all those usernames and passwords.

LockNote® by Steganos® is a basic program that will encrypt any amount of text with a password. The great thing about LockNote is how simple it is. You don't have to install or configure anything. Even the newest of computer users can pick it up right away. It uses 256-bit AES so you don't have to worry about it being cracked. Let's look at a simple example.

1. Download LockNote from http://sourceforge.net/projects/locknote/.
2. Click Download.
3. Click Save.
4. Select your C:\security folder.
5. If the program doesn't automatically open, browse to your C:\security folder.
6. Right-click the locknote-1.0.5-src+binary-win32.zip file and select Extract All. (The version number will change with new releases. Download the latest version.)
7. Browse to C:\security\locknote-1.0.5-src+binary-win32\LockNote 1.0.5.
8. Copy LockNote.exe.
9. Paste LockNote.exe onto your Desktop.

Note: In this example, we saved LockNote to your desktop to make it easier for you to access your usernames and passwords when you need them. You can save it in any directory you'd like.

10. Double-click the LockNote icon on your desktop.
11. Click Run.
12. Delete the text in the LockNote window.
13. Enter YourName and the words "Username and Password" three times. (In this example, it was Randy Boyle.) (See Figure 16-1.)
14. Click File, Exit, and Yes.
15. Enter a password you can remember. (In this example, we entered "tiger1234" for the password.) (See Figure 16-2.)
16. Click OK.
17. Double-click the LockNote icon on the desktop again to see the text you just saved.

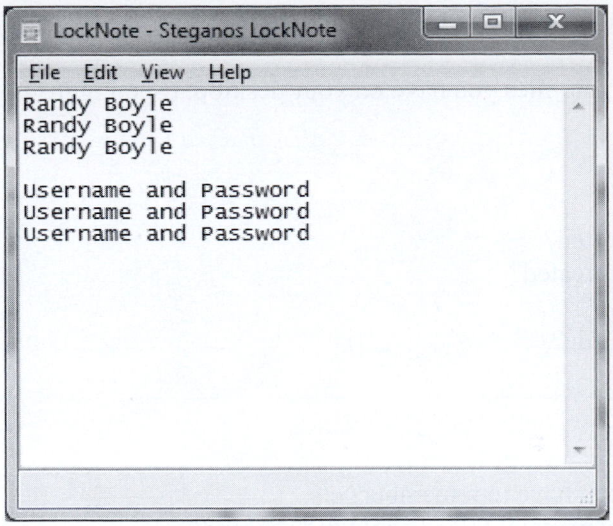

Figure 16-1: Entering text into LockNote.

Figure 16-2: Choose a password.

18. Enter the password you used (in this example, "tiger1234" without quotes). (See Figure 16-3.)
19. Click OK.
20. Take a screenshot of the unlocked LockNote screen.
21. Click File, and Save As.
22. Enter YourNameLockNote and leave the file type blank. (In this example, it was RandyBoyleLockNote.)
23. Save it to your desktop.
24. Enter the same password you used in the prior example when prompted.
25. Take a screenshot of your desktop showing both the original LockNote.exe program and the new YourNameLockNote file. (See Figure 16-4.)

Figure 16-3: Enter your password.

Figure 16-4: New LockNote file.

Figure 16-5: New LockNote file.

26. Right-click on your desktop.
27. Select New, and Text Document.
28. Name the new text file YourNameSecrets.txt. (Don't forget to add the .txt extension. In this case, the file name was RandyBoyleSecrets.txt.)
29. Double-click on the text document you just created.
30. Enter YourName and the words "Secret Stuff" in the text document.
31. Click File, and Save.
32. Click File, and Exit.
33. Drag-and-drop the file named YourNameSecrets.txt on top of the LockNote.exe icon.
34. Click Yes.

35. Enter the same password again (in this case, "tiger1234" without quotes).
36. Click OK, and OK.
37. Take a screenshot showing all three LockNote files you have on your desktop. (See Figure 16-5.)

PROJECT QUESTIONS

1. What was the name of the first file you created?
2. What was the name of the second file you created?
3. What was the password you used?
4. How big was your new "secret" LockNote file?

THOUGHT QUESTIONS

1. How many usernames and passwords do you have to remember?
2. If someone "discovered" your password, how many logins could they access?
3. If you lost the paper with all your passwords on it, could you remember them all?
4. Do people other than yourself have physical access to your computer?

16.2 AXCRYPT®

In the prior example, we looked at encrypting simple text within a single file. What would you do if you had to encrypt more than just text? Do you have sensitive files, such as databases, documents, spreadsheets, images, programs, logs, etc., that you need to keep confidential? Most businesses have files on their computers that they know must be encrypted. They just don't know how to encrypt them. Once you see how easy encrypting files can be, you might start using it on a regular basis.

AxCrypt® is a simple and powerful encryption tool. To use it, you select the files you want encrypted, enter your password, and you're done. It is even available as an option when you right-click a file. If you open an encrypted file for editing, AxCrypt will automatically re-encrypt the file after you are done editing it. It also has the ability to permanently "shred" files. It is an open source application that uses 128-bit AES.

1. Download AxCrypt from http://www.axantum.com/AxCrypt/.
2. Click Download.
3. Click on the appropriate version for your operating system. (In this case, it was AxCrypt-1.7.2931.0-Setup.exe. Download the latest version available.)
4. Click Save.
5. Select the C:\security folder.
6. If the program doesn't automatically open, browse to your C:\security folder.
7. Right-click on AxCrypt-Setup.exe.
8. Click Run as administrator.
9. Click Yes, if prompted.
10. Click I Agree.
11. Click Custom Installation.
12. Deselect all the bloatware from Amazon.
13. Click Install.
14. Deselect Register.
15. Click Finish.

Note: At this point, you will need to save all your work, exit all other programs, and reboot your computer. Once your computer is rebooted, you can continue on to the next step.

16. Open Windows Explorer.
17. Browse to C:\security.
18. Right-click the file named YourName.txt. (You can create the file if necessary.) (See Figure 16-6.)
19. Select AxCrypt, and Encrypt.
20. Enter the password "tiger1234" without quotes.
21. Click OK.

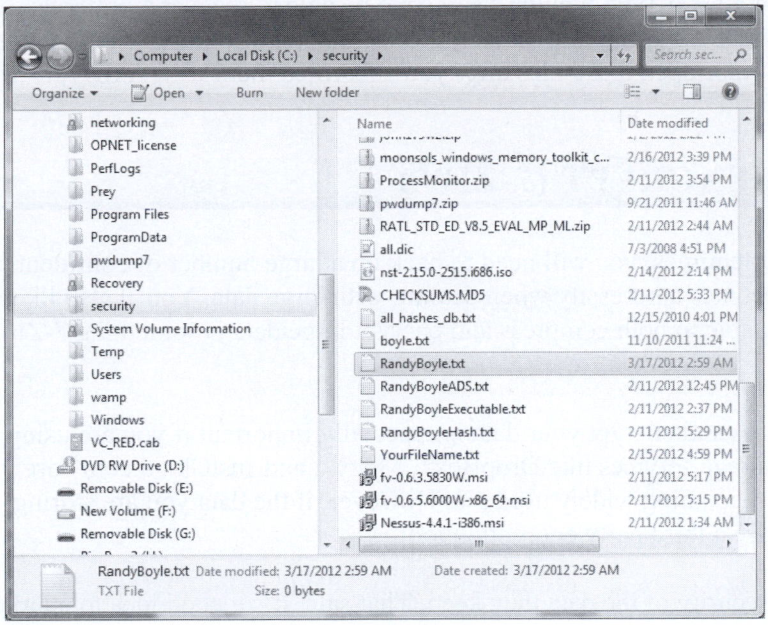

Figure 16-6: Select file to encrypt.

22. Double-click the new YourName-txt.axx file you just created.
23. Enter the password "tiger1234" without quotes.
24. Click OK.
25. Close the text file that you just opened.
26. In Windows Explorer, highlight the YourName-txt.axx file.
27. Take a screenshot.
28. Right-click the file named YourName-txt.axx.
29. Select AxCrypt, and Decrypt.
30. Enter the password "tiger1234" without quotes.
31. Click OK.
32. Right-click the file named YourName.txt. (This time you're going to make an executable file that can be opened by anyone. Axcrypt won't be necessary to be able to open the .exe.)
33. Select AxCrypt, and Encrypt copy to .EXE.
34. Enter the password "tiger1234" without quotes.
35. Click OK.
36. In Windows Explorer, highlight the YourName-txt.exe file.
37. Take a screenshot.

PROJECT QUESTIONS

1. What was the name of the first file you encrypted?

2. What password did you use to encrypt the file?
3. What was the name of the executable you created?
4. How big was the executable you created?

THOUGHT QUESTIONS

1. Why would you need an encrypted file that self-extracts (i.e., an .EXE)?
2. Will AxCrypt work on multiple files, or entire directories or folders?
3. Even if you encrypted a file with AxCrypt, wouldn't someone be able to recover a previous version of the file with a file recovery program? (Hint: AxCrypt has a built-in shredder.)
4. Could your network administrator open these files after you encrypted them with AxCrypt? Why not?

16.3 COMPRESS AND ENCRYPT (7-ZIP®)

Backing up data is a common task. Oftentimes, you will need to back up a large number of confidential files and directories. Compression becomes a necessity when dealing with large data. You'll also likely need to store the data securely. Being able to both compress and encrypt large data is something 7-Zip® can do well.

Using a program like 7-Zip to compress and encrypt your data is especially important if you are using cloud-based online storage. Online storage services like DropBox®, Mozy®, and JustCloud.com® are innovative and feature-rich. They are becoming widely used too. However, if the data you are storing online is sensitive, you may want to use a third party encryption tool.

All online storage providers tout the security of the data they keep. That said, it's a good idea to encrypt all of your data regardless of their security procedures. Encrypting the data twice won't hurt. Personally ensuring the security of your own data is preferred. 7-Zip allows you to do this easily and quickly.

1. Download 7-Zip from http://www.7-zip.org.
2. Click Download.
3. Click on the appropriate version for your operating system. (In this case, it was the 64-bit Windows version. Download the latest version available.)
4. Click Save.
5. Select the C:\security folder.
6. If the program doesn't automatically open, browse to your C:\security folder.
7. Right-click on 7z920-x64.msi.
8. Click Install, Run, Next, I accept, Next, Next, Install, and Finish.
9. Click Start, All Programs, 7-Zip, and 7-Zip File Manager.
10. Double-click Computer, C:, and your C:\security folder. (You should see several files in this directory with your name on them.)
11. Right-click any file and select Create File.
12. Name the file YourNameSecretFile.txt. (In this case, it was RandyBoyleSecretFile.txt.)
13. Select the file you just created and one other larger file. (You can select as many other files as you'd like. In this case, the Nessus installer and the new text file were chosen.)
14. Click the Add button. (See Figure 16-7.)
15. In the upper text box, name the archive YourNameSecureBackup. (In this case, it was RandyBoyleSecureBackup.7z.)
16. Enter a password twice.
17. Note the encryption method used. (In this case, AES-256.)
18. Select the "Encrypt file names" option.

19. Take a screenshot. (See Figure 16-8.)

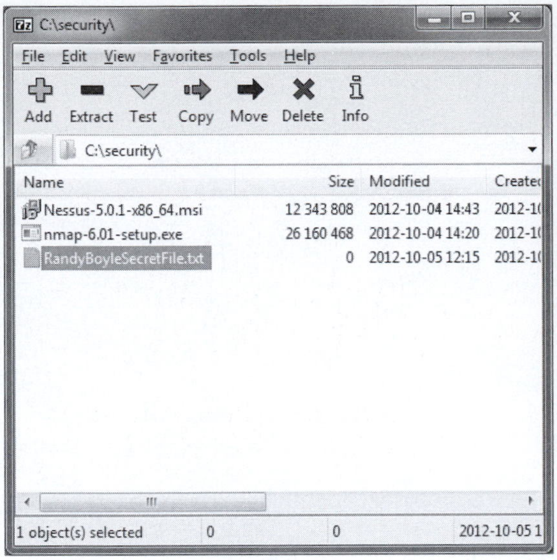

Figure 16-7: Creating a new secret text file.

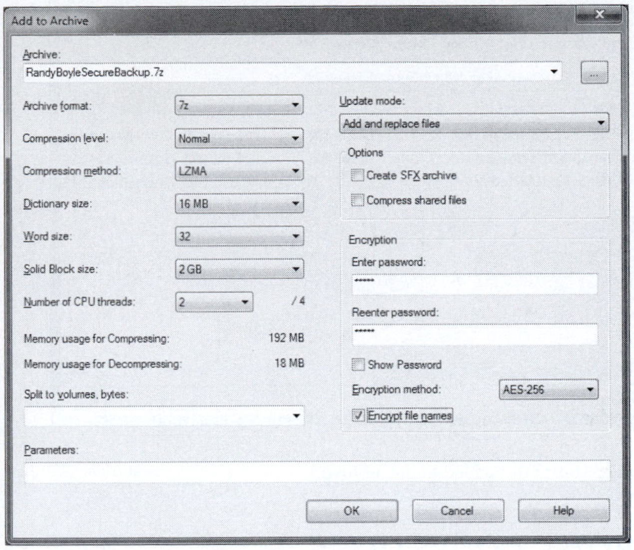

Figure 16-8: Encrypting the backup file.

20. Click OK.
21. Close the 7-Zip File Manager window.
22. Open Windows Explorer.
23. Browse to your C:\security folder.
24. Right-click the file labeled YourNameSecureBackup.7z. (In this case, it was RandyBoyleSecureBackup.7z.)
25. Select 7-Zip, and Extract to YourNameSecureBackup\. (In this case, it was RandyBoyleSecureBackup\.
26. Enter your password.
27. Click OK. (Note that a new folder was created in your C:\security folder containing the compressed files.)
28. Right-click any other file in your C:\security folder. (In this case, it was the Nmap installer.)
29. Select 7-Zip, and Add to archive.
30. Change the upper Archive drop-down to show your secure backup file named YourNameSecureBackup.7z. (In this case, it was RandyBoyleSecureBackup.7z.)
31. Click OK.
32. Enter the password you set.
33. Click OK.
34. Right-click the file named YourNameSecureBackup.7z.
35. Select 7-Zip, and Open archive.
36. Enter the password you set.
37. Click OK.
38. Take a screenshot showing the additional file in the secure backup file. (In this case, the Nmap installer was added to the archive.) (See Figure 16-9.)

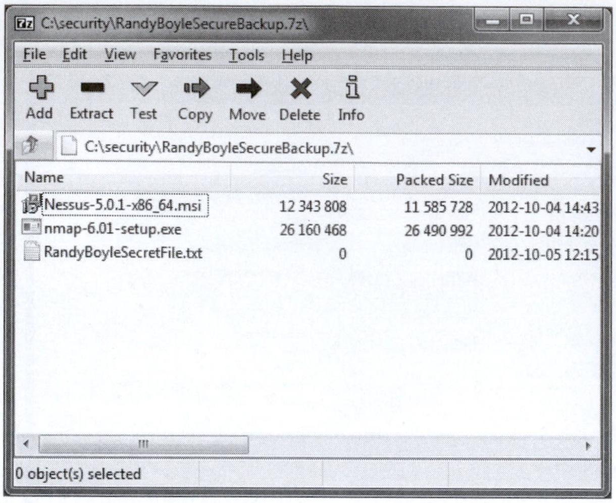

Figure 16-9: Files added to the archive.

PROJECT QUESTIONS

1. What was the name of the secret file you created?
2. What was the name of the secure backup file (i.e., the .7z) you created?
3. How many characters were in your password?
4. Which file did you add to the secure backup file?

THOUGHT QUESTIONS

1. Why is it important to encrypt all archive or backup files?
2. Why is it important to encrypt file names?
3. Is it still important to use a strong password, even if you are using AES-256 encryption? Why?
4. Why might it be important to encrypt your own backup files, rather than relying on a third party?

16.4   ENIGMA®

Below is an illustration of the Enigma® machine simulator, which functions exactly like the Enigma encryption machines used during WWII. This example has been included to help you better understand how encryption actually worked in the early days, and to inspire you to learn more about cryptography.

This project is more for learning, entertainment, and historical purposes. It's a great learning tool when you first start exploring the subject of cryptography and how it actually works. Young children find this project fairly interesting after you show them how they can send messages to their friends (as long as they both have access to the same simulator, of course). This project will use an online Enigma simulator, but you can download a much more realistic looking simulator, with interchangeable rotors, from here: http://users.telenet.be/d.rijmenants/en/enigmasim.htm.

Enigma machines provided fairly good encryption strength for their day. Modern cryptographic systems are much more secure than Enigma machines. However, Enigma machines are more fun to watch. Let's look at the basic functionality of an Enigma machine.

1. Open a Web browser and go to http://enigmaco.de/enigma/enigma.swf.
2. Use the left and right arrows to move each of the top three rotors so that each has the letter "A" selected in blue. (See Figure 16-10.)
3. Click in the Input text box in the bottom of your screen.
4. Slowly type your first name and last name without a space. (In this case, it was RandyBoyle. If you make a typing error, you can start over by pressing the Backspace key.)
5. Take a screenshot. (See Figure 16-11.)

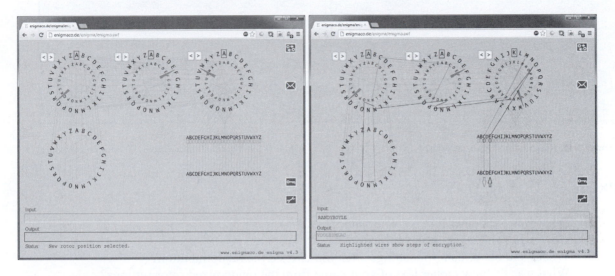

Figure 16-10: Start Enigma with "AAA" settings.   Figure 16-11: Your name encrypted.

Note: Pay attention to the colored paths as you type. The red path goes through the three rotors, bounces off the reflector, becomes green, and then goes back through the three rotors. The right rotor moves with each keystroke. If it completes one full cycle, it will advance the middle rotor and subsequently the left rotor.

Note: The text in the Input text box is what you typed. The text in the Output text box is what you would send. You are now going to reset the dials to their original position (in this case, AAA) and type the *encrypted* text (or cipher text) you produced in the Output text box. You can copy the cipher text from the screenshot you just took. Subsequently, you should see your name reproduced in the bottom box. This is the equivalent of decrypting the message.

6. Click in the Input text box and Backspace your name. (The rotors should be set back to their AAA position.)
7. Refer back to the screenshot you just took and copy down the output (i.e., the cipher text). (In this case, the cipher text for "RANDYBOYLE" was "VDOLZYMEAC.")
8. Type the cipher text into the Input text box. (Type slowly so you won't make a mistake and have to start over!)
9. Take a screenshot with your name showing in the Output text box. (See Figure 16-12.)
10. Backspace the text in the Input text box.
11. Slowly press the A key ten times and notice how a different encrypted letter is chosen as output through the rotating dials even though you are hitting the same key each time.
12. Take a screenshot. (See Figure 16-13.)
13. Click the wrench icon in the bottom right-hand of your screen.
14. Click Random.
15. Type your name again in the Input text box.
16. Take a screenshot of the new cipher text using the random rotor settings.

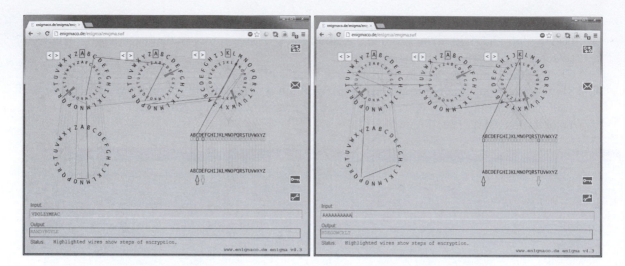

Figure 16-12: Reset dials to "AAA" settings.   Figure 16-13: Your name decrypted by entering encrypted text.

PROJECT QUESTIONS

1. What was the cipher text for your name?
2. How many characters was your name?
3. What were the three rotor settings after you clicked the random button?
4. What was the new cipher text of your name from the randomized rotor settings?

THOUGHT QUESTIONS

1. How does an Enigma machine compare with modern cryptographic systems? (Hint: If the wiring scheme is known, the number of possible combinations is 10^{23}, or about 76 bits.)
2. Could modern computers crack a message sent using an Enigma machine?
3. What factor(s) determines how long a computer would take to crack a cryptographic system?
4. Why is a different letter chosen each time even though you keep hitting the same key?

16.5   TRUECRYPT®

TrueCrypt® makes the process of securing your private files easy. Using TrueCrypt, you can create a mountable virtual drive from a file on your existing C: drive. The new virtual drive is fully encrypted. You can just drag-and-drop your files into this new drive. Once you are done using the files on the encrypted drive, you just unmount the drive with TrueCrypt.

After unmounting the drive, it will look like a normal (and big) file again. All your data is safely encrypted. If you want to access the files, you simply use TrueCrypt to mount the drive again. The ability to move files directly to another drive without having to enter a password for each individual file saves a great deal of time. TrueCrypt reduces the overall load on users. TrueCrypt is a great solution if you are working with a large number of files that need to be encrypted.

TrueCrypt can also encrypt your entire hard drive, USB, or a partition. The best part about TrueCrypt is its price. It's free.

1. Download TrueCrypt from http://www.truecrypt.org/downloads.
2. Click Download for the Windows version. (There are also versions for Mac OS and Linux.)

3. Click Save.
4. Select your C:\security folder.
5. If the program doesn't automatically open, browse to your C:\security folder.
6. Right-click on TrueCrypt Setup 7.1a.exe and select Run as administrator.
7. Click I Accept, Next, Next, Install, OK, No, and Finish.
8. Double-click the TrueCrypt icon on your desktop.
9. Click Tools, and Volume Creation Wizard.
10. Click Next, Next, and Select File.
11. Browse to your C:\security folder.
12. Select any text file with your name showing. (You can create a new text file if one doesn't exist. In this case, it's RandyBoyle.txt.)
13. Click OK.
14. Take a screenshot. (See Figure 16-14.)
15. Click Next.
16. Note the encryption algorithm used.
17. Click Next.
18. Enter 20 MB for the size of the container. (See Figure 16-15.)
19. Click Next.

Figure 16-14: Select file to act as a hidden encrypted drive.   Figure 16-15: Select the size of the new hidden drive.

20. Enter a password that you can remember. (In this case, "tiger1234" without quotes.)
21. Click Next, Format, Yes, OK, and Exit. (The TrueCrypt Volume Creation Wizard will close, but the main TrueCrypt window should still be open.)
22. Click on the Q: drive. (You can select any available drive.)
23. Click Select File.
24. Browse to your C:\security folder.
25. Select the text file you chose earlier. (In this case, it was RandyBoyle.txt.)
26. Click Open.
27. Click Mount. (See Figure 16-16.)
28. Enter the password you chose earlier.
29. Click OK.
30. Open Windows Explorer.
31. Drag-and-drop any file from your C:\security folder to the newly created drive. (In this case, the Q: drive).
32. Take a screenshot. (See Figure 16-17.)
33. Close Windows Explorer.

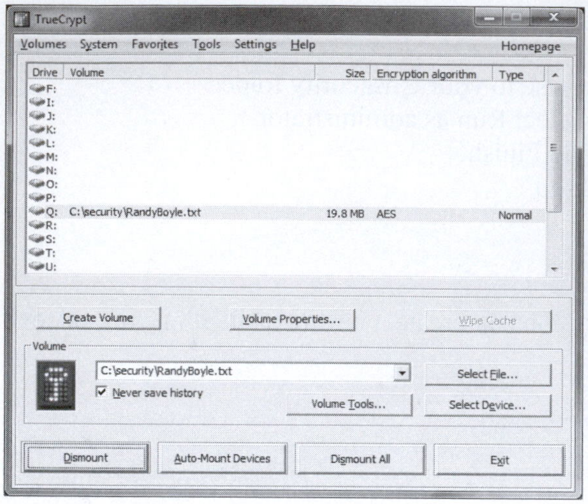

Figure 16-16: Mount the new volume.

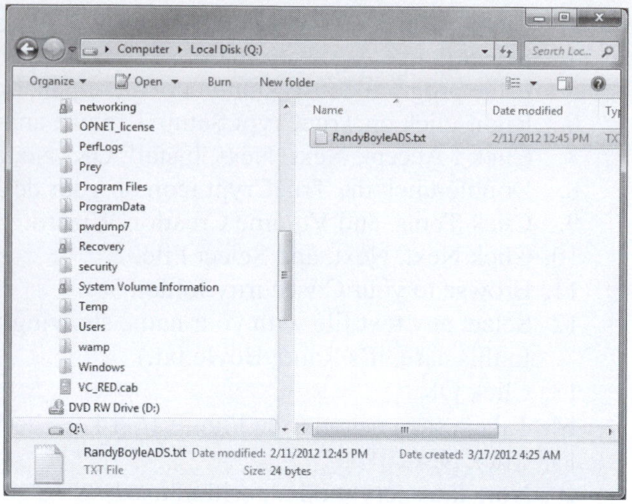

Figure 16-17: Copy file to the new drive.

34. Back in TrueCrypt, click on the Q: drive.
35. Click Dismount.
36. Open Windows Explorer.
37. Browse to your C:\security folder.
38. Note the size of the text file you selected earlier. (In this case, RandyBoyle.txt is now 20MB.)
39. Take a screenshot showing your new text file.

PROJECT QUESTIONS

1. What was the name of the file you used?
2. Which drive letter did you choose?
3. Which file did you move over to your TrueCrypt virtual drive?
4. Which encryption algorithm was used to encrypt the file?

THOUGHT QUESTIONS

1. What would you see if you opened the text file you used in this project?
2. What is the purpose of a "hidden" volume? (This was an option when you created the first volume.)
3. What are keyfiles and how do they work?
4. Can TrueCrypt encrypt an entire drive (e.g., an external hard drive)?

16.6   CRYPTOOL V2®

Cryptography can be a daunting subject for students. It has a specific terminology, lengthy history, a variety of well known ciphers, as well as numerous custom ciphers, and a necessary math component. All of these can discourage students from exploring the subject more fully.

In reality, cryptography and cryptanalysis are less cumbersome than they might appear at first glance. If students can overcome the terminology hurdle, they often find cryptography a fascinating subject. The tool shown below (CrypTool v2®) allows students to visually see how cryptography and cryptanalysis work. It shows specific cryptographic processes and their respective data flows (i.e., inputs and outputs).

In this project, you will encrypt text using a simple Caesar cipher, run a frequency test, determine the key length used to encrypt it, and then decrypt it. CrypTool v2 is a feature-rich tool with many other ciphers and cryptanalysis functions. If you find cryptography interesting, this is a fun place to start learning.

1. Download CrypTool v2 from http://www.cryptool.org/en/cryptool2.
2. Click Downloads.
3. Click on the download link for the latest stable release. (In this case, it was CrypTool 2, Beta 8b, build 4805.1. A later release might be available for download.)
4. Click Save.
5. Select your C:\security folder.
6. If the program doesn't automatically open, browse to your C:\security folder.
7. Right-click on Setup CrypTool 2.0. (Beta 8b – Build 4805.1).exe and select Run as administrator. (The build version will undoubtedly be different than the one shown here. New builds are continuously released. Download the latest version.)
8. Click OK, Next, I Agree, Next, Next, Next, Next, Install, and Close.

Note: You will need Microsoft .NET Framework 4 to run CrypTool 2. It's likely that your computer already has it. If CrypTool v2 won't run because you don't have .NET 4.0 installed, you can get it from the following link: http://www.microsoft.com/en-us/download/details.aspx?displaylang=en&id=17718. You can also do an Internet search for "Microsoft .NET Framework 4 installer".

9. Double-click the CrypTool 2.0 icon on your desktop. (You can also access it through your Start menu.)
10. Click Cryptography, Classic, and Caesar Cipher. (You can turn off the lower Log pane by clicking the Log button in the top ribbon.) (See Figure 16-18.)
11. Add the text "AAA YourName" to the beginning of the Text Input component. (In this case, it was "AAA RandyBoyle The quick brown fox jumps over the lazy dog.")
12. In the center component labeled "Caesar," change the "Key as integer" box to read zero (0). (This will prevent the text from being encrypted, or in this case, shifted.)
13. Click Play and then Stop. (See Figure 16-19.)
14. Take a screenshot. (Note that the text in the Input text box is the same as the text in the Output text box. If they are not the same, you may have forgotten to change the Key in the Caesar component to zero [0].)

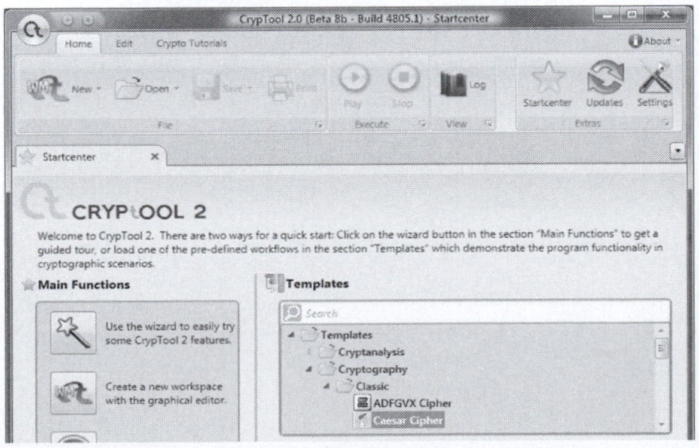

Figure 16-18: CrypTool 2 Startcenter.

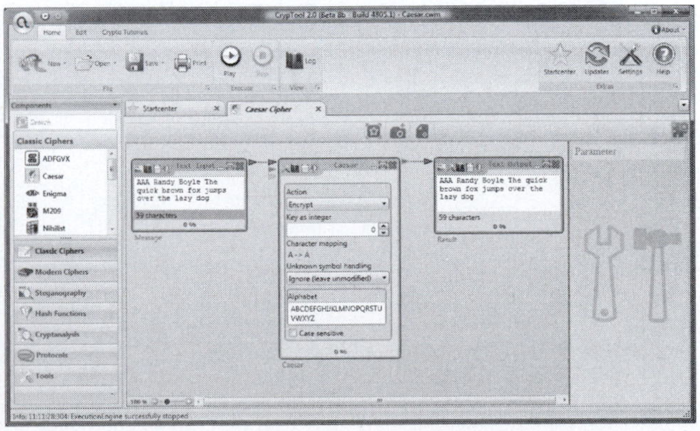

Figure 16-19: The Caesar cipher template before starting.

15. In the center component labeled "Caesar," change the "Key as integer" box to read three (3). (This will shift the text three characters to the right down the alphabet. The "AAA" will read "DDD" in the Output text box if you do it correctly.)
16. Click Play and then Stop.

17. Take a screenshot. (See Figure 16-20.)

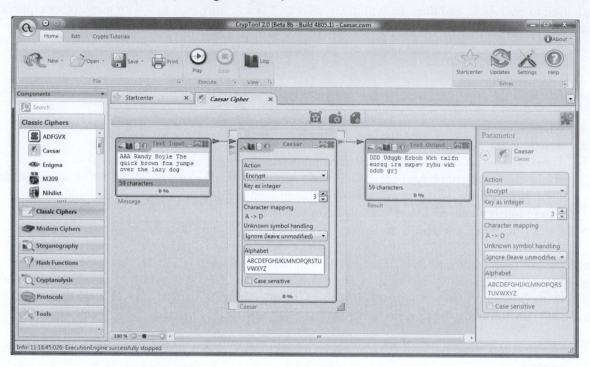

Figure 16-20: Testing the Caesar cipher.

18. Open a Web browser and go to www.Google.com.
19. Click News.
20. Click on any news story that interests you.
21. Select the text of the article.
22. Copy and paste the text from your Web browser into the Input text box in CrypTool 2. (In this case, it was an article about the Nobel Prize in Physics from CNET with 2,794 characters.)
23. Add the text "AAA YourName" to the beginning of the Text Input component showing your news article. (In this case, it was "AAA RandyBoyle Two researchers received the Nobel...")
24. Click Play and then Stop.
25. Take a screenshot. (See Figure 16-21.)

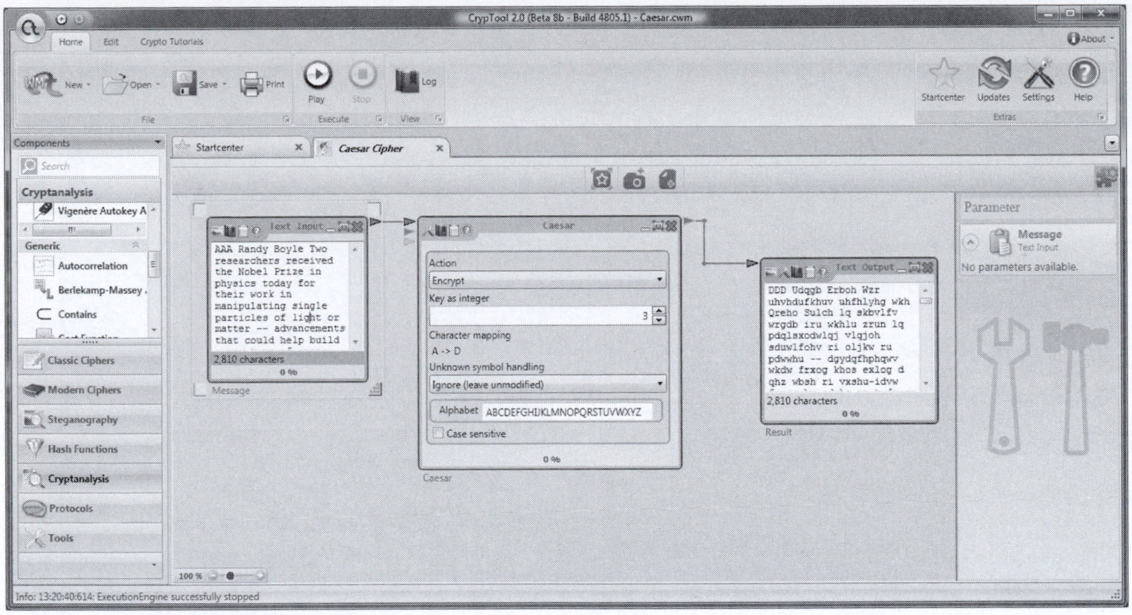

Figure 16-21: Encrypting a news article.

Note: You have successfully used the Caesar cipher to encrypt some plain text into cipher text. In the next step, you will perform some basic cryptanalysis to see if you can automatically decrypt the cipher text. You will use frequency analysis to see which letters occur most often in the cipher text. The frequency of the letters used in the message may give an indication of how many times the message was "shifted."

The letter "E" is used most commonly in the English language. Watch for a large spike in the frequency chart. This large spike should be the letter "E," and provide us with an indication of how many shifts occurred.

26. Click Cryptanalysis in the left-hand pane.
27. Drag-and-drop the Frequency Test icon onto the center workspace.
28. Resize the Frequency Test component by dragging the bottom right-hand corner until you can see the words "No data available yet" displayed. (You can move the components by grabbing the corner boxes.)
29. Drag-and-drop the triangle on the top-right corner of the Caesar Cipher component down to the top-left of the Frequency Test component. (You should see a green box telling you that this is an acceptable connection to make. You should see a path from the Caesar Cipher component to the Frequency Test component.)
30. Click Play and then Stop. (See Figure 16-22.)

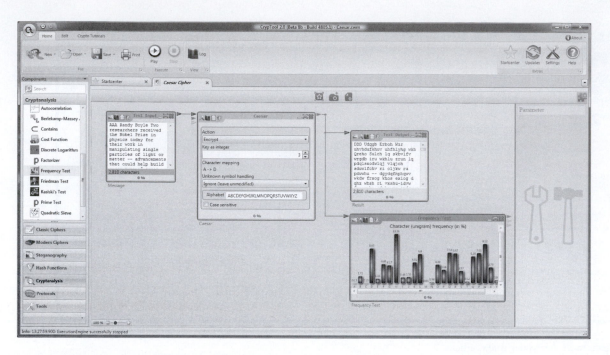

Figure 16-22: Running frequency analysis on the cipher text.

Note: Clicking on each componenet will change the changeable parameter values shown in the right-hand parameter pane.

Note: You should see a spike in the number of occurrences in the letter "H" in your cipher text. The spike should have occurred in letter "E." This leads us to believe that the entire alphabet may have been shifted three times to the right. Other letters in the alphabet have similar predictable patterns. Given these patterns, we can make a good guess about how many times the text was shifted (i.e., the key was used).

In the next step, you will use a cryptanalysis tool (Caesar Analyser) designed specifically for the Caesar cipher. It will take the frequencies from the Frequency Test and the cipher text to determine the likely number of shifts. The output of the Caesar Analyser will be an integer (in this case, 3). You will then send this integer to another Caesar cipher component for *decryption*, not encryption.

You may have to resize and move your components around. Refer to the figures below to make sure you are making the connections correctly. You will see a green progress bar at the bottom of each component telling you if it is working correctly.

31. Click Cryptanalysis in the left-hand pane.
32. Drag-and-drop the Caesar Analyser icon onto the center workspace.
33. Resize the Caesar Analyser component by dragging the bottom right-hand corner until you can see the words "Language German" displayed. (You can move the components by grabbing the corner boxes.)
34. Change the Language option to English.

Note: You can click on the Data icon on each of the components to see the data, and data type, which is associated with each input/output arrow. The Data icon is the little white chipboard in the top left-hand of each component.

35. Drag-and-drop the triangle on the top right corner of the Caesar Cipher component down to the top left of the Caesar Analyser component (upper triangle). (You should see a green box telling

you that this is an acceptable connection to make. You should see a path from the Caesar Cipher component to the Caesar Analyser component. They should both be light grey arrows.)

36. Drag-and-drop the triangle on the top right corner (top of the three, in grey) of the Frequency Test component up to the top left of the Caesar Analyser component (second arrow down, dark grey). (You should see a green box telling you that this is an acceptable connection to make. You should see a path from the Frequency Test component to the Caesar Analyser component.)

37. Click Play.

38. Hover over the turquois arrow on the right-hand side of the Caesar Analyser to see its output. (In this case, it should be "3" because the original message was shifted three times. You can change the Caesar Cipher encryption integer to something other than "3" to test and verify that the Caesar Analyser is working correctly.)

39. Click Stop.

40. Take a screenshot. (See Figure 16-23.)

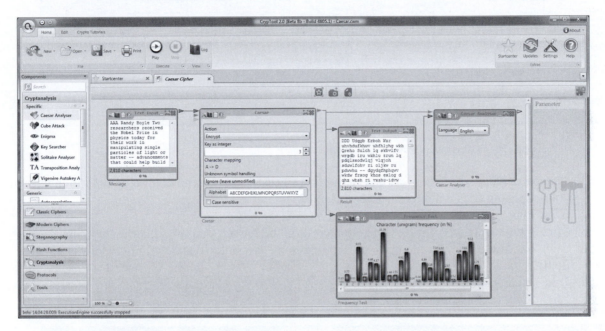

Figure 16-23: Adding the Caesar Analyzer component.

Note: You have now done the Frequency Test correctly and the Caesar Analyzer is providing us with an integer (3) that it thinks will correctly decrypt the message. You are now going to connect the output from the Caesar Analyser to another Caesar Cipher component for decryption.

41. Click Classic Ciphers in the left-hand pane.

42. Drag-and-drop the Caesar icon onto the center workspace to the right of the Caesar Analyser component.

43. Resize the Caesar Cipher component.

44. Drag-and-drop the turquois triangle on the top right corner of the Caesar Analyser component to the top left of the Caesar Cipher component (third arrow down, turquois).

45. Drag-and-drop the triangle (light grey) on the top right corner of the first Caesar Cipher component to the top left triangle (dark grey) of the second Caesar Cipher component (first arrow, dark grey).

46. Change the Action drop-down box to read Decrypt.

47. Click Tools in the left-hand pane.

48. Drag-and-drop the Text Output icon onto the center workspace and below the second Caesar cipher component.

49. Resize the Text Output component if necessary.

50. Drag-and-drop the triangle (light grey) on the top right corner of the second Caesar Cipher component to the top left of the Text Output component (purple).
51. Click Play and then Stop.
52. Take a screenshot. (See Figure 16-24.)

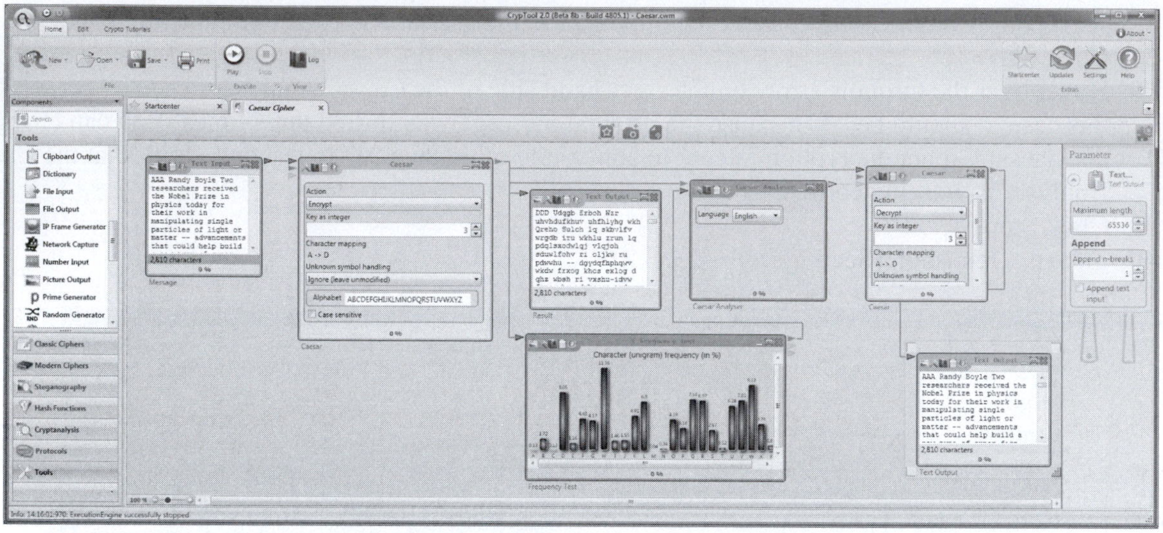

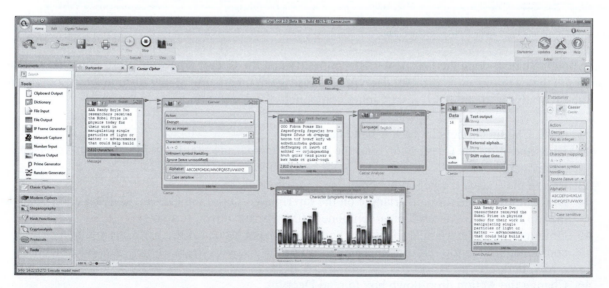

Figure 16-24: Passing the key and decrypting the text.

53. Change the Key as integer text box in the first Caesar Cipher component to a random integer of your choosing (i.e., a number between 1 and 25).
54. Click Play.
55. Click on the Data icon (little white clipboard) on the second Caesar Cipher component.
56. Click on Shift value (turquois). (You should see the key value displayed in the left-hand data field)
57. Take a screenshot.
58. Click Stop. (See Figure 16-25.)

Figure 16-25: Changing the encryption key and testing the cryptanalysis method.

PROJECT QUESTIONS

1. What was your random key value?
2. What text was displayed for your name when you shifted it three times? (Hint: Udqgb Erboh.)
3. What was the percent frequency for the letter "H" when you ran the frequency analysis the first time?
4. What was the lowest percent frequency on your chart? Which letter do you think it was?

THOUGHT QUESTIONS

1. Why would frequency analysis work on a Caesar shift?
2. What do you think are other commonly occurring letters in the English language? Why?
3. Would a Caesar shift be considered secure encryption? Why or why not?
4. Is it possible to try all possible Caesar shifts to decrypt the message? How?

16.7 ENCRYPTED USB (TRUECRYPT®)

This project will show you how to create an encrypted USB drive using TrueCrypt®. There are commercially available encrypted USB drives that you can purchase pre-configured. However, they do cost more than a typical USB. This project will show you how to use TrueCrypt to create a portable version of TrueCrypt and an encrypted TrueCrypt volume on your USB. You'll be able to take it to any computer and decrypt your files for use.

In order to create the encrypted USB, you will first need a blank USB. The size of the USB is not important. You just want to make sure it does not contain any other files. You will use half of the USB to create an encrypted volume.

Note: If you have already installed TrueCrypt, you can skip down to step 9.

1. Download TrueCrypt from http://www.truecrypt.org/downloads.
2. Click Download for the Windows version. (There are also versions for Mac OS and Linux.)
3. Click Save.
4. Select your C:\security folder.
5. If the program doesn't automatically open, browse to your C:\security folder.
6. Right-click on TrueCrypt Setup 7.1a.exe and select Run as administrator.
7. Click I Accept, Next, Next, Install, OK, No, and Finish.
8. Double-click the TrueCrypt icon on your desktop.
9. Insert a blank USB into your computer.
10. Click Tools, and Volume Creation Wizard.
11. Click Next, Next, and Select File.
12. Browse to your USB drive. (In this case, it was the G: drive)
13. In the File name text box, enter YourNameEncryptedUSB.txt for the file name. (In this case, it was RandyBoyleEncryptedUSB.txt.)
14. Click Save. (See Figure 16-26.)
15. Click Next, and Next.
16. Enter a size for the volume that is about half the size of the drive. (In this case, it was 1 GB of a 2GB USB drive.)
17. Click Next. (See Figure 16-27.)

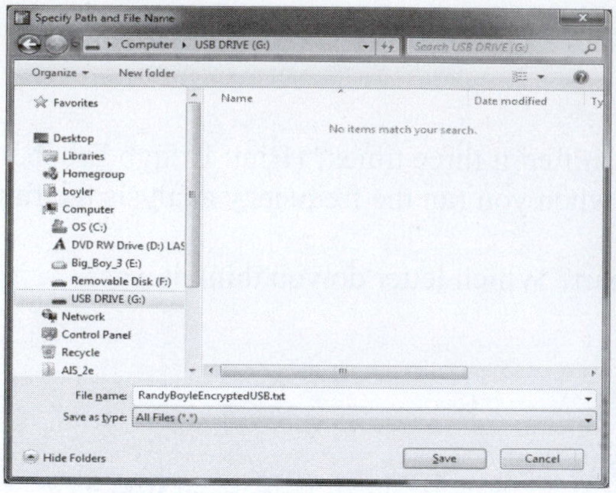

Figure 16-26: Creating a file for the encrypted USB drive. 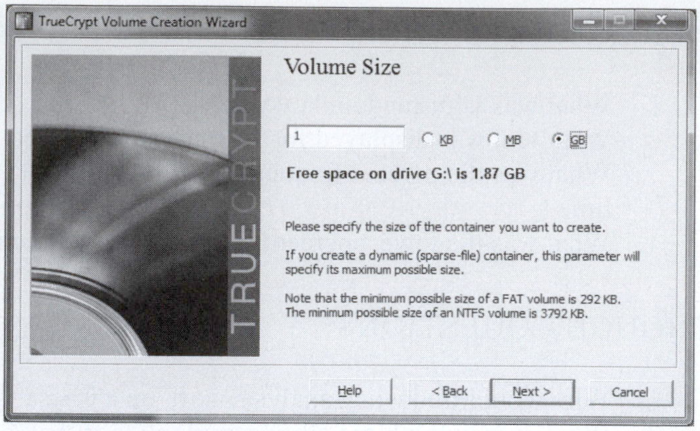   Figure 16-27: Select the size of the new volume.

18. Enter a password that you can remember. (In this case, "tiger1234" without quotes.)
19. Click Next, Format, Yes, OK, and Exit. (The TrueCrypt Volume Creation Wizard will close, but the main TrueCrypt window should still be open.)
20. Click Tools, and Traveler Disk Setup.
21. Click Browse.
22. Select your USB drive. (In this case, it was the G: drive.)
23. Click OK.
24. Select Auto-mount TrueCrypt volume, specified below.
25. Click Browse.
26. Browse to your USB.
27. Select the file named YourNameEncryptedUSB.txt. (In this case, it was RandyBoyleEncryptedUSB.txt.)
28. Click Open.
29. Take a screenshot. (See Figure 16-28.)
30. Click Create, OK, and Close.
31. Remove your USB drive.
32. Close TrueCrypt.
33. Insert your USB drive.
34. Browse to the TrueCrypt folder on your USB. (In this case, it was G:\TrueCrypt\.)
35. Double-click TrueCrypt.exe.
36. Click on any drive letter. (In this case, it was the R: drive letter.)
37. Click Select File.
38. Browse to the file labeled YourNameEncryptedUSB.txt on your USB drive. (In this case, it was G:\RandyBoyleEncryptedUSB.txt.)
39. Click Open.
40. Click Mount.
41. Enter the password you set. (In this case ,it was tiger1234.)
42. Take a screenshot. (See Figure 16-29.)

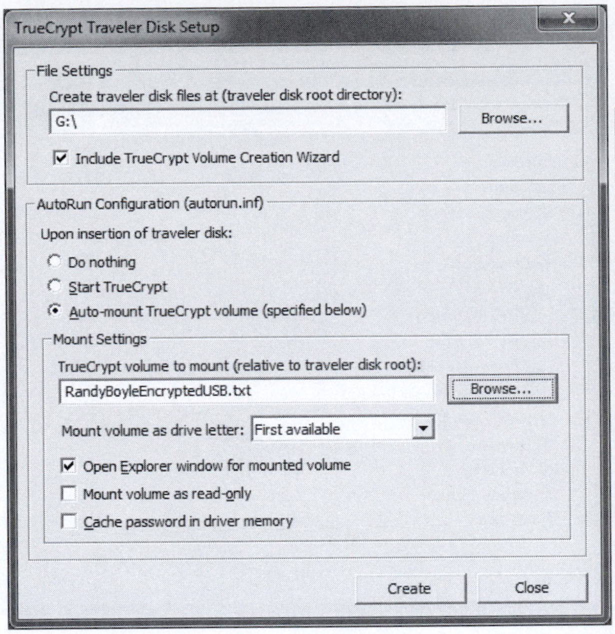

Figure 16-28: TrueCrypt Traveler Disk Setup.

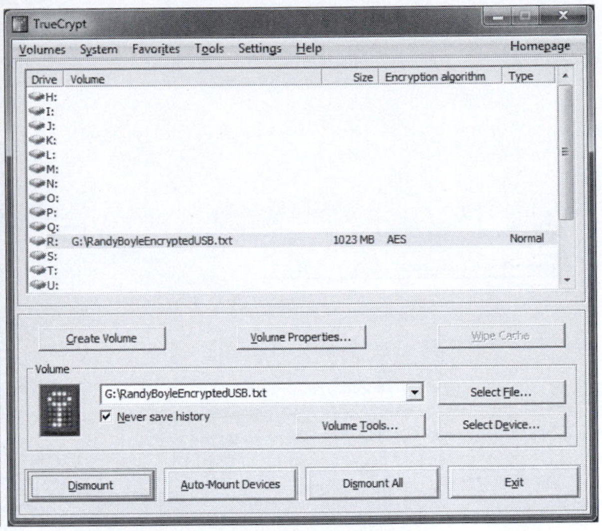

Figure 16-29: The new volume is mounted.

43. Click Favorites, and Add Mounted Volume to Favorites.
44. In the Label text box, enter "EncryptedUSB".
45. Select "Mount selected volume when its host device gets connected" and "Open Explorer window for selected volume when successfully mounted."
46. Click OK. (See Figure 16-30.)
47. Copy any file into your new encrypted drive. (In this case, the new drive was the R: drive.)
48. Click Dismount All.
49. Exit TrueCrypt.
50. Disconnect your USB drive.
51. Reconnect your USB drive. (A prompt should automatically open and ask you for the password for "Encrypted USB." If it doesn't, you can open TrueCrypt.exe located on your USB drive.)
52. Enter the password for your Encrypted USB drive. (In this case, it was tiger1234.)
53. Click OK.
54. Enter the password you chose earlier.
55. Click OK. (TrueCrypt should automatically mount the encrypted volume on your USB and open Windows Explorer.)
56. Browse your newly mounted drive to view the file you copied.
57. Take a screenshot. (See Figure 16-31.)

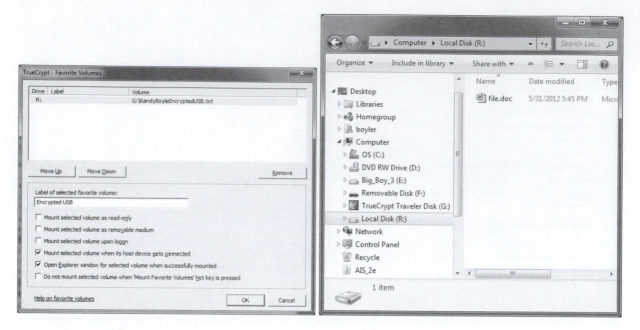

Figure 16-30: Setting mounting options for your USB.   Figure 16-31: Viewing the new volume.

PROJECT QUESTIONS

1. What was the name of your encrypted TrueCrypt volume?
2. Which letter did you assign to your encrypted USB when it loads?
3. How big was the volume you created on your USB?
4. How much space did the other TrueCrypt files take up on your USB?

THOUGHT QUESTIONS

1. Why would someone want an encrypted USB drive?
2. Could you encrypt the entire drive?
3. Would it be a good policy to have all corporate USBs encrypted? Why?
4. Why would the TrueCrypt autorun not work?

16.8 ENCRYPTED EMAIL (HUSHMAIL®)

Most people believe the emails they send are confidential and secure. This is not true. Few people realize that the emails they send are read, indexed, searched, and can be made available to authorities at any time. The emails you send can also be kept indefinitely.

Hushmail® provides confidential and secure email. You can even send secure emails to people who don't have a Hushmail account. Most encrypted email systems require both sides of the email communication (i.e., sender *and* receiver) to have certificates. Hushmail handles all key management behind the scenes.

Hushmail's basic service is free. Upgrade accounts offer email aliases (i.e., a custom email address that does not end in "@hushmail.com"), Microsoft Outlook integration, and more storage. The following project will sign you up for a basic account and send a few encrypted emails.

1. Open a Web browser and go to http://www.hushmail.com.
2. Click on the "Sign up for free email" link.

3. Enter YourName in the text box for your new email address. (In this case, it was RandyBoyle@hushmail.com.) (See Figure 16-32.)
4. Enter a strong passphrase twice. (Make sure they are both the same.)
5. Enter the numbers shown in the Captcha.
6. Agree to the Terms of Service.
7. Click the "Create YourName@hushmail.com now" button.
8. Click the "To sign in now, click here" button.
9. Click Sign In.
10. Enter your passphrase.
11. Click Sign In. (See Figure 16-33.)
12. Click Compose.

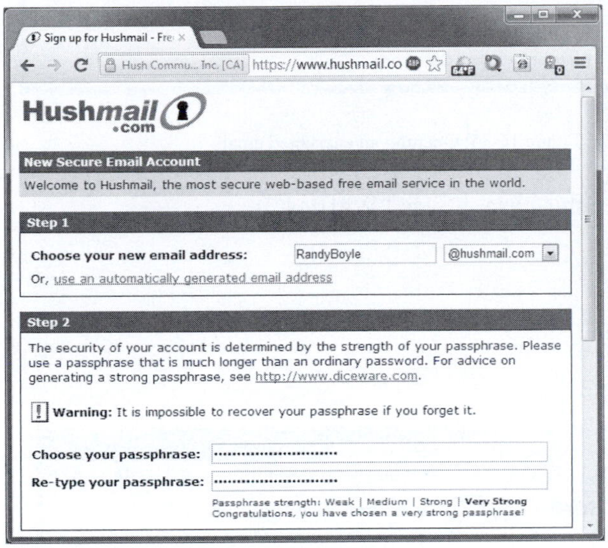

Figure 16-32: Creating a Hushmail account.

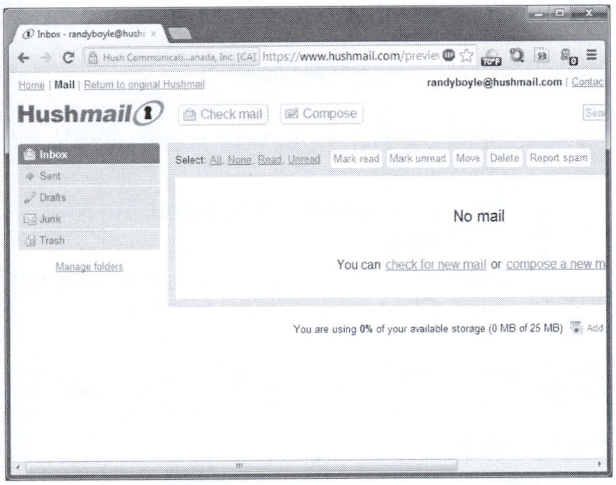

Figure 16-33: Hushmail Inbox.

13. Enter an email addresses that you regularly check. (In this case, it was Boyle.Longwood@gmail.com. You are going to open this email after you send it.)
14. Enter "Encrypted email test" in the subject line.
15. Check the Encrypted box.
16. Enter a secret question. (In this case, it was "What is my favorite food?")
17. Enter an answer to that question. (In this case, it was "Waffles.")
18. Enter your name and the words "encrypted email test" in the body of the email message.
19. Take a screenshot. (See Figure 16-34.)
20. Click Send.
21. Open the email account to which you sent the message.
22. Click on the link provided within the mail. (See Figure 16-35.)

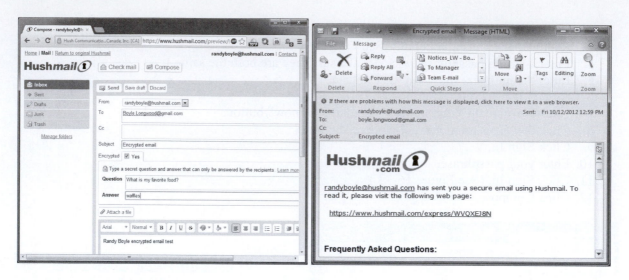

Figure 16-34: Sending an encrypted email.

Figure 16-35: Opening an encrypted email.

23. Enter the answer to your secret question. (In this case, it was "Waffles.")
24. Click Continue.
25. Take a screenshot. (See Figure 16-36.)
26. Click Reply.
27. Enter the text, "This is the return message."
28. Click Send. (See Figure 16-37.)

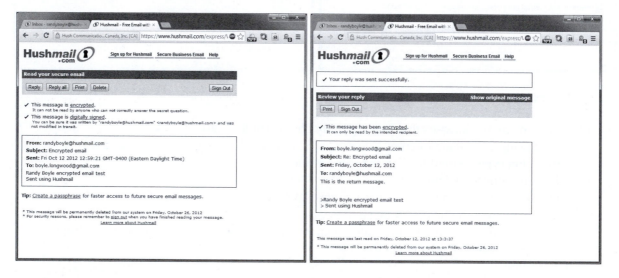

Figure 16-36: Reading an encrypted response.

Figure 16-37: Replying to an encrypted email.

29. Return to your Hushmail.com Inbox.
30. Click Check mail.
31. Click on the message you just sent yourself.
32. Take a screenshot. (See Figure 16-38.)
33. Click Compose.
34. Enter your Hushmail email address into the To box. (In this case, it was randyboyle@hushmail.com. Essentially, you are going to send yourself an email. If you are sending to another Hushmail account, you won't need to enter a secret question or answer.)
35. Enter "To Hushmail account" in the Subject box.
36. Click the Encrypted option.

37. Click Send. (See Figure 16-39.)

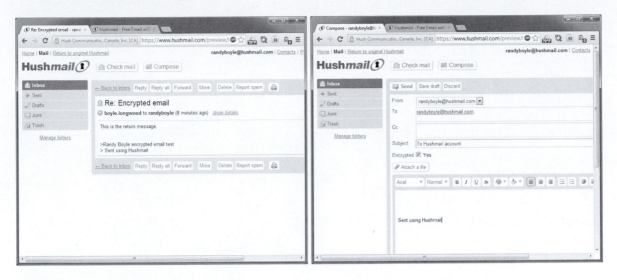

Figure 16-38: Reading another encrypted response.

Figure 16-39: Sending to another Hushmail account.

38. Click Check mail.
39. Click on the email you just sent yourself.
40. Take a screenshot.

PROJECT QUESTIONS

1. What was the name of your Hushmail.com account?
2. How many characters were in your password?
3. What was your secret question?
4. What do you think would be another good secret question?

THOUGHT QUESTIONS

1. Does Hushmail use certificates to secure your email? How?
2. Can you send secure emails to someone who does not use Hushmail? How?
3. Why would someone want to use secure email?
4. Could law enforcement force Hushmail to turn over your emails?

chapter 17

Cryptography makes messages unreadable to unintended users. Steganography goes one step further and hides the encrypted message itself. Throughout the past two thousand years, messages were hidden in a variety of different media, including images, tattoos, an innocuous-looking message, etc. More recently, digital media, email, and the Internet have allowed steganography to blossom.

Individuals can hide covert messages in a variety of different digital media (e.g., images, video, text, music, etc). They can then be posted to the Web or sent by email. The receiver can download the image/video/text/music and extract the message using a secret password. Not only is the covert message encrypted, but it is also hidden. To the casual observer, it doesn't even appear to be a covert message.

The use of steganography has some IT security professionals concerned. Criminals, terrorists, disgruntled employees, drug dealers, and other nefarious individuals could use these tools for a variety of illegal acts. It's not hard to think up a list of ways steganography could be used inappropriately. Luckily, there are ways to search for and decrypt messages hidden using steganography.

Time required to complete this chapter: 45 minutes

Chapter Objectives

Learn how to:
1. Create a digital watermark.
2. Hide text in an image.
3. Detect hidden text in an image.
4. Hide a file in multiple carriers.

Chapter Projects

Project:
17.1 Digital Watermarking
17.2 Invisible Secrets
17.3 Stegdetect
17.4 OpenPuff

Watermarking is the process of adding identifying or copyright markings to images, music, or videos. Watermarking helps prevent images from being used without proper permission. It can also prevent intellectual property theft. The watermark can be visible, hidden, or both. Visible watermarks are a quick way of displaying ownership and discouraging improper use.

Watermarking has become much more important with the advent of the Internet. Media posted on the Internet can be viewed, shared, copied, or stolen by anyone with a Web browser. In this project, you will watermark an image of yourself using a free watermarking application by ByteScout®.

1. Download ByteScout Watermarking® from http://bytescout.com/?q=/download/download_freeware.html
2. Click on the download link for Watermarking (EXE).
3. Click Save.
4. Select your C:\security folder.
5. If the program doesn't automatically open, browse to your C:\security folder.
6. Right-click on Watermarking.exe and select Run as administrator.
7. Click OK, Next, I accept, Next, Next, Next, Next, Install, and Finish.
8. Click on the Bytescout Watermarking icon on your desktop if it hasn't already started.
9. Open Windows Explorer.
10. Copy a picture of yourself to your C:\security folder. (This is the image you are going to watermark.)
11. Return to ByteScout Watermarking.
12. Click Add files.
13. Browse to your C:\security folder.
14. Select the picture you just copied into this folder.
15. Click Open.
16. Take a screenshot.
17. Select the file you just added.
18. Click Next.
19. In the Text box, enter "© Copyright 2012, YourName". (In this case, it was © Copyright 2012, Randy Boyle.)
20. Click Preview.
21. Press Escape to exit the preview.
22. Click Next, and Next.
23. Change the Output Folder to your C:\security folder.
24. Click Start, Rename, and Finish.
25. Browse to your C:\security folder.
26. Double-click the picture you just watermarked. (You should see two similar images listed. The newly watermarked image should have a "(1)" in it from the renaming process.)
27. Take a screenshot. (See Figure 17-1.)

Figure 17-1: Watermarked image.

PROJECT QUESTIONS

1. What was the name of the image you watermarked?
2. What did your watermark say?
3. How big (i.e., how many bytes) was the image you selected to be watermarked as shown in the ByteScout Watermarking screenshot?
4. What was the resolution of the image you selected to be watermarked as shown in the ByteScout Watermarking screenshot?

THOUGHT QUESTIONS

1. Could you watermark all of your images at once? How?
2. Could you change the placement of the watermark? How?
3. Would it be difficult to remove the watermark? Why?
4. How does watermarking stop theft of intellectual property?

17.2   INVISIBLE SECRETS 2.1®

Invisible Secrets® allows you to hide more than just plain text inside a variety of different image types. You can even encrypt an image inside another image, even audio or video. It also allows you to add your own encryption algorithm and add additional carrier types. It even has an integrated FTP server connection to make uploading the image easier after you have hidden your data.

For this example, we will use Invisible Secrets 2.1®, which has limited functionality but is free. Invisible Secrets 4® is an upgraded version with much more functionality. If you are working with a lot of sensitive data, it might be worth buying the full version ($40) to get some excellent additional features. Let's look at a simple example.

1. Download Invisible Secrets 2.1 from http://www.invisiblesecrets.com/ver2/index.html.
2. Click on the download link for Invisible Secrets 2.1 FREE edition.
3. Click Save.
4. Select your C:\security folder.

5. If the program doesn't automatically open, browse to your C:\security folder.
6. Right-click on invsec2.exe and select Run as administrator.
7. Click Yes, Next, Yes, Next, Next, Install, and Finish.
8. In Invisible Secrets, click Options to see that you can add additional carrier types and encryption algorithms. (See Figure 17-2.)

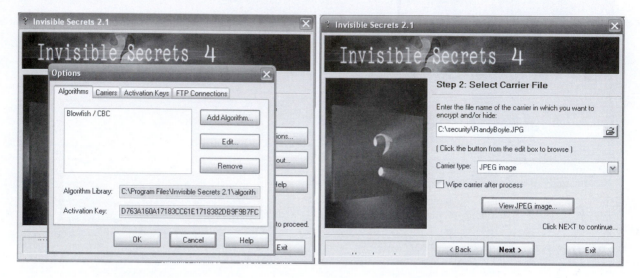

Figure 17-2: Select the algorithm you want to use.   Figure 17-3: Select the original image.

9. Click Cancel to return to the main screen.
10. Click Next, and Next.

Note: You are now going to copy any .JPG image on your computer and rename it YourName.JPG. This copy will be used as the carrier image. If you don't have any other .JPG images on your computer, you can use the Sample.JPG image located in the Invisible Secrets 2.1 program folder at C:\Program Files\Invisible Secrets 2.1. Once you have the image copy made, you will hide a small program inside the image.

11. Open Windows Explorer.
12. Select any .JPG picture on your computer. (You can use any .JPG image you would like.)
13. Copy it and rename it YourName.JPG. (In this case it was RandyBoyle.JPG.)
14. Save the new YourName.JPG image in the C:\security folder.
15. In Invisible Secrets, click on the folder next to the empty text box at the top of the screen.
16. Select the image labeled YourName.JPG in the C:\security folder. (In this case, RandyBoyle.JPG.) (See Figure 17-3.)
17. Click Next.
18. In Invisible Secrets, click Add Files.
19. Browse to your C:\security folder.
20. Select the Fport.exe program. (You can choose a different file if you would like.) (See Figure 17-4.)
21. Click Open, and Next.
22. Enter "tiger" for the password. (The free version only allows five characters.) (See Figure 17-5.)
23. Click Next.

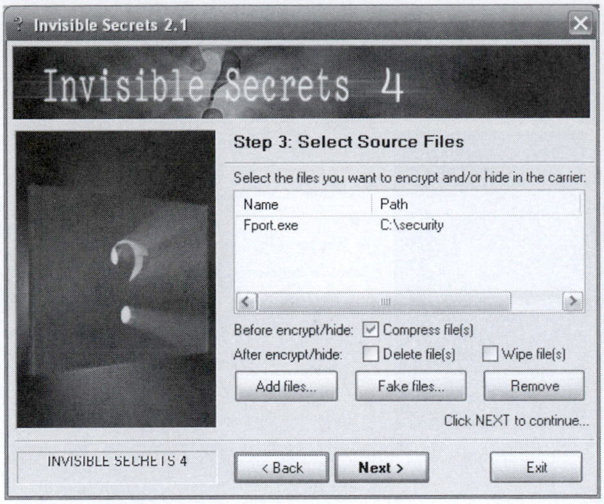

Figure 17-4: Select the file you want to hide.

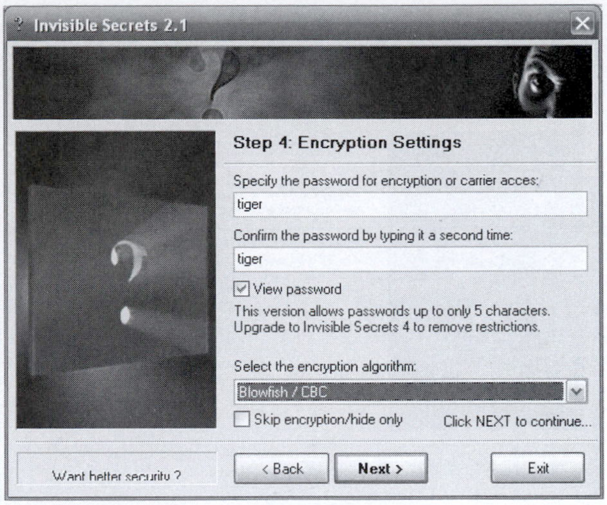

Figure 17-5: Enter the recovery password.

24. In the target file text box, enter YourNameHidden.JPG. (In this case, RandyBoyleHidden.JPG.)
25. Take a screenshot. (See Figure 17-6.)
26. Click Next, and Next.
27. Click Review Carrier File to make sure the picture wasn't distorted. (See Figure 17-7.)
28. Take a screenshot.

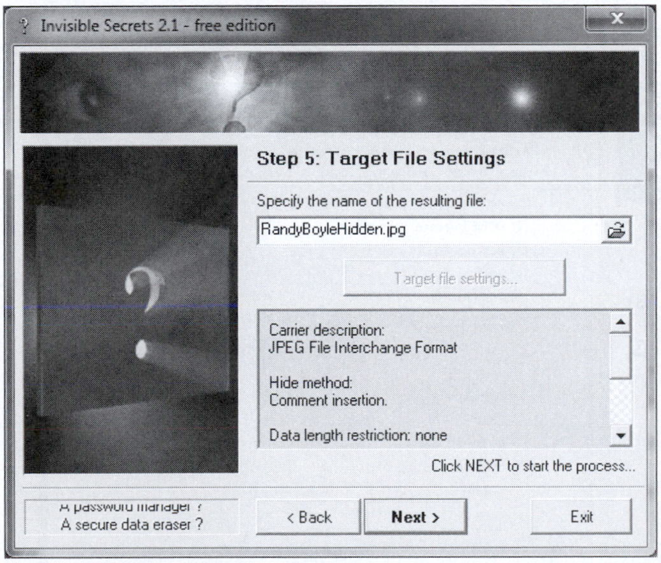

Figure 17-6: Name of the new image with hidden data.

Figure 17-7: New image with hidden data.

29. Click Finish.
30. Click Extract and/or Decrypt files from a carrier file.
31. Click Next.
32. Browse to your C:\security folder.
33. Select the image labeled YourNameHidden.JPG. (See Figure 17-8.)
34. Click Next.

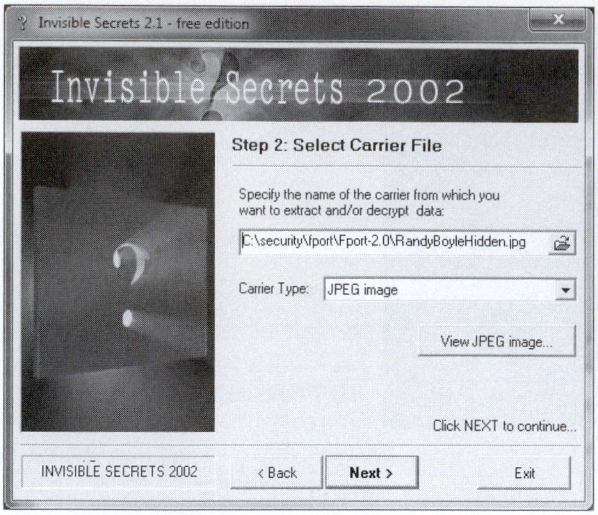

Figure 17-8: Select the image with the hidden data.

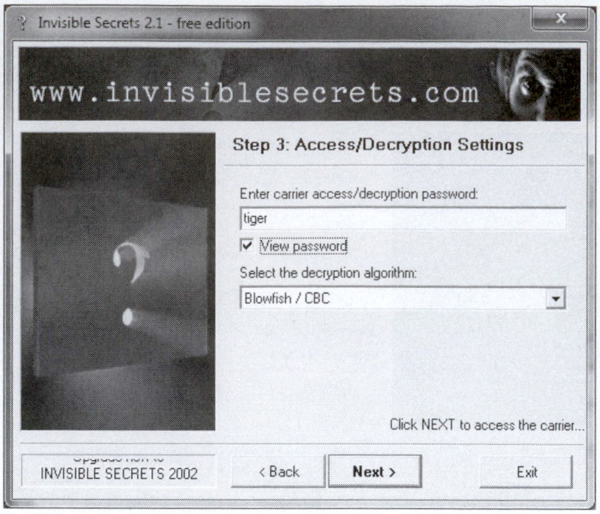

Figure 17-9: Enter the password to recover the data.

35. Enter "tiger" for the password. (See Figure 17-9.)
36. Click Next.
37. Take a screenshot showing the files that it can decrypt and unhide. (In this case, Fport.exe.) (See Figure 17-10.)
38. Click Next.
39. Click Explore Extracted Data.
40. Take a screenshot of the window showing your recovered file. (See Figure 17-11.)

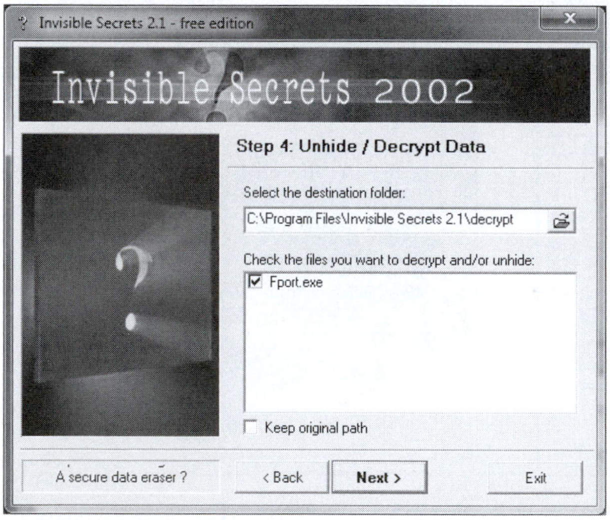

Figure 17-10: Recovered data.

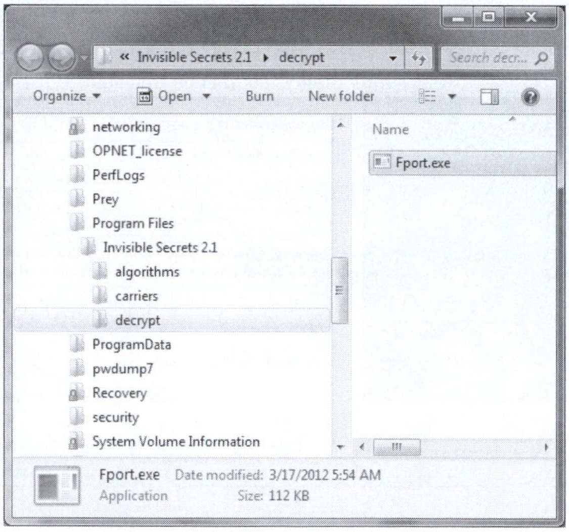

Figure 17-11: Saved data that was once hidden.

PROJECT QUESTIONS

1. What was the name of the .JPG image you used?
2. Which file did you hide inside the image?
3. What was the password you used?
4. What encryption algorithm did you use?

THOUGHT QUESTIONS

1. Why would Invisible Secrets allow you to use your own custom encryption algorithms?
2. What different carrier types would be beneficial to use? Why?
3. Could this program be used to watermark an image or other file type in order to prove ownership?
4. Could this program be used to covertly sneak secret information through a secure corporate network?

17.3 STEGDETECT®

Like most IT security tools, steganography can be used for both good and bad purposes. It's the bad purposes that are most worrisome. IT security professionals need to be able to detect images that may contain inappropriate content. Steganography detection tools are of interest to corporate security officers, law enforcement, and a variety of national security organizations (i.e., FBI, CIA, DEA, etc.).

In the previous example, you learned how to hide a file inside an image. In this example, you are going to learn how to scan your system and detect images that may have hidden payloads. Stegdetect® by Niels Provos is one of the few free tools available that can detect images with hidden content. There are other tools available to law enforcement but they are more expensive.

Let's see if Stegdetect can scan your C:\security folder and find the YourNameHidden.JPG image that has a file hidden inside of it. The xsteg.exe program we will run is the front-end GUI to the Stegdetect program.

1. Download Stegdetect from http://www.outguess.org/detection.php.
2. Click Download.
3. Click on the "Stegdetect 0.4 - Windows Binary" link below the heading.
4. Click Save.
5. Select your C:\security folder.
6. If the program doesn't automatically open, browse to your C:\security folder.
7. Right-click on stegdetect-0.4.zip.
8. Select Extract All, and Extract.
9. Browse to C:\security\stegdetect-0.4\stegdetect.
10. Right-click on xsteg.exe and select Run as administrator. (See Figure 17-12.)

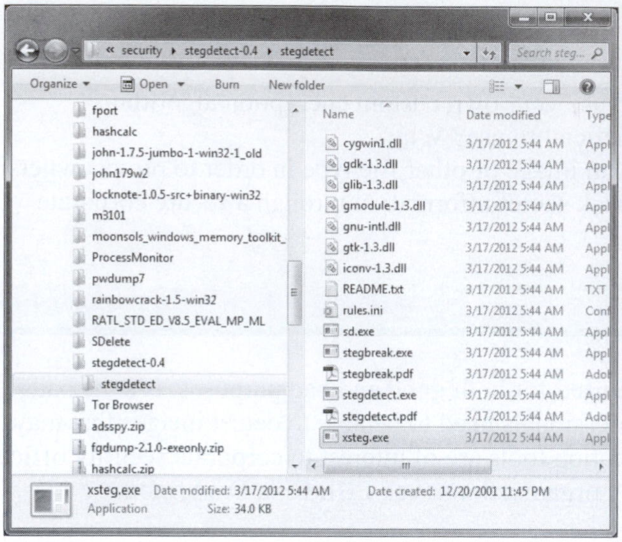

Figure 17-12: Xsteg.exe program. 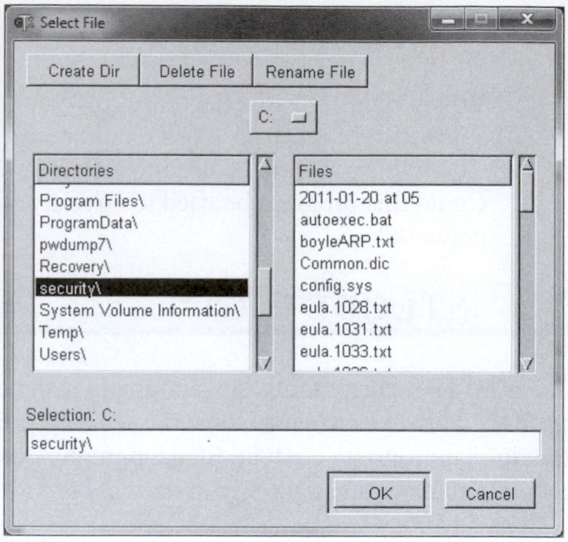   Figure 17-13: Select the directory or drive to scan.

11. In the xsteg window, click File, and Open.
12. Browse to your C:\security folder. (See Figure 17-13.)
13. Click OK.
14. Take a screenshot showing the detection of the YourNameHidden.JPG file you created in the earlier project. (If you didn't do the earlier project, you won't see any results.) (See Figure 17-14.)

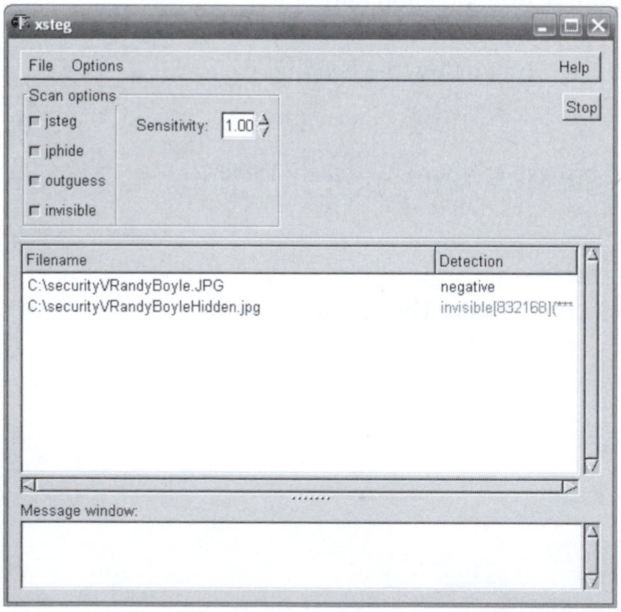

Figure 17-14: Image with hidden data is detected.

PROJECT QUESTIONS

1. How many images did the scan find?
2. Was there an image that was "negative"? Which one?
3. Was there an image that was "invisible"? Which one?

4. Did any other images have other types of detection messages? Which ones?

THOUGHT QUESTIONS

1. How would you open an image that contains hidden data?
2. Could you use the Stegbreak.exe tool to determine the password for a hidden file inside an image?
3. Could you write an automated program to scan a website, or the entire Internet, for images that may contain hidden data?
4. Could you scan all of your email attachments or images for hidden data?

17.4 OPENPUFF®

OpenPuff® is a very powerful steganography tool. It has the ability to hide the target file (i.e., the one you want to hide) across many different media file types or carriers. In others words, you may have a large file you want to hide but it's too big to hide in a single image. OpenPuff allows you to spread the contents of the large file across multiple images. These carrier files can be images, audio files, video files, or flash files (PDF). OpenPuff also allows you to protect the file with multiple passwords using advanced obfuscation (i.e., multiple layers of 256-bit encryption and hardware generated noise).

When you attempt to extract (or "unhide") a target file, you must know which carriers were used, and the order in which they were used. The sequencing of the carrier files is part of the steganographic process. If the carrier files are not in the correct order, the target file will not be extracted. You can even add a decoy into the carriers. OpenPuff is a feature-rich steganography tool that provides a secure way of hiding files within other media files.

Note: A common mistake in this project is to choose carrier files that are too small to accommodate a target file. You need to make sure you choose carrier files that are large enough to hide your target file. If you get a message saying the target file was too large to hide in the carrier files, you can choose larger carrier files or a smaller target file.

1. Download OpenPuff from http://embeddedsw.net/openpuff.html.
2. Click on the link labeled "OpenPuff" to download the program. (Always download the latest version if one is available.)
3. Click Save.
4. Select your C:\security folder.
5. If the program doesn't automatically open, browse to your C:\security folder.
6. Right-click on OpenPuff.zip.
7. Select Extract All, and Extract.
8. Browse to the C:\security\OpenPuff\OpenPuff folder.
9. Right-click the OpenPuff.exe program and select Run as administrator. (See Figure 17-15.)
10. Click Hide.
11. Uncheck Enable (B) and (C) passwords. (For this project, we will use only one password. Using multiple passwords is more secure.)
12. Enter a password into the (A) box. (In this example, the password "tiger1234" was used. See Figure 17-16.)

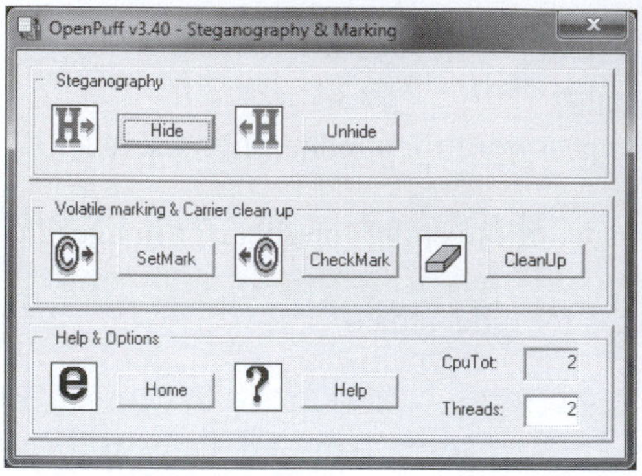

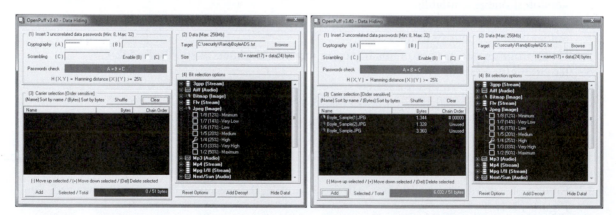

Figure 17-15: OpenPuff. 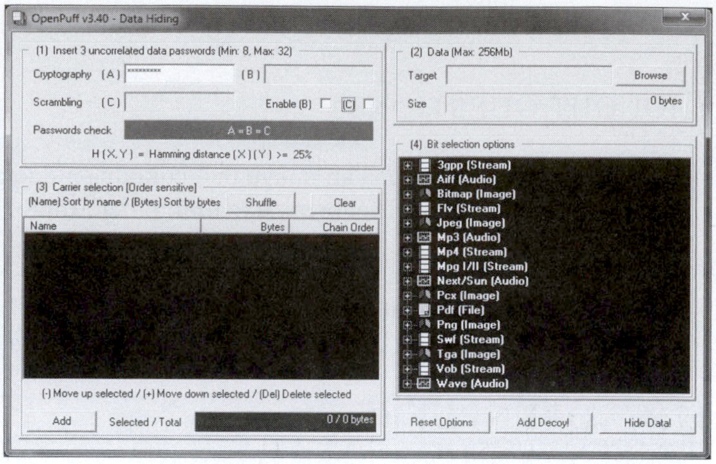   Figure 17-16: Password set.

13. Click on the Browse button to the left of the Target text box.
14. Browse to your C:\security folder.
15. Select one of the text files with your name in it. (If you don't see a text file with your name in the filename, you can create one now. In this case, it was RandyBoyle.txt.)
16. Click Open.
17. Take a screenshot. (See Figure 17-17.)
18. Click on the Add button at the bottom of the Carrier selection box.
19. Browse to your C:\security folder.
20. Select a few of the images used in the prior projects. (If you don't see any images listed, you can copy a few to your C:\security folder. You can copy PDFs to your C:\security folder as well. The listing order of the images will be important when you unhide the hidden text.)
21. Expand the Jpeg [Image] tree in the right-hand pane. (You will be able to select how much of the image will be used.)
22. Select ¼ [25%] – high. (All of the colored bars should be green now. If you selected a target file that was larger than the carriers you are going to hide it in, the bottom "Selected/Total" bar may be red. You can choose a different target file or additional carriers. A small text file with a few words, which is your target, should only be a few bytes. Most JPEG images will be much larger.)
23. Take a screenshot. (See Figure 17-18.)

Figure 17-17: Target file selected.   Figure 17-18: Carrier files loaded.

24. Click Hide Data.
25. Set the output director to your desktop. (You can delete these files later.) (See Figure 17-19.)
26. Click OK.

Note: You might see a warning message stating that only some of the carrier images were used. This is perfectly normal. It's likely that the target text file you selected was very small and the carrier image was very large. The additional carriers were not necessary. You will only load the carriers used to hide the target. In this example, only Boyle_Sample(1).JPG was used to hide RandyBoyleADS.txt. (See Figure 17-20.)

27. If you see a warning message, note how many of the carriers were used. (You will only load the carriers used when you unhide the hidden target text file. In this case, only the first image, RandyBoyleADS.txt, was used to hide the target text file.
28. Click OK, and Done.

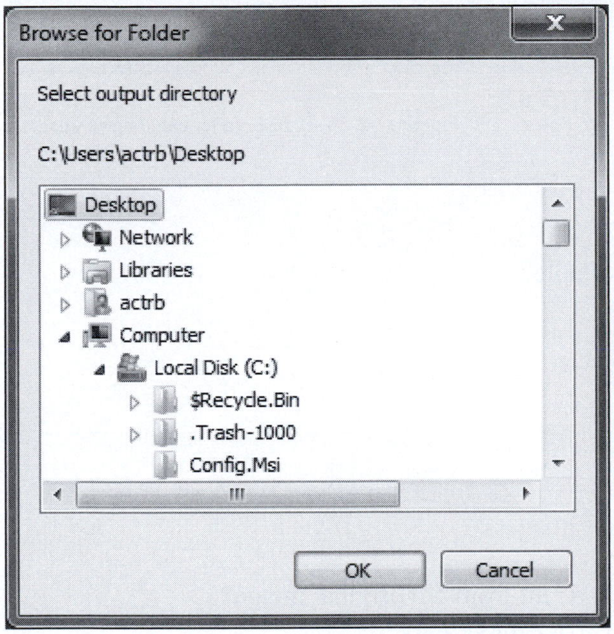

Figure 17-19: Selecting the output directory.

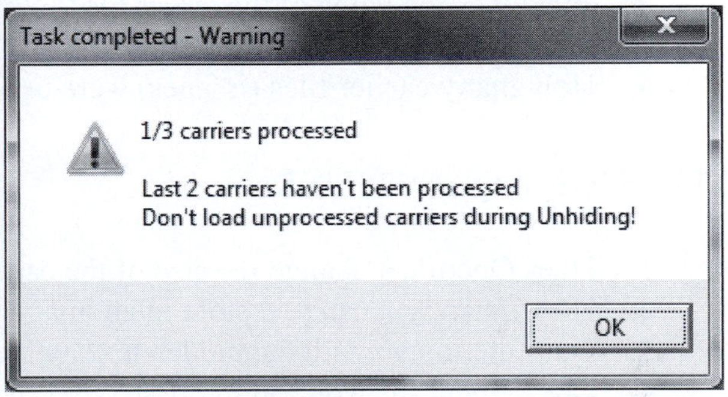

Figure 17-20: Warning message about how many carriers were processed during the hiding of the image.

29. Close the Data Hiding window.
30. Click Unhide in the OpenPuff main window.
31. Uncheck Enable (B) and (C) passwords.
32. Enter the password you chose into the (A) box. (In this example, the password "tiger1234" was used.)
33. Click Add Carriers.
34. Browse to your desktop.
35. Select the image file that was used as the carrier.
36. Click Open.
37. Take a screenshot. (See Figure 17-21.)
38. Click Unhide.
39. Select your desktop as the output directory.
40. Click OK, and OK.
41. Take a screenshot of the Task Report window showing the file that was unhidden. (In this case, the hidden file was RandyBoyleADS.txt. You should now have an image and a text file on your desktop.) (See Figure 17-22.)

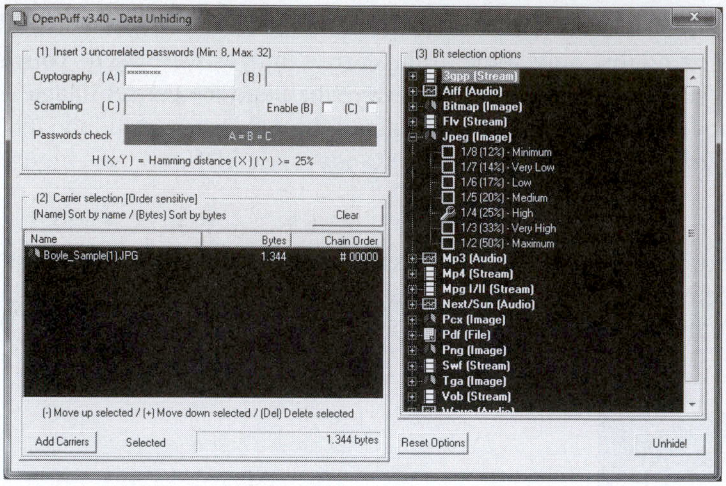

Figure 17-21: Unhiding a hidden file.

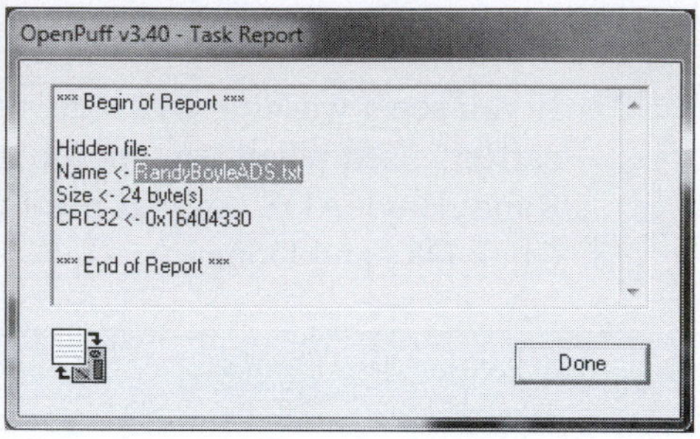

Figure 17-22: Task report after unhiding an image.

PROJECT QUESTIONS

1. What was the password you used in this example?
2. What was the name of the target file?
3. What was the name of the image file?
4. How many carrier files (images) were used?

THOUGHT QUESTIONS

1. Does OpenPuff change the size of the carrier image(s)?
2. How much text can you store in an image?
3. Does the image with the hidden text look different from the original image?
4. Does OpenPuff work on multiple types of carrier files? Why?

chapter 18

Computer forensics is not exactly like it's portrayed in the movies and on TV. Performing a computer forensic investigation requires significant levels of technical skill, patience, organization, and the ability to follow specific procedures. You need to be able to follow very specific instructions and protocols to work in the field of computer forensics.

In this section, you will see a few basic forensic tools and a forensic suite that includes a variety of tools. The forensic suite (CAINE®) is actually a Linux distribution that we will run as a virtual machine. This book has tried to focus on free Windows-based software. However, at this time, there isn't an abundance of Windows-based software available with the same functionality included in this CAINE distribution. There is excellent Windows-based forensic software available, but it is rather expensive.

The following projects are intended to give introductory exposure to computer forensics and get students excited about the field of computer forensics. You will not be ready, or qualified, to complete a forensic investigation after reading this book. You will need a great deal more experience and certified training in order to be qualified to initiate a real investigation. Again, these projects are just an introduction to the IT security field.

Time required to complete this chapter: 60 minutes

Chapter Objectives

Learn how to:
1. Display basic system information.
2. Gather digital forensic data.
3. Extract metadata.
4. Create a forensic image file.
5. Search for specific file types.

Chapter Projects

Project:
18.1   BGInfo
18.2   Metadata (TAGView)
18.3   CAINE

In general, computer forensics gathers information (or "artifacts") from a computer system while trying to explain what information is present and its origin. When people first hear the word "forensics," they put up mental roadblocks and just assume that they won't understand what is going on. We are going to start slowly with basic software that gathers general information from a computer. Then we will move on to tools with more functionality.

The first tool we will look at is BgInfo®, developed at Sysinternals by Bryce Cogswell. It shows basic system information on the computer background. Systems administrators are always running multiple DOS commands or clicking through a series of windows to get basic information that they need about the local computer. Having it displayed in the background saves administrators time and effort. Let's look at a quick example using BgInfo.

1. Download BgInfo from http://technet.microsoft.com/en-us/sysinternals/bb897557.aspx.
2. Click Download BgInfo at the bottom of the page.
3. Click Save.
4. Select the C:\security folder.
5. If the program doesn't automatically open, browse to C:\security.
6. Right-click on Bginfo.zip.
7. Select Extract All, Next, Next, and Finish.
8. Browse to C:\security\BgInfo.
9. Double-click on Bginfo.exe.
10. Click anywhere on the text to stop the ten-second timer. (It will close the program if you don't.)
11. Remove any fields you don't want to see by editing the text directly (i.e., select and delete lines).
12. Take a screenshot. (See Figure 18-1.)
13. Click OK.
14. Take a screenshot of your computer background with the system information showing. (See Figure 18-2.)

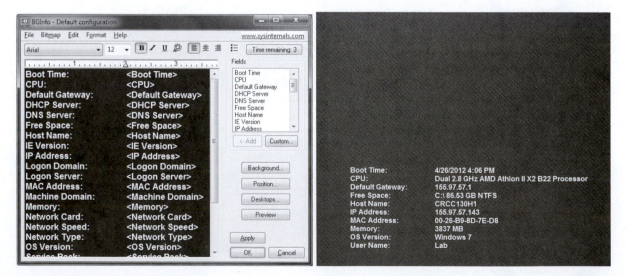

Figure 18-1: BgInfo configuration screen.   Figure 18-2: Desktop showing system details.

PROJECT QUESTIONS

1. What was your IP address as shown on your desktop?

2. What was your MAC address as shown on your desktop?
3. What time was displayed for the most recent boot time?
4. What brand CPU does your computer have?

THOUGHT QUESTIONS

1. What DOS commands would you have to enter to get the information shown by BgInfo?
2. Why would an administrator need to know the IP and MAC addresses for a given computer?
3. Can you change your MAC address?
4. What are some specific diagnostic benefits to BgInfo?

18.2 METADATA (TAGVIEW®)

When you take a digital photo, there is more information stored in the photo file than just the image. Information about the image is also stored. These data are called "metadata." Metadata are extremely valuable in forensic examinations. They can provide you with information such as the date, time, type of camera, exact GPS location, etc. Metadata are used in many criminal trials.

You should be concerned about metadata from a privacy point of view. It wasn't until recently that social networking websites started to strip metadata from their websites. It was very easy to capture that information right from their website. This project will show you some of the metadata captured in a digital photo.

1. Download TAGView® from http://www.evigator.com/store.
2. Scroll down until you see TAGView.
3. Click Add to Cart.
4. Click Checkout.
5. Provide the required basic information. (You can use any non-important email address to which you have access.)
6. Open up your email account from the information provided.
7. Follow the TAGView download link.
8. Select Click Here to download TAGView.
9. Select Save File to save the file to your C:\security folder.
10. Navigate to your download folder (C:\security).
11. Right-click on tagview.exe and select Run as administrator.
12. Click Yes, Next, I Accept the Agreement, Next, Next, Next, Install, and Finish.
13. Click the folder icon in the upper left-hand corner within TAGView.
14. Go to your My Pictures folder or anywhere you have JPGs or other image files located.
15. Select an image, preferably of yourself.
16. Click Open.
17. Look at the metadata provided.
18. Take a screenshot. (See Figure 18-3.)

Note: In the next part of this project, you will recover metadata from an image that will contain the coordinates (i.e., the GPS) where the picture was taken. Choose one or both method(s) below to recover the GPS metadata. If your mobile phone does not have this capability, you will need to choose the second option.

Smart Phone Option:

1. Be sure to enable Location Services, or the equivalent, on your phone.

2. Take a picture.
3. Email the picture to yourself.
4. Download the image file to C:\security folder.
5. On the upper left-hand corner of TAGView, select the folder icon.
6. Go to your C:\security folder and locate the image file that you took with your cell phone.
7. Select the image and click Open.
8. Look at the metadata provided.
9. Take a screenshot.

Internet Option:

1. Perform an Internet search using the keywords "Geotag example". (An example of one can be found here: http://pic.farbauti.de/geotag-example.jpg. Make sure you download the original photo, not a resized copy.)
2. Download the image to your C:\security folder.
3. Return to TAGView and click on the folder icon.
4. Go to your C:\security folder and locate the image file that you took with your cell phone.
5. Select the image and click Open.
6. Look at the metadata provided and notice the GPS coordinates.
7. Take a screenshot. (See Figure 18-4.)

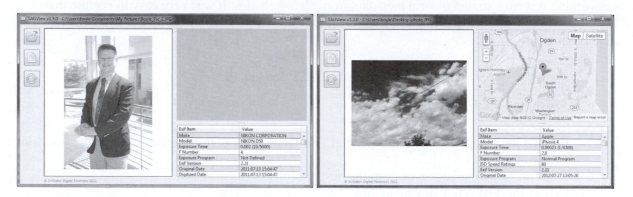

Figure 18-3: Metadata from JPG image.   Figure 18-4: Successful Geotag search with GPS coordinates.

PROJECT QUESTIONS

1. What was the file name of the first image you examined?
2. What was the file name of the second image you examined?
3. What was the original date (i.e., the date the photo was taken) listed on the second image?
4. What was the location (or GPS coordinates) of the second image you examined?

THOUGHT QUESTIONS

1. How can metadata from pictures be useful in criminal investigations?
2. How can metadata from pictures be used by attackers?
3. What recommendations would you give Web developers when allowing image content on the company website?
4. What security policies would you put in place regarding smart phone images that capture GPS location data?

CAINE® is a distribution focused on IT forensics. It is a good learning environment for beginning users. CAINE has intuitive interfaces, a variety of functionality, and good reporting and documentation tools. Most IT forensics suites are quite expensive and require a fair amount of training. A free tool like CAINE, that has good collection, analysis, and reporting tools, is invaluable for someone just starting out in the field. SANS® also provides a free forensic toolkit distribution (the SANS Investigate Forensic Toolkit®, or SIFT) that has many of the same tools.

In this exercise, you will download a "live" version of CAINE and load it on a virtual machine using Oracle VM VirtualBox. You'll then take a partial image of the virtual hard drive using the Air tool and search for specific file types using SFDumper® and Scalpel®. This is one of the longer projects in this book. The imaging and analysis components may each take several minutes. You can take breaks and come back as needed.

1. Download CAINE from http://www.caine-live.net.
2. Click DOWNLOADS.
3. Click CAINE 3.0.iso. (The .ISO image is about 1.2 GB.)
4. Click Save.
5. Select your C:\security folder.

Note: You will need Oracle VM VirtualBox to load CAINE on a virtual machine. We will install VirtualBox first, and then create the CAINE virtual machine. You should have VirtualBox already installed from a prior project. If you already have VirtualBox installed, you can skip to Step 13.

6. Download Oracle VirtualBox from http://www.oracle.com/technetwork/server-storage/virtualbox/downloads/index.html.
7. Click on the download link for latest version of Oracle VM VirtualBox for Windows. (At the time of writing, the latest version was VirtualBox-4.2.6.82870-Win.exe. Download the latest version of VirtualBox available. Versions for Mac OS X and Linux are also available.)
8. Click Save.
9. Select your C:\security folder.
10. If the program doesn't automatically open, browse to C:\security.
11. Double-click the VirtualBox-4.2.6.82870-Win.exe program. (The version number will likely be different as later versions are released.)
12. Click Run, Run, Next, Next, Next, Install, Next, and Finish. (This runs you through the installations process.)

Note: If you already have VirtualBox installed, you can start here.

13. Open Oracle VM VirtualBox by clicking Start, All Programs, Oracle VM VirtualBox, and Oracle VM VirtualBox.
14. Click New.
15. Enter CAINE_YourName for the name of the virtual machine. (Replace YourName with your first and last name. In this case, it was CAINE_RandyBoyle.)
16. Enter Linux for the operating system type.
17. Enter Ubuntu (64-bit) for the version. (If you have a 32-bit system, you can select Ubuntu.)
18. Click Next. (See Figure 18-5.)
19. Increase the amount of memory to 2000MB+. (See Figure 18-6.)

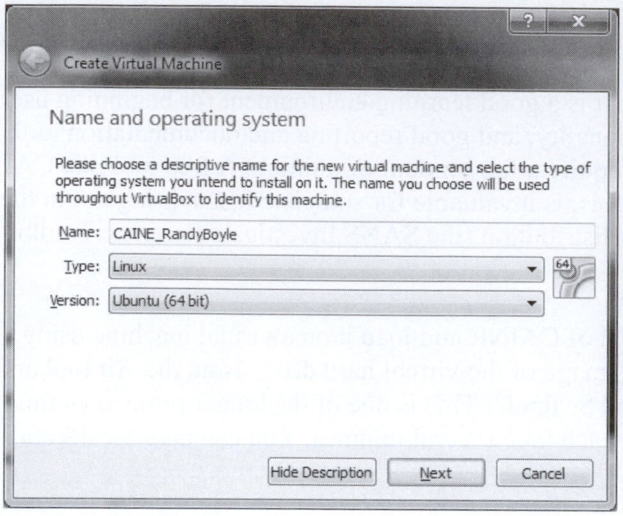

Figure 18-5: Creating virtual machine.

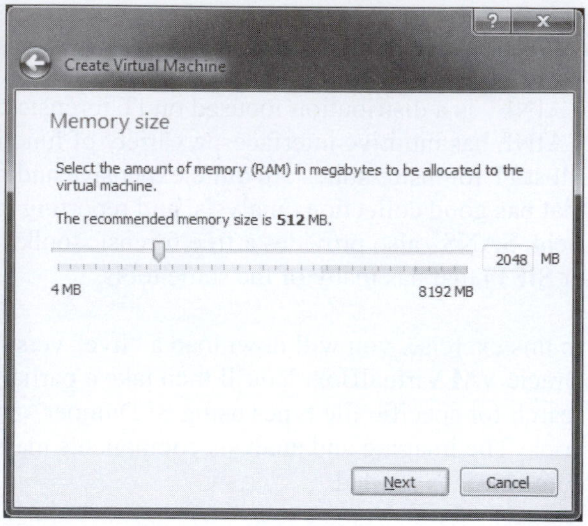

Figure 18-6: Setting the amount of RAM.

20. Click Next, Next, Next, and Next.
21. Increase the hard drive space to 18GB+.
22. Click Create.
23. Select the Virtual machine labeled CAINE_YourName. (See Figure 18-7.)
24. Click Storage in the right-hand panel.
25. Click on the "Empty" disk icon in the IDE Controller tree.
26. On the right-hand side of the window, click on the disk icon next to IDE Secondary Master.
27. Select "Choose a virtual CD/DVD disk file."
28. Browse the C:\security folder and select the downloaded ISO image labeled caine3.0.iso. (See Figure 18-8.)
29. Click Open.
30. Click OK
31. Click Start (the green arrow). (After you click Start, you will have to quickly arrow down to the Install option.)
32. Arrow down and select Install.
33. Press Enter.
34. Allow CAINE to boot. (This can take a couple of minutes.)

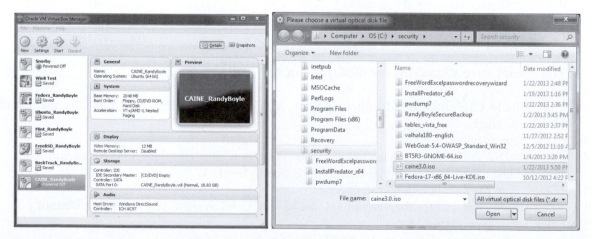

Figure 18-7: Virtual machine created.

Figure 18-8: Loading the CAINE image.

Note: You may want to use ScreenshotPilot to take the screenshots of your virtual machine. You can download ScreenshotPilot at http://www.colorpilot.com/screenshot.html.

35. Click Continue, Continue, Continue, and Install Now.
36. Select your time zone.
37. Click Continue, and Continue.
38. Enter your login information, including your name and password. (See Figure 18-9.)
39. Click Continue. (This will take several minutes to finish installing. Remember: Hold the right Ctrl key to escape out of the virtual machine.)

Note: You are now going to have to take the CAINE ISO image out of the virtual CD ROM so you don't have to go through the installation process again. If you don't take out the ISO image, the installation process will start again when you reboot the virtual machine.

40. Press the right Ctrl key to exit the virtual machine. (You may be able to skip this step on newer versions of VirtualBox. Older versions may still require it.)
41. In the VirtualBox menu, for the virtual machine you are working on, click Devices, CD-DVD ROM, and Remove disk from virtual drive. (This will unmount the CAINE ISO image.)
42. Click Force Unmount. (This should remove the ISO image from your virtual CD-DVD drive.)
43. Click Restart Now. (This will reboot your virtual machine from the virtual hard drive. You can also manually reset it in the main VirtualBox screen.)
44. Enter your username and password.
45. Press Enter.
46. Enter your password again for administrator access.
47. Click the Menu button, Forensic Tools, and Air. (See Figure 18-10.)

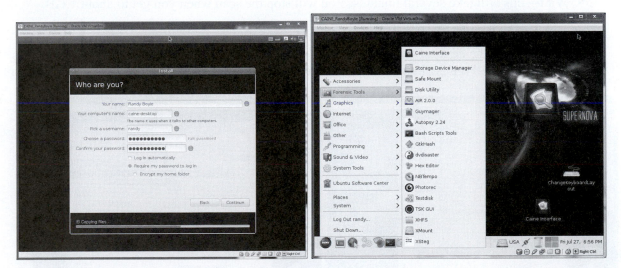

Figure 18-9: Installing CAINE.   Figure 18-10: CAINE menu.

48. Enter your password if prompted.
49. Click Cancel, if asked to delete the previous log.
50. Click on the SDA icon.
51. Click Set as Source.
52. Click the browse button for the Destination device/file in the upper right-hand corner of the window.

53. Enter YourNameImage.img for the file name (In this case, it was RandyBoyleImage.img.) (See Figure 18-11.)
54. Click Save.
55. Click Start. (See Figure 18-12.)

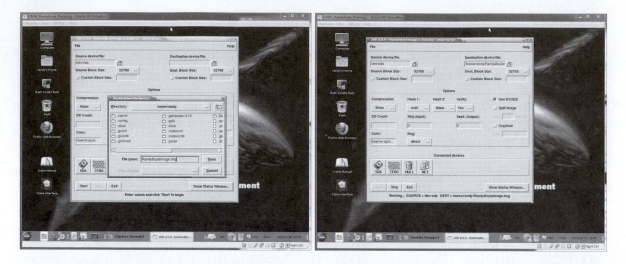

Figure 18-11: Designating destination file.   Figure 18-12: Creating image.

56. Click Show Status Window. (See Figure 18-13.)
57. Exit your virtual machine
58. Take a screenshot. (You may want to use ScreenshotPilot to take this screenshot. The link to ScreenshotPilot is located at the start of this project.)
59. Wait—this will take several minutes. You will stop the scan when you get to about 1 GB.
60. Click Stop when you get to about 1 GB.
61. Click Yes.
62. Double-click the desktop shortcut labeled YourUsername's Home. (In this case, it was randy's Home. You will see the image you just created.) (See Figure 18-14.)

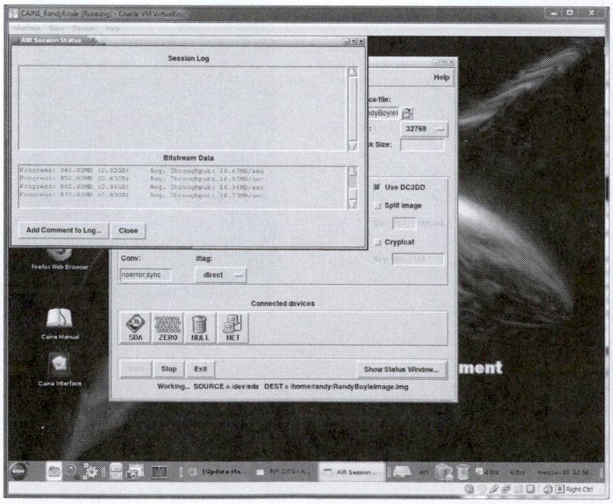

Figure 18-13: Acquiring data. 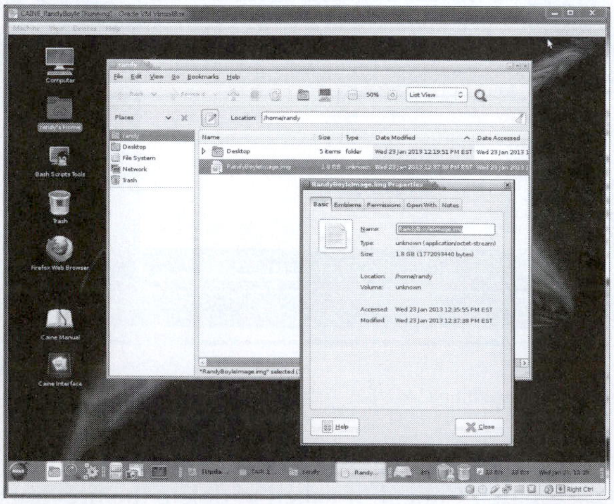   Figure 18-14: Properties of the created image.

Note: You just captured an "image" of part of the virtual hard disk used by the virtual machine you are working on. The virtual hard disk is actually a file stored on the physical hard disk in your computer. In the next part of this project, you are going to use a tool to search the image you created. You will look for certain types of files in the image you captured.

63. Click the Menu button (or the Start button in Windows), Forensic Tools, and CAINE interface.
64. Enter your password when prompted.
65. Click Create Report.
66. Enter YourNameCase as the case name. (In this case, it was RandyBoyleCase.)
67. Click OK.
68. Enter YourName as the name of the investigator. (See Figure 18-15.)
69. Click OK.
70. At the Caine interface, click on Analysis, and Scalpel. (See Figure 18-16.)

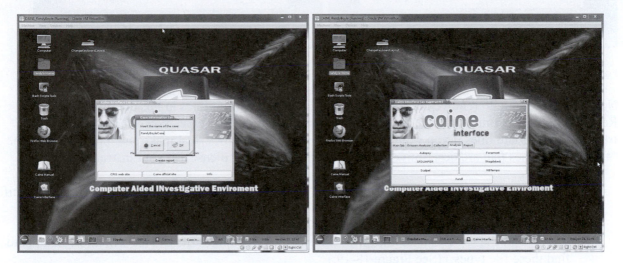

Figure 18-15: CAINE analysis tools.   Figure 18-16: CAINE interface.

71. Click Open input file.
72. Click File System, home, and YourUsername. (In this case, the username was randy.)
73. Select YourNameImage.img. (In this case, it was RandyBoyleImage.img.) (See Figure 18-17.)
74. Click OK.
75. Click Select directory.
76. Click Create Folder on the top right-hand corner.
77. Enter Scalpel in the text box.
78. Press Enter. (See Figure 18-18.)
79. Click OK.

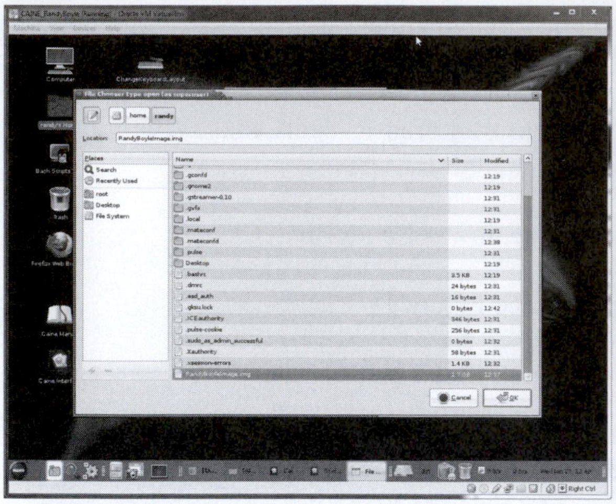

Figure 18-17: Select file to be used by Scalpel. 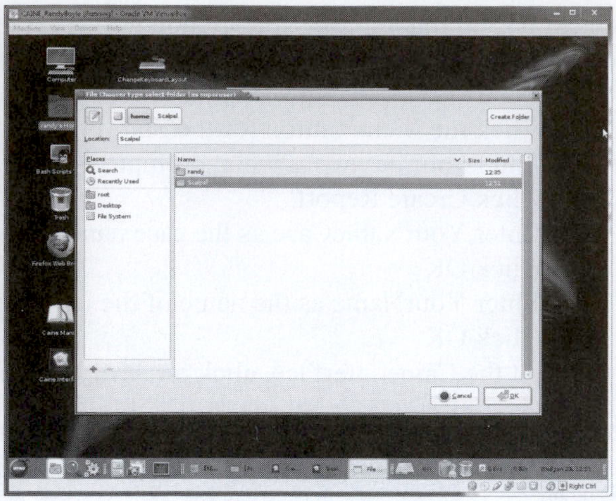　　　　　Figure 18-18: Select a target directory.

Note: You are going to remove the "#" from the beginning of several lines in this configuration file. Removing the "#" from each line allows Scalpel to search for this file type. You can remove all the "#" from the appropriate lines if you want to search for multiple file types. Just make sure not to remove the "#" from any lines that are descriptive text. If you have questions, please ask your instructor.

80. Click Edit file, to edit the configuration file. (This file will configure Scalpel to search for specific file types.)
81. Scroll down until you get to the Graphics Files section.
82. Remove all the "#" from the lines with extensions for Graphics files. (This will allow Scalpel to find these file types.) (See Figure 18-19.)
83. Scroll down until you get to the Microsoft Office section.
84. Remove all the "#" from the lines with extensions for Word documents (i.e., .doc).
85. Scroll down and remove all the "#" from the lines with extensions for HTM and PDF.
86. Click File, and Save.
87. Click File, and Quit.
88. Click Run Scalpel. (This will take a few minutes depending on the size of the image you captured.) (See Figure 18-20.)

Figure 18-19: Edit the Scalpel configuration file.　　　　　Figure 18-20: Scalpel processing data.

89. Click Quit.
90. Click Open Output Directory. (These are the folders that may contain recovered files.)
91. Double-click a folder with recovered files. (In this case, the JPG folder.) (See Figure 18-21.)
92. Take a screenshot of the contents of the folder you opened.

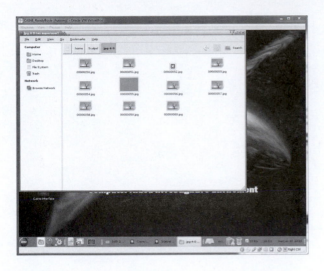

Figure 18-21: Folders that may contain recovered data.

PROJECT QUESTIONS

1. What was the name of your virtual machine?
2. What was the name of the image file you used?
3. How large was your image file?
4. About how long did it take for Scalpel to run?

THOUGHT QUESTIONS

1. Could you run Autopsy on the image you used in this exercise?
2. What advantage would the Live CD have in a forensic investigation?
3. What does the Report tab allow you to do?
4. Which programs are included in the Grissom Analyzer tab?

chapter 19

SQL injection is when someone takes advantage of database vulnerabilities by submitting malicious parameters through a Web interface. SQL injection techniques can be thwarted by using parameterized statements or by filtering the input before it is processed. Unfortunately, you are not going to learn how to protect against SQL injection attacks here.

Even mentioning SQL injection can be problematic. When is it appropriate to teach students about how SQL injection works? Most good IT security professionals know how SQL injection works and how to protect against it. Talking about SQL injection is the equivalent of having the birds-and-the-bees talk with your child. You know it has to be done sooner or later. You just don't want them to learn incorrect or inappropriate ideas from other children.

Do not use any of the information presented below on real websites. The projects below are intended to give the beginning IT security student an idea of how SQL injection works. They are not intended to be used inappropriately. Remember, everything you do on the Internet can be (and probably is) logged. You don't want to get into legal trouble for being curious.

There are several good books and a multitude of websites that have more than enough information about SQL injection. Please feel free to learn more about it. If you learn how SQL works, you'll become indispensable to companies that need to secure their databases from hackers. You will have a long and successful career.

Time required to complete this chapter: 60 minutes

Chapter Objectives

Learn how to:
1. Identify application vulnerabilities.
2. Test concurrency flaws.
3. Test XSS weaknesses.
4. Test authentication errors.
5. Perform SQL injection.

Chapter Projects

Project:
19.1 Concurrency Flaws
19.2 Cross-Site Scripting (XSS)
19.3 Authentication Errors
19.4 SQL Injection

19.1   CONCURRENCY FLAWS

This project will *not* look at automated software that analyzes an application for security vulnerabilities. Rather, it will load a training platform that can be used to see how weaknesses can be exploited and how to secure them. The aim of this book is to introduce students to basic IT security tools and how to use them – not how to break things.

This exercise demonstrates how a poorly secured website might allow online purchase transactions to be easily exploited. In this example, we will look at a basic technique that allows you to purchase merchandise for a lower price than for what it would originally be sold.

The Open Web Application Security Project® (OWASP) is an organization focused on improving the security of application software. OWASP approaches security enhancement with a transparent approach. OWASP has created training platforms that you can practice on without harming an actual website.

The training platform used in this chapter is called WebGoat®. It runs off of an installed Apache Tomcat® server that you will run on your local machine. This version contains WebGoat 5.4, Java Runtime Environment® (JRE), and Tomcat. Take some time to get familiar with WebGoat, and run through any additional exercises that interest you.

*** **Warning** *** Do NOT use any of the information presented in this text on real websites. This book is not intended to be a hacker training manual. It is intended to give beginning IT security professionals exposure to known application security vulnerabilities. Additional materials are available if you want to learn how to secure your databases and websites against attack.

Part of being a security professional is acting responsibly with the knowledge you have. Do not use the skills learned in this or the subsequent projects to do harm to other systems.

1. Download OWASP's WebGoat from http://code.google.com/p/webgoat/downloads/list.
2. Click on WebGoat-5.4-OWASP_Standard_Win32.zip.
3. On the next page, click on WebGoat-5.4-OWASP_Standard_Win32.zip.
4. Click Save.
5. Select the C:\security folder.
6. Click Save.
7. If the program doesn't automatically open, browse to C:\security.
8. Right-click on WebGoat-5.4-OWASP_Standard_Win32.
9. Click 7-Zip, and Extract to "\WebGoat…"
10. Browse to C:\security\WebGoat-5.4-OWASP_Standard_Win32.
11. Open the WebGoat-5.4 folder. (You will see 5 or 6 files.)
12. Double-click the webgoat.bat file. (This will open a runtime viewer. You can minimize this viewer, but do not close it.) (See Figure 19-1.)
13. Click Allow access, if you see a Windows Security Alert. (See Figure 19-2.)

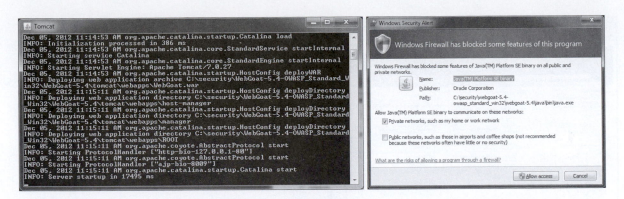

Figure 19-1: Apache Tomcat server runtime viewer.

Figure 19-2: Making an exception through Windows Firewall.

14. Open an Internet browser (e.g., Firefox or Internet Explorer).
15. Type the URL http://localhost/WebGoat/attack.
16. Type "guest" for the username and "guest" for the password, without quotation marks.
17. Click on Start WebGoat. (See Figure 19-3.)

Note: You will now see the WebGoat application running through your Internet browser. While running WebGoat, your machine is extremely vulnerable to attack. If possible, you should disconnect from the Internet while using this program.

18. With WebGoat running, open a browser and type: http://localhost/WebGoat/attack. This address is case-sensitive so be sure to capitalize the W and G in the address line.
19. Click on Start WebGoat.
20. On the left-hand side, click on Concurrency. (The links labeled "Lesson Plan" and "Solution" provide detailed explanations about why coding errors make this attack possible.)
21. Click on Shopping Cart Concurrency Flaw. (See Figure 19-4.)

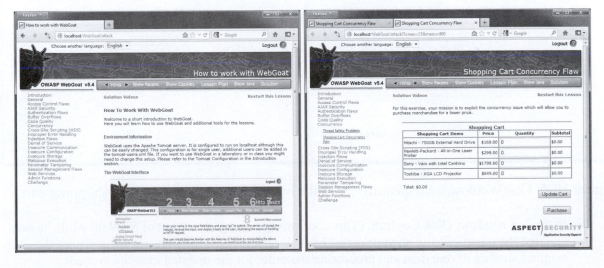

Figure 19-3: WebGoat interface.

Figure 19-4: WebGoat application on local host.

22. Right click on the Shopping Cart Concurrency Flaw link and select Open Link in New Window. (You should have two tabs open with the exact same content.)
23. Align the windows so they are side-by-side. (See Figure 19-5.)

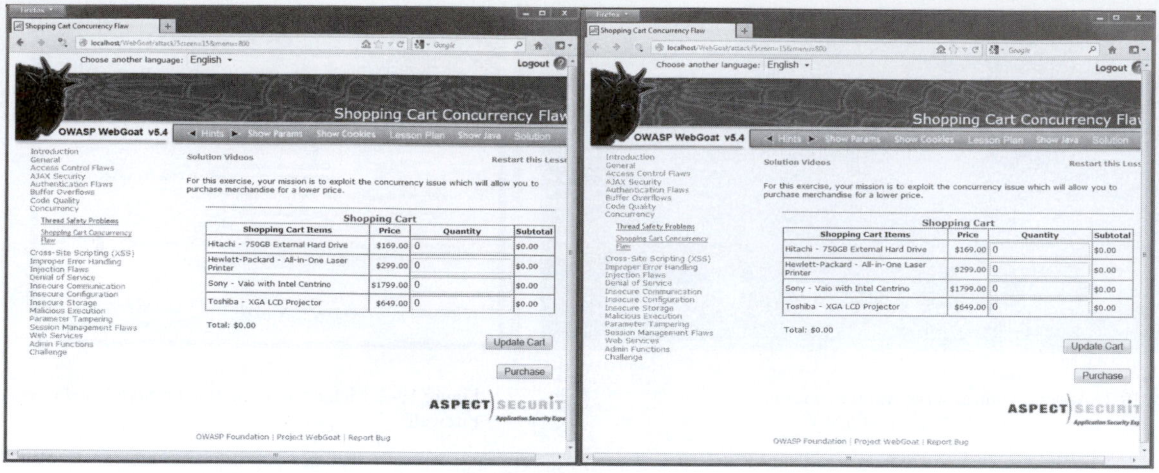

Figure 19-5: The same Web page shown in side-by-side windows.

24. In the *left* window, change the quantity of Hitachi Hard Drives from 0 to 1.
25. Click Purchase. (Do not click Confirm.)
26. In the *right* window, change the quantity of Hitachi Hard Drives from 0 to 15.
27. Click Update Cart.
28. Take a screenshot of your entire desktop showing both windows (Ctrl-PrintScreen). (See Figure 19-6.)

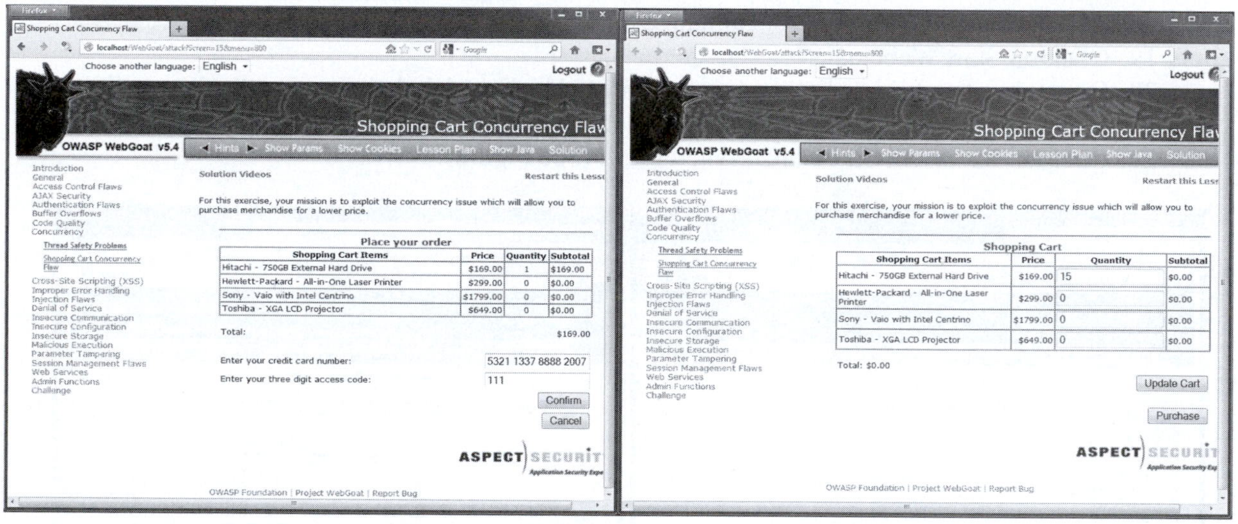

Figure 19-6: One window with quantity 1 and the other with quantity 15 in the shopping cart.

29. In the *left* window, click Confirm. (This confirms the charged amount of $169.00 while having updated the quantity to 15 in your cart! This will now process the transaction, charging the original amount of one item and processing the order for the updated quantity amount.)
30. Take a screenshot of your entire desktop showing both windows (Ctrl-PrintScreen). (See Figure 19-7.)

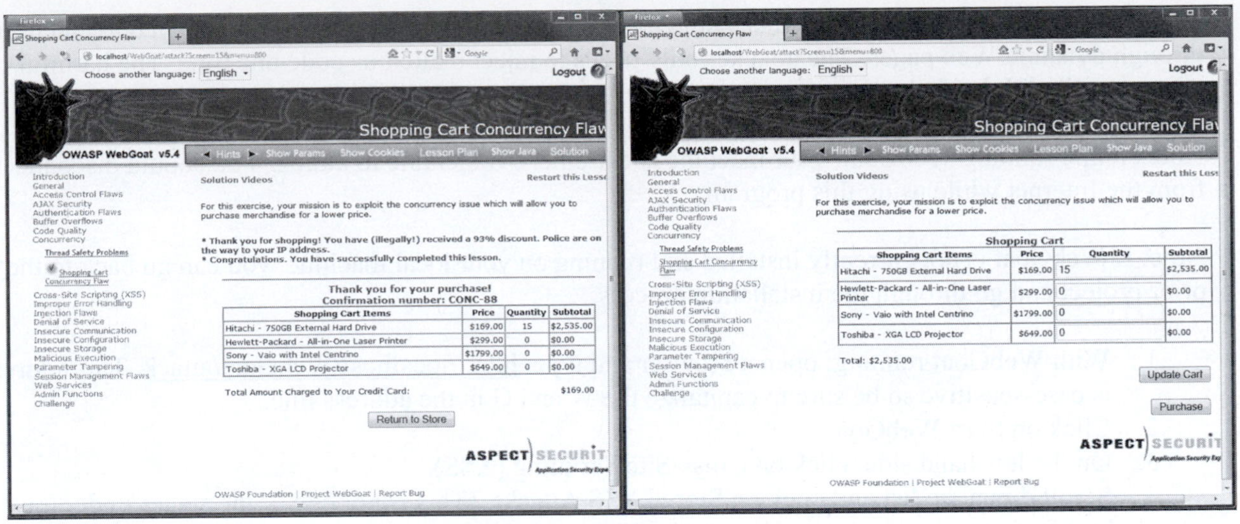

Figure 19-7: Concurrency flaw found.

31. Close the right window.
32. In the *left* window, click Restart this lesson, in the top right-hand side of the page.
33. Repeat the steps in this exercise to reproduce a similar concurrency flaw using a different product (i.e., not the Hitachi hard drive) and different quantities.
34. Take a screenshot of your entire desktop showing both windows after you have reproduced the concurrency flaw (Ctrl+PrintScreen).

PROJECT QUESTIONS

1. Which product(s) did you use when you reproduced the concurrency flaw?
2. What quantities did you use in both windows?
3. What was your subtotal in both windows?
4. What was your percent (%) discount shown at the end?

THOUGHT QUESTIONS

1. How could knowing how to use WebGoat help you either enter the IT security industry or further your career?
2. How can WebGoat run without being connected to the Internet?
3. Why would a system or computer connected to the Internet be more vulnerable to attack when running WebGoat?
4. What are the advantages of having a training environment like WebGoat?

19.2 CROSS-SITE SCRIPTING (XSS)

Cross-Site Scripting (XSS) attacks typically exploit Web applications that allow malicious code to be entered, or "injected," into a link that appears to be from a trusted source. These attacks can be carried out using client-side languages such as JavaScript, HTML, ActiveX, Flash, etc.

This project looks at a type of XSS attack known as Stored Cross-Site Scripting. This vulnerability relies on Web applications that accept unsanitized data via comment forums, blogs, Contact Us pages, etc. Typically, data processed by Web applications are legitimate; however, they can be malicious. If malicious data (or code) are injected and stored on a file system, they can then be displayed to end users through dynamic Web pages. The attacker only needs to inject malicious code one time. The harmful effects can be felt by many users.

Note: While running WebGoat, your machine is extremely vulnerable to attack. You should disconnect from the Internet while using this program.

Note: If WebGoat is not currently installed and running on your local machine, you can go back to the prior project and go through the installation process.

1. With WebGoat running, open a browser and type: http://localhost/WebGoat/attack. This address is case-sensitive so be sure to capitalize the W and G in the address line.
2. Click on Start WebGoat.
3. On the left-hand side, click on Cross-Site Scripting (XSS).
4. Scroll down the list and click on Stored XSS Attacks. (This is not one of the stages under the "LAB: Cross Site Scripting" link.) (See Figure 19-8.)
5. In the title text box, enter YourLastName XSS Test. (In this case, it was Boyle XSS Test.)
6. In the message input box, carefully type the following and replace YourLastName with your last name. (In this case, the text read: <script language="javascript" type="text/javascript">alert("You have been hacked by Boyle XSS!");</script>. This code can be copy-pasted from the Solution link.) (See Figure 19-9.)

```
<script language="javascript" type="text/javascript">alert("You have
been hacked by YourLastName XSS!");</script>
```

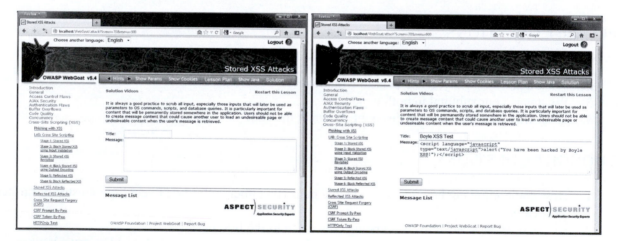

Figure 19-8: XSS – Stored Attacks.　　　　　　　Figure 19-9: XSS Title and Message.

7. Click Submit.
8. Click on the "YourLastName XSS Test" link located under the Submit button. (In this case, it was Boyle XSS Test.) (See Figure 19-10.)
9. Click on your "YourLastName XSS Test" message.
10. Take a screenshot. (See Figure 19-11.)
11. Click OK.

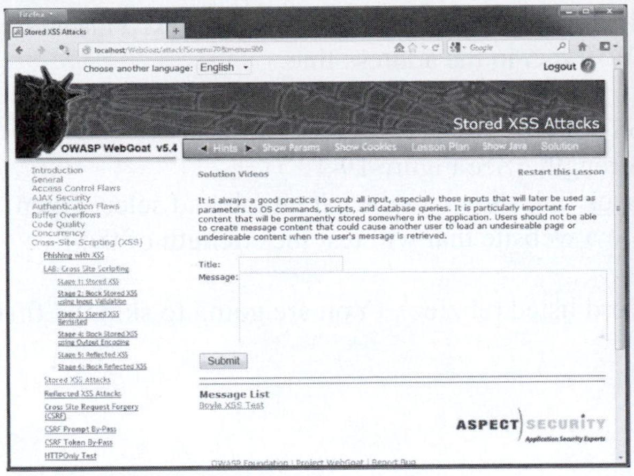

Figure 19-10: XSS – Message was posted.

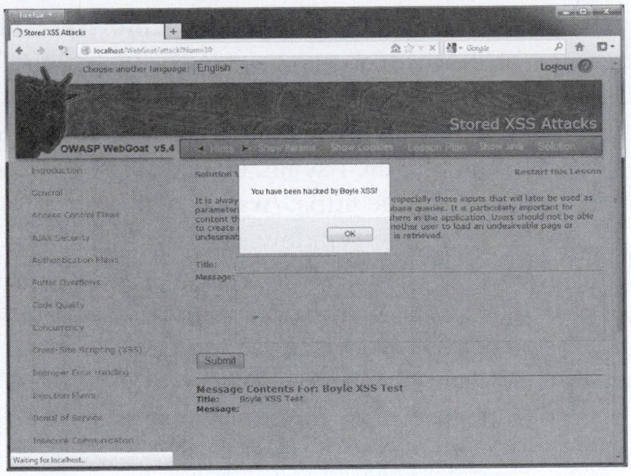

Figure 19-11: Successful XSS injection.

12. Repeat the steps in this exercise to reproduce a similar XSS injection using a different title and message. (Hint: You can copy-paste the code from the Solution link, and then alter the contents of the message. This will ensure the code works properly.)
13. Take a screenshot showing you have reproduced the XSS injection.

PROJECT QUESTIONS

1. What was the title of your first message?
2. What did your first message say?
3. What was the title of your second message?
4. What did your second message say?

THOUGHT QUESTIONS

1. Why would knowing how to perform an XSS attack make you a better security professional?
2. How would you explain XSS vulnerabilities to someone who is not tech savvy?
3. What types of code can be used to enable this type of vulnerability?
4. What websites do you visit frequently that could potentially fall victim to an XSS attack?

19.3   AUTHENTICATION ERRORS

Web applications often do not require strong password authentication. This is common even in large organizations. Strong passwords require combinations of letters, numbers, and special characters, and are not dictionary words.

Unfortunately, even if Web applications require strong passwords, attackers can figure out ways to bypass login screens if the code behind them is weak. This project will look at a couple of authentication errors that attackers might use to bypass login screens.

Note: While running WebGoat, your machine is extremely vulnerable to attack. You should disconnect from the Internet while using this program.

Note: If WebGoat is not currently installed and running on your local machine, you can go back to the prior project and go through the installation process.

1. With WebGoat running, open a browser and type: http://localhost/WebGoat/attack. This address is case-sensitive so be sure to capitalize the W and G in the address line.
2. Click on Start WebGoat.
3. On the left-hand side, click on Authentication Flaws.
4. Scroll down the list and click on Password Strength. (See Figure 19-12.)
5. Right-click the https://www.cnlab.ch/codecheck link shown in the paragraph and select Open Link in a New Window. (This will take you to a website that will test the strength of the five passwords listed on the WebGoat page.)
6. At the cnlab website, enter the *second* password listed (abzfez). (You are going to skip the first password listed for now.)
7. Click Run the check.
8. Click Yes, I want this word to be tested.
9. Click Continue.
10. Note that the website estimates it could take approximately 1,394 seconds to find the password.
11. Return to the WebGoat window.
12. Input the results (i.e., 1394) for the second password listed. (See Figure 19-13.)

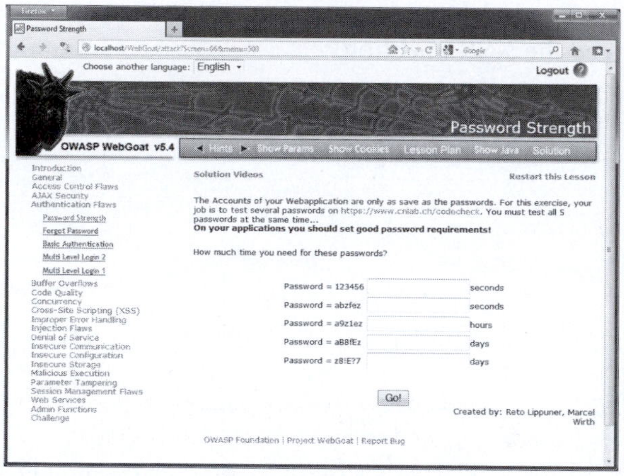

Figure 19-12: Authentication Flaws – Password Strength.

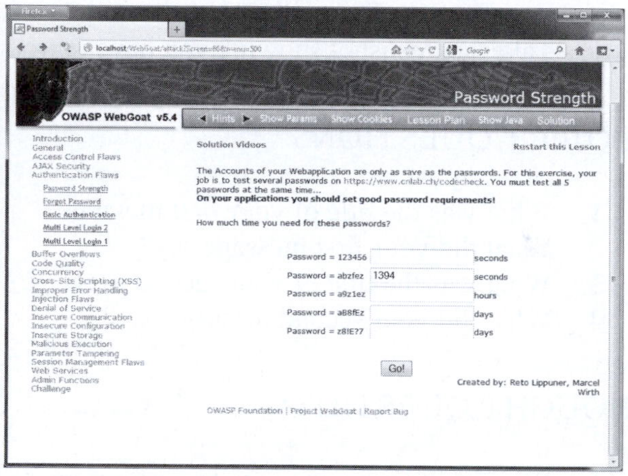

Figure 19-13: Inputting results from strength test.

13. Repeat the password strength test using the www.cnlab.ch website for the other passwords listed, and enter the values in their respective text boxes.
14. Click Go!, after you have entered all the estimated values.
15. Take a screenshot. (See Figure 19-14.)
16. Return to the www.cnlab.ch website and enter "yourfirstandlastname" without quotes and all lower case, as one word. (In this case, it was "randyboyle" without quotes.)
17. Click Run the check. (Note the length of the name you entered and the time it might take to find it.)
18. Take a screenshot.

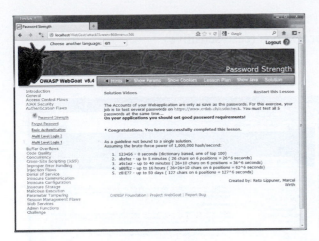

Figure 19-14: Completed password strength lesson.

Note: In the next part of this project, you are going to use an automated password reset to get a user's password. Poorly designed password reset systems can be easily manipulated.

19. Click Authentication Flaws in the left-hand menu.
20. Click on Forgot Password. (See Figure 19-15.)
21. Type "webgoat" without quotes into the User Name text box (case sensitive).
22. Click on Submit.
23. The Secret Question (also known as a Security Question) asks 'What is your favorite color?'
24. In the Answer text box, type "red" without quotes. (case sensitive)
25. Click Submit. (See Figure 19-16.)

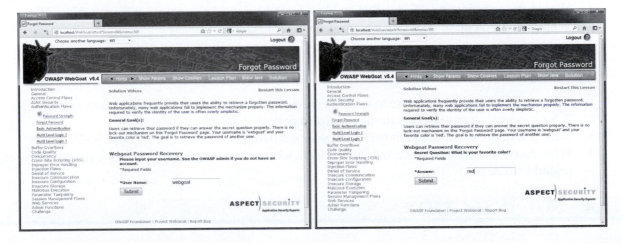

Figure 19-15: Automated password reset.   Figure 19-16: Password recovery question.

We will now go through the process of retrieving the password of another user by guessing the answer to the Secret Question:

26. Click on Forgot Password in the left-hand menu.
27. Type "admin" without quotes in the User Name text box (case-sensitive).
28. Click on Submit. (See Figure 19-17.)
29. The Secret Question (also known as a Security Question) asks, "What is your favorite color?"
30. Type "red" without quotes in the Answer text box (case-sensitive).
31. Press Enter.
32. Type "blue" without quotes in the Answer text box (case-sensitive).

33. Press Enter.
34. Type "green" without quotes in the Answer text box (case-sensitive).
35. Press Enter.
36. Take a screenshot. (See Figure 19-18.)

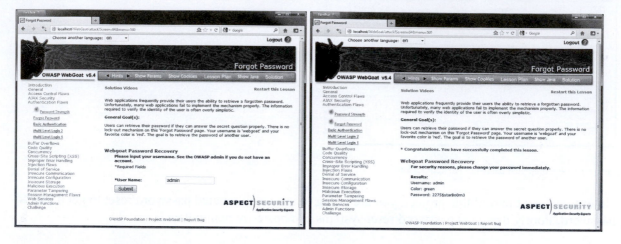

Figure 19-17: Recovering the admin's password.   Figure 19-18: The admin's password.

PROJECT QUESTIONS

1. How long was your first and last name that you entered?
2. According to the www.cnlab.ch website, how long might it take to find the password consisting of your first and last name?
3. Would the combination of your first and last name be a good password? Why or why not?
4. What might you do to make your password harder to crack?

THOUGHT QUESTIONS

1. Why do attackers often choose to crack the security question rather than the actual password?
2. Why it is important to have a strong password policy?
3. Why is it important to frequently change your password?
4. What recent events have occurred in the media where a password was cracked (e.g., celebrity, big organizations, etc.)?

19.4   SQL INJECTION

SQL injection, one of the exploits we will look at, is when someone takes advantage of database vulnerabilities by submitting malicious parameters through a Web interface. SQL injection techniques can be thwarted by using parameterized statements or by filtering the input before it is processed. Unfortunately, you are not going to learn how to protect against SQL injection attacks here.

Even mentioning SQL injection can be problematic. When is it appropriate to teach students about how SQL injection works? Most good IT security professionals know how SQL injection works and how to protect against it. Talking about SQL injection is the equivalent of having the birds-and-the-bees talk with your child. You know it has to be done sooner or later. You just don't want them to learn incorrect or inappropriate ideas from other children.

Note: While running WebGoat, your machine is extremely vulnerable to attack. You should disconnect from the Internet while using this program.

Note: If WebGoat is not currently installed and running on your local machine, you can go back to the prior project and go through the installation process.

1. With WebGoat running, open a browser and type: http://localhost/WebGoat/attack. This address is case-sensitive so be sure to capitalize the W and G in the address line.
2. Click on Start WebGoat.
3. Click on Injection Flaws in the left-hand menu.
4. Click on the XPATH Injection subheading. (See Figure 19-19.)

Note: You are now going to view the test user name to see what data is available. Notice that the database table includes the following personal attributes: Username, Account No., and Salary.

5. In the User Name data input box, type Mike (case-sensitive)
6. In the Password data input box, type test123 (case-sensitive).
7. Click Submit.
8. Take a screenshot. (See Figure 19-20.)

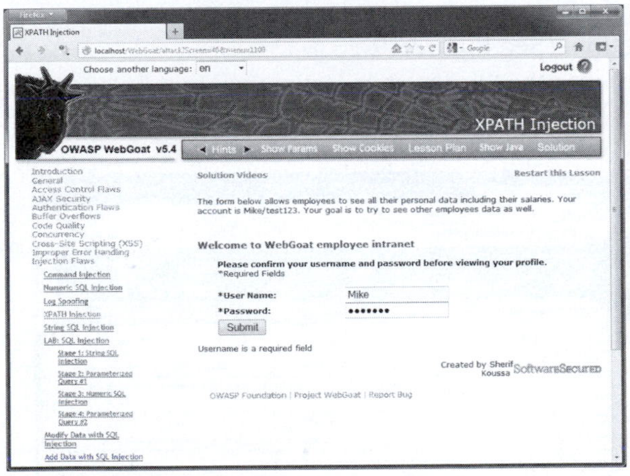

Figure 19-19: Entering the test account credentials.

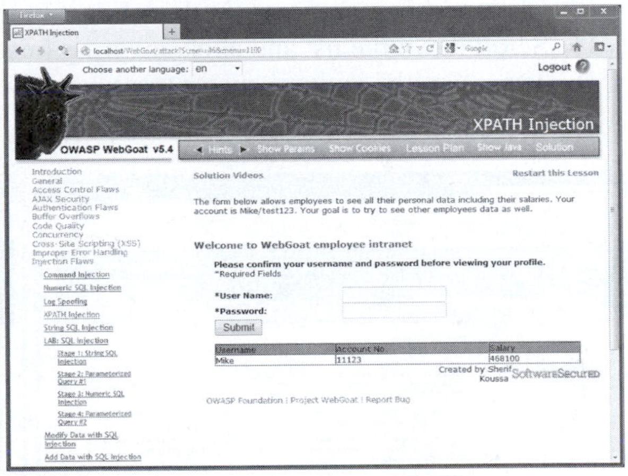

Figure 19-20: Employee information for the test account.

Note: Now you are going to attempt to extract and view all employee data including salaries using SQL injection. You need to type this in the data input box and not copy-paste it, otherwise the single quotations may not work.

9. Type the following in the User Name text box: **Mike' or 1=1 or 'a'='a**
10. In the Password data input box, type any combination of characters you want. (You must type at least one character for the injection to be successful. In this case, the letter "a" was entered.)
11. Click Submit. (See Figure 19-21.)
12. Enter your first and last names into the User Name text box.
13. Take a screenshot. (See Figure 19-22.)

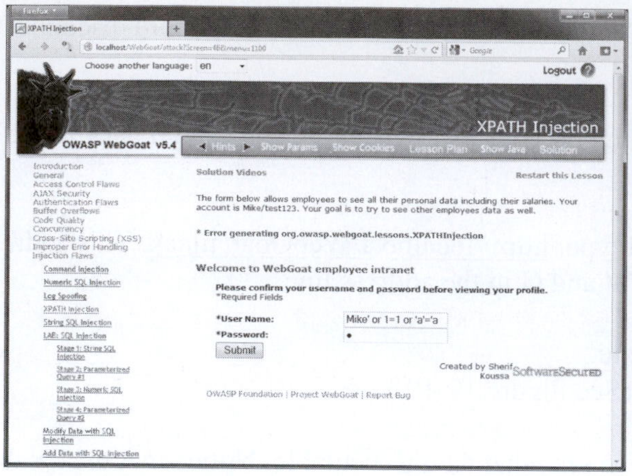

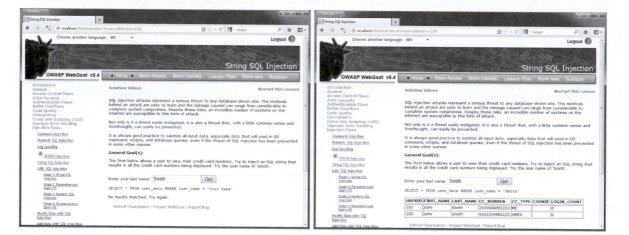

Figure 19-21: SQL injection. 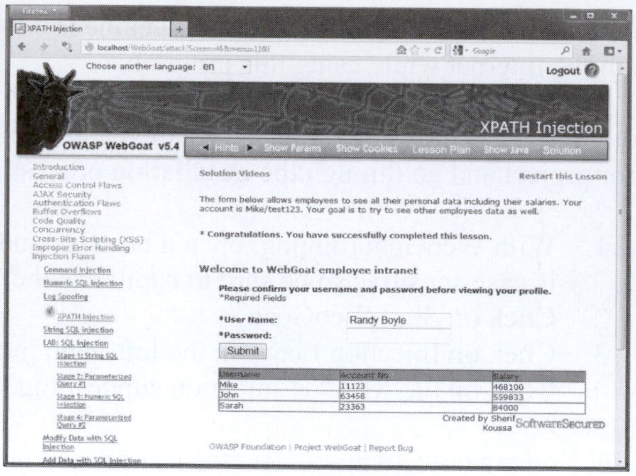   Figure 19-22: List of employee information.

Note: In this part of the project, you are going to use a similar SQL injection technique with similar syntax to get a listing of customer credit card numbers. You will enter the modified SQL syntax into a different field.

14. Click on Injection Flaws in the left-hand side menu.
15. Scroll down the list and click on String Injection. (See Figure 19-23.)
16. Type "Smith" without quotes (case-sensitive) into the "Enter your last name" text box.
17. Click Go. (See Figure 19-24.)

Figure 19-23: XPATH injection.   Figure 19-24: Viewing a test user's data.

Note: Now you are going to attempt to extract and view all IDs, names, credit card numbers, and credit card types using SQL injection. You will use similar syntax like that used in the prior example.

18. Type the following in the "Enter your last name" text box: `Smith' or 1=1 or 'a'='a`

Note: You need to type this in the data input box and not copy-paste it, otherwise the single quotations may not work.

19. Click Go. (See Figure 19-25.)
20. Scroll down to see the complete lising of user account data.
21. Enter your first and last name into the "Enter your last name" text box.
22. Take a screenshot. (See Figure 19-26.)

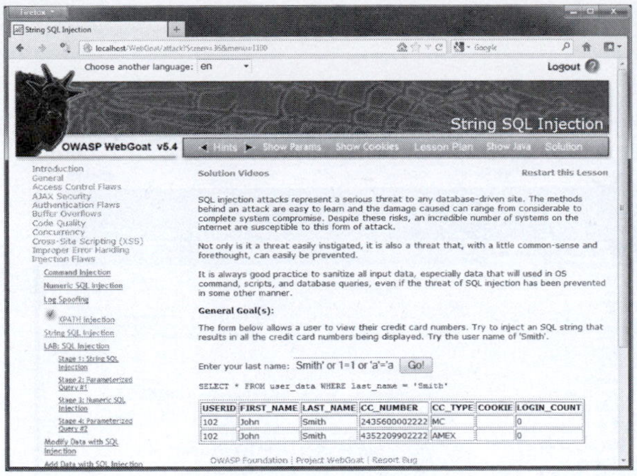

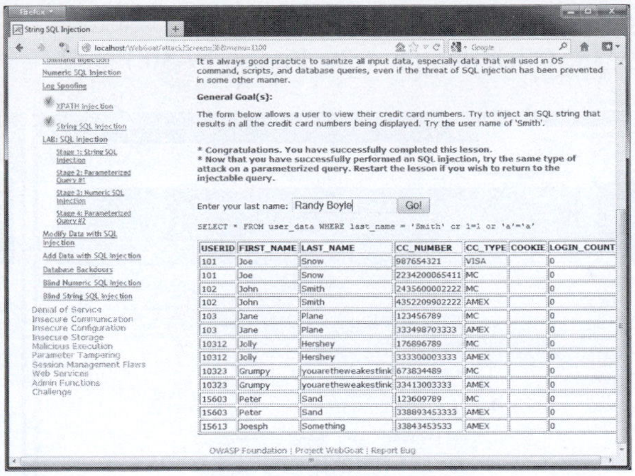

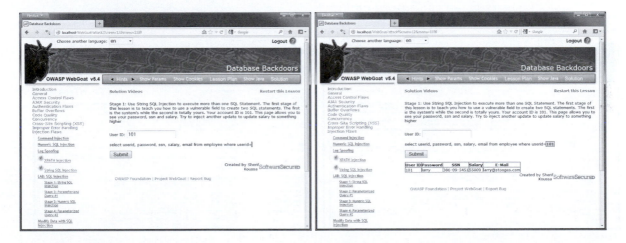

Figure 19-25: String SQL injection.   Figure 19-26: Viewing users' credit card data.

Note: In this part of the project, you are going to enter text into a text box that is normally used to query a person's user ID, password, Social Security Number, salary, and email address. Typically, one user ID is entered at a time. You will use SQL injection to get a complete listing all at once. You will also use SQL injection to give one person a hefty raise.

23. Click on Injection Flaws in the left-hand side menu.
24. Scroll down the list and click on Database Backdoors.
25. Type 101 in the User ID text box. (See Figure 19-27.)
26. Click Submit. (See Figure 19-28.)

Figure 19-27: Entering a user ID.   Figure 19-28: Viewing a test user's record.

Note: The following fields were displayed: User ID, Password, SSN, Salary, and E-Mail. In the next steps, you will update a person's salary -- in this case, a raise -- using SQL injection.

27. Type the following in the User ID text box: **101 or 1=1**
28. Click Submit.
29. Enter your first and last name into the User ID text box.
30. Take a screenshot. (See Figure 19-29.)
31. Clear the contents of the User ID text box.
32. Type the following in the User ID text box:

101;UPDATE employee SET salary=1500000 WHERE userid=101

33. Click Submit. (See Figure 19-30.)

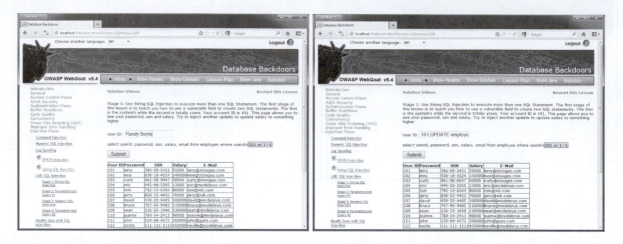

Figure 19-29: SQL injection.   Figure 19-30: List of employee information.

34. Enter your first and last name into the User ID text box.
35. Take a screenshot. (See Figure 19-31.)
36. Type the following in the User ID text box: **101 or 1=1**
37. Click Submit. (This will verify that the salary was changed.) (See Figure 19-32.)
38. Repeat these steps to raise one other person's salary by a random dollar amount.
39. Take a screenshot.

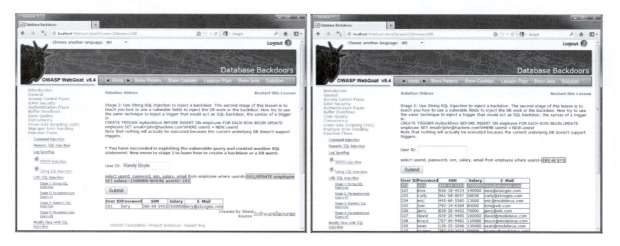

Figure 19-31: Updating a person's salary.   Figure 19-32: Updated salary list.

PROJECT QUESTIONS

1. To which user did you give a raise?
2. What was his/her user ID?
3. What was his/her email address?
4. How much was the raise?

THOUGHT QUESTIONS

1. Why are some databases vulnerable to SQL injection attacks?

2. Why do commands like `')` `or` `1=1` allow you to get past the login screen?
3. Why is the term UPDATE used in the Database Backdoor attack?
4. Could you use SQL injection to lower a person's salary or add a fictitious user?

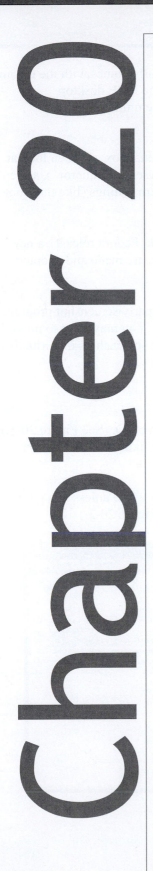

Much of the best IT security software is written for the Linux/Unix/BSD platform. Many of the top websites run their servers on Linux/Unix/BSD machines. Given the popularity of Linux as an enterprise-level operating system, it's surprising so few people have actually used Linux.

This chapter is designed to be a basic Linux primer for the average Windows user. It is not intended to be an exhaustive survey of all the functionality contained in the Linux operating system. Many books have been written that explore the Linux operating system in greater detail.

Most people are surprised at the functionality available in the various Linux distributions. You can get many of the same programs in Linux that you use in Windows, and you don't have to pay a penny. It's also likely that Linux will be more stable, more secure, faster, and easier to use, and cost less than Windows. Actually, it turns out that Linux is totally free!

Linux is like ice cream. There are lots of flavors, but in the end it's all ice cream. You will see many different "flavors" of Linux that you can download and experiment with. Each flavor, or "distro," of Linux comes with its own benefits and features but shares the same basic functionality.

This chapter was intentionally designed to introduce you to multiple Linux distributions. At the time of this writing, www.DistroWatch.com listed the following as the top 5 most popular Linux distributions over the past six months, in this order: Mint, Ubuntu, Fedora, openSUSE, and Debian.

Any IT security professional worth his or her salt will have at least a couple of Linux machines and be intimately familiar with the operating system. You need to take the time to become proficient with command-line Linux. It might be a little intimidating at first, but you will quickly get the hang of it.

Time required to complete this chapter: 60 minutes

Chapter Objectives

Learn how to:
1. Install Linux.
2. Use the Linux command line.
3. Install Linux software.
4. Use Linux networking tools.
5. Use Linux system tools.
6. Manage users and groups.
7. Use CLI network tools.
8. Use CLI file tools.
9. Capture data via a CLI.
10. Create adhoc TCP connections.
11. Create custom packets.
12. Use portable applications.

Chapter Projects

Project:
20.1 Linux Installation
20.2 Command-line Primer
20.3 Software Installation
20.4 Networking Commands
20.5 System Tools & Configuration
20.6 User and Group Management
20.7 Network CLI Utilities
20.8 File CLI Utilities
20.9 Tcpdump
20.10 Netcat
20.11 Hping
20.12 Portable Linux

20.1   LINUX INSTALLATION (FEDORA®)

In this project, you will install a flavor of Linux called Fedora®. Fedora typically comes with the Gnome® desktop environment. However, in this project, you will install Fedora with the KDE desktop environment. Both Gnome and KDE® are widely used. It's good to experience multiple desktop environments.

This project will walk you through a simple installation using Oracle VM VirtualBox and then look at some features of the KDE desktop environment. You will look at a Web browser (Konqueror®), a file manager (Dolphin®), a command prompt (Xterm®), the general desktop, system settings (like the Control Panel in Windows), and add a couple of widgets.

This project uses Fedora 17 (Beefy Miracle), but a later version will also work. Fedora releases a new version of their operating system about every six months. This means changes are made and adopted quickly. This has its advantages and disadvantages.

Note: Taking screenshots of virtual machines will be easier if you use a third party screenshot program like Screenshot Pilot, available at http://www.colorpilot.com/screenshot.html. You may have to press the right Ctrl key to exit the virtual machine and then use Screenshot Pilot to take screenshots in VirtualBox. If you didn't install Screenshot Pilot in an earlier project, you should do so now.

1. Download Fedora (KDE) from: http://fedoraproject.org.
2. Click on the Download link at the top of the page.
3. Click the link labeled "More download options" for the installable Live CD. (See Figure 20-1.)
4. Click on Download Now!, for the Fedora 17 KDE Spin. (You'll most likely need the 64-bit version.)
5. Click Save.
6. Select your C:\security folder. (This is a big download that will take a while unless you get it from your instructor or classmate. It should be about 700 MB.) (See Figure 20-2.)

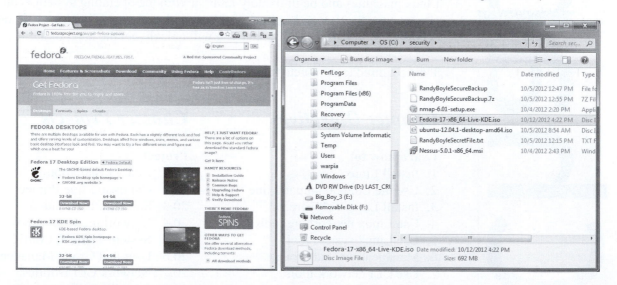

Figure 20-1: Fedora distribution page.   Figure 20-2: Fedora KDE image.

7. Open Oracle VM VirtualBox by clicking Start, All Programs, Oracle VM VirtualBox, and Oracle VM VirtualBox. (You installed VirtualBox as part of projects in an earlier chapter. If you haven't installed VirtualBox, you will need to do so now.)
8. Click New.
9. Enter "Fedora_YourName" for the Name. (In this case, it was Fedora_RandyBoyle.) (See Figure 20-3.)
10. Select Linux for the Operating System.
11. Select Fedora (64 bit) for the Version. (Select just "Fedora" if you have a 32-bit system.)
12. Click Next.
13. Increase the amount of memory to 2000 MB+. (See Figure 20-4.)

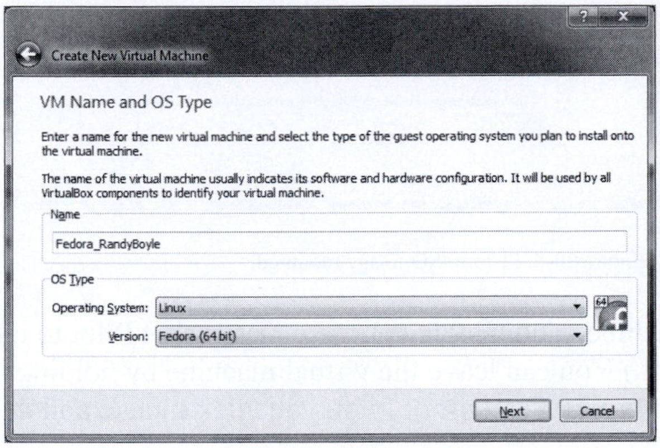

Figure 20-3: Naming the Fedora virtual machine.

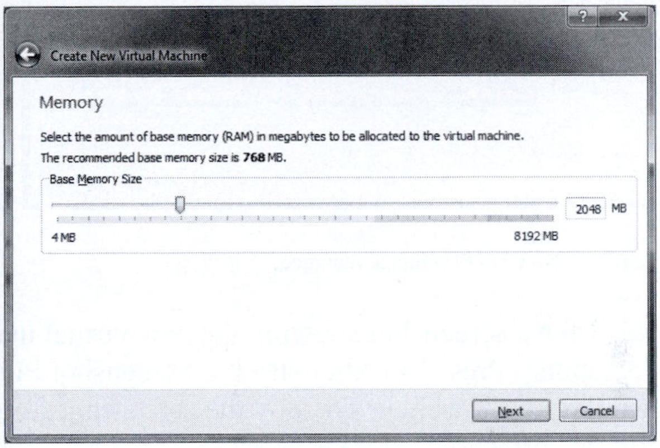

Figure 20-4: Allocating RAM to the virtual machine.

14. Click Next, Next, Next, and Next.
15. Increase the hard drive space to 15GB (or more if you have the space). (See Figure 20-5.)
16. Click Next, Create, and Create.
17. Select the Virtual machine labeled Fedora_YourName. (See Figure 20-6.)

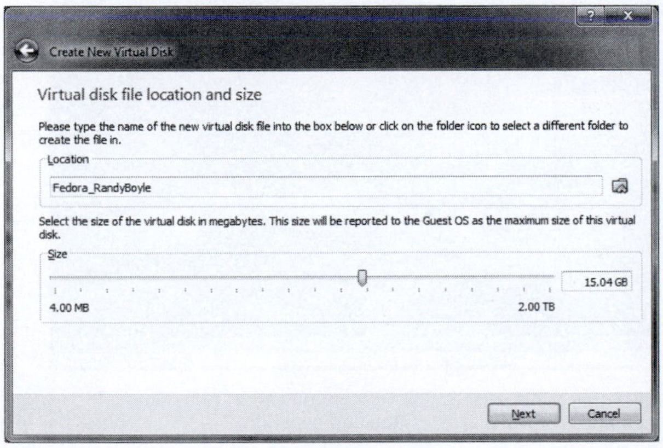

Figure 20-5: Setting the size of the virtual hard drive.

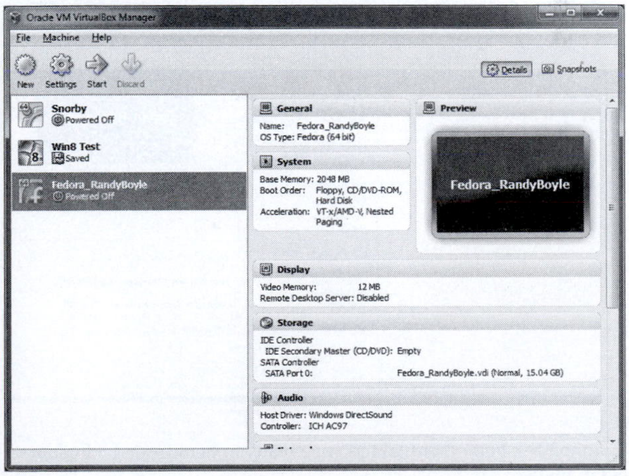

Figure 20-6: Fedora virtual machine created.

18. In the right-hand pane, click Storage, IDE Controller, and Empty. (See Figure 20-7.)
19. Click the Browse button on the right-hand side of the screen by the CD/DVD Drive drop-down box. (It looks like a little CD.)
20. Click Choose virtual CD/DVD disk file.
21. Browse to your C:\security folder.
22. Select the Fedora (KDE) image you downloaded.

23. Click Open. (See Figure 20-8.)
24. Click OK.

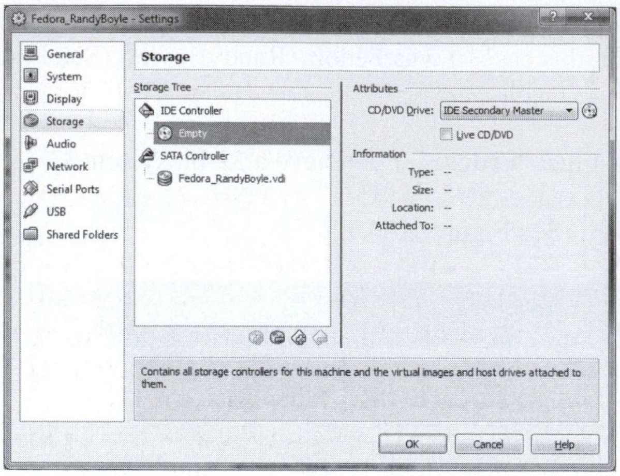

Figure 20-7: No CD/DVD image mounted.

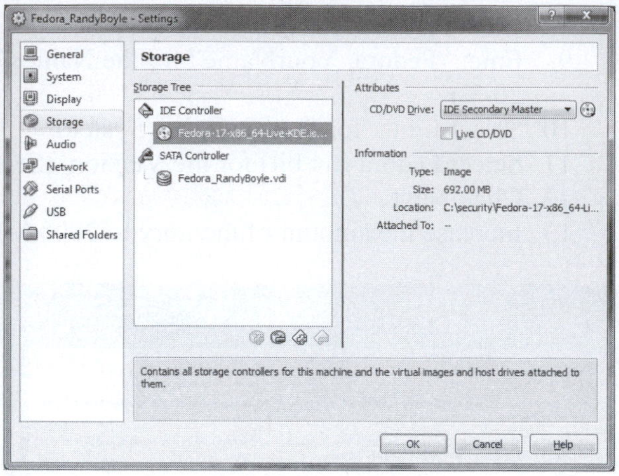

Figure 20-8: Fedora ISO image mounted.

Note: Take a screenshot showing the new virtual machine. You may have to use Screenshot Pilot to take screenshots. (Press F11 after starting Screenshot Pilot.) You can leave the virtual machine by holding down the right Ctrl key. To copy the screenshot from within Screenshot Pilot, you click Image, and then Copy to Clipboard.

25. Click Start. (It may take 3 or more minutes for Fedora to load depending on the resources allocated to the virtual machine.) (See Figure 20-9.)
26. Double-click the Install to Hard Drive icon. (See Figure 20-10.)

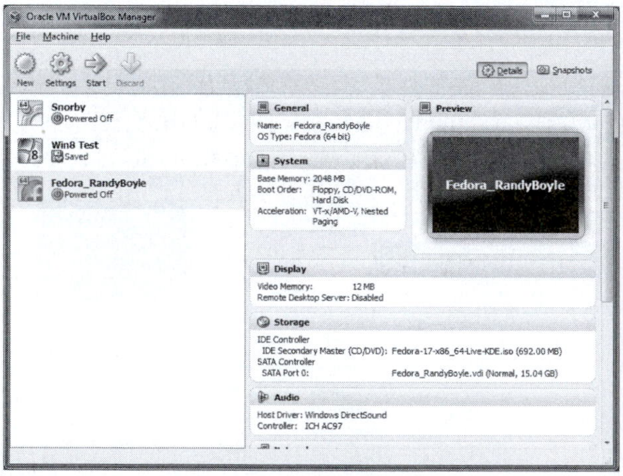

Figure 20-9: Fedora virtual machine ready to boot from the Fedora KDE image.

Figure 20-10: Fedora desktop and installer.

27. Click Next, Next, and Yes.
28. Enter "YourNameFedora" for the Hostname. (In this case, it was RandyBoyleFedora.) (See Figure 20-11.)
29. Click Next.
30. Select the closest city. (See Figure 20-12.)
31. Click Next.

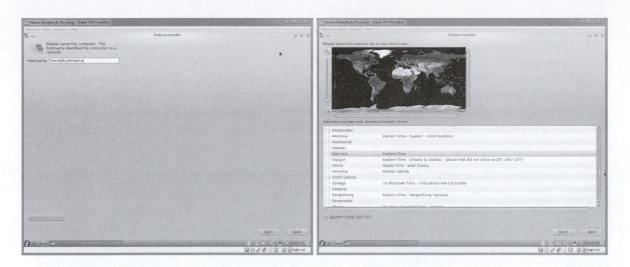

Figure 20-11: Entering a hostname.   Figure 20-12: Setting the time zone.

32. Enter a root password twice. (It's a good idea to write down your root password if you have a bad memory. You will need to know this password for later projects.) (See Figure 20-13.)
33. Press Next, Next, and Write changes to disk. (The installation process will take several minutes.)

Note: *After* the installation process finishes, you will have to remove the Fedora ISO image out of the virtual CD ROM so you don't have to go through the installation process again. If you don't take out the ISO image, the installation process will start again when you reboot the virtual machine.

34. Press the right Ctrl key to exit the virtual machine. (This step may not be necessary for most versions of VirtualBox. Older versions may require it.)
35. In the VirtualBox menu for the virtual machine you are working on, click Devices, CD-DVD ROM, and Remove disk from virtual drive. (This will unmount the Fedora ISO image.) (See Figure 20-14.)
36. Click Force Unmount. (This should remove the ISO image from your virtual CD-DVD drive.)
37. In the Fedora virtual machine, click Reboot. (This will reboot your virtual machine from the virtual hard drive. If the virtual machine hangs, you can close the window and restart the virtual machine from the VirtualBox menu.)

Figure 20-13: Entering a password for the root account.   Figure 20-14: Unmounting the Fedora installation image.

38. Click Forward, and Forward. (See Figure 20-15.)
39. Enter your first and last name. (In this case, it was Randy Boyle. The username should fill in automatically. If it doesn't, enter your first name.)
40. Enter a password you can remember twice. (It's a good idea to use the *same* password that you entered for the root account. In general, this is not good practice. However, this is only a virtual machine. You can change your password later.) (See Figure 20-16.)
41. Click Forward, Forward, Finish, and No, do not send. (Your Fedora virtual machine should reboot at this time.)

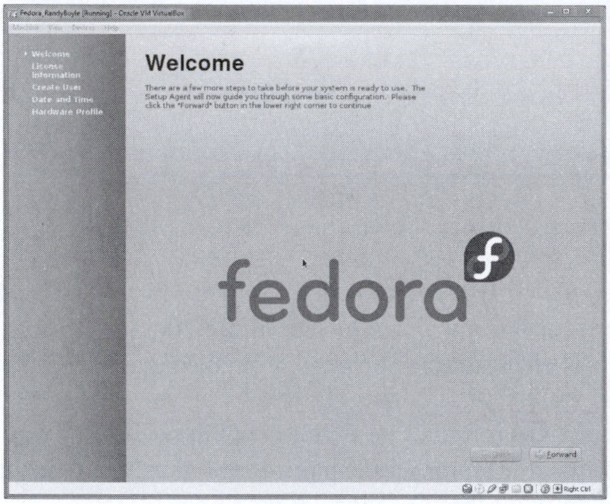

Figure 20-15: Welcome screen.

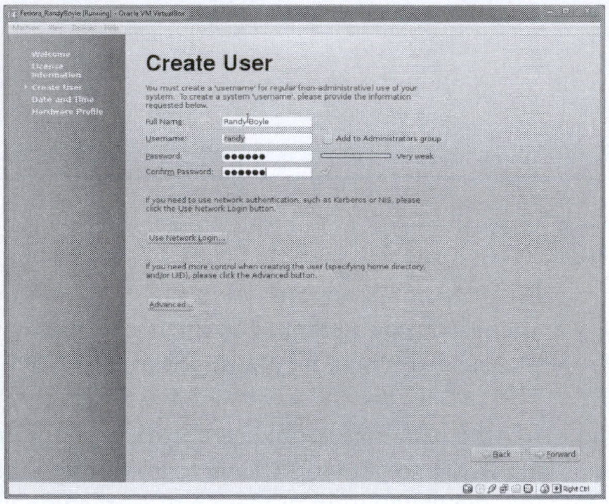

Figure 20-16: Setting username and password.

42. Enter your username. (It should be your first name. In this case, it was Randy.)
43. Take a screenshot of the login screen. (See Figure 20-17.)
44. Enter your password.
45. Click Log In.
46. Click on the Fedora menu icon on the bottom left-hand of the screen. (This is similar to the Start button in Windows.)
47. Click Applications, Internet, and Web browser. (This will open the default Web browser called Konqueror.)
48. Browse to www.Google.com.
49. Enter your name into the search box.
50. Take a screenshot of your virtual desktop showing your name in the Google search box. (See Figure 20-18.)

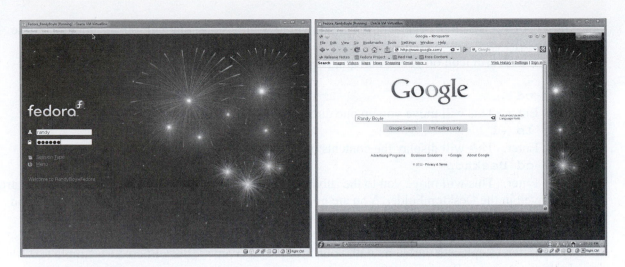

Figure 20-17: Fedora login screen.   Figure 20-18: Konqueror Web browser in Fedora.

51. Click on the Fedora menu icon on the bottom left-hand of the screen.

52. Click Applications, System, and File Manager - Dolphin. (This will open the default File browser called Dolphin. You will see your home directory. This is similar to the My Documents folder in Windows.)

53. Click on the red "root" folder in the left-hand pane. (This will show a listing of all the directories under root. This is similar in many ways to the C: drive in Windows. Your personal home directory, along with all other user directories, is located in the home directory.) (See Figure 20-19.)

54. Click on the "home" directory.

55. Click on the directory with your name on it.

56. Take a screenshot of the contents of your home directory. (See Figure 20-20.)

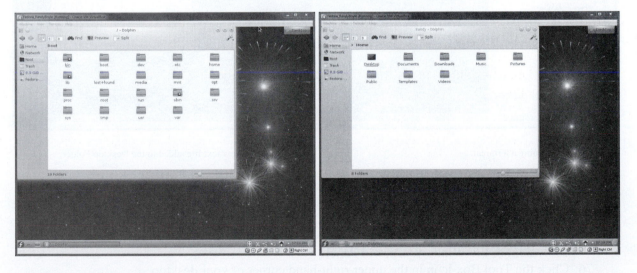

Figure 20-19: The root directory.   Figure 20-20: A user's home directory.

57. Click on the Fedora menu icon on the bottom left-hand of the screen. (This is similar to the Start button in Windows.)

58. Click Applications, and System. (You are going to create a shortcut to the Terminal application, XTerm, from this menu.)

59. Scroll down and right-click on Terminal (XTerm).

60. Select Add to Desktop. (This will add a shortcut to your desktop that will open a command-line terminal.)
61. Click the XTerm icon on your desktop. (This should open an XTerm terminal.) (See Figure 20-21.)
62. Type **cd ..**
63. Press Enter. (This will move you up one directory to your home directory.)
64. Type **ls -l**
65. Press Enter. (This will display the contents of your home directory.)
66. Type **cd Desktop**
67. Press Enter. (This will move you to the subdirectory that contains files, folders, links, etc. that are displayed in the Desktop Folder. You are going to create a text document and have it display on your desktop.)
68. Type **touch YourName.txt**
69. Press Enter. (Replace YourName with your first and last name. This will create a simple text file. In this case, it was RandyBoyle.txt.)
70. Type **ls**
71. Press Enter. (This will verify that you created the text file. You should see the new text file with your name on it. It should also appear in the Desktop Folder.)
72. Take a screenshot of your virtual machine desktop showing the XTerm terminal, and the new text file in the Desktop folder. (See Figure 20-22.)

Figure 20-21: Opening a terminal.   Figure 20-22: New text file added to the Desktop Folder.

73. Click on the Fedora menu icon on the bottom left-hand of the screen.
74. Click Applications, Settings, and System Settings. (This will open an application similar to the Control Panel in Windows.) (See Figure 20-23.)
75. Close the System Settings window. (You opened System Settings so you could see the Linux equivalent of the Windows Control Panel.)
76. Click the Tool Box icon in the upper right-hand corner of your desktop.
77. Click Add Widgets. (See Figure 20-24.)

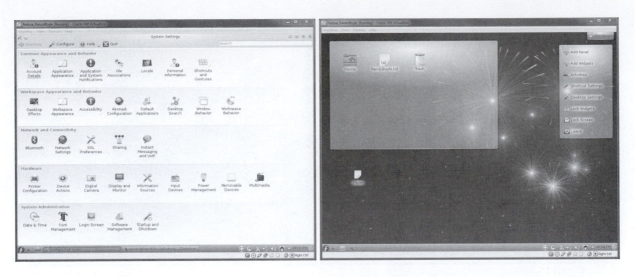

Figure 20-23: System Settings.   Figure 20-24: Adding widgets from the Tool Box.

78. Scroll to the right until you see the system monitor that looks like a graph. (See Figure 20-25.)
79. Drag-and-drop the System Monitor icon onto your desktop. (You may have to resize it bigger to see the graphs displayed in the next step.)
80. Click on each of the grayed-out icons to display the graphs below. (See Figure 20-26.)
81. Close the Add Widgets toolbar.

Figure 20-25: Adding the System Monitor widget.   Figure 20-26: System Monitor widget.

82. Right-click the taskbar along the bottom of your screen.
83. Click Panel Options, and Add Widgets.
84. Double-click the Lock/Logout icon. (It's a red, square icon. This will add it to your taskbar on the bottom of your screen.) (See Figure 20-27.)
85. Take a screenshot of your modified desktop. (See Figure 20-28.)

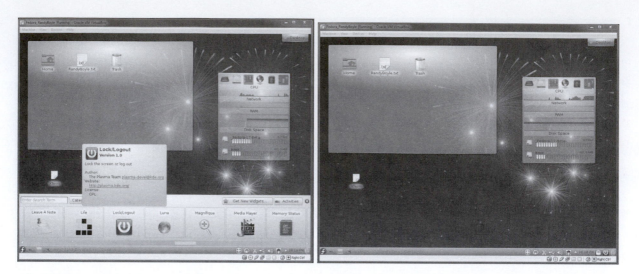

Figure 20-27: Adding the Lock/Logout widget.   Figure 20-28: Lock/Logout widget now on taskbar.

PROJECT QUESTIONS

1. What was your username?
2. What was the name of the text file you created?
3. How much disk space did your boot partition take up?
4. Do you think the Fedora KDE desktop is easy to use? Why?

THOUGHT QUESTIONS

1. Approximately how many software packages could be installed and used with Fedora?
2. What is in the /media directory?
3. Can you download additional widgets other than the ones shown?
4. Is KDE the default desktop environment for Fedora?

20.2   COMMAND-LINE PRIMER (FEDORA)

This project will go through some basic Linux command-line exercises. These commands are intended to be a short primer, *not* an exhaustive dissertation about all possible Linux command-line functionality. These are just some of the more commonly used commands. There are additional online tutorials that provide broader coverage of the command-line tools shown below.

You will need to practice these commands many times to become even moderately proficient. Only after entering them many hundreds of times will they become second nature to you. You can complete equivalent tasks using a command-line interface in a fraction of the time it would take you to complete them using a GUI interface in Windows.

Taking screenshots using the Alt-PrntScrn key sequence does not always work with virtual machines. It's better to use Ctrl-PrntScrn or download Screenshot Pilot from http://www.colorpilot.com/screenshot.html. In this project, you are going to press Enter after typing each command, unless otherwise directed.

1. Open Oracle VM VirtualBox by clicking Start, All Programs, Oracle VM VirtualBox, and Oracle VM VirtualBox.
2. Select your Fedora virtual machine.

3. Click Start.
4. Login if you are not already logged in. (Your username should be "yourname" in all lower-case. In this case, it was "randy.")
5. Click the Fedora icon, Applications, System, and Terminal. (See Figure 20-29.)
6. Type **cd ..**
7. Press Enter. (This will move you up one directory to your home directory.)
8. Type **ls**
9. Press Enter. (This displays a listing of the files in the current directory.)
10. Type **ls -l**
11. Press Enter. (This displays the listing in long format.)
12. Type **ls -al**
13. Press Enter. (This displays a listing of files including hidden files. There are many hidden files in your home directory.)
14. Take a screenshot. (See Figure 20-30.)

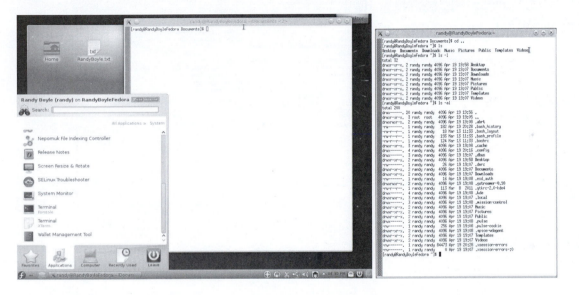

Figure 20-29: Starting a terminal.   Figure 20-30: Results from the ls command.

15. Type **man ls**
16. Press Enter. (This displays the manual page for the ls command.)
17. Type **q**
18. Press Enter. (This will exit the man page.)
19. Type **man man**
20. Press Enter. (This displays the manual page for the man command.) (See Figure 20-31.)
21. Take a screenshot.
22. Type **q**
23. Press Enter. (This will exit the man page.)
24. Type **date**
25. Press Enter. (This will display the current time and date.)
26. Type **cal**
27. Press Enter. (This will display the current month's calendar.)
28. Type **uptime**
29. Press Enter. (This will display how long the system has been up and running.)
30. Type **w**
31. Press Enter. (This will display who is logged on to the system.)
32. Type **whoami**

33. Press Enter. (This will display whom you are logged on as.)
34. Type **finger yourname**
35. Press Enter. (This will display who "randy" is.) (See Figure 20-32.)
36. Take a screenshot.
37. Type **clear**
38. Press Enter. (This will clear the screen.)

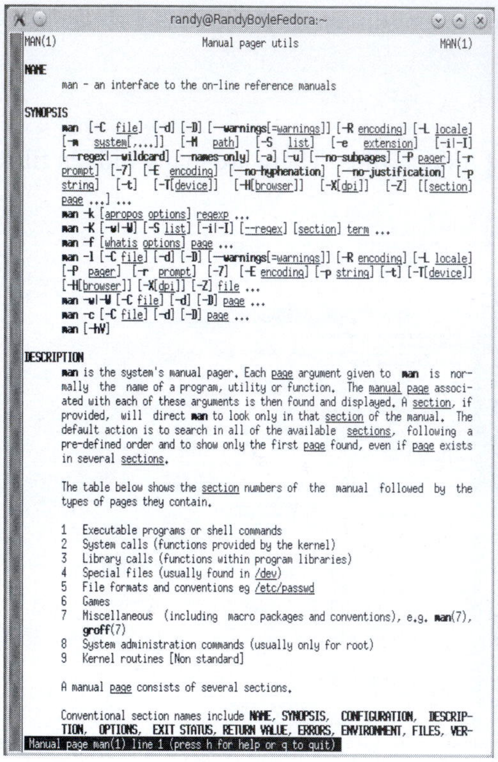

Figure 20-31: MAN page.

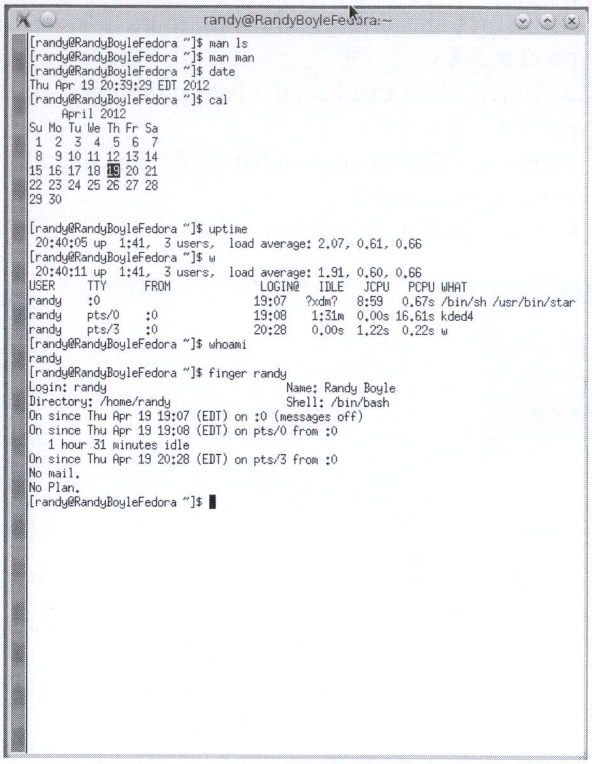

Figure 20-32: Results from the w, whoami, and finger commands.

39. Type **df**
40. Press Enter. (This will display how much of your hard disk you have used.)
41. Type **touch YourName.txt**
42. Press Enter. (This will create a simple text file. Replace YourName with your first and last name. In this case, it was RandyBoyle.txt.)
43. Type **ls**
44. Press Enter. (This will verify that you created the text file. You should see the new text file with your name on it.)
45. Type **vi YourName.txt**
46. Press Enter. (This will start the vi editor and enter text into the new file you created. You are now in the vi editor. You are not at the command prompt.)
47. Press **i**. (This will put you in "insert" mode and allow you to enter text into the document. It will say "insert" at the bottom of the screen.)
48. Enter your name three times. (In this case, "Randy Boyle" was typed three times.)
49. Press the ESC key.
50. Press **ZZ**. (This will save the text file and exit the vi editor. Note, it is case-sensitive and those are capital Zs.)
51. Type **vi YourName.txt**
52. Press Enter. (This will open the vi editor and verify that you correctly saved the text document.)
53. Take a screenshot. (See Figure 20-33.)

54. Press **ZZ.** (This will save and exit the vi editor.)
55. Type **mkdir YourNameFolder**
56. Press Enter. (This will create a folder in your home directory. The terms "folder" and "directory" are used interchangeably here, but the preferred term in Linux is directory.)
57. Type **ls**
58. Press Enter. (This will display the current directory and verify that you did create the new directory.) (See Figure 20-34.)

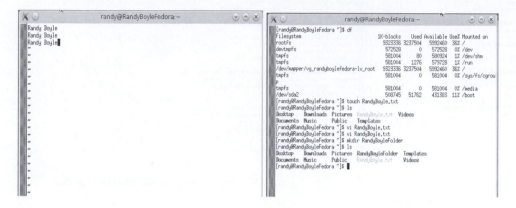

Figure 20-33: Editing a text file in vi.   Figure 20-34: Making a directory.

59. Type **cd YourN**
60. DO NOT PRESS THE ENTER KEY. Instead, press the Tab key to finish the name of the directory. (In this case, the command was "**cd RandyB**". Using the tab key can save you lots of time and prevent errors. You need to be careful though, because commands are case-sensitive. A lower-case "r" and an upper-case "R" are not the same thing.)
61. Press Enter.
62. Type **pwd**
63. Press Enter. (This will display the full path. It stands for "print working directory.")
64. Type **cd ..**
65. Press Enter. (This will move back one level in the directory structure to your home directory.)
66. Type **ls**
67. Press Enter. (This will verify you are back in your home directory.)
68. Type **cp YourName.txt YourNameCopy.txt**
69. Press Enter. (This will create a copy of your text file. In this case, YourName will be RandyBoyle for the remainder of this project.)
70. Type **ls**
71. Press Enter. (This will display the contents of the current directory and verify the copy was made correctly.) (See Figure 20-35.)
72. Type the following command to make a copy of the copy, move it into the directory you just created, and give it a new name (case-sensitive).

cp YourNameCopy.txt /home/yourname/YourNameFolder/YourNameCopy2.txt

73. Type **cd YourNameFolder**
74. Press Enter. (This will enter your subdirectory.)
75. Type **ls**
76. Press Enter. (This will view the new file you just copied over.)
77. Take a screenshot. (See Figure 20-36.)

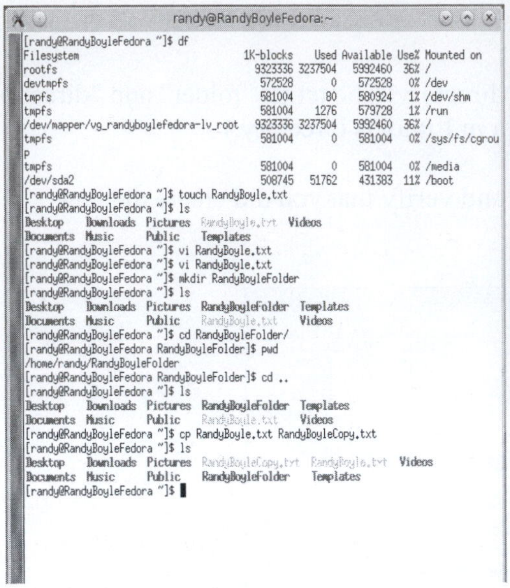

Figure 20-35: Making a copy of a file.

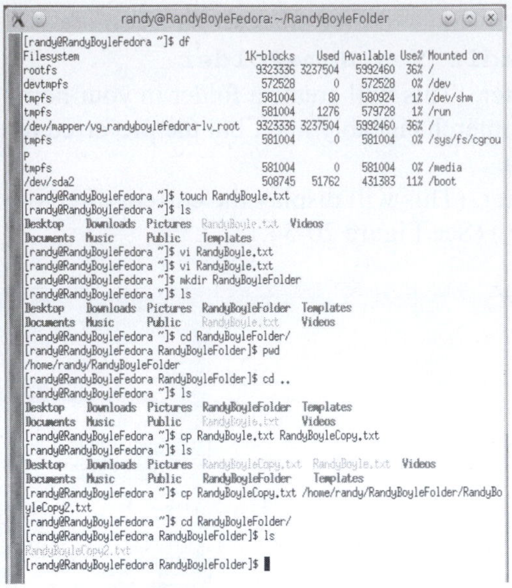

Figure 20-36: Copying a file from one directory to another.

78. Type **cd ..**
79. Press Enter. (This will move you back to your home directory.)
80. Type **ls**
81. Press Enter. (This will display the contents of your home directory.)
82. Type **rm YourNameCopy.txt**
83. Press Enter. (This will delete the copied file in your home directory.)
84. Type **ls**
85. Press Enter. (This will confirm the deletion of the YourNameCopy.txt file.)
86. Type **rm -r YourNameFolder**
87. Press Enter. (This will remove the directory and its contents.)
88. Type **ls**
89. Press Enter. (This will confirm the deletion of the directory.) (See Figure 20-37.)
90. Type **!!**
91. Press Enter. (This will repeat the last command.)
92. Type **cd ..**
93. Press Enter. (This will move you to the home directory. Directories for all users are located here.)
94. Type **cd ..**
95. Press Enter. (This will move you to the root directory. This is roughly the equivalent to the C: drive on your Windows computer.)
96. Type **ls**
97. Press Enter. (This will display a listing of all of the directories in root.)
98. Type **find -name YourName.txt**
99. Press Enter. (This will find the text file you created. You will also get plenty of "permission denied" responses, but you should see your file listed near the top. If you get too many "permission denied" responses, you can reenter the command and press Ctrl+c to stop the search after it has found your file.)
100. Take a screenshot. (See Figure 20-38.)

Figure 20-37: Deleting files and directories.   Figure 20-38: Results from the find command.

101. Type **su root**
102. Press Enter. (This will switch to the administrator account. In Linux, the administrator account is called root.)
103. Enter the password you set when you installed Fedora. (Don't worry if you can't see the characters being entered. Linux doesn't display asterisks for password characters like Windows does.)
104. Press Enter.
105. Type **find -name YourName.txt**
106. Press Enter. (This will find your text file. You won't see all of the "permission denied" errors. In this case, the command was find -name RandyBoyle.txt.)
107. Take a screenshot. (See Figure 20-39.)
108. Type **exit**
109. Press Enter. (This will exit the root account and lower your privileges. It's better to only run as root when necessary. It will keep you from inadvertently damaging your system.)
110. Type **cd home**
111. Press Enter. (This will move you into the home directory.)
112. Type **cd yourname**
113. Press Enter. (In this case, it was cd randy. This will move you into your directory.)
114. Type **ls**
115. Press Enter. (This will confirm that you are back in your directory.)
116. Type **grep lastname YourName.txt**
117. Press Enter. (This will search for instances where "lastname" appears in the YourName.txt file. In this case, the command was grep boyle RandyBoyle.txt. It will return every line of text where your lastname appears.)
118. Type **grep Lastname YourName.txt**
119. Press Enter. (This is the same as above *except* for the change in capitalization. You will see if capitalization makes a difference when using the grep command. In this case, the command was grep Boyle RandyBoyle.txt and it returned three instances where it found "Boyle" in the text file.)
120. Take a screenshot. (See Figure 20-40.)

```
[randy@RandyBoyleFedora /]$ find -name RandyBoyle.txt
./home/randy/Desktop/RandyBoyle.txt
./home/randy/RandyBoyle.txt
find: './var/lib/mlocate': Permission denied
find: './var/lib/udisks': Permission denied
find: './var/lib/pulse': Permission denied
find: './var/lib/rsyslog': Permission denied
find: './var/lib/authconfig': Permission denied
find: './var/lib/yum/history/2012-04-11/1': Permission denied
^C
[randy@RandyBoyleFedora /]$ su root
Password:
[root@RandyBoyleFedora /]# find -name RandyBoyle.txt
./home/randy/Desktop/RandyBoyle.txt
./home/randy/RandyBoyle.txt
[root@RandyBoyleFedora /]#
```

```
[randy@RandyBoyleFedora /]$ find -name RandyBoyle.txt
./home/randy/Desktop/RandyBoyle.txt
./home/randy/RandyBoyle.txt
find: './var/lib/mlocate': Permission denied
find: './var/lib/udisks': Permission denied
find: './var/lib/pulse': Permission denied
find: './var/lib/rsyslog': Permission denied
find: './var/lib/authconfig': Permission denied
find: './var/lib/yum/history/2012-04-11/1': Permission denied
^C
[randy@RandyBoyleFedora /]$ su root
Password:
[root@RandyBoyleFedora /]# find -name RandyBoyle.txt
./home/randy/Desktop/RandyBoyle.txt
./home/randy/RandyBoyle.txt
[root@RandyBoyleFedora /]# exit
exit
[randy@RandyBoyleFedora /]$ cd home
[randy@RandyBoyleFedora home]$ cd randy
[randy@RandyBoyleFedora ~]$ ls
Desktop   Downloads  Pictures  RandyBoyle.txt  Videos
Documents Music      Public    Templates
[randy@RandyBoyleFedora ~]$ grep boyle RandyBoyle.txt
[randy@RandyBoyleFedora ~]$ grep Boyle RandyBoyle.txt
Randy Boyle
Randy Boyle
Randy Boyle
[randy@RandyBoyleFedora ~]$
```

Figure 20-39: Results from the find command as root.   Figure 20-40: Results from the grep command.

121. Type **clear**
122. Press Enter. (This will clear the screen.)
123. Type **tar cf YourNameArchive.tar YourName.txt**
124. Press Enter. (This will create a compressed archive of your text file similar to a zip file. Remember to replace YourName with your first and last name. In this case, the file was named RandyBoyleArchive.tar.)
125. Type **ls**
126. Press Enter. (This will confirm the creation of the tar file.)
127. Type **rm YourName.txt**
128. Press Enter. (This will delete the text file. In this case it was RandyBoyle.txt.)
129. Type **ls**
130. Press Enter. (This will confirm the deletion of the text file.)
131. Type **tar xf YourNameArchive.tar**
132. Press Enter. (This will extract the file from the archive into your directory. In this case, the file was named RandyBoyleArchive.tar.)
133. Type **ls**
134. Press Enter. (This will confirm that the archive did extract the text file into your home directory.)
135. Take a screenshot. (See Figure 20-41.)
136. Type **top**
137. Press Enter. (This will display a listing of the processes currently running on your virtual machine. You are now in interactive mode.) (See Figure 20-42.)
138. Press q. (This will quit interactive mode and return you to the command prompt.)
139. Click on the Fedora menu icon (like the Start menu in Windows), Applications, Office, and Spreadsheet (Calligra Tables). (You can also use KSpread if it's available. Any application will work, but it will have a different process name that you will need to find.)
140. Double-click on Blank Worksheet.
141. Enter a couple of random values in a few of the cells.

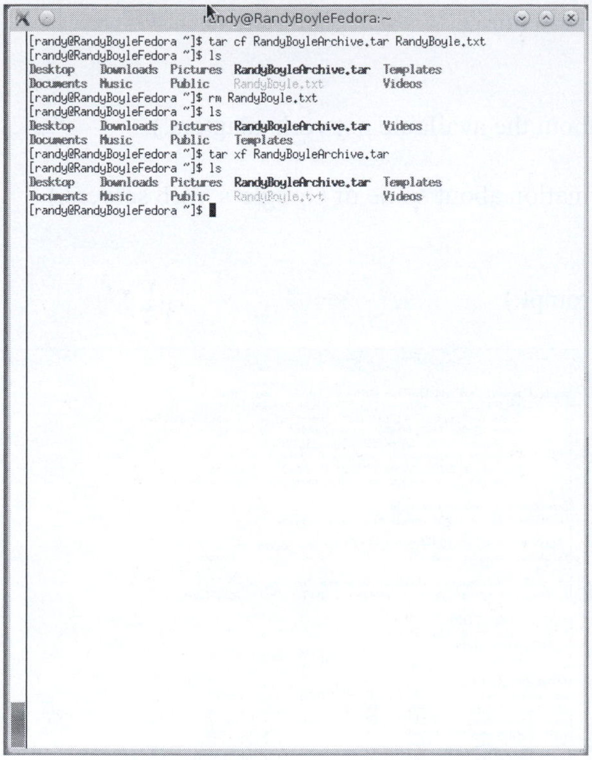

Figure 20-41: Archiving a file with the tar command.

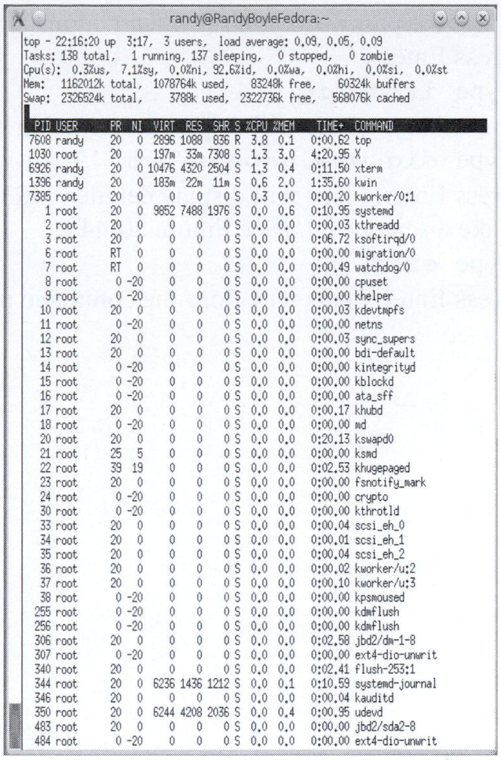

Figure 20-42: Listing processes with the top command.

142. Return to the command prompt.

143. Type **top -u yourname**

144. Press Enter. (In this case, the command was `top -u randy`. This will display only the processes you are running. You are now in interactive mode.)

145. Press M. (This is case-sensitive. This will sort the processes by the amount of memory they are using. The "calligratables" or "kspread" process should be listed near the top.)

146. Write down the process ID (PID) for calligratables. (In this case, it was the second process from the top and the PID was 7610. Your process ID will be different. You will have to correctly identify the PID for calligratables or kspread on your machine. The PID is listed on the left-hand side.)

147. Press k.

148. Press Enter. (This is will now allow you to enter the PID you want to kill.)

149. Type the calligratables pin.

150. Press Enter twice. (It is very unlikely that your PID was 7610. You need to enter your PID. You should see the process disappear and the spreadsheet window close.) (See Figure 20-43.)

151. Press q.

152. Press Enter. (This will quit the interactive mode and return you to the command prompt.)

153. Type **ping www.google.com**

154. Press Enter. (This will ping one of Google's Web servers. You will stop this command by pressing Ctrl-C.)

155. Press Ctrl-C to cancel the ping command after about four responses.

156. Press the up arrow key (↑) to scroll through prior commands until you get to the `ping www.google.com` command.

157. Press Enter.

158. Press Ctrl-C to cancel the ping command after about four responses.

159. Type **su root**

160. Press Enter. (This will switch to the root account.)

161. Enter the password you set when you installed Fedora.
162. Press Enter.
163. Type `ifconfig`
164. Press Enter. (This will display information about the available network adapters.)
165. Type `dig www.google.com`
166. Press Enter. (This will display detailed information about some of Google's Web servers.)
167. Take a screenshot. (See Figure 20-44.)
168. Type `exit`
169. Press Enter. (This will close the command prompt.)

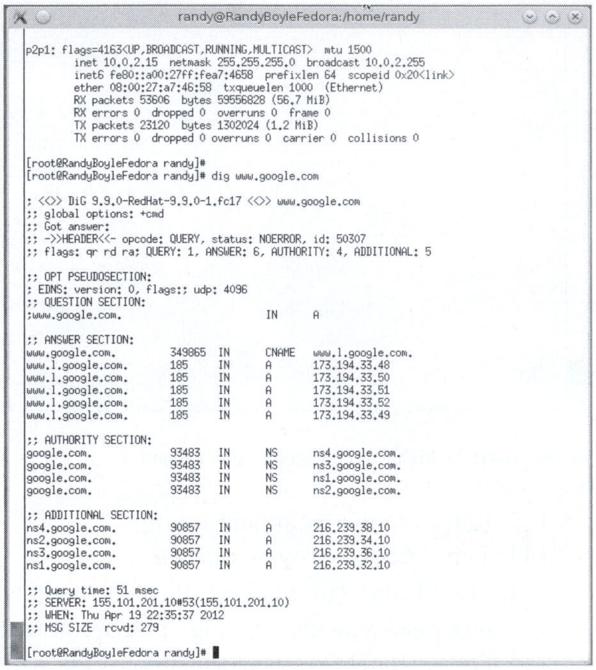

Figure 20-43: Killing a process.   Figure 20-44: Results from the dig command.

PROJECT QUESTIONS

1. What was the name of the text file you created?
2. What was the name of the directory you created?
3. What did you find using the grep command?
4. What was the process ID (PID) that you stopped?

THOUGHT QUESTIONS

1. Do these commands work on a Mac? Why or why not?
2. Are there study sheets available as a reference?
3. How can knowing command-line Linux save you time?
4. Which of the commands in this project was a compression utility?

In this project, you will install software using the Ubuntu Software Center and using the command-line. There are many thousands of pieces of software available for Linux that provide the same functionality you will find on Windows or MAC. In fact, many cutting-edge applications are developed initially for the Linux platform. There are new applications being developed every day by the open source community and being made available to everyone for free.

This project will use the Ubuntu distribution. Not only is this a different flavor of Linux, but this also uses a newer Unity desktop environment. This is a good chance to compare and contrast the differences between KDE and Unity. In later projects, you will look at the Cinnamon and Gnome desktops. You can get Ubuntu in KDE, Gnome, or Unity (default). Most applications can be run on a variety of desktops. It's all a matter of personal preference.

1. Download Ubuntu from: http://www.ubuntu.com.
2. Click the Download link at the top of the page.
3. Click the "Ubuntu desktop" link. (See Figure 20-45.)
4. Change the dropdown box to 64-bit. (You likely have a 64-bit version if you have a newer computer. If you have an older computer, you can get the 32-bit version.)
5. Click Save.
6. Select your C:\security folder. (This is a big download that will take a while unless you get it from your instructor or classmate. It should be about 700 MB.) (See Figure 20-46.)

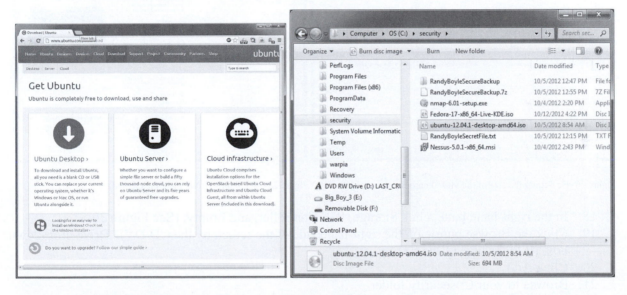

Figure 20-45: Ubuntu distribution page.   Figure 20-46: Ubuntu image.

7. Open Oracle VM VirtualBox by clicking Start, All Programs, Oracle VM VirtualBox, and Oracle VM VirtualBox. (You installed VirtualBox as part of projects in an earlier chapter. If you haven't installed VirtualBox, you will need to do so now.)
8. Click New.
9. Enter Ubuntu_YourName for the Name. (In this case, it was Ubuntu_RandyBoyle.) (See Figure 20-47.)
10. Select Linux for the Operating System.
11. Select Ubuntu (64 bit) for the Version. (Select just "Ubuntu" if you have an older 32-bit system.)
12. Click Next.
13. Increase the amount of memory to 2000 MB+. (See Figure 20-48.)

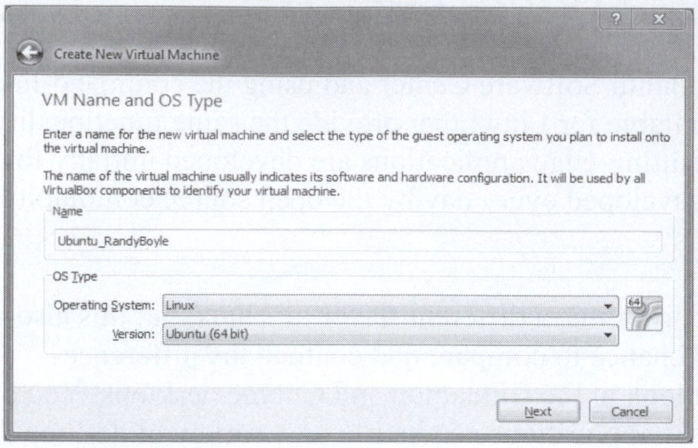

Figure 20-47: Naming the Ubuntu virtual machine.

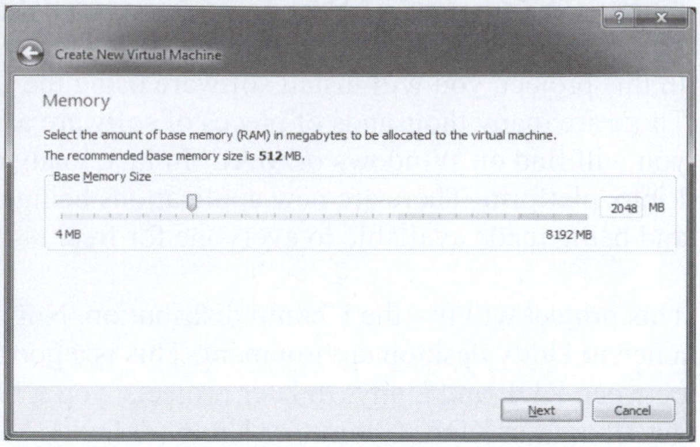

Figure 20-48: Allocating RAM to the virtual machine.

14. Click Next, Next, Next, and Next.
15. Increase the hard drive space to 15GB (or more if you have the space). (See Figure 20-49.)
16. Click Next, Create, and Create.
17. Select the Ubuntu_YourName virtual machine. (See Figure 20-50.)

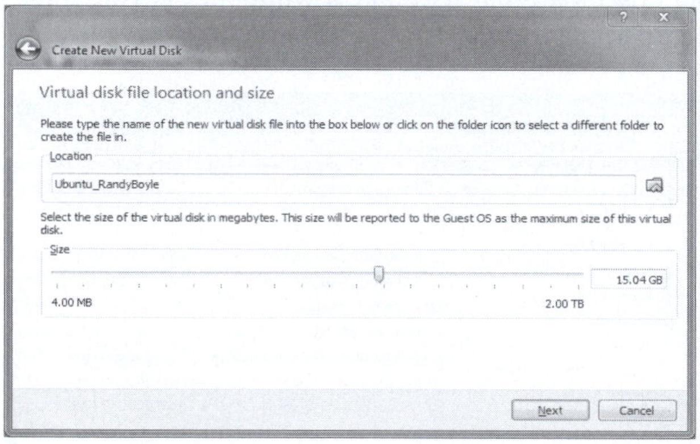

Figure 20-49: Setting the size of the virtual hard drive.

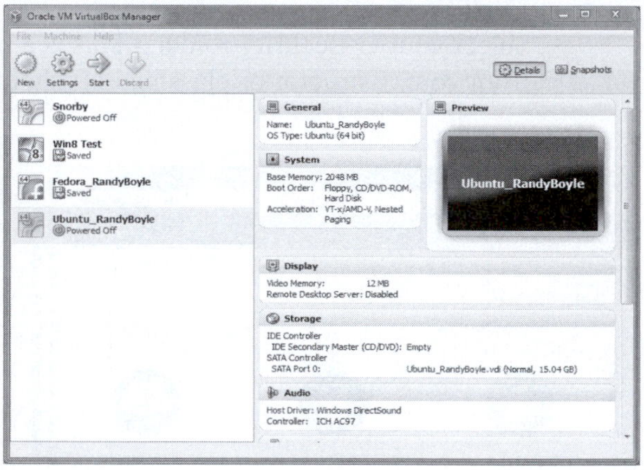

Figure 20-50: Ubuntu virtual machine created.

18. In the right-hand pane, click Storage, IDE Controller, and Empty. (See Figure 20-51.)
19. Click the Browse button on the right-hand side of the screen by the CD/DVD Drive drop-down box. (It looks like a little CD.)
20. Click Add.
21. Browse to your C:\security folder.
22. Select the Ubuntu ISO image you downloaded. (In this case, it was Ubuntu-12.04.1-desktop-amd64.iso.)
23. Click Open. (See Figure 20-52.)
24. Click OK.

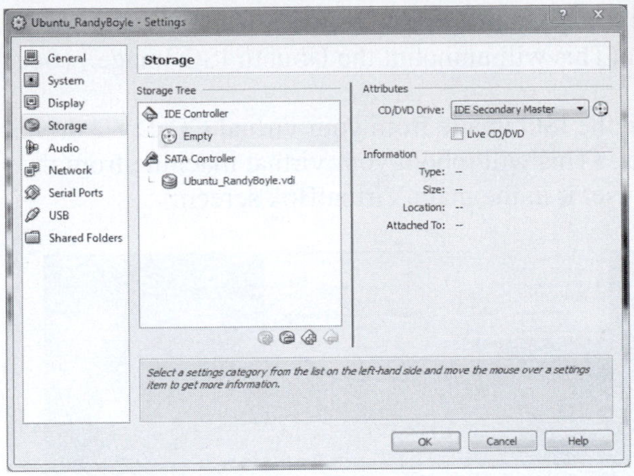

Figure 20-51: No CD/DVD image mounted.

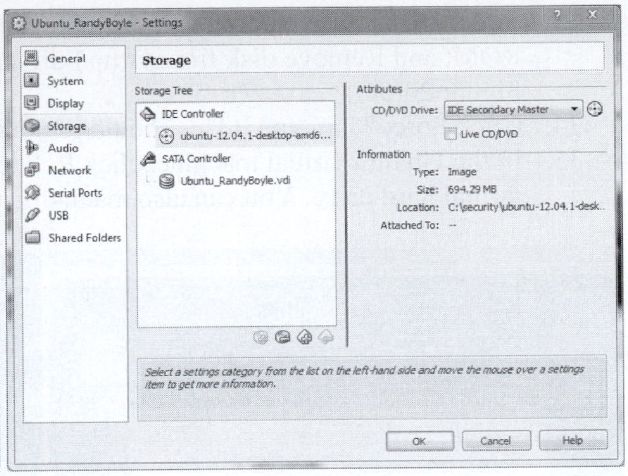

Figure 20-52: Ubuntu ISO image mounted.

25. Take a screenshot showing the new virtual machine. (You may have to use Screenshot Pilot to take screenshots. You can leave the virtual machine by holding down the right Ctrl key. To copy the screenshot from within Screenshot Pilot, you click Image, and then Copy to Clipboard.) (See Figure 20-53.)
26. Click Start. (It may take 3 or more minutes for Ubuntu to load depending on the resources allocated to the virtual machine.)
27. Click the Install Ubuntu button. (See Figure 20-54.)

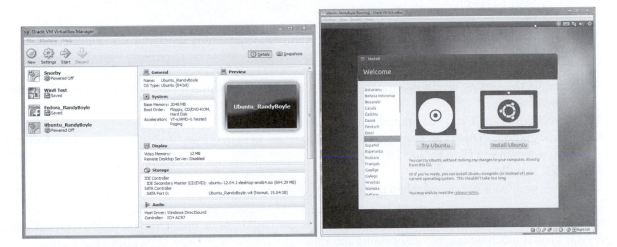

Figure 20-53: Ubuntu virtual machine ready to boot.

Figure 20-54: Ubuntu desktop and installer.

28. Click Continue, Continue, Install Now, Continue, and Continue.
29. Enter your first and last name. (Your username should be your first name.)
30. Enter a root password twice. (It's a good idea to write down your root password if you have a bad memory. You will need to know this password for later projects.) (See Figure 20-55.)
31. Click Continue. (The installation process will take several minutes.)

Note: You are now going to have to take the Ubuntu ISO image out of the virtual CD ROM so you don't have to go through the installation process again. If you don't take out the ISO image, the installation process may start again when you reboot the virtual machine.

32. Press the right Ctrl key to exit the virtual machine. (You may be able to skip this step on newer versions of VirtualBox. Older versions may still require it.)

33. In the VirtualBox menu for the virtual machine you are working on, click Devices, CD-DVD ROM, and Remove disk from virtual drive. (This will unmount the Ubuntu ISO image.) (See Figure 20-56.)
34. Click Force Unmount. (This should remove the ISO image from your virtual CD-DVD drive.)
35. In the Ubuntu virtual machine, click Reboot. (This will reboot your virtual machine from the virtual hard drive. You can also manually reset it in the main VirtualBox screen.)

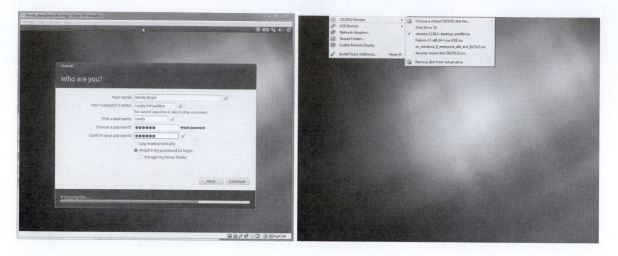

Figure 20-55: Entering a password for the root account.   Figure 20-56: Unmounting the Ubuntu installation image.

36. Enter your password.
37. Press Enter.
38. Click the Ubuntu Software Center icon (the shopping bag) on the left-hand side menu. (See Figure 20-57.)
39. Click on Sound & Video in the left-hand pane.
40. Change the sorting dropdown menu from By Top Rated to Name. (This will sort the applications alphabetically.)
41. Scroll down until you see gtkpod.
42. Click gtkpod. (This is an application that allows you to manage an iPod when it is connected to a Linux machine.) (See Figure 20-58.)
43. Click Install.
44. Enter your root password when prompted.

Note: If you get an error stating that the software packages could not be updated, you might have an issue with your virtual machine correctly accessing the Internet. Open a Web browser within your virtual machine and make sure you have Internet access.

Figure 20-57: Menu for Add/Remove Applications.   Figure 20-58: Selecting gtkpod to be installed.

45. Click All Software, Internet, and All.
46. Change the sorting dropdown menu from By Top Rated to Name. (This will sort the applications alphabetically.)
47. Scroll down until you see EtherApe. (This is a network monitoring tool that provides a graphical representation of network traffic.)
48. Click EtherApe.
49. Click Install.
50. Enter your root password when prompted.
51. Scroll down until you see Wireshark. (This is the same program you used in earlier projects. You are installing it here to show you that the same software used in earlier projects can run on Linux.)
52. Click Wireshark. (See Figure 20-59.)
53. Click Install.
54. Scroll down until you see Zenmap. (This is a GUI front end to Nmap. Nmap is a powerful network mapping, scanning, and host identification tool.)
55. Click Zenmap. (See Figure 20-60.)
56. Click Install.

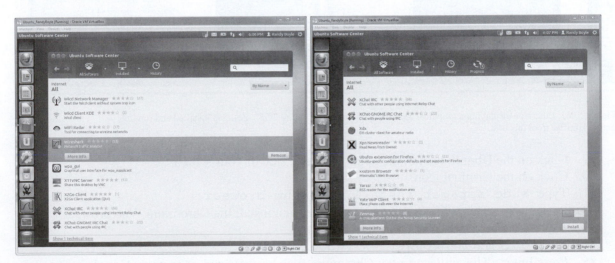

Figure 20-59: Selecting Wireshark to be installed.   Figure 20-60: Selecting Zenmap to be installed.

57. Click on the gtkpod icon on the left-hand side of your screen. (It looks like an iPod.)

58. Take a screenshot.
59. Click on the Ubuntu icon in the upper left-hand side of your screen.
60. In the search box, start typing "terminal". (It should display a terminal icon below the search box. You can click on the terminal icon, or finish typing the word "terminal" and press enter. Both actions will open a terminal.)
61. Type **sudo etherape**
62. Press Enter. (This will elevate your privileges and start EtherApe from the terminal.)
63. Enter your root password when prompted. (EtherApe will open, but the screen may remain blank. You will open a Web browser in the next step to generate some traffic.)
64. Open the Firefox Web browser by clicking on the icon on the left-hand menu.
65. Go to www.Google.com.
66. Click on News.
67. Minimize the Web browser.
68. Return to EtherApe. (You should see EtherApe changing.)
69. Take a screenshot. (See Figure 20-61.)
70. Return to the terminal window.
71. Press Ctrl-C to cancel the process.
72. Type **sudo zenmap**
73. Press Enter. (This will elevate your privileges and start Zenmap from the terminal.)
74. Enter your root password when prompted.
75. Enter "127.0.0.1" as the target.
76. Click Scan.
77. Take a screenshot after the scan completes. (See Figure 20-62.)
78. Close all applications.

Figure 20-61: EtherApe displaying a graphical representation of network traffic from this host.

Figure 20-62: Zenmap installed and running.

79. Click on the Ubuntu icon in the upper left-hand side of your screen.
80. Click on the terminal icon.
81. Type **sudo apt-get install chromium-browser**
82. Press Enter. (This will elevate your privileges and install the Chromium Web browser.)
83. Type "y" if prompted. (Wait for it to finish.)
84. Type **chromium-browser www.google.com**
85. Press Enter. (This will start your Chromium Web browser and go to www.Google.com.)
86. Type your name into the search box. (In this case, Randy Boyle.)
87. Press Enter.

88. Take a screenshot showing Google Chrome running within your virtual machine. (See Figure 20-63.)
89. Return to the terminal.
90. Press Ctrl-C to close the Chromium Web browser.
91. Type `sudo apt-get install apache2`
92. Press Enter. (See Figure 20-64.)
93. Type "y" if prompted.

Figure 20-63: Google Chrome successfully installed.   Figure 20-64: Installing Apache via a command prompt.

94. Type `sudo /etc/init.d/apache2 start`
95. Press Enter. (This will make sure Apache is running.)
96. Open the Chromium Web browser.
97. Enter "127.0.0.1" into the address bar. (This is the loopback adapter. This will direct your Web browser to request the default page on your locally installed Apache Web server.)
98. Take a screenshot. (See Figure 20-65.)

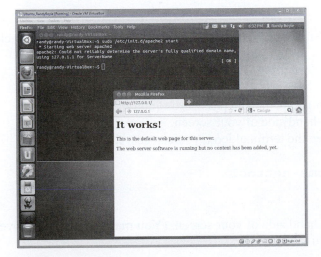

Figure 20-65: Starting Apache.

PROJECT QUESTIONS

1. What was your username?
2. Approximately how many other connections were shown in EtherApe when you took your screenshot?
3. Was it faster for you to install software graphically using the software center, or at the command prompt?
4. What was the first website displayed when you searched for your name?

THOUGHT QUESTIONS

1. Can you install Oracle VM VirtualBox on Linux and run a Windows virtual machine?
2. Why are there different software repositories and who manages them?
3. Why is it possible to install software on Linux from the command-line or through the GUI interface?
4. Can you install all Linux applications in a Unity, Gnome, or KDE desktop environment?

20.4 NET-TOOLS AND NETWORKING COMMANDS (UBUNTU)

In this project, you will look at some of the basic networking tools that come loaded with Linux. In the first part of the project, you will use an application that has several commonly used networking utilities. In the second half of this project, you will use command-line tools to produce the same results. You will see that some of the command-line tools are similar to the tools you used in the DOS prompt.

You will also use the tcpdump command to capture packets, write them to a log file, and then read the log file. This is the command-line equivalent of Wireshark, the packet capturing software you used in earlier projects. Many of the same options you used in the Wireshark projects are also available in tcpdump.

Knowing how to use the command-line tools is important because they are available on almost every computer. Experienced network administrators use them constantly. The following project is a basic primer.

1. Open Oracle VM VirtualBox by clicking Start, All Programs, Oracle VM VirtualBox, and Oracle VM VirtualBox.
2. Select your Ubuntu virtual machine.
3. Click Start.
4. If you are not already logged in, enter your username and password to log in.
5. Click on the Ubuntu icon in the upper left-hand side of your screen.
6. Click on the terminal icon. (If you don't see the terminal icon, you can search for the term "terminal" and you should see the icon.)
7. Type `sudo apt-get install gnome-nettool`
8. Press Enter.
9. Enter your password when prompted.
10. Click on the Ubuntu icon in the upper left-hand side of your screen. (You may have to hover over the top icon for it to scroll up to the Ubuntu icon.)
11. In the search box, type "network".
12. Click on the Network Tools icon.
13. Change the Network device from the loopback adapter to your network card.
14. Click on the Firefox icon on the left-hand menu.
15. Resize the Web browser so it is next to the Network Tools screen.
16. Go to www.Google.com and search for YourName. (Watch the Interface Statistics change.)

17. Leave the virtual machine and click on your desktop. (You may have to press the right Ctrl key to leave the virtual machine.)
18. Take a screenshot. (Your name should be visible in the Google search results.) (See Figure 20-66.)

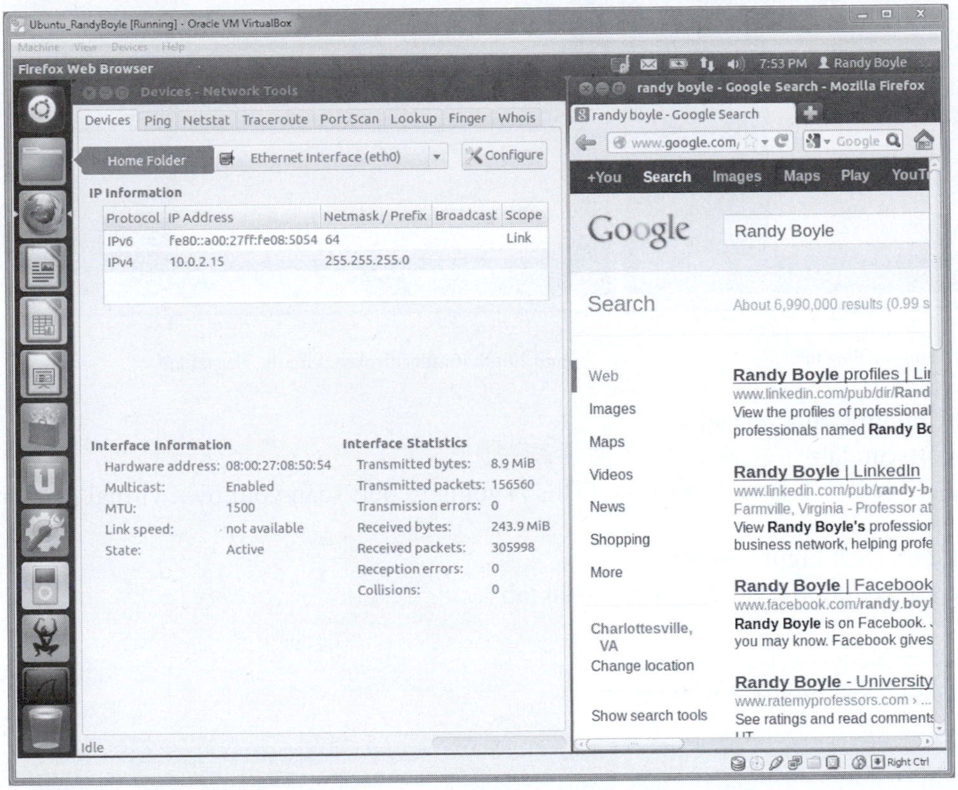

Figure 20-66: Network interface information and statistics.

19. Return to the Ubunutu virtual machine.
20. Click on the Ping tab in the Network Tools menu.
21. Enter "www.Google.com" for the Network address.
22. Click Ping.
23. Enter another hostname of your choice to ping (e.g., www.yourschool.com).
24. Click Ping.
25. Take a screenshot. (See Figure 20-67.)
26. Click on the Netstat tab.
27. Select Routing Table Information.
28. Click Netstat.
29. Take a screenshot. (See Figure 20-68.)

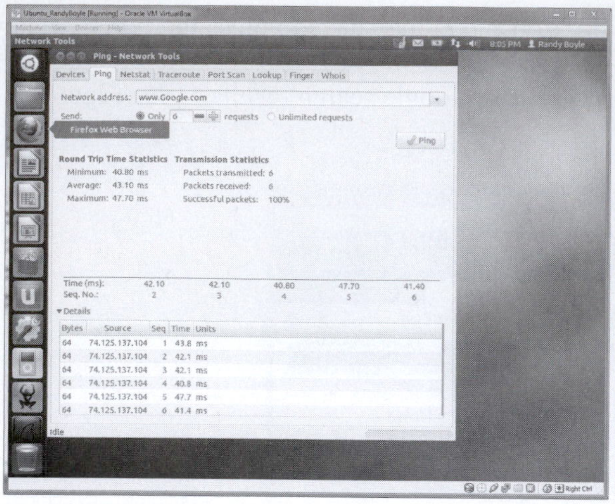

Figure 20-67: Results displayed for the Ping tab.

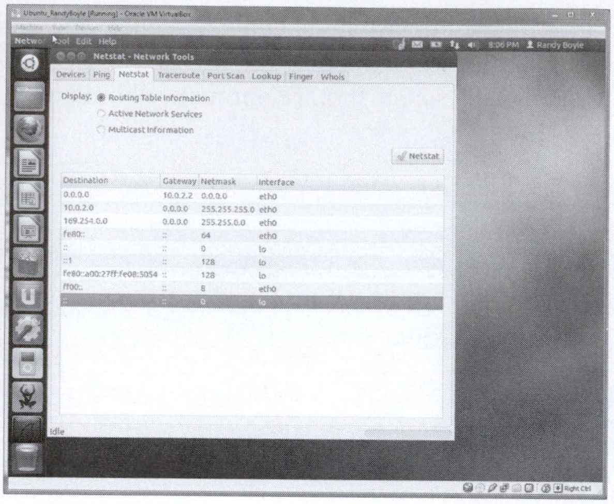

Figure 20-68: Results displayed for the Netstat tab.

30. Return to the Ubuntu virtual machine.
31. Click on the Portscan tab.
32. Enter "127.0.0.1" for the Network address. (This is going to port scan your own virtual machine.)
33. Click Scan.
34. Take a screenshot. (See Figure 20-69.)
35. Click on Active Network Services in the Netstat tab.
36. Click Netstat.
37. Click on the other Network Tools window.
38. Take a screenshot. (See Figure 20-70.)

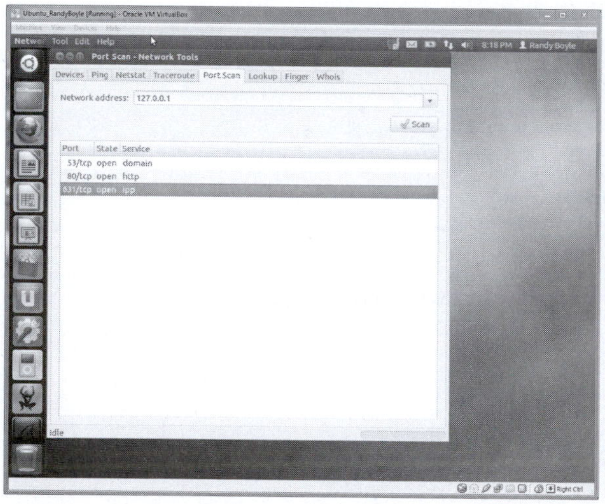

Figure 20-69: Results displayed for the Port Scan tab.

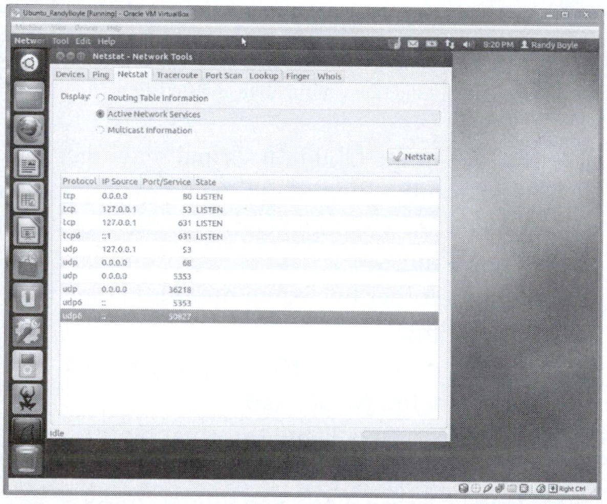

Figure 20-70: Results displayed for the Active Network Services (Netstat) tab.

39. Return to the Ubuntu virtual machine.
40. Click on the Lookup tab in the Network Tools menu.
41. Enter "www.Google.com" for the Network address.
42. Click Lookup.
43. Take a screenshot. (See Figure 20-71.)
44. Click on the other Network Tools window.
45. Click on the Whois tab.
46. Enter "www.Google.com" for the Network address.

47. Click Whois.
48. Take a screenshot showing the results in the Lookup and Whois tabs. (See Figure 20-72.)

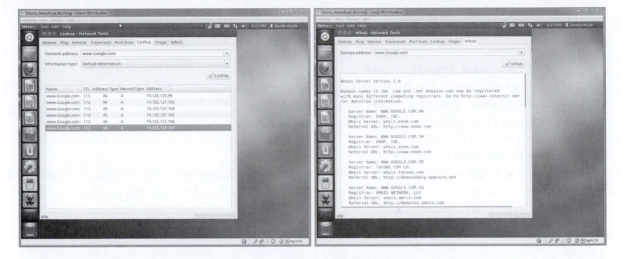

Figure 20-71: Results displayed for the Lookup tab.   Figure 20-72: Results displayed for the Whois tab.

49. Click on the Ubuntu icon in the upper left-hand side of your screen.
50. Click on the terminal icon. (If it is not displayed, you can search for it by typing "terminal" in the search box.)
51. Type **netstat --route**
52. Press Enter. (This will display the routing table.)
53. Type **netstat -r**
54. Press Enter. (This will also display the routing table. All of the commands below can be shortened to use just the first letter. For added clarity, this project will use more explicit options.)
55. Type **netstat --interfaces**
56. Press Enter. (This will display all current network interfaces on your virtual machine.)
57. Take a screenshot. (See Figure 20-73.)
58. Type **netstat --statistics --tcp**
59. Press Enter. (This will display TCP statistics.)
60. Type **netstat --statistics --udp**
61. Press Enter. (This will display UDP statistics.)
62. Take a screenshot. (See Figure 20-74.)

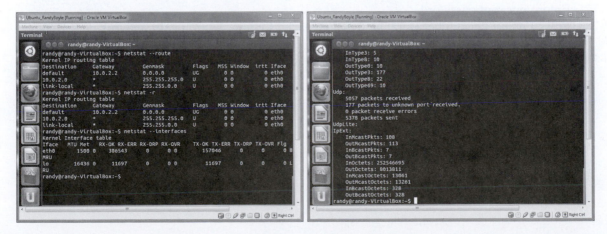

Figure 20-73: Routing table produced using the netstat command.   Figure 20-74: UDP statistics.

63. Type `ping www.google.com -c 3`
64. Press Enter. (This will display information about the ping responses.) (See Figure 20-75.)
65. Type `tracepath www.google.com`
66. Press Enter. (This will display information about the route from your virtual machine to one of Google's servers.)
67. Take a screenshot.
68. Type `host www.google.com`
69. Press Enter. (This will resolve www.Google.com into multiple IP addresses.)
70. Type `dig www.google.com`
71. Press Enter. (This will display the information provided by the host command plus additional information from DNS.)
72. Type `whois www.google.com`
73. Press Enter. (This will display the whois entry for www.Google.com. Scroll up so the command you typed and the first entry are showing in the terminal before you take the screenshot.)
74. Take a screenshot. (See Figure 20-76.)

Figure 20-75: Ping results from www.Google.com.   Figure 20-76: Results from a whois lookup.

Note: The following command (tcpdump) can capture filtered packets in a similar way Wireshark captures packets. This is the command-line equivalent. After entering each command, you will need to refresh your Web browser to produce packets. You can press the up/down arrow keys to scroll through prior commands and edit them. This can save you time and reduce syntax errors.

75. Type `sudo tcpdump -c 5`
76. Press Enter. (This command requires root-level permission to run correctly.)
77. Enter your root password.
78. Press Enter. (This will capture the first five packets going through your network card.) (See Figure 20-77.)
79. Refresh your Web browser. (This will push packets through your network card.)

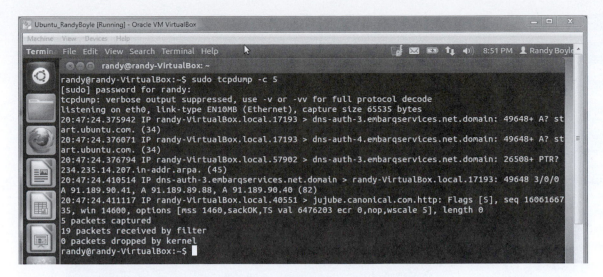

Figure 20-77: Capturing packets using the tcpdump command.

80. Type **sudo tcpdump -c 5 -n**
81. Press Enter. (This will display the five packets showing unresolved IP addresses.)
82. Refresh your Web browser.
83. Type **sudo tcpdump -c 5 -n port 80**
84. Press Enter. (This will display only those five packets going over port 80. This will only capture Web traffic.)
85. Refresh your Web browser.
86. Type **sudo tcpdump -c 5 -n port 80 -w YourNameCapture.log**
87. Press Enter. (This will write the packets you capture to a log file. In this case, the log file was RandyBoyleCapture.log.) (See Figure 20-78.)
88. Refresh your Web browser.

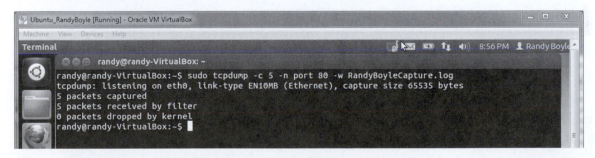

Figure 20-78: Capturing packets and writing them to a log file.

89. Type **ls**
90. Press Enter. (This will give a listing of the files in the current directory. You should see the log file that was just created.)
91. Type **sudo tcpdump –r YourNameCapture.log**
92. Press Enter. (This will display the packets you captured.)
93. Take a screenshot. (See Figure 20-79.)

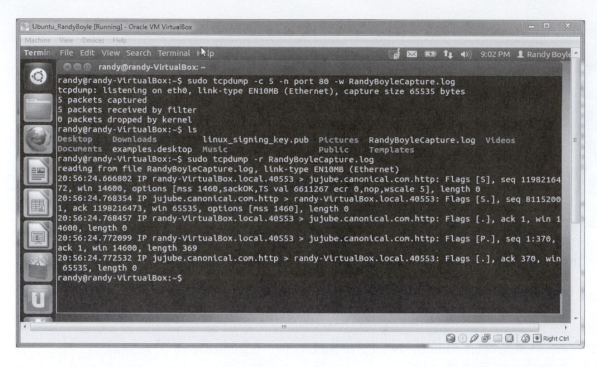

Figure 20-79: Results from the packet capture log file.

94. Type **ifconfig**
95. Press Enter. (This is similar to the ipconfig command you used in the DOS prompt.)
96. Take a screenshot. (See Figure 20-80.)

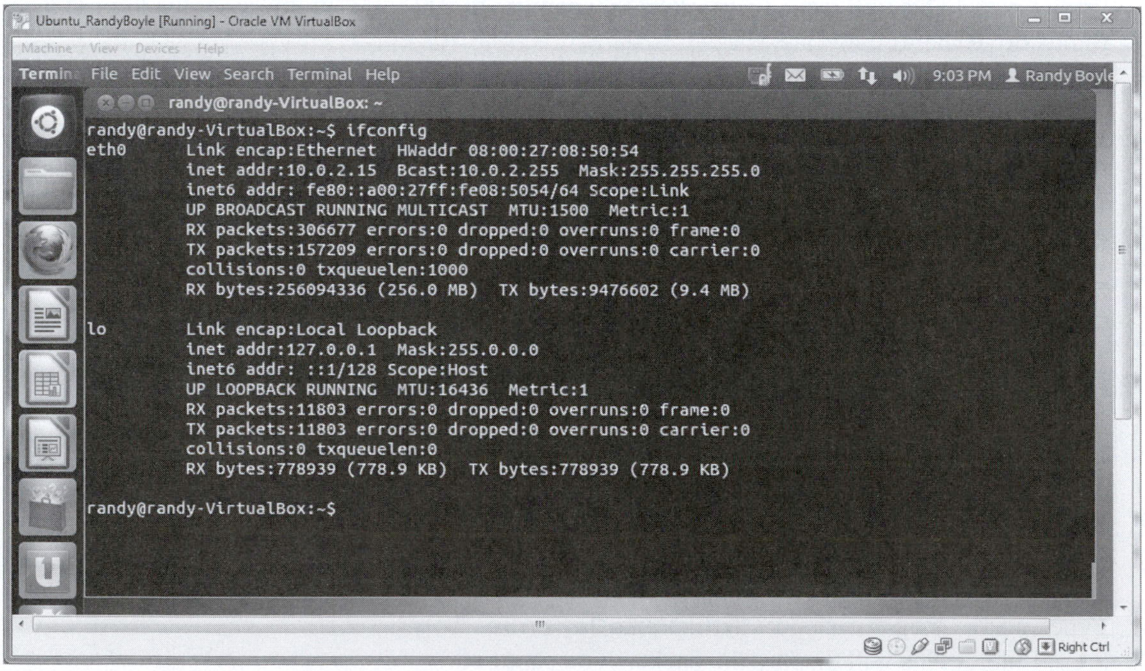

Figure 20-80: Results from the ifconfig command.

1. What was your IP address (IPv4) when you ran the `ifconfig` command?
2. What was your IP address (IPv6) when you ran the `ifconfig` command?
3. What was the name of your capture file?
4. What was the MAC address of your virtual machine?

THOUGHT QUESTIONS

1. Could you use tcpdump to capture packets for a specific IP address?
2. Why did some commands, like tcpdump and ifconfig, require root-level permission to run?
3. If you hadn't set a limit (-c 3) when you used the ping command, what would have happened?
4. Are there command-line tools that produce the same or better results than GUI tools? What would be the advantage of a GUI tool over a command-line tool?

20.5   SYSTEM TOOLS AND CONFIGURATION (UBUNTU)

This project will look at some basic system tools that Linux administrators use often. Some of these tools may look familiar. These are the Linux equivalent to the Windows tools you used in earlier projects. You will see that you can accomplish the same tasks in Linux that you can in Windows. In some instances, it can be done much more quickly and efficiently in Linux.

First, you will explore the System Monitor. This is the equivalent of the Windows Task Manager. You will identify a process and kill it. You will also look at some basic system monitors. These are the same tasks you performed with Windows Task Manager.

Next, you will change your network settings. You will change the default DHCP IP address and settings to a manually configured static IP address. You will get the necessary information to set the static IP address from a few simple commands.

Finally, you will look at a disk usage analyzer and use a terminal server client to access a Windows machine. These basic tasks will help familiarize you with the Linux operating system and help you understand how Linux can make your job as a network administrator much easier.

1. Open Oracle VM VirtualBox by clicking Start, All Programs, Oracle VM VirtualBox, and Oracle VM VirtualBox.
2. Select your Ubuntu virtual machine.
3. Click Start.
4. Login if you are not already logged in.

Note: You can install VirtualBox Guest Additions to make the virtual machine run smoother (i.e., resize the virtual machine, get better mouse integration, etc.). In the VirtualBox file menu for your virtual machine, click Devices, and Install VirtualBox Guest Additions. This will mount an ISO image in your virtual machine's CDROM drive. You can browse to the ISO image in the Ubuntu file manager. You should see a button labeled "Open Autorun Prompt," or you can run autorun.sh. Follow the prompts and then reboot your virtual machine.

5. Click the Ubuntu icon at the top of the left-hand menu.
6. Type "system".
7. Click on the System Monitor icon.
8. Click on the Processes tab.

9. Click on the Memory column heading twice to sort by memory usage in descending order.
10. Click the Firefox icon in the left-hand menu. (You should see the Firefox process show up in the list and the Firefox Web browser open.)
11. Search for your name.
12. Return to the System Monitor.
13. Right-click the row for the Firefox process.
14. Take a screenshot. (See Figure 20-81.)

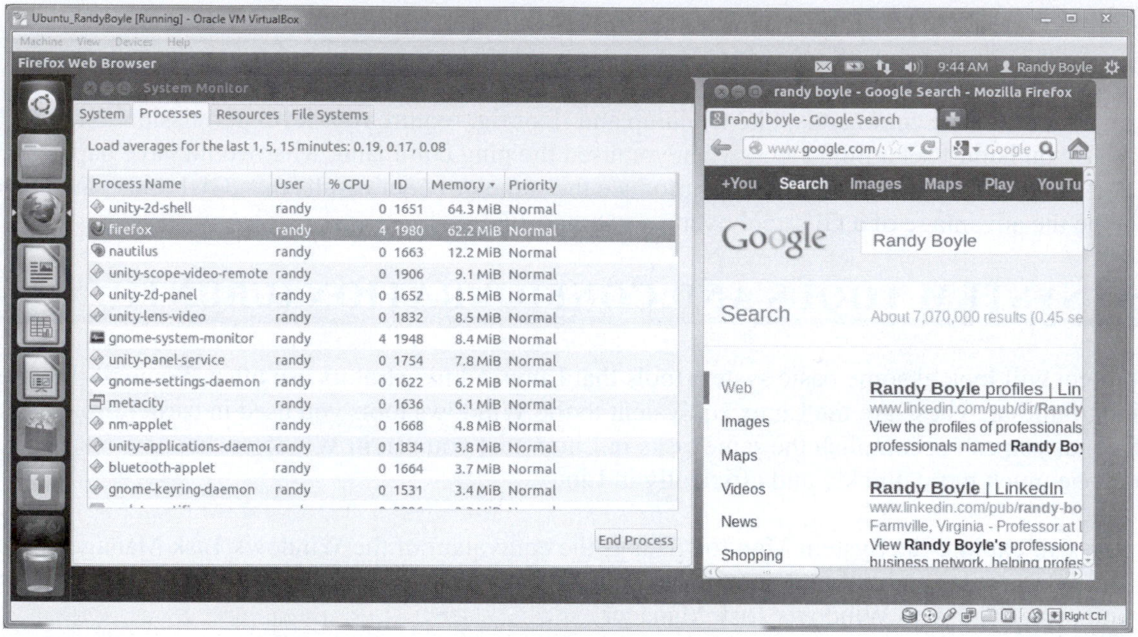

Figure 20-81: Started a Web browser.

15. Select End Process. (This is similar to the task you did in Windows Task Manager.)
16. Click on the Resources tab. (This will start the graphing functions for these resource meters.)
17. Open the Firefox Web browser again.
18. Click Refresh or press F5 5-10 times. (This will put a load on the resource meters and make changes in the graphs.)
19. Return to the System Monitor.
20. Take a screenshot showing the changes in the resource meters. (See Figure 20-82.)

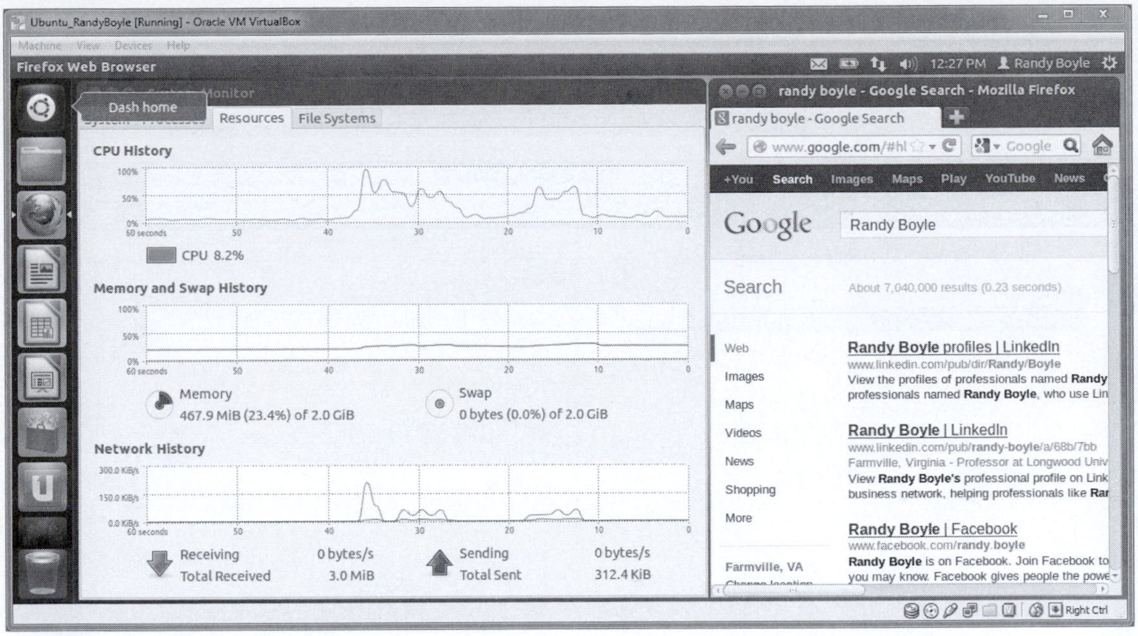

Figure 20-82: System monitors for CPU, memory, and bandwidth usage.

21. Click on the System tab.
22. Take a screenshot. (Your name should be showing in the computer name.) (See Figure 20-83.)

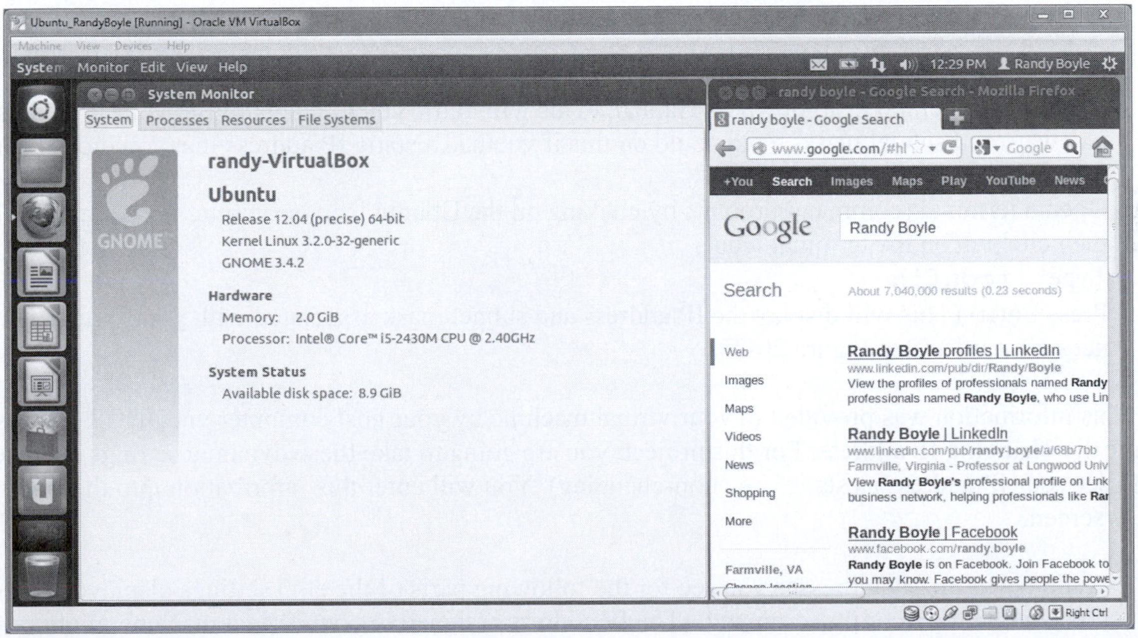

Figure 20-83: System information.

23. Close System Monitor and the Web browser.
24. Click the Ubuntu icon at the top of the left-hand menu.
25. Type "Network Connections".
26. Click on the Network Connections icon.
27. Select your wired network card. (In this case, it was labeled "Wired connection 1".)
28. Click Edit.

29. Take a screenshot showing the Wired tab and the MAC address of your virtual machine. (See Figure 20-84.)

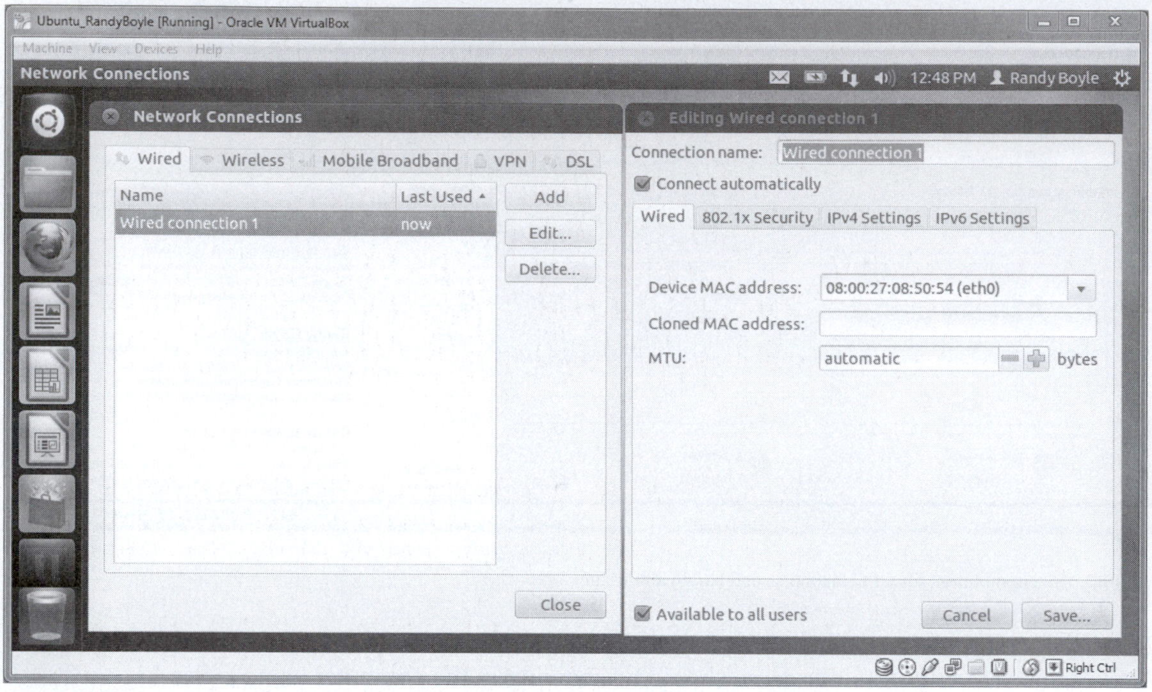

Figure 20-84: Network Connection settings.

30. Click on the IPv4 Settings tab.
31. Change the Method drop-down to Manual. (This will allow you to manually set your IP address, gateway, and subnet mask. You would do this if you had a static IP address that you didn't want to change.)
32. Open a terminal (command prompt) by clicking on the Ubuntu icon, searching for "terminal", and then clicking on the terminal icon.
33. Type **ifconfig**
34. Press Enter. (This will display the IP address and subnet mask associated with your virtual network card.) (See Figure 20-85.)

Note: This information was provided to your virtual machine by your host computer via DHCP. This is a dynamically changing IP address. For this project, you are going to take these dynamic settings and use them to set your IP address as static (i.e., non-changing). You will enter this information into the IPv4 Settings screen.

35. Write down the IP addresses you see for the following parts of the eth0 settings displayed when you entered the ifconfig command. (The IP address assigned to your virtual machine might be different than the one shown below. This information is shown in the second line down for each adapter. You want to get the information for the eth0 adapter.)

Inet addr: _____._____._____._____   (In this case, it was 10.0.2.15.)
Mask: _____._____._____._____   (In this case, it was 255.255.255.0.)

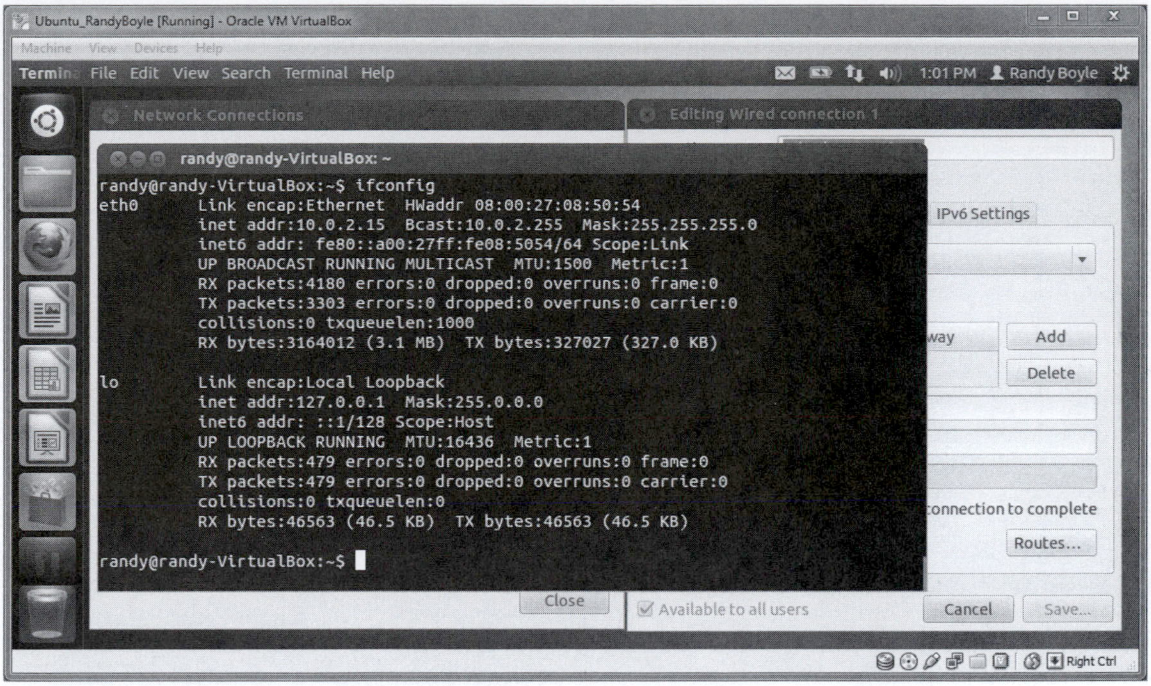

Figure 20-85: Results from the ifconfig command.

36. Return to the command prompt.
37. Type **route**
38. Press Enter. (The line of your routing table listed as "default" will display your gateway address. In this case, it was 10.0.2.2.)
39. Type **cat /etc/resolv.conf**
40. Press Enter. (This will give a listing of the DNS servers your computer uses to resolve hostnames into IP addresses. In this case, it was 127.0.0.1.)
41. Write down the correct IP addresses for your gateway and DNS.

Gateway: ____.____.____.____   (In this case, it was 10.0.2.2.)
DNS: ____.____.____.____   (In this case, it was 127.0.0.1.)

42. Enter the IP addresses for your computer, network mask, gateway, and DNS server.
43. Take a screenshot. (See Figure 20-86.)
44. Click Save.

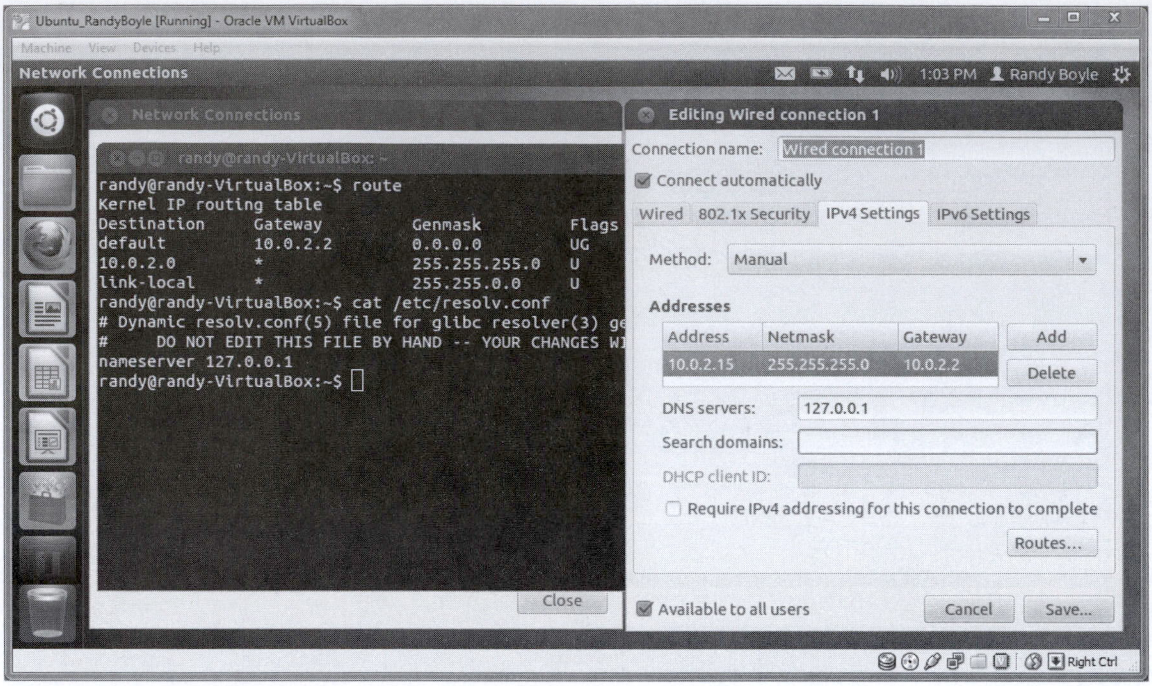

Figure 20-86: Showing the default gateway and DNS server from the route command and resolv.conf file.

45. Return to the command prompt.
46. Type **clear**
47. Press Enter. (This will clear the output displayed in the terminal.)
48. Type **sudo ifconfig eth0 down**
49. Press Enter. (This will elevate your privileges and *disable* the network interface. The number zero, not the letter "O," is used at the end of eth0.)
50. Enter your password when prompted.
51. Press Enter.
52. Type **ifconfig**
53. Press Enter. (This will display the interface configuration information. Notice that the eth0 interface is *not* shown.)
54. Type **sudo ifconfig eth0 up**
55. Press Enter. (This will elevate your privileges and *enable* the network interface.)
56. Enter your password when prompted. (It will keep your privileges elevated for a short time. You may not need to enter your password, or use the sudo command, if you work quickly enough.)
57. Press Enter.
58. Type **ifconfig**
59. Press Enter. (This will display the interface configuration information.) (See Figure 20-87.)

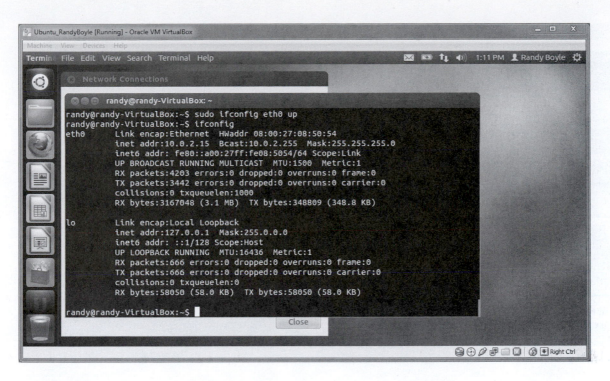

Figure 20-87: Static IP address is configured.

Note: The IP address for your computer is still the same one issued by the internal DHCP managed by VirtualBox. We can change the host IP address to confirm that it is a static IP address.

60. Return to the configuration screen for your wired connection.
61. Change your IP address by increasing the last octet by 2. (In this case, it was changed from 10.0.2.15 to 10.0.2.17.)
62. Click Save.
63. Return to the command prompt.
64. Type **sudo ifconfig eth0 down**
65. Press Enter. (This will disable the network interface.)
66. Type **sudo ifconfig eth0 up**
67. Press Enter. (This will enable the network interface.)
68. Type **ifconfig**
69. Press Enter. (This will display the interface configuration information.)
70. Take a screenshot showing the changed IP address. (See Figure 20-88.)

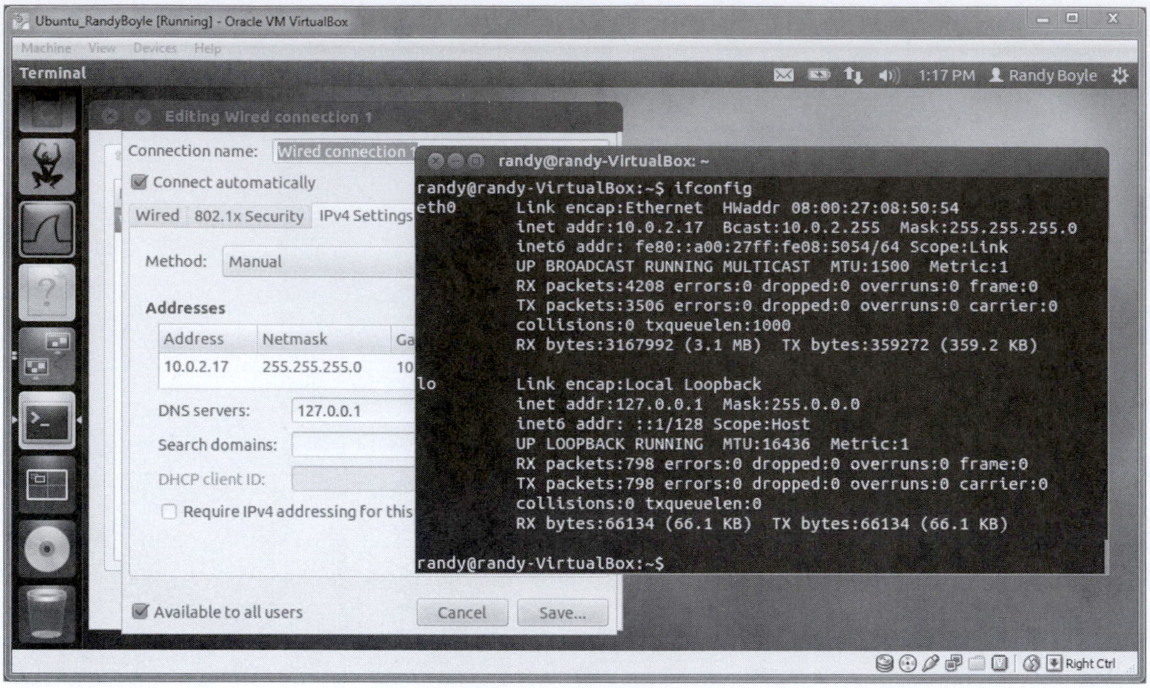

Figure 20-88: Results showing a changed static IP address.

71. Close the Terminal and Network Connections windows.
72. Click the Ubuntu icon at the top of the left-hand menu.
73. Type "disk".
74. Click on the Disk Usage Analyzer icon.
75. Click on the hard drive icon to scan your file system. (You can also press Ctrl-F.) (See Figure 20-89.)
76. Expand the tree under Home.
77. Expand the tree for your username. (In this case, it was randy.)
78. Take a screenshot. (You should see a graphical representation of which directories and/or files are using the most storage capacity on your virtual hard drive.) (See Figure 20-90.)
79. Close the Disk Usage Analyzer.

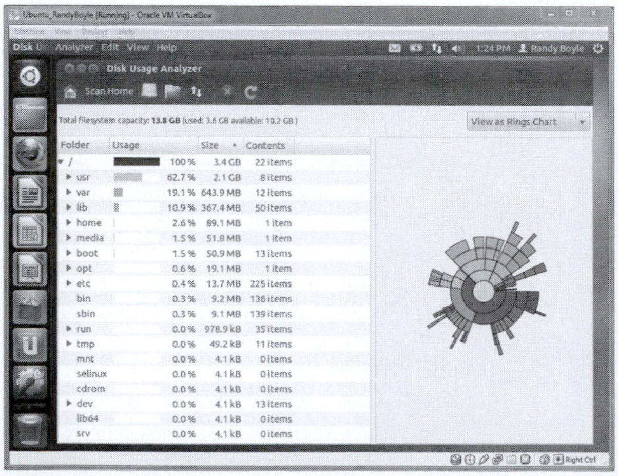

Figure 20-89: Disk usage for entire hard drive.

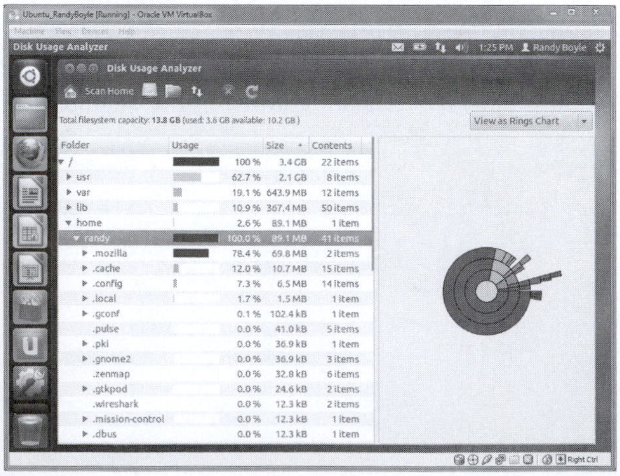

Figure 20-90: Disk usage for a specific user.

80. Click the Ubuntu icon at the top of the left-hand menu.

81. Type "remote".
82. Click on the Remmina Remote Desktop Client icon. (This is the application that will let you remotely access other computers.)
83. Click on the "Create new remote desktop file" icon with a green "+" on it.
84. Name the profile YourName. (In this case, it was RandyBoyle.)
85. Enter in the IP address of a remote Windows computer that you can access into the Server text box. (You must have a valid username and password to log in. You can use a classmate's computer, a computer set up by your instructor, or any other Windows computer to complete this project.)
86. Enter your username and password for the remote Windows computer.
87. Change the Color depth to True color (24 bpp). (You may need to adjust this setting to get the coloring correct.)
88. Click Save. (See Figure 20-91.)

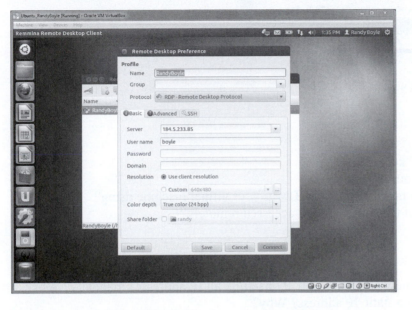

Figure 20-91: Terminal Server Client in Linux.

89. Double-click on your saved profile.
90. Click Connect.
91. Click OK if prompted.
92. Open a Web browser within the remote Windows computer.
93. Browse to www.Google.com.
94. Enter your name into the search box.
95. Take a screenshot of the remote Windows desktop *within* the Linux desktop. (Your name should appear in the search box. Note that you are accessing a remote computer from within a virtual machine that is running on your local host.) (See Figure 20-92.)

Figure 20-92: Remote desktop from Linux into Windows.

PROJECT QUESTIONS

1. What was your original IP address?
2. To what did you change your IP address?
3. Approximately how much memory (% or MB) was your virtual machine using?
4. What was the IP address of the computer you accessed remotely?

THOUGHT QUESTIONS

1. Is it easier to administer a network using DHCP or setting all IP addresses manually? Why?
2. Do certain computers need a static IP address? Why?
3. When will IPv6 be implemented (i.e., widely used)?
4. Can you have multiple concurrent users logged on to a Linux computer at the same time? Does this work in Windows?

20.6   USER AND GROUP MANAGEMENT (MINT®)

In this project, you will install another popular flavor of Linux called Mint®. Mint has become widely used in the past few years as a desktop OS. Traditionally, Mint came with the Gnome desktop environment. However, the Linux environment is dynamic and changes are commonplace. Mint is now shipping with the MATE, Cinnamon, KDE, or Xfce desktop environments. This project will install the Cinnamon desktop environment of Mint.

In this project, you will also add/remove users and groups using graphical (GUI) and command-line (CLI) interfaces. You will add users to groups, learn how to reset a password, and lock/unlock an account. These are all common tasks performed by systems administrators.

Using the graphical interface to add/remove users is fairly intuitive. However, managing users via the command-line is not. Repeated practice using the command-line will make it second nature to you. This is also a good opportunity to compare the differences between GUI and command-line administration.

1. Download Mint from: http://linuxmint.com/.
2. Click on the Download link at the top of the page.
3. Click the link for the 64-bit version of Mint with the Cinnamon desktop. (You can download the 32-bit version if you have older hardware.) (See Figure 20-93.)
4. Click on a mirror site that is close to you. (In this case, it was University of Maryland, College Park.)
5. Click Save.
6. Select your C:\security folder. (This is a big download that will take a while unless you get it from your instructor or classmate. It should be about 800 MB.) (See Figure 20-94.)

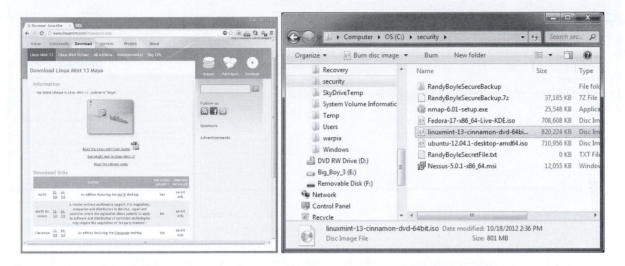

Figure 20-93: Mint distribution page.   Figure 20-94: Mint ISO image.

7. Open Oracle VM VirtualBox by clicking Start, All Programs, Oracle VM VirtualBox, and Oracle VM VirtualBox. (You installed VirtualBox as part of projects in an earlier chapter. If you haven't installed VirtualBox, you will need to do so now.)
8. Click New.
9. Enter Mint_YourName for the Name. (In this case, it was Mint_RandyBoyle.) (See Figure 20-95.)
10. Select Linux for the Operating System.
11. Select Ubuntu (64 bit) for the Version. (Select just "Ubuntu" if you have an older 32-bit system. You can use Ubuntu settings because Mint is based on Ubuntu.)
12. Click Next.
13. Increase the amount of memory to 2000 MB+. (See Figure 20-96.)

Figure 20-95: Naming the Mint virtual machine.   Figure 20-96: Allocating RAM to the virtual machine.

14. Click Next, Next, Next, and Next.
15. Increase the hard drive space to 15GB (or more if you have the space). (See Figure 20-97.)
16. Click Next, Create, and Create.
17. Select the virtual machine labeled Mint_YourName. (In this case, it was Mint_RandyBoyle.) (See Figure 20-98.)

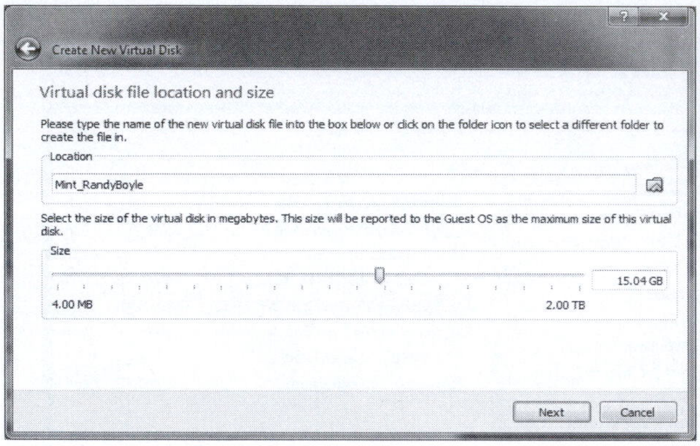

Figure 20-97: Setting the size of the virtual hard drive.

Figure 20-98: Mint virtual machine created.

18. In the right-hand pane, click Storage, IDE Controller, and Empty. (See Figure 20-99.)
19. Click the Browse button on the right-hand side of the screen by the CD/DVD Drive drop-down box. (It looks like a little CD.)
20. Click Add.
21. Browse to your C:\security folder.
22. Select the Mint (Cinnamon) image you downloaded. (In this case, it was linuxmint-13-cinnamon-dvd-64bit.iso.)
23. Click Open. (See Figure 20-100.)
24. Click OK.

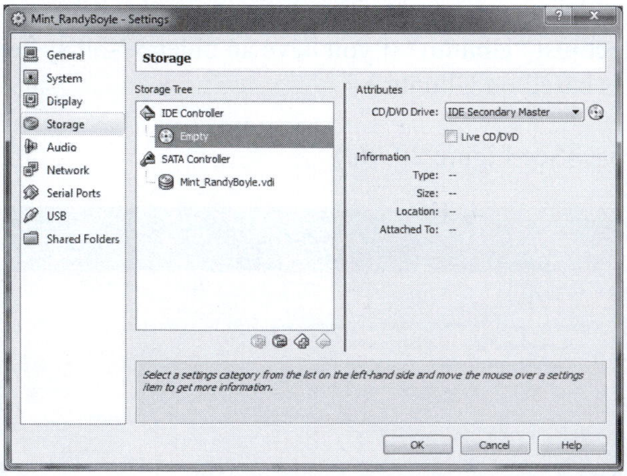

Figure 20-99: No CD/DVD image mounted.

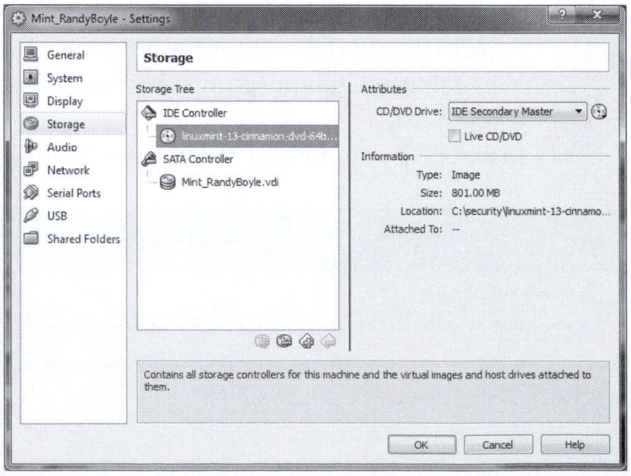

Figure 20-100: Mint ISO image mounted.

25. Take a screenshot showing the new virtual machine. (You may have to use Screenshot Pilot to take screenshots. You can leave the virtual machine by holding down the right Ctrl key. To copy

the screenshot from within Screenshot Pilot, you click Image, and then Copy to Clipboard.) (See Figure 20-101.)

26. Click Start. (It may take 3 or more minutes for Mint to load depending on the resources allocated to the virtual machine.)
27. Double-Click the Install Linux Mint icon. (See Figure 20-102.)

Figure 20-101: Mint virtual machine ready to boot.   Figure 20-102: Mint desktop.

28. Click Continue, Continue, Continue, Install Now, Continue, and Continue.
29. Enter your first and last name. (Your username should be your first name.)
30. Enter a root password twice. (It's a good idea to write down your root password if you have a bad memory. You will need to know this password for later projects.) (See Figure 20-103.)
31. Click Continue. (The installation process will take several minutes. You will see an "Installation Complete" notice when it finishes. Do *not* click Restart Now before completing the following steps.)

Note: You are now going to have to take the Mint ISO image out of the virtual CD ROM so you don't have to go through the installation process again. If you don't take out the ISO image, the installation process may start again when you reboot the virtual machine.

32. Press the right Ctrl key to exit the virtual machine. (You may be able to skip this step on newer versions of VirtualBox. Older versions may still require it.)
33. In the VirtualBox menu for the virtual machine you are working on, click Devices, CD-DVD ROM, and Remove disk from virtual drive. (This will unmount the Mint ISO image.) (See Figure 20-104.)
34. Click Force Unmount. (This should remove the ISO image from your virtual CD-DVD drive.)
35. In the Mint virtual machine, click Restart Now. (This will reboot your virtual machine from the virtual hard drive. You can also manually reset it in the main VirtualBox screen.)

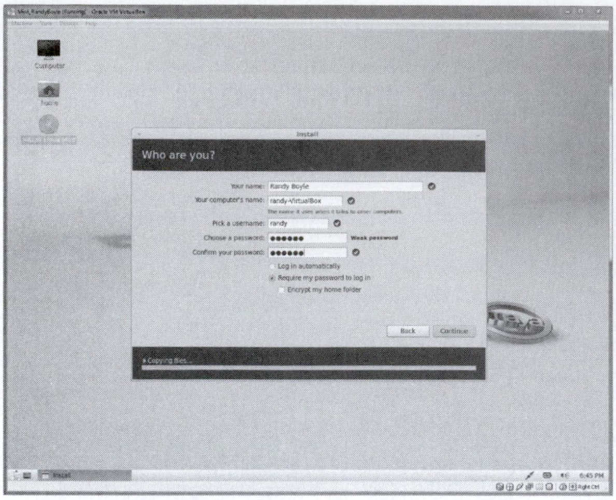

Figure 20-103: Entering a password for the root account.

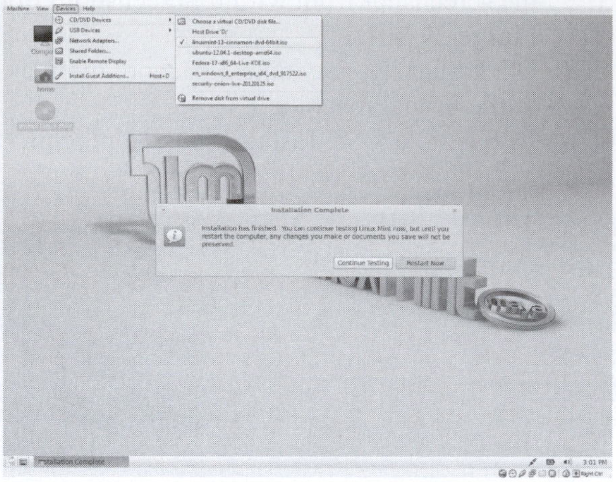

Figure 20-104: Unmounting the Mint installation image.

36. Enter your username. (It will likely be your first name. In this case, it was "randy.")
37. Enter your password.
38. Press Enter.

Note: You can install VirtualBox Guest Additions to make the virtual machine run smoother (i.e., resize the virtual machine, get better mouse integration, etc.). In the VirtualBox file menu for your virtual machine, click Devices, and Install VirtualBox Guest Additions. This will mount an ISO image in your virtual machine's CDROM drive. You can browse to the ISO image in the Ubuntu file manager. You should see a "Open Autorun Prompt" button, or you can run autorun.sh. Follow the prompts and then reboot your virtual machine.

39. Click on the Mint menu (the equivalent of the Start menu in Microsoft Windows) in the bottom left-hand of your Mint desktop.
40. Click System Tools, System Settings, and User Accounts.
41. Click the Unlock icon at the top of the screen so you can make changes.
42. Enter your root password.
43. Click Authenticate. (See Figure 20-105.)
44. Click the "+" button in the bottom left-hand of the screen to Add User.
45. Enter a name in the Full name text box. (This can be any name of your choosing. In this case, it was Noah. The Username should automatically fill in.) (See Figure 20-106.)
46. Click Create.

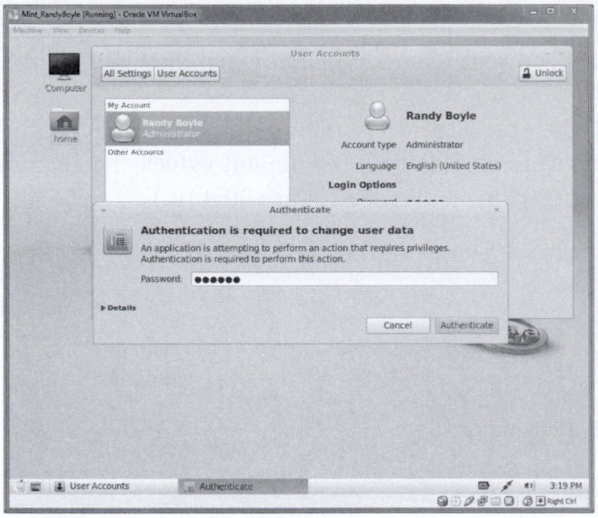

Figure 20-105: Authenticating to make changes to user accounts.   Figure 20-106: Adding a user.

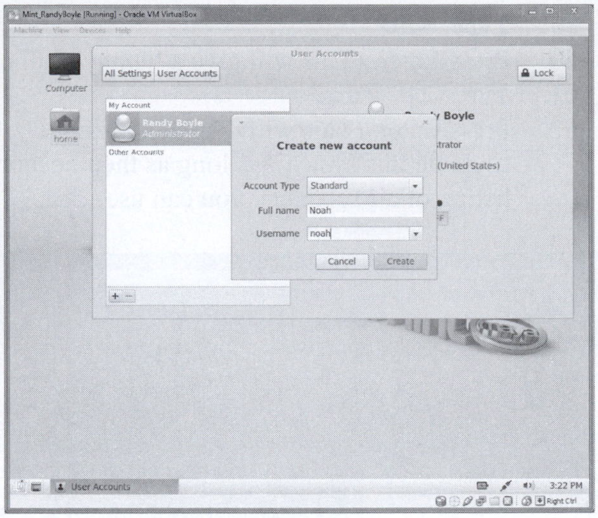

47. Select the user account you just created.
48. Click on the words "Account disabled" next to Password.
49. Enter a password twice.
50. Click Change. (See Figure 20-107.)
51. Click on the word "Standard" next to Account type.
52. Click on Administrator.
53. Take a screenshot showing you and the new user as members of the Administrator group. (See Figure 20-108.)
54. Close the User Accounts window.

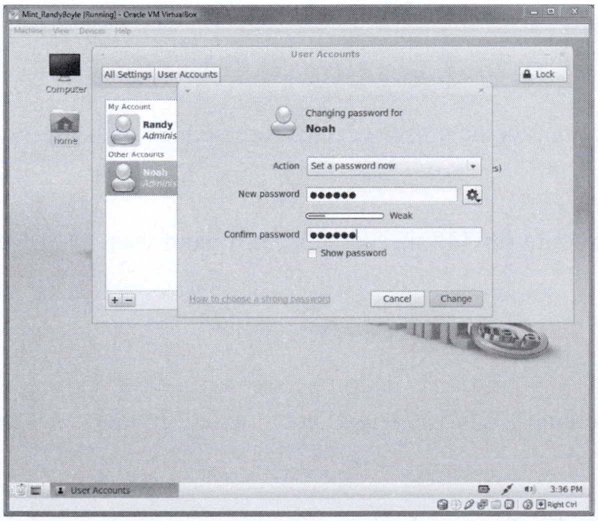

Figure 20-107: Setting the user's password. 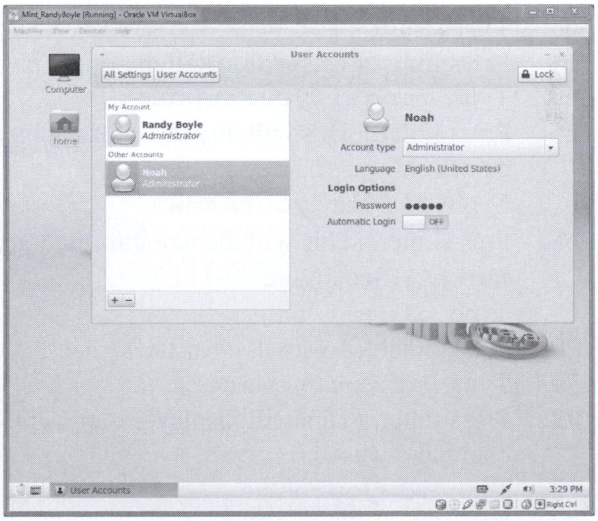   Figure 20-108: Verifying that the user's account type was changed to Administrator.

55. Click on the Mint menu (the equivalent of the Start menu in Microsoft Windows) in the bottom left-hand of your Mint desktop.
56. Click Accessories, and Terminal. (See Figure 20-109.)
57. Type **users**
58. Press Enter. (This will give a listing of all users currently logged in. Since you are likely the only user logged in, you should only see yourself listed.)

59. Type **who**
60. Press Enter. (This will give a listing of all users currently logged in and when they logged in.)
61. Type **ls /home**
62. Press Enter. (This will display a listing of all the user directories. This gives you an idea of the users on this system, as long as their accounts were created with the default values. To get a full listing of all accounts, you can use `cat /etc/passwd`.) (See Figure 20-110.)

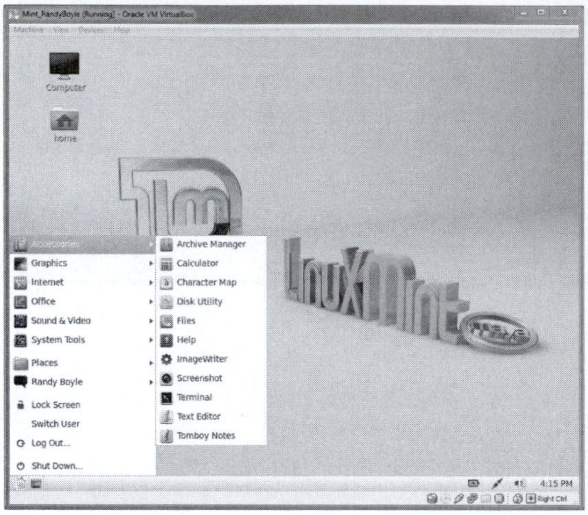

Figure 20-109: Opening a terminal.

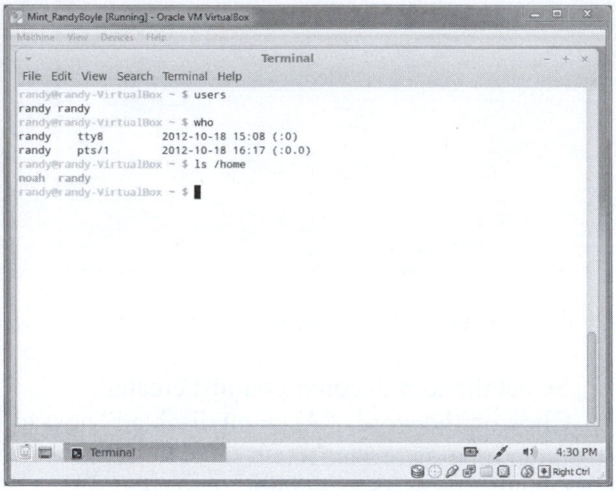

Figure 20-110: Identifying users.

Note: You are going to install the "finger" package that will gather more information about the users accessing your system. By default, it is not installed. It could pose a security risk if used inappropriately. It can be installed and uninstalled by users with administrator-level access.

63. Type **sudo apt-get install finger**
64. Press Enter. (This will install the finger package.)
65. Type **finger yournewuser**
66. Press Enter. (This will display information about the new user you just created. In this case, the command was `finger noah`.)
67. Type **finger yourname**
68. Press Enter. (This will display information about you. In this case, the command was `finger randy`.) (See Figure 20-111.)
69. Type **clear**
70. Press Enter. (This will clear the screen.)
71. Type **id yournewuser**
72. Press Enter. (This will display group membership for the new user you created. In this case, the command was `id noah`.)
73. Type **id yourname**
74. Press Enter. (This will display group membership for you. In this case, the command was `id randy`. Note the differences in group membership.) (See Figure 20-112.)

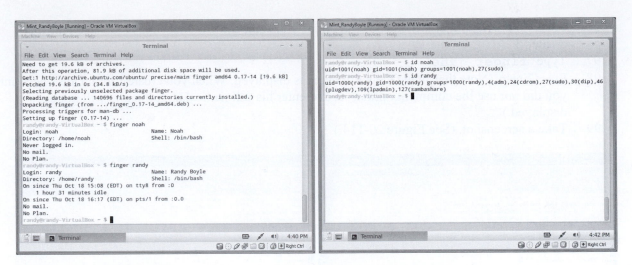

Figure 20-111: Using the finger command.   Figure 20-112: Listing group memberships.

75. Type **clear**
76. Press Enter. (This will clear the screen.)
77. Type **useradd –m john**
78. Press Enter. (This will attempt to add John Doe as a user. You will get an *error* and John's account will not be created.)
79. Type **sudo useradd –m john**
80. Press Enter. (This will add John Doe as a user. Sudo runs the command with administrator privileges and the -m option forces the creation of the user's home directory. Enter your root password if prompted to do so.)
81. Type **sudo passwd john**
82. Press Enter. (This will set John Doe's password.)
83. Enter "john1234" as the password and press enter twice.
84. Type **ls /home**
85. Press Enter. (This will display a listing of all the user directories. You should see the new "john" directory.)
86. Take a screenshot. (See Figure 20-113.)

Note: It is good practice to use "sudo" to perform administrative tasks rather than being logged in as root. This helps prevent errors and system damage. There is also a log made each time sudo is used. You could complete the rest of this tutorial by logging in as root (or su root). However, for this project you will use sudo.

87. Type **sudo useradd –c "Jane Doe" -m jane**
88. Press Enter. (This will add Jane Doe as a user and create her home directory. It will also enter her full name as a comment.)
89. Type **sudo passwd jane**
90. Press Enter. (This will set Jane Doe's password.)
91. Enter "jane4444" as the password. (This is not a typo. You are intentionally entering Jane's password this way. You will reset it to jane1234 in the next step.)
92. Type **sudo passwd jane**
93. Press Enter. (This will reset Jane's password. Resetting user passwords can be a common occurrence.)
94. Enter "jane1234" as the password.
95. Type **ls /home**

96. Press Enter. (This will provide a listing of all users and confirm that Jane Doe's account was created.)
97. Type **finger jane**
98. Press Enter. (Note that Jane Doe's full name is displayed. When you created John Doe's account, you did *not* use the comment option, -c, and enter his full name. His full name will not be displayed.)
99. Take a screenshot. (See Figure 20-114.)

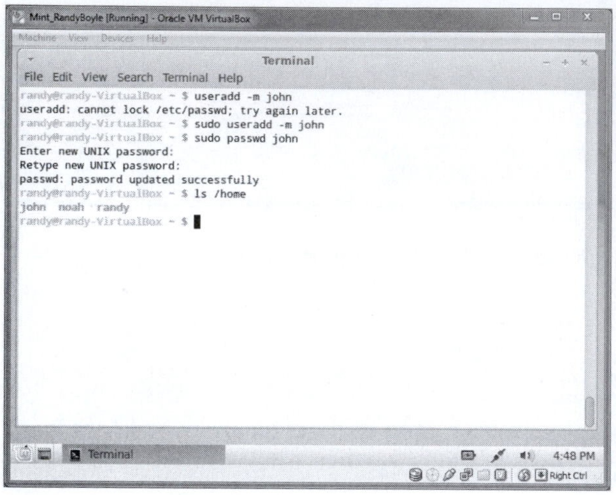

Figure 20-113: Adding a user.

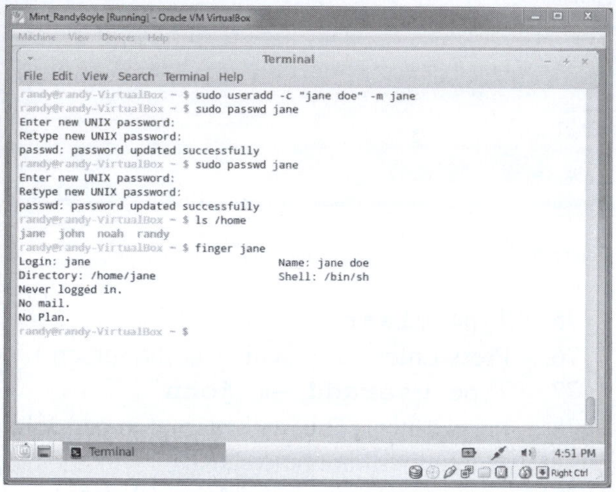

Figure 20-114: Adding a user and resetting the password.

100. Type **clear**
101. Press Enter. (This will clear the screen.)
102. Type **sudo usermod -L jane**
103. Press Enter. (This will lock Jane's account. This is useful if someone goes on vacation or needs to have their access disabled temporarily.)
104. Type **sudo passwd -S jane**
105. Press Enter. (This will provide the status of Jane's password. You will see an "L" for locked.)
106. Type **sudo usermod -U jane**
107. Press Enter. (This will unlock Jane's account.)
108. Type **sudo passwd -S jane**
109. Press Enter. (This will provide the status of Jane's password. You will see a "P" for passworded. This account is unlocked and Jane has access.)
110. Type **sudo userdel -r john**
111. Press Enter. (This will force the removal of John Doe's account and his home directory. This is useful if someone is permanently leaving the organization.)
112. Type **id john**
113. Press Enter. (You shouldn't see John listed.)
114. Type **ls /home**
115. Press Enter. (This will confirm that John Doe's account was deleted.)
116. Take a screenshot. (See Figure 20-115.)
117. Type **sudo groupadd nerds**
118. Press Enter. (This will add a group called nerds.)
119. Type **cat /etc/group**
120. Press Enter. (This will list all groups. Your new group should show up near the bottom of the list.)
121. Type **sudo groupmod -n techies nerds**
122. Press Enter. (This will change the group name from "nerds" to "techies.")

123. Type **cat /etc/group**
124. Press Enter. (You should see the new group named "techies.")
125. Type **sudo usermod -a -G techies jane**
126. Press Enter. (This will add Jane Doe to the techies group.)
127. Type **cat /etc/group**
128. Press Enter. (You should see Jane listed as a group member.)
129. Take a screenshot. (See Figure 20-116.)

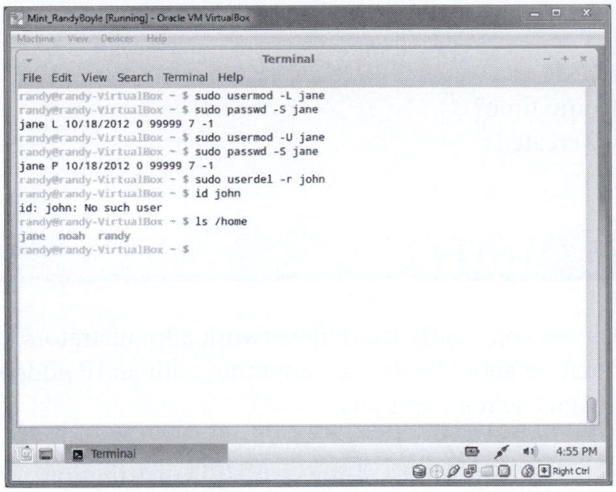

Figure 20-115: Locking/unlocking an account and deleting a user.

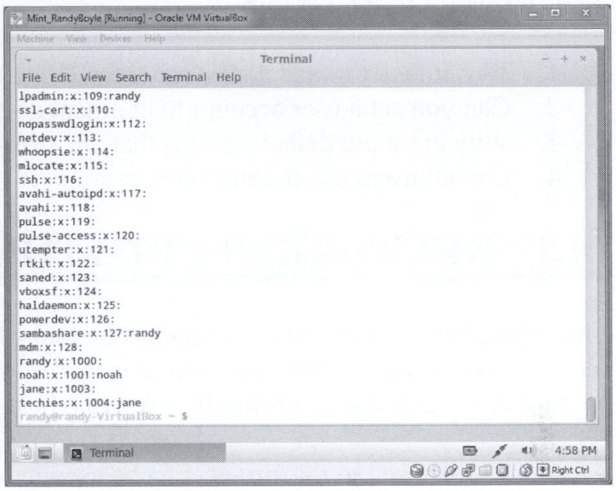

Figure 20-116: Creating a group and adding a user to that group.

130. Type **sudo groupdel techies**
131. Press Enter. (This will delete the group called techies.)
132. Type **cat /etc/group**
133. Press Enter. (You shouldn't see the techies group anymore.)
134. Type **date**
135. Press Enter. (This will display the current date and time.)
136. Take a screenshot. (See Figure 20-117.)

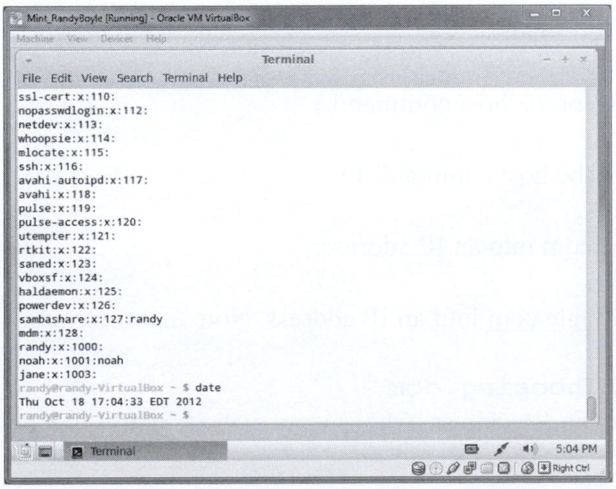

Figure 20-117: Deleting a group.

PROJECT QUESTIONS

1. What was your username?
2. What was the name of your new user?
3. What time was listed for your most recent login when you used the "who" command?
4. What was the date and time listed when you used the "date" command?

THOUGHT QUESTIONS

1. Was it faster to add a user using the GUI or CLI?
2. Can you set a user account to expire at a specific time?
3. Why are there default groups that are already created?
4. Can all users use the sudo command?

20.7   NETWORK CLI UTILITIES (MINT)

This project will cover a few command-line tools that are commonly used by network administrators and security professionals. They are used to gather information about hosts (i.e., anything with an IP address). More specifically, this project will look at the host, whois, and nmap tools.

All of the tools used in this project can be used in just about any UNIX, Linux, or BSD distribution. The "host" command is primarily used to resolve hostnames into IP addresses. It can also provide information about types of servers associated with a given hostname. The "whois" command is used to get information about the individual or group registered to a hostname or block of IP addresses.

1. Open Oracle VM VirtualBox by clicking Start, All Programs, Oracle VM VirtualBox, and Oracle VM VirtualBox.
2. Select your Linux Mint virtual machine.
3. Click Start.
4. If you are not already logged in, enter your username and password to log in.
5. Click on the Mint menu (the equivalent of the Start menu in Microsoft Windows) in the bottom left-hand of your Mint desktop.
6. Click System Tools, System Settings, and Terminal.
7. Type **man host**
8. Press Enter. (This will display the man page for the host command.)
9. Type **q**
10. Press Enter. (This will exit the man page for the host command.)
11. Type **host google.com**
12. Press Enter. (This will resolve www.Google.com into an IP address.)
13. Type **host www.google.com**
14. Press Enter. (This will also resolve www.Google.com into an IP address. Note that there are fewer entries.)
15. Type **host www.AnyWebSiteOfYourChoosing.com**
16. Press Enter. (This will resolve a website into an IP address. Choose any website you'd like. In this case, it was www.Yahoo.com.)
17. Take a screenshot. (See Figure 20-118.)

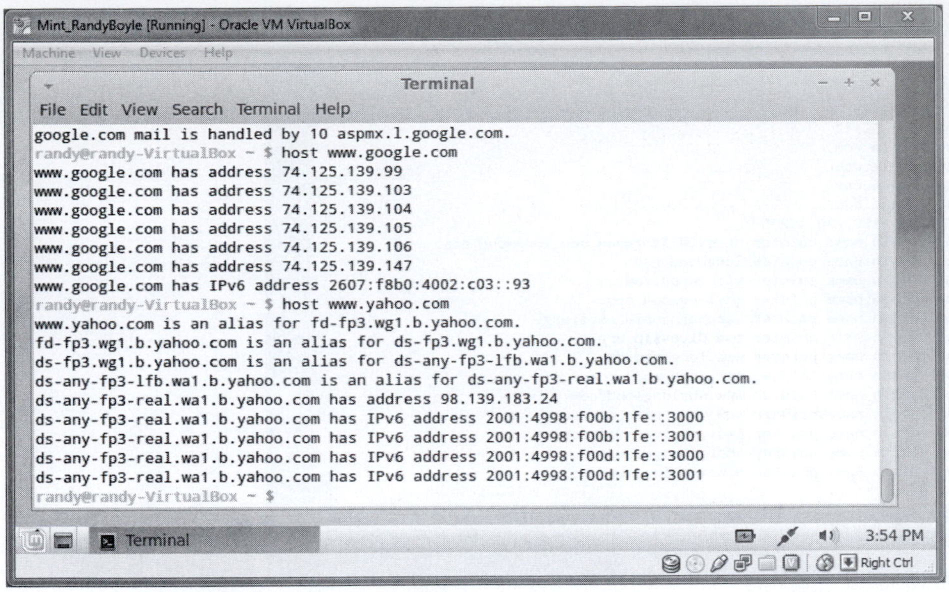

Figure 20-118: Resolved hostname.

18. Type **host longwood.edu**
19. Press Enter. (This will resolve www.Longwood.edu. You can use any other ".edu" hostname of your choosing.)
20. Type **host -t mx google.com**
21. Press Enter. (This returns a list of Google's mail exchangers.)
22. Type **host -t ns google.com**
23. Press Enter. (This returns a list of Google's name servers.)
24. Type **host -t cname news.google.com**
25. Press Enter. (This tells us that news.Google.com is actually an alias for news.l.google.com.)
26. Type **host -t any google.com**
27. Press Enter. (This returns a list of all query record types for Google.com. Note that the "any" type returned much more information than just using just the host command without any options.)
28. Type **host 159.230.4.205**
29. Press Enter. (This will return a list of hostnames associated with this IP address.)
30. Take a screenshot. (See Figure 20-119.)

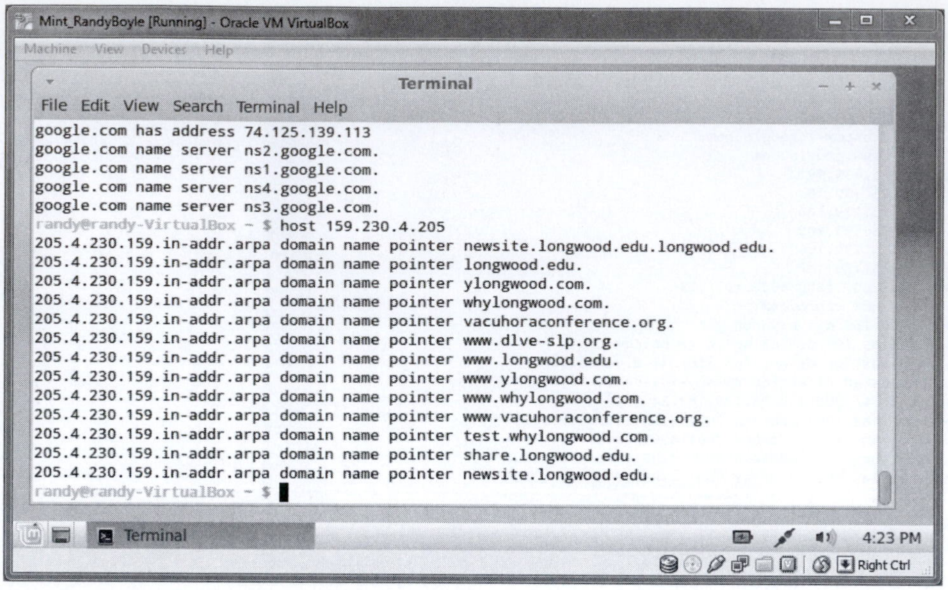

Figure 20-119: Host command used to resolve an IP address.

31. Type `man whois`
32. Press Enter. (This will display the man page for the whois command.)
33. Type `q`
34. Press Enter. (This will exit the man page for the whois command.)
35. Type `whois longwood.edu`
36. Press Enter. (This will retrieve information about the organization that registered the "longwood.edu" hostname and its corresponding IP address[es]. You can choose any other ".edu" hostname.)
37. Type `whois biadu.com`
38. Press Enter. (This will *not* return the complete listing for Biadu.com in the default whois database. It will return a listing for Whois Privacy Protection Service, Inc. You will get more detailed information about Biadu.com in the next steps.)
39. Type `host biadu.com`
40. Press Enter. (This will resolve Biadu.com into an IP address.)
41. Type `whois 116.212.117.220`
42. Press Enter. (This will return the complete listing for Biadu.com because it uses a different whois server.)
43. Take a screenshot. (See Figure 20-120.)

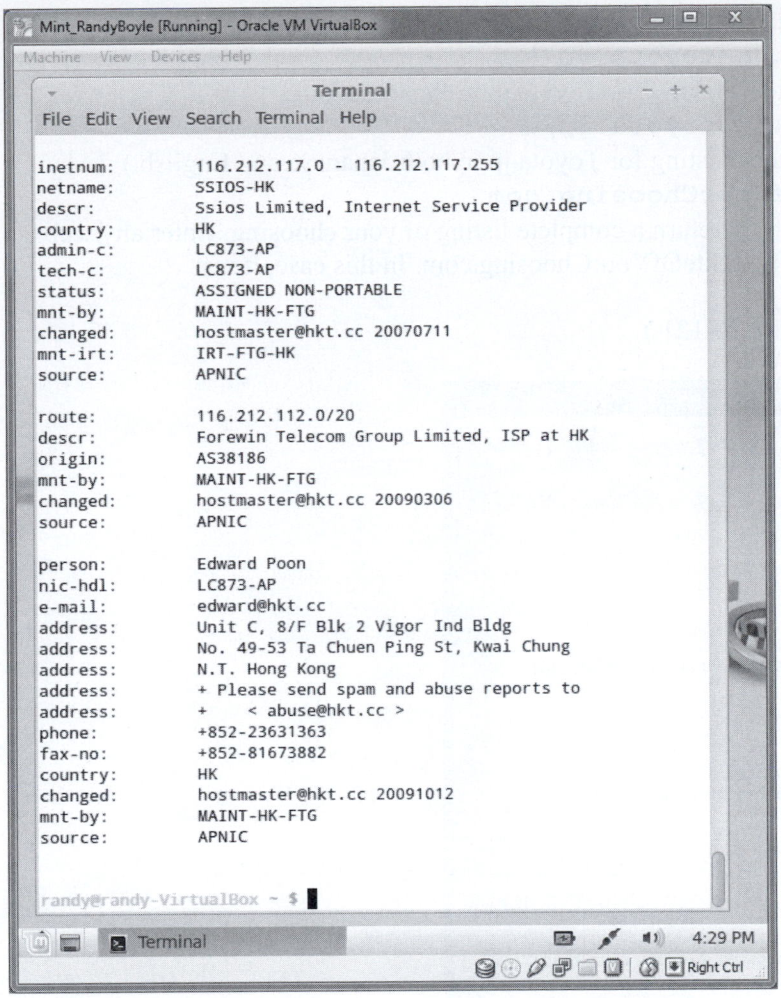

Figure 20-120: Whois information for an IP address.

Note: The country code listed for this IP address was HK. If you see a country code that you don't recognize, you can use the following command to get more information. It provides information about top-level domain (TLD) names such as com, edu, net, and all country codes. (In this case, it was "hk" for Hong Kong.)

44. Type **whois -h whois.iana.org hk**
45. Press Enter. (This will provide more information about the "hk" top-level domain.)

Hint: Pressing the up and down arrows (↑ and ↓) will scroll through previous commands. You can edit a prior command instead of typing in each command in its entirety. This should save time and reduce errors.

46. Type **whois -h whois.iana.org ru**
47. Press Enter. (This will provide more information about the "ru" top-level domain.)
48. Type **whois -h whois.iana.org com**
49. Press Enter. (This will provide more information about the "com" top-level domain. Note which company manages the .com top-level domain -- whois.verisign-grs.com.)
50. Type **whois -h whois.iana.org edu**
51. Press Enter. (This will provide more information about the "edu" top-level domain.)
52. Type **whois -h whois.kr lg.co.kr**

53. Press Enter. (This will provide a listing for LG.co.kr in both Korean and English.)
54. Type `whois -h whois.jp toyota.jp`
55. Press Enter. (This will provide a listing for Toyota.jp in Japanese.)
56. Type `whois -h whois.jp toyota.jp/e`
57. Press Enter. (This will provide a listing for Toyota.jp in both Japanese and English.)
58. Type `whois WebSiteOfYourChoosing.com`
59. Press Enter. (This will hopefully return a complete listing of your choosing. Enter any website that you want to in place of WebSiteOfYourChoosing.com. In this case, it was www.Yahoo.com.)
60. Take a screenshot. (See Figure 20-121.)

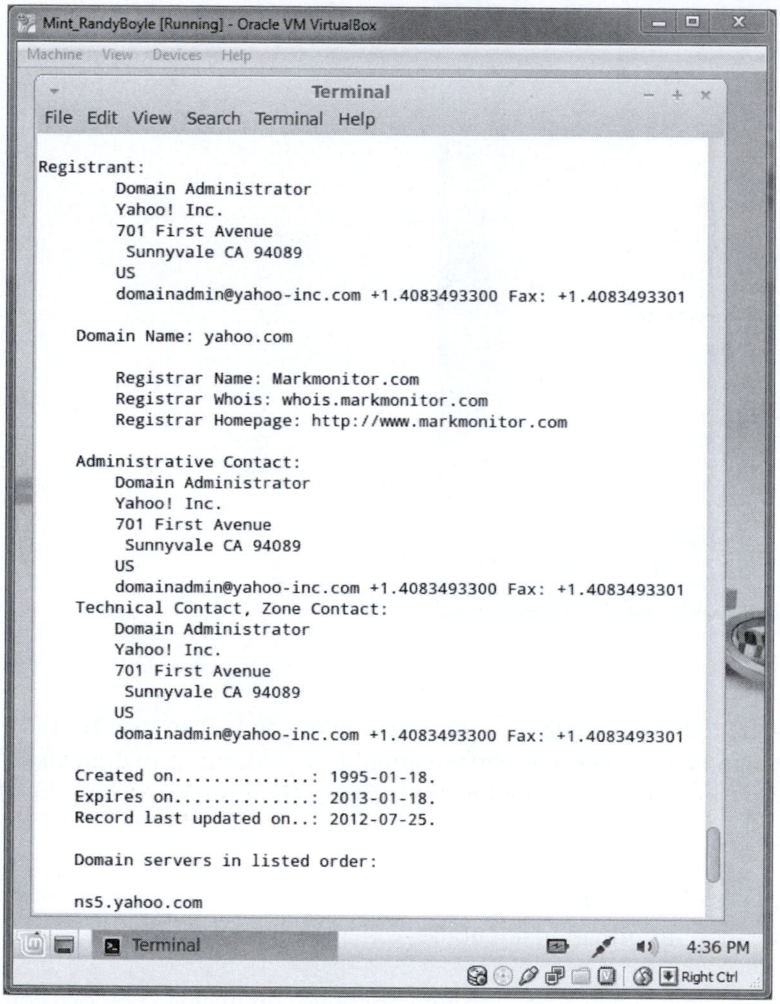

Figure 20-121: Whois information for Yahoo.com.

61. Type `sudo apt-get install nmap`
62. Press Enter. (This will install nmap.)
63. Type `man nmap`
64. Press Enter. (This will display the man page for the nmap command.)
65. Type `q`
66. Press Enter. (This will exit the man page for nmap.)
67. Type `ifconfig`

68. Press Enter. (Note your IP address on the second line down, inet addr. In this case, it was 10.0.2.15. You will need to know the IP address of your virtual machine to complete the next steps.)
69. Type **nmap [YourIPAddress]**
70. Press Enter. (This will port scan your computer/virtual machine. Replace [YourIPAddress] with the IP address assigned to your virtual machine. Your IP address was show when you entered the ifconfig command above. In this case, the command was **nmap 10.0.2.15**.)
71. Type **nmap [YourIPAddress]/24**
72. Press Enter. (This will scan 256 IP addresses on the subnet containing your computer/virtual machine. Nmap can scan any range of valid IP addresses. In this case, the command was **nmap 10.0.2.15/24**.)
73. Take a screenshot. (See Figure 20-122.)

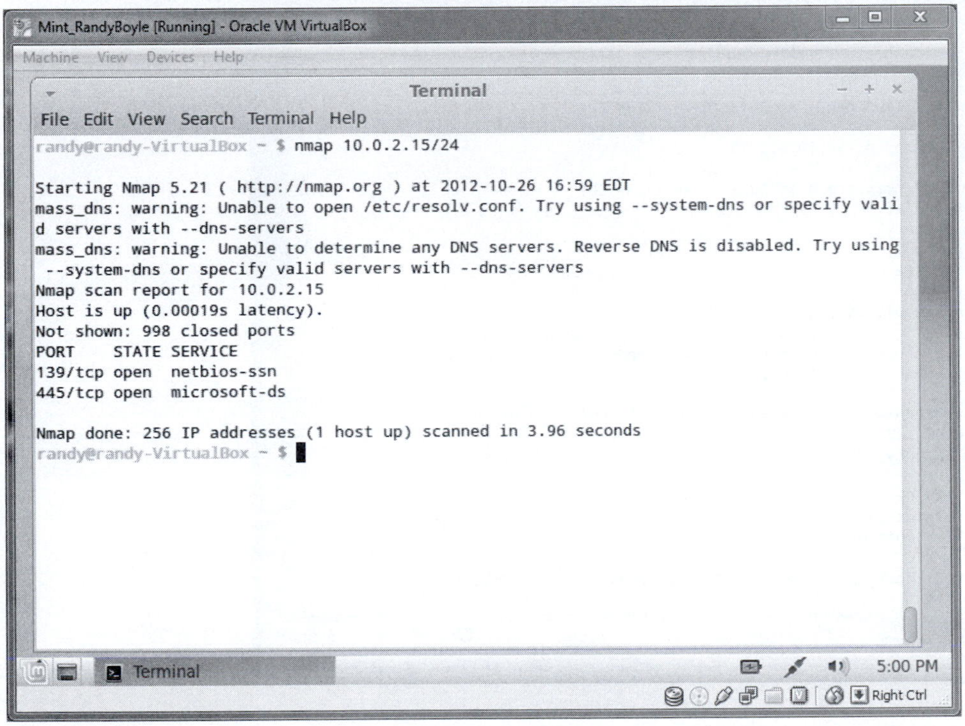

Figure 20-122: Nmap scan of your local machine.

74. Type **nmap -sn [YourIPAddress]**
75. Press Enter. (This will perform a ping scan of your computer. It will not port scan your computer.)
76. Type **nmap -n -sn [YourIPAddress]**
77. Press Enter. (The -n option will keep nmap from attempting DNS resolution. This will clean up the output so it's easier to understand.)

Note: The following are going to be commands that perform different types of scans. These commands can be combined and run at the same time. We will need root access to run some of these scans.

78. Type **su root**
79. Press Enter.
80. Type your password.
81. Press Enter. (Note the color change and the prompt changed from a $ to a #.)

82. Type **nmap -n -sS [YourIPAddress]**
83. Press Enter. (This will perform a SYN scan on your computer.)
84. Type **nmap -n -sA [YourIPAddress]**
85. Press Enter. (This will perform an ACK scan on your computer.)
86. Type **nmap -n -sU [YourIPAddress]**
87. Press Enter. (This will perform a UDP scan on your computer.)
88. Type **nmap -n -sF [YourIPAddress]**
89. Press Enter. (This will perform a FIN scan on your computer.)
90. Type **nmap -n -sX [YourIPAddress]**
91. Press Enter. (This will perform an Xmas scan on your computer.)
92. Take a screenshot. (See Figure 20-123.)

```
Mint_RandyBoyle [Running] - Oracle VM VirtualBox

Machine  View  Devices  Help

                          Terminal                        - + x

File  Edit  View  Search  Terminal  Help
Starting Nmap 5.21 ( http://nmap.org ) at 2012-10-26 17:38 EDT

randy-VirtualBox randy # nmap -n -sF 10.0.2.15

Starting Nmap 5.21 ( http://nmap.org ) at 2012-10-26 17:39 EDT
Nmap scan report for 10.0.2.15
Host is up (0.0000040s latency).
Not shown: 998 closed ports
PORT      STATE         SERVICE
139/tcp open|filtered netbios-ssn
445/tcp open|filtered microsoft-ds

Nmap done: 1 IP address (1 host up) scanned in 1.24 seconds
randy-VirtualBox randy # nmap -n -sX 10.0.2.15

Starting Nmap 5.21 ( http://nmap.org ) at 2012-10-26 17:39 EDT
Nmap scan report for 10.0.2.15
Host is up (0.0000040s latency).
Not shown: 998 closed ports
PORT      STATE         SERVICE
139/tcp open|filtered netbios-ssn
445/tcp open|filtered microsoft-ds

Nmap done: 1 IP address (1 host up) scanned in 1.24 seconds
randy-VirtualBox randy #

  Terminal                                    (1))  5:39 PM
                                                    Right Ctrl
```

Figure 20-123: Various Nmap scans.

93. Type **nmap -n -p1-500 [YourIPAddress]**
94. Press Enter. (This will scan only ports 1 to 500 on your computer.)
95. Type **nmap -n -p1-1000 [YourIPAddress]**
96. Press Enter. (This will scan only ports 1 to 1000 on your computer. Note that more open ports were reported.)
97. Type **nmap -n -O [YourIPAddress]**
98. Press Enter. (This will try to identify your OS.)
99. Type **nmap -n -O -sS -sV -T5 [YourIPAddress]**
100. Press Enter. (This will combine different types of scans and set it to run relatively quickly [i.e., -T5 rather than -T0].)
101. Type **nmap -n -A [YourIPAddress]**
102. Press Enter. (This will try to detect your OS, load many scripts for scanning, and display it all in verbose mode on the screen.)
103. Take a screenshot. (See Figure 20-124.)

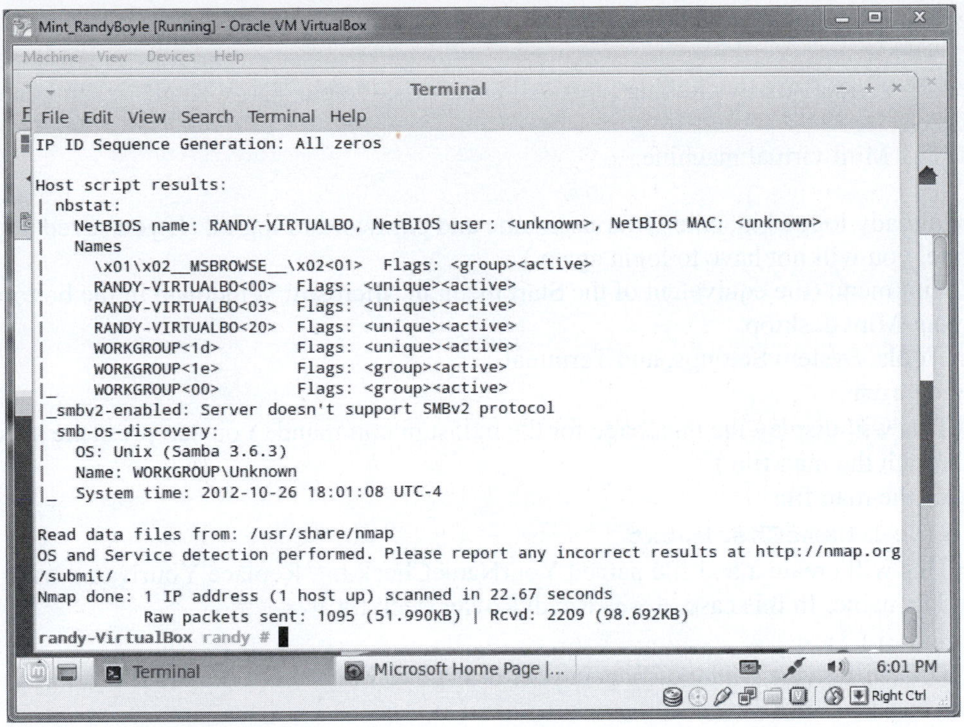

Figure 20-124: Nmap host identification.

PROJECT QUESTIONS

1. What hostname did you resolve with the host command?
2. What hostname did you use with the whois command?
3. What was your IP address for this project?
4. How long did the last nmap scan take?

THOUGHT QUESTIONS

1. Could the command-line version of nmap be faster than the GUI version? Why?
2. Why are there so many options for nmap?
3. Is it possible to make scans run faster or slower? How? (Hint: T)
4. Do you think your computer has been scanned by someone using nmap? Why?

20.8 FILE CLI UTILITIES (MINT)

In this project, you will learn how to use some commonly used command-line tools that are related to file manipulation. More specifically, you will learn how to use md5sum and sha1sum to produce hashes of text strings, individual files, or entire directories. You will change one of the files and then check the hashes to confirm which file was changed. You will also use a versatile command, lsof, to see which files are open or being accessed.

Lastly, you will learn how to recover deleted files using photorec, securely delete files using shred and srm, clear the volatile memory on your computer with sdmem, and securely wipe the free space on your hard drive using sfill. There is also a short introduction to gpg using symmetric encryption. Public key encryption will not be covered here.

This project has several steps, so read each step carefully.

1. Open Oracle VM VirtualBox by clicking Start, All Programs, Oracle VM VirtualBox, and Oracle VM VirtualBox.
2. Select your Linux Mint virtual machine.
3. Click Start.
4. If you are not already logged in, enter your username and password to log in. (If you saved your machine's state, you will not have to login again.)
5. Click on the Mint menu (the equivalent of the Start menu in Microsoft Windows) in the bottom left-hand of your Mint desktop.
6. Click System Tools, System Settings, and Terminal.
7. Type **man md5sum**
8. Press Enter. (This will display the man page for the md5sum command. You can press the space bar to page through the man file.)
9. Type **q** to exit the man file.
10. Type **touch YourNameCheck.txt**
11. Press Enter. (This will create a text file named YourNameCheck.txt. Replace YourName with your first and last name. In this case, it was RandyBoyleCheck.txt.)
12. Type **ls**
13. Press Enter. (This will give a listing of files in your directory. You should see the file you just created.)
14. Type **echo "YourName" >> YourNameCheck.txt**
15. Press Enter. (This will write your name to the text file you just created. Replace YourName with your first and last name. In this case, the command was `echo "RandyBoyle" >> RandyBoyleCheck.txt`.)
16. Type **md5sum YourNameCheck.txt**
17. Press Enter. (This will compute an MD5 hash of YourNameCheck.txt. In this case, it was RandyBoyleCheck.txt.)
18. Type **cat YourNameCheck.txt | md5sum**
19. Press Enter. (This will also compute an MD5 hash of YourNameCheck.txt. In this case, it was RandyBoyleCheck.txt. This should produce the identical hash shown in the prior command.)
20. Take a screenshot. (See Figure 20-125.)

Figure 20-125: Calculating a hash.

21. Type **echo -n "password123456" | md5sum**
22. Press Enter. (This will produce a hash of the text "password123456" without a -n trailing line.)
23. Type **echo -n "any text you want" | md5sum**
24. Press Enter. (This will produce a hash of any text you want.)
25. Type **touch text2.txt**
26. Press Enter. (This will create a new text file.)
27. Type **md5sum *.***
28. Press Enter. (This will compute hashes for all files in the current directory. You should see hashes for the two text files you created. The hashes should be different.)
29. Type **md5sum YourNameCheck.txt > YourNameHash.md5**
30. Press Enter. (This will write the hash of YourNameCheck.txt to a file named YourNameHash.md5. In this case, it wrote a hash of RandyBoyleCheck.txt to a file named RandyBoyleHash.md5.)
31. Type **ls**
32. Press Enter. (You should see the new hash file created. It will have an .md5 extension.)
33. Type **md5sum -c YourNameHash.md5**
34. Press Enter. (This will check to see if the hash recorded in the .md5 file matches a newly computed hash of the YourNameCheck.txt file. You should get an "OK" response. If there were any changes to the YourNameCheck.txt file, then the hashes would be different and the check would yield a "FAILED" response.)
35. Type **echo "additional text" >> YourNameCheck.txt**
36. Press Enter. (This will add "additional text" to your text document. When the hash is checked again, it will not be the same. In this case, the file appended was RandyBoyleCheck.txt.)
37. Type **md5sum -c YourNameHash.md5**
38. Press Enter. (You should see a "FAILED" response telling you that the md5 hashes recorded in the YourNameHash.md5 file do not match. This is expected since we appended the text file with "additional text.")
39. Take a screenshot. (See Figure 20-126.)

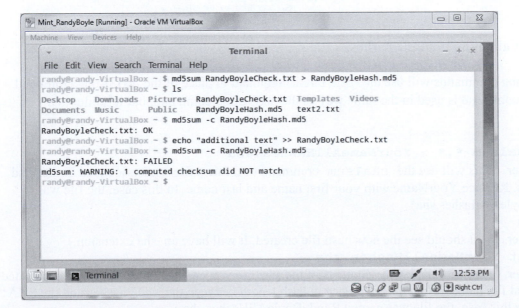

Figure 20-126: Validating a hash.

40. Type **md5sum *.* > YourNameAllHashes.md5**
41. Press Enter. (This will create hashes for all the files in the current directory. Replace YourName with your first and last name. In this case, the file was RandyBoyleAllHashes.md5.)
42. Type **ls**
43. Press Enter. (You should see the new hash file created. It will have an .md5 extension.)
44. Type **cat YourNameAllHashes.md5**
45. Press Enter. (This will display the contents of the .md5 file you created. You should see associated hashes and file names. In this case, the file was named RandyBoyleAllHashes.md5.)
46. Type **md5sum –c YourNameAllHashes.md5**
47. Press Enter. (This will check to see if any changes were made to any of the files in the current directory.)
48. Take a screenshot. (See Figure 20-127.)

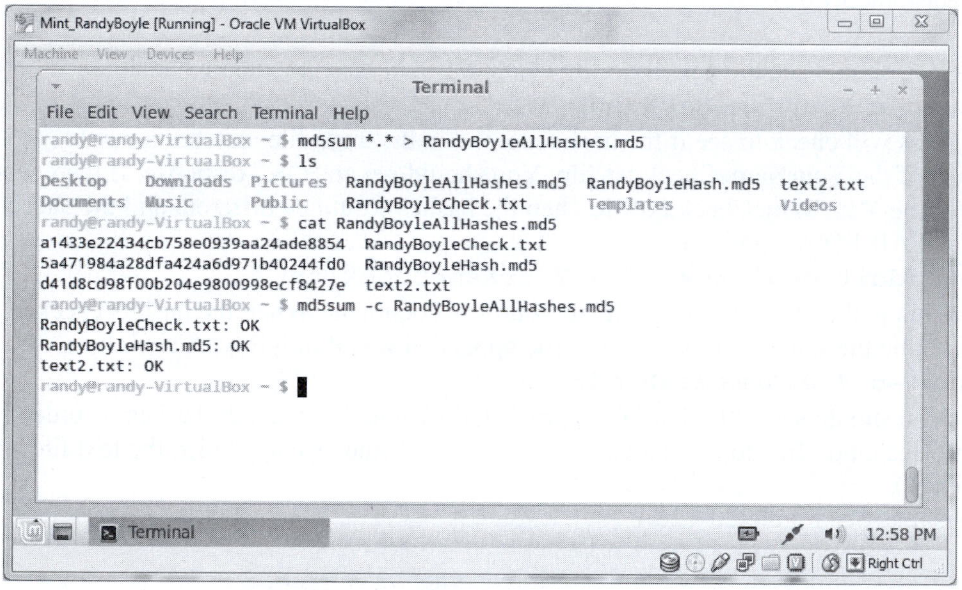

Figure 20-127: Validating multiple hashes.

Note: The following commands will use the `sha1sum` command in place of the `md5sum` command. The `sha1sum` command is used in the same way as the `md5sum` command, but it produces a different hash.

49. Type **sha1sum *.* > YourNameAllHashes.sha**
50. Press Enter. (This will use the `sha1sum` command to create a file with associated hashes and filenames. Replace YourName with your first name and last name. In this case, the file was RandyBoyleAllHashes.sha)
51. Type **ls**
52. Press Enter. (You should see the new hash file created. It will have an .sha extension.)
53. Type **cat YourNameAllHashes.sha**
54. Press Enter. (This will display the contents of the .sha file you created. You should see associated hashes and file names. Note the difference in hash length between the MD5 hashes and the SHA1 hashes. In this case, the file was named RandyBoyleAllHashes.sha.)
55. Type **sha1sum –c YourNameAllHashes.sha**
56. Press Enter.

57. Take a screenshot. (See Figure 20-128.)

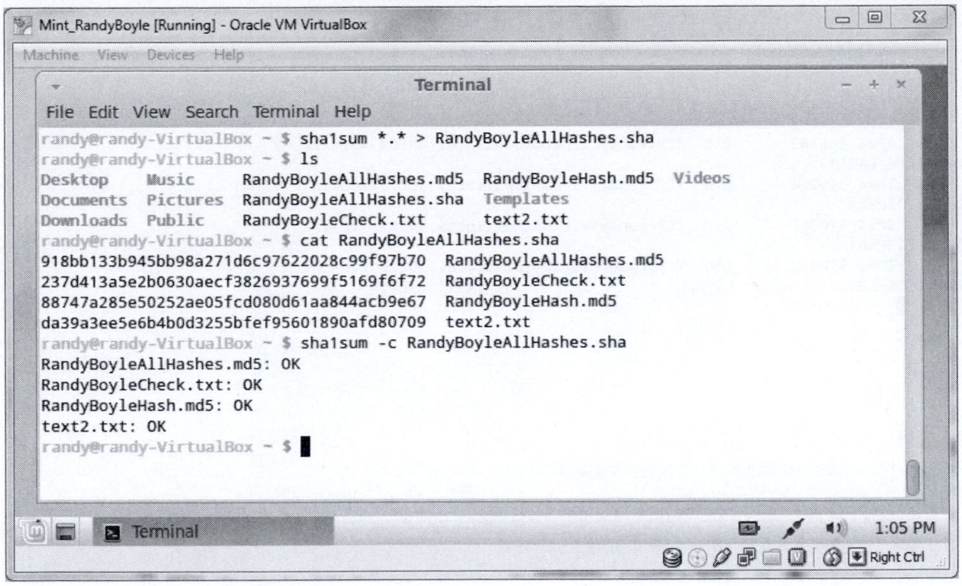

Figure 20-128: Calculating SHA hashes.

Note: The following section will cover the lsof (i.e., list of open files) command. It can be used to see who is accessing sensitive files.

58. Type **man lsof**
59. Press Enter. (This will display the man page for the lsof command. Notice the large number of options.)
60. Type **q** to exit the man page for lsof.
61. Type **lsof -i**
62. Press Enter. (This will return a listing of all Internet and x.25 network files.)
63. Click on the Mint Start menu icon.
64. Click Internet, and then Firefox.
65. Browse to www.Yahoo.com.
66. Type **lsof -i TCP**
67. Press Enter. (This will return a listing of all Internet files using TCP.)
68. Type **lsof -i TCP:80**
69. Press Enter. (This will return a listing of all Internet files using TCP port 80.)
70. Type **lsof -i -U**
71. Press Enter. (This will return a listing of all Internet files and domain sockets.)
72. Type **whoami**
73. Press Enter. (This will return your username. You will need to know your username for the next few steps.)
74. Type **lsof -u yourusername**
75. Press Enter. (This will return a listing of the open files for a specific user. In this case, the user was "randy." Replace yourusername with your actual username.)
76. Type **lsof -i -a -u yourusername**
77. Press Enter. (This will return a listing of all Internet files associated with a username. In this case, the username was "randy" and the command was lsof -i -a -u randy. Replace yourusername with your actual username.)
78. Take a screenshot. (See Figure 20-129.)

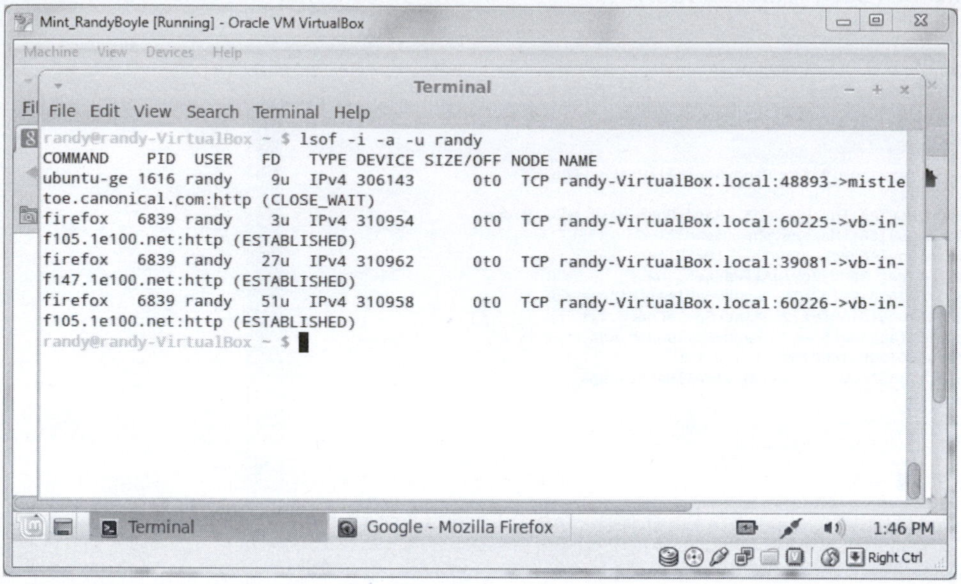

Figure 20-129: Listing files for a user.

79. Type **touch YourNameOpenFile.txt**
80. Press Enter. (This will create a text file named YourNameOpenFile.txt. In this case, it was RandyBoyleOpenFile.txt. You are going to open this file using the default text editor, gedit, and then locate it using the lsof command.)
81. Click on the Mint Start icon.
82. Click Places, and Home Folder. (You should see the file you just created named YourName OpenFile.txt.)
83. Double-click the YourNameOpenFile.txt file. (In this case, the file was named RandyBoyleOpenFile.txt.)
84. Return to the terminal.
85. Type **lsof /home/yourusername**
86. Press Enter. (This will display a listing of the open files in your home directory. In this case, it was **lsof /home/randy**. You should see a large listing. The next step will use the -c option followed by the letter "g" to limit the listing to only the files.)
87. Type **lsof -cg -a /home/yourusername**
88. Press Enter.
89. Take a screenshot. (See Figure 20-130.)

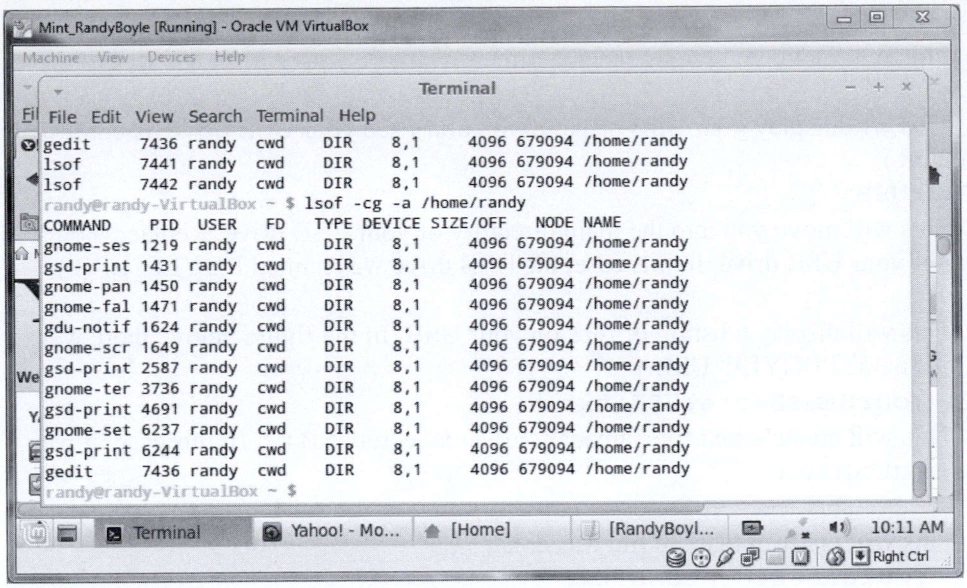

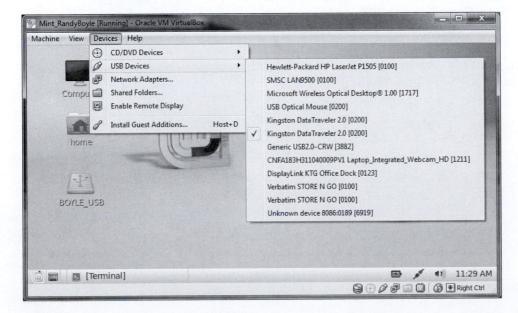

Figure 20-130: Listing files that start with "g" opened by a user.

Note: TestDisk comes with the "testdisk" command and "photorec" command. The former is for help recovering partitions, and the latter is used for recovering files.

90. Type **sudo apt-get install testdisk**
91. Press Enter. (This will install the TestDisk utility.)
92. Enter your password when prompted.
93. Press "y" if prompted.
94. Insert a USB into your computer.
95. In your VirtualBox menu, click Devices, USB Devices, and then select the USB drive you just inserted. (In this case, it was a Kingston® Data Traveler 2.0® USB drive.) (See Figure 20-131.)

Figure 20-131: Mounting a USB drive.

96. Type **cd /media**
97. Press Enter. (This will move you into the media directory where you will see your USB drive.)
98. Type **ls**
99. Press Enter. (This will display your USB drive. If you don't see your USB drive listed, it was not properly mounted.)
100. Type **cd YourUSB**
101. Press Enter. (This will move you into the main directory of your USB drive. Replace YourUSB with the name of your USB drive. In this case, the USB drive was named BOYLE_USB.)
102. Type **ls**
103. Press Enter. (This will display a listing of files on your USB. In the figure below, there were three files on the USB named BOYLE_USB.)
104. Type **touch YourNameSecretUSB.txt**
105. Press Enter. (This will create a text file named YourNameSecretUSB.txt. In this case, it was RandyBoyleSecretUSB.txt.)
106. Type **ls**
107. Press Enter. (This will confirm that the file was created.)
108. Type **gedit YourNameSecretUSB.txt**
109. Press Enter. (This will open the text file you created. In the following steps, you are going to copy your name multiple times to fill up the textfile. Later in this project, you will search for your name in the file you will recover.)
110. Type your first and last name. (In this case, it was Randy Boyle.)
111. Copy and past your name until you see a few hundred (yes, hundred) entries. (The file needs to be greater than 4K. Re-copying what you have already copied is an easy way to generate a large amount of data. You can copy one line and then just hold down Ctrl-v to repeatedly paste your name. You can see how many characters you have in the bottom right-hand of the gedit screen. Make sure you have over 4,000 characters. In this case, it was 5425.)
112. Click File, and Save.
113. Close the gedit window.
114. Type **ls -l**
115. Press Enter. (This will confirm the size of the file. In this case, it was 5425 bytes.)
116. Type **rm YourNameSecretUSB.txt**"
117. Press Enter. (This will delete the file you created.)
118. Type **ls**
119. Press Enter. (This will confirm that the file was deleted.)
120. Take a screenshot. (See Figure 20-132.)

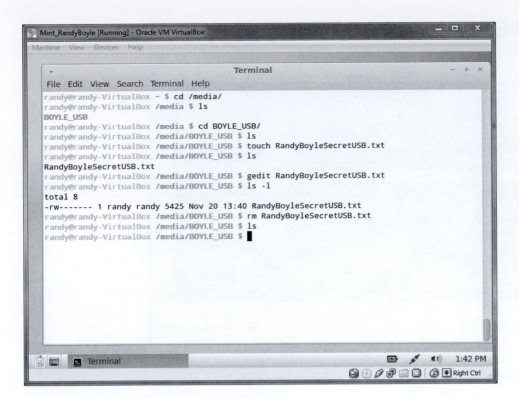

Figure 20-132: Creating and deleting a file.

121. Type **cd /**
122. Press Enter. (This will move you to the root directory.)
123. Type **sudo photorec**
124. Press Enter.
125. Enter your password if prompted. (This will start photorec and display a listing of possible drives to scan.)
126. Make sure your USB is highlighted. (You may need to arrow down. In this case, the USB drive was the second drive listed. The first drive was the virtual drive.)
127. Press Enter. (See Figure 20-133.)

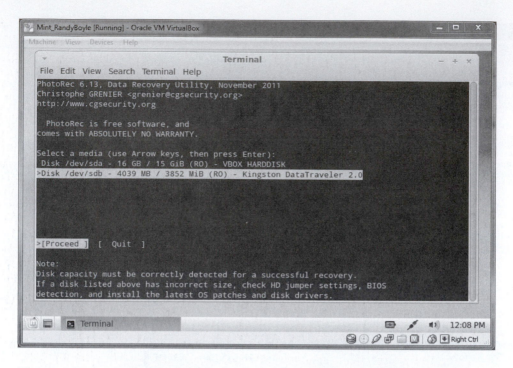

Figure 20-133: Selecting a drive to scan for recoverable files.

128. Arrow over and select File Opt.
129. Press "s" to disable all file families.
130. Scroll down until you see "txt Other text files". (Photorec can recover a large number of file
     types, so it is a long list.)
131. Press the Space bar. (This will tell photorec to only recover text files.)
132. Press "b" to save your settings. (See Figure 20-134.)
133. Press Enter, and Enter.

Figure 20-134: Selecting "txt" type files to search for.

134. Arrow over to Search. (Make sure your USB is highlighted.)
135. Press Enter.
136. Make sure "Other" file system type is selected and press Enter.
137. Make sure "Free" is selected and press Enter.
138. Arrow down until the /home directory is highlighted and press Enter.
139. Arrow down until your directory is highlighted and press Enter. (In this case, the directory name was "randy." You should see your name listed as a possible directory.)
140. Arrow down until your Documents directory is highlighted and press Enter.
141. Press C. (This will set the /home/yourusername/Documents directory as the location to store the recovered files. In this case, it was /home/randy/Documents. This should also start the scan.)
142. Take a screenshot when the scan finishes. (See Figure 20-135.)

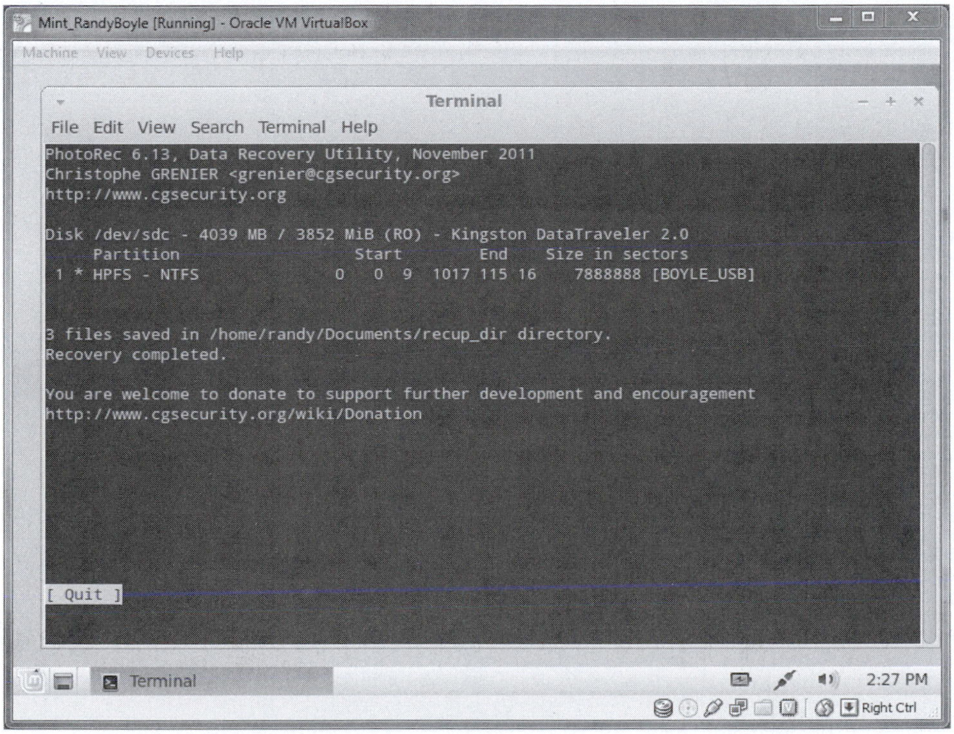

Figure 20-135: PhotoRec scan is complete.

Note: The recovery process may take several minutes. The 4GB drive used in this example took about 11 minutes to scan. Thousands of files (79,071) were recovered from this USB when it was scanned the first time because it was well used. After wiping it using sfill (used later in this project), it only recovered the file that was simply deleted. If you are using a new USB drive, it may only recover a few text files.

143. Press Enter to quit photorec.
144. Arrow over to select Quit.
145. Press Enter.
146. Type `cd /home/yourusername/Documents`
147. Press Enter. (This will move you to your Documents directory where the recovered files were stored in directories. In this case, the directory was /home/randy/Documents.)
148. Type `ls`

149. Press Enter. (This will display the directories containing the files you have recovered. In this case, there was one directory, but if you have a well-used USB it could be hundreds of directories.)
150. Type the following command:

```
sudo grep -H -r "YourLastName" /home/yourusername/Documents
```

151. Press Enter. (This will find all text files that contain the string "YourLastName" in your Documents directory and all subdirectories. The command was `sudo grep -H -r "Boyle" /home/randy/Documents`. The contents of the file you deleted should be displayed. You may see several text documents listed if you have used the USB before. If you recovered several files, it could take a few minutes to find the file containing the "YourLastName" string.)
152. Enter your password when prompted.
153. Take a screenshot. (See Figure 20-136.)

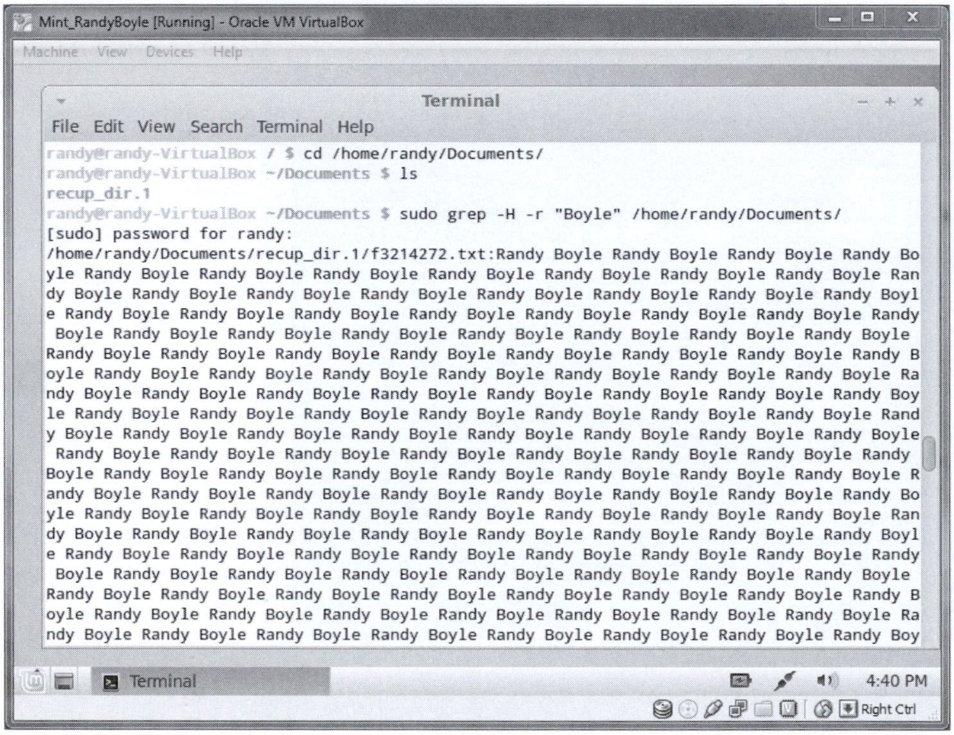

Figure 20-136: Recovered files.

154. Type `cd /home/yourusername`
155. Press Enter. (This will move you into your home directory. In this case, the command was `cd /home/randy`.)
156. Type `echo "anytext" >> ShredMe.txt`
157. Press Enter. (This will create a file named ShredMe.txt and append "anytext." You will securely delete the contents in the next steps. You will also securely delete the file itself.)
158. Type `gedit ShredMe.txt`
159. Press Enter. (This will open ShredMe.txt and confirm the contents of the file.)
160. Click File, and Quit.
161. Type `shred -v ShredMe.txt`
162. Press Enter. (This will securely delete the contents of ShredMe.txt in verbose mode. The file itself will not be deleted.)

163. Type **gedit ShredMe.txt**
164. Press Enter. (This will open ShredMe.txt and confirm that the contents of the file were deleted. You should see an error message saying there was a problem opening the file. This is good news.)
165. Click Cancel, and close gedit.
166. Type **shred -v -u ShredMe.txt**
167. Press Enter. (This will securely delete the contents of ShredMe.txt and the file itself in verbose mode.)
168. Type **ls**
169. Press Enter. (This will confirm that the file was deleted.)
170. Take a screenshot. (See Figure 20-137.)

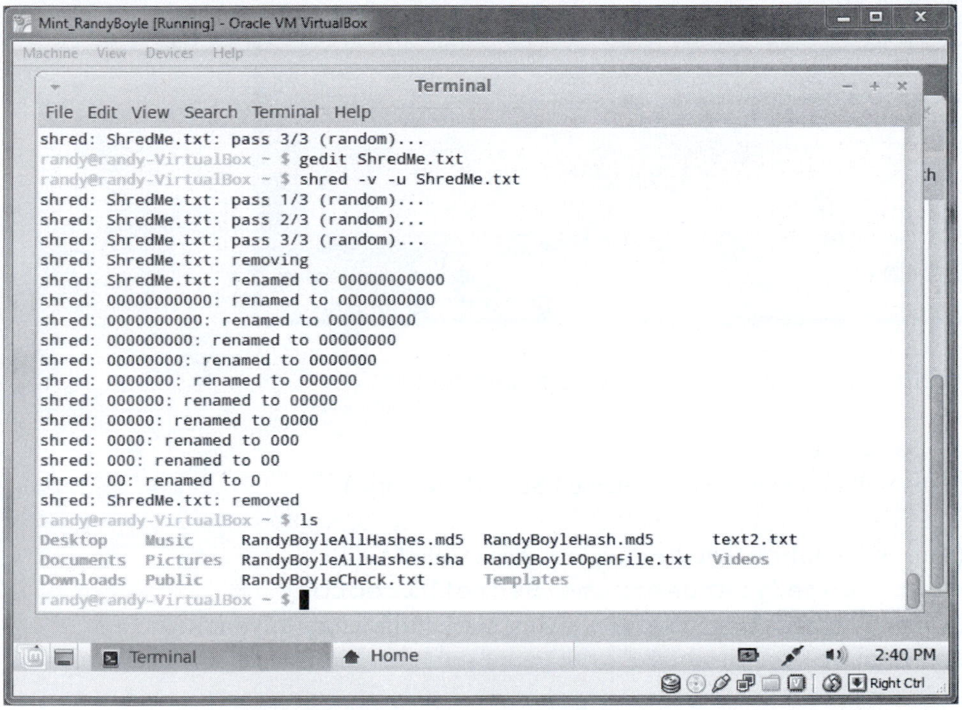

Figure 20-137: Using the shred command.

Note: In the next steps, you will install Secure Delete utilities. These utilities will allow you to delete files and directories, securely wipe your volatile memory, and wipe your free space.

171. Type **sudo apt-get install secure-delete**
172. Press Enter. (This will install the Secure Delete utilities.)
173. Type **echo "anytext" >> YourNameSecureDelete.txt**
174. Press Enter. (This will create a text file named YourNameSecureDelete.txt and append the text "anytext." In this case, the file was named RandyBoyleSecureDelete.txt.)
175. Type **ls**
176. Press Enter. (This will confirm that the file was created.)
177. Type **srm -v YourNameSecureDelete.txt**
178. Press Enter. (This will securely delete the text file named YourNameSecureDelete.txt [verbosely]. In this case, it was RandyBoyleSecureDelete.txt.)
179. Type **ls**
180. Press Enter. (This will confirm that the file was deleted.)
181. Take a screenshot. (See Figure 20-138.)

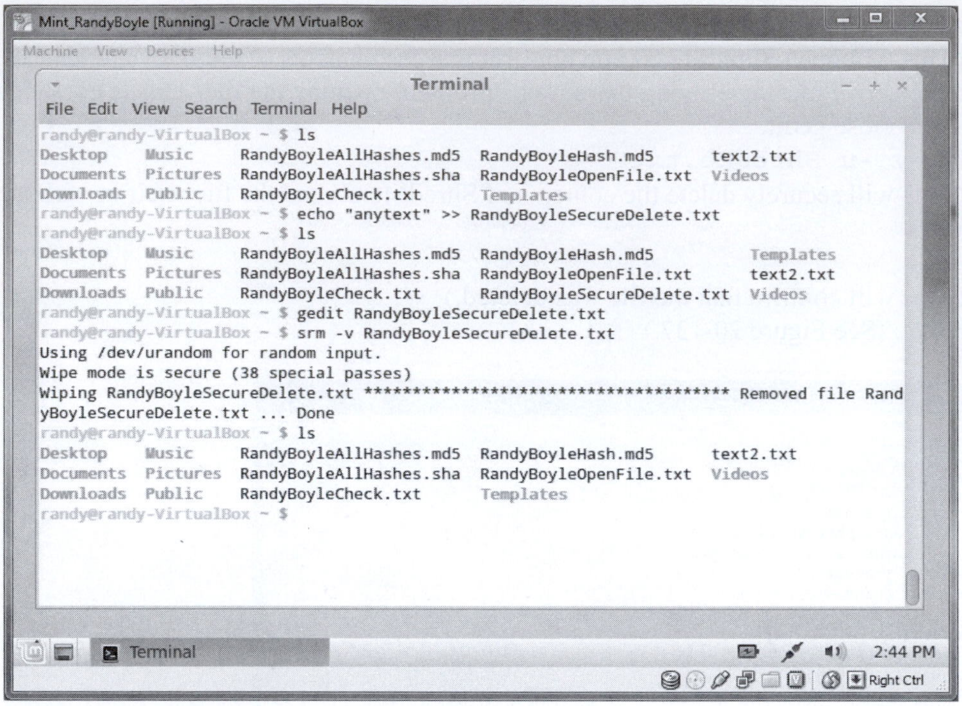

Figure 20-138: Securely deleting a file using the srm command.

182. Type **mkdir SecretDirectory**
183. Press Enter. (This will create a directory named SecretDirectory.)
184. Type **ls**
185. Press Enter. (This will confirm that the directory was created.)
186. Type **cp *.txt /home/yourusername/SecretDirectory**
187. Press Enter. (This will copy all the text files in your current directory to your new SecretDirectory. Replace "yourusername" with your username. In this case, the username was "randy.")
188. Type **ls /home/yourusername/SecretDirectory**
189. Press Enter. (This will confirm that the text files were copied into the SecretDirectory. You should see a few files listed. Replace "yourusername" with your username. In this case, the username was "randy.")
190. Type **srm –vrf /home/YourUsername/SecretDirectory**
191. Press Enter. (This will securely delete the directory and all files within it [verbose, recursive, and forced]. Replace "yourusername" with your username. In this case, the username was "randy.")
192. Type **ls**
193. Press Enter. (This will confirm that the directory and files were securely deleted.)
194. Take a screenshot. (See Figure 20-139.)

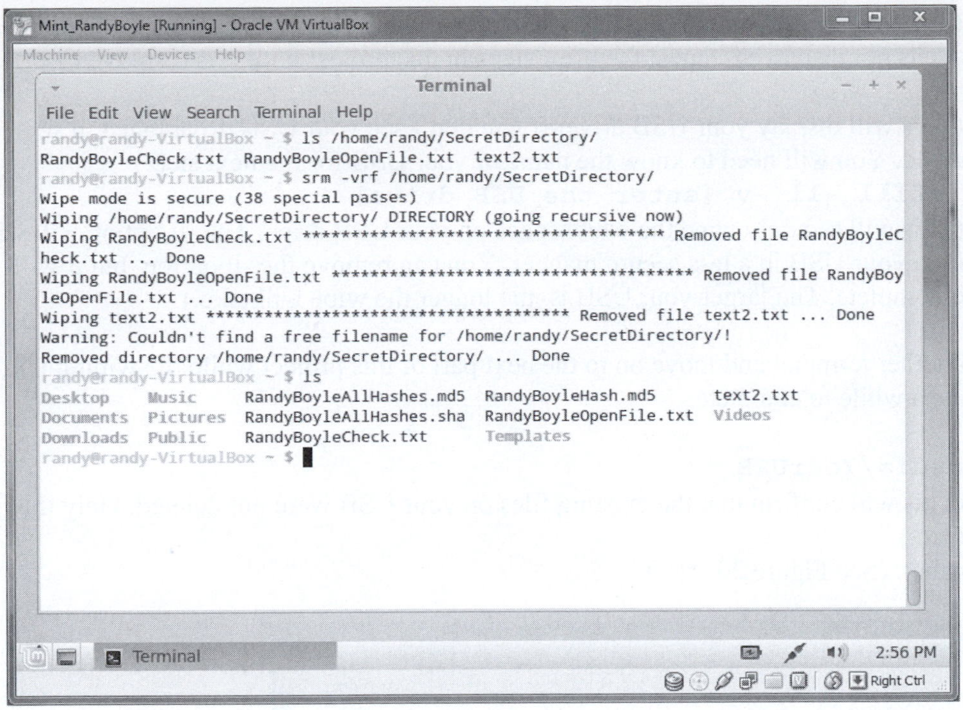

Figure 20-139: Securely deleting a directory.

195. Type **sdmem –ll -v**
196. Press Enter. (This will securely wipe your volatile memory, or RAM, in verbose mode. The command uses two letter "L"s, not two number "1"s. It may take a few minutes to complete depending on how much memory you have allocated to your virtual machine. In this case, it took a little over 2 minutes. You should see the word "Killed" displayed when it finishes.)
197. Take a screenshot. (See Figure 20-140.)

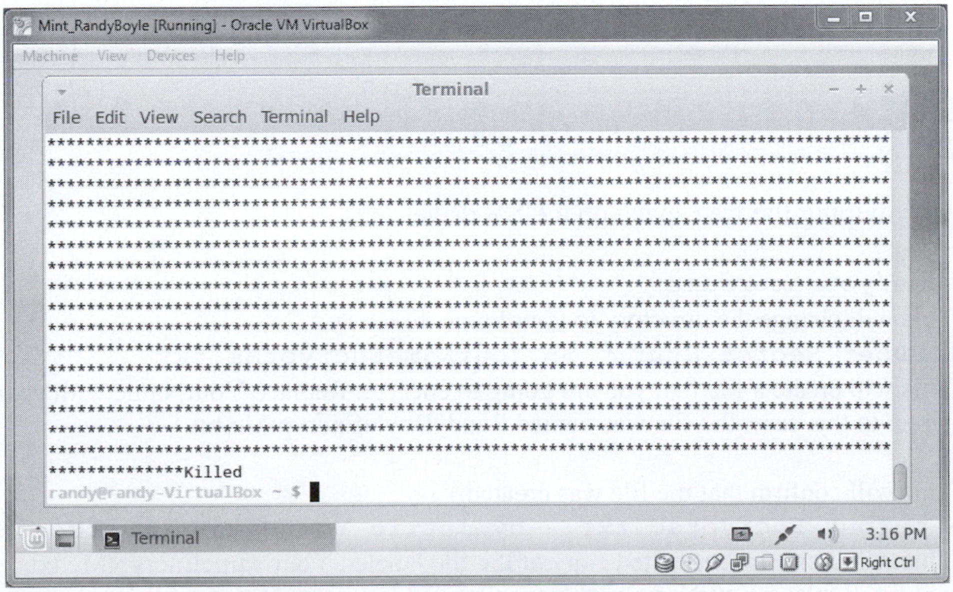

Figure 20-140: Securely wiping volatile memory.

198. Type **cd /media**

199. Press Enter. (This will move you into the media directory where you will see your USB drive. If your USB drive is not displayed, repeat the prior steps in this project until it is displayed.)
200. Type `ls`
201. Press Enter. (This will display your USB drive. If you don't see your USB drive listed, it was not properly mounted. You will need to know the name of your USB for the next step.)
202. Type `sudo sfill -ll -v [enter the USB drive]`
203. Press Enter. (This will securely wipe the white space on your USB drive. The -ll option will wipe the free space on your USB in a less secure manner. You can remove the -ll option, but it will take longer to complete. The larger your USB is, the longer the wipe will take.)

Note: You can open another terminal and move on to the next part of this project while the wiping is being done. It may take a while to complete.

204. Type `ls /media/YourUSB`
205. Press Enter. (This will confirm that the existing files on your USB were not deleted. Only the free space was wiped.)
206. Take a screenshot. (See Figure 20-141.)

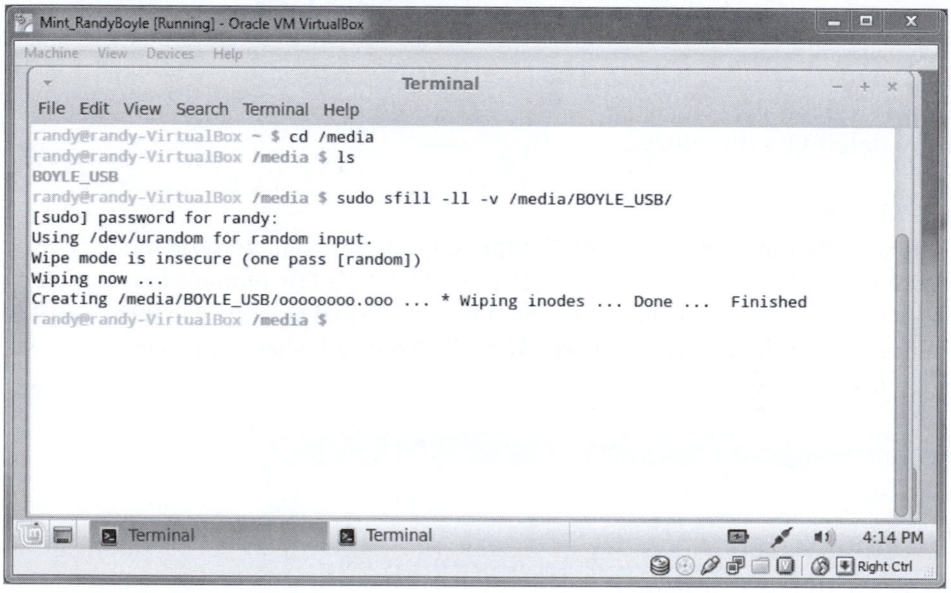

Figure 20-141: Securely wiping the free space on a USB drive.

207. Type `cd /home/yourusername`
208. Press Enter. (This will change the directory to your home directory.)
209. Type `echo "Super Secret Stuff" >> YourNameEncryptMe.txt`
210. Press Enter. (This will create a file that you are going to encrypt. Replace YourName with your first and last name. In this case, the file was named RandyBoyleEncryptMe.txt.)
211. Type `ls`
212. Press Enter. (This will confirm that the file was created.)
213. Type `gpg --output Encrypted.txt --symmetric YourNameEncryptMe.txt`
214. Press Enter. (This will create an encrypted copy of the file labeled YourNameEncryptMe.txt, called Encrypted.txt. Replace YourName with your first and last name.)
215. Enter a simple password twice. (In this case, the password was "tiger.")
216. Type `gedit Encrypted.txt`

217. Press Enter. (This will try to open the encrypted text file. You will get an error message. You will not be able to read this file because it is encrypted.)
218. Click Cancel, to close the gedit window showing the error message.
219. Type `gpg --output Decrypted.txt --decrypt Encrypted.txt`
220. Press Enter. (This will create a decrypted copy [Decrypted.txt] of the encrypted file labeled Encrypted.txt.)
221. Enter a simple password twice. (In this case, the password was "tiger.")
222. Type `ls`
223. Press Enter. (This will confirm that the decrypted file was created.)
224. Type `gedit Decrypted.txt`
225. Press Enter. (This will open the decrypted text file.)
226. Close the gedit window.
227. Take a screenshot of your current directory showing the Decrypted.txt file. (See Figure 20-142.)

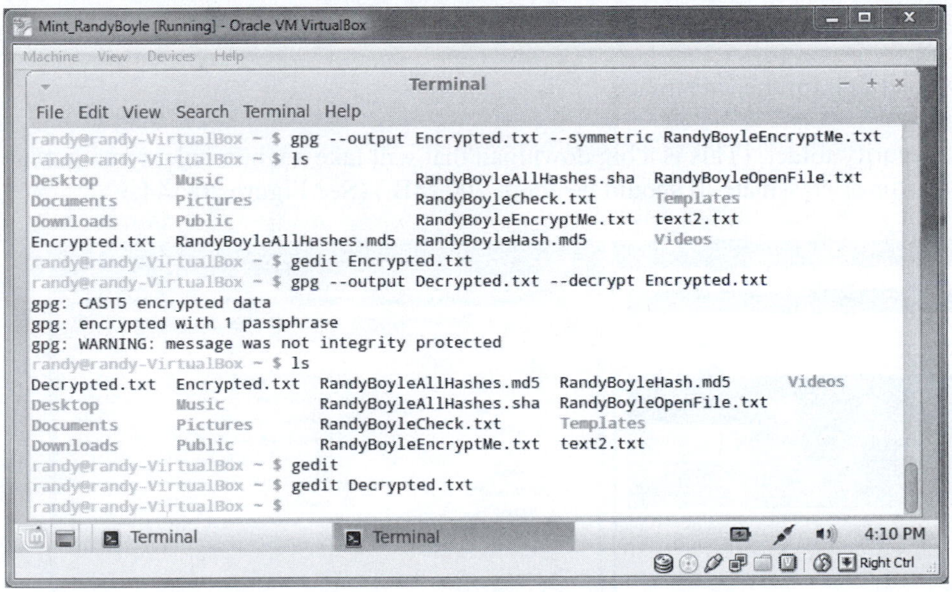

Figure 20-142: Encrypting and decrypting a file.

PROJECT QUESTIONS

1. What was the name of the file you encrypted?
2. What was the name of the file in which you stored your hashes?
3. What was the name of the file you securely deleted using srm?
4. How many files did you recover using Photorec?

THOUGHT QUESTIONS

1. Why does it take so long to wipe the empty space on a drive?
2. Would corporations be interested in securely deleting data? Why?
3. Why would you need to calculate a hash?
4. Could the lsof command be used to detect employee fraud? How?

20.9 TCPDUMP (PC-BSD®)

In an earlier chapter, you had a short introduction to tcpdump. This project will take a more in-depth look at tcpdump's functionality. You will capture specific types of traffic, traffic intended for a given hostname or IP address, view the contents of captured packets, write packets to a file, and subsequently read the capture file. You will look at more options available for tcpdump that can make it more user friendly and useful.

This project will also introduce you to another operating system – FreeBSD®. You will install a flavor of FreeBSD called PC-BSD®. FreeBSD is a Unix variant that is widely used by corporations, government entities, and large organizations. It is widely used due to its stability, security, scalability, and customizability. Incidentally, FreeBSD makes up an important part of Apple's OS X operating system.

1. Download PC-BSD (FreeBSD) from: http://www.pcbsd.org/.
2. Click on the Download link at the top of the page.
3. Click the link for the CD 64-bit version of PC-BSD. (You can download the 32-bit version if you have older hardware.) (See Figure 20-143.)
4. Click Download.
5. Click the download link for the ISO image.
6. Click Save.
7. Select your C:\security folder. (This is a big download that will take a while unless you get it from your instructor or classmate. It should be about 700 MB.) (See Figure 20-144.)

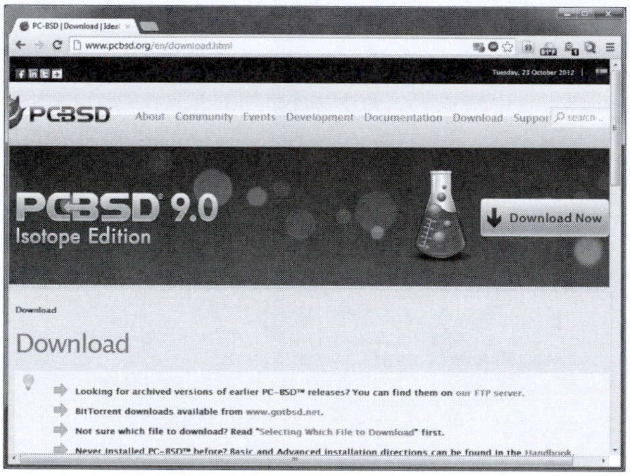

Figure 20-143: PC-BSD distribution page.

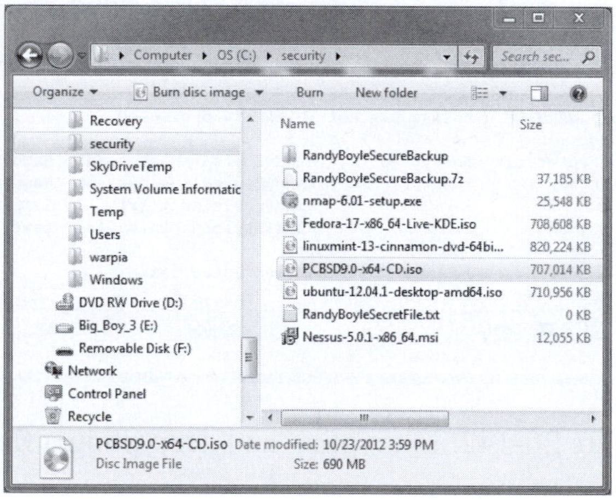

Figure 20-144: PC-BSD (FreeBSD) ISO image.

8. Open Oracle VM VirtualBox by clicking Start, All Programs, Oracle VM VirtualBox, and Oracle VM VirtualBox. (You installed VirtualBox as part of projects in an earlier chapter. If you haven't installed VirtualBox, you will need to do so now.)
9. Click New.
10. Enter "FreeBSD_YourName" for the Name. (In this case, it was FreeBSD_RandyBoyle.) (See Figure 20-145.)
11. Select BSD for the Operating System.
12. Select FreeBSD (64 bit) for the Version. (Select just "FreeBSD" if you have an older 32-bit system.)
13. Click Next.
14. Increase the amount of memory to 2000 MB+. (See Figure 20-146.)

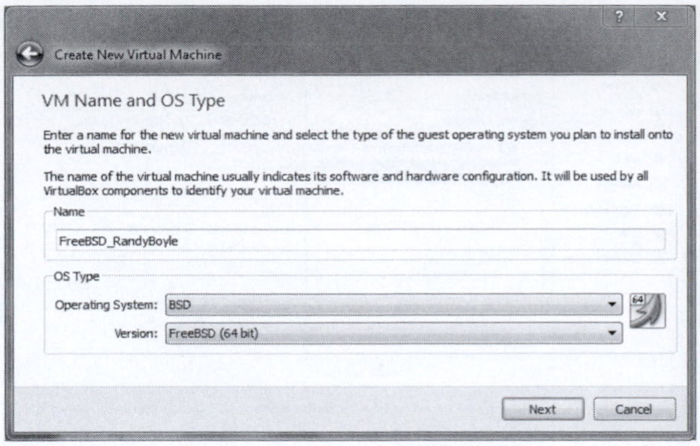

Figure 20-145: Naming the FreeBSD virtual machine.

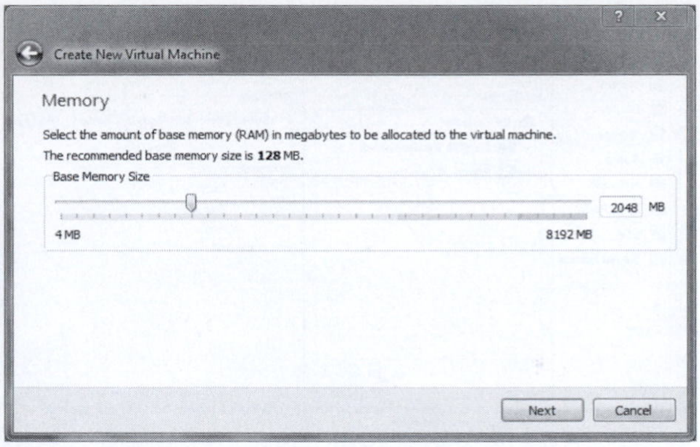

Figure 20-146: Allocating RAM to the virtual machine.

15. Click Next, Next, Next, and Next.
16. Increase the hard drive space to 15GB (or more if you have the space). (See Figure 20-147.)
17. Click Next, Create, and Create.
18. Select the virtual machine labeled FreeBSD_YourName. (In this case, it was FreeBSD_RandyBoyle.) (See Figure 20-148.)

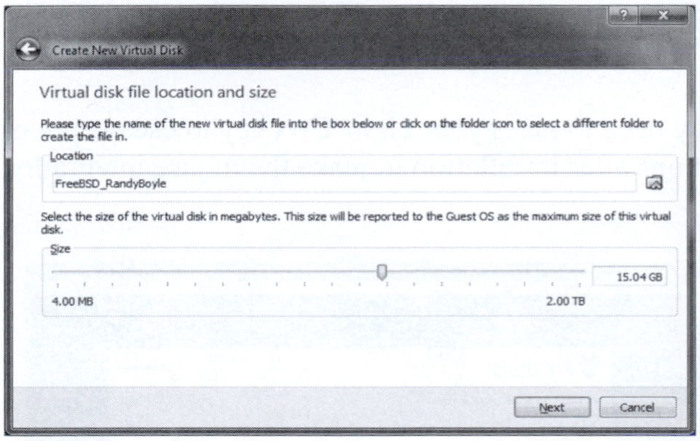

Figure 20-147: Setting the size of the virtual hard drive.

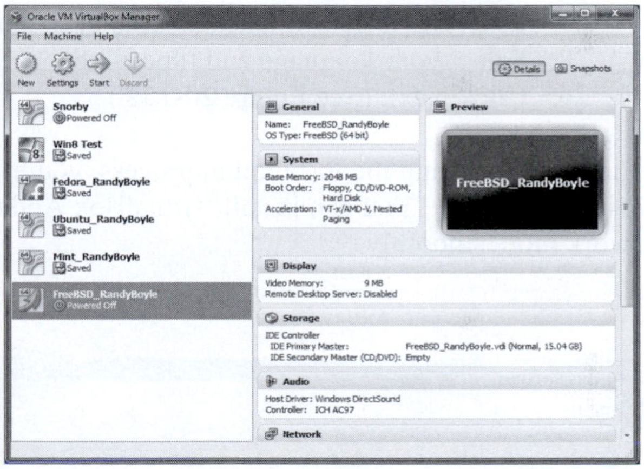

Figure 20-148: FreeBSD virtual machine created.

19. In the right-hand pane, click Storage, IDE Controller, and Empty. (See Figure 20-149.)
20. Click the Browse button on the right-hand side of the screen by the CD/DVD Drive drop-down box. (It looks like a little CD.)
21. Click Add.
22. Browse to your C:\security folder.
23. Select the PC-BSD (FreeBSD) image you downloaded. (In this case, it was PCBSD9.0-x64-CD.iso.)
24. Click Open. (See Figure 20-150.)
25. Click OK.

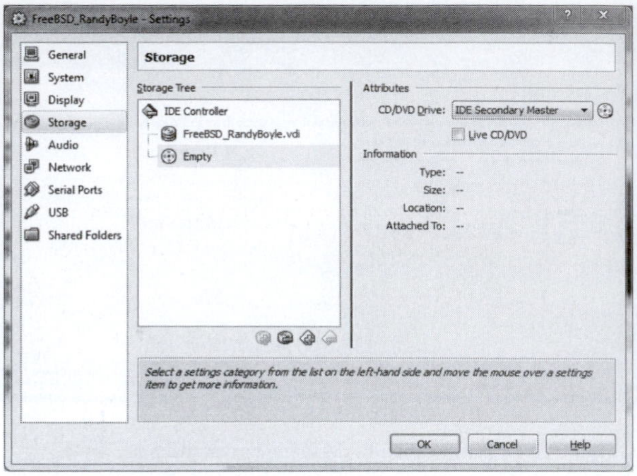

Figure 20-149: No CD/DVD image mounted.

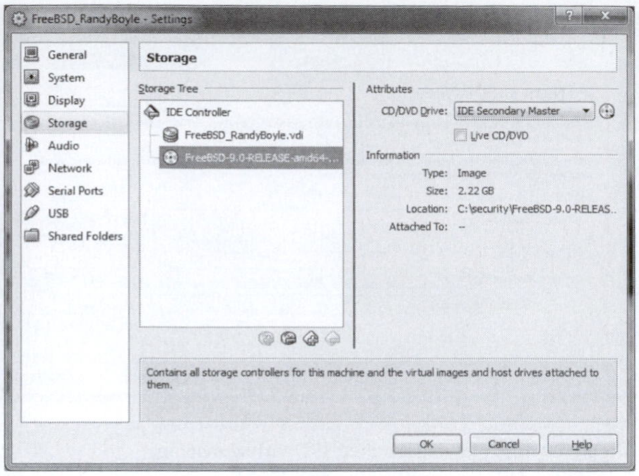

Figure 20-150: FreeBSD ISO image mounted.

26. Take a screenshot showing the new virtual machine. (You may have to use Screenshot Pilot to take screenshots. You can leave the virtual machine by holding down the right Ctrl key. To copy the screenshot from within Screenshot Pilot, you click Image, and then Copy to Clipboard.) (See Figure 20-151.)

27. Click Start. (It will take a couple of minutes to boot.)

28. Select your language and time zone.

29. Click Next. (See Figure 20-152.)

Important: During the installation process, you may need to press your **right Ctrl** key to escape out of the virtual machine. You can install VirtualBox Additions after installation to make the mouse integration work more smoothly.

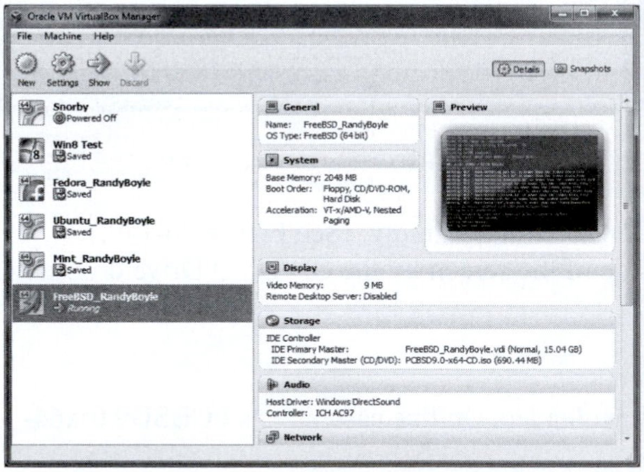

Figure 20-151: FreeBSD virtual machine ready to boot.

Figure 20-152: Language and time zone selection.

30. Click Next, and Next.

31. Select Use Entire Disk.

32. Click Next.

33. Enter a root password twice. (It's a good idea to write down your root password if you have a bad memory. You will need to know this password for later projects.) (See Figure 20-153.)

34. Enter your first name (lower-case) for your username.

35. Enter your full name (first and last name) in the Full name text box.

36. For your user password, enter the same system password you entered above twice.
37. Take a screenshot. (See Figure 20-154.)
38. Click the Add button with the green "+" next to it.
39. Click Next, Next, and Yes. (The installation process will take several minutes.)

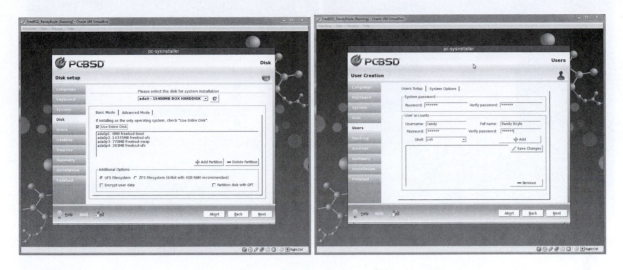

Figure 20-153: Free BSD installer.   Figure 20-154: Entering system password and a user account.

40. Do *not* press Finish to reboot your virtual machine. (You need to remove the PC-BSD ISO image before rebooting.)

Note: You are now going to have to take the PC-BSD ISO image out of the virtual CD ROM so you don't have to go through the installation process again. If you don't take out the ISO image, the installation process may start again when you reboot the virtual machine.

41. Press the right Ctrl key to exit the virtual machine. (You may be able to skip this step on newer versions of VirtualBox. Older versions may still require it.)
42. In the VirtualBox menu for the virtual machine you are working on, click Devices, CD-DVD ROM, and Remove disk from virtual drive. (This will unmount the ISO image.) (See Figure 20-155.)
43. Click Force Unmount. (This should remove the ISO image from your virtual CD-DVD drive.)
44. Return to your virtual machine.
45. Click Finish. (Your virtual machine should automatically reboot.)
46. Click Skip if you see a Display Settings dialogue box.
47. Click on your name at the Welcome screen.
48. Enter the password you set earlier.
49. Press Enter, or click Log In.
50. Click the PC-BSD start icon in the lower left-hand corner of your screen.
51. Click Preferences, and PC-BSD Control Panel.
52. Double-click the System Manager icon under the System Management section.
53. Click the System Packages tab.
54. Expand the Misc. tree.
55. Select VirtualBoxGuest. (This will make interacting with your PC-BSD virtual machine easier.)
56. Click Apply Changes, and OK. (See Figure 20-156.)
57. Expand the Desktop tree. (Note that the default desktop you are using is LXDE. You can also get GNOME, KDE, XFCE, and a few other unsupported desktops.)
58. Close the System Configuration window.

Important: To leave your virtual machine, you may have to press your **right Ctrl** key to escape out of the virtual machine.

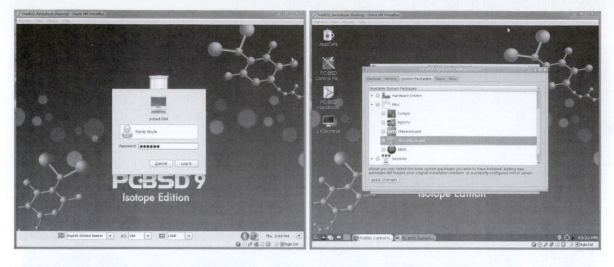

Figure 20-155: Entering a password for the root account.   Figure 20-156: System Configuration.

59. Click the PC-BSD start icon in the lower left-hand corner of your screen.
60. Click Accessories, and LXTerminal.
61. Type `su root`
62. Press Enter.
63. Enter your password.
64. Type `pkg_add -r tcpdump`
65. Press Enter. (See Figure 20-157.)
66. Type `ifconfig`
67. Press Enter. (This will list configurations for your network adapters. You will need to know which adapter your network traffic is going through. In this case, it was the first adapter listed as em0 [with a zero, not the letter "O"]. In the next step, you will see it listed as the first adapter.)
68. Type `tcpdump -D`
69. Press Enter. (This will display all of the available network adapters on your computer.) (See Figure 20-15.)
70. Take a screenshot. (See Figure 20-158.)
71. Note the Ethernet interface number. (In this case, the number 1 is listed for em0 [with a zero, not the letter "O"] that you will use for this project. You will use this number in the next step.)

Note: You will need to be able to determine which adapter you are using for the remainder of the project. In this case, the wired adapter was #1 on the list. The remaining steps will use adapter #1. However, it is possible that you are using a different adapter. You can see a listing of the available adapters by using the ifconfig command.

Figure 20-157: Elevating privileges and installing tcpdump.   Figure 20-158: Listing available network interfaces.

72. Type **pkg_add -r chromium**
73. Press Enter. (This will install the Chromium Web browser. You will use this browser to generate traffic for tcpdump to capture. You could also install Firefox, Opera, or Konqueror.)
74. Type **tcpdump -i 1**
75. Press Enter. (This will capture all packets on network interface 1. Your adapter may be *different*. Use the adapter that can access the Internet. See the note above and make sure you are using the correct network adapter.)
76. Open Chromium by clicking the PC-BSD icon, Internet, and Chromium.
77. Browse to any website. (In this case, www.Google.com)
78. Return to the terminal. (See Figure 20-159.)
79. Press Ctrl+C to stop capturing packets. (You likely captured hundreds or even a few thousand packets.)
80. Type **tcpdump -i 1 host www.longwood.edu**
81. Press Enter. (This will only capture packets that have a source or host name of www.Longwood.edu. You can substitute another URL, such as your school URL, if you'd like.)
82. In your Web browser, go to www.Longwood.edu. (Note that no packets were captured until you went to www.Longwood.edu.)
83. Press Ctrl+C to stop capturing packets.
84. Take a screenshot. (See Figure 20-160.)

Important: To leave your virtual machine, you may have to press your **right Ctrl** key to escape out of the virtual machine.

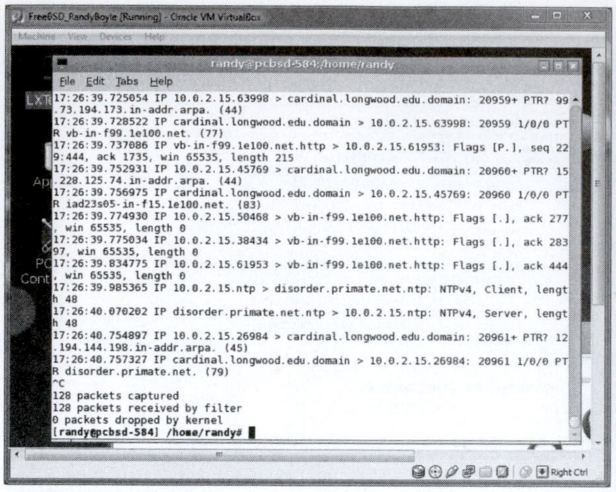

Figure 20-159: Capturing packets from a website.

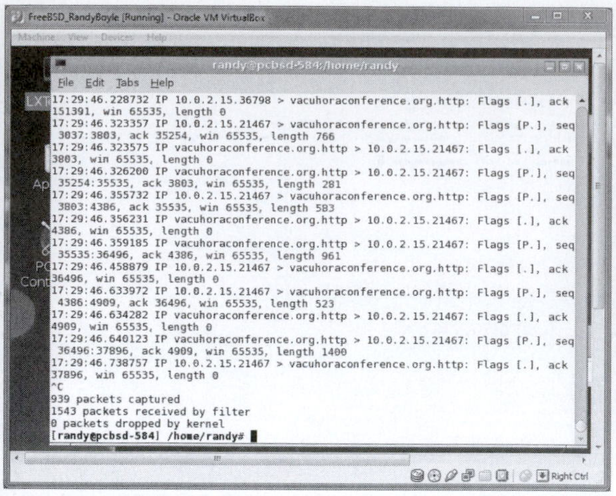

Figure 20-160: Capturing packets for a specific hostname.

Note: In the following steps, you will enter your computer's IP address. In this example, the computer's IP address was 10.0.2.15. Your IP address will be different. Use the ifconfig command to determine your IP address. It may be a local, non-routable, IP address (e.g., 10.X.X.X or 192.168.X.X), or a public IP address. Replace [type your IP address] with your actual IP address, without brackets.

85. Type **tcpdump –i 1 host [type your IP address]**
86. Press Enter. (This will capture packets on interface 1 that have a specified source or destination IP address. In this case, it was 10.0.2.15. Your IP address will be different than the one shown.)
87. In your Web browser, refresh the page you are on. (Note that only packets with your IP address were captured.)
88. Press Ctrl+C to stop capturing packets.
89. Type **tcpdump –i 1 src [type your IP address]**
90. Press Enter. (This will capture packets on interface 1 that have a specified source IP address. In this case, it was 10.0.2.15.)
91. In your Web browser, refresh the page you are on. (Note that only packets listing your IP address as the *source* were captured.)
92. Press Ctrl+C to stop capturing packets.
93. Type **tcpdump –i 1 dst [type your IP address]**
94. Press Enter. (This will capture packets on interface 1 that have a specified destination IP address. In this case, it was 10.0.2.15.)
95. In your Web browser, refresh the page you are on. (Note that only packets listing your IP address as the *destination* were captured.)
96. Press Ctrl+C to stop capturing packets.
97. Take a screenshot. (See Figure 20-161.)

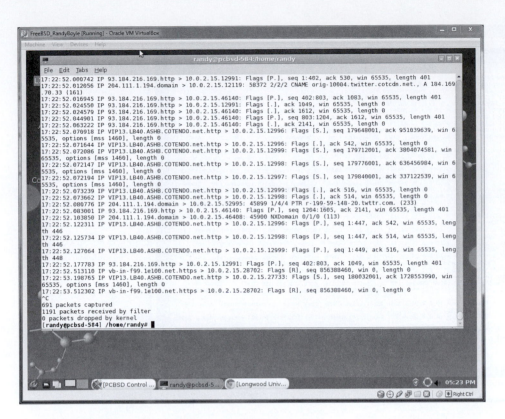

Figure 20-161: Capturing packets addressed to a specific IP address.

98. Type **tcpdump –i 1 port 53**

99. Press Enter. (This will capture DNS packets.)

100. In your Web browser, type in any URL. (In this example, it was www.Google.com.)

101. Press Ctrl+C to stop capturing packets.

102. Type **tcpdump –i 1 src port 53**

103. Press Enter. (This will capture DNS packets listing 53 in their source port field.)

104. In your Web browser, type in any other URL. (In this example, it was www.Yahoo.com.)

105. Press Ctrl+C to stop capturing packets.

106. Take a screenshot. (See Figure 20-162.)

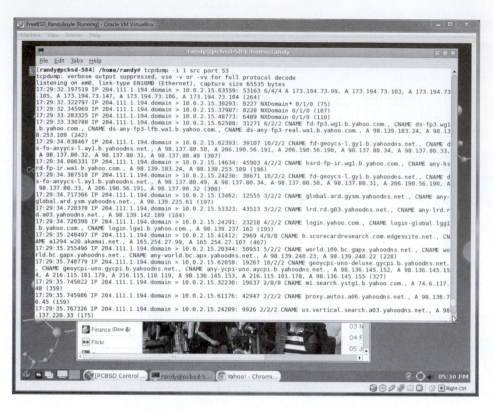

Figure 20-162: Capturing DNS packets.

107. Type **`tcpdump –i 1 dst port 53`**

108. Press Enter. (This will capture DNS packets listing 53 in their destination port field.)

109. In your Web browser, type in any other URL. (In this example, it was www.Facebook.com.)

110. Press Ctrl+C to stop capturing packets.

111. Type **`tcpdump –i 1 udp dst port 53`**

112. Press Enter. (This will capture only UDP DNS packets listing 53 in their destination port field.)

113. In your Web browser, type in any other URL. (In this example, it was www.Twitter.com.)

114. Press Ctrl+C to stop capturing packets.

115. Type **`tcpdump –n –i 1 udp dst port 53`**

116. Press Enter. (The "-n" option will force tcpdump to *not* resolve host names.)

117. In your Web browser, type in any other URL. (In this example, it was www.CNN.com. Note that IP addresses are now displayed instead of hostnames.)

118. Press Ctrl+C to stop capturing packets.

119. Type **`tcpdump –tn –i 1 udp dst port 53`**

120. Press Enter. (The "-t" option will remove timestamps.)

121. In your Web browser, type in any other URL. (In this example, it was www.Longwood.edu. Note on the right-hand side you can see some of the hostnames that were being requested.)

122. Press Ctrl+C to stop capturing packets.

123. Take a screenshot. (See Figure 20-163.)

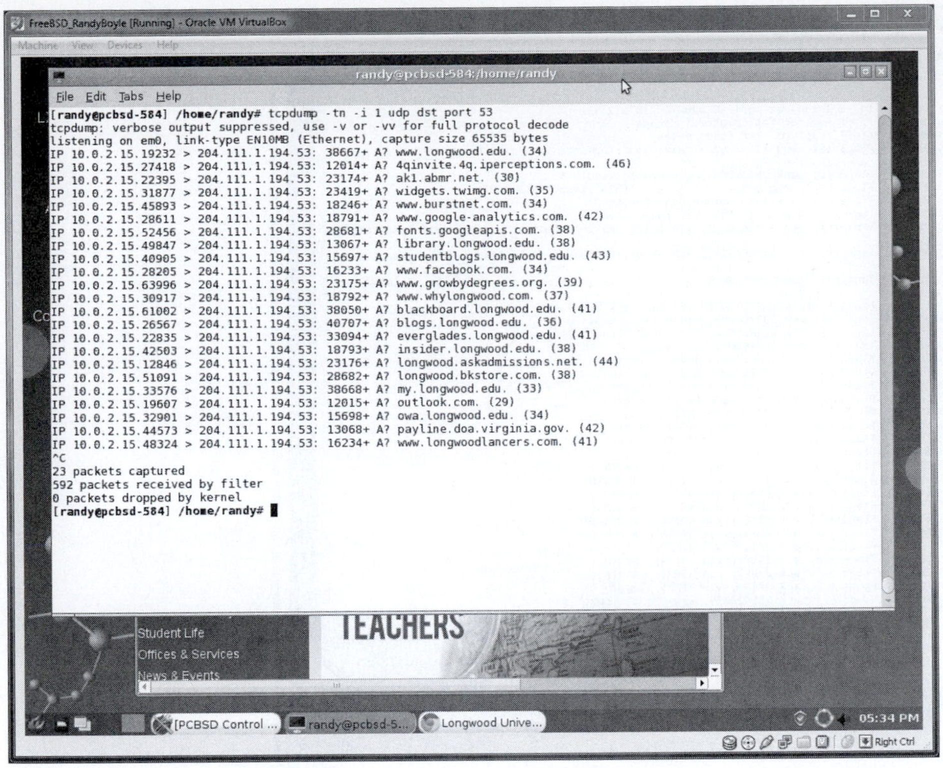

Figure 20-163: Capturing DNS packets without timestamps.

124. Type **tcpdump –Xtn –i 1 udp dst port 53**
125. Press Enter. (The "-X" option will display the contents of the packets.)
126. In your Web browser, type in any other URL. (In this example, it was www.Yahoo.com.)
127. Press Ctrl+C to stop capturing packets.
128. Type the following command:

tcpdump –tn –i 1 tcp dst port 80 and src [type your IP address]

129. Press Enter. (This will capture TCP packets with destination port 80 [Web traffic], and a specific source IP address. In this case, it was 10.0.2.15.)
130. In your Web browser, type in any other URL. (In this example, it was www.Google.com.)
131. Press Ctrl+C to stop capturing packets.
132. Take a screenshot. (See Figure 20-164.)

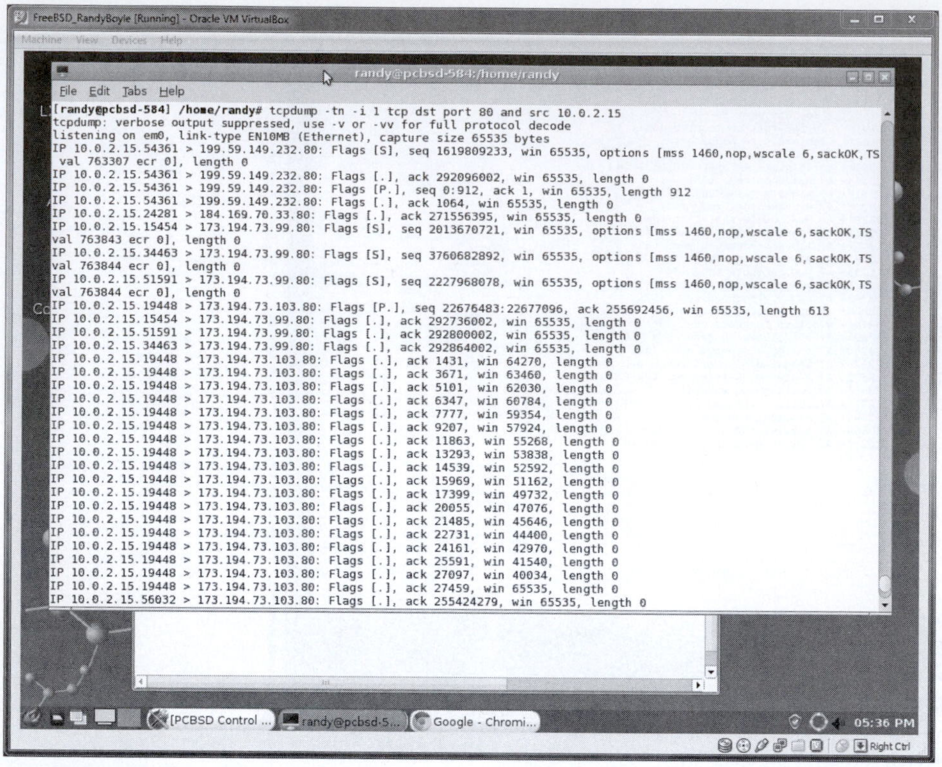

Figure 20-164: Capturing Web traffic from a specific IP address.

133. Type **tcpdump -i 1 -c 5 dst port 53**

134. Press Enter. (The "-c" option will capture a specific number of packets. In this case, it will capture 5 DNS packets. It will stop capturing packets after it captures the first five.)

135. In your Web browser, type in any other URL. (In this example, it was www.Twitter.com.)

136. Type **tcpdump -i 1 -c 5 -w YourNameCapture.txt dst port 53**

137. Press Enter. (The "-w" option will write the captured packets to a YourNameCapture.txt file. Replace "YourName" with your first and last name. In this case, it was RandyBoyleCapture.txt.)

138. In your Web browser, type in any other URL. (In this example, it was www.Google.com.)

139. Type **tcpdump -r YourNameCapture.txt**

140. Press Enter. (This will read the saved text file you just created. The five packets you captured will be displayed on the screen.)

141. Take a screenshot. (See Figure 20-165.)

Figure 20-165: Capturing packets and writing them to a text file.

PROJECT QUESTIONS

1. What was your IP address in this project?
2. What was the name of your capture file?
3. What websites did you go to during this project?
4. How many packets did you capture when you used the tcpdump command for the first time in this project?

THOUGHT QUESTIONS

1. Why would it be important to be able to capture only port 53 traffic?
2. Why would a network administrator want to only capture traffic from a specific IP address?
3. Could tcpdump be used to capture packets and write them to a text file for later analysis?
4. How could tcpdump be used to prevent internal phishing scams?

20.10 NETCAT (PC-BSD)

In this project, you are going to use a versatile tool with many different options that can be used in a variety of ways – Netcat (actually the OpenBSD Netcat variant). In order to demonstrate the basic functionality of Netcat, you are going to open two terminal windows. The terminal window on the *left* will represent a remote *server*, and the terminal window on the *right* will represent a local *client*. Netcat is obviously intended to be used between two different hosts, but for simplicity you will open two windows on the same host (i.e., your FreeBSD virtual machine).

Netcat can be used to make connections between any two hosts over any available port. In this project, you will make a connection between the two terminal windows on the same virtual machine. You will be able to transfer text, like a chat session, or the contents of entire files. More specifically, you will transfer the contents of a file from one terminal to another terminal and store the data in a new file. You will also see how to use Netcat as a simple port scanner.

You can complete this project by yourself using your virtual machine. However, it will be more interesting, and fun, if you were to complete this project with a classmate using your real IP addresses. There is a Windows version (ncat) that comes with Nmap (Zenmap) software package, which you used in an earlier project (http://nmap.org/ncat/). You can run ncat through a DOS prompt and the instructions will be similar.

Important: To leave your virtual machine, you may have to press your **right Ctrl** key to escape out of the virtual machine. Also, to quickly switch between terminal windows, you can press Alt-Tab.

1. Open Oracle VM VirtualBox by clicking Start, All Programs, Oracle VM VirtualBox, and Oracle VM VirtualBox.
2. Select your FreeBSD virtual machine.
3. Click Start.
4. If you are not already logged in, enter your username and password to log in.
5. Click on the PC-BSD start menu in the bottom left-hand of your FreeBSD desktop.
6. Click Accessories, and LXTerminal.
7. In the terminal window, click File, and New Window.
8. Resize the terminal windows so they are in a side-by-side configuration as shown below. (The terminal window on the *left* will represent a remote server, and the terminal window on the *right* will represent a local client.)
9. Type **man nc**
10. Press Enter. (This will display the man file for Netcat, which is nc.) (See Figure 20-166.)

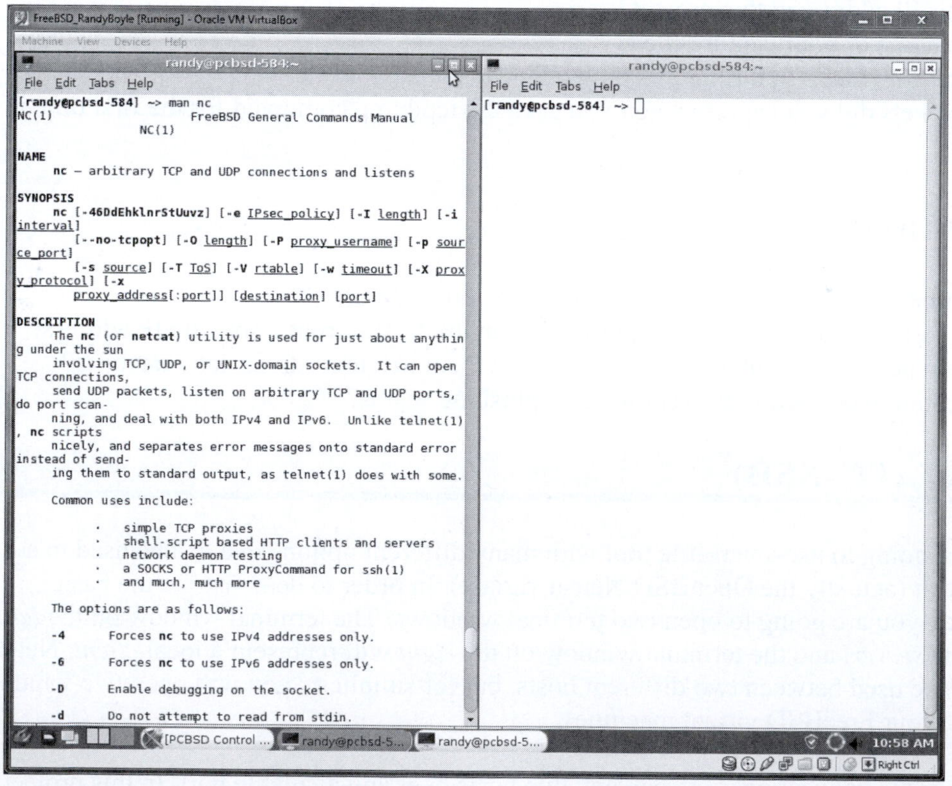

Figure 20-166: Man page for Netcat.

11. Type q to exit the man page for Netcat.
12. Type **clear**
13. Press Enter. (This will clear the display.)
14. In the *left* terminal window, type **nc -l 4444**
15. Press Enter. (This will start Netcat listening on port 4444. The option is a lower-case "L," not the number 1.)
16. In the *right* terminal window, type **nc localhost 4444**
17. Press Enter. (This will make a connection to your local computer on port 4444. Essentially, you are making a connection between the two terminal windows. It is important to note that the two terminal windows could be on two different computers. For simplicity, this project uses two terminal windows on the same computer.)
18. In the *right* terminal window, type **hello YourName**
19. Press Enter. (Due to the connection between the two terminal windows, you should see "hello YourName displayed in both windows. In this case, the text transferred was "hello Randy Boyle." Any text you type in the right-hand terminal will be displayed in the left-hand terminal.)
20. In the *right* terminal, press Ctrl+C to terminate the connection. (The server will also stop listening.)
21. Take a screenshot. (See Figure 20-167.)

Note: To quickly switch between terminal windows, you can press Alt-Tab.

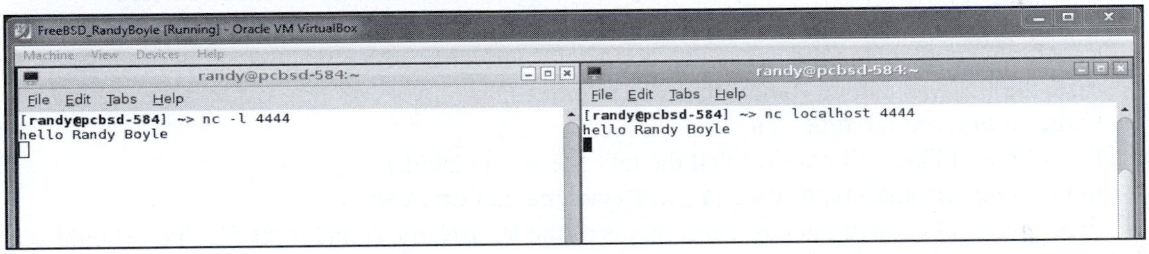

Figure 20-167: Using Netcat to make a connection and transfer some text.

22. In the *left* terminal window, type **ifconfig**
23. Press Enter. (This will display the IP address for your virtual machine. In this case, it was 10.0.2.15 [bolded below]. It is likely that your IP address will be different. Make sure you write down the IP address displayed next to the word "inet." You will need it in the next steps.)
24. In the *left* terminal window, type **nc -k -l 4444**
25. Press Enter. (This will start Netcat listening on port 4444. The -k option keeps the server listening even if the client disconnects. The -l option is a lower-case "L," not the number 1.)
26. In the *right* terminal window, type **nc [your ip address] 4444**
27. Press Enter. (This will make a connection to your computer by specifying your ip address and a port number. In this case, the IP address was 10.0.2.15.)
28. In the *right* terminal, type **hello hello hello**
29. Press Enter. (This will confirm that the connection is made using an IP address and that the text is being sent correctly.)
30. In the *right* terminal, press Ctrl+C to terminate the connection. (Note that the connection was terminated, but the other terminal window continued to listen for connections.)
31. In the *right* terminal window, type **nc [your ip address] 4444**
32. Press Enter. (This will reestablish the connection. In this case, the IP address was 10.0.2.15. Hint: You can press the up arrow to quickly repeat a prior command.)
33. In the *right* terminal, type **hello again**
34. Press Enter. (This will confirm that the connection was reestablished.)

35. In the *right* terminal, press Ctrl+C to terminate the connection.
36. In the *left* terminal, press Ctrl+C to stop Netcat listening on port 4444.
37. Take a screenshot. (See Figure 20-168.)

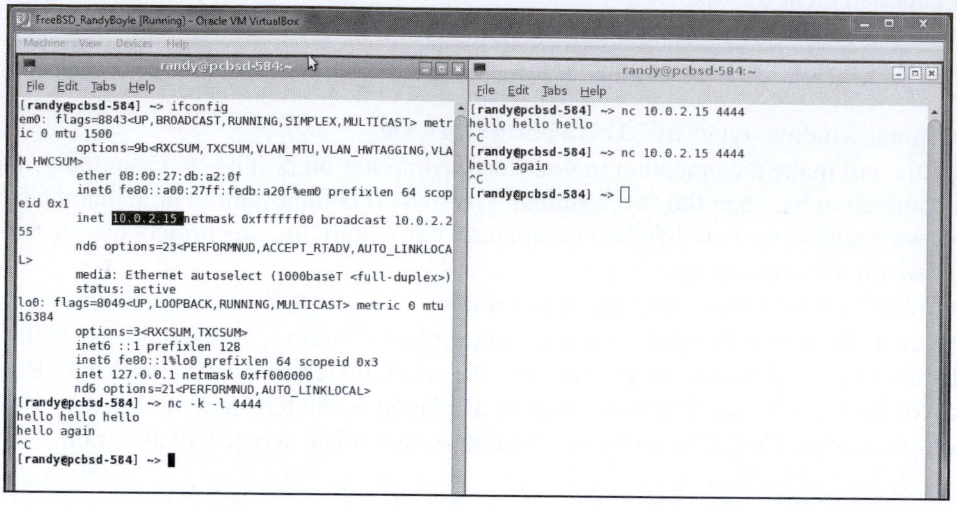

Figure 20-168: Using Netcat to make a persistent connection to a host by specifying an IP address.

38. In the *right* terminal, type `echo "anytext" >> YourNameTransfer.txt`
39. Press Enter. (This will create a file named YourNameTransfer.txt and append "anytext." You will transfer the contents in the next steps. Replace YourName with your first and last name. In this case, the file was named RandyBoyleTransfer.txt.)
40. In the *right* terminal, type `ls`
41. Press Enter. (This will confirm that the text file was created.)
42. In the *right* terminal, type `cat YourNameTransfer.txt`
43. Press Enter. (This will display the contents of the YourNameTransfer.txt file. You should see "anytext" displayed. In this case, the text file was named RandyBoyleTransfer.txt.)
44. In the *left* terminal window, type `nc -k -l 4444 > YourNameReceived.txt`
45. Press Enter. (This will start Netcat listening and write anything received to a text file named YourNameReceived.txt. Replace YourName with your first and last name. In this case, the text file was labeled RandyBoyleReceived.txt.)
46. In the *right* terminal, type the following command:

```
cat YourNameTransfer.txt | nc [your ip address] 4444
```

47. Press Enter. (This will copy the contents of the YourNameTransfer.txt file to Netcat, which is listening on the other end of the connection.)
48. In the *left* terminal, press Ctrl+C to stop Netcat from listening.
49. In the *left* terminal, type `ls`
50. Press Enter. (This will confirm that the YourNameReceived.txt file was created.)
51. In the *left* terminal, type `cat YourNameReceived.txt`
52. Press Enter. (This will display the contents of the YourNameReceived.txt file. You should see "anytext" displayed. In this case, the text file was named RandyBoyleReceived.txt.)
53. Take a screenshot. (See Figure 20-169.)

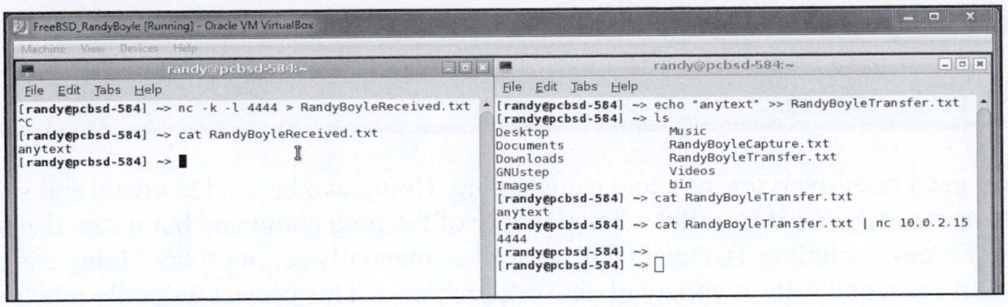

Figure 20-169: Using Netcat to transfer the contents of a file.

54. In the *left* terminal window, type `nc -k -l 4444`
55. Press Enter. (This will start Netcat listening on port 4444. In the next step, you are going to tell Netcat to scan your computer for open ports.)
56. In the *right* terminal window, type `nc -w 1 -z [your ip address] 4000-5000`
57. Press Enter. (The -z option will tell Netcat to scan ports 4000 through 5000 on the IP address listed [i.e., your computer] to see which ones are open. You should get a response that port 4444 is open. The -w 1 option limits timeouts to 1 second. In this case, the IP address was 10.0.2.15.)
58. In the *right* terminal window, type `nc -v -w 1 -z [your ip address] 4440-4450`
59. Press Enter. (This will display the results of a simple port scan for ports 4440 through 4450. The -v option displays verbose output.)
60. Take a screenshot. (See Figure 20-170.)

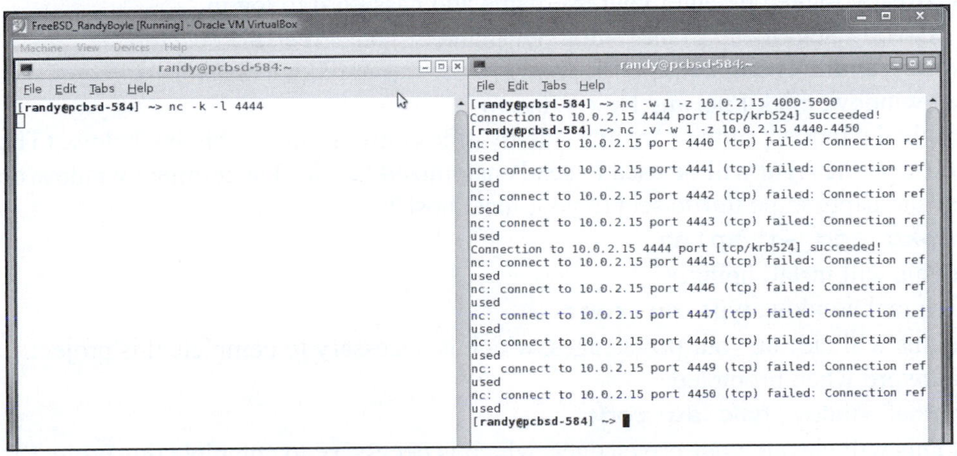

Figure 20-170: Using Netcat as a port scanner.

PROJECT QUESTIONS

1. What was the name of the file you created to transfer?
2. What was the name of the file in which you stored the received data?
3. What was your IP address for this project?
4. About how long do you think it took to scan ports 4000 through 5000?

THOUGHT QUESTIONS

1. Can Netcat be used to create connections to reserved port numbers like port 80? Why?
2. Can you transfer entire files using Netcat? How?
3. Give one example of how Netcat could be used to diagnose a network problem?

4. Could Netcat be used to send a customized packet? How?

20.11 HPING3 (PC-BSD)

In this project, you will get a brief overview of a tool called hping. Hping can be used to create and send custom packets. As its name suggests, it has all the functionality of the ping command but it can also send a variety of other packet types, including TCP and UDP, as well as manually setting flags. Hping can also be used to send data, port scan, and solve a variety of network problems. This project will only touch on a small portion of hping's functionality.

To demonstrate hping's basic functionality, you are going to open two terminal windows. The terminal window on the *left* will represent a server that will *receive* packets. The terminal window on the *right* will represent a local client you will use to *send* packets. You will use hping to send the packets in the *right* terminal, and then use tcpdump to capture the packets in the *left* terminal.

Important: To leave your virtual machine, you may have to press your **right Ctrl** key to escape out of the virtual machine. Also, to quickly switch between terminal windows, you can press Alt-Tab.

1. Open Oracle VM VirtualBox by clicking Start, All Programs, Oracle VM VirtualBox, and Oracle VM VirtualBox.
2. Select your FreeBSD virtual machine.
3. Click Start.
4. If you are not already logged in, enter your username and password to log in.
5. Click on the PC-BSD Start menu in the bottom left-hand of your FreeBSD desktop.
6. Click Accessories, and LXTerminal.
7. In the terminal window, click File, and New Window.
8. Resize the terminal windows so they are in a side-by-side configuration as shown below. (The terminal window on the *right* will be used to send customized traffic. The terminal window on the *left* will be used to capture the traffic sent to your local host.)
9. Type `sudo pkg_add -r hping`
10. Press Enter. (This will install hping.)
11. In the *right* terminal window, type `su root`
12. Press Enter. (This will elevate your priveledges, which is necessary to complete this project.)
13. Enter your password when prompted.
14. In the *left* terminal window, type `su root`
15. Press Enter. (This will elevate your priveledges, which is necessary to complete this project.)
16. Enter your password when prompted.
17. In the *left* terminal window, type `man hping`
18. Press Enter. (This will display the man file for hping.)
19. Type `q` to quit the man page. (See Figure 20-171.)

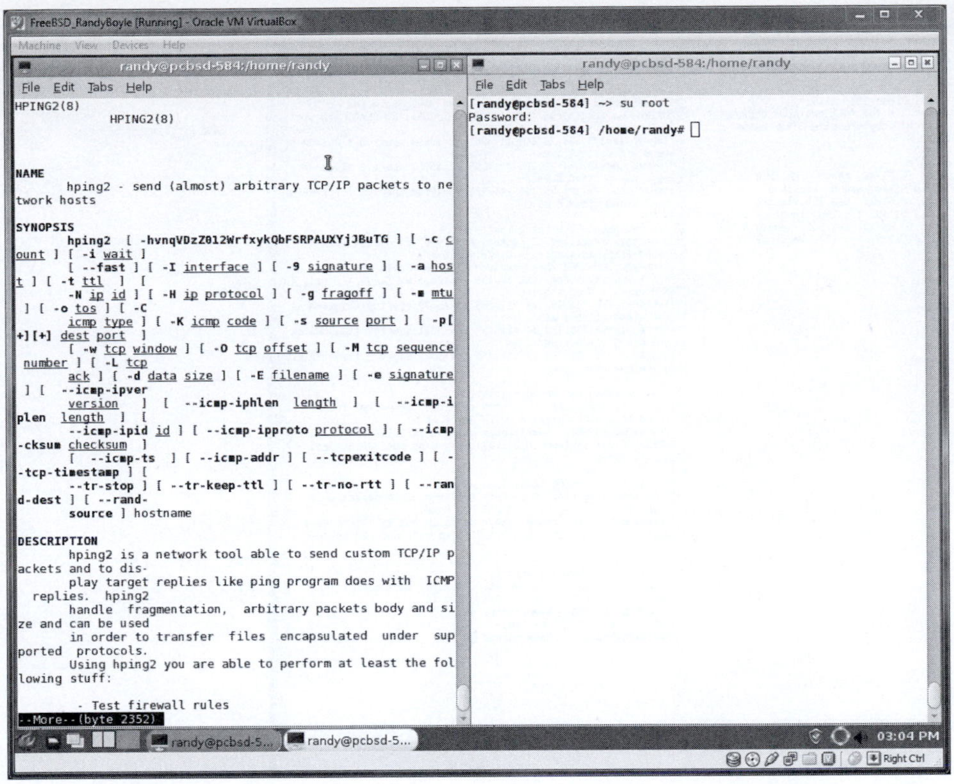

Figure 20-171: Man page for Hping.

20. In the *right* terminal window, type **hping www.Google.com -c 3**

21. Press Enter. (This will ping www.Google.com with three packets. Note that hping has similar functionality to the ping command.)

22. In the *right* terminal window, type **hping [any website] -c 3**

23. Press Enter. (This will ping any website of your choosing with three packets. In this case, it was www.Yahoo.com.)

24. In the *left* terminal window, type **tcpdump -tn -i 3 dst [your IP address]**

25. Press Enter. (This will capture packets sent to your IP address. It won't display timestamps [-t] or resolve hostnames [-n]. Replace [your IP address] with your local IP address. In this case, the IP address was 10.0.2.15. The command used was `tcpdump -tn -i 3 dst 10.0.2.15`.)

26. In the *right* terminal window, type **hping [your IP address] --udp -c 3**

27. Press Enter. (This will send three UDP packets. Note that the source and destination IP addresses are the same. In this case, the IP address was 10.0.2.15. The command used was `hping 10.0.2.15 --udp -c 3`.)

28. In the *right* terminal window, type **hping [your IP address] --icmp -c 3**

29. Press Enter. (This will send three ICMP packets. Note that the left-hand window captured six packets, including three ICMP echo requests and three ICMP echo responses. In this case, the IP address was 10.0.2.15. The command used was `hping 10.0.2.15 --icmp -c 3`.)

30. Type **date**

31. Press Enter. (This will display the time and date.)

32. Take a screenshot. (See Figure 20-172.)

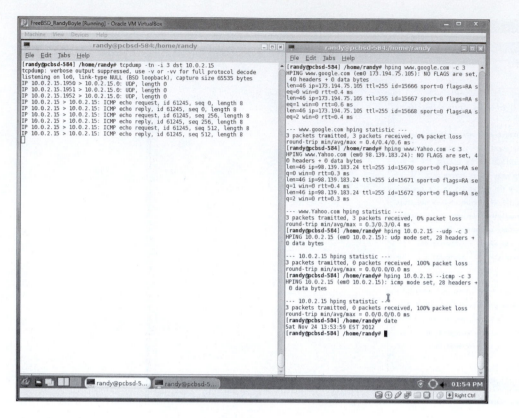

Figure 20-172: Using hping to send UDP and ICMP traffic.

33. In the *right* terminal window, type the following command:

hping [your IP address] --udp --data 300 -c 3

34. Press Enter. (This will send three UDP packets with a length of 300. In this case, the IP address was 10.0.2.15. The command used was hping 10.0.2.15 --udp --data 300 -c 3.)
35. In the *right* terminal window, type the following command:

hping [your IP address] --udp --scan 80-81

36. Press Enter. (This will scan ports 80 and 81 using UDP packets. In this case, the IP address was 10.0.2.15. The command used was hping 10.0.2.15 --udp –scan 80-81.)
37. In the *right* terminal window, type the following command:

hping [your IP address] --icmp --spoof 1.2.3.4 -c 3

38. Press Enter. (This will send three ICMP packets spoofed from a fake IP address, 1.2.3.4. In this case, the local IP address was 10.0.2.15. The command used was hping 10.0.2.15 --icmp --spoof 1.2.3.4 -c 3.)
39. In the *right* terminal window, type the following command:

hping [your IP address] --ICMP –rand-source -c 3

40. Press Enter. (This will send three ICMP packets spoofed from randomly selected fake IP addresses. In this case, the local IP address was 10.0.2.15. The command used was hping 10.0.2.15 --icmp –rand-source -c 3.)

41. Type **date**
42. Press Enter. (This will display the time and date.)
43. Take a screenshot. (See Figure 20-173.)

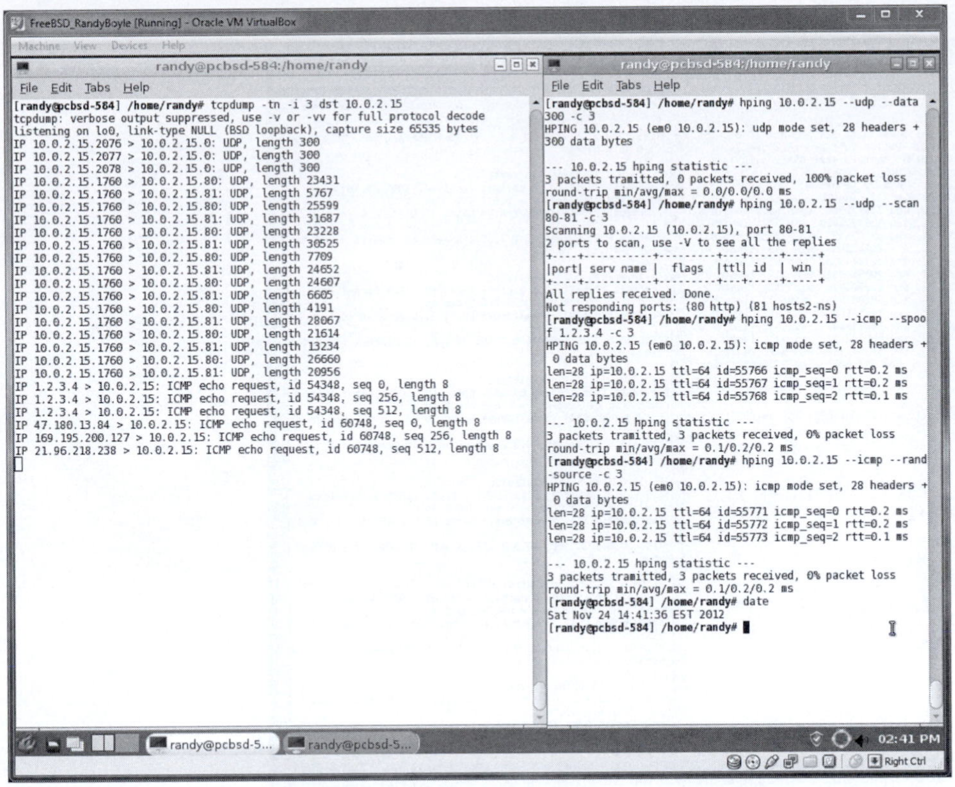

Figure 20-173: Port scanning and spoofing packets.

44. Change focus to the *left* window.
45. Press Ctrl+C to stop tcpdump.
46. In the *left* terminal window, type the following command:

tcpdump –tn –i 3 dst port 333 and dst [your IP address]

47. Press Enter. (This will capture packets sent to your IP address with a destination port of 333. Port 333 was randomly chosen. Replace [your IP address] with your local IP address. In this case, the IP address was 10.0.2.15. The command used was `tcpdump –tn –i 3 dst port 333 and dst 10.0.2.15`. You will start capturing packets in the next step.)
48. In the *right* terminal window, type **hping [your IP address] –c 3 –p 333**
49. Press Enter. (This will send three packets to your IP address using port 333 with no flags set. Note in the left-hand terminal window that the flags are empty.)
50. In the *right* terminal window, type **hping [your IP address] –S –c 3 –p 333**
51. Press Enter. (This will send three SYN packets.)
52. In the *right* terminal window, type **hping [your IP address] –A –c 3 –p 333**
53. Press Enter. (This will send three ACK packets.)
54. In the *right* terminal window, type **hping [your IP address] –F –c 3 –p 333**
55. Press Enter. (This will send three FIN packets.)
56. In the *right* terminal window, type **hping [your IP address] –R –c 3 –p 333**
57. Press Enter. (This will send three RST packets.)
58. In the *right* terminal window, type **hping [your IP address] –S –A –c 3 –p 333**

59. Press Enter. (This will send three SYN + ACK packets.)
60. Type **date**
61. Press Enter. (This will display the time and date.)
62. Take a screenshot. (See Figure 20-174.)

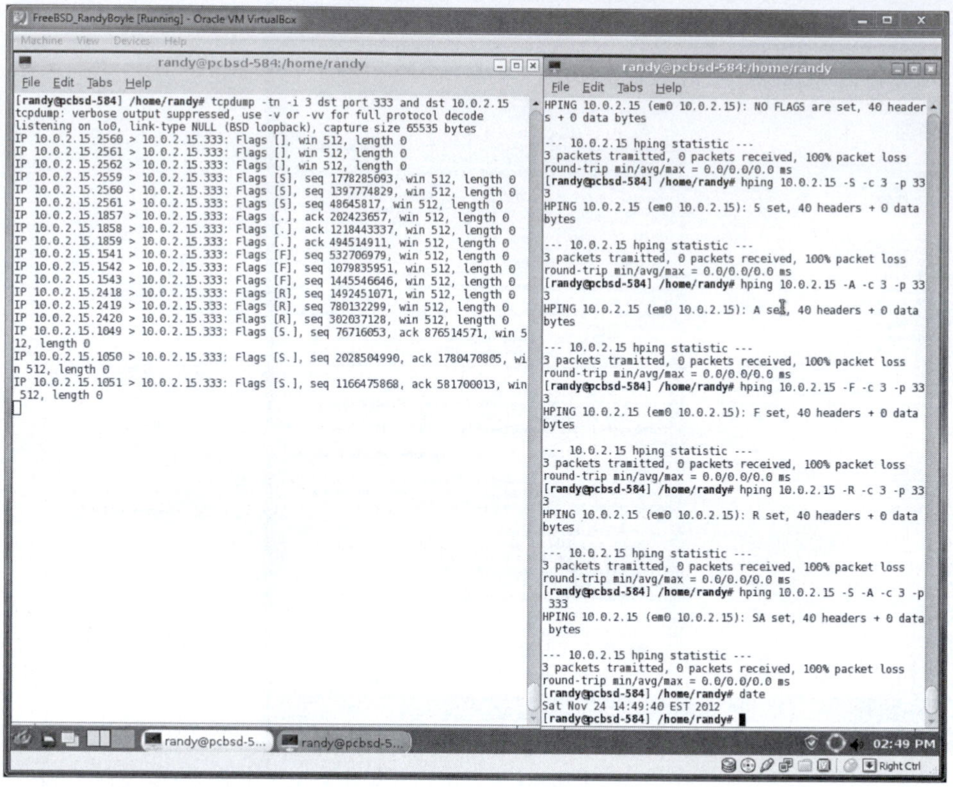

Figure 20-174: Sending different types of packets.

PROJECT QUESTIONS

1. Which website did you ping at the start of the project?
2. What was your IP address for this project?
3. What was the date you completed this project?
4. What was the approximate time of day you completed this project (shown when you used the "date" command)?

THOUGHT QUESTIONS

1. How could hping be used to bypass firewalls? Give one possible example.
2. How could hping be used to solve network issues? Give one possible example.
3. How could hping be used to resolve a server issue? Give one possible example.
4. How could hping be used maliciously? Give one possible example.

20.12 PORTABLE LINUX (DEBIAN)

In this project, you are going to create a bootable Linux (Debian) USB drive. You will be able to boot your computer and access all of your unencrypted files without having to login through your regular operating system. You will be able to transfer files between your USB drive and your hard disk. You will need a blank USB drive of at least 2GB for this project.

This project demonstrates the necessity of maintaining physical security at all times. Just because your computer is password protected via an operating system does not mean it is safe from attack. If an attacker gains access to your computer, he or she could bypass your operating system and steal (or encrypt) all of your important files.

This project will use a tool called Your Universal Multiboot Installer® (YUMI). It has the ability to install multiple Linux versions on the same USB. For simplicity's sake, we will only install one version. After installing Linux on your USB, you can treat it like any other hard drive. You can install software, transfer files, run a terminal window, etc.

1. Download YUMI from: www.pendrivelinux.com.
2. Click on the link labeled YUMI – Your Universal Multiboot Installer. (This site is updated often so the link may have moved. You can search the site or a search engine for "YUMI – Your Universal Multiboot Installer" if there is not a link on the main page.
3. Click Save.
4. Select your C:\security folder.
5. Right-click the YUMI-0.0.7.9.exe executable. (The version number will likely be later than the one listed here. Use the most current version.) (See Figure 20-175.)
6. Select Run as administrator, and Yes.
7. Click I Agree. (See Figure 20-176.)
8. Insert a blank USB drive. (It can be previously used. Make sure you back up and remove any files that may be on the drive you are going to use. You will be formatting this drive.)

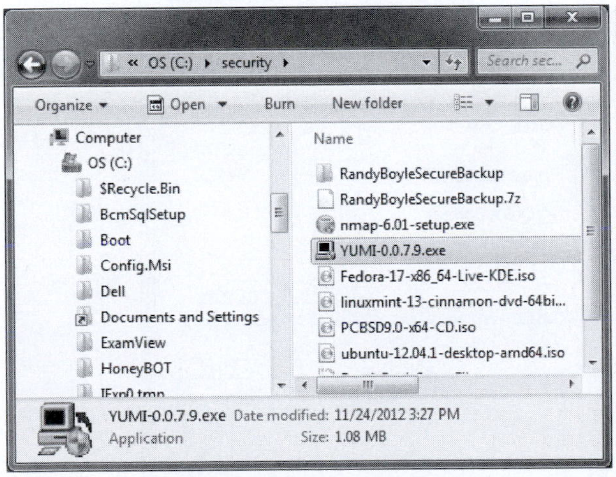

Figure 20-175: YUMI installer.

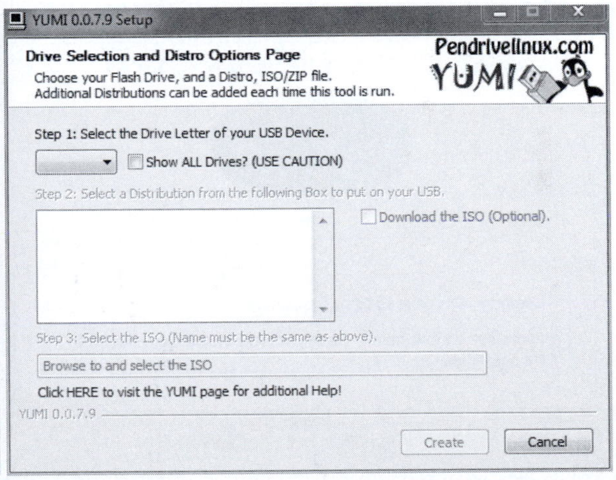

Figure 20-176: YUMI setup page.

9. Start Windows Explorer.
10. Right-click on your USB drive.
11. Select Properties.
12. Name the drive YourName. (In this case, the USB drive was labeled BOYLE_USB.)
13. Ensure that your USB is formatted with the FAT 32 file system.

STOP: If your USB is formatted using NTFS, the installation will not complete correctly (See Figure 20-177). You will need to reformat your USB using FAT32. This will completely wipe your USB. Back up any files from your USB before you proceed.

The following instructions will explain how to format your USB with the FAT32 file system. Make sure you use the correct drive letter that corresponds with your USB drive. In this case, the USB was the G: drive. Your drive letter may be different. Adjust the instructions below to match your correct drive letter.

a) Make sure your USB is inserted.
b) Open Windows Explorer.
c) Right-click on your USB drive.
d) Click Format.
e) Change the File system drop-down menu to read FAT32 (Default).
f) Make sure Quick Format is selected.
g) Click Start. (See Figure 20-178.)
h) Click OK to confirm.
i) Wait for the format to complete.
j) Click Close on the Format window.
k) Proceed with the rest of the exercise.

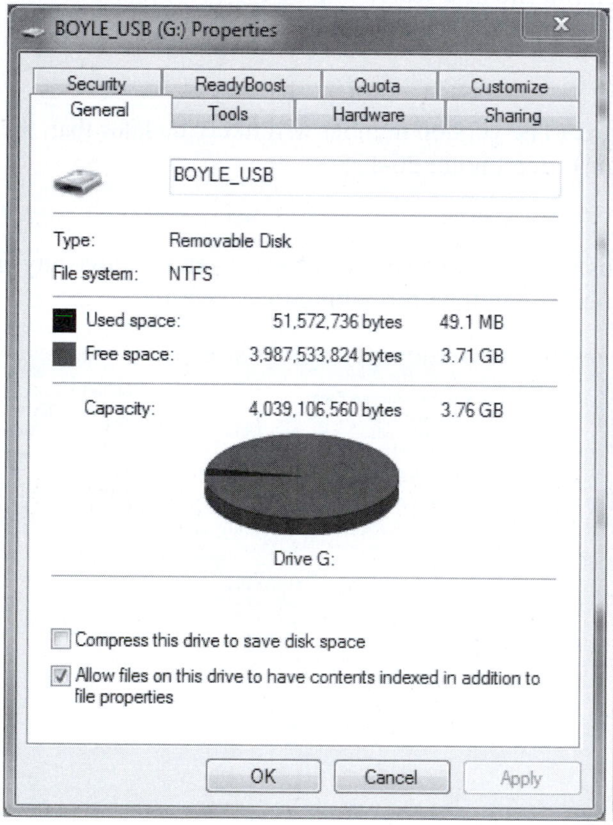

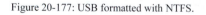

Figure 20-177: USB formatted with NTFS. 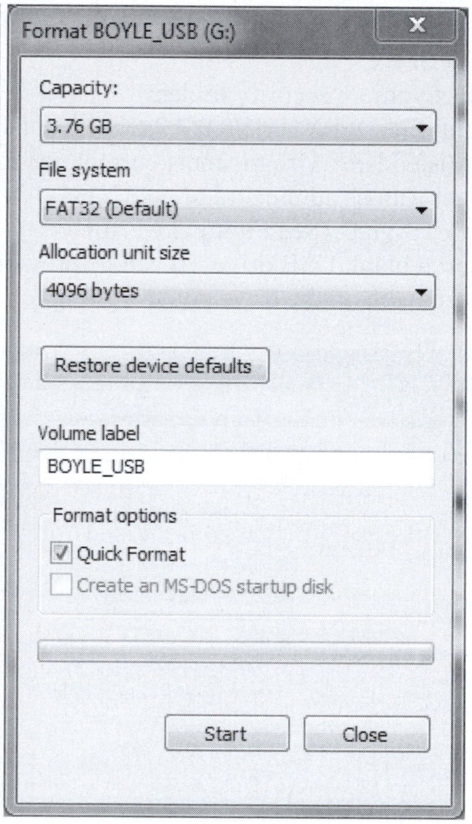   Figure 20-178: Formatting a USB drive with FAT32.

14. Return to the YUMI setup window. (It should have started as part of the installation process.)
15. Change the USB drop-down to display your drive letter. (In this case, it was the G:\ drive.)
16. Scroll down the distribution list to see how many different distributions are available for installation.
17. Select the Debian Live 6 Gnome 64bit option. (See Figure 20-179.)
18. Check the "Download the iso" option. (Alternatively, you can download the ISO image directly and then select it manually in Step 3.)

19. Click Yes, to launch the download link. (This will start downloading the Debian ISO image. Depending on the speed of your Internet connection, it could take 5 to 50 minutes. You can use an ISO image provided by your instructor to avoid the longer download time.)
20. After the download finishes, click Browse.
21. Browse to your download folder.
22. Select the Debian ISO image you just downloaded.
23. Click Open.
24. Click Create, and Yes. (See Figure 20-180.)

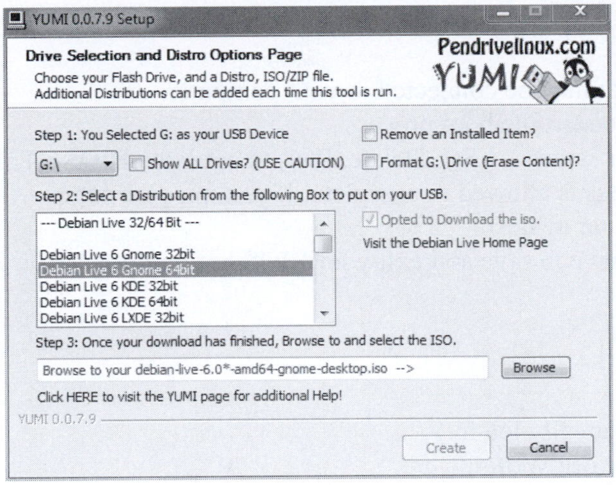

Figure 20-179: Select a drive and distribution.

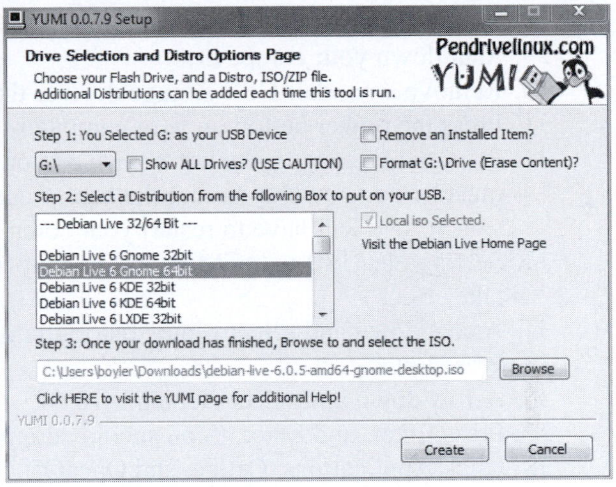

Figure 20-180: Downloaded ISO image is selected.

25. Take a screenshot while it is creating the bootable drive. (See Figure 20-181.)
26. Click Next, No, and Finish.
27. Wait for the creation to complete. (This may take several minutes.) (See Figure 20-182.)

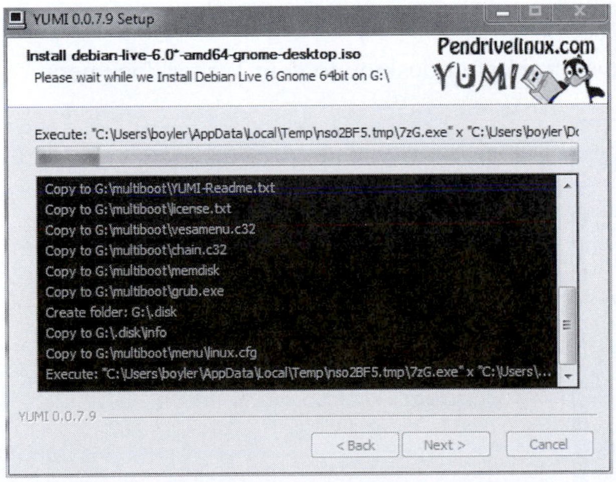

Figure 20-181: Creation of bootable USB is complete.

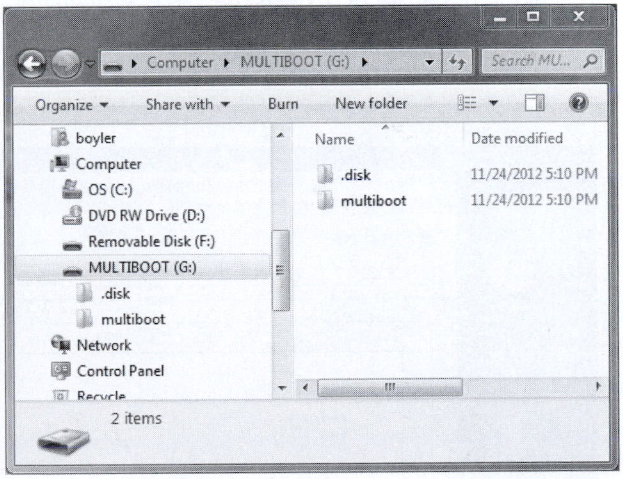

Figure 20-182: Contents of bootable USB.

Note: In the next part of this project, you are going to shut down your computer and then boot it from your USB. Your computer is likely set to boot from your hard drive. You will need to enter your BIOS and change the boot order so it will try to boot from the USB first.

Your computer may have a different BIOS than the one used in this example. This means the instructions will be slightly different. This will require you to adapt these instructions to your specific

BIOS. As your computer is booting, you will press a key to enter the BIOS and/or change the boot order. In this example, it was the F2 key. You will see a screen telling you which key to press. You may only get a couple of seconds to press the key.

Depending on your BIOS, you may have to press one of the following keys to change the boot order: F2, DEL, ESC, F12, CTRL+ALT+ESC, CTRL+ALT+S, etc. It will probably be F2, ESC, or DEL. After you press this key (or sequence of keys), you will need to navigate the BIOS menu and change the boot order. The computer used in this project was a Dell.

28. Save all documents and close all programs.
29. Shut down your computer.
30. Remove any other USB storage devices that may be connected to your computer.
31. Press the power button on your computer to start the boot process.
32. Press the F2 key (or the key shown on your screen – ESC, Delete, Etc.) to enter the BIOS. (This must be done quickly before the boot process is allowed to complete. If you miss the setup screen, you will have to restart your computer again.)
33. Select your USB to boot from. (You may have to save and exit your BIOS before the settings will take effect.)
34. Arrow down and select Linux distributions.
35. Press Enter.
36. Arrow down and select Debian Live 64.
37. Press Enter, and Enter. (You should automatically log in.)
38. Click Applications, Office, and OpenOffice.org Writer.
39. Type your name, "Bootable USB," and today's date. (In this case, it was Randy Boyle, Bootable USB and 11/26/2012.) (See Figure 20-183.)
40. Click Applications, Accessories, and Take Screenshot.
41. Click Take Screenshot. (See Figure 20-184.)
42. Make sure that "Save in folder" is set to Desktop.
43. Click Save.
44. Click Cancel, to exit the Take Screenshot window.
45. Return to the Writer document.
46. Drag-and-drop the .PNG image you just saved from your desktop to your Writer document.

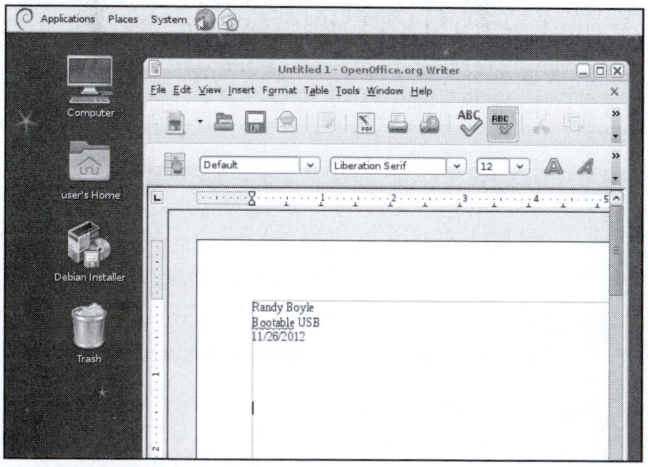

Figure 20-183: OpenOffice.org Writer.

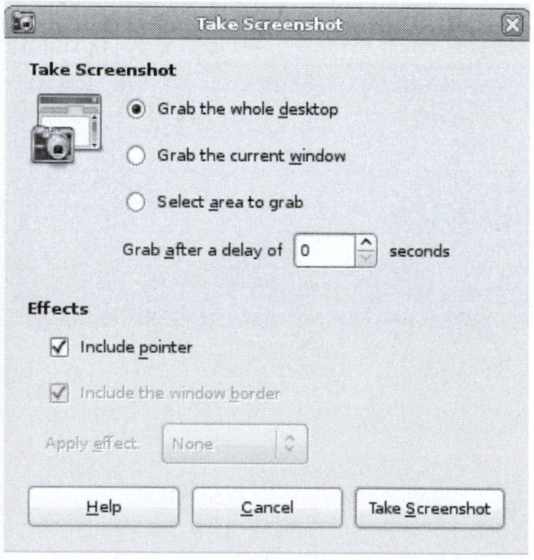

Figure 20-184: Taking a screenshot.

47. Click File, and Save As.
48. Enter "YourNameUSB" in the Name text box. (In this case, it was RandyBoyleUSB.)
49. Click Browse for other folders.

50. Select your hard drive (Windows computer) in the left-hand pane. (In this case, it was OS. It's very likely your computer will have a different name.)
51. Double-click the "security" folder. (You should have created this folder on your C: drive as part of earlier project. If you haven't created it, you can do so now.)
52. Change the drop-down labeled "Save file as type" to Microsoft Word (.doc). (See Figure 20-185.)
53. Click Save.
54. Close the document.
55. Click System, Shutdown, and Shutdown.
56. Remove your USB drive.
57. Restart your computer normally.
58. Open Windows Explorer.
59. Browse to the C:\security\ folder.
60. Open the file named YourNameUSB.doc. (In this case, it was RandyBoyleUSB.doc.)
61. Take a screenshot of this document. (The screenshot you took earlier of the Debian desktop should be visible.) (See Figure 20-186.)

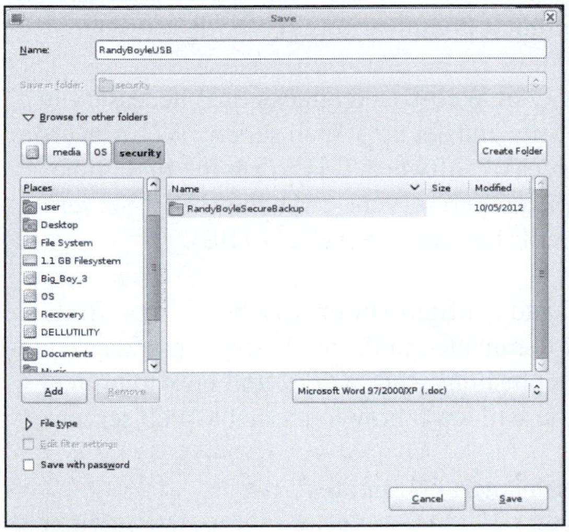

Figure 20-185: Saving the file.

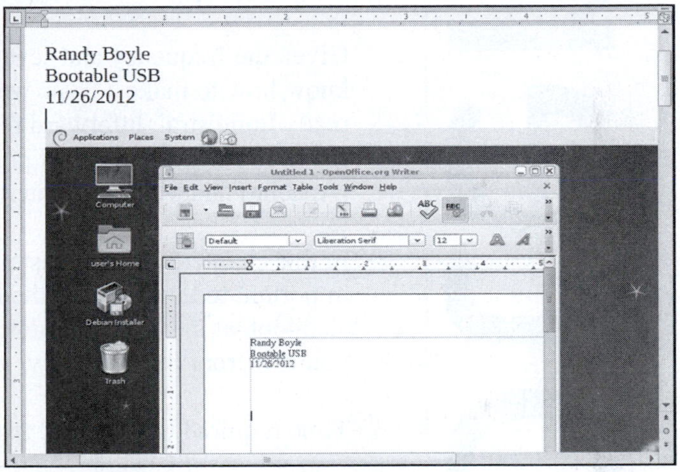

Figure 20-186: Open file in Windows from Linux.

PROJECT QUESTIONS

1. What was the name of your document?
2. What was the name on your USB drive?
3. What letter was assigned to your USB drive?
4. What date did you type in your document?

THOUGHT QUESTIONS

1. How could a bootable USB drive be used maliciously?
2. How could you protect against an attacker using a bootable USB drive?
3. How could a bootable USB drive be used for legitimate purposes?
4. Could you access your files stored on your hard drive using a bootable USB drive? Why?

chapter 21

Websites in the United States are under attack every day of the week. Major online retails are often the target of these attacks. Hackers set up fake websites to trick innocent users into giving away their private information. The number of defaced websites has grown too large to track.

In general, corporate websites are becoming bigger targets for potential criminals because they are putting more of their critical systems online. Insecure Web servers are a potential security vulnerability that can cause substantial harm to your organization.

It's imperative that IT security professionals have a good understanding of how Web servers work, and how to secure them from external attacks. Only then will they be able to protect their organizations.

Given the frequency and severity of Web-based attacks, it is necessary to know how to make a basic website and set up a Web server. Web servers are really quite straightforward pieces of software. It is worth the time to be familiar with the two most popular Web servers - Apache HTTP Server® (Apache) and Microsoft Internet Information Services® (IIS).

In this chapter, you will install and configure both Apache and IIS. Both are important to know due to their dominance in the Web server market. You will also look at the basics of how a phishing scam works, and how to protect yourself from them. Finally, you will learn how to harden a Web server.

Time required to complete this chapter: 60 minutes

Chapter Objectives

Learn how to:
1. Install and configure a Web server.
2. Create a simple Web page.
3. Host multiple websites.
4. Modify the hosts file.
5. Control access via authentication.
6. Set site limits and blocking.
7. Filter incoming URL requests.

Chapter Projects

Projects:
1. Install Apache, create a website, and host pages.
2. Internet Information Services (IIS) installation.
3. Phishing and hosts file.
4. Authentication, limits, and blocking.
5. Request filtering and logs.

21.1 INSTALL APACHE®, CREATE A WEBSITE, AND HOST PAGES

One of the more common questions asked by students and entrepreneurs is, "How do I make a website?" They are actually asking about more than just making a website. They are actually asking about hosting, maintenance, administration, connecting the website to a back end database, etc.

You can set up a basic Web server, make a website, and start serving Web pages in about five minutes. This is a good project to show what is involved in the creation, hosting, and eventual maintenance of a website. You probably won't be ready to start your own hosting company after doing this project, but it will be a good first experience.

Apache is the leading Web server in the world. It's also free! You can load Apache on your Windows box and serve pages directly from your computer. If you want to run your own website, you will have to register your IP address through a company like Network Solutions.

1. Download the Apache Web Server from http://httpd.apache.org/download.cgi.
2. Scroll down to the Apache HTTP server with Win32 binaries.
3. Click Download for the apache_2.2.22-win32-x86-no_ssl.msi file. (Make sure it has the MSI extension. At the time of this writing, the latest version was 2.2.22. Get the latest version available that is listed as a Win32 binary.)
4. Click Save.
5. Select your C:\security folder.
6. Click Run, and OK.
7. If your download doesn't automatically unzip and run, right-click the file labeled apache_2.2.22-win32-x86-no_ssl.msi and select Install.
8. Click Run, Next, I accept, Next, and Next.
9. Enter your first name and your last name followed by .com for the network domain. (In this case, it was RandyBoyle.com.)
10. Enter www.YourName.com for the server name (e.g., www.RandyBoyle.com).
11. Enter an email address. (I recommend entering a fake one.) (See Figure 21-1.)

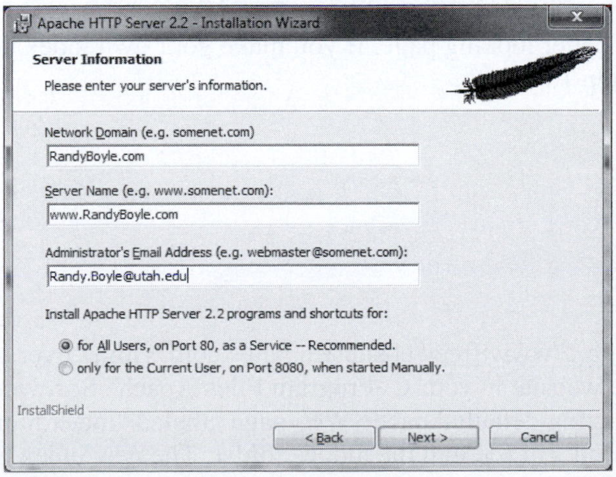

Figure 21-1: Apache configuration screen.

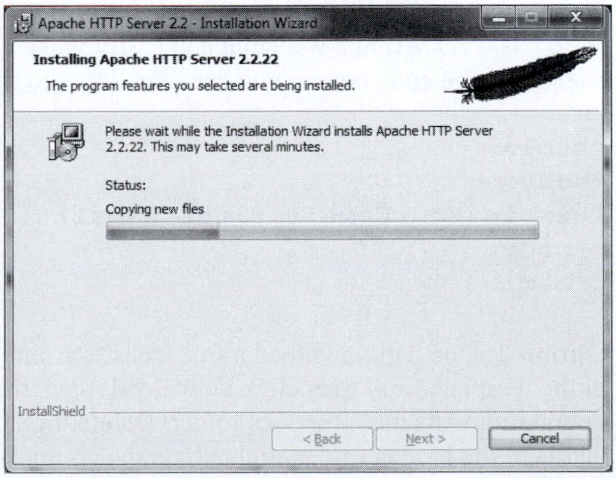

Figure 21-2: Installing Apache.

12. Take a screenshot.

13. Click Next, Next, Next, Install, and Finish. (See Figure 21-2.)
14. Open a Web browser. (In this case, it was Google Chrome.)
15. Enter "localhost" or "127.0.0.1" into the address bar. (Both of these are Web page requests to your local computer, not to an external server. The "It works!" page shown below is the default Apache Web page (index.html). (See Figure 21-3 and Figure 21-4.)

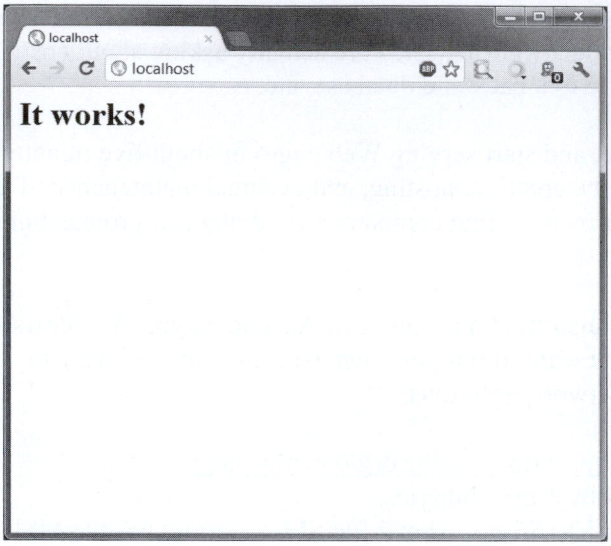

Figure 21-3: Apache on localhost.

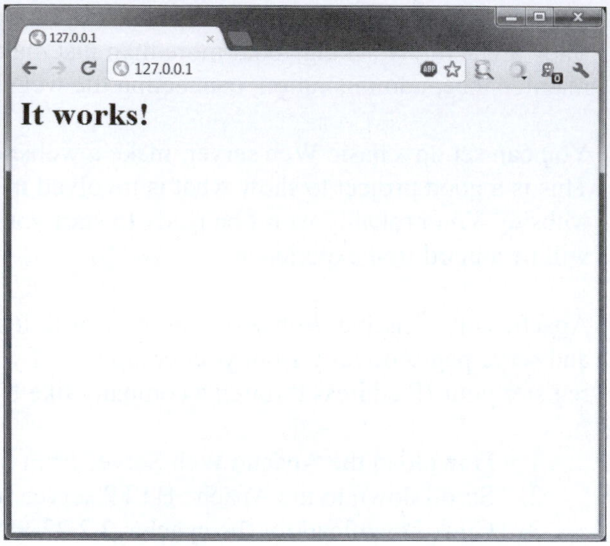

Figure 21-4: Apache on 127.0.0.1.

Note: You have just installed the Apache Web server and seen the default Apache Web page. You now need to create a more realistic looking website. You have several options when it comes to creating a website. Choose from one of the three options below and then skip down to Step 16.

Option 1: You can create a very simple website with a single page using the code below. You can copy/paste the following code into a text file, replace YourName with your first and last name, and save the text file as index.htm (*not* index.htm.txt) in your C:\Program Files\Apache Software Foundation\Apache2.2\htdocs folder. The Apache default page (index.html) will already be there. Your web page will be saved as index.htm, *not* as index.html. These are two different files.

This is simple HTML code you can use to create a basic website (actually just a main page). You can learn basic HTML in a weekend and easily make a better looking page. If you make your own index.htm page from the code below, you can skip down to Step 16.

```
<html>
<body>
This is YourName's first website!!
</body>
</html>
```

Option 2: You can download a free website from http://www.freewebsitetemplates.com. Hover over one of the templates and then click Download. Save the website in your C:\Program Files\Apache Software Foundation\Apache2.2\htdocs folder. Delete the existing default Apache Web page labeled "index.html" that is in the htdocs folder, and extract the compressed .zip file into the htdocs folder. The new index.html (main page) and its subfolders must be in the htdocs folder, not a sub directory. Once the website is extracted, you can skip down to step 16.

Option 3: You can also create an entire website from a template using Microsoft Publisher® 2007/2003 (Microsoft Publisher 2010 doesn't have this capability), or Microsoft Web Expression®. If your college or university has a DreamSpark agreement, you can get Microsoft Web Expression for free. A standard website can be made in about 28 seconds. Customizing it may take longer.

    a) Open Microsoft Publisher.
    b) In the middle pane, select Web Sites. (See Figure 21-5.)
    c) Select any template from the center pane. (In this case, the "Summer" template was chosen.) (See Figure 21-6.)
    d) Click Create.
    e) Select all the options on Your Site Goals. (See Figure 21-7.)

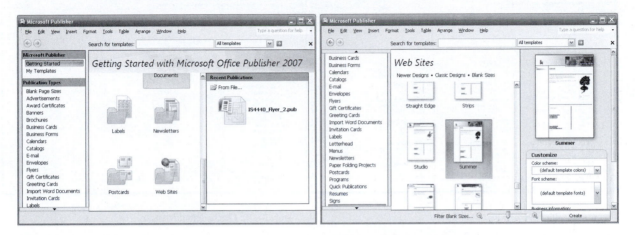

Figure 21-5: Creating a website from a template.　　　　Figure 21-6: Standard website templates.

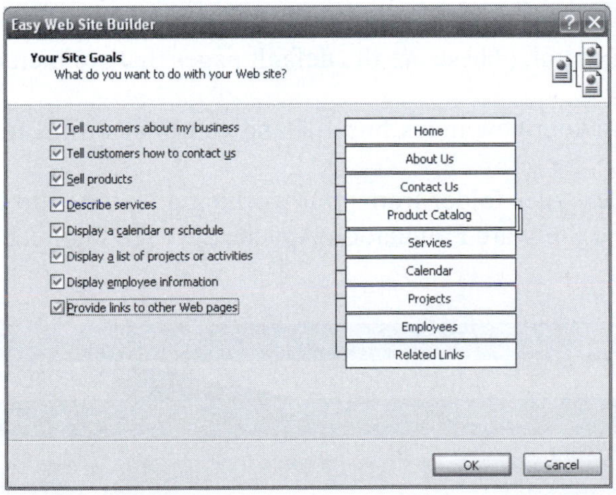

Figure 21-7: Standard pages to include in website. 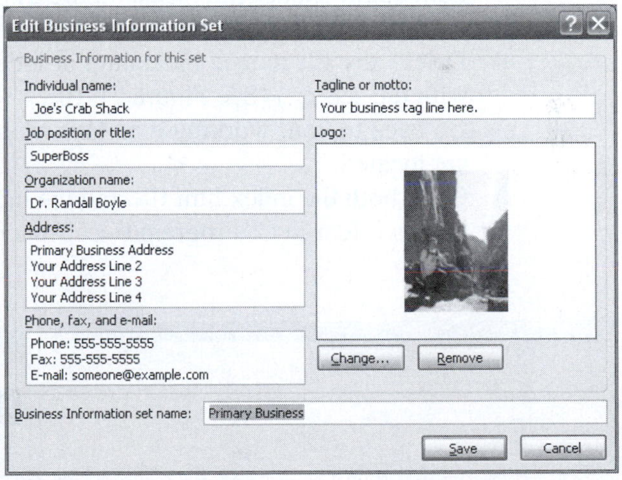　　　Figure 21-8: Business information to include on website.

    f) Click OK.
    g) On the File menu, click Insert, and Business Information.
    h) In the left-hand pane, click Organization Name, and Change Business Information.
    i) Click Edit.
    j) Change the Organization Name to your full name (e.g., Randy Boyle). (See Figure 21-8.)
    k) Click Save, and Update Publication.
    l) On the File menu, click File, Publish to the Web, and Save.
    m) Select Other location. (By default, it will save to your desktop.)

n) Click Next.

Note: You have just created a full website and saved it in your working directory. (Mine was My Documents.) Your main Web page will be called index.htm and all other pages will be in a folder called index_files located in your working directory. We are going to move your main page (index.htm) and all subsequent pages/graphics, currently located in the index_files folder, to your Apache folder named htdocs (i.e., C:\Program Files\Apache Software Foundation\Apache2.2\htdocs). Once we move these files and start your Apache Web server, the world will be able to see your new website.

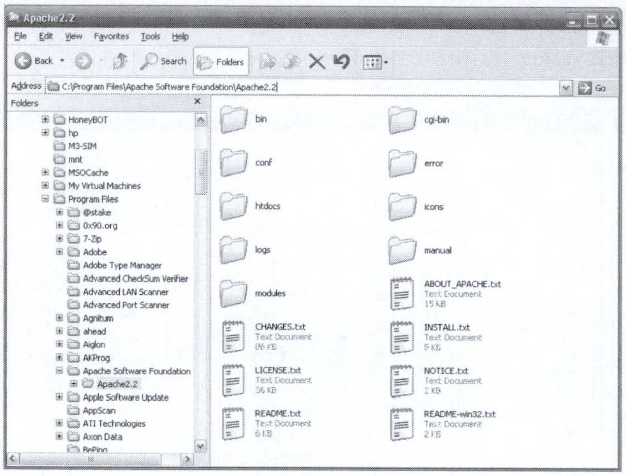

Figure 21-9: Place website in htdocs folder.

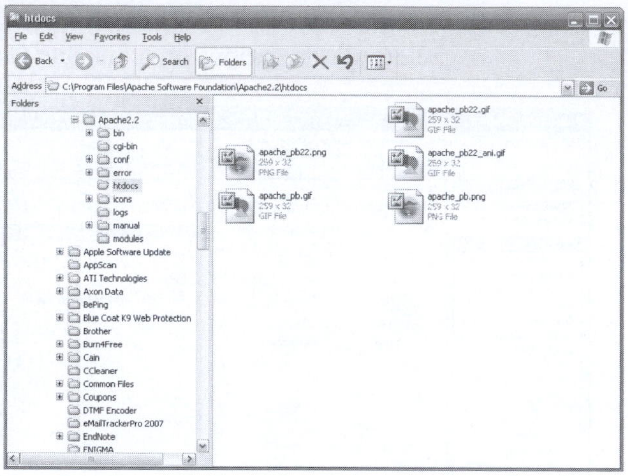

Figure 21-10: Delete default website.

o) Open Windows Explorer and navigate to C:\Program Files\Apache Software Foundation\Apache2.2. (See Figure 21-9.)
p) Open the htdocs folder.
q) Delete any file named index.htm or index.html. (These are the default pages that are included with the server.) (See Figure 21-10.)
r) Go back to your working directory where your new index.htm file and your index_files folder are located.
s) Copy both the index.htm file and the index_files folder from your working directory into the htdocs folder in C:\Program Files\Apache Software Foundation\Apache2.2. (See Figure 21-11.)

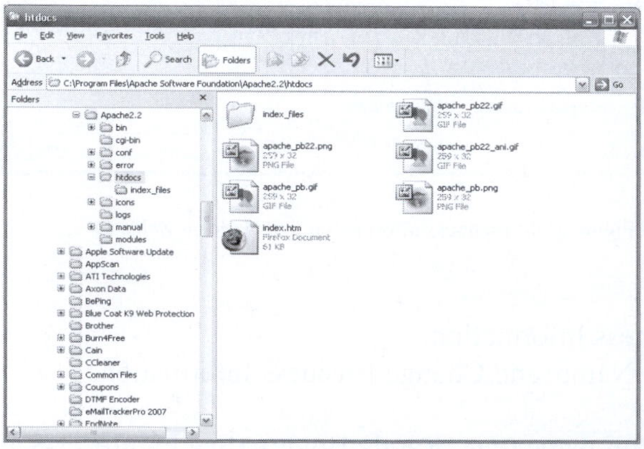

Figure 21-11: Copy your new website into the htdocs folder.

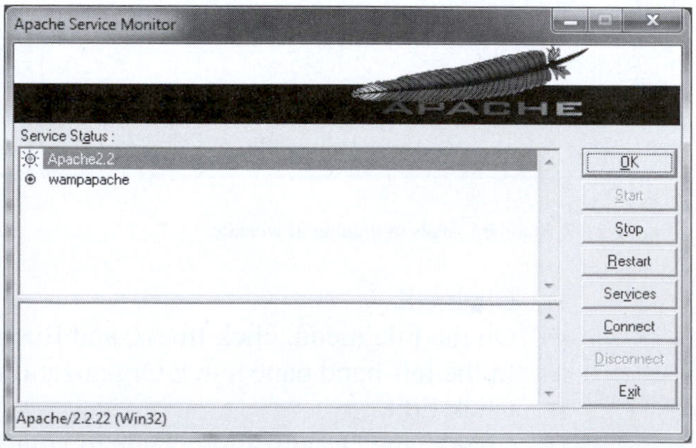

Figure 21-12: Start your Apache Web server.

16. Right-click the Apache icon in the lower right-hand corner of your screen. (It looks like a little red feather. If it's hidden, you can click on the small up arrow on the right-hand side of your taskbar.)
17. Open the Apache Monitor.
18. Select Apache 2.2.
19. Click Start. (It may already be started.) (See Figure 21-12.)
20. Open a Web browser and enter your IP address in the address bar. (If you don't know your IP address, you can enter the word localhost or 127.0.0.1.) (See Figures 22-13 and 22-14.)

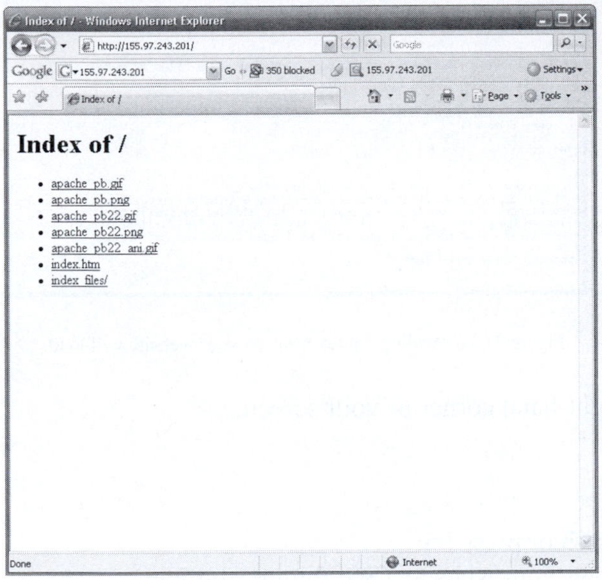

Figure 21-13: Enter your IP address into the address bar.

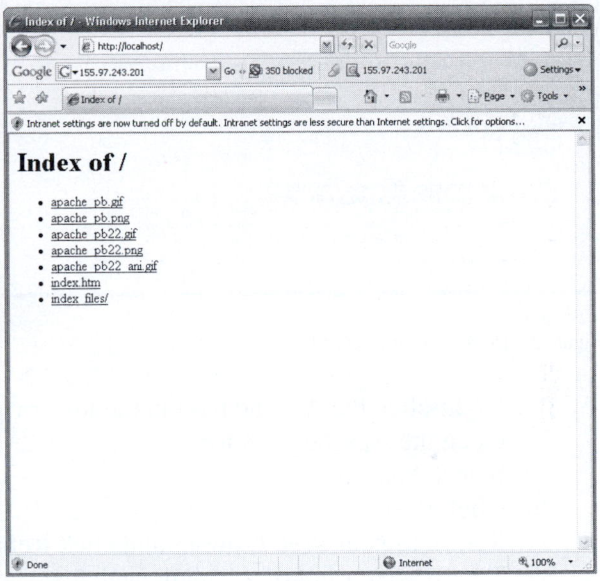

Figure 21-14: You can also enter "localhost" into the address bar.

Note: Your Web page may not have come up. Depending on the option you chose when you created your website, your main page may be index.htm or index.html. However, you were able to get a listing of all the Web pages and files that your Web server does have. You can see that your index.htm is one of them. If you click on this link, your full website will come up. However, we want it to open when people visit for the first time.

The reason it didn't open was because the default page for Apache is index.html, not index.htm. (The difference is the "l" at the end.) If you created your website using Microsoft Publisher, your main page would be index.htm. We will now change the configuration file so that Apache will open index.htm by default.

21. Open Windows Explorer and navigate to C:\Program Files\Apache Software Foundation\Apache2.2\conf folder.
22. Open the text file named httpd.conf.
23. Scroll down until you see a heading that reads # DirectoryIndex: sets the file that Apache will serve if a directory is requested. (See Figure 21-15.)
24. Change the text four lines below from:

DirectoryIndex index.html

To:

DirectoryIndex index.htm index.html

(There must be a space between index.htm and index.html.) (See Figure 21-16.)

25. On the File menu, click File, and Save.
26. Close the text file named httpd.conf.

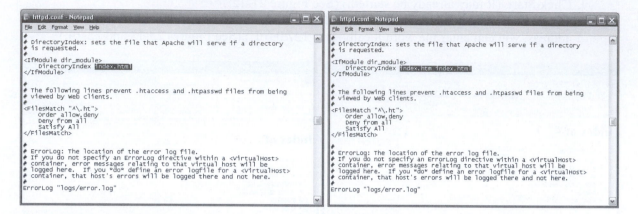

Figure 21-15: Apache httpd.conf file.   Figure 21-16: Adding "index.htm" so your website will load.

27. Right-click the Apache icon in the lower right-hand corner of your screen.
28. Open the Apache Monitor.
29. Select Apache 2.2.
30. Click Restart.
31. Return to your Web browser and click Refresh or press F5.
32. Take a screenshot of the main page that shows your website. (See Figure 21-17.)

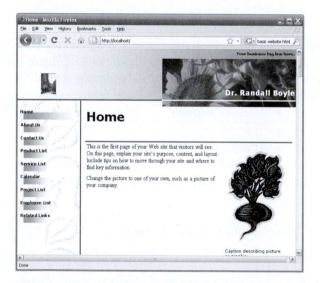

Figure 21-17: Your standard website.

Note: You have successfully loaded a Web server, created a website, edited a configuration file, and served Web pages. Anyone that enters your IP address into their web browser will see your Web pages. If you register your Web address (e.g., www.YourName.com) with your IP address, then the world can just enter your Web address without having to know your IP address.

33. In your Web browser, go to www.NetworkSolutions.com.

34. Enter "wwwYourName.com" into the Search for a Domain Name text box. (Replace YourName with your first and last name.)
35. Click Search.
36. Take a screenshot.

IMPORTANT You must STOP your Apache Web server before you do the next project so port 80 will be available. You will get an error message if you don't stop it before you get IIS up and running. Right-click the Apache icon on the taskbar and select Open Apache Monitor. Select your website and click Stop.

PROJECT QUESTIONS

1. Which method did you use to create your website?
2. Was your domain name available?
3. How much would it cost to register your domain name for a year?
4. What IP address would you use to register with your domain name?

THOUGHT QUESTIONS

1. Why did you have to edit the configuration file rather than using a GUI interface?
2. Do large companies like CNN use Apache? Why?
3. Can you host multiple websites on a single computer?
4. If you can turn your computer into a Web server, then what is the difference between your computer and the "servers" in the racks at Google?

21.2   INTERNET INFORMATION SERVICES (IIS) INSTALLATION

In this project, you will install and configure the *second* most popular Web server in use today (Apache is #1). Microsoft ships IIS with Microsoft Windows XP/Vista/7. Most people don't even know that they have the ability to run a Web server on their personal computer. Within the Windows Control Panel, you can add additional Windows components. IIS is one of many additional components that don't come installed as part of a default Windows installation.

The IIS interface is easier for beginners to learn than Apache. It comes with a nice GUI and is fairly intuitive. If you run it on Microsoft Windows Server 2008, you can run as many websites as you want! Running IIS on your Windows 7 machine is a great way to start learning the basics of administering a website. Let's look at an example.

In this project, you will create a simple Web page from a text file. You will also enter a few basic HTML tags into a text file and save it as a Web page. You will then open a Web browser and view it through your Web server.

IMPORTANT Make sure to stop your Apache Web server from the prior project so that port 80 is available for this project. Right-click the Apache icon on the taskbar and select Open Apache Monitor. Select your website and click Stop.

1. Click Start, and Control Panel.
2. Double-click Programs, and Turn Windows features on or off.

3. Select Internet Information Services. (Make sure all subcomponents are selected.) (See Figure 21-18.)

Note: Make sure all subcomponents for Common HTTP Features, Health & Diagnostics, and Security are selected under World Wide Web Services. You will be using these subcomponents in later projects. These will be important for setting the authentication and logging features.

4. Click OK.
5. In the Control Panel, double-click System and Security, and Administrative Tools.
6. Double-click Internet Information Services (IIS) Manager. (See Figure 21-19.)

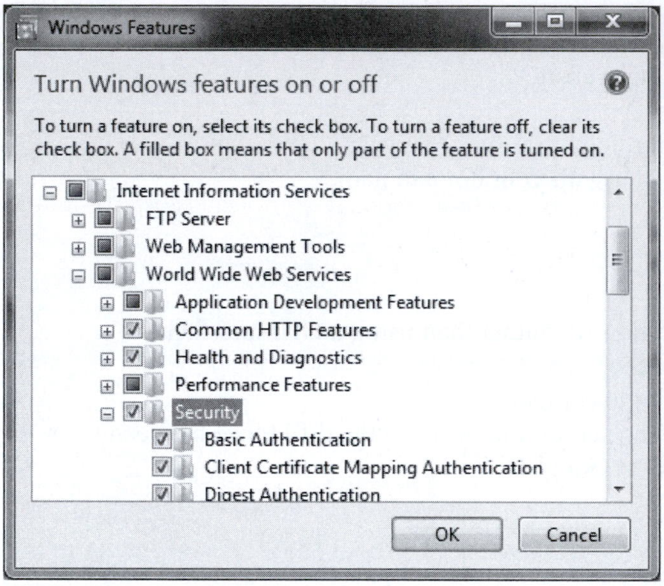

Figure 21-18: Selecting IIS components for installation.

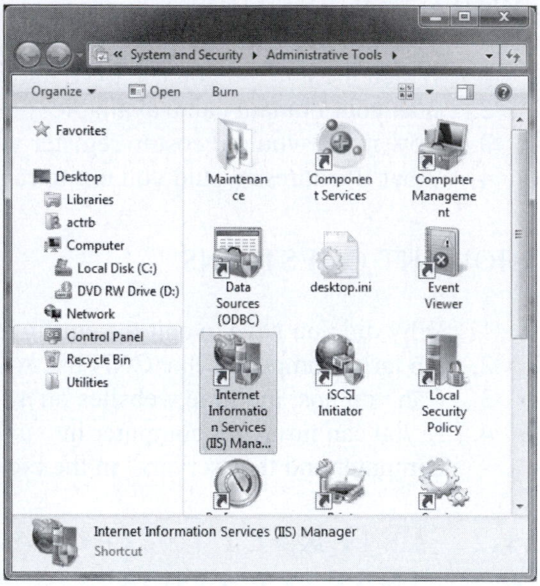

Figure 21-19: IIS shortcut in the Control Panel.

7. Expand the file tree until you see the Default Web Site.
8. Click on the Default Web Site.
9. In the right-hand pane, click Browse *:80 (http).
10. Take a screenshot of the default IIS page. (See Figure 21-20.)

Note: This will open a Web browser so you can see the default Web page being hosted on your computer. You can also manually open a Web browser and enter "localhost" or "127.0.0.1" to display this page. This step confirms that IIS is running correctly. If the default IIS page does not display in your Web browser, you may want to try reinstalling IIS and/or using a different browser. If you are using Windows XP, you may see a slightly different default page.

11. Return to IIS.
12. In the right-hand pane, click Explore. (This will take you to the C:\inetpub\wwwroot location on your computer where the default Web page/site is stored. You are going to save your new Web page in this directory.) (See Figure 21-21.)

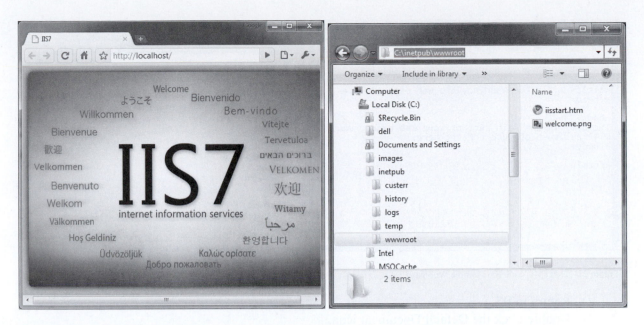

Figure 21-20: IIS 7 default Welcome page.

Figure 21-21: Default Web page (iisstart.htm) in the wwwroot directory.

13. Open Notepad by clicking Start, All Programs, and Accessories.
14. Right-click Notepad.
15. Select Run as administrator.
16. Type the following HTML code into the new text file. (Replace YourName with your first and last name. In this case, it was RandyBoyle. Be careful to enter all of the tags correctly.) (See Figure 21-22.)

```
<html>

<head>
<title> Title for YourName's Web page </title>
</head>

<body>
The body is the main part of your Web page. You will put most of your
content here.
</body>

</html>
```

17. Click File, and Save As.
18. Enter "yourname.html". (In this case, it was "randyboyle.html" all in lower-case. You are *not* going to save this as a text file. You are going to save it as an .html file. If you get an error saying you don't have permission to write to this directory, then you didn't start Notepad with administrator-level privileges.) (See Figure 21-23.)
19. Click Save.
20. Close Notepad.

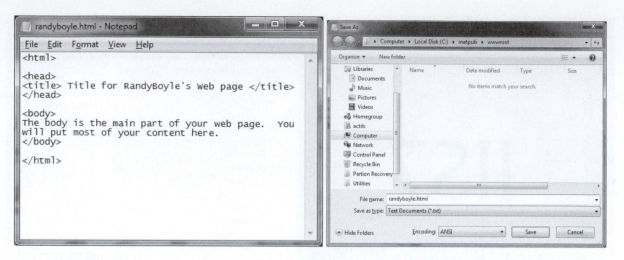

Figure 21-22: HTML code for a simple Web page.

Figure 21-23: Saving your simple Web page in the wwwroot directory.

21. Return to IIS.
22. Double-click the Default Document icon.
23. Click Add.
24. Enter "yourname.html". (In this case, it was randyboyle.html.)
25. Click OK. (You should see yourname.html at the top of the list. If you don't see it at the top of the list, you can select yourname.html and click Move Up until it is at the top of the list.) (See Figure 21-24.)
26. Click on Default Web Site in the left-hand pane.
27. Click on Browse *:80 (http). (You can also open any Web browser and enter "localhost" or "127.0.0.1" in the address bar. If your browser is already open, you can refresh the page.)
28. Take a screenshot with your name showing in the title bar. (See Figure 21-25.)

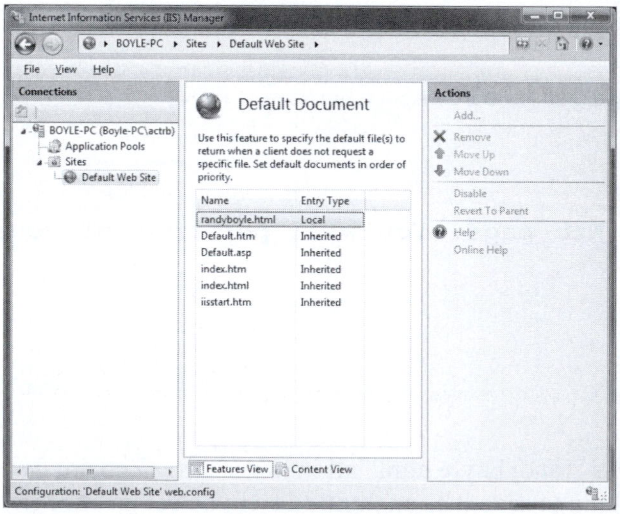

Figure 21-24: Adding yourname.html to the list of default documents in IIS.

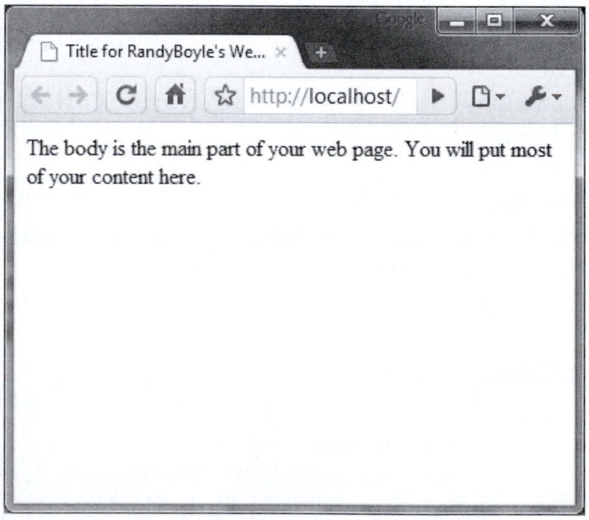

Figure 21-25: Your simple Web page displayed in a Web browser.

29. Open any Web browser and enter "127.0.0.1" in the address bar.
30. Take a screenshot with 127.0.0.1 in the address bar and your name in the title. (See Figure 21-26.)
31. Change the address to "http://127.0.0.1/iisstart.htm".
32. Take a screenshot. (See Figure 21-27.)

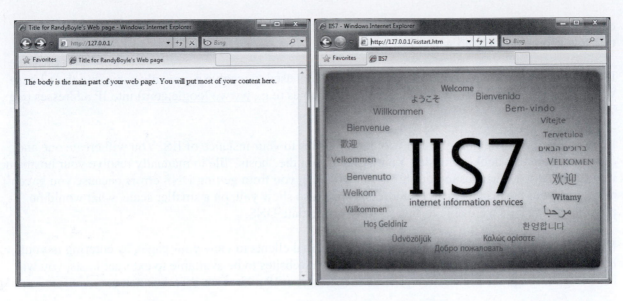

Figure 21-26: Accessing your Web page using the loopback adapter.   Figure 21-27: The IIS default Welcome page is still accessible.

Note: You have successfully installed and configured IIS. You also created a simple Web page and changed the IIS settings to have it load before iisstart.htm.

PROJECT QUESTIONS

1. What was the title for your main Web page?
2. What was the title for your default Web page?
3. What is the IP address of the computer you used for this project?
4. If you entered your IP address into a Web browser on another computer, what would you see?

THOUGHT QUESTIONS

1. If you moved index.htm above index.html in the Documents tab in ISS, which website would show?
2. If you enter a search term into the saved Google page, it won't return any results. Could you get it to work?
3. Can you password protect your website? How?
4. Can you require the use of SSL on your website?

21.3   PHISHING AND HOSTS FILE

Phishing scams are fairly easy to set up but somewhat difficult to execute. You need to copy a website (easy), host it on a machine you broke into (somewhat difficult), email out a believable link to hundreds of thousands of people (getting harder every day), get the stolen data off the machine before it is shut down (tricky), and get away without being tracked (difficult and dangerous).

One of the easiest ways of identifying phishing scams is to look at the URL. If it looks funny, don't click on it. Legitimate websites don't have funky URLs. Unfortunately, there are people who don't even know what a URL is.

In the summer of 2008, there was a major DNS vulnerability in the news. This vulnerability could have allowed malicious individuals to re-route Internet traffic to any computer they designated. IT security experts were concerned but the general public appeared ambivalent. It might have been due to the fact that few people understand what DNS actually does.

DNS is like a phone book. A traditional phone book is used to resolve a person's name into the address where they live. Similarly, DNS changes domain names (e.g., www.Google.com) into IP addresses (e.g., 74.125.19.103).

In this project, you are going to add two new websites to your instance of IIS. You will create one and copy one from this book's website. You will then edit the "hosts" file to manually resolve your hostnames into IP addresses. Changes to your hosts file will keep you from getting DNS errors because you haven't registered your hostnames to an IP address. It will also show you, on a smaller scale, what would be possible if attackers were able to successfully manipulate DNS.

Manually editing your hosts file will not allow external clients to view your pages by entering in your hostnames. This is just a shortcut. If you want these websites to be available to external hosts, you will have to go through the registration process to match your IP address to each hostname.

This project will show you 1) how your hosts file works, 2) how a single Web server can host multiple websites, and 3) how your Web server will sort each Web request based on the hostname, within the Web request. You will also get an error at the end of this project and fix it.

1. Click Start, All Programs, Accessories, and Windows Explorer.
2. Browse to your C:\inetpub\wwwroot folder.
3. Create the following folders and replace YourName with your first name and last name. (See Figure 21-28.)

    YourName_Books_Website
    YourName_Company1_Website
    YourName_Company2_Website
    YourName_Company3_Website

Note: In the next step, you are going to download three websites built from templates, and copy the website (actually just the main page) for this book. There are many websites that offer pre-made websites from templates. In a prior project, you may have used www.FreeWebsiteTemplates.com. In this project, you will use www.DoTemplate.com. You could also use www.Wix.com, or any number of other websites. The goal is to get a realistic looking website with little effort.

4. Open a Web browser and go to www.DoTemplate.com.
5. Click Free Templates.
6. Click on one of the websites shown in the Templates gallery. (You will repeat this process three times to get the three websites you will use in this project.)
7. Click Customize and Download.
8. Click Download, XHTML template, and Download your template.
9. Save the .ZIP file in your C:\inetpub\wwwroot\YourName_Company1_Website folder.
10. Right-click the .ZIP file and select Extract All, and Extract.
11. Move the contents (the new website) from the newly created folder to your C:\inetpub\wwwroot\YourName_Company1_Website folder. (See Figure 21-29.)

Note: If you completed the above steps correctly, the folder labeled YourName_Company1_Website should contain 1) the .ZIP file you downloaded, 2) the uncompressed folder, and 3) the website template. You should see an index.html file in the directory.

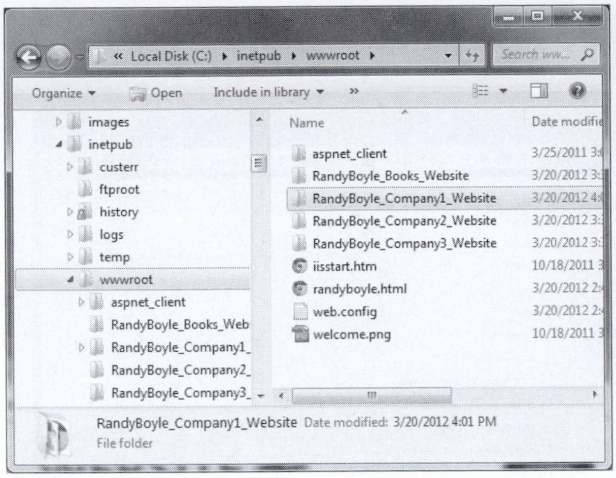

Figure 21-28: Creating website folders.

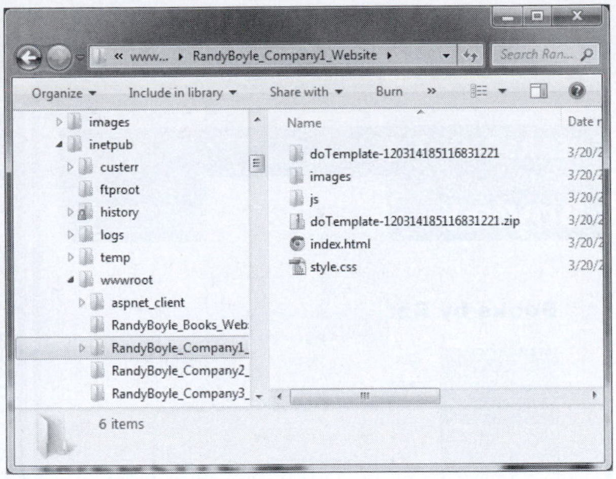

Figure 21-29: Saved website in Company1.

12. Repeat Steps 4 through 11 two more times and save the websites you download in folders YourName_Company2_Website and YourName_Company3_Website, respectively.

Note: After repeating Steps 4 through 11, you should have two additional websites in folders YourName_Company2_Website and YourName_Company3_Website, respectively. You should have a file named "index.html" in each of the three "company" folders you created. (See Figure 21-30 and Figure 21-31.)

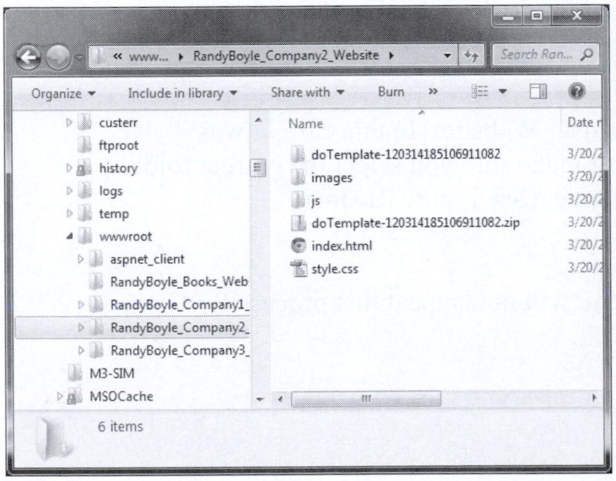

Figure 21-30: Saved website in Company2.

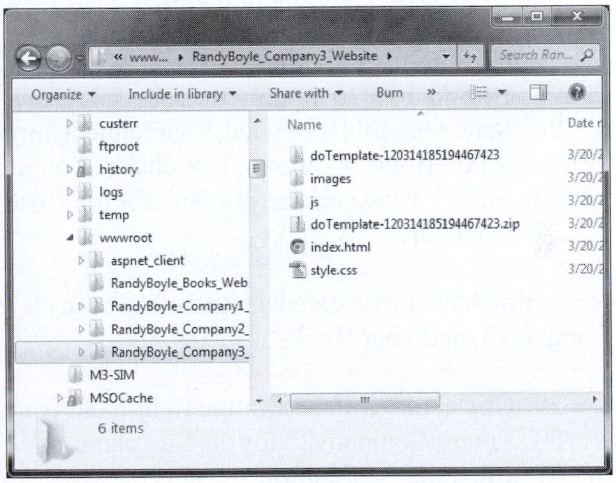

Figure 21-31: Saved website in Company3.

13. Open a Web Browser. (Chrome, Internet Explorer, or Firefox will work.)
14. Browse to http://www.pearsonhighered.com/boyle/. (This is the website for this book.)
15. Click File, and Save Page As. (See Figure 21-32.)
16. Select Complete Web Page as the type.
17. Save the file in the directory labeled C:\inetpub\wwwroot\YourName_Books_Website folder. (In this case, it was C:\inetpub\wwwroot\RandyBoyle_Books_Website.) (See Figure 21-33.)
18. Click Save.

Note: The website you just saved had a main page with a long name (Pearson-Online…). This is not one of the default documents listed when you create a new website in IIS. This will cause an error later in the project and you will need to rename this file index.htm for the page to work correctly.

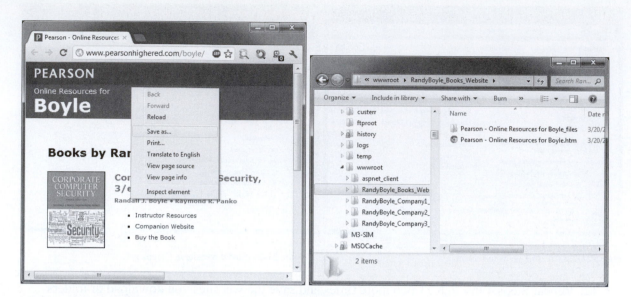

Figure 21-32: Saving a website.

Figure 21-33: Saving a website as the Books website.

19. Click Start, Control Panel, System and Security, Administrative Tools, and Internet Information Services (IIS) Manager.
20. Expand the tree in the left-hand pane until you see the Sites icon.
21. Click on the Sites icon.
22. Click Add Web Site in the right-hand pane.
23. Enter "Company1" for the Site name.
24. Click the "…" button.
25. Browse to C:\inetpub\wwwroot.
26. Select the folder labeled YourName_Company1_Website. (In this case, it was RandyBoyle_Company1_Website. You must make sure you select the correct folder.)
27. Enter "www.company1.com" for the Host name. (See Figure 21-34.)
28. Click OK.

Note: You have just created a site for Company1. You will now repeat this process for Company2, Company3, and your Books website.

29. Click Add Web Site in the right-hand pane.
30. Enter "Company2" for the Site name.
31. Click the "…" button.
32. Browse to C:\inetpub\wwwroot.
33. Select the folder labeled YourName_Company2_Website. (In this case, it was RandyBoyle_Company2_Website. You must make sure you select the correct folder.)
34. Enter "www.company2.com" for the Host name. (See Figure 21-35.)
35. Click OK.

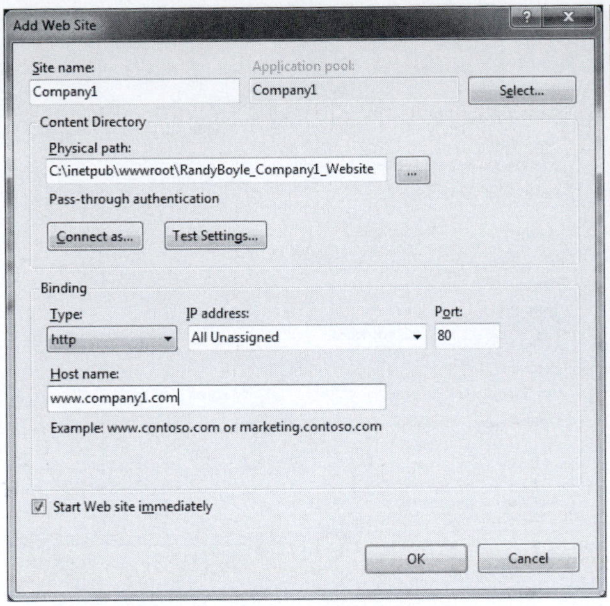

Figure 21-34: Adding the Company1 website. 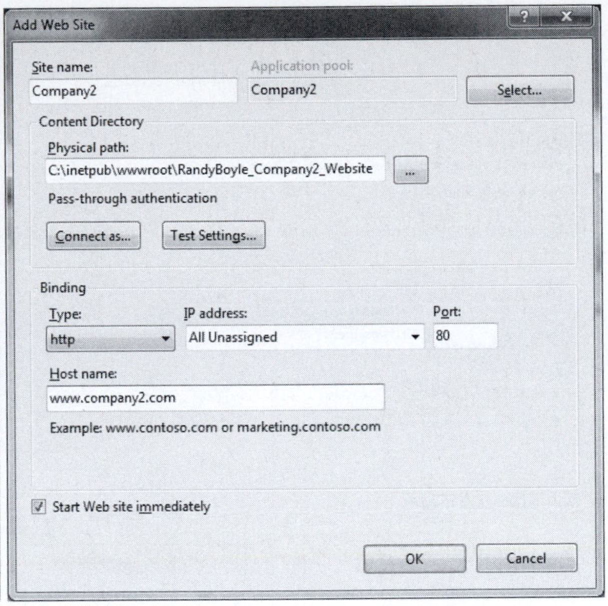   Figure 21-35: Adding the Company2 website.

36. Click Add Web Site in the right-hand pane.
37. Enter "Company3" for the Site name.
38. Click the "…" button.
39. Browse to C:\inetpub\wwwroot.
40. Select the folder labeled YourName_Company3_Website. (In this case, it was RandyBoyle_Company3_Website. You must make sure you select the correct folder.)
41. Enter "www.company3.com" for the Host name. (See Figure 21-36.)
42. Click OK.

Note: Now you are going to add the Books site.

43. Click Add Web Site in the right-hand pane.
44. Enter "YourNameBooks" for the Site name. (In this case, it was RandyBoyleBooks.)
45. Click the "…" button.
46. Browse to C:\inetpub\wwwroot.
47. Select the folder labeled YourName_Books_Website. (In this case, it was RandyBoyle_Books_Website. You must make sure you select the correct folder.)
48. Enter "www.YourNameBooks.com" for the Host name. (In this case, it was www.RandyBoyleBooks.com.) (See Figure 21-37.)
49. Click OK.

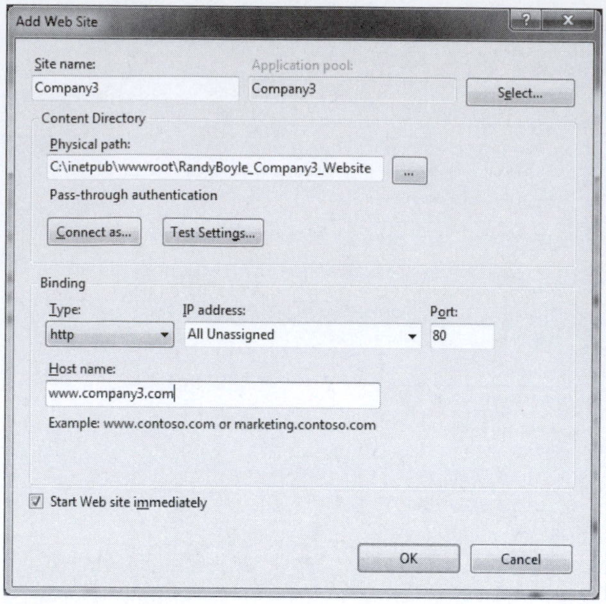

Figure 21-36: Adding the Company3 website.

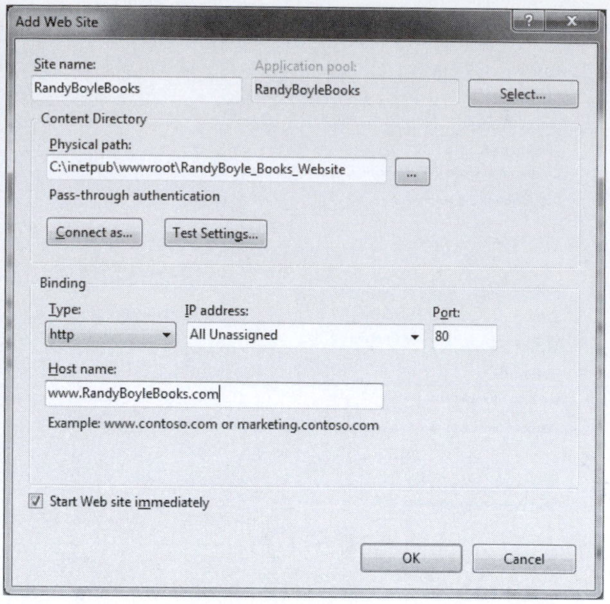

Figure 21-37: Adding the Books website.

Note: You should now have four websites (Company1, Company2, Company3, and Books) running on your Web Server. However, you have not registered your IP address and their associated host names (e.g. www.company1.com). We are going to trick your computer into thinking it resolved the hostnames by editing your "hosts" file.

Your computer will check this file *before* it makes a DNS request. After these changes are made, you can enter a hostname like www.Company1.com into your Web browser's address bar and your website will come up. This *only* works on your local computer. If you want these hostnames to work on other people's computers, you will have to register your hostnames and IP address.

50. Open Notepad by clicking Start, All Programs, and Accessories.
51. Right-click on Notepad.
52. Select Run as administrator. (If you don't start Notepad with **administrator-level privileges**, you will not be able to save the changes you are going to make to this file. The rest of the project will not work if you don't save these changes.)
53. Click File, and Open.
54. Browse to C:\Windows\System32\drivers\etc\.
55. Change the file type to All Files (*.*). (This will allow you to see the hosts file.)
56. Select the hosts file. (See Figure 21-38.)
57. Click Open.
58. Scroll to the bottom of the text file.
59. Add the following text to the bottom of the file. (Replace YourName with your first and last name so it matches the hostnames for your Books website. You can add as many blank lines as you want. It won't affect how the hostnames are processed. Make sure these host names are *exactly* the same as the host names you entered when you set up the websites.) (See Figure 21-39.)

```
127.0.0.1   www.company1.com
127.0.0.1   www.company2.com
127.0.0.1   www.company3.com
127.0.0.1   www.YourNameBooks.com
```

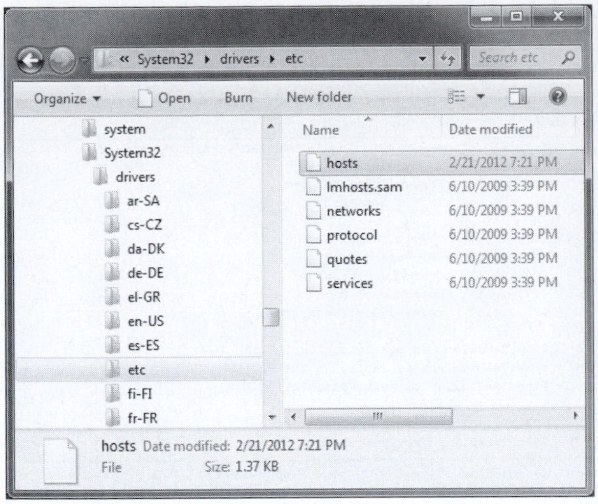

Figure 21-38: Opening the hosts file.

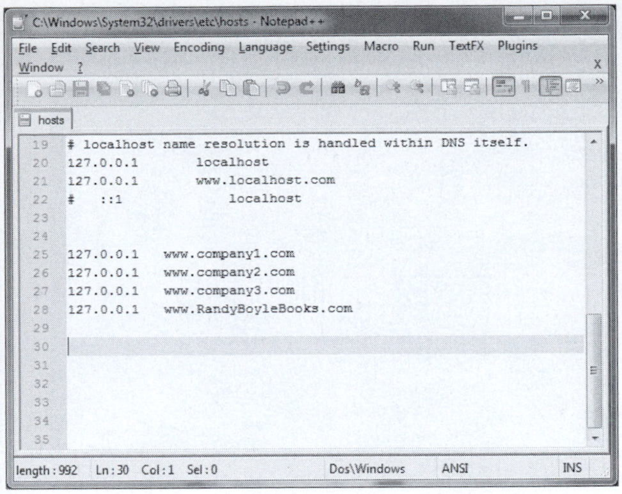

Figure 21-39: Changes made to the hosts file.

60. Open a command prompt by clicking Start, All Programs, Accessories, and Command Prompt.
61. Ping www.Yahoo.com and www.Twitter.com. (See Figure 21-40.)
62. Record the IP addresses that were resolved in each ping. (In this case, www.Yahoo.com was at 209.191.122.70 and www.Twitter.com was at 199.59.150.7.)
63. Make the following entry to your hosts file just below your previous entries. (Make sure to replace YourName with your first and last name. In this case, the first line used www.RandyBoyle.com. Lines with a "#" will not be processed. The first entry will redirect your Web browser to www.Yahoo.com if you type www.YourName.com in the address bar. The second entry will redirect your browser to www.Twitter.com if you enter www.Yahoo.com into the address bar.)

```
#www.Yahoo.com is really at 209.191.122.70
#www.Twitter.com is really at 199.59.150.7
#They are going to be reversed below!!

209.191.122.70    www.YourName.com
199.59.150.7      www.yahoo.com
```

64. Click File, and Save. (See Figure 21-41.)
65. Take a screenshot.
66. Close the hosts file.

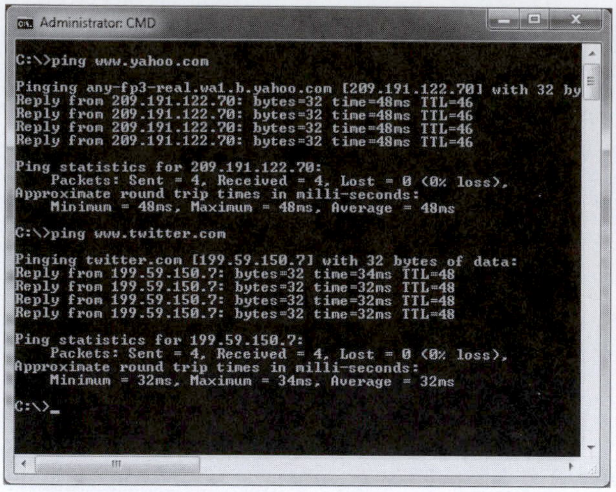

Figure 21-40: Using ping to resolve host names.

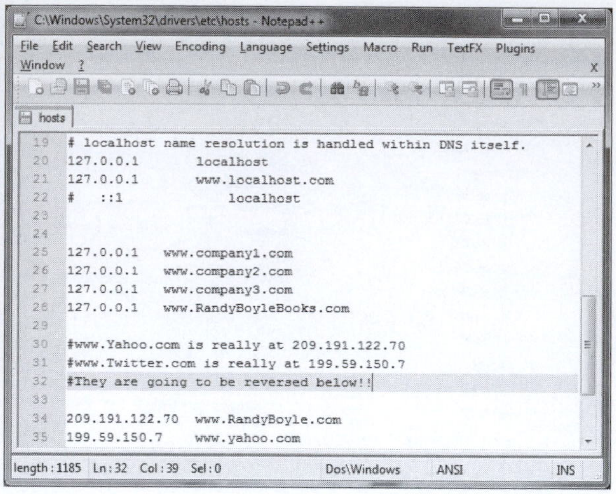

Figure 21-41: Hostname redirects.

67. Close any Web browsers you may have open.
68. Open a Web browser.
69. Enter "www.company1.com" into the address bar.
70. Take a screenshot of your website.
71. Enter "www.company2.com" into the address bar.
72. Take a screenshot of your website.
73. Enter "www.company3.com" into the address bar.
74. Take a screenshot of your website.
75. Enter "www.YourName.com" into the address bar. (This should redirect to www.Yahoo.com, but leave your name in the address bar.)
76. Take a screenshot of the website with your name showing in the address bar.
77. Enter "www.Yahoo.com" into the address bar. (This should redirect to www.Twitter.com, but leave www.Yahoo.com in the address bar.)
78. Enter "www.YourNameBooks.com" into the address bar. (You should get an error message because the main page in the folder is not listed in the list of default pages for that website.)
79. Take a screenshot of the error message. (See Figure 21-42.)
80. Open Windows Explorer.
81. Browse to C:\inetpub\wwwroot\YourName_Books_Website. (In this case, it was C:\inetpub\wwwroot\RandyBoyle_Books_Website. There should be one folder and one HTML page in that directory.)
82. Right-click on the HTML page in that directory. (There should only be one HTML page named "Pearson-Online…")
83. Select Rename.
84. Name the file "index.htm". (See Figure 21-43.)
85. Press Enter.
86. Click Yes.

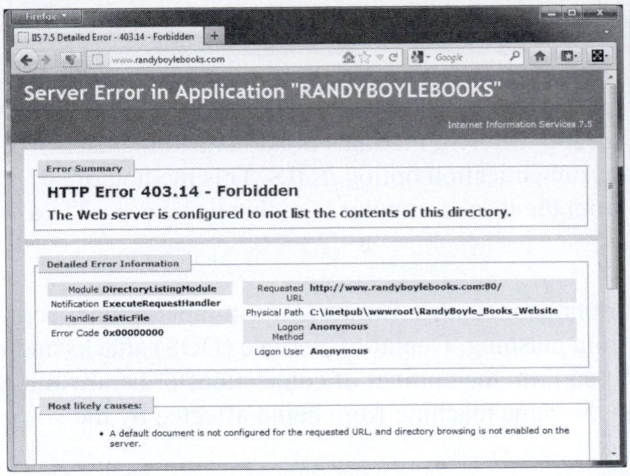

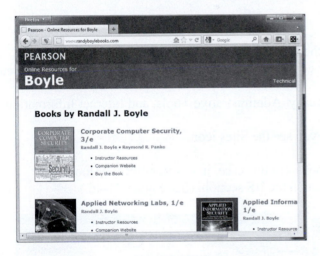

Figure 21-42: Error message for the Books website.

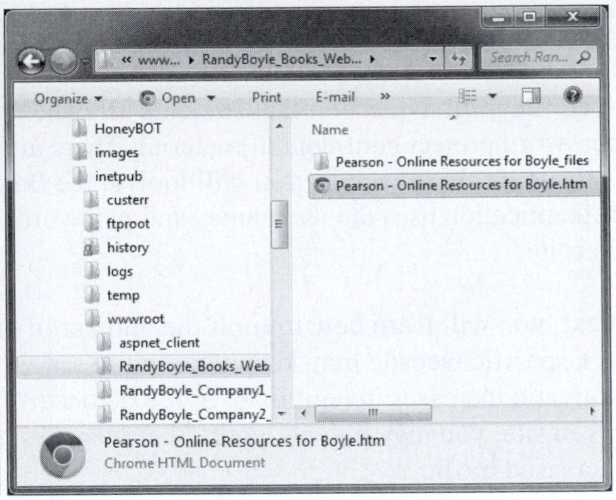

Figure 21-43: Renamed main page for the Books website.

87. Return to your Web browser.
88. Enter "www.YourNameBooks.com" into the address bar.
89. Take a screenshot of your website with your name showing in the address bar. (See Figure 21-44.)

Figure 21-44: Books website with your name in the address bar.

PROJECT QUESTIONS

1. What was the subject of your Company1 website?
2. What was the subject of your Company2 website?
3. What was the subject of your Company3 website?
4. What was the hostname for your Books website?

THOUGHT QUESTIONS

1. If a hacker or disgruntled worker was able to maliciously modify a large DNS server, could they cause problems? How?
2. How many root DNS servers are there?
3. How could you tell if you were being redirected to an incorrect website?
4. Could a virus modify your hosts file and cause you problems?

A common first question that students ask when they are beginning to learn to host Web content is how to password protect confidential material. There are several different methods of authenticating users to a website. In this example, you will look at the Basic Authentication option in IIS. This method of authentication uses the usernames and passwords from the local computer to authenticate access to a website.

Next, you will learn how to limit the number of current connections. Limiting the number of connections to a specific website may keep your entire server from crashing. Denial-of-Service (DOS) attacks and/or dramatic increases in legitimate usage do occur. If you limit the number of connections or bandwidth to a given site, you may prevent your other websites on the same machine from being affected by the increased traffic.

Finally, you will learn how to block certain IP addresses from accessing your website. Learning how to "black hole" a range of IP addresses can be useful if your website is consistently being attacked by individuals with IP addresses in the same range. Temporarily blocking a DOS attack from a specific host may be an effective short-term strategy. Blocking a competitor's IP range may also be a good idea in certain instances.

1. Open a Web browser.
2. Enter "www.YourNameBooks.com" into the address bar. (It should open correctly if you completed the prior project. If you haven't completed the prior project, you will need to complete it before continuing.) (See Figure 21-45.)
3. Click Start, Control Panel, System and Security, Administrative Tools, and Internet Information Services (IIS) Manager.
4. Expand the tree in the left-hand pane until you see the Sites icon.
5. Click on the Sites icon.
6. Click on the website labeled YourNameBooks. (In this case, it was RandyBoyleBooks.)
7. Double-click the icon labeled Authentication in the IIS section. (See Figure 21-46.)

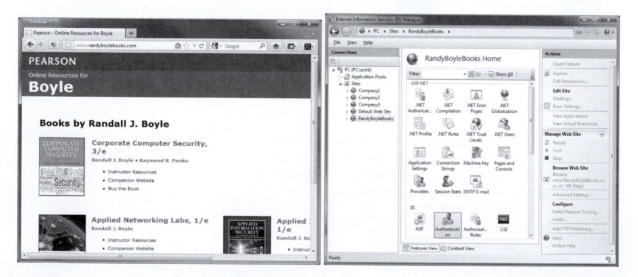

Figure 21-45: Your Books website.　　　　Figure 21-46: Authentication icon.

8. Select the row labeled Anonymous Authentication.
9. Click Disable in the right-hand pane.
10. Click on the row labeled Basic Authentication.

11. Click Enable. (Basic Authentication should be the only form of authentication enabled. See Figure 21-47.)
12. Click on the website labeled YourNameBooks in the left-hand pane.
13. Click Stop in the right-hand pane.
14. Click Start in the right-hand pane.
15. Close your Web browser.
16. Reopen your Web browser.
17. Enter "www.YourNameBooks.com" into the address bar. (In this case, it was www.RandyBoyleBooks.com. You should see a login screen. You might see your website opened in the background if your Web browser cached it. Without having it cached first, you wouldn't be able to see it without authenticating first.)
18. Enter your username and password as if you were logging into your local computer. (In this case, the user name was "actrb." This is the same username and password you use to log into your computer on a daily basis.)
19. Take a screenshot. (See Figure 21-48.)
20. Click Log In.
21. Return to the IIS Manager.
22. Click on the YourNameBooks website. (In this case, it was RandyBoyleBooks.)
23. Double-click the icon labeled Authentication in the IIS section.
24. Select the Anonymous Authentication row.
25. Click Enable in the right-hand pane.
26. Click on the Basic Authentication row.
27. Click Disable. (Anonymous Authentication should be the only form of authentication enabled.)

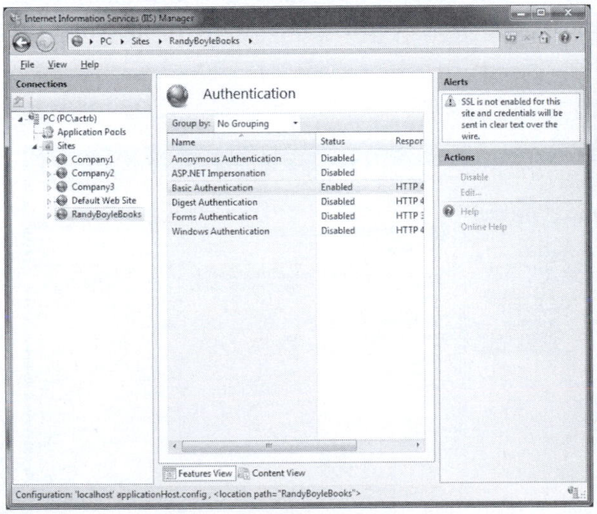

Figure 21-47: Changing authentication for the website.

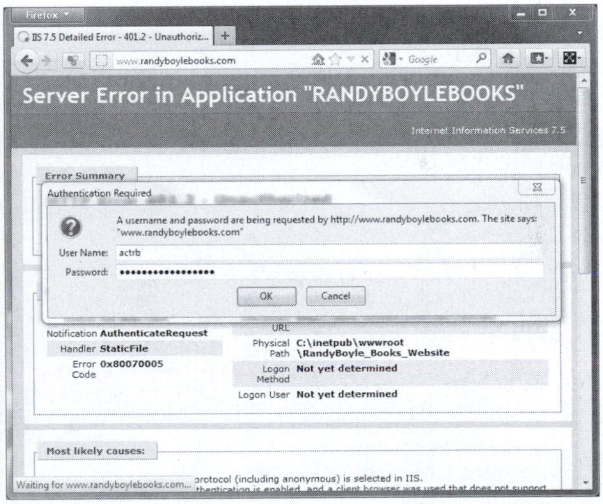

Figure 21-48: Login screen for access to the website.

28. Return to the IIS Manager.
29. Click on the YourNameBooks website. (In this case, it was RandyBoyleBooks.)
30. Click Limits in the right-hand pane.
31. Select Limit number of connections.
32. Enter "2" for the number of connections. (See Figure 21-49.)
33. Click OK.
34. Return to your Web browser. (The main page or a sub page should be showing.)
35. Copy the URL into the address bar. (You can copy it by pressing Ctrl-C.)
36. Press Ctrl-T three times to open three additional tabs.
37. Paste the copied URL from your Web page into each of the tabs.
38. Press enter on each of the tabs to start loading the page.

39. Keep refreshing each tab (F5) quickly until you start seeing parts of the page fail to load.
40. Take a screenshot of one of the tabs that failed to load properly. (See Figure 21-50.)
41. Return to the IIS Manager.
42. Change the limits back to unlimited connections.

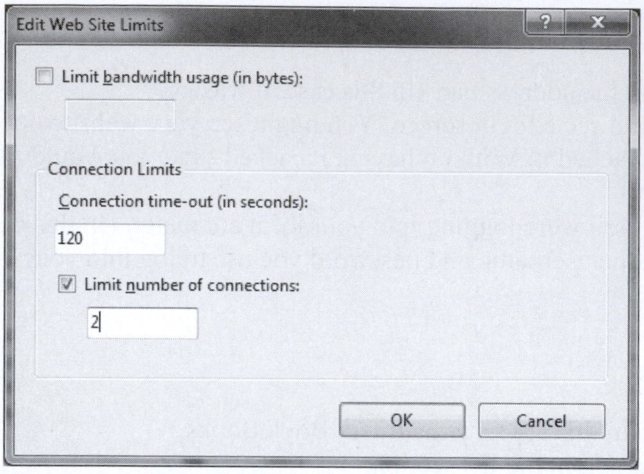

Figure 21-49: Limiting the number of connections.

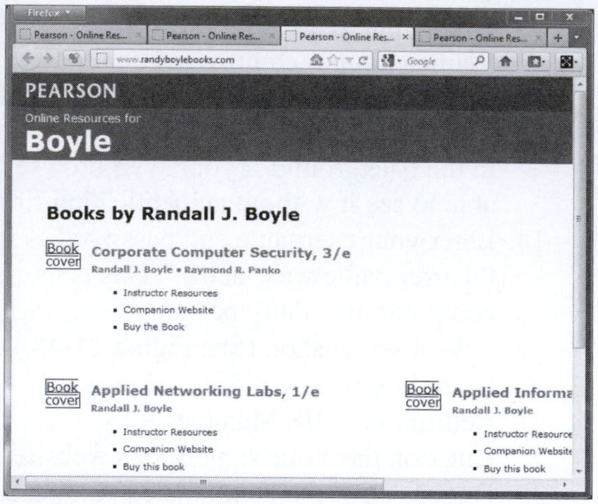

Figure 21-50: Page elements failing to load correctly due to limitations on the number of connections.

43. Return to the IIS Manager.
44. Click on the website labeled YourNameBooks. (In this case, it was RandyBoyleBooks.)
45. Click on the icon labeled IP Address and Restrictions in the center pane in the IIS section. (See Figure 21-51.)
46. Click Add Deny Entry. (See Figure 21-52.)

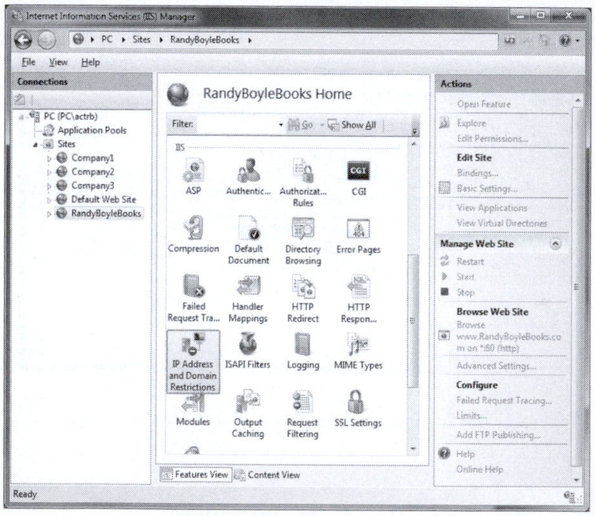

Figure 21-51: IP Address and Domain Restrictions icon.

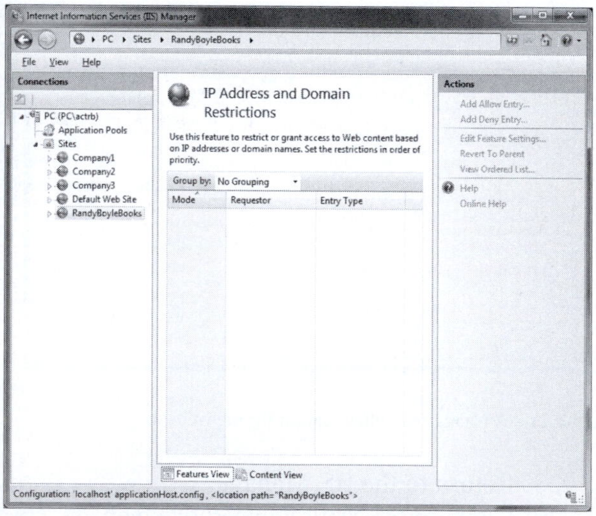

Figure 21-52: IP Address and Domain Restrictions pane.

47. Click on the icon labeled IP Address and Restrictions in the center pane in the IIS section.
48. Click Add Deny Entry.
49. Enter "127.0.0.1" in the text box under Specific IP address. (This will block your local loopback IP address. Blocking your loopback IP address is only useful as a demonstration. More realistically, you could enter any IP address, or block of IP addresses, you might want to block. This could include competitors, IPs that are known to be sources of attacks, or a block from an entire country.)

50. Click OK. (See Figure 21-53.)
51. Take a screenshot of the IP address and Domain Restrictions listing. (See Figure 21-54.)

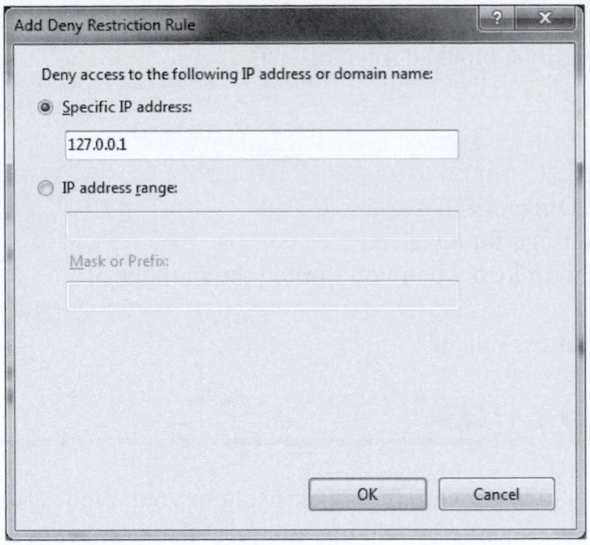

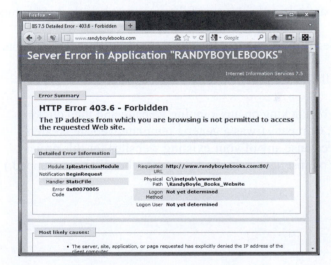

Figure 21-53: Denying access to 127.0.0.1. 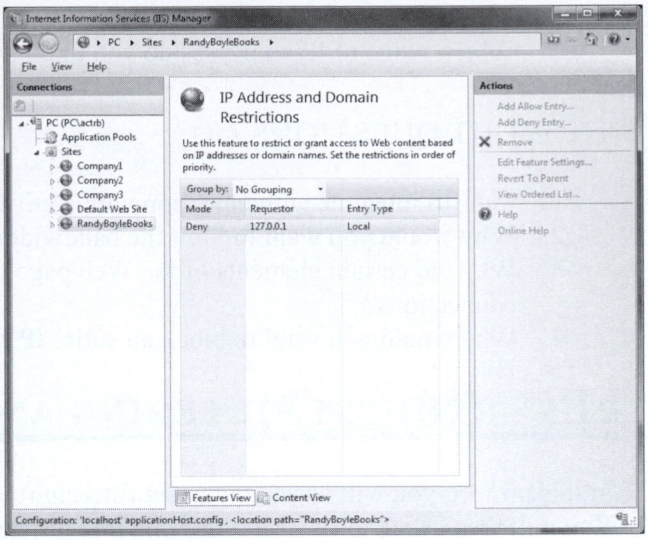   Figure 21-54: Listing of IP Address and Domain Restrictions.

52. Click on the website labeled YourNameBooks in the left-hand pane.
53. Click Stop in the right-hand pane.
54. Click Start in the right-hand pane.
55. Return to your Web browser.
56. Click refresh (F5) if you are still on www.YourNameBooks.com or go to www.YourNameBooks.com.
57. Take a screenshot of the "forbidden" error message. (See Figure 21-55.)
58. Return to IIS Manager and remove the 127.0.0.1 restriction.

Figure 21-55: Access denied due to an IP restriction.

PROJECT QUESTIONS

1. What was the hostname of your Books website?
2. What was the username you entered to access your website?
3. Is there another user with access to the computer you used who would also have access to your website? If so, which one?
4. Which range of IP addresses do you think might be blocked most often?

THOUGHT QUESTIONS

1. Can IIS integrate authentication with Active Directory?
2. Why would you want to limit the bandwidth usage for a website?
3. Why did certain elements of the Web page fail to load when you limited the number of connections?
4. Why would you want to block an entire IP address range?

21.5 REQUEST FILTERING AND LOGS

In this project, you will learn how to set filtering rules to block certain requests sent to your Web server. You will then check to see if the filtering rule has been effective by making a request that you believe should be blocked. You will get error messages specific to the filtering rule you set. In the last step of this project, you will look at the error logs that recorded these blocked requests.

You will set specific filtering rules that will block characters sequences (".."), file types (.exe), directories on your Web server (/private), and keywords you may specify. You will also limit the overall length of incoming URLs. Effective use of filtering rules will make your Web server more secure by blocking incoming attacks. Using a combination of filtering rules will likely yield the most secure configuration.

1. Click Start, Control Panel, Programs, and Turn Windows features on or off.
2. Expand the tree under Internet Information Services, World Wide Web Services, and Security. (See Figure 21-56.)
3. Make sure all the options under Security are selected. (Request Filtering must be selected for this project to work.)
4. Click Start, Control Panel, System and Security, Administrative Tools, and Internet Information Services (IIS) Manager.
5. Expand the tree in the left-hand pane until you see the Sites icon.
6. Click on the Sites icon.
7. Stop all websites *except* Company1.com by clicking on any running website and then clicking Stop in the right-hand pane. (In this case, Company1 was a generic template website created using Microsoft Expression Web 4. You can use any of your existing websites for this project. Company1.com was randomly chosen. You just need to make sure your other sites are stopped.) (See Figure 21-57.)

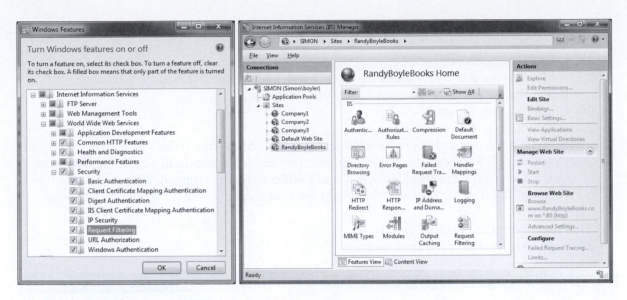

Figure 21-56: Ensure IIS options are enabled.   Figure 21-57: Stopping all other websites.

8. Open a Web browser.
9. Enter "www.Company1.com" into the address bar. (It should open *correctly* if you completed the prior project. If you haven't completed the prior project, you will need to complete it before continuing. One of your local websites must be displayed before moving on to the next step.)
10. Enter "www.Company1.com/index.html" into the address bar. (Your website should *correctly* load and display your main page – index.html.)
11. Press Enter. (See Figure 21-58.)
12. Enter "www.Company1.com/index.htm" into the address bar. (Note that the lower-case letter "l" is missing at the end of index.htm. This should cause you to get a common 404.0 error. Your website should *not* load correctly.)
13. Press Enter. (See Figure 21-59.)

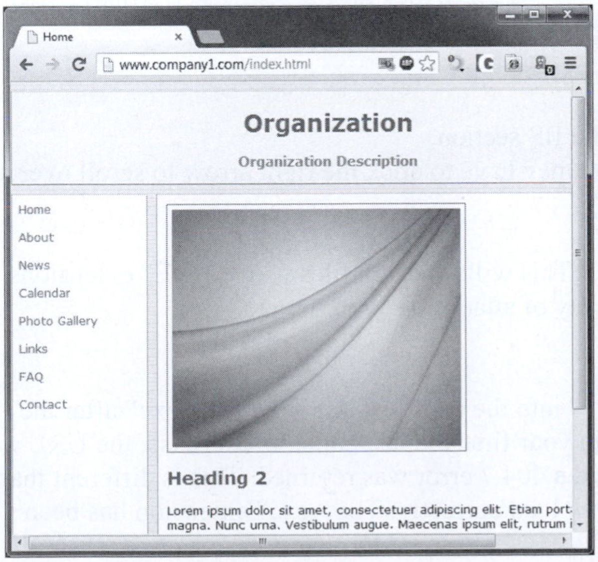

Figure 21-58: Website correctly loads the main page. 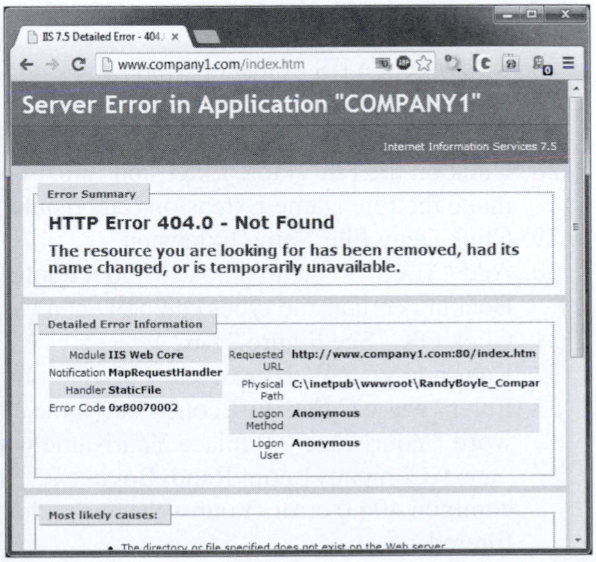   Figure 21-59: A generic 404.0 error.

14. Return to the IIS Manager window.
15. Click on the Company1 website. (You can use any of your websites for this project.)
16. Double-click the Request Filtering icon in the IIS section.

17. Click on the URL tab. (You may have to click the right arrow to scroll over and make the URL tab visible.)
18. Click Deny Sequence.
19. Add ".." to the text box, without quotes. (This will block URL sequences that contain ".." in them. The use of ".." is common in transversal attacks.)
20. Click OK. (See Figure 21-60.)
21. Return to your Web browser.
22. Enter "www.Company1.com/YourName.." into the address bar. (Note the ".." after the word "YourName". Replace YourName with your first and last name. In this case, the URL was "www.Company1.com/RandyBoyle.." and a 404.5 error was returned. This is different than a common 404.0 error. Your website should *not* load correctly. The ".." sequence has been filtered.)
23. Press Enter. (See Figure 21-61.)
24. Take a screenshot of the error message.

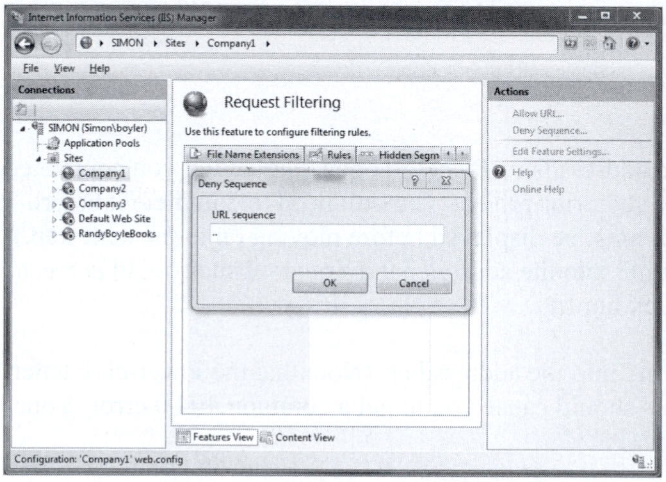

Figure 21-60: Adding a sequence of characters that will be denied.

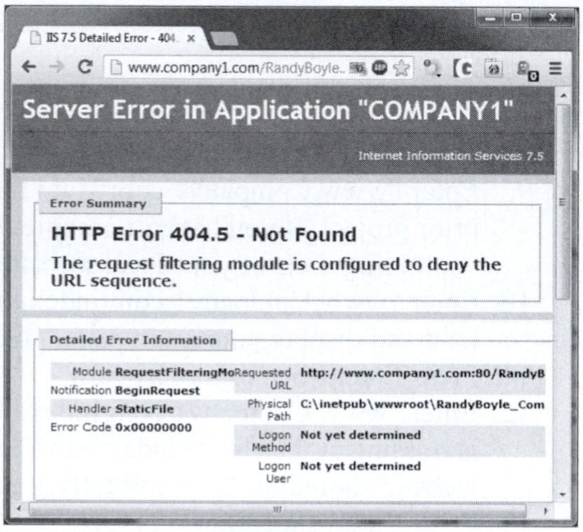

Figure 21-61: A 404.5 error due to a denied URL sequence.

25. Return to the IIS Manager window.
26. Click on the Company1 website.
27. Double-click the Request Filtering icon in the IIS section.
28. Click on the File Name Extensions tab. (You may have to click the right arrow to scroll over and make the File Name Extensions tab visible.)
29. Click Deny File Name Extension.
30. Add ".EXE" to the text box, without quotes. (This will block all files with ".EXE" extensions. Bocking certain file types can prevent a variety of attacks on Web servers.)
31. Click OK. (See Figure 21-62.)
32. Return to your Web browser.
33. Enter "www.Company1.com/YourName.exe" into the address bar. (Note the ".exe" after the word "YourName". Replace YourName with your first and last name. In this case, the URL was "www.Company1.com/RandyBoyle.exe" and a 404.7 error was returned. This is different than a common 404.0 error. Your website should *not* load correctly. The ".exe" extension has been filtered.)
34. Press Enter. (See Figure 21-63.)
35. Take a screenshot of the error message.

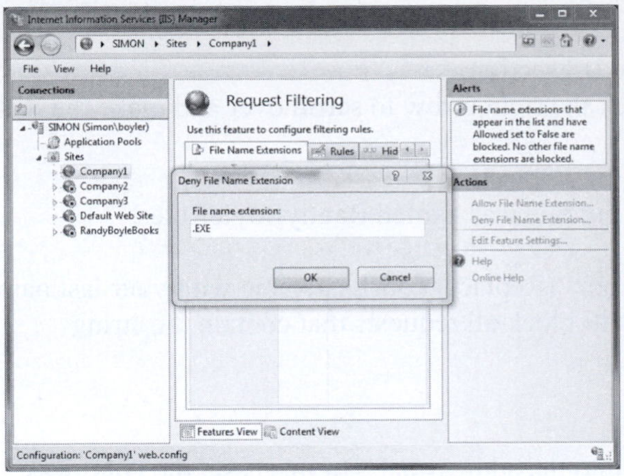

Figure 21-62: Adding a file extension that will be denied.

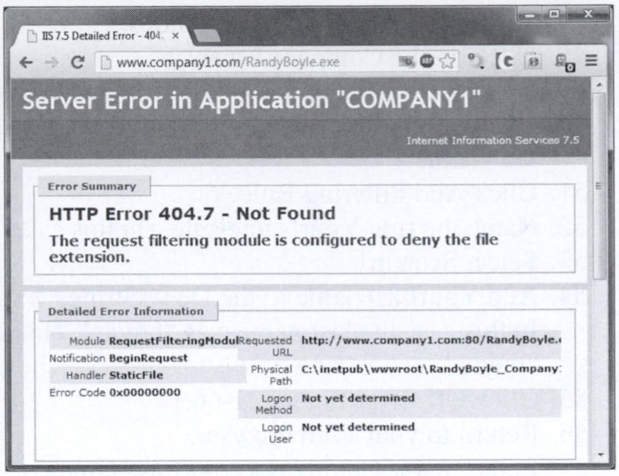

Figure 21-63: A 404.7 error returned due to an extension being denied.

36. Return to the IIS Manager window.
37. Click on the Company1 website.
38. Double-click the Request Filtering icon in the IIS section.
39. Click on the Hidden Segments tab. (You may have to click the right arrow to scroll over and make the Hidden Segments tab visible.)
40. Click Add Hidden Segment.
41. Add "private" to the text box, without quotes. (This will block all requests made to a directory named "private.")
42. Click OK. (See Figure 21-64.)
43. Return to your Web browser.
44. Enter "www.Company1.com/private/" into the address bar. (In this case, the URL was "www.Company1.com/private/" and a 404.8 error was returned. This is different than a common 404.0 error. Your website should *not* load correctly. The request to access the "private" directory was denied.)
45. Press Enter. (See Figure 21-65.)
46. Take a screenshot of the error message.

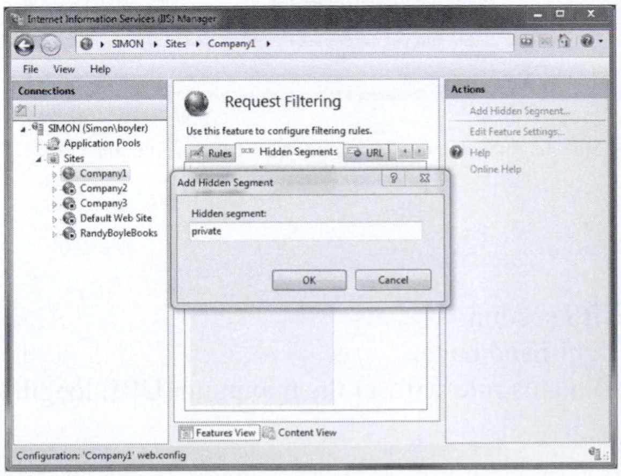

Figure 21-64: Adding a folder (segment) name that will be hidden.

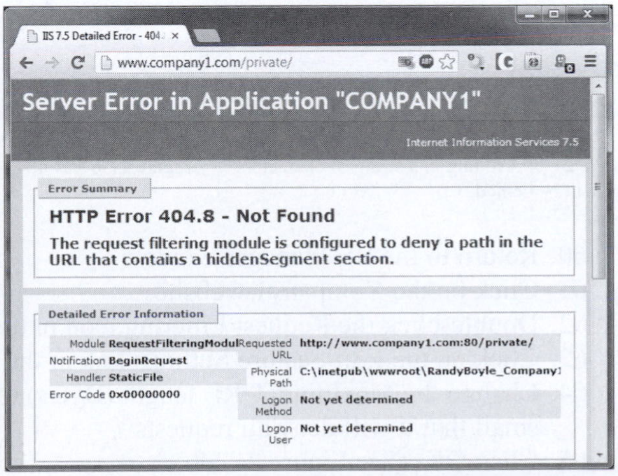

Figure 21-65: A 404.8 error returned after requesting a hidden folder.

47. Return to the IIS Manager window.
48. Click on the Company1 website.
49. Double-click the Request Filtering icon in the IIS section.
50. Click on the Rules tab. (You may have to click the right arrow to scroll over and make the Rules tab visible.)
51. Click Add Filtering Rule.
52. Name the rule YourNameRule. (In this case, the rule was named RandyBoyleRule.)
53. Select Scan url.
54. Add YourLastName to the Deny Strings text box. (Replace YourLastName with your last name. In this case the last name was "boyle." This will block all requests that contain the string "boyle.")
55. Click OK. (See Figure 21-66.)
56. Return to your Web browser.
57. Enter "www.Company1.com/LastName.txt" into the address bar. (In this case, the URL was "www.Company1.com/boyle.txt" and a 404.19 error was returned. This is different than a common 404.0 error. Your website should *not* load correctly. The request was denied because it contained the prohibited string.)
58. Press Enter. (See Figure 21-67.)
59. Take a screenshot of the error message.

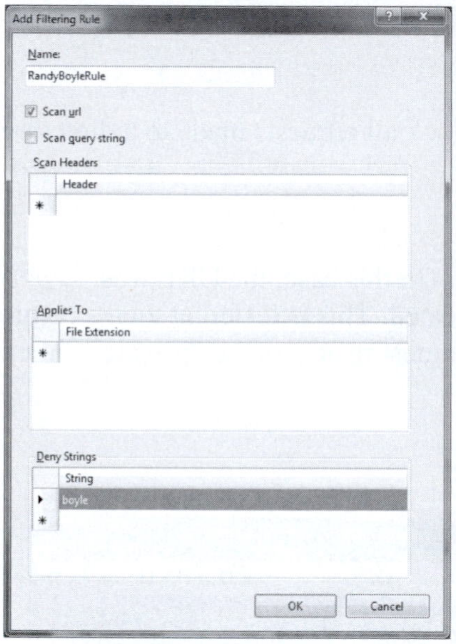

Figure 21-66: Adding in a string of characters that will be denied.

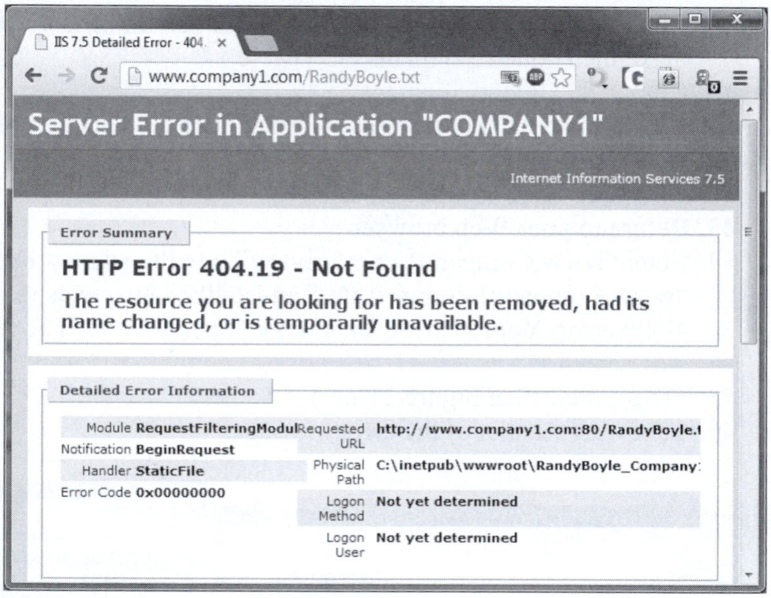

Figure 21-67: A 404.19 error returned due to a restricted string being sent in the URL.

60. Return to the IIS Manager window.
61. Click on the Company1 website.
62. Double-click the Request Filtering icon in the IIS section.
63. Click on the Edit Feature Settings link in the right-hand pane.
64. Change the Maximum URL length (Bytes) to 5. (This rule will set the maximum URL length so small that it will deny all requests.)
65. Click OK. (See Figure 21-68.)
66. Return to your Web browser.
67. Enter "www.Company1.com" into the address bar. (In this case, the URL was "www.Company1.com" and a 404.14 error was returned. This is different than a common 404.0 error. Your website should *not* load correctly. Reducing the maximum URL length can prevent

attacks that rely on the ability to send in very long URLs. You can change the Maximum URL length back to 4,096 so your site will load properly.)

68. Press Enter. (See Figure 21-69.)
69. Take a screenshot of the error message.

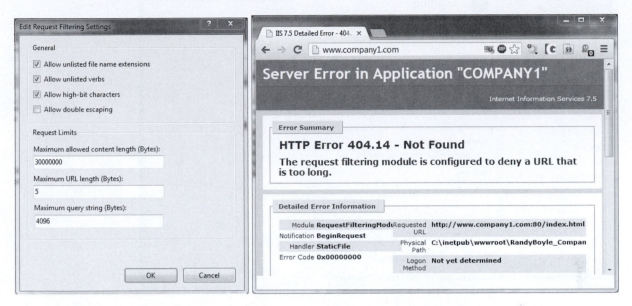

Figure 21-68: Setting the Maximum URL length arbitrarily low.

Figure 21-69: A 404.14 error returned due to a URL that is too long.

70. Return to the IIS Manager window.
71. Click on the Company1 website.
72. Double-click the Logging icon in the IIS section.
73. Note the directory in which the logs are stored. (In this case, it was C:\inetpub\logs\LogFiles.) (See Figure 21-70.)

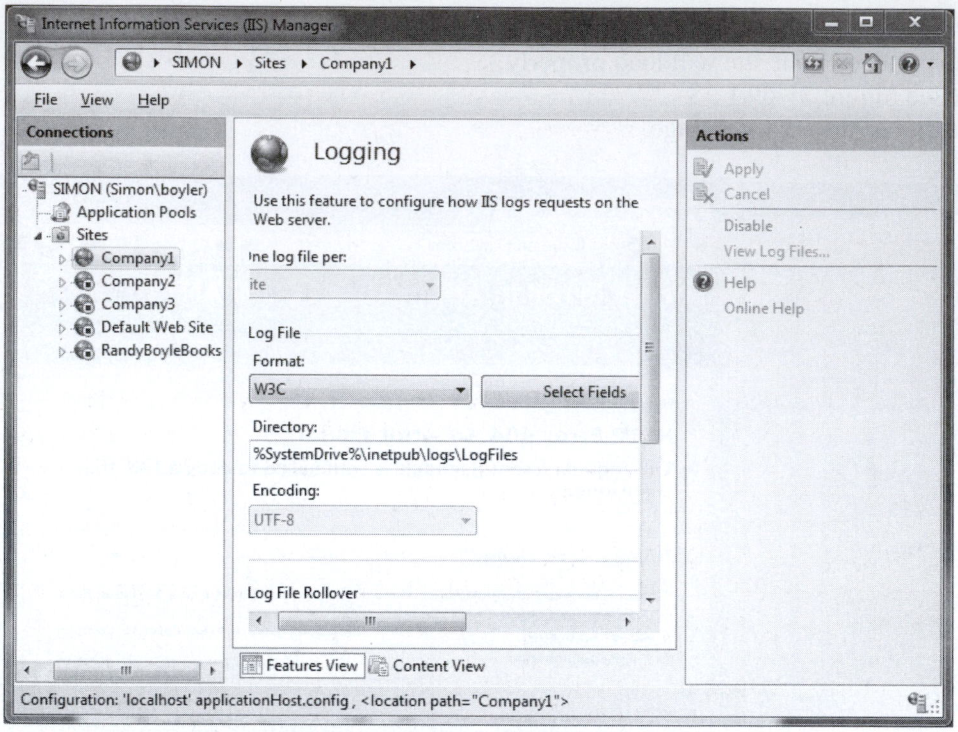

Figure 21-70: IIS logging configuration screen.

74. Click Start, Accessories, and Windows Explorer.
75. Browse to C:\inetpub\logs\LogFiles.
76. Open the folder that was most recently modified.
77. Open the text file with the most recent Date modified.
78. Expand your text window so you can completely see each entry.
79. Take a screenshot of your log file showing your errors. (Note the timestamps, files requested, information about the browser making the request, and the specific error message sent at the end of the entry.) (See Figure 21-71.)

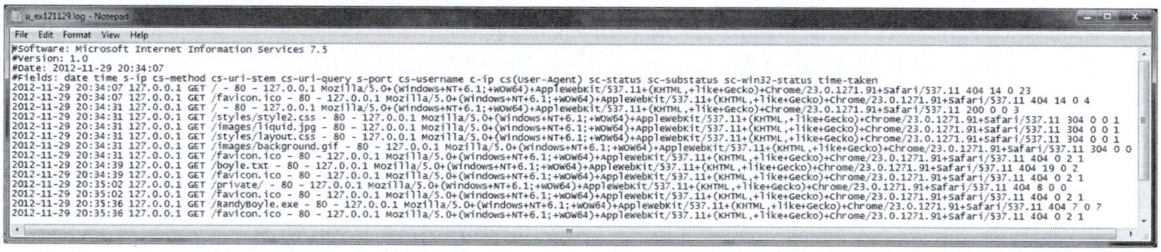

Figure 21-71: IIS error log.

PROJECT QUESTIONS

1. What was the path where your website was stored?
2. What was the name of your website?
3. What was the name of the .exe file you entered into the URL?
4. What was the name of the .txt file you entered into the URL?

THOUGHT QUESTIONS

1. How could filtering certain extension types help secure your Web server?
2. How could filtering certain directories help secure your Web server?
3. How could filtering certain key words help secure your Web server?
4. How could setting a limit to the length of URL requests help secure your Web server?

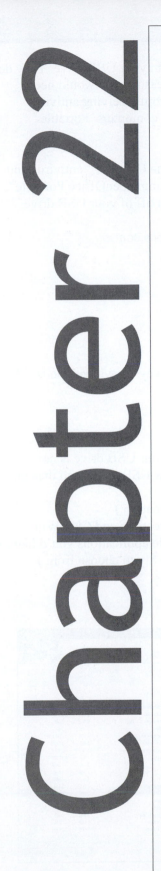

Below are a few miscellaneous tools that are important for IT security students to learn how to use. IT security professionals use them every day and you'll need to know them. This is just a small sampling of the vast number of additional IT security tools available. A large number of books could be written about the litany of useful IT security tools. We wish there was room for all of them.

Having an array of useful tools and knowing how to use them will increase your personal IT skill set and the value you add to an organization. Reading and actively searching for new IT security tools should be a daily event. You just need to get into the habit of reading about, testing, and implementing new tools. IT security professionals are lucky to be in such a dynamic field that is changing every day. You'll never be bored.

Time required to complete this chapter: 60 minutes

Chapter Objectives

Learn how to:
1. Run portable applications.
2. Remotely access a computer.
3. Identify running processes.
4. Change a MAC address.
5. Use a binder to create an executable.
6. Cause and prevent a buffer overflow.
7. Split and recombine a large file.
8. Use a USB to secure a computer.

Chapter Projects

Project:
22.1 Portable Applications
22.2 Remote Desktop
22.3 Process Explorer
22.4 Change MAC Address
22.5 Binders (IExpress)
22.6 Buffer Overflow
22.7 File Splitting
22.8 USB Lock (Predator)

22.1 PORTABLE APPLICATIONS

In this project, you will load a set of portable applications that can be run from your USB drive. They do not have to be installed on the local computer. Viruses are one of the many reasons you would need portable applications. Some of the more recent virus variants prevent users from receiving antivirus updates, visiting antivirus websites, and installing antivirus software on their computers. Portable applications solve all of these issues.

We will only look at a small number of applications. You are going to load the ClamAV® antivirus and run a scan of your local machine. You are also going to create a document using OpenOffice Portable®, delete it, and then use Recuva to recover the document. All of this will be run off of your USB drive.

Feel free to browse the entire list of portable applications at www.PortableApps.com.

1. Insert a USB drive with 2 GB or more of free space.
2. Open a Web browser.
3. Download PortableApps® from http://portableapps.com.
4. Click Download.
5. Click Download Now.
6. Save the download in your C:\security folder.
7. Right-click on the PortableApps.com_Platform_Setup_11.2.exe. (Always download the latest version available. There will likely be a newer version available.)
8. Click Run as administrator.
9. Click Yes, if prompted.
10. Click OK, Next, and I Agree.
11. Make sure your USB drive is selected as the Destination Folder. (If your USB drive is not selected as the Destination Folder, you must click Browse, select your USB drive, and then click OK. In this case, the USB drive was the E: drive.) (See Figure 22-1.)
12. Click Install, and Finish. (This should launch the Portable Apps application.)
13. Scroll down and select Notepad++ Portable under the Development section, and ClamWin Portable under the Security section. (You can select any other portable applications you'd like to load on your USB before continuing on to the next step. There are plenty to choose from.)
14. Click Next. (See Figure 22-2.)
15. Click OK when it finishes.

Figure 22-1: Choosing an installation location.   Figure 22-2: Portable application directory.

16. Click the PortableApps icon on the taskbar. (It is also available as a notification icon.)
17. Click Notepad++ Portable. (See Figure 22-3.)
18. Type your name, then "Notepad++ Portable", and the date. (In this case, it was Randy Boyle, Notepad++ Portable, and 12/1/2012.)
19. Take a screenshot with your name showing. (See Figure 22-4.)

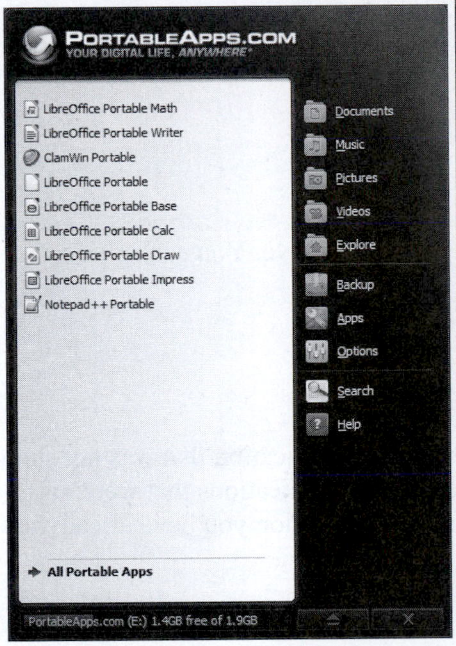

Figure 22-3: Installed portable applications. 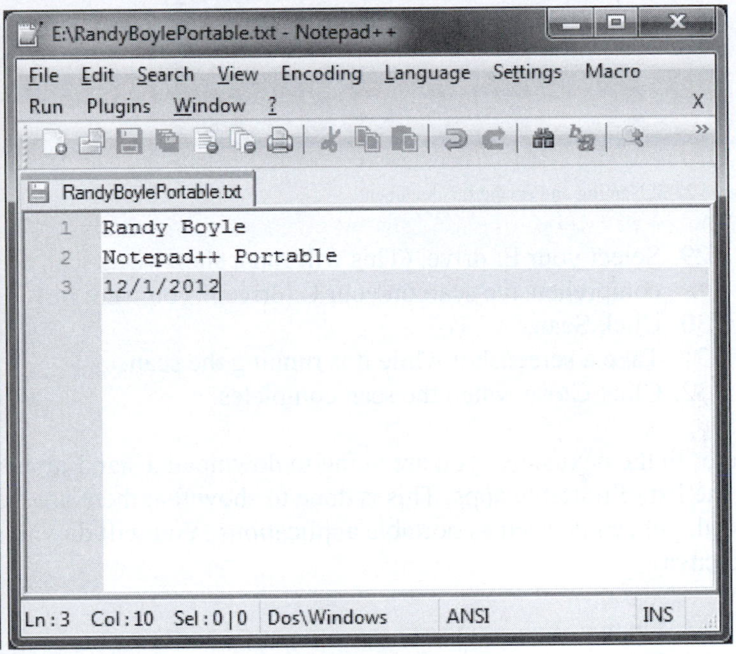   Figure 22-4: Notepad++ document.

20. Click File, and SaveAs.
21. Select your USB drive as the location. (In this case, it was the E: drive.)
22. Name the file YourNamePortable.txt. (In this case, it was RandyBoylePortable.txt.)
23. Click Save. (You are going to delete and recover this file later in this project.)
24. Close the Notepad++ window. (See Figure 22-5.)
25. Click the PortableApps icon on the taskbar. (It is also available as a notification icon.)
26. Click the ClamWin Portable icon.
27. Click Yes, if you are asked to download the virus definitions database. (The first time you run ClamWin, it will take several minutes to download all of the virus definitions. It won't require substantial updates each time.)
28. Click Close, when it finishes.

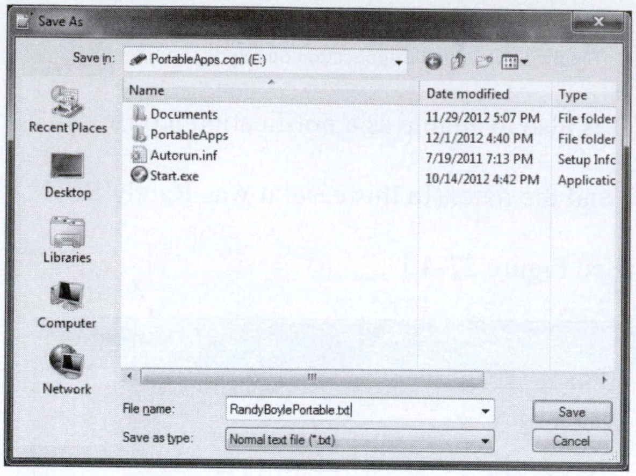

Figure 22-5: Naming and saving the document.

29. Select your E: drive. (This will run a short virus scan on your USB drive. You can run a more comprehensive scan on your C: drive if you want to.)
30. Click Scan.
31. Take a screenshot while it is running the scan.
32. Click Close, when the scan completes.

Note: In the next steps, you are going to download a stand-alone portable application that was not shown in the list of portable apps. This is done to show that there are many other applications that were not listed, yet can be used as portable applications. You will download an application you have already used (Recuva).

33. Open a Web browser.
34. Browse to http://www.Pendrivepps.com.
35. Search for "Recuva" in the Google Custom Search box within www.Pendriveapps.com.
36. Click on the first link. (It should point to the page listing Recuva – Portable File Recovery Tool.)
37. Scroll down and click on the Download link.
38. Save the download to your USB drive.
39. Open Windows Explorer.
40. Browse to your E: drive.
41. Right-click on the rcsetup144.zip file. (The version number will undoubtedly be different when you download your version of Recuva.)
42. Click Extract All, and Extract.
43. Browse to the Recuva directory on your USB. (In this case, it was E:\rcsetup144.)
44. Right-click on Recuva64.exe (or recuva.exe if you have a 32-bit system). (See Figure 22-6.)
45. Click Run as administrator.
46. Click Yes.
47. Select Do not show this Wizard on startup.
48. Click Cancel.
49. Select your USB drive. (In this case, it was the E: drive.) (See Figure 22-7.)

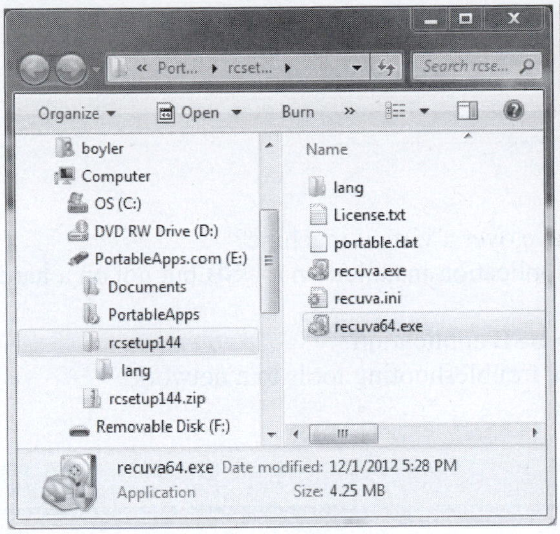

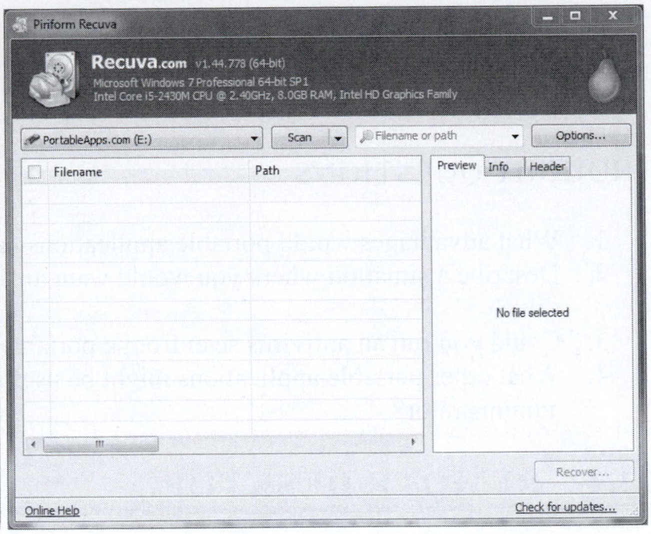

Figure 22-6: Recuva options.

Figure 22-7: Recuva Wizard.

50. Return to Windows Explorer.
51. Delete the file you just saved in Notepad++. (In this case, it was RandyBoylePortable.txt.)
52. Return to Recuva.
53. Click Scan.
54. Select the file you just deleted.
55. Take a screenshot of the Recuva window with your deleted document showing. (See Figure 22-8.)
56. Click Recover.
57. Select your USB drive.
58. Click OK, Yes, and OK.
59. Take a screenshot of the recovered document in your USB drive. (See Figure 22-9.)

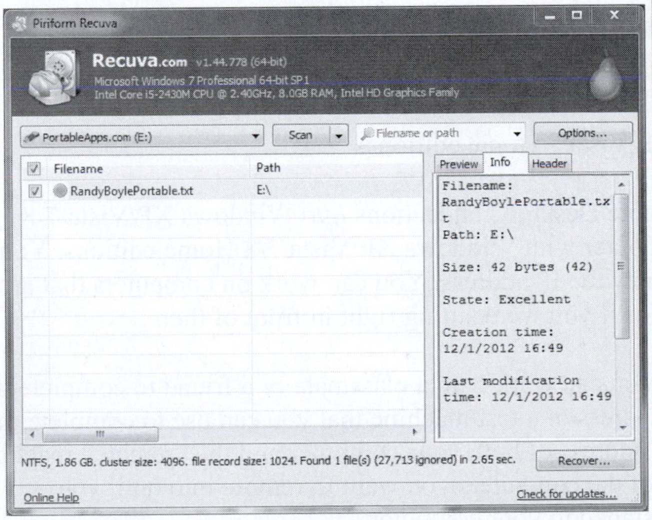

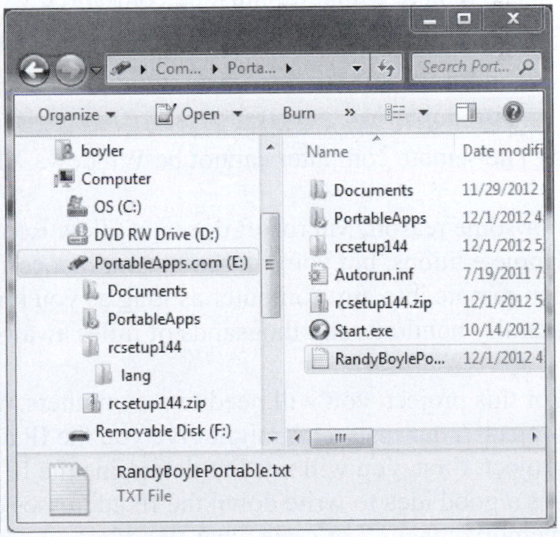

Figure 22-8: Recovered file on a USB drive.

Figure 22-9: Recovered document.

PROJECT QUESTIONS

1. What date was listed in the file you created?

2. What was the name of the file you deleted and recovered?
3. Did Recuva find any other files? How many?
4. About how long did the antivirus scan take?

THOUGHT QUESTIONS

1. What advantages would portable applications have over a virtual machine?
2. Describe a situation where you would want an application installed on a USB but not on a hard drive.
3. Could you run an antivirus scan from a portable USB application?
4. What other portable applications might be useful troubleshooting tools to a network administrator?

22.2   REMOTE DESKTOP®

Remote Desktop® is an extremely useful tool for IT professionals. It allows you to log in to a remote computer as if it were a local machine. You would then have access to drives and printers on both machines. Remote Desktop comes pre-loaded on all Windows-based computers that have Microsoft Windows XP, Windows 7, or Windows 8. The ability to remotely administer a computer or system is nice because an administrator can work in multiple machines in different locations simultaneously without having to physically access the console of each server.

Many employees and employers are taking advantage of working remotely from home. The cost savings for all parties involved are tremendous (e.g., reduced commercial office space, no commute, flexible hours, environmentally friendly, etc.). Remote Desktop is also compatible with Mac OS and most Linux distributions. In order for Remote Desktop to work correctly, make sure you check the following:

1) The remote computer must be turned on.

2) The remote computer must be configured with a password protected user account.

3) The remote computer must have Remote Desktop connections enabled.

4) The firewall of the remote computer must be configured to allow Remote Desktop connections through port 3389.

5) The remote computer cannot be Windows XP/Vista/7 Home editions.

For some reason, Microsoft does not allow Remote Desktop connections *into* Windows XP/Vista/7/8 Home editions, but you can remote *out of* a computer with Windows XP/Vista/7/8 Home editions. You can remote into any computer as long as you know the IP address. You can work on computers that are literally hundreds and thousands of miles away as if you were sitting right in front of them.

For this project, you will need two computers. You can work with a classmate or a friend to complete the project. Your instructor might give you the IP address of a test machine that you can use to complete this project. First, you will need to determine the IP address of both your computer and the "remote" machine. It's a good idea to write down the IP addresses of the computers you want to remote into until you memorize them. Let's see what IP address is assigned to your computer.

1. Click Start, Control Panel, System and Security, System, and Remote Settings.
2. Click on the Remote tab.
3. Select "Allow connections from computers running any version of Remote Desktop (less secure)." (See Figure 22-10.)
4. Click OK.

5. Click Start, Control Panel, System and Security, and Windows Firewall.
6. Click "Allow a program or feature through Windows Firewall."
7. Scroll down and make sure Remote Desktop is selected. (See Figure 22-11.)
8. Click OK.
9. Open a command prompt by clicking Start, All Programs, Accessories, and Command Prompt.
10. Type `ipconfig /all`
11. Write down your IP address. (In this example, it was 10.0.1.14. This is a non-routable IP address that is not accessible over the Internet. In this case, RDP was being used on a local private network. Your IP address will be different.)
12. Go to another computer. (This could be a friend's computer or another computer in your house.)

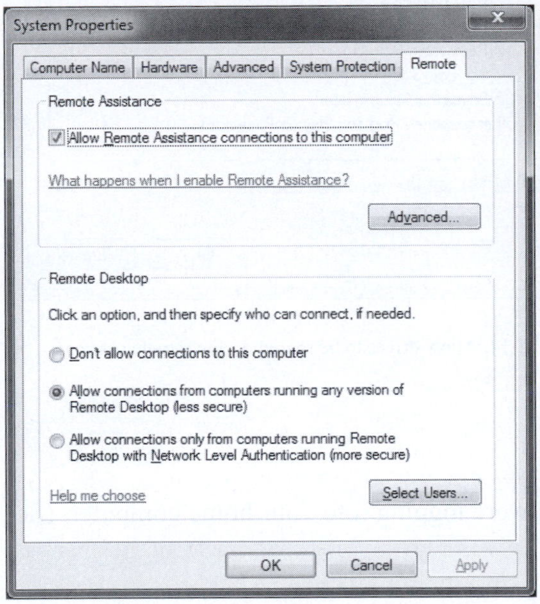

Figure 22-10: Windows remote settings.

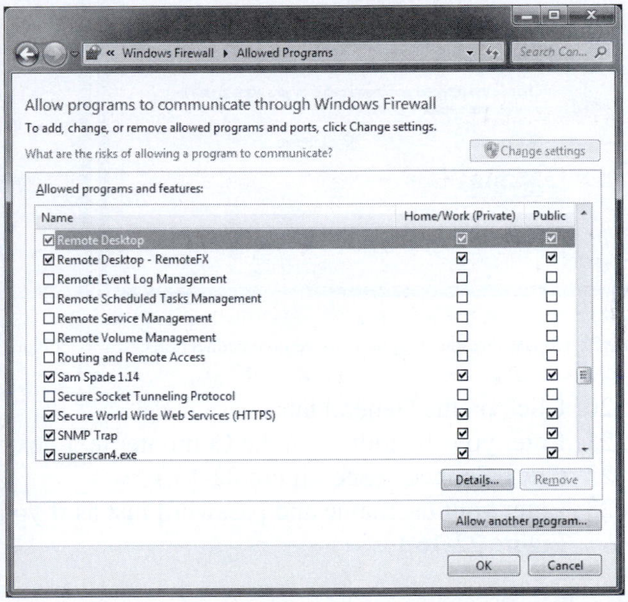

Figure 22-11: Allow Remote Desktop through your firewall.

Figure 22-12: Remote Desktop connection.

13. Click Start, All Programs, Accessories, and Remote Desktop Connection. (See Figure 22-12.)
14. Click Show Options.
15. Click Local Resources. (See Figure 22-13.)
16. Select Printers, and Clipboard.
17. Click More.
18. Select all of the options for Drives. (See Figure 22-14.)
19. Click OK.

Figure 22-13: Local resource options for remote connections.

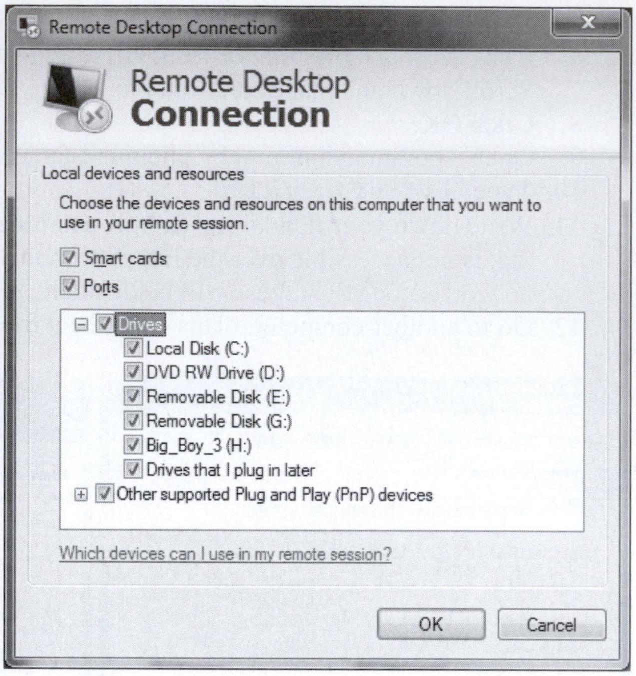

Figure 22-14: Allow drives to be shared during remote sessions.

20. Click on the General tab.
21. Enter your IP address in the Computer text box.
22. Click Connect. (See Figure 22-15.)
23. Enter your username and password just as if you were logging into your home computer. (See Figure 22-16.)

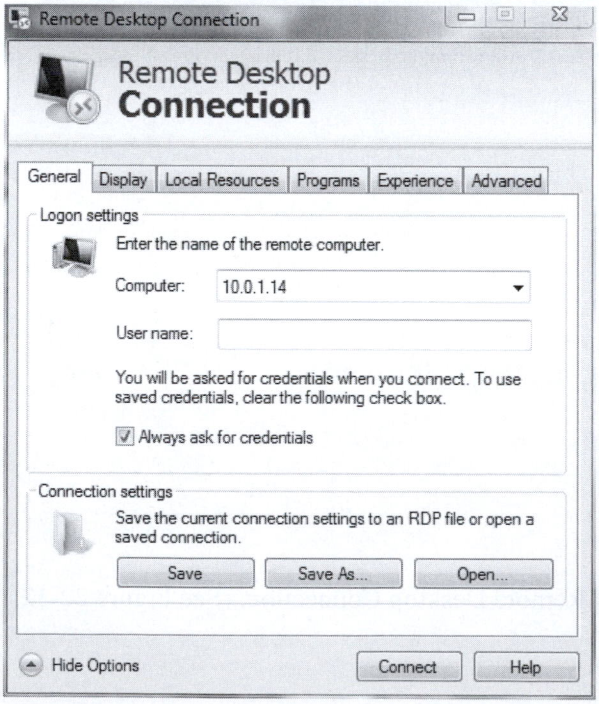

Figure 22-15: Remote Desktop connection.

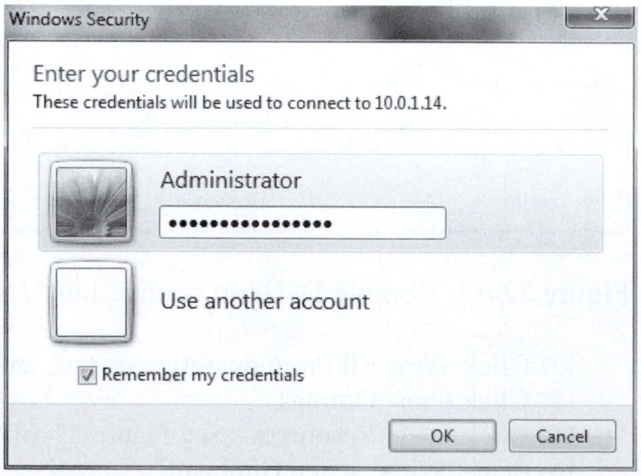

Figure 22-16: Login for remote connection.

24. Click the Restore Down button in the top right-hand corner of the window so the remote desktop will be a smaller window, and so you can take a screenshot of the whole window.
25. Take a screenshot of your whole local desktop with the Remote Desktop window in the middle using the Ctrl+PrintScreen key sequence. (See Figure 22-17.)

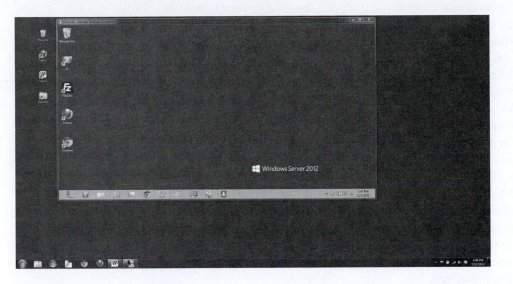

Figure 22-17: Working remotely.

PROJECT QUESTIONS

1. What was the IP address of the local computer you used?
2. What was the IP address of the remote computer you accessed?
3. What was the username you used?
4. Were the clocks synchronized on both the remote and local computers?

THOUGHT QUESTIONS

1. Can you remote into more than one computer at a time?
2. Can you remote through a chain of multiple computers?
3. Can you copy files from a remote desktop and paste them to the local desktop?
4. What keeps the bad guys from using remote desktop to access your computer?

22.3 PROCESS EXPLORER®

Even though you may only be running two programs (i.e., MS Word and Firefox) you will likely have a couple dozen processes running behind the scenes. Viruses, worms, and malware can run as processes without the user even knowing they are loaded into memory. Faulty programs can also take up large amounts of physical memory or CPU speed. It's critical to have the ability to identify the offending program and/or process and kill it.

IT security professionals use Process Explorer® (or a program similar to it) all the time. They need to know exactly which programs and processes are running. They also need to know which DLLs are being used, the location of the process, what the process does, who made it, if it's sending or receiving information, etc. Process Explorer turns out to be an invaluable diagnostic tool. Let's go through a simple example to see just a few of the more basic functionalities.

1. Download Process Explorer from http://technet.microsoft.com/en-us/sysinternals/bb896653.aspx.
2. Click Download Process Explorer.
3. Click Save.
4. Select your C:\security folder.
5. If the program doesn't automatically open, browse to your C:\security folder.
6. Right-click on ProcessExplorer.zip.
7. Select Extract All, and Extract.
8. Browse to C:\security\ProcessExplorer.
9. Right-click on procexp.exe and select Run as administrator. (If you find this to be a useful tool, you might want to make it a shortcut on your desktop.)
10. Open a Web browser. (In this case, it was Google Chrome.)
11. Scroll down the list of open processes until you find your Web browser.
12. Select your Web browser. (See Figure 22-18.)
13. Take a screenshot.
14. Double-click the line with your Web browser highlighted. (See Figure 22-19.)
15. Take a screenshot.
16. Click on the TCP/IP tab.
17. Click Refresh in your Web browser. (You can also press F5.)
18. Note the local computer and ports listed. (You can watch them slowly disappear as the TCP connections are closed.)
19. Click on the Image tab.
20. Click Kill Process, to close your browser.
21. Click Yes, if prompted.
22. Click OK, to close the properties window for that process.

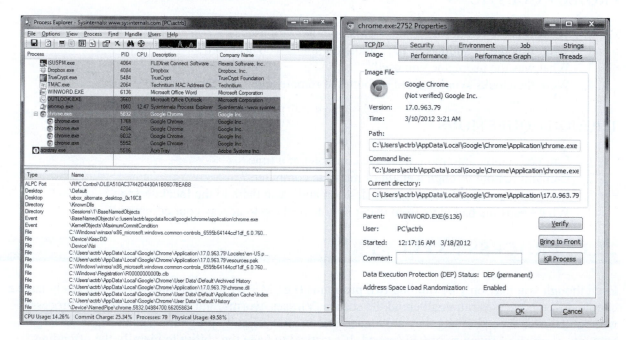

Figure 22-18: Processes shown with chrome.exe highlighted.   Figure 22-19: Details for chrome.exe.

23. In Process Explorer, click View, and System Information. (See Figure 22-20.)
24. Take a screenshot.
25. Click OK to close the System Information window.
26. Click View, Lower Pane View, and DLLs. (See Figure 22-21.)
27. Take a screenshot.

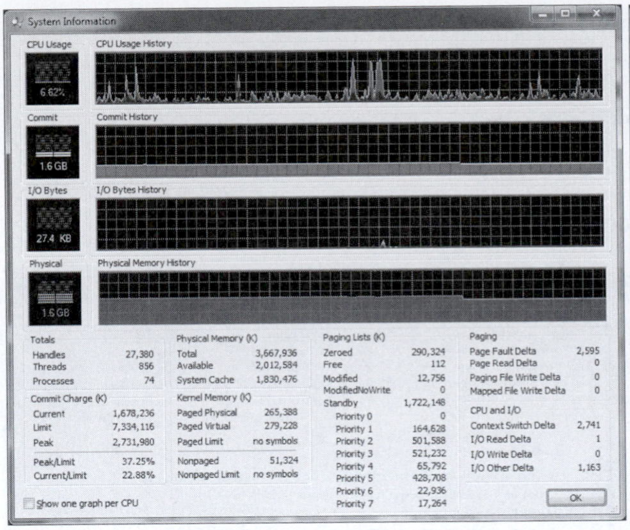

Figure 22-20: System information.

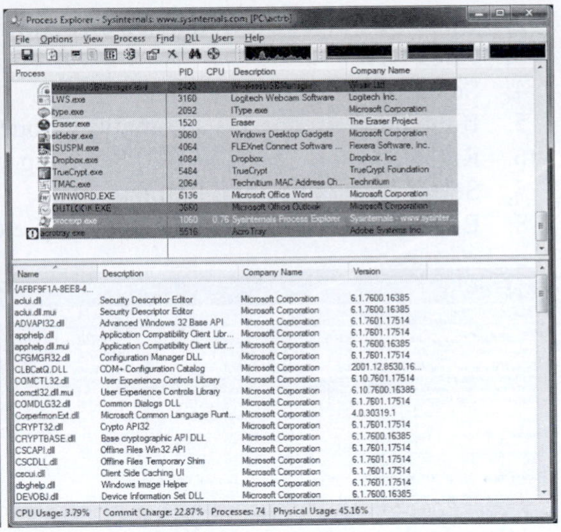

Figure 22-21: Detailed DLL information.

PROJECT QUESTIONS

1. Which Web browser did you open?
2. What was the process number for your Web browser, shown in the main Process Explorer window?
3. How much CPU power are you using?
4. How much total physical memory does your computer have?

THOUGHT QUESTIONS

1. Why are all these processes started?
2. Can you keep these processes from starting? How?
3. Are there any processes you recognize or don't recognize?
4. What do DLLs do and why are they associated with a specific process?

22.4   CHANGE MAC ADDRESS

A security concern with wireless networks is that packets are tagged with each sender's MAC address. Bad guys can use a promiscuous packet sniffer and learn the MAC addresses of all wireless clients on a network. This information could pose a potential security risk. A malicious person could redirect wireless traffic from any host.

There are also privacy concerns. User activity can be monitored and tracked by any number of organizations based on MAC addresses. Privacy advocates worry that tracking information based on MAC addresses could be used inappropriately and violate basic civil rights.

Being able to change MAC addresses can facilitate an exact copy of an existing system for a hot-site backup. If a company is using an application that requires specific registered MAC addresses, then an exact duplicate would be necessary. Being able to change MAC addresses is also a great tool to help troubleshoot network problems. Let's look at a tool that can change your MAC address.

1. Download MAC Address Changer v6.0.3® from http://tmac.technitium.com/tmac/index.html.

2. Click Download Now, and Download Link 1.
3. Click Save.
4. Select your C:\security folder.
5. If the program doesn't automatically open, browse to your C:\security folder.
6. Right-click on TMACv6.0.3_Setup.zip.
7. Select Extract All, and Extract.
8. Browse to C:\security\TMACv6.0.3_Setup.

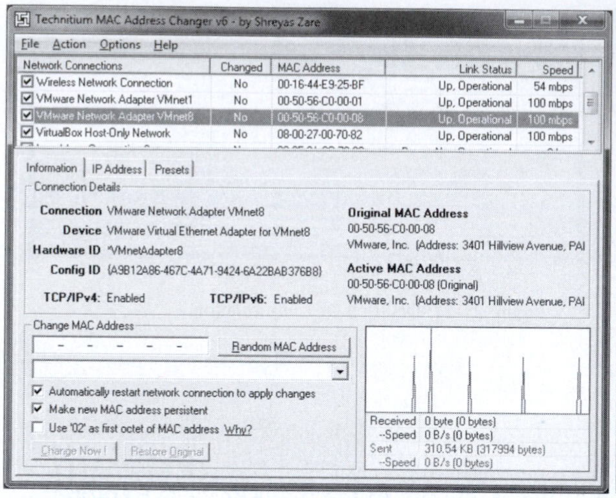

Figure 22-22: List of your network adapters.

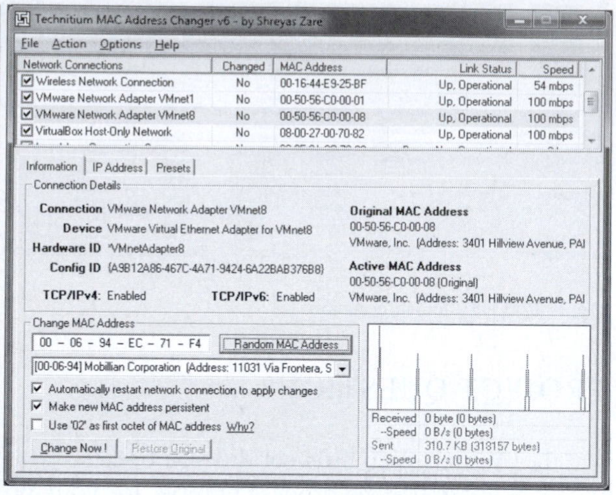

Figure 22-23: Changing your MAC address.

9. Right-click on TMACv6.0.3_Setup.exe and select Run as administrator.
10. Click Next, I Agree, Next, Next, Next, Finish.
11. Right-click the TMACv6 icon on your desktop and select Run as administrator.
12. Click on one of the VMware virtual network adapters. (You should have at least one of them visible from the prior VMware project. If not, you can use any existing NIC.) (See Figure 22-22.)
13. Click Random MAC Address. (See Figure 22-23.)
14. Click Change Now!
15. Click OK.
16. Click on the adapter you just changed.
17. Take a screenshot.

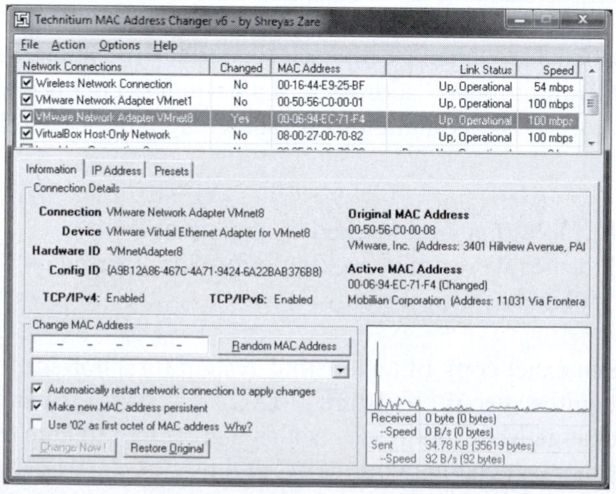

Figure 22-24: Change your MAC address back.

18. Select the same network adapter you just changed.
19. Click Restore Original. (See Figure 22-24.)
20. Click OK.
21. Take a screenshot.

PROJECT QUESTIONS

1. Which network adapter did you choose?
2. What was the original MAC address of the adapter you chose?
3. What was the new MAC address?
4. What was the approximate network speed for the adapter you chose?

THOUGHT QUESTIONS

1. How could a large organization benefit from changing their MAC addresses?
2. Do certain Web-based applications filter requests based on MAC address?
3. Why do we need MAC addresses? Aren't IP addresses sufficient?
4. What would happen if there were two computers with the same MAC address on the same network?

22.5   BINDERS (IEXPRESS®)

A binder is a tool that can combine multiple separate programs into a single executable. Typical binders can bind any file type or program, encrypt/decrypt files, move each file to a designated directory on extraction, run each program on extraction, add bound programs to startup, and self-destroy itself on extraction. Binders can save a system administrator time if he or she has to configure many different hosts. A single executable can install and run several disparate programs with a single click.

Binders are also important to study in a security setting because they are one of the tools that can be used to create malicious software. Showing you that binders do exist, and can potentially be used to bind malicious software with legitimate software, helps you learn not to click on every executable program you get as an attachment in an email. Binders, like any tool, can be used for good or bad purposes.

In this example you will not use a fully functional binder (or "dropper"). Instead, you will use a simple application (IExpress®) that comes with Windows and performs some of the functionality listed above. This application can be useful if you are installing software across multiple machines. If you are working with less experienced users, it will really speed up the installation process.

Creating your own installation program gives you more control over the installation process. It can also force your users to reboot their computers if necessary. This project will create a simple installer that will run two applications (iexplore.exe and explorer.exe) that come with Windows.

1. Click Start.
2. Type "iexpress" into the search box in the Start menu.
3. Press Enter. (IExpress Wizard should start automatically.)
4. Make sure "Create new Self Extracting Directive file" is selected. (See Figure 22-25.)
5. Click Next.
6. Make sure "Extract files and run an installation command" is selected.
7. Click Next.
8. Enter YourNameInstaller for the package title. (In this case, it was RandyBoyleInstaller.)

9. Take a screenshot. (See Figure 22-26.)

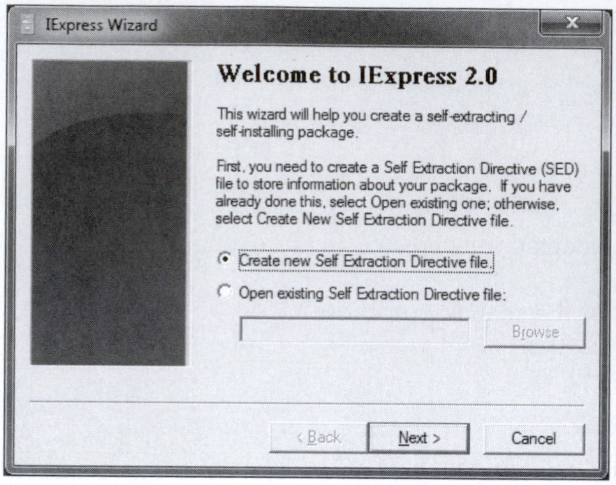

Figure 22-25: Creating the SED.

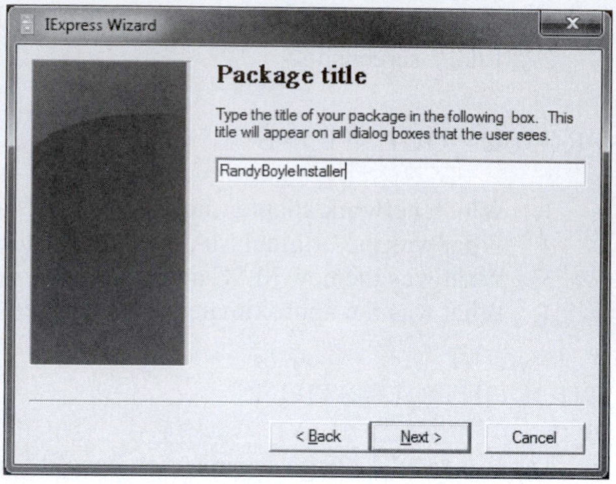

Figure 22-26: Naming the package.

10. Make sure "No prompt" is selected.
11. Click Next.
12. Make sure "Do not display a license" is selected.
13. Click Next.
14. Click Add.
15. Browse to C:\Program Files\Internet Explorer.
16. Select iexplore.exe. (See Figure 22-27.)
17. Click Open.
18. Click Add (again).
19. Browse to C:\Windows.
20. Select explorer.exe. (See Figure 22-28.)
21. Click Open.

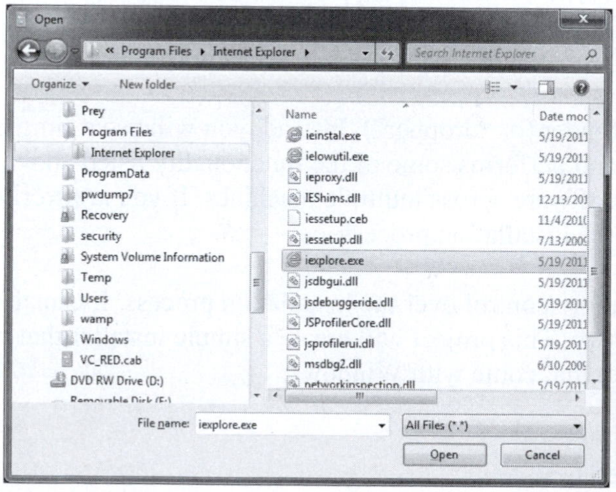

Figure 22-27: Selecting iexplore.exe.

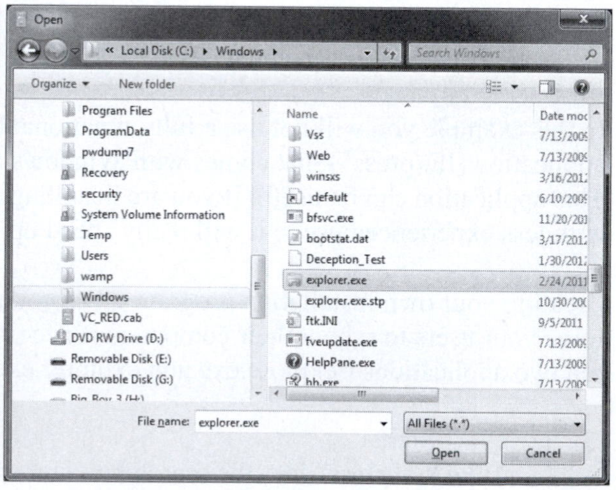

Figure 22-28: Selecting explorer.exe.

22. Click Next. (See Figure 22-29.)
23. Click Add.
24. Select iexplore.exe as the install program selection.
25. Select explorer.exe as the post install command. (See Figure 22-30.)

26. Click Next, and Next.

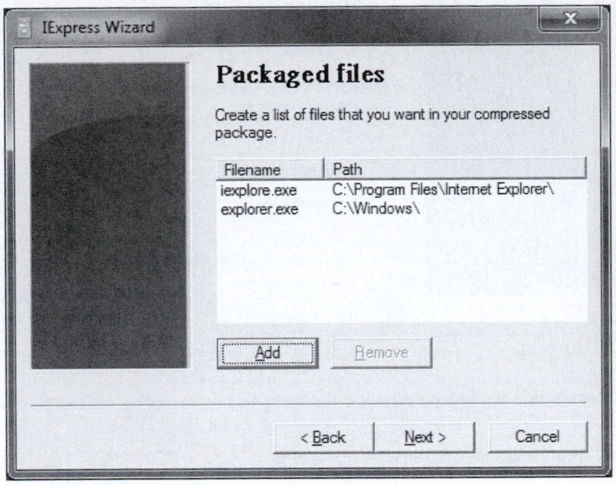

Figure 22-29: List of files in the SED.

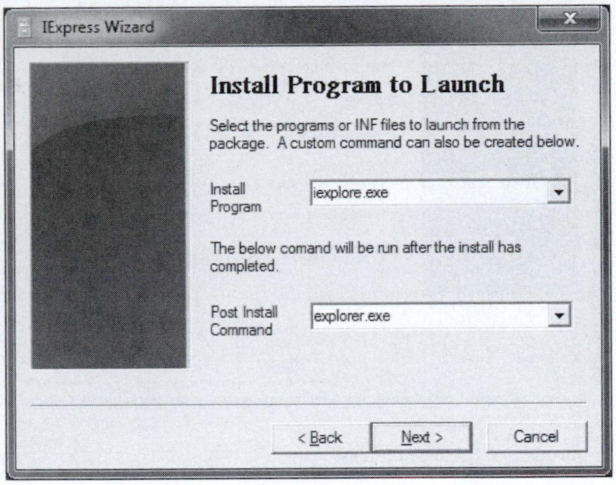

Figure 22-30: Designating the program to run at launch.

27. Select Display message.
28. Enter "YourName created a self-extracting file!" for the message, replacing YourName with your first and last name. (See Figure 22-31.)
29. Take a screenshot.
30. Click Next.
31. Click Browse.
32. Browse to C:\security\.
33. Name the file YournameInstaller.exe. (See Figure 22-32.)
34. Click Save.

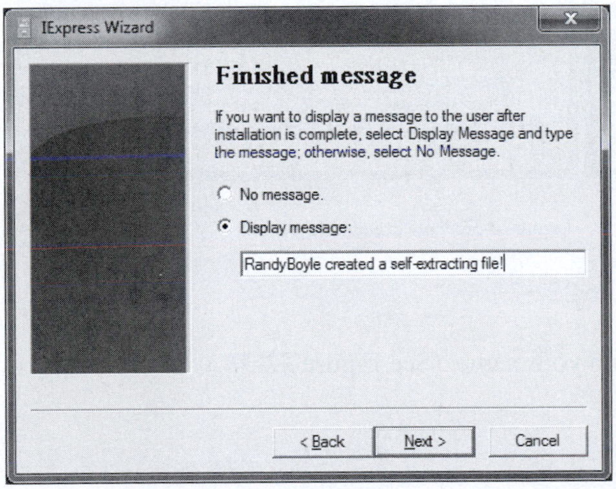

Figure 22-31: Message to display after installation.

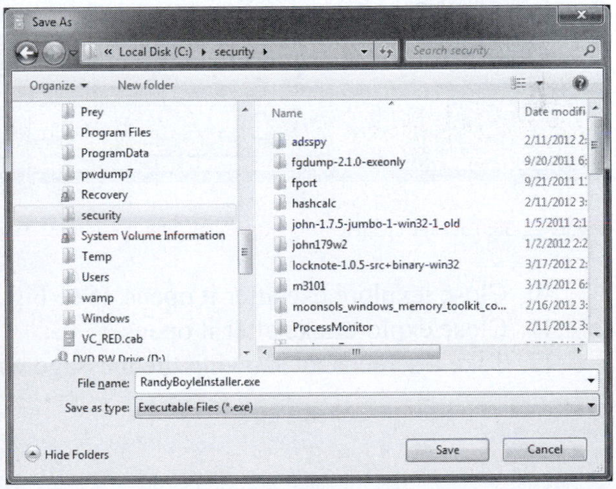

Figure 22-32: Naming the executable.

35. Click Next. (See Figure 22-33.)
36. Select No Restart. (See Figure 22-34.)
37. Click Next, Next, Next, and Finish. (See Figure 22-35.)

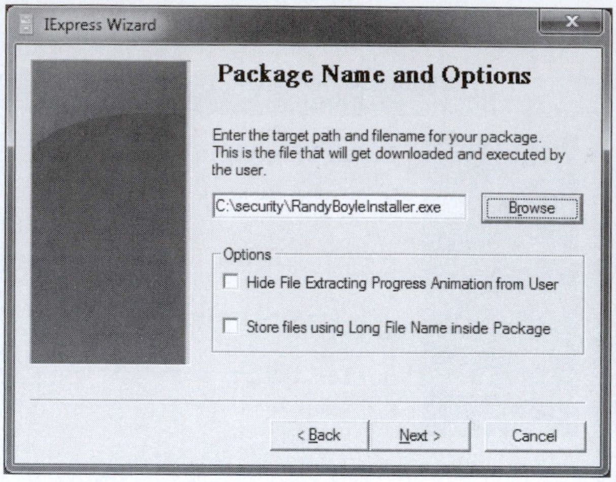

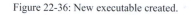

Figure 22-33: Package options.

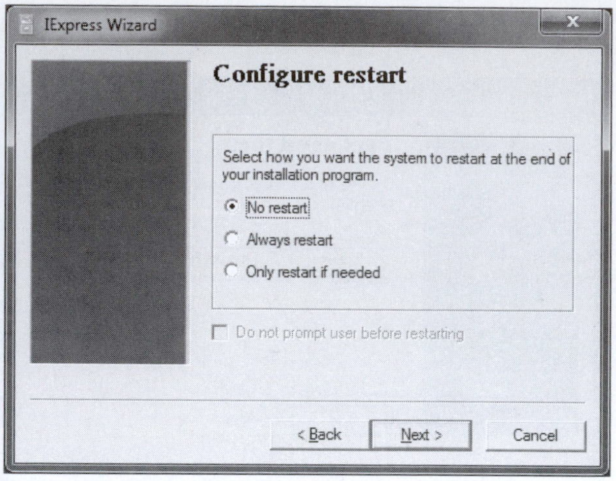

Figure 22-34: Options for restarting.

38. Browse to C:\security.
39. Double-click the YournameInstaller.exe file. (See Figure 22-36.)

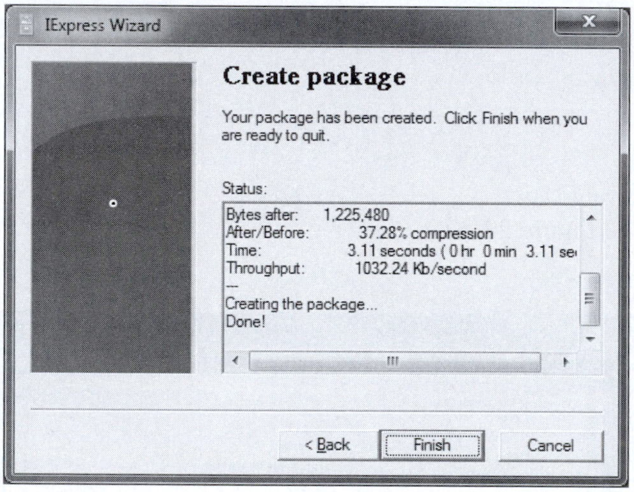

Figure 22-35: Package created.

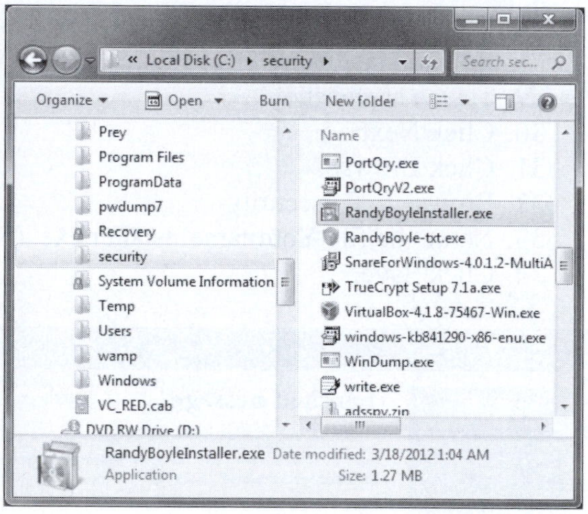

Figure 22-36: New executable created.

40. Close iexplore.exe after it opens. (See Figure 22-37.)
41. Close explorer.exe after it opens.
42. Take a screenshot showing the message with your name. (See Figure 22-38.)

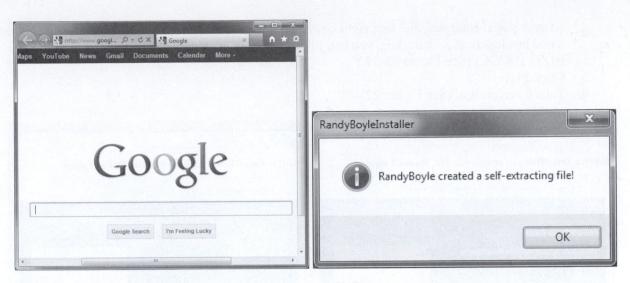

Figure 22-37: Internet Explorer.

Figure 22-38: Confirmation that file was created.

PROJECT QUESTIONS

1. What was the name of the executable you created?
2. What did the message say after the installer was done?
3. How long did it take to create the executable as shown in the screenshot you took?
4. What was the default website in the browser that opened?

THOUGHT QUESTIONS

1. Can you add more than just .exe files to the list of installation files?
2. Why do some installations require you to reboot your computer?
3. Give an example of when a network administrator might use this tool.
4. In addition to the .exe file, another file was created. What is in this second file?

22.6 BUFFER OVERFLOW

Buffer overflows are a fairly common vulnerability. They can crash an application, allow unauthorized access, process unintended payloads, etc. Most students who are new to the field of IT security have heard about buffer overflows but may not understand how they work.

The following online example is a demonstration of how a buffer overflow actually works. It really helps students understand how buffer overflows work if they can see a graphical representation of what is happening. They can better visualize the memory space, and how the overflow may affect the underlying code. The buffer overflow example shown below is just one example of a buffer overflow, written by Dr. Susan Gerhart.

1. Open a Web browser and go to http://nsfsecurity.pr.erau.edu/bom/. (Additional buffer overflow examples [e.g., BOallDemos.zip and BOallDemos.tar] are archived and available for download on this same page.)
2. Scroll down and click on the Spock link.
3. Click Play, or Run this time, if prompted.

4. After it stops, enter *only* the first eight characters of your last name as the password. (If your last name has less than 8 characters, you can fill in the last characters with "X"; in this case, BOYLEXXX.) (See Figure 22-39.)
5. Click Play.
6. Take a screenshot. (See Figure 22-40.)

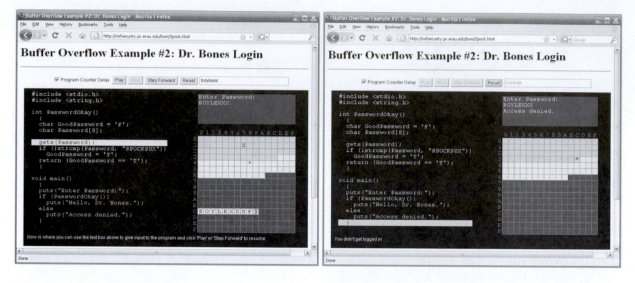

Figure 22-39: Entering an incorrect password.   Figure 22-40: Denied access.

7. Click Reset.
8. Click Play.
9. After it stops, enter *only* the first eight characters of your last name as the password *and* the upper-case letter "T" at the end. (If your last name has less than 8 characters, you can fill in the last characters with "X;" in this case, BOYLEXXXT.) (See Figure 22-41.)
10. Click Play.
11. Take a screenshot. (See Figure 22-42.)

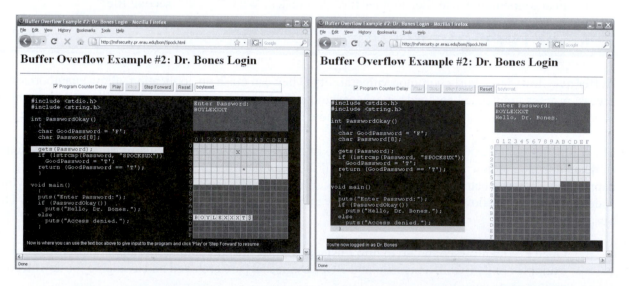

Figure 22-41: Incorrect password with "T" at the end.   Figure 22-42: Access granted.

PROJECT QUESTIONS

1. How long (in characters) is your last name?
2. What did you enter for your last name in Step 4?
3. What did you enter for your last name in Step 9?
4. What happened after you clicked Play in Step 10?

THOUGHT QUESTIONS

1. Why did the addition of the letter "T" allow you to bypass the login with a fake password?
2. What would happen if you entered a 15-character password consisting of all X's?
3. Could the code behind this login be fixed to stop this buffer overflow? How?
4. Are there different overflow attacks? (Hint: Look at the other examples shown.)

22.7 FILE SPLITTING

In this project, you are going to use 7-Zip to split a large file (an ISO image) into many smaller files. You will then delete the original file and recombine the split parts back into the original whole file. You can use any large file of your choosing. You should have several large Linux ISO images stored in your C:\security folder from prior projects.

Large data are becoming much more common. Cyber forensic investigators often store hundreds of hard drive images gathered as part of investigations. Corporations regularly store and transfer large data files between distributed corporate websites. Online retailers can gather terabytes, and even petabytes, of data on a daily basis. This tutorial will cover one simple tool that can be used to manage larger data files.

1. Download 7-Zip from http://www.7-zip.org.
2. Click Download.
3. Click on the appropriate version for your operating system. (In this case, it was the 64-bit Windows version. Download the latest version available.)
4. Click Save.
5. Select the C:\security folder.
6. If the program doesn't automatically open, browse to your C:\security folder.
7. Right-click on 7z920-x64.msi.
8. Click Install, Run, Next, I accept, Next, Next, Install, and Finish
9. Click Start, All Programs, 7-Zip, and 7-Zip File Manager.
10. Double-click Computer, C:, and your C:\security folder. (You should see several files in this directory with your name on them.)
11. Right-click on any file that is larger than 100MB. (In this case, it was a 710 MB Ubuntu ISO image. You should have several large ISO images available from prior projects. If you don't have any large files in that directory, you can copy any large file to this directory. You can get a number of large ISO images from www.DistroWatch.com.) (See Figure 22-43.)
12. Click Rename.
13. Rename it to YourNameBigFile.iso. (In this case, it was RandyBoyleBigFile.iso.) (See Figure 22-44.)

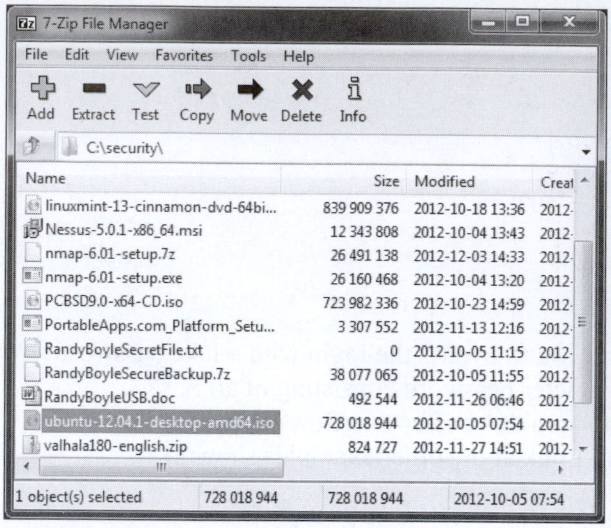

Figure 22-43: Selecting a large file to rename.

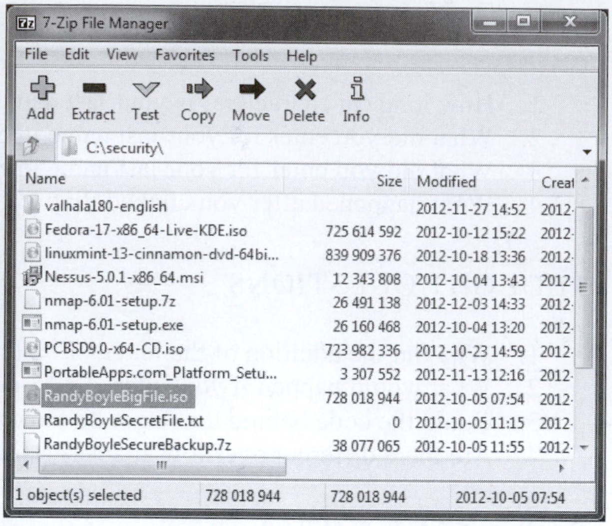

Figure 22-44: Large file is renamed.

14. Right-click on the YourNameBigFile.iso file. (In this case, it was RandyBoyleBigFile.iso.)
15. Click Split file, and OK. (This will split the large ISO image into smaller 10MB chunks.) (See Figure 22-45.)
16. Scroll down to the last of the new files created.
17. Take a screenshow showing the last of the new split files. (In this case, there were 70 files created.) (See Figure 22-46.)

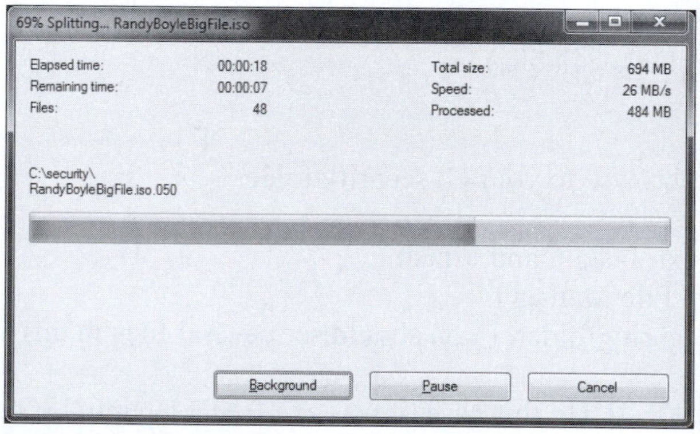

Figure 22-45: Splitting a large file.

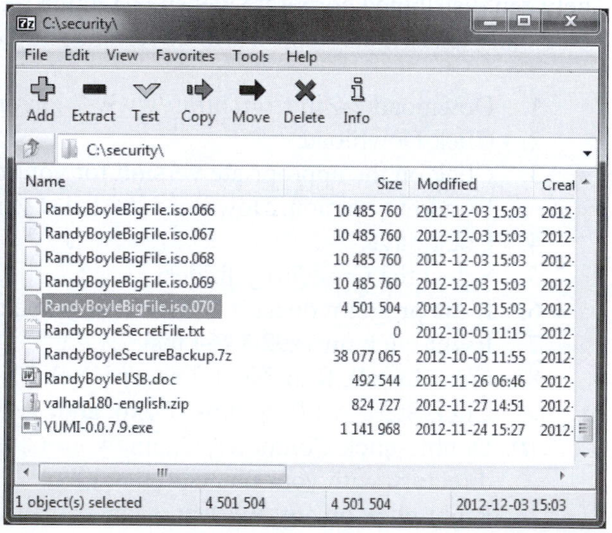

Figure 22-46: Split files created.

18. Scroll up and delete the original large ISO image you split.
19. Right-click on the first file created. (It should be labeled YourNameBigFile.iso.001. In this case, it was RandyBoyleBigFile.iso.001.)
20. Click Combine files.
21. Click OK. (This will recombine the split files. The newly recombined file will have a more recent creation date than the split files.)
22. Take a screenshow showing the newly combined ISO image. (See Figure 22-47.)

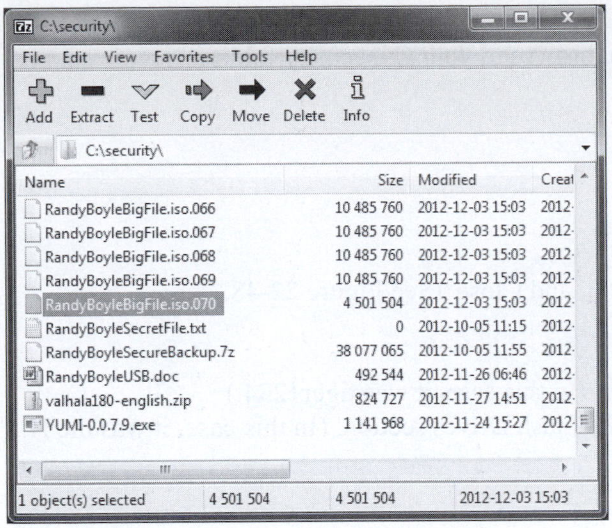

Figure 22-47: File recreated from split files.

PROJECT QUESTIONS

1. What was the name of your large file?
2. How many split files were created?
3. How big was the last file made during the splitting process?
4. About how long did it take to split the file?

THOUGHT QUESTIONS

1. Why would you need to know how to split a file?
2. Are some files so big that they cannot be stored on certain storage media?
3. How could you use a file splitter to secure important data?
4. Is it possible to both encrypt and split a file? How?

22.8   USB LOCK (PREDATOR®)

In this project, you will learn how to create a USB drive that will lock your computer when taken out. This USB lock can be a useful security tool in office workpaces. Modern office environments have large amounts of foot traffic around workplaces without locked doors. Workers oftentimes leave their desks without logging out.

Predator® is an application that will lock your USB when you step away from your workplace. In fact, it has the ability to lock multiple computers with a single USB drive. It can also allow multiple USB drives, carried by separate users, to access the same computer. If there is a need to control access to internal computing resources without spending a lot of money, Predator might be a viable option.

1. Download Predator from http://www.predator-usb.com.
2. Click Download.
3. Click Download Predator Free Edition.
4. Click Download Predator Free Edition for 64-bit Windows. (If you have a 32-bit system, you should download the 32-bit version. Most newer computers are 64-bit.)
5. Click Save.

6. Select your C:\security folder.
7. If the program doesn't automatically open, browse to your C:\security folder.
8. Right-click on InstallPredator_x64.zip.
9. Select Extract All, and Extract.
10. Browse to C:\security\InstallPredator_x64.
11. Right-click on InstallPredator.exe.
12. Select Run as administrator.
13. Click Yes, if prompted.
14. Click Next, I Agree, Next, Next, Next, Next, and Close. (See Figure 22-48.)
15. Insert a USB drive into your computer.
16. Click OK.
17. Enter a password you can easily remember. (In this case, it was tiger1234.)
18. Make sure your USB drive is selected in the Flash Drives section. (In this case, it was the H: drive.)
19. Click Create Key.
20. Take a screenshot. (See Figure 22-49.)
21. Click OK, and OK.

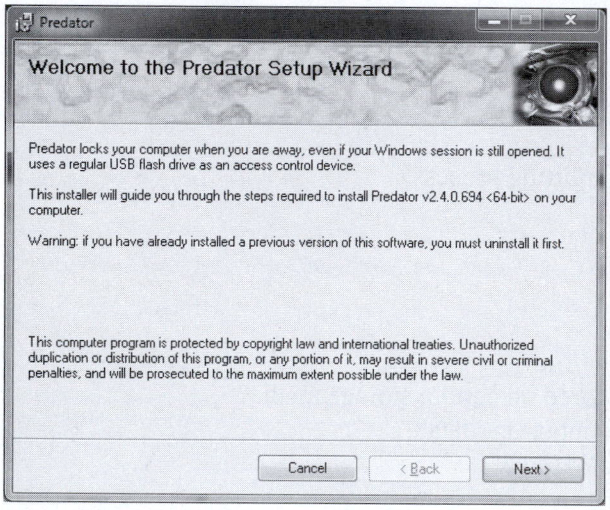

Figure 22-48: Predator setup.

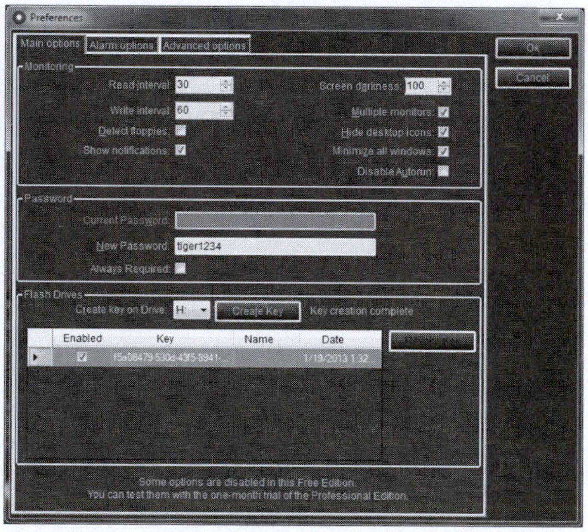

Figure 22-49: Predator Preferences screen.

Note: Predator should now be running. If it isn't running, you can double-click the Predator icon that was created on your desktop. You should see a green monitoring icon in your Notification Area Icons.

22. Remove your USB drive. (Your computer should go dark in a few seconds.)
23. Reinsert your USB drive. (Your computer should come back fairly quickly.)
24. Right-click the gree Predator icon in the Notification Area at the bottom-right-hand of your screen. (It may be hidden. If it is hidden, you can click on the small triangle to see the hidden notification icons.)
25. Click Show Log.
26. Take a screenshot. (See Figure 22-50.)
27. Close the Predator log.

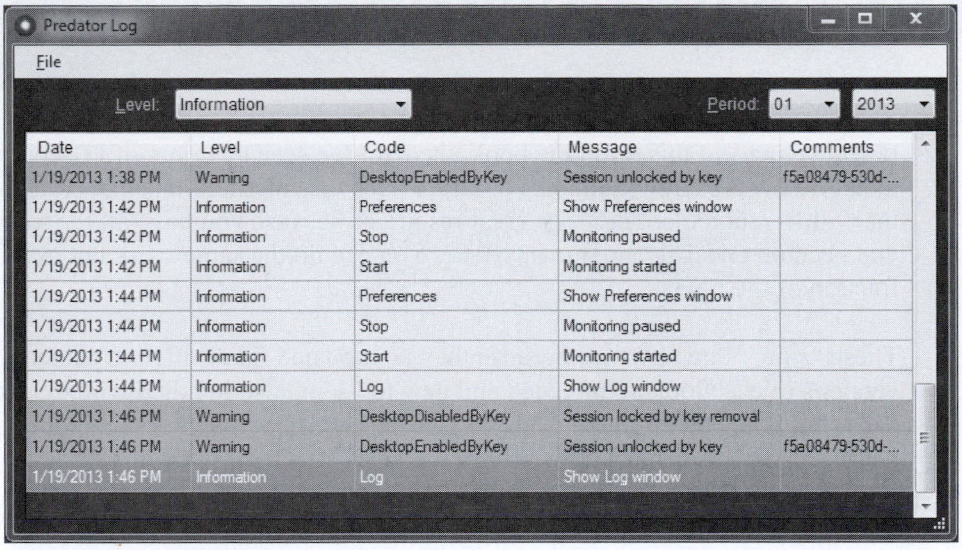

Figure 22-50: Predator log file.

Note: You may want to uninstall Predator at this point. The instructions below walk you through the uninstallation process.

1. Right-click the green Predator icon in the Notification Area at the bottom-right-hand of your screen. (It may be hidden. If it is hidden, you can click on the small triangle to see the hidden notification icons.)
2. Click Exit.
3. Click Start, Control Panel, and Uninstall a program.
4. Scroll down and select Predator.
5. Click Uninstall.
6. Right click your taskbar.
7. Select Start Task Manager.
8. Click Show processes from all users.
9. Scroll down and select PredatorACE.exe.
10. Click End Process.
11. Return to the Predator Uninstallation program.
12. Click OK.

PROJECT QUESTIONS

1. What was the drive letter for your USB drive?
2. How long was the password you used?
3. What were the first two charcters of your Key?
4. What time was shown in the Predator log when you removed your USB drive?

THOUGHT QUESTIONS

1. When might a USB locking application be appropriate?
2. Do you often leave your computer logged in and unattended?
3. Do you work with people whom you would not want accessing your computer?
4. Why can Predator lock multiple computers with a single USB?

chapter 23

If you've made it this far in the book, then you've seen a variety of IT security tools. Below are a few examples of larger packages/distributions that contain many different tools. These are great resources because you have all the tools you need on one disk and one interface. You can do the same work but in a fraction of the time.

These "suites" are also nice because they are updated fairly often. Updated versions of each tool are included and new tools are also bundled with existing software. Some distributions come as live disks, virtual machines, and/or can be loaded directly from a USB drive.

These are powerful tools that are worth burning to a disk and learning how to use. If you are going to be involved in penetration testing for your job, these are the tools to get.

Time required to complete this chapter: 120 minutes

Chapter Objectives

Learn how to:
1. Look up exploits.
2. Gather DNS information.
3. Run a fuzzer.
4. Fingerprint a Web server.
5. Test for vulnerabilities.
6. Check cached passwords.
7. Sniff login credentials.

Chapter Projects

Project:
23.1 Kali I
23.2 Kali II
23.3 Cain & Able

One of the best Linux distributions focused on IT security tools is Kali® Linux. Kali Linux is the new fork of the now depreciated BackTrack® distribution, but contains all of the tools that were included with BackTrack. Kali comes with over 300 tools focused specifically on IT security and penetration testing. There is also a bootable USB version. If you had to learn one suite of security tools, this would probably be it. As of this writing, the latest version is Kali 1.0. By the time you read this, there will likely be a newer version.

This project will not cover all of the tools included with Kali. In this project, you will go through the Kali installation process and then look at two tools. You will look at a few exploits in Armitage (the GUI for Metasploit) but won't use them against another computer. You will then use Maltego to gather information about your IP address.

The Kali ISO image is a large download. It may be faster to get it from your instructor or a fellow classmate.

1. Download Kali from: http://www.kali.org/.
2. Click on the Downloads link at the top of the page.
3. Click on the Download link. (You don't have to register.)
4. Select the latest release version. (In this case, it was Kali 1.0.)
5. Select Gnome desktop.
6. Select your chip architecture. (In this case, it was AMD 64-bit. Most newer computers will be 64-bit.)
7. Click on the Download Kali button.
8. Click Save.
9. Select your C:\security folder. (This is a big download that will take a while unless you get it from your instructor or classmate. It should be about 2.5 GB.)

Note: You are now going to create a Kali virtual machine using Oracle VirtualBox.

10. Open Oracle VM VirtualBox by clicking Start, All Programs, Oracle VM VirtualBox, and Oracle VM VirtualBox. (You installed VirtualBox as part of projects in an earlier chapter. If you haven't installed VirtualBox, you will need to do so now.)
11. Click New.
12. Enter "Kali_YourName" for the Name. (In this case, it was Kali_RandyBoyle.) (See Figure 23-1.)
13. Select Linux for the Operating System.
14. Select Debian (64 bit) for the Version. (Select just "Debian" if you have an older 32-bit system. The Kali distribution is based on Debian.)
15. Click Next.
16. Increase the amount of memory to 2000 MB+. (See Figure 23-2.)

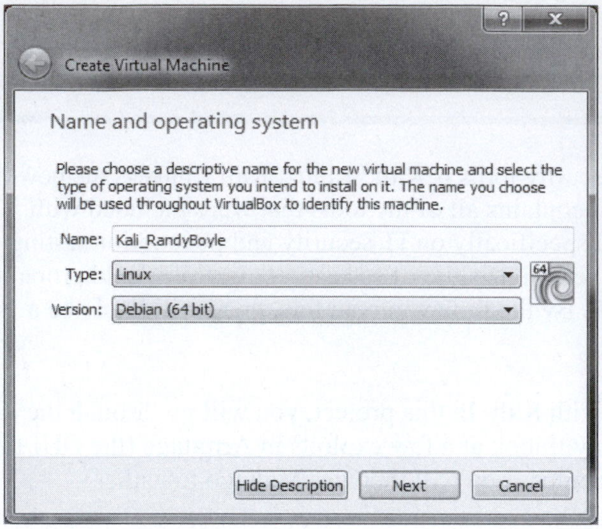

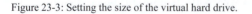

Figure 23-1: Naming the Kali virtual machine. 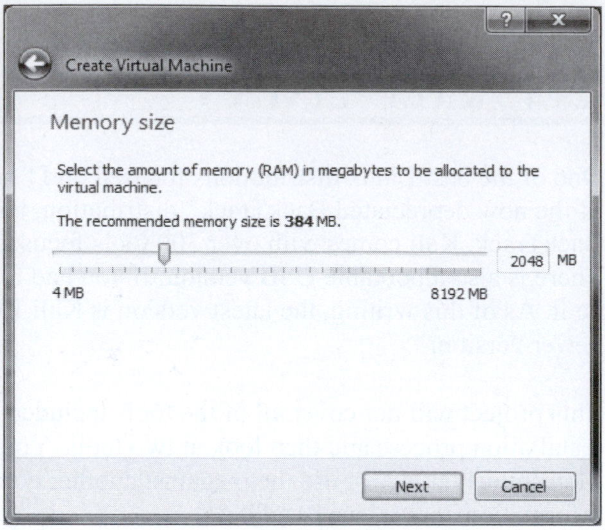   Figure 23-2: Allocating RAM to the virtual machine.

17. Click Next, Create, Next, and Next.
18. Increase the hard drive space to 15GB (or more if you have the space). (See Figure 23-3.)
19. Click Create.
20. Select the Virtual machine labeled Kali_YourName. (See Figure 23-4.)

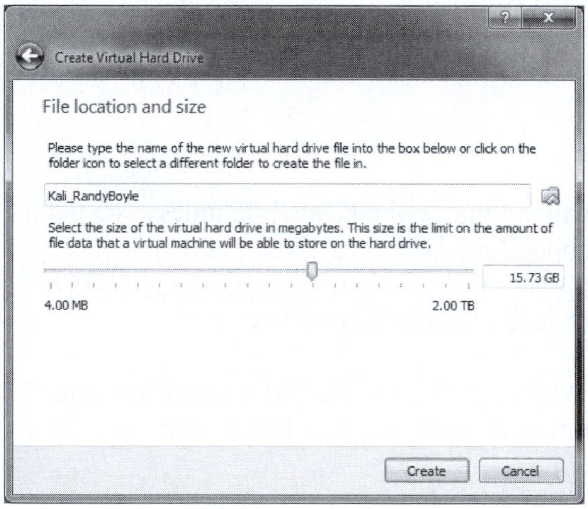

Figure 23-3: Setting the size of the virtual hard drive. 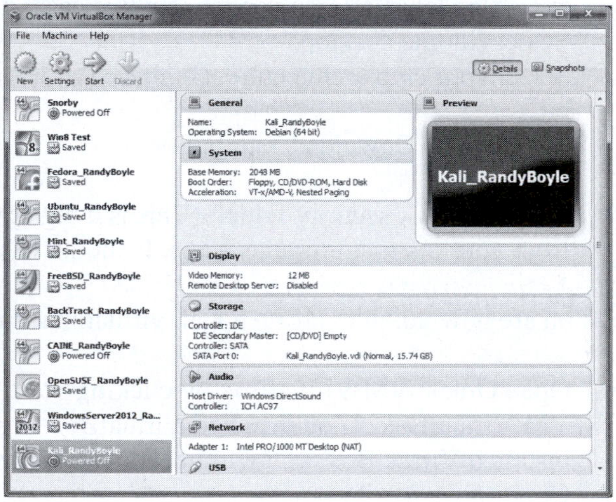   Figure 23-4: Kali virtual machine created.

21. In the right-hand pane, click Storage, IDE Controller, and Empty. (See Figure 23-5.)
22. Click the Browse button on the right-hand side of the screen by the CD/DVD Drive drop-down box. (It looks like a little CD.)
23. Click Add.
24. Browse to your C:\security folder.
25. Select the Kali ISO image you downloaded. (In this case, it was kali-linux-1.0.4-amd64.iso.)
26. Click Open. (See Figure 23-6.)
27. Click OK.

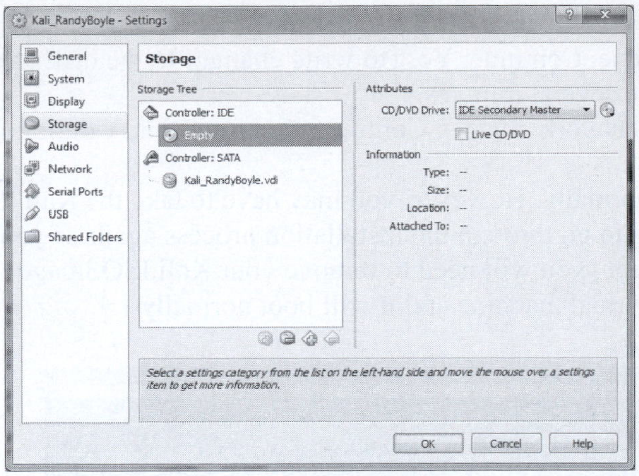

Figure 23-5: No CD/DVD image mounted.

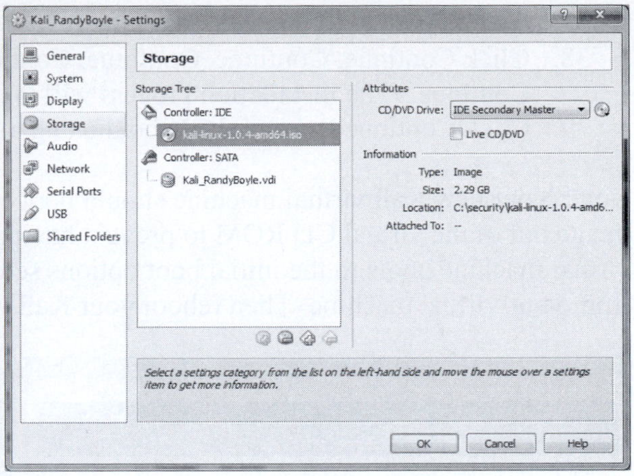

Figure 23-6: Kali ISO image mounted.

28. Take a screenshot showing the new virtual machine. (You may have to use Screenshot Pilot to take screenshots. You can leave the virtual machine by holding down the right Ctrl key. To copy the screenshot from within Screenshot Pilot, you click Image, and then Copy to Clipboard.) (See Figure 23-7.)

29. Click Start. (It may take 3 or more minutes for Kali to load depending on the resources allocated to the virtual machine.)

30. In the Kali virtual machine arrow down and select Graphical Install.

31. Press Enter. (See Figure 23-8.)

Note: Alternate boot methods shown in the initial splash screen are available but won't be used in this project. If your version of Kali boots to a command prompt, you can type "startx" to start the graphical interface.

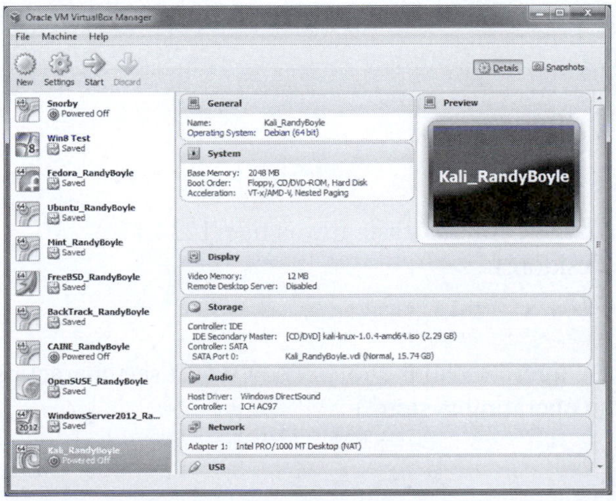

Figure 23-7: Kali virtual machine ready to boot.

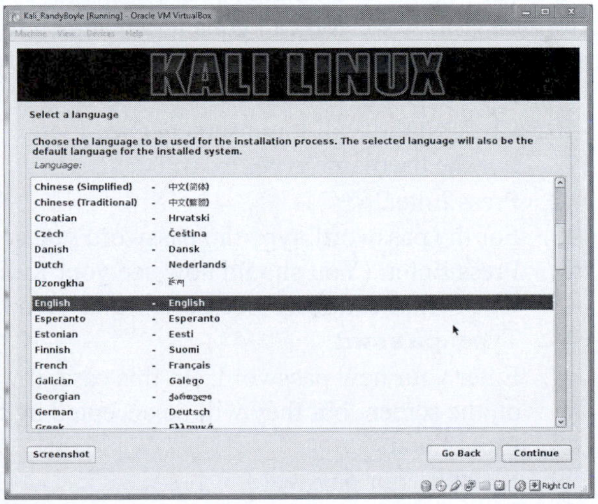

Figure 23-8: Kali installation options.

32. Select your desired language and click Continue.

33. Select your location and click Continue.

34. Select your keyboard and click Continue.

35. Enter your first name as the host name and click Continue. (In this case, it was "randy.") (See Figure 23-9.)

36. Click Continue, at the configure network screen.

37. Enter a password you can remember twice. (In this case, it was tiger1234.)
38. Click Continue, Continue, Continue, Continue, Continue, Yes (to write changes to the disk), and Continue. (The installation process will take several minutes.)
39. Click Continue (when asked about using a network mirror), Continue, Continue, and Continue.

Note: Your new Kali virtual machine should boot normally. However, you may have to take the Kali ISO image out of the virtual CD ROM to prevent having to go through the installation process again. If your virtual machine boots to the initial boot options screen, you will need to remove your Kali ISO image from your virtual machine. Then reboot your Kali virtual machine and it will boot normally.

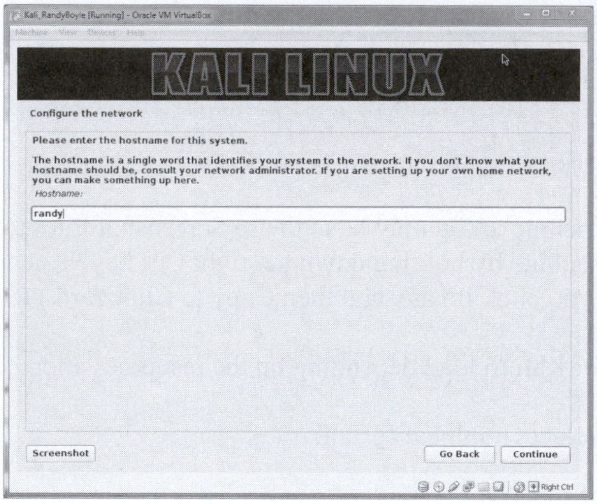

Figure 23-9: Installing Kali. 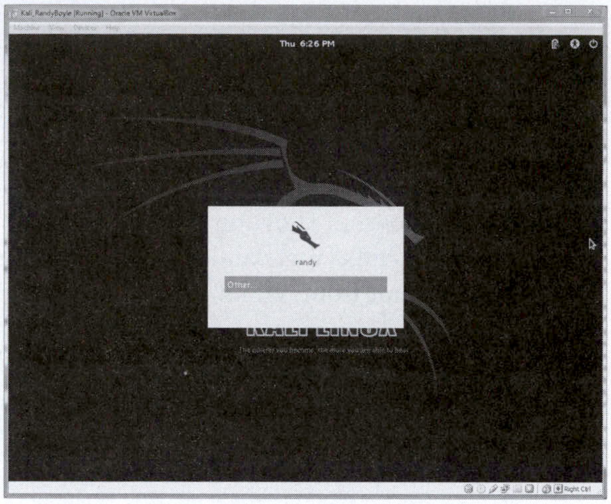   Figure 23-10: Kali Login screen.

Note: You are going to enter the default username (root) and your password to log in. You will then go through the process of changing your password. Changing your password in Linux is a commonly performed task. Also, you can get a larger screen for your virtual machine if you install Guest Additions through the VirtualBox menu.

40. Click on the Kali login screen. (See Figure 23-10.)
41. For the username type **root**.
42. Press Enter.
43. For the password, type the password you set earlier. (In this case, it was tiger1234.)
44. Press Enter. (You should now see your Kali desktop.)
45. Click Applications, Accessories, and Terminal.
46. Type **passwd**
47. Enter your new password. (In this case, it was "tiger" without quotes. You won't see characters on the screen, but they will be accepted by the operating system.)
48. Press Enter.
49. Reenter your password.
50. Press Enter. (See Figure 23-11.)
51. Close the terminal.
52. Click Applications, Kali Linux, Exploitation Tools, Network Exploitation Tools, and Armitage. (See Figure 23-12.)
53. Click Connect, and Yes.

Note: If you have problems starting Armitage, you can update your Metasploit installation by typing "msfupdate" at a command prompt. This will update the Metasploit framework and should resolve potential conflicts with Armitage.

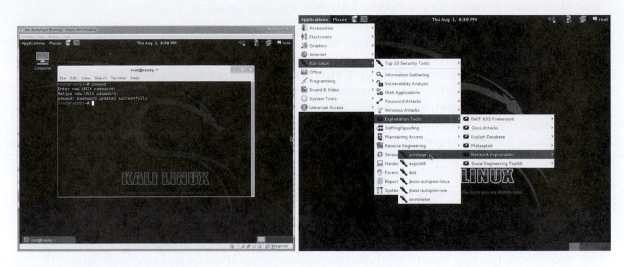

Figure 23-11: Changing your password.   Figure 23-12: Kali menu.

54. Click Exploit, Windows, and Antivirus.
55. Double-click on one of the exploits.
56. Take a screenshot. (See Figure 23-13.)
57. Close the attack window.
58. Open any other exploit category under Windows.
59. Double-click on any exploit that interests you.
60. Take a screenshot. (See Figure 23-14.)
61. Close the attack window.
62. Close Armitage.

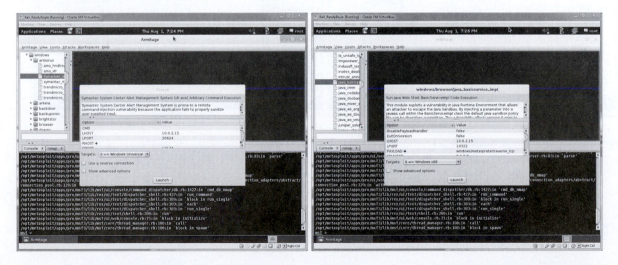

Figure 23-13: Windows exploit.   Figure 23-14: Another exploit.

63. Click Applications, Kali Linux, Information Gathering, DNS Analysis, and Maltego®.
64. Click Next.
65. Click the blue "Register here" link.
66. Enter any user information on the Paterva site. (It's necessary to register to be able to use Maltego. You could enter a temporary email account, or one that you don't use very often. Do *not* enter the real password that corresponds to the email account you enter.)
67. Enter any email address, any password, and solve the CAPTCHA.
68. Click Register.

69. Wait about a minute for the Paterva activation email to arrive.
70. Click on the Activation link within the Paterva email.
71. Click Activate Account after being directed to the Paterva activation screen. (You should now be registered.)
72. Return to the Maltego window in your virtual machine.
73. Enter the email address you used, password, and solve the CAPTCHA.
74. Click Next, Next, Next, and Finish.
75. Close the "Start a Machine" window by clicking Cancel.
76. Click the Matego icon in the upper left-hand corner of the screen, and click New. (You can also press Ctrl+T.)
77. Expand the Infrastructure tree in the left-hand menu. (It might already be expanded.)
78. Drag-and-drop the IPv4 Address icon from the left-hand pane to the center of the screen.
79. Click on the icon you just moved over.
80. In the bottom right-hand pane labeled Property View, change the IP address to your current IP address. (In this case, it was 159.230.216.145. Do *not* use this IP address for your project. You can use the ipconfig command to determine your current IP address. Enter your current IP address.) (See Figure 23-15.)
81. Right-click on the icon with your IP address showing.
82. Select Run Transform, All Transforms, and To Netblock [Using whois info]. (See Figure 23-16.)

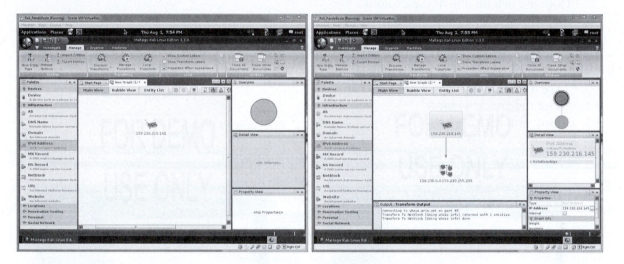

Figure 23-15: Enter your IP address.   Figure 23-16: Your block of IP addresses.

83. Right-click on the icon with your IP address showing.
84. Select Run Transform, DNS from IP, and To DNS Name [Reverse DNS]. (See Figure 23-17.)
85. Right-click on the DNS icon that appeared.
86. Select Run Transform, Convert to Domain, and To Domains [DNS].
87. Take a screenshot. (See Figure 23-18.)

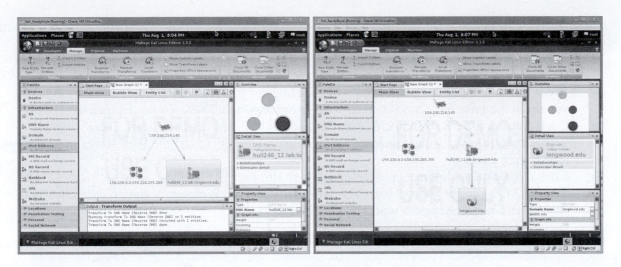

Figure 23-17: Resolved DNS names for the IP.   Figure 23-18: Resolved to domains.

PROJECT QUESTIONS

1. What was the name of your Kali virtual machine?
2. How long was your new root password?
3. Which exploit did you click on?
4. What was your IP address during this project?

THOUGHT QUESTIONS

1. Are most of the tools included in Kali GUI or command-line? Why?
2. What does Metasploit do?
3. Why would someone use Maltego?
4. Where would you go to learn about all the tools in Kali?

23.2   KALI LINUX II

In this project, you are going to look at three applications from Kali. You are going to get a very high-level preview of what these tools can do. They have more functionality than is shown here. In fact, there are hundreds of additional applications included with Kali. Some of them will be familiar to you from earlier projects.

The first application you will look at is BED. The acronym "BED" stands for Bruteforce Exploit Detector. You will start a Web server on your local Kali virtual machine that you will test for vulnerabilities. This scan will take a very long time. You do not have to wait for it to finish.

The next application you will look at is called whatweb. It is a Web fingerprinting tool that will give you key Web server configuration information. Knowing the type of Web server that's hosting a website is the first step in knowing which vulnerabilities might exist.

Finally, you will use lynis to scan your local virtual machine for vulnerabilities. Please feel free to try any of the other tools in Kali. Use caution and only target your local machine or one provided to you by your instructor.

1. Open Oracle VM VirtualBox by clicking Start, All Programs, Oracle VM VirtualBox, and Oracle VM VirtualBox.
2. Select your Kali virtual machine.
3. Click Start.
4. If you are not already logged in, you will need to enter your username (root) and the password you set in the prior project. (The default password was "toor" before you changed it.)
5. Click Applications, Kali Linux, System Services, HTTP, and apache 2 start. (This will start a Web server on your virtual machine. You will use a "fuzzer" to test the Web server in later steps.) (See Figure 23-19.)
6. Click Applications, Internet, and Iceweasel Web Browser.
7. Type 127.0.0.1 in the address bar. (This will verify that the Web server started correctly. You should see a page saying, "It works!") (See Figure 23-20.)
8. Press Enter.

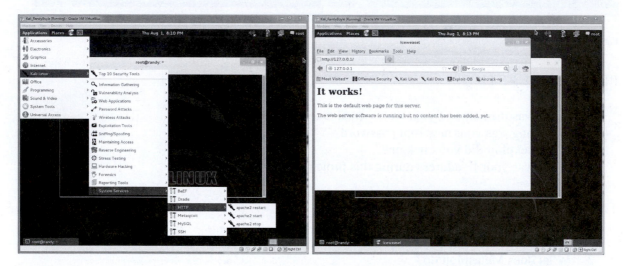

Figure 23-19: Starting your Apache Web server.   Figure 23-20: Verifying the server is started.

9. Click Applications, Kali Linux, Vulnerability Analysis, Fuzzing Tools, and bed. (The acronym "bed" stands for Bruteforce Exploit Detector.) (See Figure 23-21.)
10. Type `bed -s http -t 127.0.0.1 -p 80`
11. Press Enter. (This will check your local Web server for common vulnerabilities. Some students have noted that they had to type "`./bed.pl -s http -t 127.0.0.1 -p 80`" to get bed to work correctly. Others did not.)
12. Take a screenshot. (See Figure 23-22.)
13. Minimize the bed terminal. (The scan will take a long time. You can check its progress at the end of this project.)

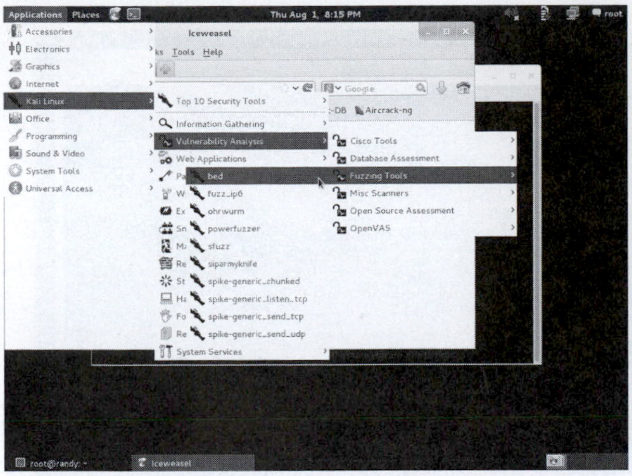

Figure 23-21: Starting bed. 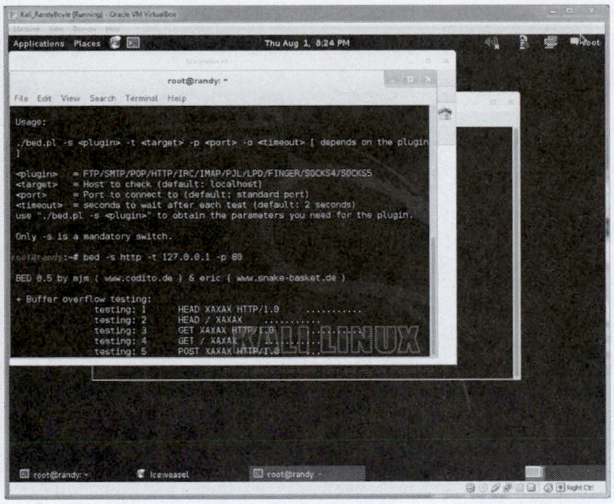   Figure 23-22: Bed assessment is started.

14. Click Applications, Kali Linux, Web Applications, Web Vulnerability Scanners, and whatweb. (See Figure 23-23.)
15. Type **whatweb www.google.com**
16. Press Enter. (Note the hostname in blue, the title in green, and the Web server in turquois.)
17. Type **whatweb www.microsoft.com**
18. Press Enter. (Note that two entries were returned this time, and that the Web server is now IIS.)
19. Type **whatweb www.microsoft.com www.google.com**
20. Press Enter. (This shows that you can get information about multiple hostnames at the same time.) (See Figure 23-24.)

Figure 23-23: Starting whatweb.   Figure 23-24: Fingerprinting websites.

21. Type **whatweb -v www.google.com**
22. Press Enter. (This shows the verbose output.) (See Figure 23-25.)
23. Type **whatweb -v [any web site you'd like]**
24. Press Enter. (In this case, it was www.BBC.com in the UK.)
25. Take a screenshot. (See Figure 23-26.)
26. Close the terminal.

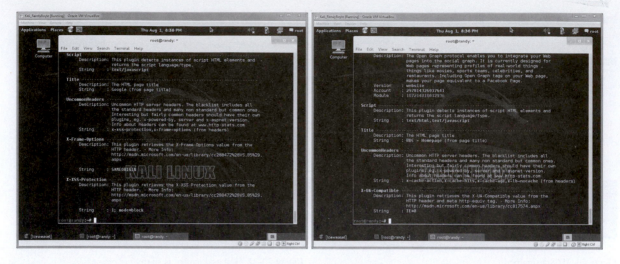

Figure 23-25: Whatweb results for www.Google.com.   Figure 23-26: Whatweb results for www.BBC.com.

27. Click Applications, Kali Linux, Vulnerability Analysis, Misc Scanners, and lynis. (See Figure 23-27.)

Note: A few students have had difficulty running the following application. However, after reinstalling lynis, it seems to work fine. The instructions below install lynis before running a vulnerability scan on the local machine.

28. Type `sudo apt-get install lynis`
29. Press Enter. (If it is already installed and working fine, the above command will be irrelevant.)
30. Type `lynis --check-all --quick`
31. Press Enter. (This will go through the scan without asking you for input. You can run this command without the --quick command and see each test it performs.)
32. Type `lynis --check-all --quick --quiet`
33. Press Enter. (This will only show problems.)
34. Take a screenshot. (See Figure 23-28.)

Figure 23-27: Starting lynis.   Figure 23-28: Results from lynis assessment.

PROJECT QUESTIONS

1. Which website did you query using the whatweb command?
2. What Web server were they using to host their site?
3. What was the IP address of the website you querried?
4. In what country was the website located?

THOUGHT QUESTIONS

1. What do fuzzers do?
2. What does fingerprinting help you identify?
3. Did you notice tools in Kali that you have used in prior projects? Which ones?
4. What background knowledge would increase your ability to learn the tools in Kali?

23.3   CAIN & ABLE

Cain & Able integrates many of the tools you have seen in prior chapters into a single application. It's fairly easy to use once you become familiar with all of the components. If you were able to do the previous projects, you will find many of the applications familiar. Some of the tools are interdependent. For example, Cain & Able can sniff packets and then send the results directly to a password auditor. Integrating tools can add additional value that neither tool had as a stand-alone tool.

WARNING Cain & Able does have certain functionality that could cause network problems if you randomly start pushing buttons. Do NOT push buttons if you're not sure what they do. It is worth the time and effort to learn more about the tool before you use it. Many of the most useful tools in the world (e.g.. knife, hammer, etc.) can be used improperly. Do not use Cain & Able improperly. If you follow the instructions, you will be fine.

1. Download Cain & Able from http://www.oxid.it/cain.html.
2. Click "Download Cain & Abel v4.9.43 for Windows NT/2000/XP." (Always download the latest version available.)
3. Click Save.
4. Select the C:\security folder.
5. If the program doesn't automatically open, browse to C:\security.
6. Double-click on ca_setup.exe.
7. Click Next, Next, Next, Next, Finish, Install, Next, Next, and I Agree.
8. If you see a window indicating that you have a prior version installed, just click Yes.
9. Click OK, and Finish.
10. Click Start, All Programs, Cain, and Cain.
11. Click on the Decoders tab.
12. Click on Wireless Passwords.
13. Click the "+" button. (If you are using a desktop, this might not return any results. You won't take a screenshot here because it may reveal stored passwords for the wireless networks you use.)
14. Click on LSA Secrets. (See Figure 23-29.)
15. Click the "+" button.
16. Take a screenshot of the results.
17. Click on the Network Tab.
18. Expand the Microsoft Windows Network until you get to your computer.
19. Click Users.
20. Click Yes, to enumerate users.
21. Select your username. (See Figure 23-30.)

22. Take a screenshot.

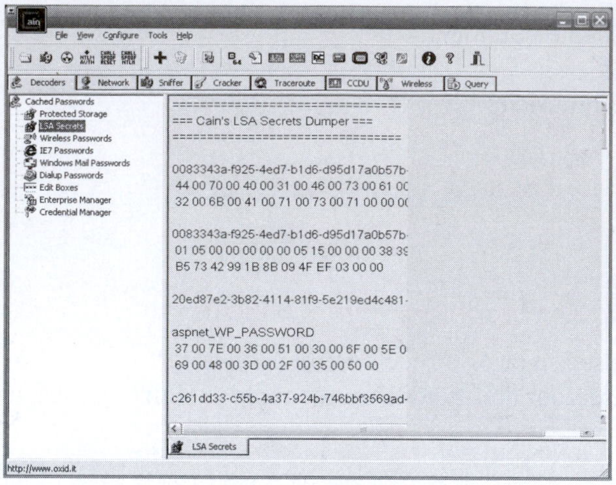

Figure 23-29: Cain's LSA Secrets Dumper. 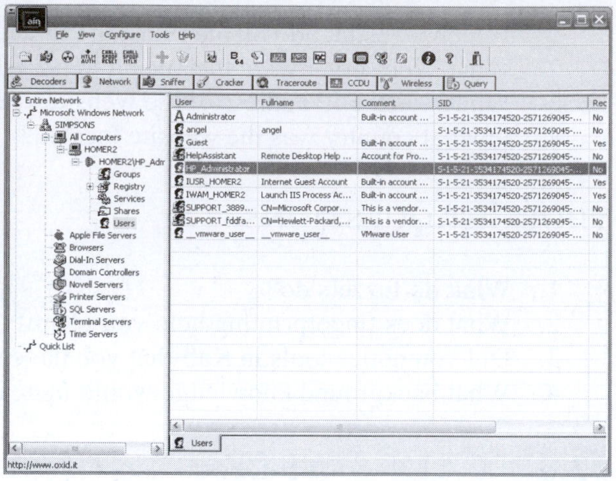   Figure 23-30: Viewing users on your computer.

23. Click on Configure, in the file menu.
24. Select your network card with your IP address. (In this case, it was 155.97.243.201.)
25. Click OK. (See Figure 23-31.)
26. Click on the Start/Stop Sniffer icon. (It looks like a little green NIC.)
27. Click on the Sniffer tab.
28. Click on the Passwords tab at the bottom of the screen. (See Figure 23-32.)
29. Open a Web browser.
30. Go to several websites that you know have logon capabilities (i.e., they are not encrypted).
31. Take a screenshot of the results.

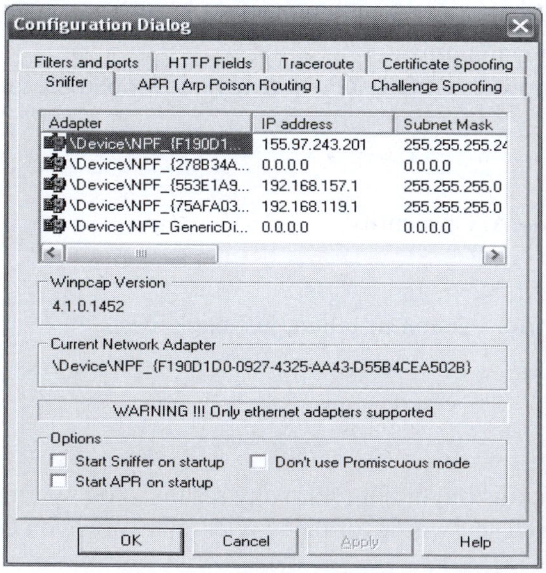

Figure 23-31: Cain sniffer configuration. 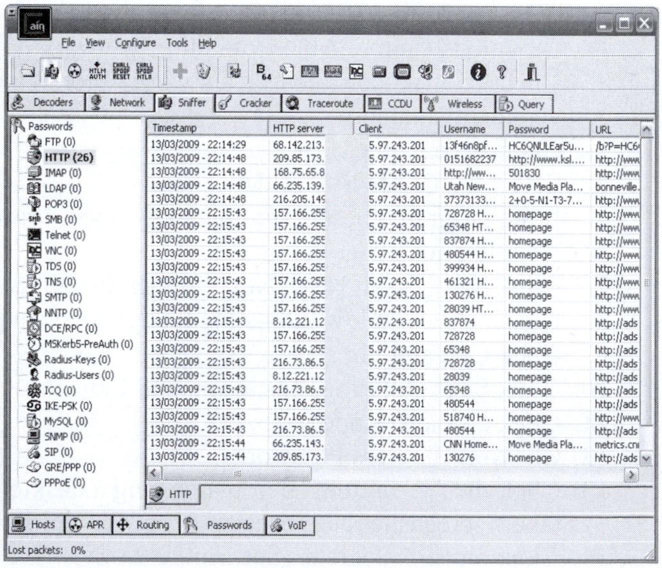   Figure 23-32: Sniffing passwords automatically.

32. Click on the Traceroute tab. (See Figure 23-33.)
33. Enter www.Google.com.
34. Click Start.
35. Take a screenshot.

36. Click on Tools, and Tcp/Udp Tables. (See Figure 23-34.)
37. Take a screenshot.
38. Click Close.
39. Click Tools, and Hash Calculator.
40. Enter YourName in the text box that will be hashed. (In this case, it was Randy Boyle, and the resulting hash was 0AEA63CAC85E0326985424E7EAD9E995.)
41. Click Calculate. (See Figure 23-35.)
42. Take a screenshot.
43. Click Cancel.

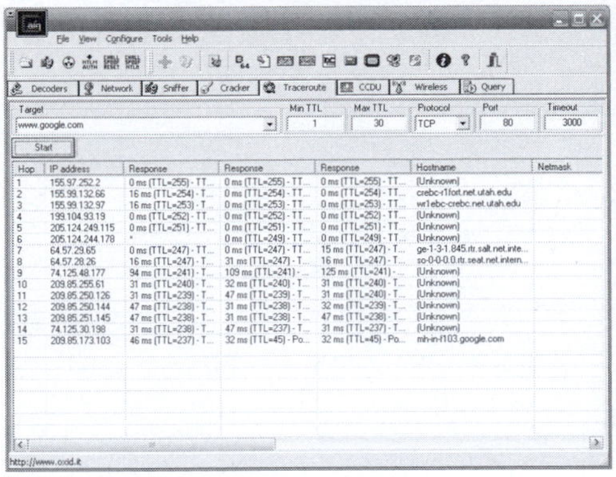

Figure 23-33: Cain's traceroute function.

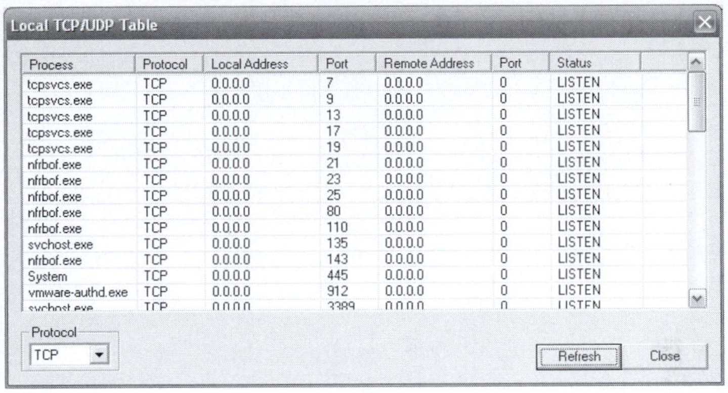

Figure 23-34: Programs and their associated local ports.

44. Click on the Cracker tab.
45. Click on the LM & NTLM Hashes icon on the left-hand menu. (See Figure 23-36.)
46. Click the "+" button.
47. Click Next.
48. Take a screenshot.

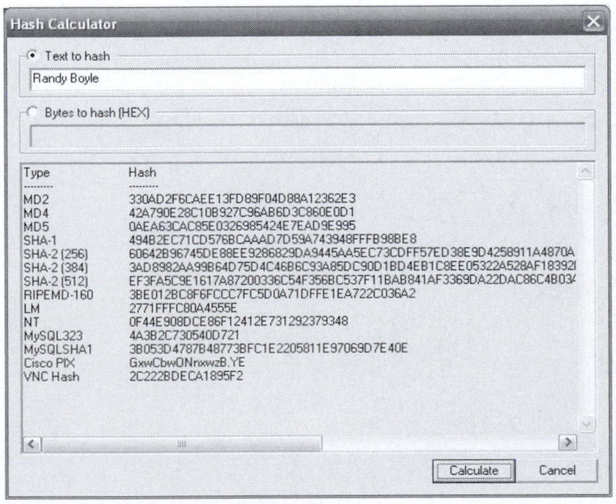

Figure 23-35: Built-in hash calculator.

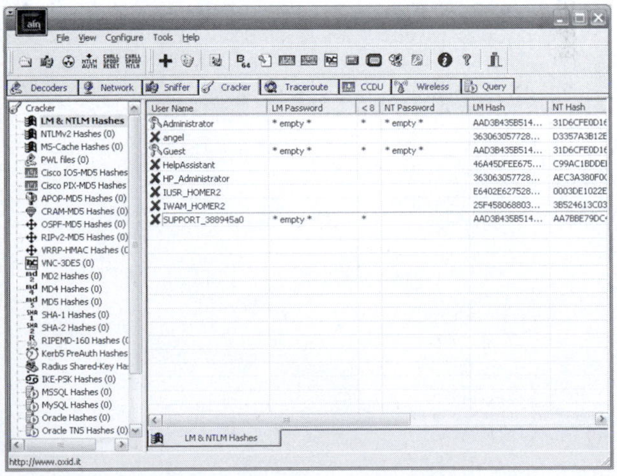

Figure 23-36: Cain's password cracker.

PROJECT QUESTIONS

1. What results were shown when you looked for cached passwords (e.g., LSA Secrets)?
2. Which wireless networks were displayed when you looked for cached passwords?
3. Which usernames were shown on the Network tab?

4. What was the MD5 hash of your name?

THOUGHT QUESTIONS

1. What is "ARP poisoning"?
2. Does Cain & Able come with wireless tools?
3. What does the Query tab do?
4. What is "spoofing" and why would someone want to do it?

chapter 24

In the last several years, the number of mobile devices has grown substantially. They have also increased in functionality, and connectivity. Mobile phones are more like small computers that hold valuable information. As such, they are susceptible to attack

Security professionals must be aware of the potential risks and challenges associated with managing personal and corporate mobile devices. As the mobile market continues to mature, it is possible that we could see similar debilitating viruses attack the mobile platform.

Every mobile device represents a potential access point for attack. They may have the ability to connect to corporate networks, access company resources, store confidential information, and even take high resolution pictures and videos. Companies should include detailed policies and procedures for the appropriate use of mobile devices. It is especially important for companies to prohibit the use of these devices in secure areas such as server and file rooms.

Along with the growth of mobile devices, there has been an increase in the number of applications that can address mobile security issues. Users can often download antivirus, VPN, and file encryption applications for not cost. Every mobile device should have an antivirus application.

In this chapter, you will look at a few applications available for mobile security. This is not an exhaustive list. It may be worthwhile to identify other applications you might want for personal or enterprise use.

Time required to complete this chapter: 60 minutes

Chapter Objectives

Learn how to:
1. Take a screenshot on your phone.
2. Track your phone if it is lost.
3. Identify wireless networks.
4. Tether a wireless device to your phone.
5. Scan other wireless devices connected to your phone.
6. Make an encrypted phone call.
7. Encrypt a file on your mobile phone.

Chapter Projects

Project:
24.1 Screenshot (DroidAtScreen)
24.2 Mobile Security (LookOut)
24.3 Wardriving (WiGLE)
24.4 Tethering
24.5 Mobile Net Tools (Fing)
24.6 Encrypted Calls (RedPhone)
24.7 Encryption (FileLocker)

24.1 SCREENSHOT (DROIDATSCREEN)

Competition within the mobile phone marketplace is fierce and the devices are diverse. There are multiple phone makes, models, and operating systems. If you have an Android® or other device that doesn't require these steps, you can skip to the next project.

Look up your phone to determine if it already has a screenshot application built in. Most phones have manufacturer shortcuts to take screenshots. Some are as simple as swiping your hand across the screen, or holding down your home and power button at the same time. If you have an Android 4.0 or later device, you may be able to take a screenshot by holding down the down volume and home keys at the same time.

If you cannot find a manufacturer screenshot shortcut for your phone, you will need to follow the following instructions. It is important to note that some Android devices require root in order to take screenshots. In order to get around it, you can download the software development kit (SDK) and allow your mobile device to display on a desktop or laptop computer. You will need to connect your device to your laptop or desktop via USB.

Using the SDK to connect a mobile phone to a computer could have multiple uses. It could be used by corporate trainers to walk employees through security best practices for their mobile devices. It could also be used to create training materials or give presentations.

1. Go to Settings on your device.
2. Scroll down to Applications.
3. Go to Development. (See Figure 24-1.)

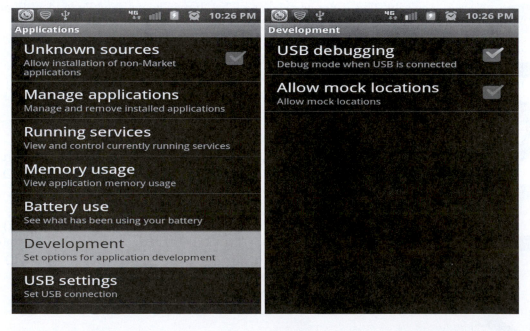

Figure 24-1: Development menu.   Figure 24-2: Selecting USB debugging.

4. Check the USB debugging and select OK. (See Figure 24-2.)
5. Attach your phone to your computer via USB.
6. Open a Web browser on your computer and search Android SDK. (See Figure 24-3.)

7. Select the download for your particular platform, android-sdk_r18-windows.zip. (In this case, it was Microsoft Windows.) (See Figure 24-4.)

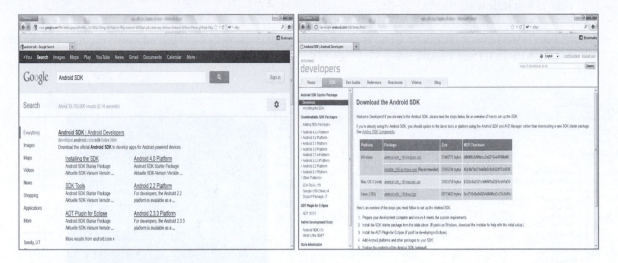

Figure 24-3: Search results for Android SDK.   Figure 24-4: SDK downloads.

8. Save it in your C:\security folder.
9. When the file is complete, right click on the file and select Extract All.
10. Open your Web browser and go to http://blog.ribomation.com/droid-at-screen/.

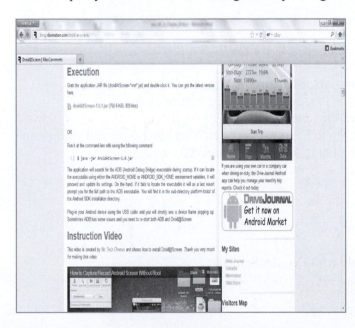

Figure 24-5: DroidAtScreen download below execution.

11. Scroll down to execution and select droidAtScreen-1.0.jar. (See Figure 24-5.)
12. Save the file in your C:\Security folder.
13. Select droidAtScreen-1.0.jar.
14. Click the "…" box in the bottom right corner.
15. Click the down arrow.
16. Go to Local Disk (C:), security, and android-sdk_r18-windows.

17.   Leave
that window open and in *another* window go to your Start menu, Computer, C:\security\android-sdk_r18-windows.
18. Select SDK Manager.exe and wait for it to open.
19. Make sure to check Tools so that Android SDK Platform-tools is selected, and uncheck Android 4.0.3 (API 15). (See Figure 24-6.)

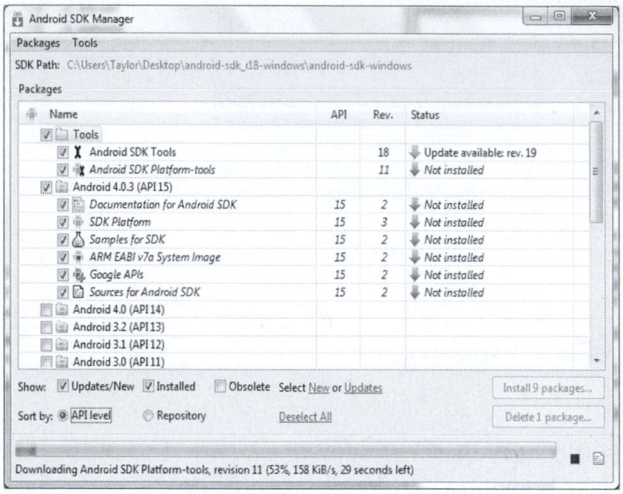

Figure 24-6: Selecting tools in SDK Manager.    Figure 24-7: Phone screen displayed on laptop.

20. Select Install, Install, and Exit.
21. Go back to DroidAtScreen.
22. Select android-sdk-windows, platform-tools, adb.exe, and Open.
23. You should be able to see your phone on the screen now. (See Figure 24-7.)
24. On the left-hand side, there is a camera for screenshots.
25. When you want to return after exiting, go to C:\Security\droidAtScreen-1.0.jar and your phone image will appear again. Make sure to plug in your phone via USB.

PROJECT QUESTIONS

1. What operating system did your phone use?
2. What phone model do you have?
3. Was your particular device compatible with DroidAtScreen?
4. What time is displayed on your screenshot?

THOUGHT QUESTIONS

1. Why do some phones have a built in shortcut for taking a screenshot, and others do not?
2. What other features can you add to your phone using the Android SDK?
3. Why do cellular providers discourage users from rooting their phones?
4. What can you do with a rooted phone as opposed to standard provider configurations?

24.2   MOBILE SECURITY (LOOKOUT®)

Lookout® provides a simple way to protect your mobile device. It offers antivirus, backup, and GPS locating if you lose your mobile device. Every mobile device should be protected with *at least* antivirus protection. Lookout allows you to scan your apps and automatically updates with the latest virus definitions. It also allows you to setup automatic backups on a daily or weekly basis.

You will need to set up an account to use Lookout. You can use www.Lookout.com to access and edit your security settings. It's important that you remember your password. You will need your password to locate your device if it is lost. There are many different apps that provide this same function, but Lookout also provides features such as Signal Flare and Lock Cam, to give you a better chance of finding your device. With the upgraded account, you can add safe browsing, remote lock, remote wipe, and increased security options.

1. Go to your app market.
2. Search Lookout Antivirus.
3. Select the Lookout Security & Antivirus application.
4. Select Install.
5. Select Accept, on the application permissions.
6. When downloading is complete, open Lookout. (See Figure 24-8.)
7. Select Next, Next, and Done.
8. Set a password for your online account. (This should not be the same password you use to access the email account shown on the registration screen.)
9. Click Start Protecting.

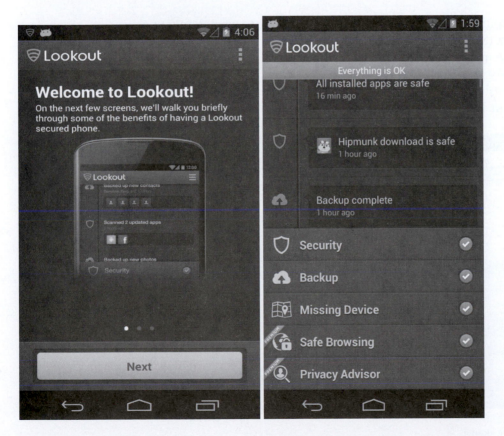

Figure 24-8: Lookout welcome screen.   Figure 24-9: Lookout scan.

10. Click No Thanks. (You can upgrade later if you choose to do so.)
11. Click Continue to Lookout Free. (You can upgrade later if you choose to do so.)
12. Deselect Enable the Mobile Threat Network. (You can re-enable this option later if you chose to do so.)
13. Click Done. (Lookout will scan all of your apps.)

14. Take a screenshot. (See Figure 24-9.)
15. Select Backup.
16. Take a screenshot. (See Figure 24-10.)

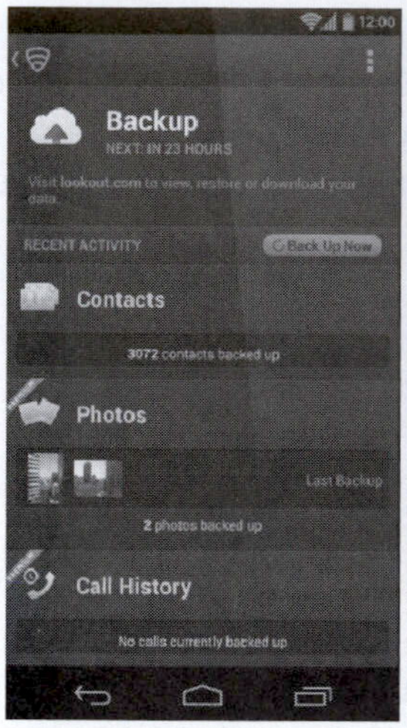

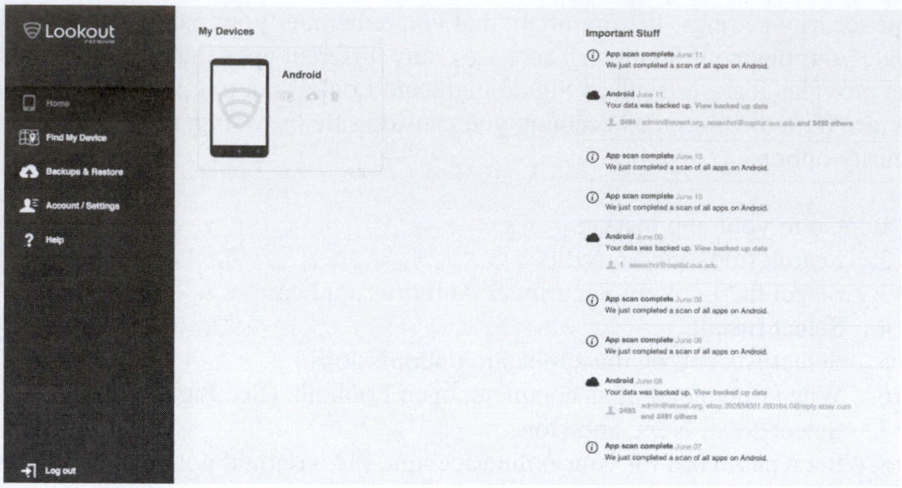

Figure 24-10: Backup options.   Figure 24-11: Logged in at www.Lookout.com.

17. Go to your computer, open your Web browser, and go to www.Lookout.com.
18. Click Log In. (See Figure 24-11.)
19. Login with your email address and password that you set earlier.
20. Click Find My Device.
21. Take a screenshot. (See Figure 24-12.)
22. Select Scream, and listen for your device.

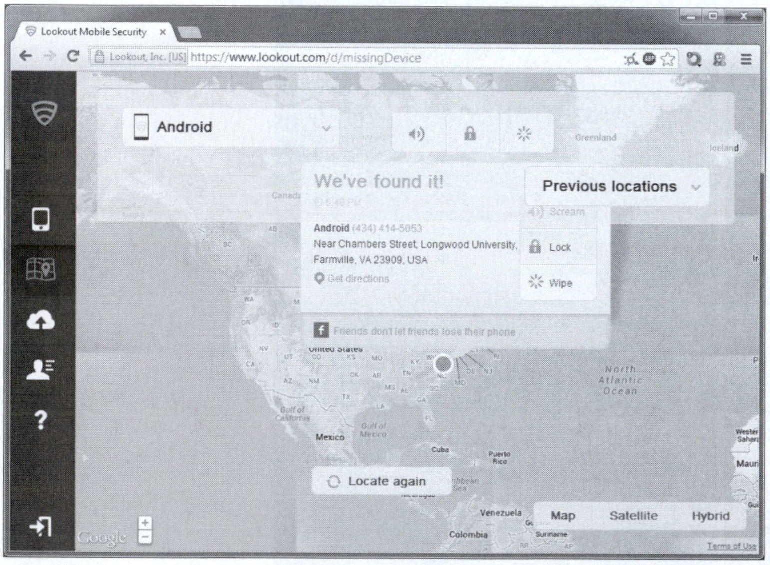

Figure 24-12: Mobile device location.

PROJECT QUESTIONS

1. Did the antivirus scanner find any rogue programs on your phone?
2. How long did the antivirus scan take?
3. Was the location of your phone as identified on the GPS map?

4. How accurate was the GPS location?

THOUGHT QUESTIONS

1. Why is antivirus necessary for mobile devices?
2. In what other situations could you use this app (e.g., children, spouse, etc.)?
3. What is the benefit for a company to upgrade to a premium account?
4. Does your device contain information that would need to be wiped if it was lost?

24.3   WARDRIVING (WIGLE WIFI®)

Www.WiGLE.net has been around since 2001. The website provides geographical maps using GPS to locate and identify wireless networks. In recent years, this website has branched out to the mobile application world and now provides WiGLE Wifi Wardrriving®—an effective wardriving tool.

This app allows users to participate in identifying and uploading new wireless networks to www.WiGLE.net. In April of 2012, the website topped 60 million documented wireless networks. With wardriving tools being so accessible today, it is important for security professionals to understand the potential threats to wireless networks.

1. Go to your app market.
2. Search for "Wigle Wifi Wardriving".
3. Select Download, and Accept.
4. When downloading is complete, open WiGLE Wifi Wardriving.
5. You will be prompted to turn on Wifi and GPS.
6. After turning on Wifi and GPS, the app will quickly begin locating all SSIDs within close proximity.
7. Take a screenshot. (See Figure 24-13.)

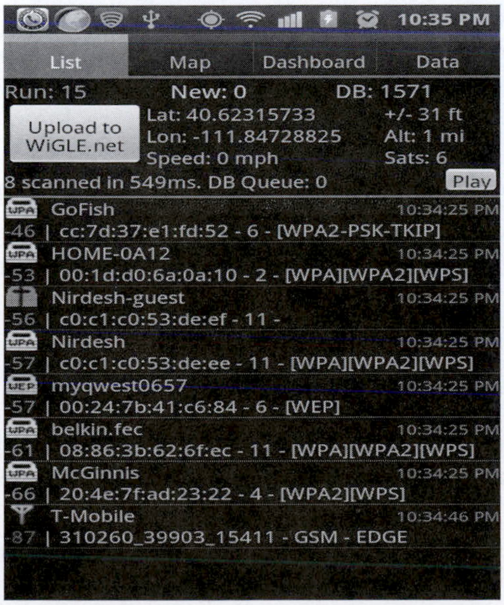

Figure 24-13: WiGLE locating access points.

8. To temporarily stop the text to speech voice, press the small Mute button. (It will say "Play" when muted.)
9. Select List, to view SSIDs being broadcast close to your device. (You will see the device's SSID, security configurations, and MAC address.)
10. Select Map, to view the GPS location of each device with SSID being displayed.

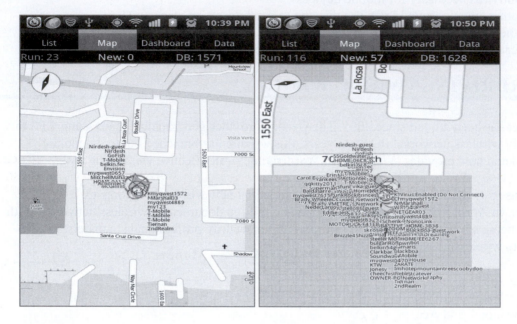

Figure 24-14: WiGLE GPS map.   Figure 24-15: WiGLE GPS map after walking down street.

11. Take a screenshot. (See Figure 24-14.)
12. Return to List and select Upload to WiGLE.net.
13. Select OK and OK.
14. Scroll down and select Time between audio speech.
15. Select the down arrow and scroll down to Off. (This will stop the TTS voice. If you want to be notified by the TTS but want to specify how and when, select the speech configuration screen at the bottom and select or deselect which events you want to be notified of by the TTS voice. You can also select Mute on the List interface.)
16. Return to the WiGLE Wifi Settings.
17. Scroll down to Exit at this battery level, and select 20%. (Wigle Wifi can drain your battery rather quickly. It is important that you shut it down with task manager when you're done using it. Otherwise, it will operate behind the scenes. In addition to the configurations mentioned, feel free to make other adjustments.)
18. Select Map and go walk or drive down your street.
19. Take a screenshot. (See Figure 24-15.)

Note: This example was done in an apartment complex. There were several wireless routers using WEP and their associated default SSID names. Using "List," you can determine what security configurations are in place (e.g., WEP, WPA, WPA2).

20. Exit WiGLE Wardriving by going to your Task Manager and selecting Exit. (If you don't exit, it will continue to operate and drain your battery.)

PROJECT QUESTIONS

1. How many WEP networks did you find?
2. What was the SSID for one of the WEP networks?
3. What was the SSID for a secured (WPA) network?
4. Were there any open networks?

THOUGHT QUESTIONS

1. Why is it important to change the default SSID name and password?
2. Why is it important to change the default security?
3. With WEP cracking technology, how fast can an attacker enter a WEP secured network?
4. How can businesses and homeowners prevent Wardrivers from gaining access to their networks?

24.4   TETHERING

Tethering is a fairly new way of networking that allows Internet-capable devices, such as laptops, tablets, or mobile phones, to share an Internet connection by creating a temporary local wireless network. Most new mobile phone operating systems have the ability to tether other wireless devices. However, older mobile operating systems, and in some cases phones that are not jailbroken or rooted, cannot use tethering.

There are several options for tethering. In this example, you will use a wireless LAN (WiFi) to create an access point (AP) that will be broadcast to your wireless network connections (SSIDs). You could also use a USB cable or Bluetooth to tether.

It is important to think about how tethering could be used by attackers to fool users in public WiFi areas. Many computers (personal and corporate) are configured to automatically connect with a specific SSID. When there are multiple SSIDs with the same name, a computer will automatically connect with the strongest broadcast SSID.

1. Go to Settings.
2. Select Wireless and Network.
3. Select Tethering and portable hotspot. (See Figure 24-16.)

Figure 24-16: Options in Tethering and portable hotspot. Figure 24-17: Naming your mobile AP.

4. Select Mobile AP settings. (You will use this to setup a new access point.)
5. Select Configure Mobile AP.
6. Enter your first and last name as your SSID. (In this case, it was Randy Boyle.)
7. Take a screenshot. (See Figure 24-17.)
8. Leave the security Open, leave "Hide my device" unchecked, and press Save.
9. In the Mobile AP settings, select the Mobile AP.
10. Select OK. (You may be asked to disconnect from WiFi. If so, select OK.)
11. Your phone should now be broadcasting as an AP.
12. Now use your computer to view other wireless connections (SSIDs).
13. Disconnect from your current wireless network.
14. Select your name and connect to your access point.
15. Take a screenshot. (See Figure 24-18.)
16. Open a Web browser and go to www.Google.com.
17. Notice the speed of your browsing.

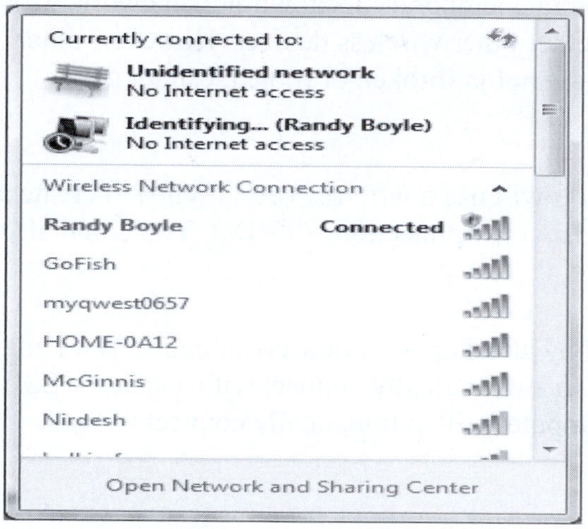

Figure 24-18: New AP broadcasted in wireless network connections.

PROJECT QUESTIONS

1. What was the name of your SSID?
2. Name one other SSID that was displayed?
3. What other options were available for tethering your device besides using the Mobile AP settings?
4. What options could you use to secure your AP if you wanted to prevent others from using it?

THOUGHT QUESTIONS

1. Where could you use tethering and what are the benefits and limitations of using tethering?
2. How fast was your connection when connected to your tethered device?
3. How can you tell the difference between an attacker's AP in a public area and a genuine AP, if both have the same SSID?
4. How are tethering and man-in-the-middle attacks similar?

24.5 MOBILE NET TOOLS (FING®)

A major part of securing information systems is identifying vulnerabilities. Fing® can help you identify unsecured ports on authorized hosts, or rogue hosts attached to your network without permission. Fing is a simple application that provides basic port scanning, network host identification, and integrated commands such as Ping and Traceroute.

Fing will identify all hosts on your network with WiFi capability, including cell phones, laptops, iPods, tablets, etc. In this project, you will identify all hosts on your network, port scan each host, and use Ping and Traceroute to test if a host will respond.

1. Go to your app market.
2. Search "Fing – Network Tools".
3. Select Accept, and Download.
4. When the app finishes downloading, open it.
5. Connect to WiFi if you are not connected.
6. When Fing opens, it will show all devices connected to your LAN and will provide their IP addresses, MAC addresses, and the devices' name or manufacturer. (From this view, you can see if a rogue device is connected to your network.)
7. Take a screenshot. (See Figure 24-19.)

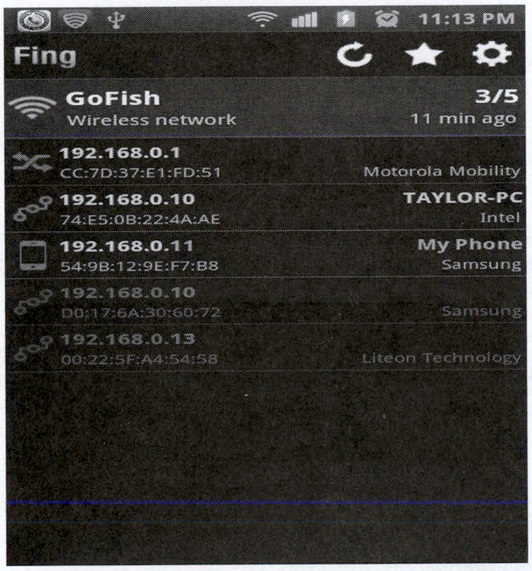

Figure 24-19: Fing opening window.

8. Select the settings (gear shaped) in the upper right hand corner.
9. Under Host Tools, select Ping.
10. In the text box, type www.Google.com, and press OK.
11. Take a screenshot. (See Figure 24-20.)

Note: Using Ping, you can see if a host is reachable or to troubleshoot networking problems. Many companies block ICMP because it is commonly used by hackers. If a company blocks ICMP, you will receive 100% packet loss.

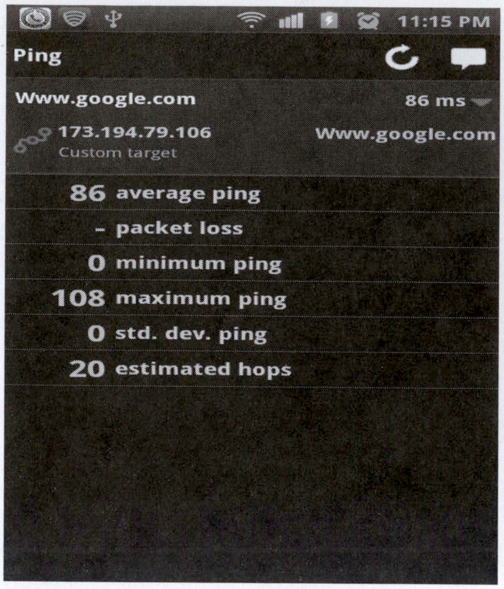

Figure 24-20: Using Ping with Fing. 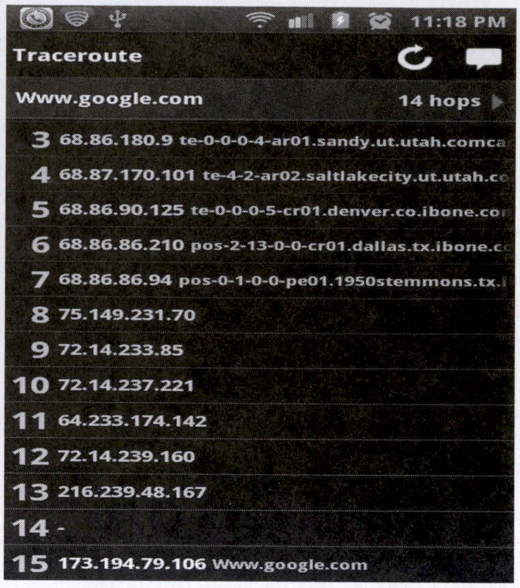   Figure 24-21: Using Traceroute with Fing.

12. Go back to Tools.
13. Select Traceroute.
14. In the text box, type www.Google.com, and press OK.
15. Take a screenshot. (See Figure 24-21.)

Note: Using Traceroute, you can see all of the hops between you and a different network. You can also use it to troubleshoot a network. If ICMP is blocked, or there is a problem in routing, you will receive an "unreachable" message.

16. Go back to Tools and scroll down to Edit TCP Services.
17. From here, you can see all of the TCP ports and their associated port number.
18. Take a screenshot. (See Figure 24-22.)

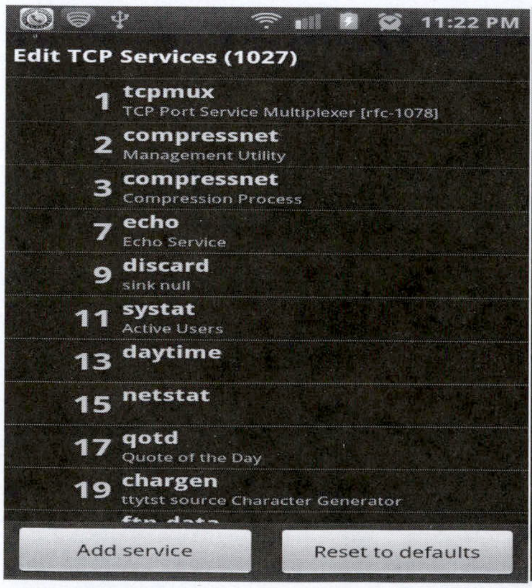

Figure 24-22: View all well-known TCP ports. 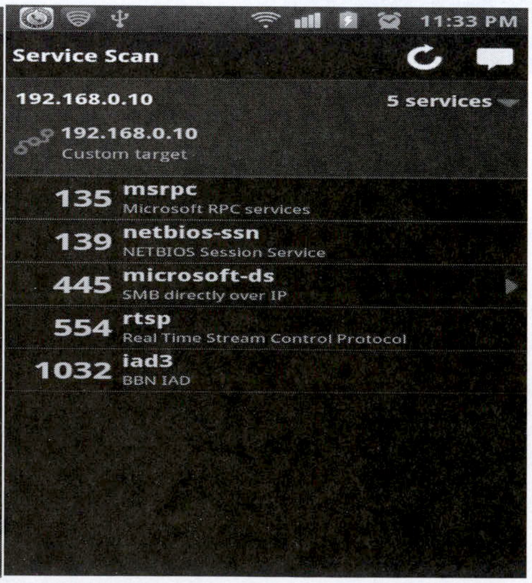   Figure 24-23: Results from service port scan.

19. Go back to Tools and select Scan TCP Services.

20. Enter a laptop or desktop computer IP address that was identified on your network and select OK. (In this case, it was 192.168.0.10.)
21. Take a screenshot of the results. (See Figure 24-23.)

Note: The results will return what TCP ports are open on your devices. With the returned ports, you can determine if a particular host on your network is leaving ports open that are vulnerable to attack. The results from this scan show a laptop with five open ports.

PROJECT QUESTIONS

1. What was the IP address of the device you scanned?
2. What ports were open on your devices?
3. Are there security issues with these ports?
4. How many hosts were on your network and what were their associated IP and MAC addresses?

THOUGHT QUESTIONS

1. Why is it important to know which ports you have open?
2. How can Ping or Traceroute help you identify network problems?
3. How can opened ports be used by attackers?
4. What steps can you take initially to prevent users from accessing your network and devices?

24.6   ENCRYPTED CALLS (REDPHONE®)

The Zimmermann Real-Time Transport Protocol (ZRTP) was primarily created by Phil Zimmerman, the creator of the Pretty Good Protocol (PGP). ZRTP is a cryptographic key exchange for SRTP and is based upon the Diffie-Hellman or elliptic curve Diffie-Hellman algorithms. It provides end-to-end VoIP security.

In addition to using Diffie-Hellman or elliptic curve Diffie-Hellman for key exchange, ZRTP uses 256-bit AES symmetric encryption for confidentiality and HMAC-SHA1 for authentication. Like PGP, ZRTP is open source. ZRTP was submitted to the Internet Engineering Task Force (IETF) in March 2006. In April 2011, ZRTP was published as RFC 6189.

RedPhone® allows you to make fully encrypted telephone calls using your cell phone. Both the sender and receiver must have the RedPhone app on their phones. RedPhone was one of the first effective implementations of secure calling via cellular phones. At the time of writing, it was only available on Android devices. PrivateGSM®, a similar app, is available for both Android and iPhone, but is not free.

1. Go to your app market.
2. Search for "RedPhone".
3. Select "RedPhone :: Secure Calls."
4. Press Install, and Accept.
5. When the download is complete, press Open.
6. Select Register, and Continue. (When the test completes, you should see a contact list.)

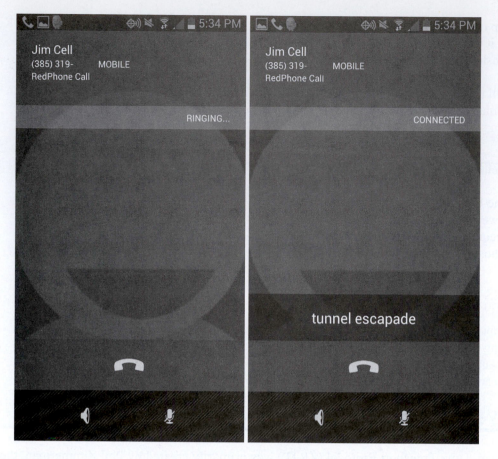

Figure 24-24: Making a call with RedPhone.   Figure 24-25: Secure connection.

7. In order for RedPhone to work, the application must be on both the sender's and receiver's phone. Invite another student or friend to download the application. Both users must be connected to the Internet via WiFi.
8. When both devices have RedPhone installed, start the RedPhone app.
9. Tap on the receiver's contact number.
10. Be patient since the connection will take a few extra seconds to connect. When the connection has been made, a phrase will appear at the bottom of your screen. (See Figure 24-24.)
11. View the Verify Security Phrase and share it with the other user. If the phrases are the same, the connection is secure and encrypted. Also note that the phrase changes for every call.
12. Take a screenshot. (See Figure 24-25.)
13. Since you are using a VoIP (data) line and not your voice line, there may be some latency or delay. Note any latency.

PROJECT QUESTIONS

1. What time of day did you make the call?
2. How strong was your VoIP connection?
3. Did you notice any latency? How much?
4. Were your security phrases the same on both ends?

THOUGHT QUESTIONS

1. Why can't the RedPhone application be used with PSTN connections?

2. Why do you think ZRTP is controversial?
3. When might you want to use ZRTP?
4. Should ZRTP be more readily available through mobile phone communications?

24.7   ENCRYPTION (FILE LOCKER®)

File Locker® is an application that can be used to protect your confidential material from being read, seen, watched, or accessed. It is fairly simple to use and can provide decent protection with a strong password. One problem with File Locker is that it encodes the file name once it is encrypted. This provides stronger protection, but also makes it difficult to remember which file is which.

File Locker can encrypt text files, pictures, and even videos. It is important that you don't forget your password since there is no password recovery. After locking a file, the content and file name will be encoded.

1. Go to your app market.
2. Search for "Jota Text Editor".
3. Select Install, and then Accept, and Download.
4. When the download is complete, open it.
5. Type "Secret Stuff" three times.
6. Take a screenshot.
7. Save it as your first initial and last name and select OK. In this case, it was Rboyle.txt.
8. Return to your app market.
9. Search for "File Locker".
10. Select Install, and then Accept, and Download.
11. Open File Locker when the download is complete.
12. When File Locker is open, scroll down to the bottom.
13. Select your file. (In this case, it was Rboyle.txt.)
14. Take a screenshot.
15. Press down for a moment until you receive additional options.
16. Select Lock.
17. Enter a password that you'll remember and select Lock.
18. Your file will now show a locked padlock and your text will change color and names.
19. Select your locked file and enter your password.
20. When the correct password is entered, the file will unlock and you'll see a key.
21. Take a screenshot.
22. Exit out of File Locker and go to your camera.
23. Take a picture and return to File Locker.
24. Select All files, and scroll down to DCIM.
25. Open DCIM and then Camera.
26. Scroll down to the bottom and select the newest picture. (The files are listed from oldest to newest, by date.)
27. Again, select the file and hold it until you receive additional options.
28. Select Lock, Create a password, and Lock.
29. Once again, your file name will be changed and the padlock will be closed.
30. Take a screenshot.
31. You can open it again by the password. When a file is left unlocked, your phone will display a key in the upper right-hand side of your phone, reminding you to lock it again.

PROJECT QUESTIONS

1. Were you able to easily find the files that you wanted to encrypt?
2. What was the name of the file you encrypted?
3. How long was the password you used?
4. Did you find that encoding the file name made it difficult to know which file was encrypted?

THOUGHT QUESTIONS

1. What information do you currently have on your phone that should be protected?
2. How many mobile devices do you think use encryption even when it's free and accessible?
3. What other file utilities come with File Locker?
4. Can File Locker encrypt the file name as well?

Appendix

None of the programs listed in this book are viruses, worms, or malware. If your antivirus software gives you a warning that any of the programs are viruses, you'll need to create an exception folder.

An antivirus program will not scan the files/programs in the exception folder you will create. Instructions on how to get McAfee® and Norton® antivirus scanners to create exception folders are shown below.

Most common antivirus scanners will have the ability to create an exception folder. If they don't have this option, you may want to get a better antivirus scanner. It may take a small amount of effort to figure out how to make an exception folder if you are using an antivirus scanner that is not listed below.

Avast!®, AVG Free®, and Microsoft Security Essentials are good antivirus programs that are free to download and use.

A.1   CREATING A VIRUS SCAN EXCEPTION FOLDER (MCAFEE)

Some of the programs shown in the projects may show up as viruses by well known virus scanners. They aren't viruses. They just have functionality that the antivirus company decided most users don't need and could be used to harm them. There are legal battles currently under way to get certain pieces of software off their virus lists.

The instructions below show you how to create a folder that will not be scanned by your antivirus software. Basically, you create an exception folder that you can place all your security software in, and then tell the antivirus scanner to ignore this folder when it scans for viruses. There are usually online instructions on how to create exceptions folders for most antivirus products.

These are the instructions for McAfee Antivirus. The instructions may vary depending on differences between versions and changes since the publication of this book.

1. Make a folder called "security" in C:\.
2. Open the McAfee VirusScan Console.
3. Open the On-Access Scanner.
4. Click All Processes.
5. Click on the Detection tab.
6. Click Exclusions.
7. Click Add.
8. Click Browse.
9. Select the "security" folder on your C: drive. If you don't see a "security" folder, you'll need to create one first.
10. Keep clicking OK until you are done.
11. McAfee VirusScan will not scan that folder.

These are the instructions for Avast! Antivirus. Again, the instructions may vary depending on differences between versions, and changes since the publication of this book.

1. Open Avast!.
2. Click on the Real-Time Sheilds tab.
3. Click Expert Settings.
4. Click Exclusions.
5. Click Browse.
6. Browse to your C:\security folder.
7. Select your C:\security folder.
8. Click OK, and Add.

These are the instructions for Norton Antivirus. Again, the instructions may vary depending on difference between versions, and changes since the publication of this book.

1. Make a folder called "security" in C:\.
2. Open your Norton Antivirus software.
3. Click on Norton Security Options.
4. Click Exclusions (on the left side).
5. Add the C:\security folder to the exclusions list.

6. Keep clicking OK until you close Norton.

Appendix

The software used in this book will be available for download on the Internet, or will be available on Canvas®/Blackboard® if your teacher chooses to upload them. If one of the links listed doesn't appear to be working, please check www.Google.com or Canvas/Blackboard for a current link. Almost all of the programs listed below can be found by searching on www.Google.com. They are all well known and virus/worm free. All of the programs in this manual were tested on a Microsoft Windows 7 Professional (64-bit) desktop machine.

We recommend you make a folder labeled "security" on your C: drive to store all the software that you will download. Creating this folder will make software organization and operation easier. This book is written with the understanding that you did create a security folder on your C: drive. All the programs in this manual will match the directions in the book if you create the C:\security folder on your C: drive.

The list of software will change every year, as new software becomes freeware. If you know of a piece of free Windows-based software that is more useful and easier to use than the ones listed below, please feel free to email a link to BoyleRJ@Longwood.edu and it might get included in the next edition.

B.1 SOFTWARE LINKS

Below is a listing of the software, and accompanying URLs, used in this book. Web links don't last forever and it's likely that by the time you pick up this book, at least one of the links listed below is out-of-date.

If a link below is broken, chances are good that you will be able to find the software listed somewhere on the main page of the listed hostname. You can also search for the name of the software through Google or Yahoo!.

Name	Company	Link
7-Zip	Igor Pavlov	http://www.7-zip.org
ADS Spy	Merijn	http://www.bleepingcomputer.com/files/adsspy.php
Advanced LAN Scanner	Famatech	http://www.advanced-ip-scanner.com/
AnyWho	YP Intellectual Property LLC	http://www.anywho.com/reverse-lookup
Apache	Apache Software Foundation	http://httpd.apache.org/
AppScan	IBM	http://www.ibm.com/developerworks/downloads/r/appscan/
AVG	AVG Technologies	http://free.avg.com/
AxCrypt	Axantum Software AB	http://www.axantum.com/AxCrypt/
Kali	Kali.org	http://www.kali.org/
BgInfo	Microsoft	http://technet.microsoft.com/en-us/sysinternals/bb897557.aspx
Buffer Overflow	Dr. Susan Gerhart	http://nsfsecurity.pr.erau.edu/bom/
Butterfat.net	Butterfat, LLC	http://map.butterfat.net/emailroutemap/
ByteScout	ByteScout	http://bytescout.com/?q=/download/download_freeware.html
Cain & Able	Massimiliano Montoro	http://www.oxid.it/cain.html
CAINE	Giancarlo Giustini	http://www.caine-live.net/
CCleaner	Piriform Ltd	http://www.piriform.com/ccleaner
Computerworld	Computerworld Inc.	http://www.computerworld.com/
CrypTool 2	Cryptool.org	http://www.cryptool.org/en/cryptool2
Default Passwords	phenoelit	http://www.phenoelit-us.org/dpl/dpl.html
Disk Wipe	Diskwipe.org	http://diskwipe.org/
Ekahau HeatMapper	Ekahau, Inc.	http://www.ekahau.com/products/heatmapper/overview.html
Enigma Simulator	Frank Spiess	http://enigmaco.de/enigma/enigma.swf

Eraser	Heidi Computers Ltd.	http://www.heidi.ie
Event Viewer	Microsoft	www.Microsoft.com
Naked Security	Sophos Ltd.	http://nakedsecurity.sophos.com/
Fedora	Red Hat Inc.	http://fedoraproject.org/
File Checksum Integrity Verifyer	Microsoft	http://support.microsoft.com/kb/841290
File Verifier++	Tom Bramer	http://www.programmingunlimited.net/siteexec/content.cgi?page=fv
Firefox	Mozilla	http://www.Mozilla.com/en-US/firefox/
Forensic Toolkit (FTK)	AccessData	http://www.accessdata.com/support/product-downloads
Free Word and Excel Password Recovery Wizard	Mastermen Pty Ltd.	http://www.freewordexcelpassword.com/
GoDaddy.com	GoDaddy.com	www.GoDaddy.com
Google	Google.com	www.Google.com
HashCalc	SlavaSoft Inc.	http://www.slavasoft.com/hashcalc/
HoneyBOT	Atomic Software Solutions	http://www.atomicsoftwaresolutions.com
Hotmail	Microsoft	www.Hotmail.com
HTTPS Everywhere	EFF.org	https://www.eff.org/https-everywhere
Hushmail	Hush Communications Canada Inc.	http://www.hushmail.com/
IIS	Microsoft	http://www.iis.net/
inSSIDer	MetaGeek, LLC	http://www.metageek.net/products/inssider
Internet Explorer	Microsoft	www.Microsoft.com
Invisible Secrets	NeoByte Solutions	http://www.invisiblesecrets.com/ver2/index.html
John the Ripper	Openwall Project	http://www.openwall.com/john/
K9	Blue Coat Systems	http://www1.k9webprotection.com/getk9/index.php
Linux Mint	Linuxmint.com	http://linuxmint.com/
LockNote	Steganos GmbH	https://www.steganos.com/us/products/for-free/locknote/overview/
MAC Address Changer v5	Technitium	http://tmac.technitium.com/tmac/index.html
McAfee Antivirus	McAfee Inc.	http://www.mcafee.com/us/
Microsoft Publisher	Microsoft	http://office.microsoft.com/en-us/publisher/default.aspx
Microsoft Security Essentials	Microsoft	http://windows.microsoft.com/en-US/windows/security-essentials-download
Nessus	Tenable Network Security	http://www.tenable.com/products/nessus

494 | P a g e

Nmap	Gordon Lyon	http://nmap.org
NotePad	Microsoft	www.Microsoft.com
Network Security Toolkit	networksecuritytoolkit.org	http://networksecuritytoolkit.org/nst/index.html
OpenPuff	Cosimo Oliboni	http://embeddedsw.net/OpenPuff_Steganography_Home.html
OpenSUSE	Novell®	http://www.opensuse.org/en/
Ophcrack	Objectif Sécurité	http://ophcrack.sourceforge.net/
Outlook	Microsoft	http://office.microsoft.com/en-us/outlook/default.aspx
Password Evaluator	George Shaffer	http://geodsoft.com/cgi-bin/pwcheck.pl
Password Generator	George Shaffer	http://geodsoft.com/cgi-bin/password.pl
PC-BSD	iXsystems, Inc	http://www.pcbsd.org/
Pendriveapps	USB Pen Drive Apps	http://www.pendriveapps.com/
Phrase Password Generator	VaultMate Software	http://www.vaultmate.com/freewaregifts.php
Ponemon Institute	Ponemone Institute, LLC	http://www.ponemon.org/
PortableApps	PortableApps.com	http://portableapps.com/
PortQry	Microsoft	http://www.microsoft.com/en-us/download/details.aspx?displaylang=en&id=17148
Predator	Richard Goutorbe	http://www.predator-usb.com
Prey	Fork, Ltd.	http://preyproject.com/
Process Explorer	Microsoft	http://technet.microsoft.com/en-us/sysinternals/bb896653.aspx
Process Monitor	Microsoft	http://technet.microsoft.com/en-us/sysinternals/bb896645.aspx
PwC	PwC	http://www.pwc.com/gx/en/consulting-services/information-security-survey/index.jhtml
Pwdump7	Tarasco.org	http://www.tarasco.org/security/pwdump_7/index.html
RainbowCrack	RainbowCrack Project	http://project-rainbowcrack.com/
Recuva	Piriform Ltd.	http://www.piriform.com/recuva
Refog Keylogger	Refog	http://www.refog.com
Remote Desktop	Microsoft	www.Microsoft.com
Sam Spade	Steve Atkins	http://www.softpedia.com/get/Network-Tools/Network-Tools-Suites/Sam-Spade.shtml
SANS	The SANS™ Institute	www.sans.org
Screenshot Pilot	Two Pilots	http://www.colorpilot.com/screenshot.html
SDelete	Microsoft	http://technet.microsoft.com/en-us/sysinternals/bb897443
Shields Up	Gibson Research Corporation	http://www.grc.com

SNARE for Windows	InterSect Alliance	http://www.intersectalliance.com/
Spector 360	SpectorSoft Corporation	http://www.spector360.com/Resources/OnlineDemos/
Steg Detect	Niels Provos	http://www.outguess.org/detection.php
TAGView	EviGator Digital Forensics	http://www.evigator.com/store/
The Register	The Register	http://www.theregister.co.uk/security/
Tor	The Tor Project	https://www.torproject.org/
TrueCrypt	TrueCrypt	http://www.truecrypt.org/
Ubuntu	Canonical Ltd.	http://www.ubuntu.com/
Untangle	Untangle, Inc.	http://www.untangle.com
Virtual Box	Oracle Corp.	http://www.oracle.com
WhatIsMyIPAddress	WhatIsMyIPAddress.com	http://whatismyipaddress.com/
WebGoat	OWASP	http://code.google.com/p/webgoat/
Whitepages.com	Whitepages.com	http://www.whitepages.com/
WiFiDEnum	Aruba Networks, Inc.	https://labs.arubanetworks.com/wifidenum
Wi-Fi Inspector	Xirrus, Inc.	Xirrus is the leading provider of high-performance wireless networks. The Xirrus Array and Access Point always perform under the most demanding circumstances. Their wired-like reliability and superior security allow our customers the confidence to take their business-critical applications and operations mobile. Our solutions are unique in the industry, transforming enterprises and organizations around the world. At a time when everyone expects to connect wirelessly anywhere and business is increasingly done in the cloud, Xirrus wireless solutions are providing a vital strategic business and IT infrastructure advantage in thousands of deployments worldwide. With headquarters in Thousand Oaks, CA, Xirrus is a privately held enterprise, designing and manufacturing its products and solutions in the USA. More information: www.xirrus.com.
WiGLE.net	arkasha & bobzilla	http://www.wigle.net/
WinDump	Riverbed Technology	http://www.winpcap.org
Winrtgen	Massimiliano Montoro	http://www.oxid.it/projects.html
Wireshark	Wireshark Foundation	http://www.wireshark.org
You Get Signal	Kirk Ouimet Design	http://www.yougetsignal.com/tools/visual-tracert/
Zabasearch	ZABA Inc.	http://www.zabasearch.com/